Lecture Notes in Computer Science

Vol. 219: Advances in Cryptology – EUROCRYPT '85. Proceedings, 1985. Edited by F. Pichler. IX, 281 pages. 1986.

Vol. 220: RIMS Symposia on Software Science and Engineering II. Proceedings, 1983 and 1984. Edited by E. Goto, K. Araki and T. Yuasa. XI, 323 pages. 1986.

Vol. 221: Logic Programming '85. Proceedings, 1985. Edited by E. Wada. IX, 311 pages. 1986.

Vol. 222: Advances in Petri Nets 1985. Edited by G. Rozenberg. VI, 498 pages. 1986.

Vol. 223: Structure in Complexity Theory. Proceedings, 1986. Edited by A.L. Selman. VI, 401 pages. 1986.

Vol. 224: Current Trends in Concurrency. Overviews and Tutorials. Edited by J.W. de Bakker, W.-P. de Roever and G. Rozenberg. XII, 716 pages. 1986.

Vol. 225: Third International Conference on Logic Programming. Proceedings, 1986. Edited by E. Shapiro. IX, 720 pages. 1986.

Vol. 226: Automata, Languages and Programming. Proceedings, 1986. Edited by L. Kott. IX, 474 pages. 1986.

Vol. 227: VLSI Algorithms and Architectures – AWOC 86. Proceedings, 1986. Edited by F. Makedon, K. Mehlhorn, T. Papatheodorou and P. Spirakis. VIII, 328 pages. 1986.

Vol. 228: Applied Algebra, Algorithmics and Error-Correcting Codes. AAECC-2. Proceedings, 1984. Edited by A. Poli. VI, 265 pages. 1986.

Vol. 229: Algebraic Algorithms and Error-Correcting Codes. AAECC-3. Proceedings, 1985. Edited by J. Calmet. VII, 416 pages. 1986.

Vol. 230: 8th International Conference on Automated Deduction. Proceedings, 1986. Edited by J.H. Siekmann. X, 708 pages. 1986.

Vol. 231: R. Hausser, NEWCAT: Parsing Natural Language Using Left-Associative Grammar. II, 540 pages. 1986.

Vol. 232: Fundamentals of Artificial Intelligence. Edited by W. Bibel and Ph. Jorrand. VII, 313 pages. 1986.

Vol. 233: Mathematical Foundations of Computer Science 1986. Proceedings, 1986. Edited by J. Gruska, B. Rovan and J. Wiedermann. IX, 650 pages. 1986.

Vol. 234: Concepts in User Interfaces: A Reference Model for Command and Response Languages. By Members of IFIP Working Group 2.7. Edited by D. Beech. X, 116 pages. 1986.

Vol. 235: Accurate Scientific Computations. Proceedings, 1985. Edited by W.L. Miranker and R.A. Toupin. XIII, 205 pages. 1986.

Vol. 236: TEX for Scientific Documentation. Proceedings, 1986. Edited by J. Désarménien. VI, 204 pages. 1986.

Vol. 237: CONPAR 86. Proceedings, 1986. Edited by W. Händler, D. Haupt, R. Jeltsch, W. Juling and O. Lange. X, 418 pages. 1986.

Vol. 238: L. Naish, Negation and Control in Prolog. IX, 119 pages. 1986.

Vol. 239: Mathematical Foundations of Programming Semantics. Proceedings, 1985. Edited by A. Melton. VI, 395 pages. 1986.

Vol. 240: Category Theory and Computer Programming. Proceedings, 1985. Edited by D. Pitt, S. Abramsky, A. Poigné and D. Rydeheard. VII, 519 pages. 1986.

Vol. 241: Foundations of Software Technology and Theoretical Computer Science. Proceedings, 1986. Edited by K.V. Nori. XII, 519 pages. 1986.

Vol. 242: Combinators and Functional Programming Languages. Proceedings, 1985. Edited by G. Cousineau, P.-L. Curien and B. Robinet. V, 208 pages. 1986.

Vol. 243: ICDT '86. Proceedings, 1986. Edited by G. Ausiello and P. Atzeni. VI, 444 pages. 1986.

Vol. 244: Advanced Programming Environments. Proceedings, 1986. Edited by R. Conradi, T.M. Didriksen and D.H. Wanvik. VII, 604 pages. 1986

Vol. 245: H.F. de Groote, Lectures on the Complexity of Bilinear Problems. V, 135 pages. 1987.

Vol. 246: Graph-Theoretic Concepts in Computer Science. Proceedings, 1986. Edited by G. Tinhofer and G. Schmidt. VII, 307 pages. 1987.

Vol. 247: STACS 87. Proceedings, 1987. Edited by F.J. Brandenburg, G. Vidal-Naquet and M. Wirsing. X, 484 pages. 1987.

Vol. 248: Networking in Open Systems. Proceedings, 1986. Edited by G. Müller and R.P. Blanc. VI, 441 pages. 1987.

Vol. 249: TAPSOFT '87. Volume 1. Proceedings, 1987. Edited by H. Ehrig, R. Kowalski, G. Levi and U. Montanari. XIV, 289 pages. 1987.

Vol. 250: TAPSOFT '87. Volume 2. Proceedings, 1987. Edited by H. Ehrig, R. Kowalski, G. Levi and U. Montanari. XIV, 336 pages. 1987.

Vol. 251: V. Akman, Unobstructed Shortest Paths in Polyhedral Environments. VII, 103 pages. 1987.

Vol. 252: VDM '87. VDM – A Formal Method at Work. Proceedings, 1987. Edited by D. Bjørner, C.B. Jones, M. Mac an Airchinnigh and E.J. Neuhold. IX, 422 pages. 1987.

Vol. 253: J.D. Becker, I. Eisele (Eds.), WOPPLOT 86. Parallel Processing: Logic, Organization, and Technology. Proceedings, 1986. V, 226 pages. 1987.

Vol. 254: Petri Nets: Central Models and Their Properties. Advances in Petri Nets 1986, Part I. Proceedings, 1986. Edited by W. Brauer, W. Reisig and G. Rozenberg. X, 480 pages. 1987.

Vol. 255: Petri Nets: Applications and Relationships to Other Models of Concurrency. Advances in Petri Nets 1986, Part II. Proceedings, 1986. Edited by W. Brauer, W. Reisig and G. Rozenberg. X, 516 pages. 1987.

Vol. 256: Rewriting Techniques and Applications. Proceedings, 1987. Edited by P. Lescanne. VI, 285 pages. 1987.

Vol. 257: Database Machine Performance: Modeling Methodologies and Evaluation Strategies. Edited by F. Cesarini and S. Salza. X, 250 pages. 1987.

Vol. 258: PARLE, Parallel Architectures and Languages Europe. Volume I. Proceedings, 1987. Edited by J.W. de Bakker, A.J. Nijman and P.C. Treleaven. XII, 480 pages. 1987.

Vol. 259: PARLE, Parallel Architectures and Languages Europe. Volume II. Proceedings, 1987. Edited by J.W. de Bakker, A.J. Nijman and P.C. Treleaven. XII, 464 pages. 1987.

Vol. 260: D.C. Luckham, F.W. von Henke, B. Krieg-Brückner, O. Owe, ANNA, A Language for Annotating Ada Programs. V, 143 pages. 1987.

Vol. 261: J. Ch. Freytag, Translating Relational Queries into Iterative Programs. XI, 131 pages. 1987.

Vol. 262: A. Burns, A.M. Lister, A.J. Wellings, A Review of Ada Tasking. VIII, 141 pages. 1987.

Vol. 263: A.M. Odlyzko (Ed.), Advances in Cryptology – CRYPTO '86. Proceedings. XI, 489 pages. 1987.

Vol. 264: E. Wada (Ed.), Logic Programming '86. Proceedings, 1986. VI, 179 pages. 1987.

Vol. 265: K.P. Jantke (Ed.), Analogical and Inductive Inference. Proceedings, 1986. VI, 227 pages. 1987.

Vol. 266: G. Rozenberg (Ed.), Advances in Petri Nets 1987. VI, 451 pages. 1987.

Vol. 267: Th. Ottmann (Ed.), Automata, Languages and Programming. Proceedings, 1987. X, 565 pages. 1987.

Vol. 268: P.M. Pardalos, J.B. Rosen, Constrained Global Optimization: Algorithms and Applications. VII, 143 pages. 1987.

Vol. 269: A. Albrecht, H. Jung, K. Mehlhorn (Eds.), Parallel Algorithms and Architectures. Proceedings, 1987. Approx. 205 pages. 1987.

Lecture Notes in Computer Science

Edited by G. Goos and J. Hartmanis

300

H. Ganzinger (Ed.)

ESOP '88

2nd European Symposium on Programming
Nancy, France, March 21–24, 1988
Proceedings

Springer-Verlag
Berlin Heidelberg New York London Paris Tokyo

Editor

Harald Ganzinger
Fachbereich Informatik, Universität Dortmund
Postfach 50 05 00, D-4600 Dortmund 50

CR Subject Classification (1987): D.1.1–3, D.2–3, F.3

ISBN 3-540-19027-9 Springer-Verlag Berlin Heidelberg New York
ISBN 0-387-19027-9 Springer-Verlag New York Berlin Heidelberg

Printed in Germany

Printing and binding: Druckhaus Beltz, Hemsbach/Bergstr.
2145/3140-543210

Preface

This volume contains the papers selected for presentation at the 2nd European Symposium on Programming, Nancy, March 21-24, 1988. The first conference in this series was held at Saarbrücken in March 1986 (see LNCS 213) as a successor to the "Colloque sur la Programmation" and the GI Conference on "Programmiersprachen und Programmentwicklung". ESOP '88 has been held in conjunction with CAAP '88.

The theme of the ESOP conference is the design, specification and implementation of programming languages and systems. Emphasis is on work in which an implemented system embodies an important concept or formal model of programming in such a way that its usefulness is demonstrated. It was therefore decided that the conference be accompanied by an exhibition of software systems in the area. This volume also contains a short description of some of the systems that have been demonstrated. The program committee has selected 23 papers out of a total of 75 submitted papers. In addition, the volume contains a paper from one of the two invited speakers.

The program committee has consisted of the following persons:

S. Abramsky, London
E. Astesiano, Genova
M. Bruynooghe, Leuven
G. Cousineau, Paris
H. Ganzinger, Dortmund (chairman)
J. Hughes, Glasgow
Th. Johnsson, Gøteborg
N. Jones, København
G. Kahn, Sophia-Antipolis
P. Klint, Amsterdam
P. Lescanne, Nancy
T. Reps, Madison, WI
B. Robinet, Paris
M. Sintzoff, Louvain-la-Neuve
R. Wilhelm, Saarbrücken
M. Wirsing, Passau

The following people have served as additional referees:

J.A.S. Alegria, L. Augustsson, D. Bert, A. Callebaut, L. F. del Cerro, A. Ciepielewski, D. Clement, G. Costa, J. Crammond, P.-L. Curien, O. Danvy, J. O'Donnell, D. Galmiche, R. Giegerich, C. V. Hall, M. Hanus, L. Hascoet, R. Heckmann, P. van Hentonxyck, R. Hennicker, N. Hermann, K. Holm, P. Jacquet, R. Jacquiert, J. Jaray, K. Karlsson, A. van Lamsweerde, J. Maluszynski, D. Maurer, D. Mery, T. Mogensen, A. Pettorossi, L. Pierron, A. Poigné, A. Quere, Th. Rauber, H. P. Sander, D. de Schreye, T. Streicher, A. Suarez, P. Wadler, A. Waern and P. Wolper.

I would like to express my sincere gratitude to all the members of the program committee, as well as to the many other referees listed above for their care and advice.

Moreover, I am grateful to Astrid Baumgart at Dortmund and to Jean-Luc Rémy, Corinne Hally and all the other people of the Local Arrangement Committee at Nancy who have helped in preparing and organizing this conference.

Dortmund, March 1988 H. Ganzinger

Table of Contents

---

* Manuscript not received in time for publication

5. Implementation of Programming Languages

Semantics-Based Program Integration

THOMAS REPS and SUSAN HORWITZ
University of Wisconsin – Madison

The need to integrate several versions of a base program into a common one arises frequently, but it is a tedious and time consuming task to integrate programs by hand. To date, the only available tools for assisting with program integration are variants of *text-based* differential file comparators; these are of limited utility because one has no guarantees about how the program that is the product of an integration behaves compared to the programs that were integrated.

Our recent work addresses the problem of building a *semantics-based* tool for program integration; this paper describes the techniques we have developed, which provide the foundation for creating such a tool. Semantics-based integration is based on the assumption that a difference in the *behavior* of one of the variant programs from that of the base program, rather than a difference in the *text*, is significant and must be preserved in the merged program. Although it is undecidable to determine whether a program modification actually leads to such a difference, it is possible to determine a safe approximation by comparing each of the variants with the base program. To determine this information, the integration algorithm employs a program representation that is similar (although not identical) to the *program dependence graphs* that have been used previously in vectorizing compilers. The algorithm also makes use of the notion of a *program slice* to find just those statements of a program that determine the values of potentially affected variables.

---

1. INTRODUCTION

Our concern is the development of a semantics-based tool for *integrating program variants*. The goal is to create a system that will either automatically combine several different but related variants of a base program, or else determine that the variants incorporate interfering changes.

The need to integrate several versions of a program into a common one arises frequently, but it is a tedious and time consuming task to integrate programs by hand. Anyone who has had to reconcile divergent lines of development will identify with the need for automatic assistance. Unfortunately, at present, the only available tools for integration are variants of differential file comparators, such as the Unix utility *diff*.

Portions of this paper are excerpted from [10] and [12].

This work was supported in part by the National Science Foundation under grants DCR-8552602 and DCR-8603356 as well as by grants from IBM, DEC, Siemens, and Xerox.

Authors' address: Computer Sciences Dept., Univ. of Wisconsin, 1210 W. Dayton St., Madison, WI 53706.

The problem with current tools is that they implement an operation for merging files as strings of text. This approach has the advantage that such tools are as applicable to merging documents, data files, and other text objects as they are to merging programs. However, these tools are necessarily of limited utility for integrating programs because the manner in which two programs are merged is not *safe*. One has no guarantees about the way the program that results from a purely *textual* merge behaves in relation to the behaviors of the three programs that are the arguments to the merge. The merged program must, therefore, be checked carefully for conflicts that might have been introduced by the merge.

Recently, in collaboration with J. Prins, we developed a radically different approach to integrating programs [10]. Our method is based on the assumption that any change in the *behavior* of one of the variant programs from that of the base program, rather than a difference in the *text*, is significant and must be preserved in the merged program. Although it is undecidable to determine whether a program modification actually leads to such a difference, it is possible to determine a safe approximation by comparing each of the variants with the base program. To determine this information, the integration algorithm employs a program representation that is similar, although not identical, to the *program dependence graphs* that have been used previously in vectorizing compilers. The algorithm also make use of the notion of a *program slice* to find just those statements of a program that determine the values of potentially affected variables.

Our integration algorithm takes as input three programs A, B, and $Base$, where A and B are two variants of $Base$; whenever the changes made to $Base$ to create A and B do not "interfere" in a certain well-defined sense, the algorithm produces a program M that integrates A and B. A number of uses for this operation in a system to support programming in the large are described in Section 2. The integration algorithm itself is described and illustrated in Section 3 (it is described in full detail in [10]).

In order to study the integration problem in a simplified setting, we have initially restricted our attention to a programming language with only the most basic data types and control constructs; in particular, we assume that expressions contain only scalar variables and constants, and that the only statements used in programs are assignment statements, conditional statements, and while-loops. Current work, described in Section 4, concerns how to extend the set of language constructs to which the program-integration algorithm is applicable, as well as the construction of a prototype integration facility.

2. APPLICATIONS TO PROGRAMMING IN THE LARGE

An environment for programming in the large addresses problems of organizing and relating designs, documentation, individual software modules, software releases, and the activities of programmers. The manipulation of related versions of programs is at the heart of these issues. In many respects, the operation of integrating program variants is the key operation in an environment to support programming in the large.

One situation in which the integration operation would be employed is when a base version of a system is enhanced along different lines, either by users or maintainers, thereby creating a number of related versions with slightly different features. To create a new version that incorporates several of the enhancements simultaneously, the integration operation is applied to the base version and its variants. If no conflicts are found, the versions are merged to create an integrated version that combines their separate features.

Pictorially, we can represent this situation by the following diagram, where *O* represents the original program, *A* and *B* represent the enhanced versions, and *M* represents the integrated program:

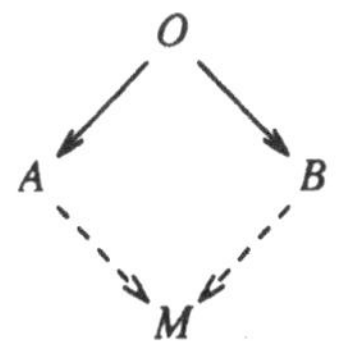

Besides the basic program integration scenario described above, there are a number of other applications for program integration; three such applications are discussed below.

2.1. Propagating Changes Through Related Versions

The program-integration problem arises when a family of related versions of a program has been created (for example, to support different machines or different operating systems), and the goal is to make the same change (*e.g.* an enhancement or a bug-fix) to all of them. One would like to be able to change the base version of the system and to have the change propagated automatically to all other versions. Of course, the change cannot be blindly applied to all versions since the differences among the versions might alter the effects of the change; one has to check for conflicts in the implementations of the different versions. Our program-integration algorithm provides a way for changes made to the base version to be automatically installed in the other versions.

For example, consider the diagram shown in Figure 1, where Figure 1(a) represents the original development tree for some module (branches are numbered as in RCS [20]). In Figure 1(b), the variant numbered "1.1.2.1" represents the enhanced version of the base program "1.1." Variant "1.1.2.2," which is obtained by integrating "1.1," "1.1.2.1," and "1.2," represents the result of propagating the enhancement to "1.2." Figure 1(c) represents the new development history after all integrations have been performed and the enhancement has been propagated to all versions.

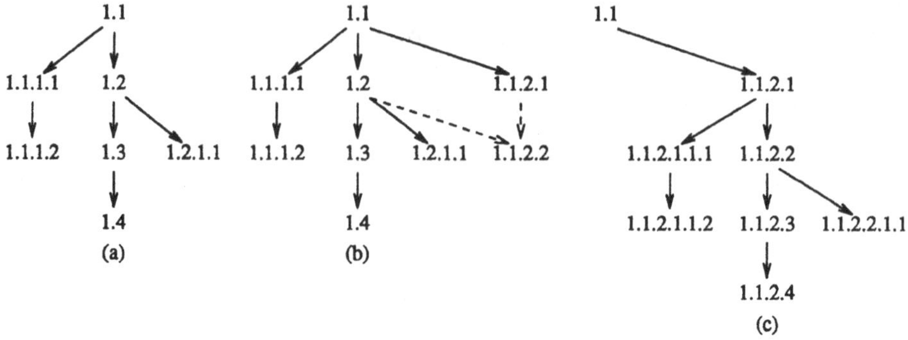

Figure 1. Propagating changes through a development-history tree.

2.2. Separating Consecutive Program Modifications

Another application of program integration permits separating consecutive edits on the same program into individual edits on the original base program. For example, consider the case of two consecutive edits to a base program O; let $O+A$ be the result of the first modification to O and let $O+A+B$ be the result of the modification to $O+A$. Now suppose we want to create a program $O+B$ that includes the second modification but not the first. This is represented by situation (a) in the following diagram:

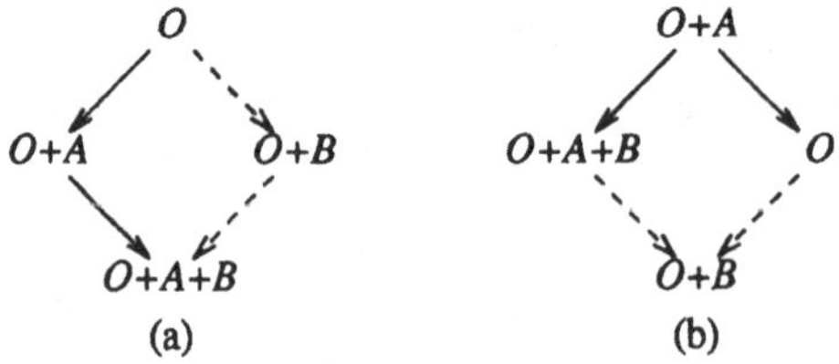

By re-rooting the development-history tree so that $O+A$ is the root, the diagram is turned on its side and becomes a program-integration problem (situation (b)). The base program is now $O+A$, and the two variants of $O+A$ are O and $O+A+B$. Instead of treating the differences between O and $O+A$ as changes that were made to O to create $O+A$, they are now treated as changes made to $O+A$ to create O. For example, when O is the base program, a statement s that occurs in $O+A$ but not in O is a "new" statement arising from an insertion; when $O+A$ is the base program, we treat the missing *s* in *O* as if a user had deleted *s* from *O*+*A* to create *O*. Version *O*+*A*+*B* is still treated as being a program version derived from *O*+*A*.

2.3. Optimistic Concurrency Control

An environment for programming in the large must provide concurrency control, *i.e.* it must resolve simultaneous requests for access to a program. Traditional database approaches to concurrency control assume that transactions are very short-lived, and so avoid conflict using locking mechanisms. This solution is not acceptable in programming environments where transactions may require hours, days, or weeks.

An alternative to locking is the use of an *optimistic concurrency control* strategy: grant all access requests and resolve conflicts when the transactions complete. The success of an optimistic concurrency control strategy clearly depends on the existence of an automatic program integration algorithm to provide acceptable conflict resolution.

3. DESCRIPTION OF THE INTEGRATION METHOD

The information used by our program integration method is encapsulated by a program representation called a *program dependence graph* (PDG). Different definitions of program dependence representations have been given, depending on the intended application; nevertheless, they are all variations on a theme introduced in [15], and share the common feature of having explicit representations of both control dependencies and data dependencies. The definition presented here has been adapted to the particular needs of the program-integration problem; it is similar, but not identical, to the program dependence representations used by others, such as the "program dependence graphs" defined in [7] and the "dependence graphs" defined in [16].

For program integration, there are two reasons to represent programs using program dependence graphs: (1) PDG's capture only relevant orderings of statements within control structures; (2) PDG's are a convenient representation on which to perform program slicing, which is used in the integration algorithm to determine the changes in behavior of each variant with respect to the base program.

3.1. The Program Dependence Graph

The definition of program dependence graph presented below is for a language with scalar variables, assignment statements, conditional statements, while loops, and a restricted kind of "output statement" called an *end statement*. An end statement, which can only appear at the end of a program, names one or more of the variables used in the program; when execution terminates, only those variables will have values in the final state. Intuitively, the variables named by the end statement are those whose final values are of interest to the programmer.

The program dependence graph for a program *P*, denoted by G_P, is a directed graph whose vertices are connected by several kinds of edges.[1] The vertices of G_P represent the assignment statements and control predicates that occur in program P. In addition, G_P includes three other categories of vertices:

a) There is a distinguished vertex called the *entry vertex*.

b) For each variable x for which there is a path in the standard control-flow graph for P [1] on which x is used before being defined, there is a vertex called the *initial definition of* x. This vertex represents an assignment to x from the initial state. The vertex is labeled "x := *InitialState* (x)."

c) For each variable x named in P's end statement, there is a vertex called the *final use of* x. This vertex represents an access to the final value of x computed by P, and is labeled "*FinalUse* (x)".

The edges of G_P represent *dependencies* between program components. An edge represents either a *control dependency* or a *data dependency*. Control dependency edges are labeled either **true** or **false**, and the source of a control dependency edge is always the entry vertex or a predicate vertex. A control dependency edge from vertex v_1 to vertex v_2, denoted by $v_1 \longrightarrow_c v_2$, means that during execution, whenever the predicate represented by v_1 is evaluated and its value matches the label on the edge to v_2, then the program component represented by v_2 will be executed (although perhaps not immediately). A method for determining control dependency edges for arbitrary programs is given in [7]; however, because we are assuming that programs include only assignment, conditional, and while statements, the control dependency edges of G_P can be determined in a much simpler fashion. For the language under consideration here, the control dependency edges reflect a program's nesting structure; a program dependence graph contains a *control dependency edge* from vertex v_1 to vertex v_2 of G_P iff one of the following holds:

i) v_1 is the entry vertex, and v_2 represents a component of P that is not subordinate to any control predicate; these edges are labeled **true**.

ii) v_1 represents a control predicate, and v_2 represents a component of P immediately subordinate to the control construct whose predicate is represented by v_1. If v_1 is the predicate of a while-loop, the edge $v_1 \longrightarrow_c v_2$ is labeled **true**; if v_1 is the predicate of a conditional statement, the edge $v_1 \longrightarrow_c v_2$ is labeled **true** or **false** according to whether v_2 occurs in the **then** branch or the **else** branch, respectively.[2]

---

[1]A *directed graph* G consists of a set of *vertices* $V(G)$ and a set of *edges* $E(G)$, where $E(G) \subseteq V(G) \times V(G)$. Each edge $(b, c) \in E(G)$ is directed from b to c; we say that b is the *source* and c the *target* of the edge.

[2]In other definitions that have been given for control dependency edges, there is an additional edge for each predicate of a **while** statement – each predicate has an edge to itself labeled **true**. By including the additional edge, the predicate's outgoing **true** edges consist of every program element that is guaranteed to be executed (eventually) when the predicate evaluates to **true**. This kind of edge is left out of our

A data dependency edge from vertex v_1 to vertex v_2 means that the program's computation might be changed if the relative order of the components represented by v_1 and v_2 were reversed. In this paper, program dependence graphs contain two kinds of data-dependency edges, representing *flow dependencies* and *def-order dependencies*.

A program dependence graph contains a flow dependency edge from vertex v_1 to vertex v_2 iff all of the following hold:

i) v_1 is a vertex that defines variable x.

ii) v_2 is a vertex that uses x.

iii) Control can reach v_2 after v_1 via an execution path along which there is no intervening definition of x. That is, there is a path in the standard control-flow graph for the program [1] by which the definition of x at v_1 reaches the use of x at v_2. (Initial definitions of variables are considered to occur at the beginning of the control-flow graph, and final uses of variables are considered to occur at its end.)

A flow dependency that exists from vertex v_1 to vertex v_2 will be denoted by $v_1 \longrightarrow_f v_2$.

Flow dependencies are further classified as *loop independent* or *loop carried*. A flow dependency $v_1 \longrightarrow_f v_2$ is carried by loop L, denoted by $v_1 \longrightarrow_{lc(L)} v_2$, if in addition to i), ii), and iii) above, the following also hold:

iv) There is an execution path that both satisfies the conditions of iii) above and includes a backedge to the predicate of loop L; and

v) Both v_1 and v_2 are enclosed in loop L.

A flow dependency $v_1 \longrightarrow_f v_2$ is loop independent, denoted by $v_1 \longrightarrow_{li} v_2$, if in addition to i), ii), and iii) above, there is an execution path that satisfies iii) above and includes *no* backedge to the predicate of a loop that encloses both v_1 and v_2. It is possible to have both $v_1 \longrightarrow_{lc(L)} v_2$ and $v_1 \longrightarrow_{li} v_2$.

A program dependence graph contains a def-order dependency edge from vertex v_1 to vertex v_2 iff all of the following hold:

i) v_1 and v_2 both define the same variable.

ii) v_1 and v_2 are in the same branch of any conditional statement that encloses both of them.

iii) There exists a program component v_3 such that $v_1 \longrightarrow_f v_3$ and $v_2 \longrightarrow_f v_3$.

iv) v_1 occurs to the left of v_2 in the program's abstract syntax tree.

A def-order dependency from v_1 to v_2 is denoted by $v_1 \longrightarrow_{do(v_3)} v_2$.

---

definition because it is not necessary for our purposes.

```
program Main
   sum := 0;
   x := 1;
   while x < 11 do
      sum := sum + x;
      x := x + 1
   od
end(x, sum)
```

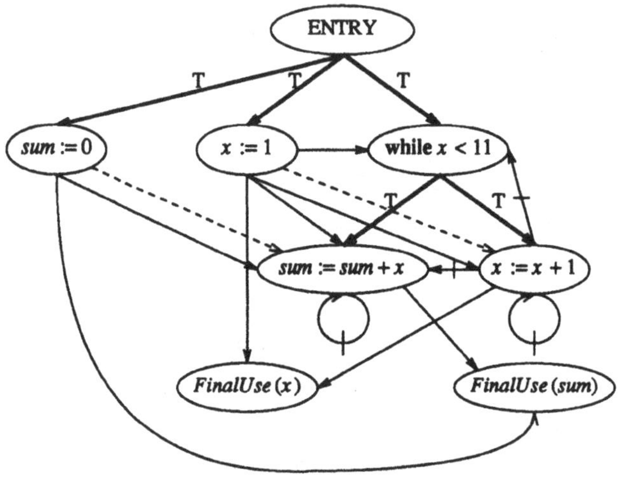

Figure 2. An example program, which sums the integers from 1 to 10 and leaves the result in the variable *sum*, and its program dependence graph. The boldface arrows represent control dependency edges, dashed arrows represent def-order dependency edges, solid arrows represent loop-independent flow dependency edges, and solid arrows with a hash mark represent loop-carried flow dependency edges.

Note that a program dependence graph is a multi-graph (*i.e.* it may have more than one edge of a given kind between two vertices). When there is more than one loop-carried flow dependency edge between two vertices, each is labeled by a different loop that carries the dependency. When there is more than one def-order edge between two vertices, each is labeled by a vertex that is flow-dependent on both the definition that occurs at the edge's source and the definition that occurs at the edge's target.

Example. Figure 2 shows an example program and its program dependence graph. The boldface arrows represent control dependency edges; dashed arrows represent def-order dependency edges; solid arrows represent loop-independent flow dependency edges; solid arrows with a hash mark represent loop-carried flow dependency edges.

The data-dependency edges of a program dependence graph (PDG) are computed using dataflow analysis. For the restricted language considered in this paper, the necessary computations can be defined in a syntax-directed manner (see [8]).

We shall assume that elements of PDG's are also labeled with some additional pieces of information. We assume that the editor used to modify programs provides a unique-naming capability so that statements and predicates are identified consistently in different versions. Each component that occurs in a program is an object whose identity is recorded by a unique identifier that is guaranteed to persist across different editing sessions and machines. It is these identifiers that are used to determine "identical" vertices when we perform operations on components from different PDG's (*e.g.* $V(G') \cap V(G)$).

3.2. Program Slices

For a vertex s of a PDG G, the *slice* of G with respect to s, written as G / s, is a graph containing all vertices on which s has a transitive flow or control dependence (*i.e.* all vertices that can reach s via flow or control edges): $V(G / s) = \{ w \mid w \in V(G) \wedge w \longrightarrow^{*}_{c,f} s \}$. We extend the definition to a set of vertices $S = \bigcup_i s_i$ as follows: $V(G / S) = V(G / (\bigcup_i s_i)) = \bigcup_i V(G / s_i)$. It is useful to define $V(G / v) = \varnothing$ for any $v \notin G$.

The edges in the graph G / S are essentially those in the subgraph of G induced by $V(G / S)$, with the exception that a def-order edge $v \longrightarrow_{do(u)} w$ is included only if G / S contains the vertex u that is directly flow dependent on the definitions at v and w. In terms of the three types of edges in a PDG we define

$$
\begin{aligned}
E(G/S) = \; & \{ (v \longrightarrow_f w) \mid (v \longrightarrow_f w) \in E(G) \wedge v, w \in V(G/S) \} \\
\cup & \{ (v \longrightarrow_c w) \mid (v \longrightarrow_c w) \in E(G) \wedge v, w \in V(G/S) \} \\
\cup & \{ (v \longrightarrow_{do(u)} w) \mid (v \longrightarrow_{do(u)} w) \in E(G) \wedge u, v, w \in V(G/S) \}
\end{aligned}
$$

3.3. Program Dependence Graphs and Program Semantics

The relationship between a program's PDG and the program's execution behavior has been addressed in [11] and [19]. The results from these papers are summarized below.

In [11] it is shown that if the program dependence graphs of two programs are isomorphic then the programs have the same behavior. The concept of "programs with the same behavior" is formalized as the concept of *strong equivalence*, defined as follows:

Definition. Two programs P and Q are *strongly equivalent* iff for any state σ, either P and Q both diverge when initiated on σ or they both halt with the same final values for all variables. If P and Q are not strongly equivalent, we say they are *inequivalent.*

The main result of [11] is the following theorem: (we use the symbol $\approx$ to denote isomorphism between program dependence graphs.)

THEOREM. (EQUIVALENCE THEOREM). *If P and Q are programs for which $G_P \approx G_Q$, then P and Q are strongly equivalent.*

Restated in the contrapositive the theorem reads: Inequivalent programs have non-isomorphic program dependence graphs.

We say that G is a *feasible* program dependence graph iff G is the program dependence graph of some program P. For any $S \subseteq V(G)$, if G is a feasible PDG, the slice G / S is also a feasible PDG; it corresponds to the program P' obtained by restricting the syntax tree of P to just the statements and predicates in $V(G / S)$ [19].

THEOREM. (FEASIBILITY OF PROGRAM SLICES). *For any program P, if G_S is a slice of G_P (with respect to some set of vertices), then G_S is a feasible PDG.*

The significance of a slice is that it captures a portion of a program's behavior. The programs P' and P, corresponding to the slice G / S and the graph G, respectively, compute the same final values for all variables x for which $FinalUse(x)$ is a vertex in S [19].

THEOREM. (SLICING THEOREM). *Let Q be a slice of program P with respect to a set of vertices. If σ is a state on which P halts, then for any state σ' that agrees with σ on all variables for which there are initial-definition vertices in G_Q: (1) Q halts on σ', (2) P and Q compute the same sequence of values at each program point of Q, and (3) the final states agree on all variables for which there are final-use vertices in G_Q.*

3.4. An Algorithm for Program Integration

An algorithm for integrating several related, but different variants of a base program (or determining that the variants incorporate interfering changes) has been presented in [10]. The algorithm presented there, called *Integrate*, takes as input three programs A, B, and $Base$, where A and B are two variants of $Base$. Whenever the changes made to $Base$ to create A and B do not "interfere" (in a certain well-defined sense), Integrate produces a program M that exhibits the changed behavior of A and B with respect to $Base$ as well as the behavior preserved in all three versions.

We now describe the steps of the integration algorithm. The first step determines slices that represent the changed behaviors of A and B and the behavior of $Base$ preserved in both A and B; the second step combines these slices to form the merged graph G_M; the third step tests G_M for interference. The integration algorithm is illustrated with an example on which the algorithm succeeds (*i.e.* the variants do not interfere).

Step 1: Determining changed and preserved behavior

If the slice of variant G_A at vertex v differs from the slice of G_{Base} at v, then G_A and G_{Base} may compute different values at v. In other words, vertex v is a site that potentially exhibits changed behavior in the two programs. Thus, we define the *affected points* of G_A with respect to G_{Base}, denoted by $D_{A,Base}$, to be the subset of vertices of G_A whose slices in G_{Base} and G_A differ $D_{A,Base} = \{ v \mid v \in V(G_A) \wedge (G_{Base} / v \neq G_A / v) \}$. We define $D_{B,Base}$ similarly. It follows that the slices $G_A / D_{A,Base}$ and $G_B / D_{B,Base}$ capture the respective behaviors of A and B that differ from *Base*.

Example. Figure 2 shows a program that sums the integers from 1 to 10 and its corresponding program dependence graph. We now consider two variants of this program: In variant A two statements have been added to the original program to compute the product of the integer sequence from 1 to 10; In variant B one statement has been added to compute the mean of the sequence. These two programs represent non-interfering extensions of the original summation program.

Variant *A*

```
program Main
  prod := 1;
  sum := 0;
  x := 1;
  while x < 11 do
    prod := prod * x;
    sum := sum + x;
    x := x + 1
  od
end(x, sum, prod)
```

Variant *B*

```
program Main
  sum := 0;
  x := 1;
  while x < 11 do
    sum := sum + x;
    x := x + 1
  od;
  mean := sum / 10
end(x, sum, mean)
```

The program dependence graphs for these two programs are shown in Figure 3.

The set $D_{A,Base}$ contains three vertices: the assignment vertices labeled "*prod* := 1" and "*prod* := *prod* * *x*" as well as the final-use vertex for *prod*. Similarly, $D_{B,Base}$ contains two vertices: the assignment vertex labeled "*mean* := *sum* / 10" and the final-use vertex for *mean*. Figure 4 shows the slices $G_A / D_{A,Base}$ and $G_B / D_{B,Base}$, which represent the changed behaviors of A and B, respectively.

The preserved behavior of *Base* in A corresponds to the slice $G_{Base} / \overline{D}_{A,Base}$, where $\overline{D}_{A,Base}$ is the complement of $D_{A,Base}$: $\overline{D}_{A,Base} = V(G_A) - D_{A,Base}$. We define $\overline{D}_{B,Base}$ similarly. Thus, the unchanged behavior common to both A and B is captured by the following slice: $G_{Base} / (\overline{D}_{A,Base} \cap \overline{D}_{B,Base})$.

Example. In our example, the slice $G_{Base} / (\overline{D}_{A,Base} \cap \overline{D}_{B,Base})$ consists of G_{Base} in its entirety. That is, the graph that represents the behavior of the original program that is preserved in both variant A and variant B is identical to the graph shown in Figure 2.

Step 2: Forming the merged graph

The merged program dependence graph, G_M, is formed by unioning the three slices that represent the changed and preserved behaviors of the two variants:

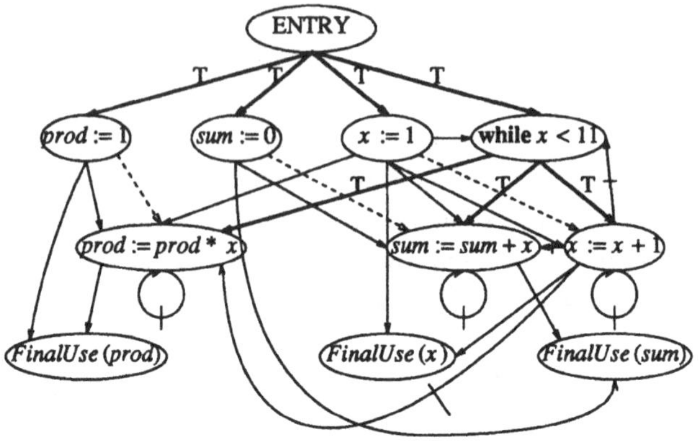

(a) The program dependence graph for variant *A*

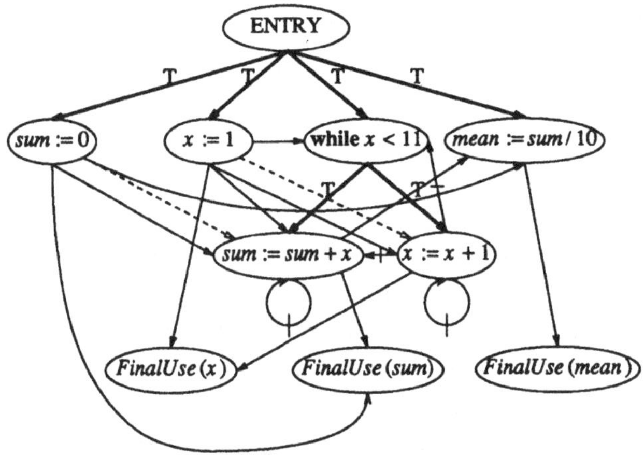

(b) The program dependence graph for variant *B*

Figure 3. The program dependence graphs for variants *A* and *B*.

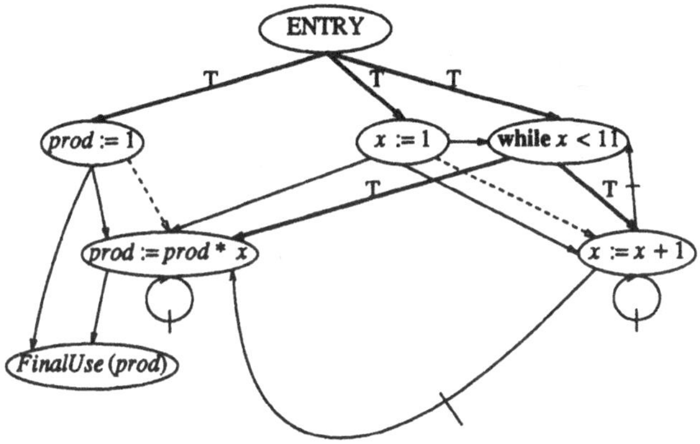

(a) The slice $G_A / D_{A,Base}$.

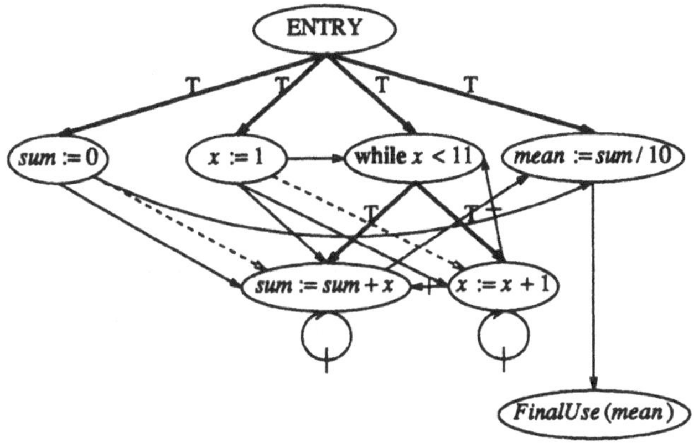

(b) The slice $G_B / D_{B,Base}$.

Figure 4. The slices that represent the changed behaviors of A and B.

$G_M = (G_A / D_{A,Base}) \cup (G_B / D_{B,Base}) \cup (G_{Base} / (\overline{D}_{A,Base} \cap \overline{D}_{B,Base}))$.

Example. The union of the slices from Figures 2 and 4 gives the program dependence graph G_M shown in Figure 5.

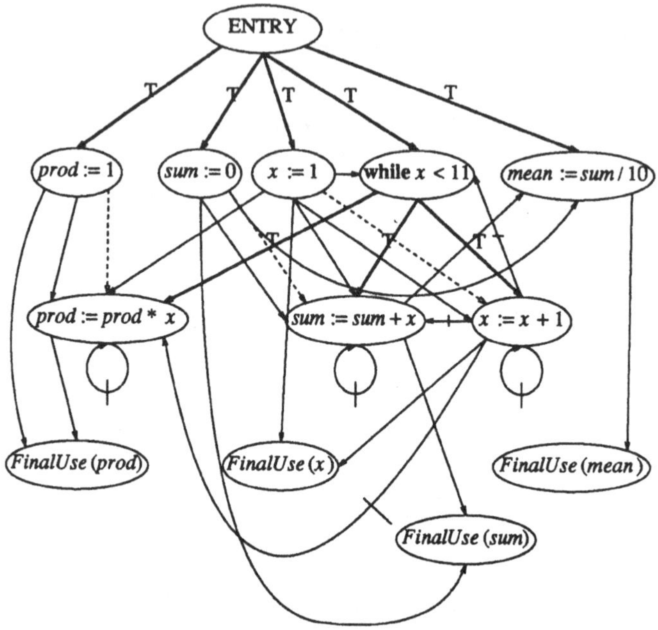

Figure 5. G_M is created by taking the union of the slices shown in Figures 2 and 4.

Step 3: Testing for interference

There are two possible ways by which the graph G_M may fail to represent a satisfactory integrated program; both types of failure are referred to as "interference." The first interference criterion is based on a comparison of slices of G_A, G_B, and G_M. The slices $G_A / D_{A,Base}$ and $G_B / D_{B,Base}$ represent the changed behaviors of programs A and B with respect to *Base*. A and B interfere if G_M does not preserve these slices; that is, there is *no* interference of this kind if $G_M / D_{A,Base} = G_A / D_{A,Base}$ and $G_M / D_{B,Base} = G_B / D_{B,Base}$.

Example. An inspection of the merged graph shown in Figure 5 reveals that there is no interference; the slices $G_M / D_{A,Base}$ and $G_M / D_{B,Base}$ are identical to the graphs that appear in Figures 4(a) and 4(b), respectively.

The final step of the integration method involves reconstituting a program from the merged program dependence graph. However, it is possible that there is no such program; that is, the merged graph may be an infeasible program dependence graph. This is the second kind of interference that may occur.

Because we are assuming a restricted set of control constructs, each vertex of G_M is immediately subordinate to at most one predicate vertex, *i.e.* the control dependencies of G_M define a tree T rooted at the entry vertex. The crux of the program-reconstitution problem is to determine, for each predicate vertex v (and for the entry vertex as well), an ordering on v's children in T. Once all vertices are ordered, T corresponds closely to an abstract-syntax tree.

Unfortunately, as we show in [8], the problem of determining whether it is possible to order a vertex's children is NP-complete. We have explored two approaches to dealing with this difficulty:

a) For graphs created by merging PDG's of actual programs, it is likely that problematic cases rarely arise. We have explored ways of reducing the search space, in the belief that a backtracking method for solving the remaining step can be made to behave satisfactorily.

b) It is possible to side-step completely the need to solve an NP-complete problem by performing a limited amount of variable renaming. This technique can be used to avoid any difficult ordering step that remains after applying the techniques outlined in approach a).

The reader is referred to [8] and [10] for more details about feasibility testing, as well as a description of a method to reconstruct a program from the merged program dependence graph.

If neither kind of interference occurs, one of the programs that corresponds to the graph G_M will be returned as the result of the integration operation.

Example. The program dependence graph shown in Figure 5 corresponds to the program:

```
program Main
  prod := 1;
  sum := 0;
  x := 1;
  while x < 11 do
    prod := prod * x;
    sum := sum + x;
    x := x + 1
  od;
  mean := sum / 10
end(x, sum, prod, mean)
```

Using the Slicing Theorem and the definition of the merged graph G_M, we can show the following theorem, which characterizes the execution behavior of the integrated program in terms of the behaviors of the base program and the two variants [19]:

THEOREM. (INTEGRATION THEOREM). *If A and B are two variants of Base for which integration succeeds (and produces program M), then for any initial state σ on which A, B, and*

Base all halt (1) M halts on σ, (2) if x is a variable on which the final states of A and Base agree, then the final state of M agrees with the final state of B on x, and (3) if y is a variable on which the final states of B and Base agree, then the final state of M agrees with the final state of A on y.

Restated less formally, M preserves the changed behaviors of both A and B (with respect to *Base*) as well as the unchanged behavior of all three.

4. WILL LANGUAGE-BASED PROGRAM INTEGRATION SCALE UP?

It remains to be seen how often integrations of real changes to programs of substantial size can be automatically accommodated by our integration technique. Due to fundamental limitations on determining information about programs via data-flow analysis and on testing equivalence of programs, both the procedure for determining the program elements that may exhibit changed behavior and the test for interference had to be made *safe* rather than *exact*. Consequently, the integration algorithm will report interference in some cases where no real conflict exists. The issue of whether fully automatic integration turns out to be a realistic proposition will only be resolved once we have built the components for creating program dependence graphs, slicing them, and testing the merged graph for interference.

In any case, some integrations will report interference. For these situations it is not enough merely to detect interference; one needs a tool for *semi-automatic, interactive integration* so that the user can guide the integration process to a successful completion. Through such a tool, it will be possible for the user to examine sites of potential conflicts, which may or may not represent actual conflicts. The tool will make use of the merged program dependence graph that is built by the integration algorithm; this graph is a product of interfering as well as non-interfering integrations.

In many respects the interactive integration tool will be similar to PTOOL, an interactive tool developed by Kennedy's group at Rice [3]. PTOOL makes use of a program dependence representation to provide programmers with diagnostic information about potential problems that arise in parallelization.

In a similar fashion, the integration tool we are building will display information about individual program elements and program slices that indicate potential integration conflicts. By highlighting collections of program elements, it will indicate such information as: the affected points in the two variant programs, the slices with respect to the affected points, and slices of the two variants that become "intertwined" in the merged graph. The tool will also provide capabilities for the user to resolve conflicts and create a satisfactory merged program.

A preliminary implementation of a program-integration tool has been embedded in a program editor created using the Synthesizer Generator [17, 18]. Data-flow analysis on programs is carried out according to the editor's defining attribute grammar and used to construct their program dependence graphs. A slice command added to the editor makes it possible to highlight the elements of program slices. An integration command invokes the integration algorithm on the program dependence graphs and reports whether the variant programs interfere.

We plan to experiment with ways of incorporating other integration facilities in this system. In particular, it may be desirable for users to be able to supply pragmas to the program-integration system. For instance, a user-supplied assertion that a change to a certain module in one variant does not affect its functionality (only its efficiency, for example) could be used to limit the scope of slicing and interference testing.

As to the practicality of our techniques, the basic techniques used in the integration algorithm (dependence analysis and slicing) are ones that have been applied successfully to programs of substantial size. Many of the techniques that are needed in order to adapt the integration algorithm to handle realistic languages (see below) have also been used in production-quality systems; these techniques include analysis of array index expressions to provide sharper information about actual dependencies among array references [2, 4, 22] and interprocedural data-flow analysis to determine "may-summary" information [5, 6].

4.1. Applicability to Realistic Languages

We have recently made progress towards extending the integration technique to handle languages with procedure calls and pointer-valued variables. The major stumbling block when making such extensions is devising a suitable extension of the program dependence representation. Our recent work in this direction is summarized below.

4.1.1. Interprocedural slicing using dependence graphs

As a first step toward extending our integration algorithm to handle languages with procedures, we have devised a multi-procedure dependence representation and have developed a new algorithm for interprocedural slicing that uses this representation [9]. The algorithm generates a slice of an entire system, where the slice may cross the boundaries of procedure calls. It is both simpler and more precise than the one previous algorithm given for interprocedural slicing [21].

The method described in [21] does not generate a precise slice because it fails to account for the calling context of a called procedure. The imprecision of the method can be illustrated using the following example:

```
program A              procedure B(y)        procedure C(z)
   x := 0;                y := y + 1             call B(z);
   w := 0;             return                    z := z + 1
   call B(x);                                 return
   call C(w);
end(w,x)
```

Using the algorithm from [21] to slice this system with respect to variable x at the end of program A, we obtain the following:

```
program A
    x := 0;
    w := 0;
    call B(x)
    call C(w);
end(x)

procedure B(y)
    y := y + 1
return

procedure C(z)
    call B(z);
return
```

However, further inspection shows that the value of x at the end of program A is not affected by the initialization of w in A, nor by the call on C in A, nor by procedure C. The reason these components are included in the slice is (roughly) the following: The statement "**call** $B(x)$" in program A causes the slice to "descend" into procedure B. When the slice reaches the beginning of B it "ascends" to *all* sites that call B, both the site in A at which it "descended" and the (irrelevant) site in C. Similarly, the slice in C ascends to the call site in A.

By contrast, our algorithm for interprocedural slicing correctly accounts for the calling context of a called procedure; on the example given above, procedure C is left out of the slice. A key element of this algorithm is an auxiliary structure that represents calling and parameter-linkage relationships. This structure, called the *linkage grammar*, takes the form of an attribute grammar. The context free part of the linkage grammar models the system's procedure-call structure; it includes one nonterminal and one production for each procedure in the system. If procedure P contains no calls, the right-hand side of the production for P is ε; otherwise, there is one right-hand side nonterminal for each call site in P. The attributes in the linkage grammar represent the parameters, globals, and return values that are transferred across procedure boundaries. Attribute dependencies, expressed via the attribute equations of the linkage-grammar's productions are used to model intraprocedural dependencies among these elements.

Transitive dependencies between attributes due to procedure calls are then determined using a standard attribute-grammar construction: the computation of the nonterminals' *subordinate characteristic graphs*. These dependencies are the key to the slicing algorithm; they permit the algorithm to "come back up" from a procedure call (*e.g.* from procedure B in the above example) without first descending to slice the procedure (it is placed on a queue of procedures to be sliced later). This strategy prevents the algorithm from ever ascending to an irrelevant call site.

4.1.2. Dependence analysis for pointer variables

We have devised a method for determining data dependencies between program statements for programming languages that have pointer-valued variables (*e.g.* Lisp and Pascal). The method determines data dependencies that reflect the usage of heap-allocated storage in such languages, which permits us to build (and slice) program dependence graphs for programs written in such languages. The method accounts for destructive updates to fields of a structure and thus is *not* limited to simple cases where all structures are trees or acyclic graphs; the method is applicable to programs that build up structures that contain cycles.

For scalar variables, one way to compute *flow dependencies* is in the form of *use-definition chains*. To do this one first computes a more general piece of information: the set of *reaching definitions* for each program point [1, 14]. A definition of variable x at some program point p *reaches* point q if there is an execution path from p to q such that no other definition of x appears on the path. The set of reaching definitions for a program point q is the set of program points that generate definitions that reach q. Program point q is *flow dependent* on all members of the reaching-definition set that define variables used at q.

To extend the concept of flow dependence for languages that manipulate heap-allocated storage, it is necessary to rephrase the definition in terms of *memory locations* rather than *variables*.

> Program point q is flow dependent on point p if p writes to a memory location that may be read by q.

Unlike the situation that exists for programs with (only) scalar variables, where there is a fixed "layout" of memory, for programs that manipulate heap-allocated storage not all accessible memory locations are named by program variables. In the latter situation new memory locations are allocated dynamically in the form of cells taken from the heap.

To compute data dependencies between constructs that manipulate and access heap-allocated storage, our starting point is the method described in [13], which, for each program point q, determines a set of structures that approximate the different "layouts" of memory that can possibly arise at q during execution. We extend the domain employed in the Jones-Muchnick abstract interpretation so that the (abstract) memory locations are labeled by the program points that set their contents. Flow dependencies are then determined from these memory layouts according to the component labels found along the access paths that must be traversed to evaluate the program's statements and predicates during execution.

ACKNOWLEDGEMENTS

Several others have participated in the development of the ideas described above. We are indebted to J. Prins for many pleasurable discussions and for his contributions to the development of the program-integration algorithm. Subsequent work to extend the integration algorithm's range of applicability has been carried out in collaboration with D. Binkley, P. Pfeiffer, and W. Yang.

REFERENCES

1. Aho, A.V., Sethi, R., and Ullman, J.D., *Compilers: Principles, Techniques, and Tools*, Addison-Wesley, Reading, MA (1986).
2. Allen, J.R., "Dependence analysis for subscripted variables and its application to program transformations," Ph.D. dissertation, Dept. of Math. Sciences, Rice Univ., Houston, TX (April 1983).
3. Allen, R., Baumgartner, D., Kennedy, K., and Porterfield, A., "PTOOL: A semi-automatic parallel programming assistant," Tech Rep. COMP TR86-31, Dept. of Computer Science, Rice Univ., Houston, TX (January 1986).
4. Bannerjee, U., "Speedup of ordinary programs," Ph.D. dissertation and Tech. Rep. R-79-989, Dept. of Computer Science, University of Illinois, Urbana, IL (October 1979).

5. Banning, J.P., "An efficient way to find the side effects of procedure calls and the aliases of variables," pp. 29-41 in *Conference Record of the Sixth ACM Symposium on Principles of Programming Languages,* (San Antonio, TX, Jan. 29-31, 1979), ACM, New York (1979).

6. Cooper, K.D. and Kennedy, K., "Interprocedural side-effect analysis in linear time," Tech. Rep. COMP TR87-62, Dept. of Computer Science, Rice Univ., Houston, TX (October 1987).

7. Ferrante, J., Ottenstein, K., and Warren, J., "The program dependence graph and its use in optimization," *ACM Transactions on Programming Languages and Systems* **9**(3) pp. 319-349 (July 1987).

8. Horwitz, S., Prins, J., and Reps, T., "Integrating non-interfering versions of programs," TR-690, Computer Sciences Department, University of Wisconsin, Madison, WI (March 1987).

9. Horwitz, S., Reps, T., and Binkley, D., "Interprocedural slicing using dependence graphs," Extended abstract, Computer Sciences Department, University of Wisconsin, Madison, WI (November 1987).

10. Horwitz, S., Prins, J., and Reps, T., "Integrating non-interfering versions of programs," in *Conference Record of the Fifteenth ACM Symposium on Principles of Programming Languages,* (San Diego, CA, January 13-15, 1988), ACM, New York (1988).

11. Horwitz, S., Prins, J., and Reps, T., "On the adequacy of program dependence graphs for representing programs," in *Conference Record of the Fifteenth ACM Symposium on Principles of Programming Languages,* (San Diego, CA, January 13-15, 1988), ACM, New York (1988).

12. Horwitz, S., Prins, J., and Reps, T., "Support for integrating program variants in an environment for programming in the large," in *Proceedings of the International Workshop on Software Version and Configuration Control 88,* (Grassau, W. Germany, Jan. 28-29, 1988), (1988).

13. Jones, N.D. and Muchnick, S.S., "Flow analysis and optimization of Lisp-like structures," in *Program Flow Analysis: Theory and Applications,* ed. S.S. Muchnick and N.D. Jones,Prentice-Hall, Englewood Cliffs, NJ (1981).

14. Kennedy, K., "A survey of data flow analysis techniques," in *Program Flow Analysis: Theory and Applications,* ed. S.S. Muchnick and N.D. Jones,Prentice-Hall, Englewood Cliffs, NJ (1981).

15. Kuck, D.J., Muraoka, Y., and Chen, S.C., "On the number of operations simultaneously executable in FORTRAN-like programs and their resulting speed-up," *IEEE Trans. on Computers* **C-21**(12) pp. 1293-1310 (December 1972).

16. Kuck, D.J., Kuhn, R.H., Leasure, B., Padua, D.A., and Wolfe, M., "Dependence graphs and compiler optimizations," pp. 207-218 in *Conference Record of the Eighth ACM Symposium on Principles of Programming Languages,* (Williamsburg, VA, January 26-28, 1981), ACM, New York (1981).

17. Reps, T. and Teitelbaum, T., "The Synthesizer Generator," *Proceedings of the ACM SIGSOFT/SIGPLAN Software Engineering Symposium on Practical Software Development Environments,* (Pittsburgh, PA, Apr. 23-25, 1984), *ACM SIGPLAN Notices* **19**(5) pp. 42-48 (May 1984).

18. Reps, T. and Teitelbaum, T., *The Synthesizer Generator: Reference Manual,* Dept. of Computer Science, Cornell Univ., Ithaca, NY (August 1985, Second Edition: July 1987).

19. Reps, T. and Yang, W., "The semantics of program slicing," Tech. Rep. in preparation, Computer Sciences Department, University of Wisconsin, Madison, WI ().

20. Tichy, W.F., "RCS: A system for version control," *Software – Practice & Experience* **15**(7) pp. 637-654 (July 1985).

21. Weiser, M., "Program slicing," *IEEE Transactions on Software Engineering* **SE-10**(4) pp. 352-357 (July 1984).

22. Wolfe, M.J., "Optimizing supercompilers for supercomputers," Ph.D. dissertation and Tech. Rep. R-82-1105, Dept. of Computer Science, University of Illinois, Urbana, IL (October 1982).

A semantics driven temporal verification system

G. D. Gough and H. Barringer*
Department of Computer Science
University of Manchester
Oxford Road
Manchester, M13 9PL

Abstract

We present an overview of SMG, a *generic* state machine generator, which interfaces to various temporal logic model checkers and provides a practical generic temporal verification system. SMG transforms programs written in user-definable languages to suitable finite state models. thus enabling fast verification of temporal properties of the input program. It can be applied, in particular, to the verification of temporal properties of concurrent and reactive systems.

1 Introduction

Over the past decade, it has been widely acknowledged that temporal logics can form a suitable basis for formal techniques for the analysis, specification and development of systems. In particular, temporal logics lend themselves well to the specification of both *safety* and *liveness* properties of concurrent computing systems. We refer the reader to [Pnu77,OL82,Lam83b,MP82] for extensive examples. More recently, compositional specification techniques based on temporal logics have been developed, for example [Lam83a,BKP84,Lam84,Bar87]; these techniques enable hierarchic (top-down) system development in the temporal framework.

To encourage the widespread use of such formally based development approaches, it is most important that support tools are available (cf. the requirement of interpreters, compilers, debuggers, source-code control systems, etc. for programming languages). Such tools range from the more mundane lexical and syntactic tools, e.g. syntax analysers, pretty printers and even proof checkers, through general book-keeping tools (at various levels), to semantic analysis tools, e.g. type checkers, interpreters, transformers and theorem provers. Not surprisingly, there are strong beliefs that formal development will only be widely adopted when practicable proof assistants and theorem provers exist to support the dischargement of proof obligations (because formal proof by hand is too tedious, time consuming and error prone for the average non-logician). It seems, therefore, crucial that mechanised verification support is investigated and developed for the logics underlying any potential/putative formal approach to system development. To this end, the TEMPLE project has been investigating the mechanisation of temporal logics. Indeed, in the report [BG87], we present a survey of different techniques for "mechanising" various forms of temporal logic; these range through decision procedures, model checkers, resolution-based theorem proving, direct execution and program synthesis.

In this article, we outline a *generic* system for the verification of temporal properties of finite state programming languages that we have developed at Manchester. The system couples the verification paradigm based on model checking [CES86] of finite state programs, with language presentation via formal semantic description such as Structural Operational Semantics [Plo81]. We have structured our

*Research supported under Alvey/SERC grant GR/D/57492

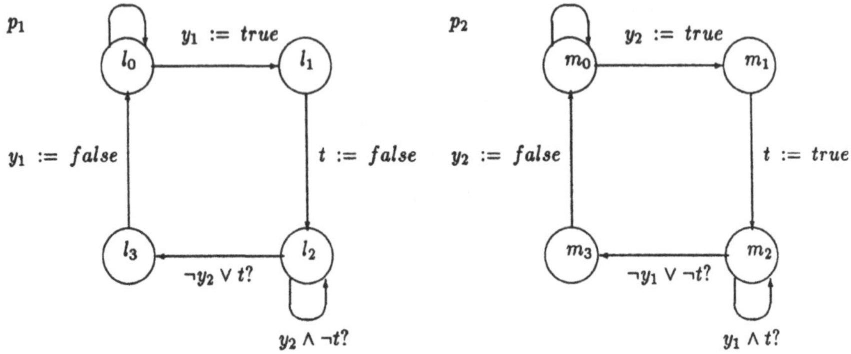

Figure 1: Mutual Exclusion Algorithm

presentation as follows. Section 2 reviews two approaches to temporal verification of programs; it highlights the impracticability of using decision procedures and the apparent viability of model checking. Section 3 provides a overview of the architecture of our verification system, in particular, it is concerned with the generic aspects of the model (or state machine) generator, SMG. Finally in section 4 we discuss the application domain for our prototype verification system, its current limitations and the future directions in which the work is proceeding.

2 Mechanised temporal verification

Given a program $\mathcal{P}$ in a finite state language $\mathcal{L}$ (see section 3.1.1) with given operational semantics, one approach to the problem of verifying its temporal behaviour, i.e. deciding whether its execution behaviour satisfies a given temporal formula ϕ, is to work entirely within the temporal framework. This means giving a temporal semantics for $\mathcal{L}$, equivalent to the operational semantics; the meaning of $\mathcal{P}$ is then a temporal formula ψ and the verification problem is then reduced to proving the validity of the formula $\psi \Rightarrow \phi$. The proof of this, usually lengthy, formula can either be tackled by hand or, if the logic used is a propositional linear time logic, can be proved mechanically by use of a decision procedure such as those of [Gou84]. Typically, a temporal logic decision procedure will validate a formula by attempting to create a model for the negation of the given formula; if a model does not exist then the formula is valid. Because of the complexities involved, this approach is not always viable.

An alternative approach of much lower complexity is to use the operational semantics to build a finite state model of the program and then use a model checker to test the truth of ϕ on the model. This approach has been used with some success in a branching time logic framework [BCDM84,CES86,BC86,Bro86].

2.1 Verification Example

We exemplify the two approaches outlined above, and justify our choice of direction, with the verification of the exclusion property of a simple mutual exclusion algorithm [Pet81,Pnu84]. Figure 1 below presents the algorithm as two concurrent finite state machines. The states labelled l_0 and m_0 are the initial states and the states l_3 and m_3 are the critical regions. Each process p_i has a variable y_i used to signal its desire to enter its critical section. The processes "share" a variable t used to arbitrate in situations of conflict.

2.1.1 Using a Decision procedure

The semantics is given in terms of a propositional, discrete linear time, temporal logic. The logic consists of a set of propositions, the standard propositional connectives and the temporal operators $\Box$, $\Diamond$ and $\bigcirc$. The intuitive interpretation of these operators is that, if ϕ is a formula, then

- $\Box\phi$ is true if ϕ is true *always* in the future (including the current moment).
- $\Diamond\phi$ is true if ϕ is true *sometime* in the future (or at the current moment).
- $\bigcirc\phi$ is true if ϕ is true at the *next* moment in the future.

The semantics of the parallel composition of the concurrent state machines p_1 and p_2 of Figure 1 is encoded as follows.

- The form of the formula describing the semantics is

$$\begin{array}{l}(\text{Initial conditions})\wedge\\ \Box((w \Rightarrow (\text{Disjunction of } p_1 \text{ transitions}))\wedge\\ \quad(\neg w \Rightarrow (\text{Disjunction of } p_2 \text{ transitions}))\wedge\\ \quad\Diamond w \wedge \Diamond\neg w)\end{array}$$

  The auxiliary proposition w is used to determine which process makes a step, so that when w is true p_1 makes a step and when $\neg w$, p_2. The final clause, $\Diamond w \wedge \Diamond\neg w$, ensures that each process takes a step infinitely often, i.e. we have a *weakly fair* parallel composition.

- Each transition is described by a formula of the form

$$\text{Old location } \wedge \bigcirc(\text{New location}) \wedge \text{State change}$$

  The locations l_0, l_1, l_2 and l_3 are encoded using auxiliary propositions c_1 and c_2 as below.

$$\begin{array}{ll} l_0 \Leftrightarrow \neg c_1 \wedge \neg c_2 & l_1 \Leftrightarrow c_1 \wedge \neg c_2\\ l_2 \Leftrightarrow \neg c_1 \wedge c_2 & l_3 \Leftrightarrow c_1 \wedge c_2\end{array}$$

  The locations of the second process, i.e. m_0, m_1, m_2 and m_3, are similarly encoded using propositions d_1 and d_2.
  Thus, for example, the p_1 transition from l_1 to l_2 is described by the formula

$$((c_1 \wedge \neg c_2) \wedge \bigcirc(\neg c_1 \wedge c_2) \wedge \bigcirc\neg t \wedge (y_1 \Leftrightarrow \bigcirc y_1))$$

We now express the desired properties of the algorithm, in this case the mutual exclusion property, as a formula in the same logic. Thus, we wish to encode "Always not (in l_3 and in m_3)", which in terms of the auxiliary control propositions is

$$\Box\neg(c_1 \wedge c_2 \wedge d_1 \wedge d_2)$$

Hence the formula for validation is that presented in Figure 2. Establishing the validity of this formula (which has 159 subformulae) with our decision procedure executing on a Sun 3/50 took about 2 minutes. Our original temporal logic encoding for this example was a slightly less obvious one, in an attempt to reduce the size of the formula to be proved; this "clever" encoding did in fact result in a slightly smaller formula (145 subformulae), but unfortunately took over 20 minutes to prove!

The above example shows quite clearly the intractability of this use of decision procedures in full-scale program verification.

$(t \wedge \neg y_1 \wedge \neg y_2 \wedge \neg c_1 \wedge \neg c_2 \wedge \neg d_1 \wedge \neg d_2) \wedge$
$\Box((w \Rightarrow ((d_1 \Leftrightarrow \bigcirc d_1) \wedge (d_2 \Leftrightarrow \bigcirc d_2) \wedge (y_2 \Leftrightarrow \bigcirc y_2) \wedge$
$\qquad (((\neg c_1 \wedge \neg c_2) \wedge \bigcirc(\neg c_1 \wedge \neg c_2) \wedge (y_1 \Leftrightarrow \bigcirc y_1) \wedge (t \Leftrightarrow \bigcirc t)) \vee$
$\qquad ((\neg c_1 \wedge \neg c_2) \wedge \bigcirc(c_1 \wedge \neg c_2) \wedge \bigcirc y_1 \wedge (t \Leftrightarrow \bigcirc t)) \vee$
$\qquad ((c_1 \wedge \neg c_2) \wedge \bigcirc(\neg c_1 \wedge c_2) \wedge \bigcirc \neg t \wedge (y_1 \Leftrightarrow \bigcirc y_1)) \vee$
$\qquad ((\neg c_1 \wedge c_2) \wedge \bigcirc(\neg c_1 \wedge c_2) \wedge (y_2 \wedge \neg t) \wedge (y_1 \Leftrightarrow \bigcirc y_1) \wedge (t \Leftrightarrow \bigcirc t)) \vee$
$\qquad ((\neg c_1 \wedge c_2) \wedge \bigcirc(c_1 \wedge c_2) \wedge (\neg y_2 \vee t) \wedge (y_1 \Leftrightarrow \bigcirc y_1) \wedge (t \Leftrightarrow \bigcirc t)) \vee$
$\qquad ((c_1 \wedge c_2) \wedge \bigcirc(\neg c_1 \wedge \neg c_2) \wedge \bigcirc \neg y_1 \wedge (t \Leftrightarrow \bigcirc t)))))$
$\wedge$
$(\neg w \Rightarrow ((c_1 \Leftrightarrow \bigcirc c_1) \wedge (c_2 \Leftrightarrow \bigcirc c_2) \wedge (y_1 \Leftrightarrow \bigcirc y_1) \wedge$
$\qquad (((\neg d_1 \wedge \neg d_2) \wedge \bigcirc(\neg d_1 \wedge \neg d_2) \wedge (y_2 \Leftrightarrow \bigcirc y_2) \wedge (t \Leftrightarrow \bigcirc t)) \vee$
$\qquad ((\neg d_1 \wedge \neg d_2) \wedge \bigcirc(d_1 \wedge \neg d_2) \wedge \bigcirc y_2 \wedge (t \Leftrightarrow \bigcirc t)) \vee$
$\qquad ((d_1 \wedge \neg d_2) \wedge \bigcirc(\neg d_1 \wedge d_2) \wedge \bigcirc t \wedge (y_2 \Leftrightarrow \bigcirc y_2)) \vee$
$\qquad ((\neg d_1 \wedge d_2) \wedge \bigcirc(\neg d_1 \wedge d_2) \wedge (y_1 \wedge t) \wedge (y_2 \Leftrightarrow \bigcirc y_2) \wedge (t \Leftrightarrow \bigcirc t)) \vee$
$\qquad ((\neg d_1 \wedge d_2) \wedge \bigcirc(d_1 \wedge d_2) \wedge (\neg y_1 \vee \neg t) \wedge (y_2 \Leftrightarrow \bigcirc y_2) \wedge (t \Leftrightarrow \bigcirc t)) \vee$
$\qquad ((d_1 \wedge d_2) \wedge \bigcirc(\neg d_1 \wedge \neg d_2) \wedge \bigcirc \neg y_2 \wedge (t \Leftrightarrow \bigcirc t)))))$
$\wedge$
$\Diamond w \wedge \Diamond \neg w))$

$\Rightarrow \Box \neg(c_1 \wedge c_2 \wedge d_1 \wedge d_2)$

Figure 2: Mutual Exclusion Verification Obligation

procedure $p_1()$
$\qquad$ [**true** $\rightarrow y_1 :=$ **true**; $t :=$ **false**; $p_{11}()$ $\Box$ **true** $\rightarrow p_1()$].
procedure $p_{11}()$
$\qquad$ [$\neg y_2 \vee t \rightarrow p_{12}()$ $\Box$ $y_2 \wedge \neg t \rightarrow p_{11}()$].
procedure $p_{12}()$
$\qquad crit_1 :=$ **true**; $crit_1 :=$ **false**; $y_1 :=$ **false**; $p_1()$.

procedure $p_2()$
$\qquad$ [**true** $\rightarrow y_2 :=$ **true**; $t :=$ **true**; $p_{21}()$ $\Box$ **true** $\rightarrow p_2()$].
procedure $p_{21}()$
$\qquad$ [$\neg y_1 \vee \neg t \rightarrow p_{22}()$ $\Box$ $y_1 \wedge t \rightarrow p_{21}()$].
procedure $p_{22}()$
$\qquad crit_2 :=$ **true**; $crit_2 :=$ **false**; $y_2 :=$ **false**; $p_2()$.

program
$\qquad y_1 :=$ **false**; $y_2 :=$ **false**; $t :=$ **true**;
$\qquad crit_1 :=$ **false**; $crit_2 :=$ **false**;
$\qquad p_1() \parallel p_2()$.

Figure 3: SMG program for Peterson Algorithm

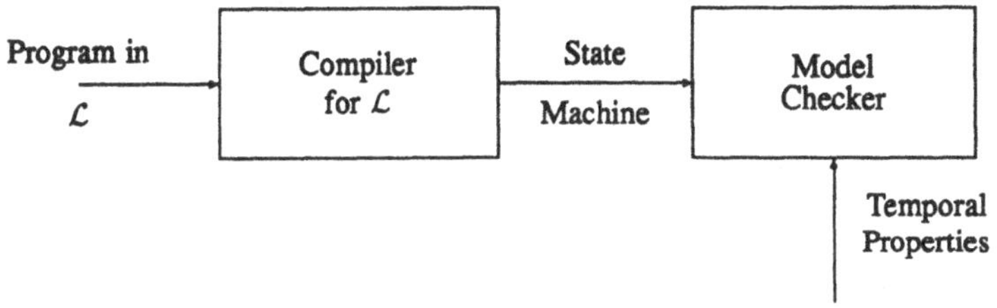

Figure 4: Architecture of Model Checking approach.

2.1.2 Using a Model checker

The alternative approach is to describe the algorithm in a high level language (see section 3.2) as shown in Figure 3. In this program, the variables $crit_1$ and $crit_2$ are used to flag the entry and exit from the critical sections; the variables y_1, y_2 and t are as above. This program is then compiled into a state machine with 32 states and we can verify that the program has the required mutual exclusion property using a temporal logic model checker. One such is `mcb` [Bro86], a model checker for *computation tree logic* (CTL), a branching time temporal logic. In CTL the mutual exclusion property is given by the formula $AG(\neg(crit_1 \wedge crit_2))$. The CTL operator AG is analogous to the linear time operator $\Box$, and the formula $AG\phi$ is true if and only if for every path, at every node on that path ϕ is true. The compilation time, again on a Sun 3/50, was less than 5 seconds and the mutual exclusion property for the resulting state machine was established in considerably less than 1 second. We have also checked the linear time form of the mutual exclusion property, i.e. $\Box\neg(crit_1 \wedge crit_2)$, using a model checker for linear time temporal logic; again the time taken for the verification was less than 1 second. Of course, once the state machine is generated we are able to use the model checker to test other temporal properties without recompilation, whereas the decision procedure approach would entail proving each property entirely separately, a substantial task in each case.

3 Verification System Architecture

We agree with the conclusions of [BC86,BCDM84,CES86] that the use of model checkers provides an attractive and tractable approach to automatic verification of temporal properties. This then leads to the basic architecture of figure 4. Indeed, this is the basic architecture underlying the verification system of Clarke et al. and the system CESAR (and later XESAR) of Sifakis et al. [QS82]. In both cases, a specific high-level programming language, SML [BC86] and CESAR respectively, have been devised for describing finite state systems. The compiler for SML (`ltd`) produces a state machine as output; this then serves as input not only to `mcb` but also to various VLSI design tools. It is possible, of course, to interface model checkers for different temporal logics to the compiler. Properties of CESAR programs are also verified by use of a model checker for a branching time temporal logic.

The formal semantics for SML is presented in terms of *conditional rewrite rules* in the style of S.O.S. [Plo81]. In our system, rather than produce specific compilers for various languages, we use such a semantics directly to drive a *generic* state machine generator. This means that the system can operate on programs written in a language for which the user can supply both the parser and semantics.

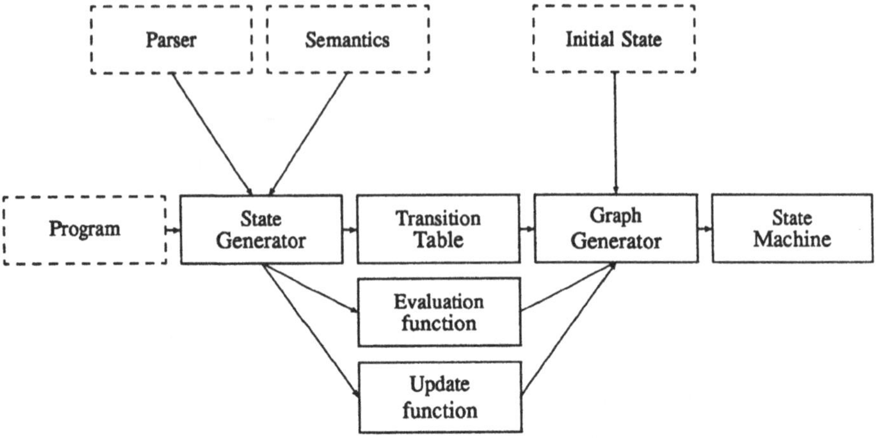

Figure 5: SMG architecture

3.1 State Machine Generator: SMG

Figure 5 outlines the basic structure of the state machine generator (compiler).

SMG takes as input a parser and operational rewrite rule semantics for the user's language $\mathcal{L}$, together with a program in $\mathcal{L}$ and an initial state assignment for the program variables. It then constructs a *transition table* for the program $\mathcal{P}$ by instantiating, for the parse tree of $\mathcal{P}$ the transition rules given in the semantics. Using the given initial states of $\mathcal{P}$, together with evaluation and state update functions obtained from the rewrite rule semantics, a *state transition graph* is then generated for $\mathcal{P}$. An illustration of this process is given in section 3.2.3.

The semantics is given, in S.O.S. style, as a set of labelled transition rules of the form

$$S_1 \xrightarrow{ec,\ sm,\ em} S_2$$

and inference rules of the form

$$\frac{R_1 \ldots R_n}{R}$$

where S_1,S_2 are program phrases, ec is a boolean expression defining the enabling condition for the transition, sm is the state modification effected by the transition, em the environment modification and R, $R_1 \ldots R_n$ are transition rules.

The parser input in the current system is given via a `yacc` grammar [Joh79].

The output format of the state transition graph can be chosen as appropriate for the model checker to be used, in particular for `mcb` or a linear time temporal logic model checker.

3.1.1 Input Language Restriction

Clearly, we can only build state transition graphs for finite state programs, i.e. programs that will only use, during their finite or infinite execution, a finite state space. Typically we refer to those languages, whose programs are always finite state, as finite state languages (e.g. as we did in section 2). In this first prototype of SMG we make no checks on finiteness of input language and assume that all variables are global, and all procedures use a call by name mechanism for parameter substitution.

3.2 An example language for SMG

The Peterson algorithm given in Fig. 3 was written in a language generated for small demonstrations of the SMG system. It consists of Boolean variables and expressions, assignment, guarded commands, sequential composition, parallel composition and tail-recursive procedures; its syntax and semantics are given below.

3.2.1 Language Syntax

We describe the syntax (omitting the syntax of expressions) using a BNF-like notation. Assuming the syntactic classes *Var*, *Expression* and *Name* for the obvious entities, we have

$$\begin{array}{lcl}
\mathit{Prog} & ::= & \mathit{Decl\text{-}list}\ \mathit{Body} \\
\mathit{Decl\text{-}list} & ::= & \mathit{Decl} \mid \mathit{Decl}\ \mathit{Decl\text{-}list} \\
\mathit{Decl} & ::= & \mathbf{procedure}\ \mathit{Name}\ (\mathit{Var\text{-}list})\ \mathit{Statement}. \\
\mathit{Var\text{-}list} & ::= & \quad \mid \mathit{NVar\text{-}list} \\
\mathit{NVar\text{-}list} & ::= & \mathit{Var} \mid \mathit{Var}, \mathit{NVar\text{-}list} \\
\mathit{Body} & ::= & \mathbf{program}\ \mathit{Statement}. \\
\mathit{Statement} & ::= & \mathit{Var} := \mathit{Expression}\ ;\ \mathit{Statement} \mid \\
 & & [\mathit{Choice}] \mid \mathit{Call} \mid \mathit{Parallel} \\
\mathit{Choice} & ::= & \mathit{Expression} \rightarrow \mathit{Statement} \mid \\
 & & \mathit{Expression} \rightarrow \mathit{Statement}\ \Box\ \mathit{Choice} \\
\mathit{Call} & ::= & \mathit{Name}(\mathit{Var\text{-}list}) \\
\mathit{Parallel} & ::= & \mathit{Call} \parallel \mathit{Call}
\end{array}$$

Note that this is not the current form of parser input, as mentioned above, SMG currently requires the user to define or modify a Yacc based parser. However it is intended to interface a parser-generator to SMG that will accept such BNF-like input.

3.2.2 Language Semantics

The dynamic semantics intended for the language's use in Fig. 3, is given below in the SOS style described in section 3.1. We assume

$$S, S_i \in \mathit{Statement}, x \in \mathit{Var}, \overline{x} \in \mathit{Var\text{-}list}$$
$$e, e_i \in \mathit{Expression} \text{ and } p \in \mathit{Name}$$

For clarity of exposition, we omit the environment component.

$$\mathbf{program}\ S. \xrightarrow{\mathbf{true},\ [\,]} S$$

$$x := e; S \xrightarrow{\mathbf{true},\ [x/e]} S$$

$$[\Box\ e_i \rightarrow S_i] \xrightarrow{e_i,\ [\,]} S_i$$

$$[\Box\ e_i \rightarrow S_i] \xrightarrow{\bigwedge \neg e_i,\ [\,]} [\Box\ e_i \rightarrow S_i]$$

$$p(\overline{x}) \xrightarrow{\mathbf{true},\ [\,]} \mathcal{E}(p)(\overline{x})$$

(where $\mathcal{E}(p)$ is the body of p in the current environment) and the inference rules

$$\frac{S_1 \xrightarrow{ec,\ sm} S_1'}{S_1 \parallel S_2 \xrightarrow{ec,\ sm} S_1' \parallel S_2}$$

$$\frac{S_1 \xrightarrow{ec,\ sm} S_1'}{S_2 \parallel S_1 \xrightarrow{ec,\ sm} S_2 \parallel S_1'}$$

These rules are fairly self explanatory, however, we briefly explain the assignment and guarded choice rules.

- If a program remaining to be executed is of the form $x := e; S$ then, since the enabling condition of the matching rule is **true**, it can *unconditionally* rewrite to the program S, using the state modification $[x/e]$ to update the global state by overwriting the current value of x by that of e.
- A guarded choice may nondeterministically rewrite to any of its choices whose guarding condition is open, i.e. true. Thus, in the graph construction, the node corresponding to the guarded choice construct in this state may have several outgoing edges, each corresponding to an open choice. If none of the guarding conditions evaluate to true, then the statement rewrites to itself; a blocked process thus appears to be idling. Alternative semantics for guarded choice are given in section 3.2.4 below.

The current version of SMG has a built in evaluation mechanism for handling Boolean expressions.This may appear to be a limitation on the user's ability to alter the input language semantics. However, although it is possible to present the semantics of Boolean expression evaluation within the SOS framework, the state explosion that would occur seems an unnecessary price to pay for such a common semantic entity. This strategy of mixed compilation and interpretation will be extended for handling other common semantic entities, however the user will be given some ability to modify or override the built in mechanisms.

3.2.3 State machine generation

To illustrate the operation of SMG, consider the program fragment

$$t := \textbf{false}; p_{11}()$$

of the example program of Fig. 3. Matching this fragment with the semantic rewrite rules given above results in the transition rules

$$
\begin{array}{llcl}
1) & t := \textbf{false}; p_{11}() & \xrightarrow{\textbf{true},\ [t/\textbf{false}]} & p_{11}() \\
2) & p_{11}() & \xrightarrow{\textbf{true},\ [\,]} & [\neg y_2 \vee t \to p_{12}() \ \square \ y_2 \wedge \neg t \to p_{11}()] \\
3) & [\neg y_2 \vee t \to p_{12}() \ \square \ y_2 \wedge \neg t \to p_{11}()] & \xrightarrow{\neg y_2 \vee t,\ [\,]} & p_{12}() \\
4) & [\neg y_2 \vee t \to p_{12}() \ \square \ y_2 \wedge \neg t \to p_{11}()] & \xrightarrow{y_2 \wedge \neg t,\ [\,]} & p_{11}() \\
5) & [\neg y_2 \vee t \to p_{12}() \ \square \ y_2 \wedge \neg t \to p_{11}()] & \xrightarrow{\neg(\neg y_2 \vee t) \wedge \neg(y_2 \wedge \neg t),\ [\,]} & [\neg y_2 \vee t \to p_{12}() \ \square \ y_2 \wedge \neg t \to p_{11}()]
\end{array}
$$

The procedure calls $p_{11}()$ occurring in rules 1 and 4 are replaced by the procedure body as given by rule 2, similarly for the call to $p_{12}()$. The final rule is of course never actually used, since its transition condition is always false; such redundant rules can be detected by use of a propositional calculus decision procedure and eliminated. This gives the following rules which are installed in the *transition table* mentioned in section 3.

$$\begin{array}{lrcl} 1) & t := \textbf{false}; p_{11}() & \xrightarrow{\textbf{true},\ [t/\textbf{false}]} & [\neg y_2 \vee t \rightarrow p_{12}()\ \Box\ y_2 \wedge \neg t \rightarrow p_{11}()] \\ 2) & [\neg y_2 \vee t \rightarrow p_{12}()\ \Box\ y_2 \wedge \neg t \rightarrow p_{11}()] & \xrightarrow{\neg y_2 \vee t,\ [\,]} & \text{Body of } p_{12}() \\ 3) & [\neg y_2 \vee t \rightarrow p_{12}()\ \Box\ y_2 \wedge \neg t \rightarrow p_{11}()] & \xrightarrow{y_2 \wedge \neg t,\ [\,]} & [\neg y_2 \vee t \rightarrow p_{12}()\ \Box\ y_2 \wedge \neg t \rightarrow p_{11}()] \end{array}$$

The transition table is used together with the evaluation and state update functions to generate the final state graph.

Consider the graph generation from the above fragment, given the a state in which

$$y_1 = \textbf{true},\ y_2 = \textbf{true},\ t = \textbf{true},\ crit_1 = \textbf{false},\ crit_2 = \textbf{false}$$

which we abbreviate to

$$S_0 = tttff,\ t := \textbf{false}; p_{11}()$$

Applying the first transition rule gives the new state

$$S_1 = ttfff,\ [\neg y_2 \vee t \rightarrow p_{12}()\ \Box\ y_2 \wedge \neg t \rightarrow p_{11}()]$$

Rules 2 and 3 now match, but rule 2 cannot be used since its enabling condition is false. Applying rule 3 then yields a state, say S_2,

$$S_2 = ttfff,\ [\neg y_2 \vee t \rightarrow p_{12}()\ \Box\ y_2 \wedge \neg t \rightarrow p_{11}()]$$

which is of course the same as state S_1. Thus the graph construction for this initial fragment terminates.

3.2.4 Alternative semantics

Given the flexibility or tailorability of SMG, it is easy for a user developing his own application language to experiment with different semantics and its effects on verification. For example, if we impose a restriction that procedures may only modify variables that they own, i.e. a distributed variables language [BKP86], then the semantics of the parallel construct can be altered to that of lock-step parallelism by replacing the two derived rules by the single rule

$$\frac{S_1 \xrightarrow{ec_1,\ sm_1} S_1',\ S_2 \xrightarrow{ec_2,\ sm_2} S_2'}{S_1 \parallel S_2 \xrightarrow{ec,\ sm} S_1' \parallel S_2'}$$

where

$$\begin{array}{rcl} ec & = & ec_1 \wedge ec_2 \\ sm & = & sm_1 \cup sm_2 \end{array}$$

and $sm_1 \cup sm_2$ is union of maps.

With the semantics given above, a set of guarded commands all of whose guards are false will idle until one of them becomes true. An alternative approach is given by introducing a new statement **skip** , with the semantics

$$\textbf{skip}\ ; S \xrightarrow{\textbf{true},\ [\,]} S$$

and replacing the existing rules for guarded commands with

$$[\Box\ e_i \rightarrow S_i] \xrightarrow{x_i,\ [\,]} S_i$$

$$[\Box\ e_i \rightarrow S_i] \xrightarrow{\bigwedge \neg x_i,\ [\,]} \textbf{skip}$$

3.3 Fairness

With the interleaving model of parallelism implied by the first SMG semantics shown, the generated state transition graph will contain all possible interleavings, even though the desired language semantics might include some notion of fairness. For example the program in figure 3 could always take a p_1 step and completely ignore p_2. In this example the presence or absence of fairness does not affect mutual exclusion, a safety property, but would affect liveness properties such as ensuring entry to each critical section. To ensure that only fair execution paths are considered by the model checker we need some mechanism for describing such paths. One approach is to describe such paths by use of additional variables. The model checker mcb includes a mechanism for expressing fairness constraints as a set of CTL formulae that are infinitely often true on each "fair" path, and such constraints can be expressed directly within the logic if a linear time model checker is being used. In the present implementation of SMG it is necessary to explicitly include these extra variables within the program. In the above example we could replace the definition of p_1 by

procedure $p_1()$
    f_1 := **true** ; f_1 := **false** ;
    y_1 := **true** ; t := **false** ; $p_{11}()$.
procedure $p_2()$
    f_2 := **true** ; f_2 := **false** ;
    y_2 := **true** ; t := **true** ; $p_{21}()$.

Fair paths are then those on which the formulae f_1,$\neg f_1$,f_2 and $\neg f_2$ are true infinitely often. Thus using mcb we impose the fairness constraints f_1,$\neg f_1$,f_2 and $\neg f_2$, and using a linear time model checker to check a property ϕ we need to check the formula

$$\Box(\Diamond f_1 \land \Diamond\neg f_1 \land \Diamond f_2 \land \Diamond\neg f_2) \Rightarrow \phi$$

The obligation on the programmer to include extra information that is actually a consequence of the language semantics is obviously unsatisfactory. Two approaches to overcome this limitation are currently under investigation. The first is to use the above approach but to generate automatically the necessary extra variables and fairness conditions for transmission to the model checker. This has the disadvantage of increasing the size of each state in the finite state machine and increasing the number of states. The second approach is to attach some form of process labelling to the edges of the state machine and to modify the model checker to use this labelling to restrict that search space to fair paths.

4 Discussion

SMG coupled with a temporal logic model checker provides a powerful tool for the verification of temporal properties of (concurrent) programs. Of course the combination is not intended to replace existing validation tools, but to supplement the tools that the systems engineer has at his disposal. The restriction, mentioned earlier, on finiteness may seem severe; however, we feel that most system structures that require temporal verification fall into this category. Applications to which we believe the tool most appropriate range from communications protocol verification (at software, e.g. LOTOS, and hardware, e.g. ELLA, levels), through process control verification to verification of temporal aspects of hardware systems. Existing experience gained with SML has certainly demonstrated the practicality of model checking and our approach of using a generic front end to model checker quickens and simplifies state model generator or "compiler" construction in much the same way as compiler generators aid compiler construction. SMG is also a most useful tool for teaching environments where it is desirable to give students the ability to design their own languages for particular verification applications.

SMG is, at present, a prototype and was constructed to investigate the feasibility and usefulness of a semantics driven approach to state transition graph generation. As such, there are several unnecessary limitations, which will not be present in future implementations. For example, all variables must be Boolean, the parameter mechanism for procedures is by name, the input language parser is given as YACC grammar and fairness is handled crudely.

There is, however, a limitation that is rather more serious, but for which we believe there there may be some hope in particular cases. The major problem with the model checking approach to program verification is *state explosion.* Consider a system consisting of 12 parallel asynchronous processes, each process represented by a 10 state automaton. The combined automaton would have an upper bound of a 10^{12} states, well beyond our current capabilities. The work of [CGB86] on concurrent system that are composed of many identical processes suggests that special techniques can be applied in certain commonly occurring circumstances. At present, we are investigating the use of compositional and inductive techniques as a possible means to control the explosion.

In summary, though, we have been sufficiently encouraged by our early experience with SMG for us to continue its development. In particular, we are interfacing the system to propositional linear-time temporal logic model checkers (enabling greater flexibility with respect to fairness), extending its language capabilities and improving the parser input mechanism.

References

[Bar87] H. Barringer.
Using Temporal Logic in the Compositional Specification of Concurrent Systems.
In A. P. Galton, editor, *Temporal Logics and their Applications*, chapter 2, pages 53–90, Academic Press Inc. Limited, London, December 1987.

[BC86] M.C. Browne and E.M. Clarke.
SML - a high level language for the design and verification of finite state machines.
In *From H.D.L. descriptions to guaranteed correct circuit designs*, IFIP, September 1986.

[BCDM84] M.C. Browne, E.M. Clarke, D. Dill, and B. Mishra.
Automatic Verification of Sequential Circuits using Temporal Logic.
Technical Report CS–85–100, Department of Computer Science, Carnegie-Mellon University, 1984.

[BG87] H. Barringer and G.D. Gough.
Mechanisation of Temporal Logics. Part 1: Techniques.
Temple internal report, Department of Computer Science, University of Manchester, 1987.

[BKP84] H. Barringer, R. Kuiper, and A. Pnueli.
Now You May Compose Temporal Logic Specifications.
In *Proceedings of the Sixteenth ACM Symposium on the Theory of Computing*, 1984.

[BKP86] H. Barringer, R. Kuiper, and A. Pnueli.
A Really Abstract Concurrent Model and its Temporal Logic.
In *Proceedings of the Thirteenth ACM Symposium on the Principles of Programming Languages*, St. Petersberg Beach, Florida, January 1986.

[Bro86] M.C. Browne.
An improved algorithm for the automatic verification of finite state systems using temporal logic.
Technical Report , Department of Computer Science, Carnegie-Mellon University, December 1986.

[CES86] E. M. Clarke, E. A. Emerson, and A. P. Sistla.
Automatic verification of finite-state concurrent systems using temporal logic specifications.
ACM Transactions on Programming Languages and Systems, 8(2):244–263, 1986.

[CGB86] E. M. Clarke, O. Grümberg, and M. C. Browne.
Reasoning about networks with many identical finite-state processes.
In *Proceedings of the Fifth Annual ACM Symposium on Principles of Distributed Computing*, ACM, August 1986.

[Gou84] G. D. Gough.
Decision Procedures for Temporal Logic.
Master's thesis, Department of Computer Science, University of Manchester, October 1984.

[Joh79] Stephen C. Johnson.
Yacc: Yet another compiler-compiler.
Unix Programmer's Manual Vol 2b, 1979.

[Lam83a] L. Lamport.
Specifying concurrent program modules.
ACM Transactions on Programming Languages and Systems, 5(2):190–222, July 1983.

[Lam83b] L. Lamport.
What good is temporal logic.

In R. E. A. Mason, editor, *Information Processing 83*, pages 657–668, IFIP, Elsevier Science Publishers B.V. (North-Holland), 1983.

[Lam84] L. Lamport.
An Axiomatic Semantics of Concurrent Programming Languages.
In Krysztof Apt, editor, *Logics and Models of Concurrent Systems*, pages 77–122, NATO, Springer-Verlag, La Colle-sur-Loup, France, October 1984.

[MP82] Z. Manna and A. Pnueli.
Verification of Concurrent Programs: The Temporal Framework.
In Robert S. Boyer and J. Strother Moore, editors, *The Correctness Problem in Computer Science*, Academic Press, London, 1982.

[OL82] S. Owicki and L. Lamport.
Proving Liveness Properties of Concurrent Programs.
ACM Transactions on Programming Languages and Systems, 4(3):455–495, July 1982.

[Pet81] G. L. Peterson.
Myths about the mutual exclusion problem.
Information Processing Letters, 12(3):115–116, 1981.

[Plo81] G. D. Plotkin.
A structural approach to operational semantics.
Technical Report DAIMI FN-19, Department of Computer Science,Aarhus University, September 1981.

[Pnu77] A. Pnueli.
The Temporal Logic of Programs.
In *Proceedings of the Eighteenth Symposium on the Foundations of Computer Science*, Providence, November 1977.

[Pnu84] A. Pnueli.
In transition from global to modular temporal reasoning about programs.
In Krysztof Apt, editor, *Logics and Models of Concurrent Systems*, pages 123–144, NATO, Springer-Verlag, La Colle-sur-Loup, France, October 1984.

[QS82] J. P. Queille and J. Sifakis.
Specification and verification of concurrent systems in CESAR.
Lecture Notes in Computer Science, 137, April 1982.

Algebraic Formalisation of Program Development by Transformation[1]

Bernd Krieg-Brückner

FB3 Mathematik und Informatik, Universität Bremen
Postfach 330 440, D 2800 Bremen 33, FR Germany
email: mcvax!unido!ubrinf!bkb

A uniform treatment of algebraic specification is proposed to formalise data, programs, transformation rules, and program developments. It is shown by example that the development of an efficient transformation algorithm incorporating the effect of a set of transformation rules is analogous to program development: the transformation rules act as specifications for the transformation algorithms.

1. Introduction

Various authors have stressed the need for a formalisation of the software development process: the need for an automatically generated transcript of a development "history" to allow re-play upon re-development when requirements have changed, containing goals of the development, design decisions taken, and alternatives discarded but relevant for re-development [1]. A *development script* is thus a formal object that does not only represent a documentation of the past but is a plan for future developments. It can be used to abstract from a particular development to a class of similar developments, a *development method*, incorporating a certain strategy. Approaches to formalise development descriptions contain a kind of development program [1], regular expressions over elementary steps [2], functional abstraction [3], and composition of logical inference rules [4, 5].

In Program Development by Transformation [6-8], the approach taken in the PROSPECTRA project [9, 10], an elementary development step is a *program transformation*: the application of a transformation rule that is generally applicable; a particular development is then a sequence of rule applications. The question is how to best formalise rules and application (or inference) strategies.

The approach taken in this paper is to regard transformation rules as equations in an algebra of programs (chapters 2, 3), to derive basic transformation operations from these rules (chapter 4), to allow composition and functional abstraction (chapters 5, 6), and to regard development scripts as (compositions of) such transformation operations (chapter 7). Using all the results from program development based on algebraic specifications we can then reason about the development of transformation programs or development scripts in the same way as about programs: we can define requirement specifications (development goals) and implement them by various design strategies, and we can simplify ("optimise") a development or development method before it is first applied or re-played.

2. The Algebra of Programs

2.1. The Algebra of Data and the Algebra of Programs

In the PROSPECTRA project, loose algebraic specifications with partial functions and conditional equations [11, 12] are used to specify the properties of data and associated operations in PAnndA-S, the

[1] The research reported herein has been partially funded by the Commission of the European Communities under the ESPRIT Programme, Project #390, PROSPECTRA (PROgram development by SPECification and TRAnsformation)

PROSPECTRA Anna/Ada specification language [9, 10]. For example, the fact that, for the mathematical integers INT, (INT, *, 1) is a monoid could be specified as in (2.1-1).

Similarly, we can define the Abstract Syntax of a programming language such as PAnndA-S by an algebraically specified Abstract Data Type: trees in the Abstract Syntax correspond to terms in this algebra of (PAnndA-S) programs, non-terminals to sorts, tree constructor operations to constructor operations, etc. Most constructor operations are free, except for all operations corresponding to List or Sequence concatenation, see & in (2.1-2). In the case of STMT_SEQ, Empty corresponds to **null**; in Ada and & would correspond to ; in the concrete syntax for Pascal-like languages; cf. [13].

(2.1-1) Example: Algebra of Data: Monoid (INT, *, 1)

```
axiom ∀ X,Y,Z : INT ⇒
  (X * Y) * Z = X * (Y * Z),    1 * X = X,    X * 1 = X
```

(2.1-2) Example: (Syntactic) Algebra of Programs: Monoid (STMT_SEQ, &, Empty)

```
axiom ∀ R, S, T : STMT_SEQ ⇒
  ( R & S) & T = R & (S & T),    Empty & R = R ,    R & Empty = R
```

2.2. Concrete and Abstract Syntax; Notation

Although we are interested in the abstract syntactic algebra of programs, it is often more convenient to use a notation for *phrases* (program fragments with schema variables) of the *concrete syntax* corresponding to appropriate *terms* (with variables) in the algebra, see (2.2-1). Schema variables (such as *P, E, EList, V*) are written with capital initials in the sequel, auxiliary and transformation functions in italics (cf. *OccursIn* in (3.3-2) and section 4.1). The brackets ⌈ ⌋ are used whenever a (nested) fragment of concrete syntax is introduced. Variables correspond in the example, repetition of (possibly distinct) actual parameter expressions *E* in ⌈ {*E*, } ⌋ corresponds to the list *EList* of expressions (simplified parameter associations), etc. In this paper, we are not concerned with notational issues at the concrete syntax level nor with the (non-trivial) translation of phrases from concrete to abstract syntax. Also, the typing and universal quantification of variables in equational axioms is usually omitted for brevity; it should be apparent from the context. The suffixes *List* and *Seq* are used to avoid ambiguity with variables for elements, , and ; are used to indicate list and sequence concatenation in the concrete syntax.

(2.2-1) Example: Correspondence between Concrete and Abstract Syntax: Procedure Call

```
⌈ P({E, } V); ⌋   ≈   Call(P, EList & Exp(V))
```

2.3. Algebraic Semantics

In the approach of the algebraic definition of the semantics of a programming language (cf. [14]), an evaluation function or interpretation function from syntactic to semantic domains is axiomatised. The equational axioms of such functions induce equivalence classes on (otherwise free) constructor terms. In other words, we can prove that two (syntactic) terms are *semantically equivalent,* in a context-free way or possibly subject to some syntactic or semantic pre-conditions. Such a proof can of course also be made with respect to some other style of semantic definition for the language. Thus we obtain a *semantic algebra* of programs in which transformation rules are equations as a quotient algebra of the *abstract syntactic algebra* in which only equations for & exist.

Note that the semantic specification may be intentionally loose, that is some semantic aspects such as the order of evaluation of expressions in a call may be intentionally left unspecified. From an algebraic point of view this means that several distinct semantic models exist for the loose semantic specification. Usually, these form a lattice between the initial model on top (where all terms are distinct that cannot be proven to equal) and the terminal model at the bottom (where all terms are the same that cannot be proven to differ). In some cases, unique initial and terminal models may not exist: if expressions may have side-effects, for example, several (quasi-terminal) models exist according to particular sequentialisations of evaluation (see sections 3.3, 3.5 below). Each choice of model (each choice of sequentialisation by a compiler) is admissible. (In Ada, a program is erroneous, if the quasi-terminal semantic models for this program do not coincide.)

3. Transformation Rules

3.1. Examples of Transformation Rules

Consider the examples below; the transformation rules specify part of the transition from an applicative to an imperative language style, cf. [15-18]: the mapping of a function declaration to a procedure declaration with an additional result parameter (**out**), and the transformation of all calls (the body is not treated here).

(3.1-1) is actually a specialisation of a more general rule for the (arbitrary) Introduction ⇔ Elimination of a Declaration: here an additional declaration of a procedure P is introduced in the beginning of the transformation process, and an analogous rule would eliminate the declaration of F at the end.. Rule (3.1-2) transforms function calls on the right-hand-side of an assignment statement into procedure calls with out parameters. Rule (3.1-3) unnests expressions that might contain a call to F such that rule (3.1-2) can be applied. We are assuming a (sub)language (of Ada) where expression have no side-effects (see also section 3.2). Note that, in a proper formulation for these rules, the context has to be taken into account, for example to ensure that (3.1-2) is applied in the context of declarations for F and P as introduced by (3.1-1), or that the compatibility of declarations can be checked, for example the proper introduction of a new identifier P or X in (3.1-1). For lack of space, we are ignoring these considerations here; see [17,18] for a particular approach to a specification of context in an algebraic framework.

(3.1-1) Trafo Rule: Introduction ⇔ Elimination of Procedure Declaration

```
declare
   {D1}
   function F({FP1;}) return R;

   {D2}
begin
   {S}
end;
```

such that
- *P does not occur in any of the D2, S*
- *P is not in conflict with other declarations*

```
declare
   {D1}
   function F({FP1; }) return R;
   procedure P({FP1; }X: out R);
   {D2}
begin
   {S}
end;
```

(3.1-2) Trafo Rule: Assignment with Function Call ⇔ Procedure Call with **out** Parameter

```
V := F({E, });
```

```
P({E, } V);
```

(3.1-3) Trafo Rule: Nested ⇔ Sequential Evaluation of Expressions in Statements

```
( return E;
| if E then {S1} [else {S2} ] end if;
| while E loop {S1} end loop;
| W := G({E1, } E {, E2});
| Q({E1, } E {, E2}); )
```

such that
- *V does not occur in any of the E1, E, E2, S1, S2*
- *V is not in conflict with other declarations*

```
declare
   V: T;
begin
   V := E;
( return V;
| if V then {S1} [else {S2} ] end if;
| while V loop {S1} V := E; end loop;
| W := G({E1, } V {, E2});
| Q({E1, } V {, E2}); )
end;
```

Assuming suitable context conditions (in particular for (3.1-2)), each rule is applicable by itself and correct as an individual rule. In a combined transformation (or "development"), all these rules are taken together and applied exhaustively in reverse order; they will then transform the function F and all its calls to the procedure P and F can be eliminated. Before we come to the issue of application strategies etc. in chapter 6, let us consider some rules in more detail.

3.2. Uni-Directional Rules: Relations

If the evaluation of an expression might have side-effects, that is for a semantics with distinct quasi-terminal models (see section 2.2 above), the rules (3.1-1) to (3.1-3) would have to be interpreted from left to right. A *uni-directional* transformation rule is a relation between semantic models such that each model in the range is a robustly correct implementation of some model in the domain; thus it corresponds to a semantic inclusion relation in a model-oriented sense. Again this notion is taken from the theory of algebraic specification (cf. [11]) and formalises the intuitive notion of correctness with respect to some implementation decision that narrows implementation flexibility or chooses a particular implementation. These rules are of course not invertible (a decision cannot be reversed) and, interpreted as rewrite rules, are not confluent in general. In this paper, we restrict our attention to bi-directional rules although most considerations generalise.

3.3. Bi-Directional Rules: Equations

The major kind of transformation rules we are interested in is the *bi-directional transformation rule*, a pair of semantically equivalent terms (in sense of section 2.2 above): an *equation* in the algebra of programs that is provable by deductive or inductive reasoning against the semantics. All rules in this paper are of this kind (indicated by ⇔). All considerations about interpreting equations as rewrite rules apply (confluence, termination, completion [12], etc.), cf. section 4.2.

(3.3-1) shows rule (3.1-2) as an equation and as a translation of the concrete syntax to terms in the semantic algebra of programs, cf. also (2.2-1); a similar translation for (3.1-1) would look very involved. (3.3-2) shows the assignment case of (3.1-3); applicability conditions have been formalised using auxiliary functions; they make the equation conditional (cf. section 4.1 for auxiliary functions having an implicit context parameter, such as TypeNameOf or TypeOf).

(3.3-1) Trafo Rule: Assignment with Function Call ⇔ Procedure Call: as Equation

AssignStmt(*V*, Call(*F*, *EList*)) = Call(*P*, *EList* & Exp(*V*))

⌈ V := F (EList); ⌋ = ⌈ P (EList, V); ⌋

(3.3-2) Trafo Rule: Collateral ⇔ Sequential Evaluation of Expressions

¬ *OccursIn(* V, ⌈ EList1, E, EList2 ⌋*)* ∧ *TypeNameOf(* E *)* = T ∧ ¬ *EqName(* V, W *)* →
⌈ W := G (EList1, E, EList2); ⌋ = ⌈ **declare** V: T; **begin** V := E; W := G (EList1, V, EList2); **end**; ⌋

3.4. Sets of Transformation Rules

We may have already noticed in section 3.1 that each rule in a set of rules achieves a certain (sub)goal (possibly only when applied exhaustively) that makes another rule applicable. We will come back to this issue in section 7.2. For the time being let us consider different sets of rules that achieve the same effect.

(3.3-2) is a rule analogous to a rule for the sequentialisation of collateral (or multiple) assignments into sequences of individual assignments (cf. [19]).The efficiency of the result depends on the sequence of application to subexpressions, and on the choice between two alternatives if an alternative analogous to (3.4-3) is added.

(3.4-1) is a simple-minded specialisation that forces a sequentialisation from left to right. This way, it does not avoid auxiliary variables, but it has the advantage of being simple to apply, with a fixed non-deterministic strategy (see section 7).

(3.4-1) Trafo Rule: Collateral ⇔ Sequential Evaluation of Expressions (Left to Right)

```
¬ OccursIn( V, ⌈ VList, E, EList ⌋) ∧ TypeNameOf( E ) = T ∧ IsVarList( VList ) ∧ ¬ IsVar( E ) →
  ⌈ W := G ( VList, E, EList ); ⌋ ≡ ⌈ declare V: T; begin V := E; W := G ( VList, V, EList ); end; ⌋
```

(3.4-2) is a generalisation of (3.3-2) that combines its effect with an "elimination" of common subexpressions in (3.5-1). If the desired goal is to unnest all function calls, then the effect is achieved by either rule (if applied exhaustively); (3.4-2), however, yields a more efficient result. Similarly, (3.4-3) combined to a rule set with (3.4-2), or, analogously, with (3.4-1) or (3.3-2), further enhances efficiency.

(3.4-3) is a specialisation of the assignment case that avoids introduction of variables. It is typical that a further strengthening of an applicability condition might lead to a specialisation that allows an improvement in efficiency. One might wish to add an additional condition ¬ *IsVar(* E *)* in (3.3-2), 3.4-2, 3), (3.5-1, 2) that restricts the application of the rule such that no trivial assignments (corresponding to renamings of program variables) are produced.

(3.4-2) Trafo Rule: Nested ⇔ Sequential Evaluation of Expressions

```
OccursIn( E, Exp ) ∧ ¬ OccursIn( V, Exp ) ∧ TypeNameOf( E ) = T ∧ ¬ EqName( V, W ) →
  ⌈ W := Exp; ⌋ ≡ ⌈ declare V: T; begin V := E; W := SubstByIn( E, V, Exp ); end; ⌋
```

(3.4-3) Trafo Rule: Nested ⇔ Sequential Evaluation of Expressions (Re-Use of Variables)

```
OccursIn( E , Exp ) ∧ ¬ OccursIn( V, Exp ) ∧ TypeOf( E) = TypeOf( V ) →
  ⌈ V := Exp; ⌋ ≡ ⌈ V := E; V := SubstByIn( E, V, Exp ); ⌋,
```

The important observation is that all these (sets of) rules, when applied exhaustively, yield semantically equivalent sequentialisations. With respect to some efficiency metrics where minimisation of assignments and variable usage is a concern, however, they behave quite differently. Moreover, the order of application of a general rule (rather than simple-minded application from left-to-right) becomes of great importance. Each application strategy yields a different syntactic (normal) form.

3.5. Derivation of Transformation Rules

Let us now derive (3.4-2) from the generally applicable rule (3.5-1) as a start, see (3.5-2). We apply the usual derivation steps of substitution, application of an equational law, renaming of variables, etc.

(3.5-1) Trafo Rule: Multiple ⇔ Single Evaluation of Same Subexpression

```
IsSimpleStmt( S ) ∧ OccursIn( E, S ) ∧ ¬ OccursIn( V, S ) ∧ TypeNameOf( E ) = T →
  S ≡ ⌈ declare V: T; begin V := E; SubstByIn( E, V, S ) end; ⌋
```

(3.5-2) Trafo Rule Derivation: Nested ⇔ Sequential Evaluation of Expressions

```
IsSimpleStmt( ⌈ W := Exp; ⌋) ∧ OccursIn( E, ⌈ W := Exp; ⌋) ∧ ¬ OccursIn( V, ⌈ W := Exp; ⌋)
  ∧ TypeNameOf( E ) = T →
  ⌈ W := Exp; ⌋ ≡ ⌈ declare V: T; begin V := E; SubstByIn( E, V, ⌈ W := Exp; ⌋) end; ⌋
```

```
OccursIn( E, Exp ) ∧ ¬ OccursIn( V, Exp ) ∧ ¬ EqName( V, W ) ∧ TypeNameOf( E ) = T →
  ⌈ W := Exp; ⌋ ≡ ⌈ declare V: T; begin V := E; W := SubstByIn( E, V, Exp ); end; ⌋
```

We continue in (3.5-3) by instantiating E in (3.5-2) by a call to F and therefore restricting the application of the general rule to only those cases that are necessary for the subsequent application of rule (3.3-1).

(3.5-3) Trafo Rule Derivation: Nested ⇔ Sequential Evaluation of Call to F

OccursIn(⌈ F (EList) ⌋, Exp *)* ∧ ¬ *OccursIn(* V, Exp *)* ∧ ¬ *EqName(* V, W *)* ∧ *TypeNameOf(* ⌈ F (EList) ⌋ *)* = T → ⌈ W := Exp; ⌋ = ⌈ **declare** V: T; **begin** V := F (EList); W := *SubstByIn(* ⌈ F (EList) ⌋, V, Exp *)*; **end;** ⌋

Now we apply an equational law, namely the transformation rule (3.3-1), to the function call to F on the right hand side. This way we finally end up with rule (3.5-4) that combines the effect of rules (3.1-2) and (3.1-3).

(3.5-4) Trafo Rule Derivation: Nested Evaluation of Function Call ⇔ Procedure Call

OccursIn(⌈ F (EList) ⌋, Exp *)* ∧ ¬ *OccursIn(* V, Exp *)* ∧ ¬ *EqName(* V, W *)* ∧ *TypeNameOf(* ⌈ F (EList) ⌋ *)* = T → ⌈ W := Exp; ⌋ = ⌈ **declare** V: T; **begin** P (EList, V); W := *SubstByIn(* ⌈ F (EList) ⌋, V, Exp *)*; **end;** ⌋

4. Transformation Operations

4.1. Auxiliary Operations, Applicability Predicates

We note a number of auxiliary functions and predicates in the above equations, such as *OccursIn* or *TypeOf*. These can be structurally defined (cf. [19]) and must hold over subterms or over a larger context of the actual rule application. Such functions correspond to derived or inherited attributes, resp., in an implementation of transformation rules by attributed tree transformations. They could be considered as auxiliary functions and predicates that are pre-defined in a transformation system for the language in question. The precise role of the implicit context parameter in these equations is presently unresolved (see also [17])

Analogously, additional auxiliary functions and predicates can be defined and tailored to the transformation rules and operations under consideration. Consider (4.1-1) and (4.1-2): they define applicability conditions of the rules (3.3-1) and (3.5-3), resp. In (4.1-2), the occurrence of a call to F (F shall be fixed by the context of the rule application) with some actual parameter list EList is postulated in X; in effect, EList is existentially quantified.

(4.1-1) Auxiliary Operation: Applicability Predicate *IsAssignFCall*

IsAssignFCall(⌈ V := G(EList) ⌋ *)* = *EqName(F, G)*,
¬ *IsCall(* Exp *)* → *IsAssignFCall(* ⌈ V := Exp ⌋ *)* = FALSE,
¬ *IsAssignStmt(* Stmt *)* → *IsAssignFCall(* Stmt *)* = FALSE

(4.1-2) Auxiliary Operation: Applicability Predicate *ContainsNestedFCall*

ContainsNestedFCall(X *)* = *OccursIn(* ⌈ F(EList) ⌋, X *)*

4.2. Transformation Operations: Homomorphisms

An elementary transformation operation can be constructed from (transformation rules, that is) equations in the semantic algebra in a straightforward way as a partial function in the ***abstract syntactic algebra***, see (4.2-1): it maps to a normal form in the quotient algebra corresponding to the equations. Each equation is considered as a rewrite rule from left to right (or from right to left), and, if the system of rewrite rules is confluent, yields a corresponding normal form. The function corresponds to an identity in the semantic algebra and achieves a normalisation in the syntactic algebra.

(4.2-1) Trafo Operation: Assignment with Function Call to Procedure Call

TFCallToProc(⌈ V := F (EList); ⌋) = ⌈ P (EList, V); ⌋

4.3. Extension of the Domain

If we want to apply elementary transformations over a larger context with some tactics (see chapter 6.2, 7), we need to extend the domain of a partial function to larger terms, as in (4.3-1) for TFCallToProc. The first equation corresponds to the previous definition for TFCallToProc. The second extends the definition to the identity over STMT , negating the applicability condition denoted by the predicate IsAssignFCall, see (4.1-1); cf. also Try in section 7.3.

(4.3-1) Trafo Operation: Extension to STMT

	TFCallToProc(⌈ V := F (EList); ⌋) = ⌈ P (EList, V); ⌋,
¬ *IsAssignFCall*(Stmt) →	*TFCallToProc*(Stmt) = Stmt

5. Development of Transformation Operations

5.1. Loose Specification

(5.1-1) Trafo Operation: Extension to STMT (Loose Specification)

(*TFCallToProc*(⌈ V := F (EList); ⌋) = ⌈ P (EList, V); ⌋) ∨ (*TFCallToProc*(Stmt) = Stmt)

Compared with (4.3-1), the compact definition of (5.1-1) is also semantically correct since TFCallToProc is a homomorphism and therefore all values in the equivalence class denoted by the original rule are acceptable. Loose specifications allow several distinct (that is non-isomorphic) models. In this case the ∨ operator between equations has been used to allow an additional degree of freedom over classical horn-clause specifications, analogous to non-determinacy (for one approach cf. [20]). This version specifies a class of functions (one being the "syntactic" identity in the term algebra); the more explicit definition of (4.3-1) specifies a single function mapping to a canonical form: for each non-trivial application the function call is actually changed to a procedure call.

Such a simple definition is often convenient at the start of the development of a transformation operation to characterise its effect before turning to considerations of termination, efficiency etc.

5.2. Requirement and Design Specifications

In general, we would like to start with a *requirement specification* of a transformation operation before considering a particular *design specification*, possibly several design alternatives (cf. also section 3.5). The same kind of reasoning as in program development can be applied. Any of the designs is then either formally derived from or proved to be a (robustly) correct implementation of the requirement specification (cf. [10-12]).

As an example, consider the extension of the effect of TFCallToProc over STMT_SEQ. We can characterise the desired effect as in (5.2-1): TFCallToProc should be applied to every element of a sequence (alternatively: to some arbitrary element). (5.2-2) and (5.2-3) show two divide and conquer strategies for achieving this (cf. [21]), depending on the basic operations available on STMT_SEQ, a partition or left linear structural decomposition strategy is applied. In fact, we can abbreviate such strategies by functional abstraction using a functional as in (5.2-4), see section 6.1.

(5.2-1) Trafo Operation: Extension over STMT_SEQ: *Requirement Specification*

TFCallStmts (*Empty*) = *Empty*,
0 < I ∧ I ≤ *Length*(SSeq) → *Select* (*TFCallStmts* (SSeq), I) = *TFCallToProc* (*Select* (SSeq, I))

(5.2-2) Trafo Operation: Extension over STMT_SEQ: *Design Specification:* Partition

```
TFCallStmts (Empty) = Empty,
TFCallStmts (SSeq1 & S & SSeq2) = TFCallStmts (SSeq1) & TFCallToProc (S) & TFCallStmts (SSeq2)
```

(5.2-3) Trafo Operation: Extension over STMT_SEQ: *Design Specification:* Linear Decomposition.

```
TFCallStmts (Empty) = Empty,
TFCallStmts (Add(S,R)) = Add(TFCallToProc (S), TFCallStmts (R))
```

(5.2-4) Trafo Operation: Extension over STMT_SEQ: *Design Specification:* Functional

```
TFCallStmts (SSeq) = MapStmtSeq (TFCallToProc)(SSeq)
```

6. Functionals

6.1. Restricted Functionals

Let us focus on this issue of functional abstraction in more detail. Higher order functions allow a substantial reduction of re-development effort (in analogy to parameterised data type specifications), just as in program development (cf. [22-24]).

Thus we can abstract the homomorphic extension over statement sequences in (5.1-1) to (5.1-3) to a (partially parameterised or "Curry'd") functional MapStmtSeq. (6.1-1) shows the signature, an abstract requirement specification and a particular design specification by partition.

(6.1-1) Functional: Extension over STMT_SEQ

```
function MapStmtSeq ( G: function (S: STMT) return STMT )
                    return function (SSeq: STMT_SEQ) return STMT_SEQ;
---------------------------------------------------------------------------
axiom for all G: function (S: STMT) return STMT; SSeq, SSeq1, SSeq2: STMT_SEQ; I: NATURAL ⇒
   MapStmtSeq (G)(Empty) = Empty,
   0 < I ∧ I ≤ Length(SSeq) → Select ( MapStmtSeq (G)(SSeq), I) = G (Select (SSeq, I));
---------------------------------------------------------------------------
   MapStmtSeq (G)(Empty) = Empty,
   MapStmtSeq (G)(SSeq1 & S & SSeq2) = MapStmtSeq (G)(SSeq1) & G(S) & MapStmtSeq (G)(SSeq2)
```

It is an interesting observation that most definitions of such functionals have a restricted form: the functional argument is unchanged in recursive calls. A functional together with its (fixed) functional parameters can then always be considered as a new function symbol (corresponding to an implicit instantiation), or it can be explicitly expanded; therefore the conformance to the theory of algebraic specification is evident in the restricted case. (Functionals of this restricted form can be transformed to Ada generics; instantiation is then explicit, cf. [19].) In the sequel, we will restrict ourselves to this case. In the presence of overloading, a functional that is locally defined to a parameterised specification has the same effect as a polymorphic functional.

6.2. Homomorphic Extension Functionals

In fact, most of these functionals have the nature of *homomorphic extension* functionals (see [25]), in this case the structural extension of the effect of a (local) transformation or predicate over larger terms. In (6.2-2,3), *SomeWhere* and *SomeWherePred* extend a total function *F* or predicate *P* on simple statements over compound statements and statement sequences; they would be similarly defined for, and over, other kinds of terms. *SomeWhere* is a homomorphic extension functional from terms to terms, and *SomeWherePred* from terms to BOOLEAN.

Compare the differences in the definition of the homomorphic extension functionals *SomeWhere* and *EveryWhere:* note that the ∨ operator between equations has been used (cf. section 5.1) to indicate arbitrary choice between then or else part, for example. Thus the function denoting a particular occurrence of an application of *F* is in the specified class of functions. *AnyWherePred* is analogous to *SomeWherePred* but uses **and** instead of **or**.

(6.2-2) Functional: *SomeWhere* over Statements

```
IsSimpleStmt(Stmt) → SomeWhere (F) (Stmt) = F (Stmt),
( SomeWhere (F)(   ⌈ SSeq1; SSeq2 ⌋) = ⌈ SomeWhere (F) (SSeq1); SSeq2 ⌋ ) ∨
  (SomeWhere (F)( ⌈ SSeq1; SSeq2 ⌋) = ⌈ SSeq1; SomeWhere (F) (SSeq2) ⌋ ),
( SomeWhere (F)(   ⌈ if B then SSeq1 else SSeq2 end if; ⌋ ) =
                   ⌈ if B then SomeWhere (F) (SSeq1) else SSeq2 end if; ⌋ ) ∨
  ( SomeWhere (F)( ⌈ if B then SSeq1  else SSeq2  end if; ⌋ ) =
                   ⌈ if B then SSeq1  else SomeWhere (F) (SSeq2)  end if; ⌋ ),
SomeWhere (F)(     ⌈ while B loop SSeq  end loop; ⌋ ) =
                   ⌈ while B loop SomeWhere (F) (SSeq) end loop; ⌋
```

(6.2-3) Functional: *SomeWherePred* over Statements

```
IsSimpleStmt(Stmt) → SomeWherePred (P) (Stmt) = P (Stmt),
SomeWherePred (P)(⌈SSeq1; SSeq2 ⌋) =
      SomeWherePred (P) (SSeq1) or SomeWherePred (P) (SSeq2),
SomeWherePred (P)( ⌈ if B then SSeq1 else SSeq2 end if; ⌋ ) =
      SomeWherePred (P) (SSeq1) or SomeWherePred (P) (SSeq2),
SomeWherePred (P)( ⌈ while B loop SSeq end loop; ⌋ ) = SomeWherePred (P) (SSeq)
```

(6.2-4) Functional: *EveryWhere* over Statements

```
IsSimpleStmt(Stmt) → EveryWhere (F) (Stmt ) = F (Stmt),
EveryWhere (F)( ⌈ SSeq1; SSeq2 ⌋) = ⌈ EveryWhere (F) (SSeq1) ; EveryWhere (F) (SSeq2) ⌋
EveryWhere (F)( ⌈ if B then SSeq1 else SSeq2 end if; ⌋ ) =
                ⌈ if B then EveryWhere (F) (SSeq1)  else EveryWhere (F) (SSeq2) end if; ⌋ ,
EveryWhere (F)( ⌈ while B loop SSeq  end loop; ⌋ ) =
                ⌈ while B loop EveryWhere (F) (SSeq) end loop; ⌋
```

7. Developments

7.1. Development Scripts: Composite Transformation Functions

Since we can regard every elementary program development step as a transformation, we may conversely define a *development script* to be a composition of transformation operations (including application strategies for sets of elementary transformation operations). In this view we regard a development script as a *development transcript* (of some constant program term) to formalise a concrete development history, possibly to be re-played, or as a *development method* abstracting to a class of analogous programs.

7.2. Development Goals: Requirement Specifications

We have already stated in chapter 3.6 that the application of some set of rules often requires the satisfaction of some pre-condition established by (exhaustive application of) some other set of rules. Conversely, this condition can be considered to be a required post-condition of the previous set of rules, or a characteristic predicate for the respective transformation function. Let us call such a condition a *development goal*: it is a requirement specification for a function yet to be designed; see example in section 7.5 below.

If these conditions can be defined structurally (or "syntactically"), as we indeed hope will mostly be the case, then they characterise certain *normal forms*. This leads to a substantial improvement in the modularisation of sets of rules and separation of concerns, consequently ease of verification. Note that intermediate conditions never need to be checked operationally as long as it can be shown that they are established by previous application of other rules. Transformation functions having structural normal forms as applicability conditions correspond to Wile's syntax directed experts [26].

7.3. Development Tactics: Transformals

In analogy to tacticals in [27], we might call some transformation functionals *transformals* since they embody application tactics or strategies, cf. *SomeWhere* and *EveryWhere* in section 6.2 above. Consider for example (7.3-1): if some transformation function *F* and its applicability condition *C* (including structural applicability, see section 7.2) are given, then *Try* provides a totalisation or extension to identity if *C* does not hold (cf. section 4.3).

(7.3-1) Functional: *Try*

¬ *C(X)* → *Try (F, C) (X) = X,* *C(X)* → *Try (F, C) (X) = F(X)*

IterateWhile can be used to apply a transformation function *F* as long as some condition *C* holds. Similarly, *IterateSomeWhile* iterates a local transformation function *F* as long as some local condition *C* holds somewhere.

(7.3-2) Functional: *IterateWhile, IterateSomeWhile*

¬ *C(X)* → *IterateWhile (F, C) (X) = X,* *C(X)* → *IterateWhile (F, C) (X) = IterateWhile (F, C) (F(X))*
TrySomeWhere(F, C) (X) = SomeWhere(Try (F, C)) (X), *IterateSomeWhile (F, C) (X) = IterateWhile (TrySomeWhere(F, C), SomeWherePred(C)) (X)*

Note that we are dealing with loose specifications here (see section 5.1 above). *F* is applicable iff *C* holds and *Try* yields the identity otherwise. Thus *SomeWhere(Try (F, C))* includes a lot of unwanted identity solutions even if *F* was applicable somewhere since *SomeWhere* may not pick the right position for the application of *F*. We would expect a stronger specification such as *TrySomeWhere* in (7.3-3) which does indeed yield a proper application of *F* if it is applicable anywhere, that is a kind of *Try(SomeWhere(F),SomeWherePred(C))* in which *SomeWhere(F)* is always well-defined. Note that *TrySomeWhere* is still loosely specified if, for example, *F* can be successfully applied in several subsequences; also, it still yields the identity if *F* can nowhere be applied. This conforms with the original specification and intentions.

(7.3-3) Functional: *TrySomeWhere* over Statements

¬*SomeWherePred(C) (X)* → *TrySomeWhere (F, C) (X) = X,*
IsSimpleStmt(Stmt) ∧ *C(Stmt)* → *TrySomeWhere (F) (Stmt) = F (Stmt),*
(*SomeWherePred(C) (SSeq1)* →
    TrySomeWhere (F, C)(⌈ SSeq1; SSeq2 ⌋) = ⌈ TrySomeWhere (F, C) (SSeq1); SSeq2 ⌋) ∨
  (*SomeWherePred(C) (SSeq2)* →
    TrySomeWhere (F, C)(⌈ SSeq1; SSeq2 ⌋) = ⌈ SSeq1; TrySomeWhere (F, C) (SSeq2) ⌋),
... and so on analogously

As far as possible, we would like to achieve the same strategic effect (the same development goal) by transformals such as *IterateSomeWhile(F, C), Sweep(Try (F, C))* or even *EveryWhere(Try (F, C))* by different, increasingly more efficient, application tactics (cf. (7.3-3, 4), (6.2-3)). A transformation from one tactic to another is possible by development rules, see the next section and an example in section 7.5.

(7.3-4) Functional: *Sweep* over Statements

```
IsSimpleStmt(Stmt) → Sweep (F) (Stmt ) = F (Stmt),
Sweep (F)( ⌈ SSeq1; SSeq2 ⌋) = F (⌈ Sweep (F) (SSeq1) ; Sweep (F) (SSeq2) ⌋),
Sweep (F)( ⌈ if B then SSeq1 else SSeq2 end if; ⌋) =
        F( ⌈ if B then Sweep (F) (SSeq1) else Sweep (F) (SSeq2) end if; ⌋),
Sweep (F)( ⌈ while B loop SSeq end loop; ⌋) =
        F( ⌈ while B loop Sweep (F) (SSeq) end loop; ⌋)
```

7.4. Development Rules: Equational Properties

Development rules, that is equational properties of development scripts, allow us to express and to reason about design alternatives or *alternative development tactics* (see (7.5-4) below), and to *simplify developments* by considering them as algebraic terms in the usual way. (7.4-1) gives us some simple properties of *Try*. The second follows immediately from the associativity of *AND* . Similarly, (7.4-2) follows from the definition of *Try* and *Iterate*. (7.4-3) shows the development of such a rule step by step, using rule (7.4-2). It may be used to simplify iterated application into bottom-up one-sweep application.

(7.4-1) Development Rule: "Associativity" of *Try*

```
Try(Try(F, AND(C1, C2)) (X) = Try(Try(F, C1), C2) (X),
AND(C1, C2) (X) = C1(X) and C2(X)
--------------------------------------------------
Try(Try(F, C1), C2) (X) = Try(Try(F, C2), C1) (X)
```

(7.4-2) Development Rule: Elimination of *Try* and *IterateWhile*

```
C(X) ∧¬ C(F(X)) →  Try (F, C) (X) = F(X),
C(X) ∧¬ C(F(X)) →  IterateWhile (F, C) (X) = F(X)
```

(7.4-3) Development Rule Derivation: *Iterate* ⇔ *Sweep*

```
IterateSomeWhile (F, C) (X) = IterateWhile (TrySomeWhere(F, C), SomeWherePred(C)) (X)
```

```
IterateSomeWhile (F, C) (X) = IterateWhile(Sweep(Try(F, C)), SomeWherePred(C)) (X)
```

```
SomeWherePred(C) (X) ∧¬ SomeWherePred(C) ( Sweep(Try(F, C)) (X) ) →
  IterateWhile(Sweep(Try(F, C)), SomeWherePred(C)) (X) = Sweep(Try(F, C)) (X)
```

```
SomeWherePred(C) (X) ∧¬ SomeWherePred(C) ( Sweep(Try(F, C)) (X) ) →
  IterateSomeWhile (F, C) (X) = Sweep(Try(F, C)) (X)
```

(7.4-4) shows an example: *SwapIf* swaps the then and else parts of a conditional if the condition is of the form **not** *B*. If *B* is not normalised, that is if it may contain further **not** prefixes, then an iteration is necessary. Otherwise a sweep suffices; we can prove the pre-condition of (7.4-3), that is that a single application at every node is enough.

(7.4-4) Trafo Function: *SwapIf*

```
SwapIf ( ⌈ if not B then SSeq1 else SSeq2 end if; ⌋) =
        ⌈ if B then SSeq2 else SSeq1 end if; ⌋
SwapIfApplicable (⌈ if B then SSeq1 else SSeq2 end if; ⌋) = IsUnaryNotExp(B),
SwapIfApplicable (⌈ while B loop SSeq end loop; ⌋) = FALSE, ...
--------------------------------------------------
SwapEveryIf(X) = IterateSomeWhile (SwapIf, SwapIfApplicable) (X)
```

¬ *SomeWherePred (SeveralNots) (X) → SwapEveryIf(X) = Sweep (Try(SwapIf, SwapIfApplicable)) (X)*

(7.4-5) shows the transition from sweep application to application at the "leaves" of a term only, if (we can prove that) the applicability condition of a transformation function *F* implies that it is applicable at "leaves" only (denoted by *IsSimple*). Here, a "leaf" is a subterm that is not further broken down by *EveryWhere*. *EveryWhere* is simpler than *Sweep* since the (structure of the) term itself is untouched and needs not be reconstructed, only "leaves" are transformed. We can think of it as simultaneous application at all "leaves", and, indeed, a parallel implementation would be possible.

(7.4-5) Development Rule: *Sweep* ⇔ *EveryWhere* over Simple Construct

Sweep(Try(F, IsSimple)) (X) = EveryWhere(F) (X)
Sweep(Try(Try(F, C), IsSimple)) (X) = EveryWhere(Try(F, C)) (X)

(7.4-6) looks not very meaningful just by itself. However, we may be able to simplify considerably by introducing specialised functions with local iteration tactics for each case, see example (7.5-5) below. In particular, local iteration can then often be expressed by explicit structural recursion in the range of one iteration step.

(7.4-6) Development Rule: Global ⇔ Local Iteration

IterateSomeWhile (F, C) (X) = Sweep(IterateSomeWhile (F, C)) (X)

7.5. A Development of a Development Script

As an example of a particular development, consider the development goals in (7.5-1), based on the applicability predicates in (4.1-1, 2). *NoNestedCall(F)* is a development goal for a transformation functional *TUnnestEveryCall(F)* in (7.5-2) corresponding to exhaustive application of rule (3.1-3) or the various rules for unnesting of expressions in the assignment statement, (3.3-2) to (3.4-3). These are not specific for *F*, but achieve the desired goal nevertheless since they unnest every call. (3.5-3) is specific; it could be made even more specific by insisting in *NoNestedCall* on nestedness, excluding that the assigned expression is a direct call to *F*. This way, the goal is satisfied with minimal changes.

At the same time, *NoNestedCall(F)* is part of *NoCall(F)* and thus pre-condition for *TElimFunctDecl(F)*. We can easily prove that *TEveryCallToProc(F, P)* and *IntroProcDecl(F, P)* are invariant w.r.t. *NoNestedCall(F)*, thus it is satisfied as a pre-condition of *TElimFunctDecl(F)*. This way, *TFunctToProc(F, P)* is correctly defined in (7.5-2) as a composition of the separate transformation functions. We assume that *F* is well-defined in *Block*.

(7.5-1) Development Goals: Function to Procedure

NoNestedCall(F)(X) = ¬ SomeWherePred(ContainsNestedCall(F))(X), *NoCall(F)(X) = NoNestedCall(F)(X) ∧ ¬ SomeWherePred(IsAssignCall(F))(X)*

(7.5-2) Development Script: Function to Procedure

TUnnestEveryCall(F)(Block) =	*IterateSomeWhile (TUnnestCall(F), ContainsNestedCall(F))(Block),*
TEveryCallToProc(F, P)(Block) =	*IterateSomeWhile (TCallToProc(F, P), IsAssignCall(F))(Block),*
NoCall(F)(Block) →	
TElimFunctDecl(F)(Block) =	*SomeWhere (TElimDecl(F))(Block)*
TFunctToProc(F, P)(Block) = *TElimFunctDecl(F) (TEveryCallToProc(F, P) (IntroProcDecl(F, P) (TUnnestEveryCall(F) (Block))))*	

Let us now try to apply some of the development rules of section 7.4 above to simplify iteration. Indeed, *TEveryCallToProc* can be simplified to *EveryWhere* iteration on simple statements since we can show that *IsAssignCall* implies *IsAssignStmt*, therefore *IsSimpleStmt*, see (4.1-1) and (7.5-3).

(7.5-3) Development Script Derivation: Simplification of *TEveryCallToProc*

TEveryCallToProc(F, P) (Block) = *EveryWhere(Try(TCallToProc(F, P), IsAssignCall(F))) (Block)*

We can try to specialise to local iteration analogously to (7.4-6), see (7.5-4) for the major cases. Note that explicit recursion on *TUnnest* instead of "deep" iteration is used for loops, *Init*, and particularly for assignments. As a minor point, *TUnnest* is not yet quite complete since the obligation to find some *F* that is not in conflict still has to be fulfilled. Improvements analogously to (3.5-3) could still be made, avoiding the unnesting of the whole expression in favour of those subexpressions containing a call to *F*.

(7.5-4) Functional: *TUnnestEveryCall*: Local Iteration

TUnnestEveryCall(F) (Block) = *Sweep(Try(TUnnest(F), ContainsNestedCall(F))) (Block)*
ContainsNestedCall(F) (E) ∧ ¬ *OccursIn(V, E)* →   *TUnnest(F)* (⌈ **return** *E* ; ⌋) = *Init(V, E)* (⌈ **return** *V* ; ⌋),   *ContainsNestedCall(F) (E)* ∧ ¬ *OccursIn(V, E)* ∧ ¬ *OccursIn(V, SSeq1)* ∧ ¬ *OccursIn(V, SSeq2)* →   *TUnnest(F)* (⌈ **if** *E* **then** *SSeq1* **else** *SSeq2* **end if**; ⌋) =   *Init(V, E)* (⌈ **if** *V* **then** *SSeq1* **else** *SSeq2* **end if**; ⌋),   *ContainsNestedCall(F) (E)* ∧ ¬ *OccursIn(V, E)* ∧ ¬ *OccursIn(V, SSeq)* →   *TUnnest(F)* (⌈ **while** *E* **loop** *SSeq* **end loop**; ⌋) =   *Init(V, E)* (⌈ **while** *V* **loop** *SSeq*; *TUnnest(F)* (⌈ *V* := *E*; ⌋) **end loop**; ⌋),   *OccursIn*(⌈ *F*(*EList*) ⌋, *Exp*) ∧ ¬ *OccursIn(V, Exp)* →   *TUnnest(F)* (⌈ *W* := *Exp*; ⌋) = *Init(V,*⌈ *F*(*EList*) ⌋,) (⌈ *W* := *SubstByIn*(⌈ *F*(*EList*) ⌋, *V*, *Exp*); ⌋),   ... analogously for procedure call
¬ *OccursIn(V, E)* ∧ ¬ *OccursIn(V, Stmt)* ∧ *TypeNameOf(E)* = *T* →   *Init(V, E) (Stmt)* = ⌈ **declare** *V* : *T*; **begin** *TUnnest(F)* (⌈ *V* := *E*; ⌋) *Stmt* **end**; ⌋

We note that it makes no difference in (7.5-2) whether to introduce the procedure declaration before or after normalisation of the function calls. This can been expressed by a re-ordering property as in (7.5-4). Thus we can combine *TEveryCallToProc(F, P) TUnnestEveryCall(F)* into one functional by unfold-fold of *TEveryCallToProc*, in other words by applying *TEveryCallToProc* to every call to F in the range of *TUnnestEveryCall* directly. This combination had been done for assignments in (3.5-4); the only change in (7.5-4) would be to unfold *Init* in the assignment case and to replace the assignment to *V* by a procedure call.

(7.5-5) Development Rule: Reordering Property of Transformations

TUnnestEveryCall(F) (IntroProcDecl(F, P) (Block)) = *IntroProcDecl(F, P) (TUnnestEveryCall(F) (Block))*

We have converged more and more to the development of a complete specification of a set of efficient transformation functions that can be directly translated into a recursive applicative program in some language, cf. [9,10,15]. Intermediate loose specifications could be made operational by some functional language with non-deterministic pattern matching and backtracking. Such a language is presently designed and implemented in the PROSPECTRA project; see [16] for a first approach.

8. Conclusion

It has been demonstrated that the methodology for program development based on the concept of algebraic specification of data types and program transformation can be applied to the development of transformation algorithms; in the semantic algebra of programs, equations correspond to bi-directional transformation rules. Starting from small elementary transformation rules that are proved correct against the semantics of the programming language, we can apply the usual equational and inductive reasoning to derive complex rules; we can reason about development goals as requirement specifications for transformation operations in the syntactic algebra and characterise them as structural normal forms; we can implement transformation operations by various design alternatives; we can optimise them using algebraic properties; we can use composition and functional abstraction; in short, we can develop *correct*, efficient, complex transformation operations from elementary rules stated as algebraic equations.

Moreover, we can regard development scripts as formal objects: as (compositions of) such transformation operations. We can specify development goals, implement them using available operations, simplify development terms, re-play developments by interpretation, and abstract to development methods, incorporating formalised development tactics and strategies. The abstraction from concrete developments to methods and the formalisation of programming knowledge as transformation rules + development methods will be a challenge for the future.

Many questions remain open at the moment. One is a suitable separation of a large set of known rules into subsets such that each can be handled by dedicated tactics with an improved efficiency over the general case, and coordinated by an overall strategy; these correspond to the "syntax-directed experts" of [26]. Another is the strategy questions: the selection of a development goal (sometimes expressible as a normal form) based on some efficiency or complexity criteria.

There is a close analogy to the development of efficient proof strategies for given inference rules (transformation rules in the algebra of proofs). Perhaps the approach can be used to formalise rules and inference tactics in knowledge based systems.

Since every manipulation in a program development system can be regarded as a transformation of some "program" (for example in the command language), the whole system interaction can be formalised this way and the approach leads to a uniform treatment of programming language, program manipulation and transformation language, and command language.

Acknowledgements

I wish to thank M. Broy, H. Ganzinger, B. Gersdorf, S. Kahrs, D. Plump, and Z. Qian for helpful criticism and comments.

References

[1] Wile, D. S..: Program Developments: Formal Explanations of Implementations. *CACM 26:* 11 (1983) 902-911. *also in:* Agresti, W. A. (ed.): *New Paradigms for Software Development.* IEEE Computer Society Press / North Holland (1986) 239-248.

[2] Steinbrüggen, R..: Program Development using Transformational Expressions. Rep. TUM-I8206, Institut für Informatik, TU München, 1982.

[3] Feijs, L.M.G., Jonkers, H.B.M, Obbink, J.H., Koymans, C.P.J., Renardel de Lavalette, G.R., Rodenburg, P.M.: A Survey of the Design Language Cold. *in:* Proc. ESPRIT Conf. 86 (Results and Achievements). North Holland (1987) 631-644.

[4] Sintzoff, M.: Expressing Program Developments in a Design Calculus. *in:* Broy, M. (ed.): *Logic of Programming and Calculi of Discrete Design.* NATO ASI Series, Vol. F36, Springer (1987) 343-365.

[5] Jähnichen, S., Hussain, F.A., Weber, M.: Program Development Using a Design Calculus. *in:* Rogers, M. W. (ed.): *Results and Achievements,* Proc. ESPRIT Conf. '86 . North Holland (1987) 645-658.

[6] Bauer, F.L., Berghammer, R., Broy, M., Dosch, W., Geiselbrechtinger, F., Gnatz, R., Hangel, E., Hesse, W., Krieg-Brückner, B., Laut, A., Matzner, T., Möller, B., Nickl, F., Partsch, H., Pepper, P., Samelson, K., Wirsing, M., Wössner, H.: The Munich Project CIP, Vol. 1: The Wide Spectrum Language CIP-L. *LNCS 183,* 1985.

[7] Bauer, F. L., Wössner, H.: *Algorithmic Language and Program Development.* Springer 1982.

[8] Pepper, P.: A Simple Calculus of Program Transformations (Inclusive of Induction). *Science of Computer Programming 9: 3* (1987) 221-262.

[9] Krieg-Brückner, B., Hoffmann, B., Ganzinger, H., Broy, M., Wilhelm, R., Möncke, U., Weisgerber, B., McGettrick, AA.D., Campbell, I.G., Winterstein, G.: Program Development by Specification and Transformation. *in:* Rogers, M. W. (ed.): *Results and Achievements,* Proc. ESPRIT Conf. '86 . North Holland (1987) 301-312.

[10] Krieg.Brückner, B.: Integration of Program Construction and Verification: the PROSPECTRA Project. in: Habermann, N., Montanari, U. (eds.): Innovative Software Factories and Ada. Proc. CRAI Int'l Spring Conf. '86. *LNCS 275* (1987) 173-194.

[11] Broy, M., Wirsing, M.: Partial Abstract Types. *Acta Informatica 18* (1982) 47-64.

[12] Ganzinger, H.: A Completion Procedure for Conditional Equations. Techn. Bericht No. 243, Fachbereich Informatik, Universität Dortmund, 1987 (to appear in *J. Symb. Comp.*)

[13] Hoare, C.A.R., Hayes, I.J., He, J.F., Morgan, C.C., Roscoe, A.W., Sanders, J.W., Sorensen, I.H., Spivey, J.M., Sufrin, B.A.: Laws of Programming. *CACM 30: 8* (1987) 672-687.

[14] Broy, M., Pepper, P., Wirsing, M.: On the Algebraic Definition of Programming Languages. *ACM TOPLAS 9* (1987) 54-99.

[15] Krieg-Brückner: Systematic Transformation of Interface Specifications. *in:* Meertens, L.G.T.L. (ed.): *Program Specification and Transformation,* Proc. IFIP TC2 Working Conf. (Tölz '86). North Holland (1987) 269-291

[16] Heckmann, R.: A Functional Language for the Specification of Complex Tree Transformation. *this volume.*

[17] Qian, Z.: Structured Contextual Rewriting. Proc. Int'l Conf. on Rewriting Techniques and Applications (Bordeaux). *LNCS 256* (1987) 168-179.

[18] Qian, Z.: Recursive Presentation of Program Transformation. PROSPECTRA Report M.1.1.S1-SN-17.1, Universität Bremen (1986).

[19] Krieg-Brückner: Formalisation of Developments: An Algebraic Approach. *in:* Rogers, M. W. (ed.): *Achievements and Impact.* Proc. ESPRIT Conf. 87. North Holland (1987) 491-501.

[20] Broy, M.: Predicative Specification for Functional Programs Describing Communicating Networks. *IPL 25* (1987) 93-101.

[21] Smith, D.R.: Top-Down Synthesis of Divide-and-Conquer Algorithms. *Artificial Intelligence 27:*1 (1985) 43-95.

[22] Bird, R.S.: Transformational Programming and the Paragraph Problem. *Science of Computer Programming 6* (1986) 159-189.

[23] Broy, M.: Equational Specification of Partial Higher Order Algebras. *in:* Broy, M. (ed.): *Logic of Programming and Calculi of Discrete Design.* NATO ASI Series, Vol. F36, Springer (1987) 185-241.

[24] Möller, B.: Algebraic Specification with Higher Order Operators. *in:* Meertens, L.G.T.L. (ed.): *Program Specification and Transformation,* Proc. IFIP TC2 Working Conf. (Tölz '86). North Holland (1987) 367-398.

[25] von Henke, F.W.: An Algebraic Approach to Data Types, Program Verification and Program Synthesis. *in:* Mazurkiewicz, A. (ed.): Mathematical Foundations of Computer Science 1976. *LNCS 45* (1976) 330-336.

[26] Wile, D. S.: Organizing Programming Knowledge into Syntax Directed Experts. USC/ISI manuscript (1987).

[27] Gordon, M., Milner, R., Wadsworth, Ch.: Edinburgh LCF: A Mechanised Logic of Computation. *LNCS 78* .

QPC: QJ-based Proof Compiler
– Simple Examples and Analysis –

Yukihide Takayama

Institute for New Generation Computer Technology
4-28, Mita 1-chome, Minato-ku, Tokyo 108, Japan
takayama@icot.jp

Abstract

This paper presents a formulation of program extraction system from constructive proofs. It is designed as a simple system and is very similar to the ordinary Gentzen style of natural deduction as compared to other constructive logics to clarify the relationship between constructive proofs and programs. Proofs and λ-expressions are regarded as different things, and they are linked by the notion of proof compilation based on realizability.

The program extraction algorithm is given explicitly, and two simple examples, simulation of course of value induction by mathematical induction and, by using this as a user-defined rule of inference, extraction of a gcd program, are investigated to check how the well known method of proof normalisation works as an optimisation technique and what kinds of inefficiency remain after the proof normalisation. Subtle points about the execution of extracted codes are also discussed. Finally, modified $\vee$-code is introduced as an easy but powerful optimisation technique,

1. Introduction

Constructive proofs can be seen as a very high level description of algorithm, as has been discussed by many computer scientists and logicians in terms of the relationship between intuitionism and computation, and programming systems such as the Nuprl system [Constable 86] and the PX system [Hayashi 87] have been implemented. These systems have the facility to extract executable codes from constructive proofs, and are based on the notion of formulae-as-types or realizability interpretation. Their main purpose is to pursue high level expressive power of constructive logic. However, studying techniques to extract good code is also an important research problem.

This paper presents another formulation of the program extraction system which is obtained from a subset of Sato's constructive logic QJ [Sato 85]. It is quite simple compared to Martin-Löf's theory of types [Martin-Löf 84] and Hayashi's PX. Roughly, it is an intuitionistic version of a Gentzen-type system of natural deduction with a simple induction schema. It has some program constructs such as λ-expressions and primitive type structures. Primitive types such as natural number type and natural number list type are provided as built-in types, so that types cannot be manipulated as objects. This simple system, however, provides a very clear insight on the relationship between proofs and programs, and makes it much easier to work on the proof transformation technique and efficient code generation. In addition, a second order feature is introduced to write user-defined rules of inference, although this system does not pursue polymorphism as investigated in [Coquand 85].

Section 2 gives our formalism of programs and logic and the algorithm of proof compilation. Section 3 gives the method of user-defined rules description and program scheme extraction by introducing predicate variables and the second order universal quantifier, $\forall^2$. Section 4 shows the extraction of a gcd program by using a user-defined course of value induction rules. Section 5 outlines the operational semantics of the extracted codes. Section 6 works on the optimisation technique based on normalisation of proof trees, and introduces another powerful optimisation technique, the modified $\vee$-code. The conclusion and future problems are given in Section 7.

2. Proof Compiler

This section gives the formalization and the naive version of the program extraction algorithm based on the notion of *q-realizability*. They are based on a subset of the 1985 version of QJ [Sato 85], except for the higher order features, predicate variable and second order $\forall^2$-I/E rules.

2.1 Notational Preliminaries

(1) Type expressions

1) nat ··· Type expression of natural number.

2) $prop$ ··· Type expression of proposition. $P : prop$ means that P is a well formed formula.

3) $Type_1 \rightarrow Type_2$ ··· The type of function from type $Type_1$ to type $Type_2$.

4) $Type_1 \times \cdots \times Type_n$ ··· the Cartesian product type.

(2) Term expressions

1) $0, 1, 2, ...$ ··· Elements of type nat.

2) $left/right$ ··· Constants.

3) $x, y, z, ...$ Individual variables are written in lower case letters. All the variables have types, and $x : Type$ is read as "variable x has type $Type$".
Type declarations are usually omitted in the following description.

4) $(Term_0, .., Term_n)$ or simply $Term_0, .., Term_n$
Sequence of terms. If $Term_i$ are of types $Type_i$ $(0 \leq i \leq n)$, then the above terms are seen to be of Cartesian product type: $Type_1 \times \cdots \times Type_n$.
Sequences of variables are denoted as $\overline{x}, \overline{y}, \overline{z}, ...$

5) $\lambda(x_0,..,x_n).\ Term$ $(0 \leq n)$ $\cdots$ Lambda abstraction.

6) $if\ A\ then\ Term_1\ else\ Term_2$ $\cdots$ A is a higher order equation or inequation defined in (3) 1).

7) $\mu(z_0,..,z_n).\ A(z_0,..,z_n)$ $(0 \leq n)$ $\cdots$ μ is the fixed point operator.

8) $Term(Term_0)(Term_1)...(Term_n)$ $\cdots$ Application. Associate to left.

9) $x\ mod\ y$ $\cdots$ Residue of fraction of x by y.

10) $proj(i)$ $\cdots$ Projection function of type $Type_0 \times \cdots \times Type_i \times \cdots Type_n \rightarrow Type_i$ where $(0 < n, 0 \leq i \leq n)$

11) $l(SEQUENCE)$ $\cdots$ Length of the sequence, $SEQUENCE$.

12) $any[N]$ $\cdots$ Sequence of arbitrary N codes. $(N > 0)$

13) $succ/pred$ $\cdots$ Successor/predecessor function on nat

14) $f(x_0,\cdots,x_n)$ $(0 \leq n)$ $\cdots$ Term which contains free variables $x_0,\cdots,x_n$.

(3) Formulae

1) $Term_1 = Term_2,\quad Term_1 \leq Term_2,\quad Term_1 < Term_2$
Higher order equation/inequation of terms.

2) $P, Q, ...$ $\cdots$ Predicate variables. These are of type $prop$.

3) $P(x)$, $Q(x)$,... Predicates that have x as free variables. $P(x)$ is also denoted in an abstraction formula, $\Lambda x.\ P$. Substitution of a term, t, to x that occurs free in P is defined as a kind of β-reduction: $(\Lambda x.\ P)(t) \rightarrow P(t)$

4) $\perp$ $\cdots$ Contradiction. Note that $\neg A \stackrel{def}{=} A \supset \perp$.

5) Definition of formulae

1. Higher order equations and inequations of terms are atomic formulae.
2. $\perp$ is an atomic formula.
3. If P and Q are formulae, $P \wedge Q$, $P \vee Q$, $P \supset Q$ are formulae.
4. If $P(x)$ is a formula containing x free, $\forall x : Type.\ P(x)$, $\exists x : Type.\ P(x)$ are formulae where $Type$ can be any type other than $prop$.
5. If Q is a predicate variable $\forall^2 Q : prop.\ P(Q)$ is a formula.

Formulae are regarded as of type $prop$.

(4) Proof trees

Proof trees are written in the ordinary natural deduction style as in [Prawitz 65]. Subtrees are often abbreviated as Π_i or, when the free variable, x, in the subtree should be stressed, $\Pi_i(x)$.

2.2 Inference Rules on Logical Constants and Equalities

The inference rules used in this paper are listed here.

(1) Introduction Rules

$$\frac{A \quad B}{A \wedge B} \qquad \frac{A}{A \vee B} \qquad \frac{B}{A \vee B} \qquad \frac{\begin{matrix}[A]\\ B\end{matrix}}{A \supset B} \qquad \frac{\begin{matrix}[x : Type]\\ A(x)\end{matrix}}{\forall x : type.\ A(x)} \qquad \frac{t : Type \quad A(t)}{\exists x : Type.\ A(x)}$$

(2) Elimination Rules

$$\frac{A \wedge B}{A} \qquad \frac{A \wedge B}{B} \qquad \frac{A \vee B \quad \begin{matrix}[A]\\ C\end{matrix} \quad \begin{matrix}[B]\\ C\end{matrix}}{C} \qquad \frac{A \quad A \supset B}{B}$$

$$\frac{t : Type \quad \forall x : Type.A(x)}{A(t)} \qquad \frac{\exists x : Type.A(x) \quad \begin{matrix}[x : Type, A(x)]\\ C\end{matrix}}{C} \qquad \frac{\perp}{A}$$

(3) Induction Rule

$$\frac{A(0) \quad \begin{matrix}[x : nat, A(x), x > 0]\\ A(succ(x))\end{matrix}}{\forall x : nat.\ A(x)}(nat\text{-}ind)$$

(4) Rules on Equalities

$$\frac{t = s\ (in\ Type)\ A(t)}{A(s)}(=1) \qquad \frac{t : Type}{t = t\ (in\ Type)}(=2) \qquad \frac{t = s\ (in\ Type)}{s = t\ (in\ Type)}(=3)$$

$$\frac{p = q\ (in\ Type)\ q = r\ (in\ Type)}{p = r\ (in\ Type)}(=4)$$

QJ also has rules of arithmetic, formation of terms and formulae, and type inferences. However, these rules are not necessary as far as program extraction is concerned. The names of these rules are abbreviated to * in the following description.
The following additional rules are of higher order logic and are not contained in the original version of QJ.

$$\frac{\begin{matrix}[P : prop]\\ F(P)\end{matrix}}{\forall^2 P : prop.\ F(P)}(\forall^2\text{-I}) \qquad \frac{Q : prop \quad \forall^2 P : prop.F(P)}{F(Q)}(\forall^2\text{-E})$$

2.3 Program Extraction Algorithm

The program extraction algorithm is given here. This algorithm performs q-realizability interpretation of QJ and the soundness of the extracted code, realizer, is proved in [Sato 85].
(1) Additional notations for algorithm description
• $Rv(A)$
Realizing variable sequence. Realizing variables are sequences of variables to which realizer codes for the formula are assigned. $Rv(A)$ is defined as follows:

1. $Rv(A) \stackrel{def}{=} (nil)$, if A is atomic.
2. $Rv(A \wedge B) \stackrel{def}{=}$ concatenation of Rv(A) and $Rv(B)$.
3. $Rv(A \vee B) \stackrel{def}{=}$ concatenation of a new variable, z, $Rv(A)$, and $Rv(B)$.
4. $Rv(A \supset B) \stackrel{def}{=} Rv(B)$.
5. $Rv(\forall x : Type.\ A(x)) \stackrel{def}{=} Rv(A(x))$.
6. $Rv(\exists x : Type.\ A(x)) \stackrel{def}{=}$ concatenation of a new variable, z, and $Rv(A(x))$.
7. $Rv(P) \stackrel{def}{=} Rv(P(x))$, if $P : prop$ has x as free variables.

• $Ext(\frac{A}{B}(Rule))$
Top level procedure (function) of program extraction. It is often abbreviated to $Ext(B)$ in the situation where A and $Rule$ are clear. When a conclusion, B, depends on a list of formulae, Γ, this procedure is denoted by $Ext(\Gamma \vdash B)$. When $Ext(A)$, where A is a formula in Γ, is needed in $Ext(\Gamma \vdash B)$, $Rv(A)$ is used as the value of $Ext(A)$.
• σ, τ,..
Substitution. These are defined as $\{x_0/Term_0, .., x_n/Term_n\}$, which means to substitute $Term_i$ for x_i $(0 \leq i \leq n)$ that occurs free in a given expression. Application of σ is denoted as $Term\sigma$.
• (nil)
Denotes empty code.
(2) Definition of Ext procedure

$$Ext(\frac{A \quad B}{A \wedge B}(\wedge\text{-I})) \stackrel{def}{=} Ext(A), Ext(B)$$

$$Ext(\frac{A \wedge B}{A}(\wedge\text{-E})) \stackrel{def}{=} proj(0)(A \wedge B) \qquad Ext(\frac{A \wedge B}{B}(\wedge\text{-E})) \stackrel{def}{=} proj(1)(A \wedge B)$$

$$Ext(\frac{A}{A \vee B}(\vee\text{-I})) \stackrel{def}{=} left, Ext(A) \qquad Ext(\frac{B}{A \vee B}(\vee\text{-I})) \stackrel{def}{=} right, Ext(B)$$

$$Ext(\frac{A \vee B \quad \begin{matrix}[A]\\ C\end{matrix} \quad \begin{matrix}[B]\\ C\end{matrix}}{C}(\vee\text{-E}))$$

$$\stackrel{def}{=} \begin{cases} Ext(A \vdash C)\sigma_0 & \text{if } proj(0)(Ext(A \vee B)) = left; \\ Ext(B \vdash C)\sigma_1 & \text{if } proj(0)(Ext(A \vee B)) = right; \\ if\ left = proj(0)(Ext(A \wedge B))\ then\ Ext(A \vdash C)\sigma_0 \\ \qquad\qquad\qquad\qquad\qquad\quad else\ Ext(B \vdash C)\sigma_1 & \text{otherwise} \end{cases}$$

where $\sigma_0 \stackrel{def}{=} \{Rv(A)/proj(1)(Ext(A \vee B))\}$ $\quad \sigma_1 \stackrel{def}{=} \{Rv(B)/proj(1)(Ext(A \vee B))\}$

$$Ext(\frac{\begin{matrix}[A]\\ B\end{matrix}}{A \supset B}(\supset\text{-I})) \stackrel{def}{=} \begin{cases} Ext(B) & \text{if Rv(A) = (nil);} \\ \lambda\ Rv(A).\ Ext(A \vdash B) & \text{otherwise} \end{cases}$$

$$Ext(\frac{A \quad A \supset B}{B}(\supset\text{-E})) \stackrel{def}{=} Ext(A \supset B)(Ext(A))$$

$$Ext(\frac{\begin{matrix}[x : Type]\\ A(x)\end{matrix}}{\forall x : Type.\ A(x)}(\forall\text{-I})) \stackrel{def}{=} \lambda\ x.\ Ext(A(x))$$

$$Ext(\frac{t : Type \quad \forall x : Type.\ A(x)}{A(t)}(\forall\text{-E})) \stackrel{def}{=} Ext(\forall x : Type.\ A(x))(t)$$

$$Ext(\frac{t : Type \quad A(t)}{\exists x : Type.\ A(x)}(\exists\text{-I})) \stackrel{def}{=} t, Ext(A(t))$$

$$Ext(\frac{\exists x : Type.\ A(x) \qquad \begin{matrix}[x : Type, A(x)]\\ C\end{matrix}}{C}(\exists\text{-E})) \stackrel{def}{=} Ext(x : Type, A(x) \vdash C)\sigma$$

where $\sigma \stackrel{def}{=} \{x/proj(0)(Ext(\exists x : Type.\ A(x))), Rv(A(x))/proj(1)(Ext(\exists x : Type.\ A(x)))\}$

$$Ext(\frac{A(0) \qquad \begin{matrix}[x : nat, A(x)]\\ A(succ(x))\end{matrix}}{\forall x : nat.\ A(x)}(nat\text{-}ind))$$

$$\stackrel{def}{=} \begin{cases} \mu\ \overline{z}.\ \lambda\ x.\ if\ x = 0\ then\ Ext(A(0))\ else\ Ext(x : nat, A(x) \vdash A(succ(x)))\sigma \\ \qquad\qquad\qquad\qquad \text{where } \overline{z} = Rv(A(x)), \text{and } \sigma = \{\overline{z}/\overline{z}(pred(x))\} \\ \lambda\ x.\ if\ x = 0\ then\ Ext(A(0))\ else\ Ext(x : nat, A(x) \vdash A(succ(x))) \\ \quad \text{if } Rv(A(x)) \text{ does not occur in } Ext(x : nat, A(x) \vdash A(succ(x))) \end{cases}$$

$$Ext(\frac{\perp}{A}(\perp\text{-E})) \stackrel{def}{=} \begin{cases} (nil) & \text{if } Rv(A) \text{ is } (nil); \\ any[l(Rv(A))] & \text{otherwise} \end{cases}$$

$$Ext(\frac{t = s\ (in\ Type) \quad A(t)}{A(s)}(=1)) \stackrel{def}{=} Ext(A(t))$$

$$Ext(\frac{t : Type}{t = t\ (in\ Type)}(=2)) \stackrel{def}{=} (nil) \qquad Ext(\frac{t = s\ (in\ Type)}{s = t\ (in\ Type)}(=3)) \stackrel{def}{=} (nil)$$

$$Ext(\frac{p = q\ (in\ Type) \quad q = r\ (in\ Type)}{p = r\ (in\ Type)}(=4)) \stackrel{def}{=} (nil) \quad Ext(\frac{A}{B}(*)) \stackrel{def}{=} (nil)$$

(3) The *Ext* procedure for ($\forall^2$-I/E) will be given in the next section.

3. Proof Schema Using Propositional Variables

3.1 Proof of Course of Value Induction

As is well known in mathematical logic, the course of value induction schema

$$\forall^2 P : prop.\ (\forall x : nat.(\forall y : nat.(y < x \supset P(y)) \supset P(x)) \supset \forall z : nat.P(z)) \qquad \text{[COV-IND]}$$

can be proven by mathematical induction in second order logic. Any proof tree of the first order theorem that uses the course of value induction rule can be transformed into one that uses the mathematical induction rules as follows. Let Q be an individual predicate. The proof of $\forall x : nat.\ \forall y : nat.((y < x \supset Q(y)) \supset Q(x))$ is called *course of value proof* in the following descriptions.

$$\frac{\begin{array}{c}\Pi_0\\ \forall x : nat.(\forall y : nat.(y < x \supset Q(y)) \supset Q(x))\end{array}}{\forall z : nat.Q(z)}(course\ of\ value\ induction)$$

This tree is transformed into the following tree, called COV-TREE:

$$\frac{\begin{array}{c}\Pi_0\\ \forall x : nat.(\forall y : nat.(y < x \supset Q(y)) \supset Q(x))\end{array} \quad \Pi_0}{\forall z : nat.Q(z)} \qquad \text{[COV-TREE]}$$

where Π_0 is as follows:

$$\frac{\begin{array}{c}\Pi_1\\ Q : prop\end{array} \quad \dfrac{\begin{array}{c}\Pi_2\\ \forall x : nat.(\forall y : nat.(y < x \supset P(y)) \supset P(x)) \supset \forall z : nat.P(z)\end{array}}{\text{COV-IND}}(\forall^2\text{-I})}{\forall x : nat.(\forall y : nat.(y < x \supset Q(y)) \supset Q(x)) \supset \forall z : nat.Q(z)}(\forall^2\text{-E}$$

Π_2 is shown in detail **Appendix 1.**

3.2 Proof Compilation Algorithm for ($\forall^2$-I/E)

The predicate variables and $\forall^2$-I/E rules are used to handle user-defined rules of inference such as the course of value induction schema explained in 3.1.
The proof compilation algorithm for $\forall^2$-I/E rules is a native extension of that for first order logic.

$$Ext(\frac{\begin{array}{c}[P : prop]\\ F(P)\end{array}}{\forall^2 P : prop.\ F(P)}(\forall^2\text{-I})) \stackrel{def}{=} \Lambda RV(P).\ Ext(P/RV(P) \vdash F(P))$$

$RV(P)$ is the variable to which $Rv(Q)$, where Q is a particular first order formula, is to be substituted. The intentional meaning of Λ is similar to ordinal lambda notation. Λ is used simply to distinguish the above case. $Ext(P/RV(P) \vdash F(P))$ means that if $Ext(P)$ is needed in the procedure of proof compilation of $F(P)$, $RV(P)$ should be used as the value of $Ext(P)$.

$$Ext(\frac{Q : prop \quad \forall^2 P : prop.\ F(P)}{F(Q)}(\forall^2\text{-E})) \stackrel{def}{=} \beta\text{-reduction on } Ext(\forall^2 P : prop.\ F(P))(Rv(Q))$$

$Ext(\forall^2 P : prop.\ F(P))$ must be of the form $\Lambda RV(P).Ext(P/RV(P) \vdash F(P))$, so that by β-reduction of the Λ-expression, the above code is $Ext(F(Q))$. This corresponds to the following normalisation of second order logic:

$$\frac{\begin{array}{c}\Pi_0\\ Q : prop\end{array} \quad \dfrac{\begin{array}{c}[P : prop]\\ \Pi_1(P)\\ F(P)\end{array}}{\forall^2 P : prop.F(P)}}{F(Q)} \Longrightarrow \begin{array}{c}\Pi_0\\ [Q : prop]\\ \Pi_1(Q)\\ F(Q)\end{array}$$

3.3 Proof Compilation of Course of Value Schema

The following code is generated from the proof of COV-IND given in 3.1 by the proof compilation algorithm given in 2.3 and 3.2. AA and $CODE_1$ are extracted from Π_{21} and *Theorem 1* in Appendix 1.

$$\Lambda RV(P).\lambda RV(P(x)).\lambda z.\ RV(P(x))(z)(A_0(z)) \qquad \text{[COV-CODE]}$$

where

$A_0 \stackrel{def}{=} \mu RV(P(y)).\lambda x.\ if\ x = 0\ then\ \lambda\ y.\ any[l(RV(P(y)))]$
$\qquad else\ \lambda\ y.\ if\ left = AA(x)(y)\ then\ RV(P(y))(pred(x))(y)$
$\qquad\qquad else\ RV(P(x))(x)(RV(P(y))(pred(x)))$

$AA \stackrel{def}{=} \mu z.\lambda x.\ if\ x = 0\ then\ \lambda\ y.\ if\ y = 0\ then\ right\ else\ any[1]$
$\qquad else\ \lambda y.\ if\ left = CODE_1(y)\ then\ left$
$\qquad\qquad else\ \ if\ left = z(pred(x))(pred(y))\ then\ left\ else\ right$

$CODE_1 \stackrel{def}{=} \mu z.\ \lambda k.\ if\ k = 0\ then\ left\ else\ if\ left = z\ then\ right\ else\ right$

The code $left = AA(x)(y)$ in A_0 is the conditional equation which is logically equivalent to $y < x$. $RV(P(x))$ is equal to $RV(\forall x : nat.(\forall y : nat.(y < x \supset P(y)) \supset P(x)))$. The proof of this part must be given as a course of value proof, and the proof contains the computational meaning of how to construct the justification of $P(x)$ by using the justifications of $P(y)$ (for all y s.t. $y < x$). $RV(P(y))$ denotes the realizing variables of $\forall y : nat.(y < x \supset P(y))$.

4. Simple Example: GCD Program

The GCD program is taken as a simple example which uses COV-IND.

4.1 GCD Proof

The specification of GCD program is as follows:

$$\forall n : nat.\ \forall m : nat.\ \exists d : nat.(d \mid n \wedge d \mid m)$$

where for $p : nat$ and $q : nat$, $p \mid q \stackrel{def}{=} \exists r : nat.q = r \cdot p$.

The specification and proof that the constructed natural number is actually a maximal one which satisfies the specification is omitted here for simplicity. However, the natural number which satisfies this condition is constructed in the proof given below. The proof is called *proof of GCD program* or *GCD proof* in the following description.

The course of value proof of this specification is shown in **Appendix 2**.

4.2 Proof Compilation of GCD Proof

The proofs in Appendices 1 and 2 give a gcd program. The following code is obtained by the method given in 3.1 and the proof compilation.

$gcd_0 \stackrel{def}{=} f(g)$

where

$f \stackrel{def}{=}$ {*The code obtained from* COV-CODE($Rv(Q)$) *by applying* β-*reduction*}

$g \stackrel{def}{=} \lambda n.\lambda\ (z_0, z_1, z_2).\ if\ left = CODE_1(n)\ then\ CODE_2\ else\ CODE_3$

$CODE_2 \stackrel{def}{=} \lambda m.\ (m, (\lambda p.\ 0)(m), (\lambda q.\ 1)(m))$

$$CODE_{3,n} \stackrel{def}{=} \lambda m.\ (\ z_0(m\ mod\ n)(n), z_2(m\ mod\ n)(n),$$
$$z_1(m\ mod\ n)(n) + z_2(m\ mod\ n)(n) \cdot \frac{m-(m\ mod\ n)}{n})$$

Here, $Q \stackrel{def}{=} \Lambda x.\ \forall m : nat.\ \exists d : nat.(d \mid x \wedge d \mid m)$, and $(z_0, z_1, z_2) \stackrel{def}{=} Rv(\forall l.(l < n \supset Q(l)))$. Let $(w_0, w_1, w_2) \stackrel{def}{=} Rv(Q(x))$. Then

$$f \stackrel{def}{=} \lambda(w_0, w_1, w_2).\lambda z.\ (w_0, w_1, w_2)(z)(A_1(z))$$

where

$$\begin{aligned} A_1 \stackrel{def}{=} \mu(z_0, z_1, z_2).\lambda x.\ & if\ x = 0\ then\ \lambda y.\ any[3] \\ & else\ \lambda y.\ \ if\ left = AA(x)(y)\ then\ (z_0, z_1, z_2)(pred(x))(y) \\ & \qquad\qquad else\ (w_0, w_1, w_2)(x)((z_0, z_1, z_2)(pred(x))) \end{aligned}$$

5. Execution of the Extracted Codes

5.1 Tiny Quty Interpreter

Tiny Quty is a subset of Quty [Sato 87]. It is a non-typed sequential functional language to describe executable codes extracted from constructive proofs. The syntax of **Tiny Quty** is given in Section 2 as the definition of term expressions and higher order (in)equations. For simplicity, the language presented here has no syntax for list structure. The chief difference from ordinal functional languages is that it allows sequences of variables as parameters of the fixed point operator, μ, i.e., multi-valued functions can be written.

The interpreter of **Tiny Quty** is an ordinal call-by-value evaluator of λ-expressions. However, the following features should be noted.

(1) $f \stackrel{def}{=} \mu(z_0, .., z_n).t(z_0, .., z_n)$ is regarded as a sequence of single-valued functions $f_0, .., f_n$, and $f_i \quad (0 \le i \le n)$ is defined as $proj(i)(f)$. The following reduction can be performed on f:

$$\mu(z_0, .., z_n).t(z_0, .., z_n) \longrightarrow t(f_0, .., f_n)$$

(2) $\lambda(x_0, .., x_n).\ t(x_0, \cdots, x_n)$ is regarded as another description of $\lambda x_0 ..., \lambda x_n.\ t(x_0, \cdots, x_n)$.

(3) $(\lambda(x_0, ..., x_n).\ t_0(x_0, .., x_n))(t_1)$ can be reduced to $t_0(A_0, .., A_n)$ where $(A_0, .., A_n) = SPLIT(t_1)$. The function, $SPLIT$, is the procedure that splits terms into sequences of terms if it is possible.

(4) $any[N](Term)$ is reduced to $Term$.

5.2 Evaluation of the GCD Code

The code extracted in Section 4 is a program that takes two natural numbers as inputs and returns the sequence of three natural numbers. The first element of the pair is the gcd of the inputs, and the other two elements are verification information that can be seen as the decoded proof to show that the first element of the pair is actually the gcd. If one is interested in only the value of gcd, the extracted code should be properly transformed into a single-valued function.

5.3 Problem of ⊥-E Code

The code, $\lambda y.\ any[l(Rv(P(y)))]$, which occurs in [COV-CODE] and is extracted from the proof which uses ⊥-E rule, is evaluated when the whole code is executed. The reason is as follows: $\forall x.\forall y.\ (y < x \supset P(y))$ in Main Proof Tree of Appendix 1 is proved by (*nat-ind*), and the

base case is proved by ⊥-E rule. The base case proof corresponds to the termination condition in terms of proof compilation, so that it must always be evaluated just before the execution terminates.
The extraction algorithm for ⊥-E rule is defined as follows in 2.3:

$$Ext(\frac{\bot}{A}(\bot\text{-E})) \stackrel{def}{=} \begin{cases} (nil) & \text{if } Rv(A) \text{ is a nil sequence;} \\ any[l(Rv(A))] & \text{otherwise} \end{cases}$$

The operational semantics of $any[..]$ code is defined as $any[N](Term) \longrightarrow Term$ in 5.1. However, it is an experimental treatment.
The treatment around the realizer code of ⊥-E rule is clearer when the ⊥-contraction rules [Troelstra 83] are performed on proof trees using ⊥-E rule. The tree, Π_1 in Appendix 1, is the base case proof of $\forall x.\ \forall y.(y < x \supset P(y))$.

Let $P(x) \stackrel{def}{=} \forall m : nat.\ \exists d : nat.\ (d \mid x \wedge d \mid m)$ in Π_1. After a sequence of ⊥-contractions, Π_1 is as follows. Note that d, p and q can be any elements of nat.

$$\dfrac{\dfrac{\dfrac{\overline{d}^{(*)} \quad \dfrac{\dfrac{\overline{p}^{(*)} \quad \dfrac{\dfrac{[y<0] \quad \dfrac{[y:nat]}{\neg(y<0)}(*)}{\bot}}{y=p\cdot d}}{d \mid y}(\exists\text{-I}) \quad \dfrac{\overline{q}^{(*)} \quad \dfrac{\dfrac{[y<0] \quad \dfrac{[y:nat]}{\neg(y<0)}(*)}{\bot}}{m=q\cdot d}}{d \mid m}(\exists\text{-I})}{d \mid y \wedge d \mid m}(\wedge\text{-I})}{\exists d.\ d \mid y \wedge d \mid m}(\exists\text{-I})}{\dfrac{P(y)}{\dfrac{y<0 \supset P(y)}{\forall y : nat.(y<0 \supset P(y))}(\forall\text{-I})}(\supset\text{-I})}(\forall\text{-I})$$

Any proof in which ⊥-E rule is used to derive a formula which contains at least one logical constant can be transformed into the proof in which the ⊥-rule is not used except to derive an atomic formula by using the same method. Consequently, the following Ext procedure suffices to extract codes from the ⊥-rule.

$$Ext(\frac{\bot}{A}(\bot\text{-E})) \stackrel{def}{=} (nil) \qquad \text{where } l(A) = 0.$$

The extracted code with this procedure is $\lambda y.\ \lambda m.\ (d, p, q)$. d, p and p can be any natural number, so that they can be m because $m : nat$ is an assumption of the (∀-I) rule application. Consequently, $\lambda y.\ any[l(Rv(P(y)))]$ is actually $\lambda y.\lambda m.(m, m, m)$.
This problem can be avoided if the mathematical induction on $x - 1$ is used in combination with divide and conquer strategy on $x = 0 \vee x > 1$. In this case, Π_1 should be as follows:

$$\dfrac{\dfrac{\dfrac{\dfrac{[y:nat] \quad [y<1]}{y=0}(*) \quad \begin{matrix}\Pi_0 \\ P(0)\end{matrix}}{P(y)}(=1)}{y<1 \supset P(y)}(\supset\text{-I})}{\forall y : nat.(y<1 \supset P(y))}(\forall\text{-I})$$

This proof gives the termination condition of the recursive call program, and the code for ⊥-E rule which is extracted from the proof of the case $x = 0$ is never executed.

6. Optimisation Technique

In the **PX** system [Hayashi 87], the optimisation of extracted codes proceeds as follows: if the code of the form $(\lambda x.\ A)(B)$ is extracted in the process of proof compilation, then perform β-reduction of the code immediately. The optimisation technique of proof compilation can be presented more systematically.

6.1 Proof Normalisation and Partial Evaluation of Programs

Normalisation of proofs corresponds to partial evaluation of extracted codes from the proofs. The following are the normalisation rules given in [Prawitz 65].

(1) ∀-normalisation

$$\dfrac{\dfrac{\begin{array}{c}\Pi(a)\\ P(a)\end{array}}{\forall x.P(x)}(\forall\text{-I})}{P(t)}(\forall\text{-E}) \quad\Longrightarrow\quad \begin{array}{c}\Pi(t)\\ P(t)\end{array}$$

(2) ⊃ normalisation

$$\dfrac{\begin{array}{c}\Pi_0\\ A\end{array} \quad \dfrac{\begin{array}{c}[A]\\ \Pi_1\\ B\end{array}}{A\supset B}(\supset\text{-I})}{B}(\supset\text{-E}) \quad\Longrightarrow\quad \begin{array}{c}\Pi_0\\ [A]\\ \Pi_1\\ \hline B\end{array}$$

There are other rules of normalisation such as the $\exists$, $\wedge and \vee$-normalisation rules; however, they are not effective for the optimisation in proof compilation as can be seen by the definition of the *Ext* procedure. Rules (1) and (2) correspond to β-reduction of λ-expressions.
Note that in terms of proof compilation, the following diagram commutes:

$$\begin{array}{ccccccc}
Proof_0 & \xrightarrow{Norm_0} & Proof_1 & \xrightarrow{Norm_1} & \cdots & \xrightarrow{Norm_n} & Proof_n \\
\big\downarrow{\scriptstyle Ext} & \circlearrowright & \big\downarrow{\scriptstyle Ext} & & & \circlearrowleft & \big\downarrow{\scriptstyle Ext} \\
Code_0 & \xrightarrow{\beta\text{-red.}} & Code_1 & \xrightarrow{\beta\text{-red.}} & \cdots & \xrightarrow{\beta\text{-red.}} & Code_n
\end{array}$$

Following this diagram, optimisation facilities can be realized in either of two ways:

1. By implementing a proof normaliser. Proofs are normalized first, and then compiled.
2. By implementing a partial evaluator built in the proof compiler. Proofs are compiled first, then the partial evaluation method of the functional programming language is applied to the extracted codes.

From an aesthetic point of view, both proofs and codes should be transformed simultaneously to maintain a clear correspondence between proofs and programs in terms of proof compilation. The order of applying the normalisation rules can be arbitrary. If the normalisation rules are applied from the leaves of proof trees, this corresponds to call-by-value evaluation of the programs extracted from the proof trees. If they are applied from the bottom of proof trees, it means call-by-name evaluation. Tiny Quty programs are evaluated with call-by-value strategy. However, this is just for efficiency of runtime evaluation.

6.2 Example of Proof Normalisation

For the GCD proof given in 4.1, first, the ∀-normalisation rule can be applied to the proof of $m \mid 0$ and $m \mid m$ in Π_1 in Appendix 2, as follows.

$$\dfrac{[m:nat] \quad \dfrac{\dfrac{\dfrac{}{0:nat}(*) \quad \dfrac{\dfrac{}{0:nat}(*)\quad [p:nat]}{0=0\cdot p}}{\exists d':nat.0=d'\cdot p}}{\forall p:nat.p\mid 0}}{m\mid 0} \quad\Rightarrow\quad \dfrac{\dfrac{}{0:nat}(*) \quad \dfrac{\dfrac{}{0:nat}(*)\quad [m:nat]}{0=0\cdot m}}{m\mid 0}$$

$$\dfrac{[m:nat] \qquad \dfrac{\dfrac{\dfrac{\overline{1:nat}^{(*)} \qquad \dfrac{\overline{1:nat}^{(*)} \quad [q:nat]}{1 = 1 \cdot q}}{\exists d'':nat.q = d'' \cdot q}}{\forall q:nat.q \mid q}}{}}{m \mid m} \quad \Rightarrow \quad \dfrac{\overline{1:nat}^{(*)} \qquad \dfrac{\overline{1:nat}^{(*)} \quad [m:nat]}{m = 1 \cdot m}}{m \mid m}$$

By this normalisation, $CODE_2$ is translated to the following $CODE_{22}$:

$$CODE_{22} \stackrel{def}{=} \lambda m.\ (m, 0, 1)$$

As the ($\supset$ -E) rule is used in the course of value induction schema given in 3.1, the $\supset$-normalisation rule can be applied:

$$\dfrac{\dfrac{\Pi_0}{\forall x.(\forall y.(y < x \supset Q(y)) \supset Q(x))} \qquad \dfrac{\begin{matrix}[\forall x.(\forall y.(y < x \supset Q(y)) \supset Q(x))] \\ \Pi' \\ \forall z.Q(z)\end{matrix}}{\forall x.(\forall y.(y < x \supset Q(y)) \supset Q(x)) \supset \forall z.Q(z)}(\supset\text{-I})}{\forall z.Q(z)}(\supset\text{-E})$$

$\Longrightarrow$

$$\begin{matrix}\dfrac{\Pi_0}{\forall x.(\forall y.(y < x \supset Q(y)) \supset Q(x))}(\forall\text{-I}) \\ \Pi' \\ \forall z.Q(z)\end{matrix}$$

where
Π_{11} is the course of value proof, and

$$\dfrac{\begin{matrix}[\forall x.(\forall y.(y < x \supset Q(y)) \supset Q(x))] \\ \Pi' \\ \forall z.Q(z)\end{matrix}}{\forall x.(\forall y.(y < x \supset Q(y)) \supset Q(x)) \supset \forall z.Q(z)}$$

is the proof of course of value schema by mathematical induction.
By this transformation, β-reduction of f(g) is performed, and the $\forall$-normalisation rule can also be applied to Π_{22} and Π_3 in Appendix 1 combined with the course of value proof given in Appendix 2, then the code is as follows:

$gcd_1 \stackrel{def}{=} \lambda z.\lambda(z_0, z_1, z_2).\ if\ left = CODE_1(z)\ then\ CODE_{22}\ else\ CODE_{3,z})(A_2(z))$

where $A_2 \stackrel{def}{=} A_1\{(w_0, w_1, w_2)/\lambda(z_0, z_1, z_2).\ if\ left = CODE_1(x)\ then\ CODE_{22}\ else\ CODE_{3,x}\}$

6.3 Modified $\vee$-Code

$left = CODE_1(y)$ in code AA corresponds to the proof of $y = 0 \vee y > 0$. However, none of the normalisation rules in 6.1 can be applied. Most of the execution of the gcd program is that of AA, the code extracted from the proof of $y < x + 1 \vdash y < x \vee y = x$, and $left = AA(x)(y)$ is logically equivalent to $y < x$, as explained in 4.2.
On the other hand, as given in 4.1, $n = 0 \vee n > 0 \quad (n : nat)$ and $y < x + 1 \vdash y < x \vee y = x$ are proved by mathematical induction. However, in practical situations, it is not efficient if we must always prove well known properties of natural numbers of this kind strictly by induction. For these reasons, the following modification is introduced in the proof compilation:

$$Ext\left(\frac{A \vee B \quad \begin{matrix}[A]\\ C\end{matrix} \quad \begin{matrix}[B]\\ C\end{matrix}}{C}(\vee\text{-E})\right) \stackrel{def}{=} if\ A\ then\ Ext(A \vdash C)\ else\ Ext(B \vdash C)$$

when A and B are equations or inequations of natural numbers.
In this case, the proof of $A \vee B$ can be omitted by declaring this formula as an axiom.
By this optimisation, the gcd code obtained in 6.2 is changed as follows:

$$gcd_2 \stackrel{def}{=} \lambda z.\lambda(z_0, z_1, z_2).\ if\ z = 0\ then\ CODE_{22}\ else\ CODE_{3,z})(A_3(z))$$

where

$$\begin{aligned} A_3 \stackrel{def}{=} \mu(z_0, z_1, z_2).\lambda x.\ & if\ x = 0\ then\ \lambda y.\ any[3] \\ & else\ \lambda y.\ if\ y < x\ then\ (z_0, z_1, z_2)(pred(x))(y) \\ & \qquad else\ (\lambda(z_0, z_1, z_2).\ if\ x = 0\ then\ CODE_{22} \\ & \qquad\qquad else\ CODE_{3,x})((z_0, z_1, z_2)(pred(x))) \end{aligned}$$

7. Conclusion

This paper presented a simple proof compiler system based on the notion of realizability. A higher order feature was introduced to handle the description of user-defined rules of inference. Optimisation was handled with the notion of proof normalisation. Modified $\vee$-code was also introduced as a powerful technique of optimisation.

Acknowledgments

Thanks must go to Dr. Aiba, Dr. Murakami, and Mr. Sakai of ICOT, and to Mr. Kameyama and Professor Sato at Tohoku University, who gave me many useful suggestions.

REFERENCES

[Constable 86] Constable, R. L. et al., "*Implementing Mathematics with the Nuprl Proof Development System*", Prentice-Hall, 1986

[Coquand 85] Coquand. T, and Huet. G, "Constructions: A Higher Order Proof System for Mechanizing Mathematics", *EUROCAL* 85, Linz, Austria, 1985

[Hayashi 87] Hayashi, S. and Nakano, H., "**PX**: *A Computational Logic*", RIMS-573, Research Institute for Mathematical Sciences, Kyoto University, 1987

[Martin-Löf 84] Martin-Löf, P., "*Intuitionistic Type Theory*", Bibliopolis, Napoli, 1984

[Prawitz 65] Prawitz, D., "*Natural Deduction*", Almqvist & Wiksell, 1965

[Sato 85] Sato, M., "*Typed Logical Calculus*", TR-85-13, Department of Computer Science, University of Tokyo, 1985

[Sato 87] Sato, M., "**Quty**: A Concurrent Language Based on Logic and Function", *Proceedings of the Fourth International Conference on Logic Programming*, Melbourne, 1987

[Troelstra 73] A. S. Troelstra, " Mathematical Investigation of Intuitionistic Arithmetic and Analysis", *Lecture Notes in Mathematics Vol.* 344, Springer-Verlag, 1973

Appendix 1 Proof of COV-IND
Main Proof Tree:

$$\dfrac{\dfrac{\dfrac{[z : nat] \quad \dfrac{\Pi_1 \quad \Pi_2}{\forall x : nat.\forall y : nat.(y < x \supset P(y))}(nat\text{-}ind)}{\forall y : nat.(y < z \supset P(y))} \quad \Pi_3}{P(z)}(\supset\text{-E})}{\dfrac{\forall z : nat.\ P(z)}{\forall x : nat.(\forall y : nat.(y < x \supset P(y)) \supset P(x)) \supset \forall z : nat.\ P(z)}}$$

Π_1 : (Base case proof of induction)

$$\dfrac{\dfrac{\dfrac{\dfrac{[y<0]\quad \dfrac{[y:nat]}{\neg(y<0)}(*)}{\bot}}{P(y)}}{y<0\supset P(y)}}{\forall y:nat.(y<0\supset P(y))}$$

Π_2 : (Step case proof of induction)

$$\dfrac{\dfrac{\begin{matrix}[x:nat]\\ [y:nat]\\ [y<succ(x)]\\ \Pi_{21}\end{matrix}\quad \dfrac{[y<x]\quad \dfrac{[y:nat]\quad [HYP]}{y<x\supset P(y)}(\forall\text{-E})}{P(y)}\quad \dfrac{[y=x]\quad \dfrac{[HYP]\quad \Pi_{22}}{P(x)}(\supset\text{-E})}{P(y)}}{\dfrac{P(y)}{y<succ(x)\supset P(y)}}(\vee\text{-E})}{\forall y:nat.(y<succ(x)\supset P(y))}$$

$$\text{where } HYP \overset{def}{=} \forall y:nat.(y<x\supset P(y))$$

Π_{21} (Proof of $x:nat,\ y:nat,\ y<succ(x)\vdash y<x\vee y=x$)

$$\dfrac{[y<succ(x)]\quad \dfrac{[y:nat]\quad \dfrac{[x:nat]\quad \dfrac{\Pi_{211}\quad \dfrac{\dfrac{\dfrac{\Pi_{212}\quad \Pi_{213}\quad \Pi_{214}}{y<x+1\vee y=x+1}(\vee\text{-E})}{y<x+2\supset y<x+1\vee y=x+1}}{\forall y:nat.\ y<x+2\supset y<x+1\vee y=x+1}}{\forall x:nat.\forall y:nat.\ y<x+1\supset y<x\vee y=x}(nat\text{-}ind)}{\forall y:nat.\ y<x+1\supset y<x\vee y=x}}{y<x+1\supset y<x\vee y=x}}{y<x\vee y=x}$$

Π_{211} (Base case proof of nat-ind)

$$\dfrac{\dfrac{\dfrac{\dfrac{\dfrac{\dfrac{\dfrac{}{0}(*)}{0=0}\quad [0<1]}{0=0\wedge 0<1}}{0=0}}{0<0\vee 0=0}}{0<1\supset 0<0\vee 0=0}\quad \dfrac{\dfrac{\dfrac{\dfrac{[y+1<1]}{y<0}(*)\quad \dfrac{[y:nat]}{\neg(y<0)}(*)}{\bot}}{y+1<0\vee y+1=0}}{y+1<1\supset y+1<0\vee y+1=0}}{\forall y:nat.\ y<1\supset y<0\vee y=0}(nat\text{-}ind)$$

Π_{212}

$$\dfrac{[y:nat]\quad \textit{Theorem 1}}{y=0\vee y>0}(\forall\text{-E})$$

Theorem 1 is a simple theorem of number theory that states *any natural number is equal to 0 or larger than 0.* This can be proved by mathematical induction as follows:

$$\dfrac{\dfrac{\dfrac{\dfrac{}{0}(*)}{0=0}}{0=0\vee 0>0}\quad \dfrac{[k=0\vee k>0]\quad \dfrac{\dfrac{\dfrac{[k=0]}{k+1=1}(*)\quad \dfrac{}{1>0}(*)}{k+1>0}}{k+1=0\vee k+1>0}\quad \dfrac{\dfrac{\dfrac{[k>0]}{k+1>1}(*)\quad \dfrac{}{1>0}(*)}{k+1>0}}{k+1=0\vee k+1>0}}{k+1=0\vee k+1>0}}{\forall k:nat.\ k=0\vee k>0}(nat\text{-}ind)$$

Π_{213}

$$\dfrac{\dfrac{[y=0] \quad \dfrac{[x:nat]}{0<x+1}(*)}{y<x+1}}{y<x+1 \lor y=x+1}$$

$\Pi_{214} : (y>0,\ y<x+2,\ HYP" \vdash y<x+1 \lor y=x+1)$

$$\dfrac{\Pi_{2141} \quad \dfrac{\dfrac{[y-1<x]}{y<x+1}(*)}{y<x+1\lor y=x+1} \quad \dfrac{\dfrac{[y-1=x]}{y=x+1}(*)}{y<x+1\lor y=x+1}}{y<x+1\lor y=x+1}$$

$\Pi_{2141} : (y>0,\ y<x+2,\ HYP" \vdash y-1<x \lor y-1=x)$

$$\dfrac{\dfrac{[y>0]\quad [y<x+2]}{y-1<x+1}(*) \quad \dfrac{\dfrac{[y>0]}{y-1:nat}(*) \quad [HYP'']}{y-1<x+1 \supset y-1<x \lor y-1=x}(\forall\text{-E})}{y-1<x\lor y-1=x}$$

where $HYP'' \stackrel{def}{=} \forall y:nat.\ (y<x+1 \supset y<x \lor y=x)$.

Π_{22} : (Application of the hypothesis)

$$\dfrac{[x:nat] \quad [\forall x:nat.(\forall y:nat.(y<x \supset P(y)) \supset P(x))]}{\forall y:nat.(y<x \supset P(y)) \supset P(x)}(\forall\text{-E})$$

Π_3 : (Application of the hypothesis)

$$\dfrac{[z:nat] \quad [\forall x:nat.(\forall y:nat.(y<x \supset P(y)) \supset P(x))]}{\forall y:nat.(y<z \supset P(y)) \supset P(z)}(\forall\text{-E})$$

Appendix 2: The course of value proof of the GCD Proof

Let $Q(x) \stackrel{def}{=} \forall m:nat.\ \exists d:nat.\ (d \mid x \land d \mid m)$.

Main Proof Tree:

$$\dfrac{\dfrac{\dfrac{\dfrac{[n:nat] \quad Theorem\ 1}{n=0 \lor n>0}(\forall\text{-E}) \quad \Pi_1 \quad \Pi_2}{Q(n)}(\lor\text{-E})}{\forall l:nat.(l<n \supset Q(l)) \supset Q(n)}}{\forall n:nat.(\forall l:nat.(l<n \supset Q(l)) \supset Q(n))}$$

$\Pi_1 : (n=0 \vdash Q(n))$

$$\dfrac{[n=0] \quad \dfrac{\dfrac{[m:nat] \quad \dfrac{\dfrac{[m:nat] \quad Theorem\ 2}{m \mid 0} \quad \dfrac{[m:nat] \quad Theorem\ 3}{m \mid m}}{m \mid 0 \land m \mid m}}{\exists d:nat.\ (d \mid 0 \land d \mid m)}}{Q(0)}(\forall\text{-I})}{Q(n)}(=\text{E})$$

Theorem 2 and 3 is simple theorems of number theory:

Theorem 2 :
(0 can be divided by any natural number)

$$\dfrac{\dfrac{\dfrac{}{0:nat}(*) \quad \dfrac{\dfrac{}{0:nat}(*) \quad [p:nat]}{0=0\cdot p}(*)}{\exists d':nat.\ 0=d'\cdot p}}{\forall p:nat.\ p \mid 0}(\forall\text{-I})$$

Theorem 3 :
(any natural number can divides itself)

$$\dfrac{\dfrac{\dfrac{}{1:nat}(*) \quad \dfrac{\dfrac{}{1:nat}(*) \quad [q:nat]}{q=1\cdot q}(*)}{\exists d'':nat.\ q=d''\cdot q}}{\forall q:nat.\ q \mid q}(\forall\text{-I})$$

$\Pi_2 : (\ \forall l : nat.\ (l < n \supset Q(l)),\ n > 0,\ m : nat,\ n : nat \vdash Q(n))$

$$\dfrac{\dfrac{\dfrac{[n:nat] \quad \Pi_{21}}{\exists d : nat.\ d \mid (m\ mod\ n) \wedge d \mid n}(\forall\text{-E}) \qquad \dfrac{[d:nat] \quad \Pi_{22}}{\exists d : nat.\ d \mid n \wedge d \mid m}(\exists\text{-I})}{\exists d : nat.\ d \mid n \wedge d \mid m}(\exists\text{-E})}{Q(n)}(\forall\text{-I})$$

$\Pi_{21} : (\forall l.(l < n \supset Q(l)),\ n > 0,\ m : nat,\ n : nat \vdash Q(m\ mod\ n))$

$$\dfrac{\dfrac{[n > 0] \quad [n : nat] \quad [m : nat]}{(m\ mod\ n) < n}(*) \qquad \dfrac{\dfrac{[n > 0], \quad [n : nat] \quad [m : nat]}{(m\ mod\ n) : nat}(*) \qquad [\forall l : nat.(l < n \supset Q(l))]}{(m\ mod\ n) < n \supset Q(m\ mod\ n)}}{Q(m\ mod\ n)}$$

$\Pi_{22} : (d : nat,\ d \mid (m\ mod\ n) \wedge d \mid n,\ n > 0,\ m : nat,\ n : nat \vdash d \mid n \wedge d \mid m)$

$$\dfrac{\dfrac{[d \mid (m\ mod\ n) \ \wedge\ d \mid n]}{d \mid n} \qquad \Pi_{221}}{d \mid n \wedge d \mid m}(\wedge\text{-I})$$

$\Pi_{221} : (d : nat,\ d \mid (m\ mod\ n) \wedge d \mid n,\ n > 0,\ m : nat,\ n : nat \vdash d \mid m)$

$$\dfrac{\dfrac{\dfrac{[m : nat] \quad [n : nat] \quad [n > 0]}{(m - (m\ mod\ n))/n : nat} \qquad \dfrac{[m : nat] \quad [n : nat] \quad [n > 0]}{m = n \cdot ((m - (m\ mod\ n))/n) + (m\ mod\ n)}}{\exists d_0 : nat.\ m = n \cdot d_0 + (m\ mod\ n)} \qquad \Pi_{2211}}{d \mid m}(\exists\text{-E})$$

$\Pi_{2211} : (\Gamma_1,\ d_0 : nat,\ m = n \cdot d_0 + (m\ mod\ n) \vdash d \mid m$, where Γ_1 is the hypothesis of Π_{221}.)

$$\dfrac{[m = n \cdot d_0 + (m\ mod\ n)] \qquad \dfrac{\dfrac{[d \mid (m\ mod\ n) \wedge d \mid n]}{d \mid (m\ mod\ n)} \qquad \dfrac{\Pi_{22111} \quad \Pi_{22112}}{d \mid n \cdot d_0 + (m\ mod\ n)}(\exists\text{-E})}{d \mid n \cdot d_0 + (m\ mod\ n)}(\exists\text{-E})}{d \mid m}(= 1)$$

where $d \mid (m\ mod\ n) \overset{def}{=} \exists d_1 : nat.\ (m\ mod\ n) = d_1 \cdot d$

$\Pi_{22111} : (\Gamma_2,\ d_1 : nat,\ (m\ mod\ n) = d_1 \cdot d \vdash d \mid n \cdot d_0$, where Γ_2 is the hypothesis of Π_{2211})

$$\dfrac{\dfrac{[d \mid (m\ mod\ n) \wedge d \mid n]}{d \mid n} \qquad \dfrac{\dfrac{[d_0 : nat] \quad [d_3 : nat]}{d_3 \cdot d_0 : nat} \qquad \dfrac{[n = d_3 \cdot d] \quad [d_0 : nat] \quad [d_1 : nat]}{n \cdot d_0 = d_3 \cdot d_0 \cdot d}}{d \mid n \cdot d_0}}{d \mid n \cdot d_0}(\exists\text{-E})$$

where $d \mid n \cdot d_0 \overset{def}{=} \exists d_2 : nat.\ n \cdot d_0 = d_2 \cdot d \qquad d \mid n \overset{def}{=} \exists d_3 : nat.\ n = d_3 \cdot d$

$\Pi_{22112} : (\Gamma_3,\ d_2 : nat,\ n = d_3 \cdot d \vdash d \mid n \cdot d_0 + (m\ mod\ n)$, where Γ_3 is the hypothesis of Π_{22111})

$$\dfrac{\dfrac{[d_1 : nat] \quad [d_2 : nat]}{d_1 + d_2} \qquad \dfrac{[n \cdot d_0 = d_2 \cdot d] \quad [(m\ mod\ n) = d_1 \cdot d]}{n \cdot d_0 + (m\ mod\ n) = (d_1 + d_2) \cdot d}}{d \mid n \cdot d_0 + (m\ mod\ n)}(\exists\text{-I})$$

Implementation of Modular Algebraic Specifications

(extended abstract)

N.W.P. van Diepen
Centre for Mathematics and Computer Science
P.O. Box 4079, 1009 AB Amsterdam, The Netherlands

The foundation of implementation of algebraic specifications in a modular way is investigated. Given an algebraic specification with visible and hidden signature an *observing* signature is defined. This is a part of the visible signature which is used to observe the behaviour of the implementation.
Two correctness criteria are given for the implementation with respect to the observing signature. An algebraic correctness criterion guarantees initial algebraic semantics for the specification as seen through the observing signature, while allowing freedom for other parts of the signature, to the extent that even final semantics may be used there. A functional correctness criterion allows one to prove the correctness of the implementation for one observing function in Hoare logic. The union over all observing functions of such implementations provides an actual implementation in any programming language with semantics as described above.
Note: Partial support has been received from the European Communities under ESPRIT project no. 348 (Generation of Interactive Programming Environments - GIPE).

1. Introduction

An algebraic specification is a mathematical structure consisting of sorts, functions (and constants) over these sorts, and equations describing the relation between the functions and constants. It is a convenient tool to specify static and dynamic semantics of programming languages, see e.g. Goguen and Meseguer ([GM82], [GM84], [MG85]) for more detail on algebraic specification, and [BHK85], [BDMW81] and [Die86] for examples. The implementation of an algebraic specification usually consists of the conversion of the equations into a *term rewriting system*, either directly or through the completion procedure of Knuth-Bendix. More detail can be found in [HO80] and [ODo85]. The performance of such an implementation is rather slow in general, compared with algorithms written in conventional programming languages, while the specification must have certain properties to be implemented in this way at all. The aim of this paper is to provide another implementation strategy, based on pre- and postconditions, allowing the application of more classical programming and optimization techniques.

1.1. Modular algebraic specifications

Algebraic specifications have been introduced to provide a description style for data types in an algebraically — mathematically — nice way. The mathematical notion of a (many-sorted) *algebra* used here is a structure consisting of carrier sets and typed functions (including constants) over these sets, together with a set of equations, specifying the behaviour of the functions. The combination of a set of sorts (the names of the carrier sets) and a set of functions (which include constants, unless stated otherwise), is called the *signature* of the algebra.

The algebraic specifications studied in this paper have additional organization primitives, prompted by both theoretical and practical considerations. Central issue is the *modular structure* imposed on the algebraic specifications. An algebraic specification can import another algebraic specification as a *module*, meaning that it adds the sorts, functions and equations of the imported specification to its own. Sorts or functions with the same name are only allowed when they are the same (they must originate in the same module), otherwise they must be renamed.

The modular approach naturally leads to two other primitives, a *parameter* mechanism, and the occurrence of *hidden* (local, auxiliary) sorts and functions. Hidden sorts and functions (hiddens) are used in the equations of the module in which they are defined, but they are not included in the exported or *visible* sorts and functions. Only the latter are included in the algebra associated with the module. Hiddens make it easier to write many specifications by providing local definitions, and they are necessary to specify properties needing an infinite number of equations (when defined without hiddens) in a finite way ([BT83], [BT82]).

The equations used are *conditional equations*, i.e. equations which are valid only when certain conditions are satisfied. The semantics provided are of an *initial* nature, which will be explained and modified in the paper. These semantics are usually intuitively clear.

1.2. Implementation of algebraic specifications

Once an algebraic specification has been written there is no clearcut way to derive a working program from it. In general, any model of the algebra can be seen as an implementation. Certain models are preferable, though.

A strategy followed quite often to implement a model satisfying initial semantics (an initial model) is to transform the specification into a *term rewriting system*. The easiest way to do this is to give every equation a direction, say from left to right, and to view the set of directed equations as a set of *rewrite rules*, transforming one term over the signature into another. This system can be found in various places in the literature ([BK86], [DE84], [FGJM85], [GMP83], [ODo85], [Die86]), but the success of this method depends on the properties of the directed version of the (in principle undirected) set of equations, combined with the technique used for rewriting. Turning an equation around (writing B=A instead of A=B) or writing the equations in a different order may have significant consequences for the behaviour (both in speed and in termination) of the implementation, while the specification has not been changed, except textually.

An additional problem is what to do with the modular structure when fitting a modular specification in a term rewriting system. Transparent semantics can be obtained by a *normalization step* (as described by Bergstra, Heering and Klint [BHK86]), flattening all imports into one module (renaming hidden functions and sorts where necessary). The approach above can be applied to the normalized module. It may be debated whether the loss of the structure in the specification is sufficiently motivated by the transparency of the semantics.

The present paper aims at a more module-oriented implementation, giving semantics to implement an *observing signature* (a signature through which one can observe the visible signature, of which it is a subsignature) in a functional way, using descriptions of the observing functions in *Hoare logic* (see e.g. the text books [LS84], [Bac86]). The significance for the semantics of the import construct will be touched upon briefly. The main advantage of this approach is that it permits the implementation of modules in a, possibly low-level, efficient way from the high-level specification. This allows the construction of a library of efficient basic modules upon which more sophisticated algebraic specifications may depend.

1.3. Related work

Implementation techniques for pure initial semantics are burdened with the obligation to implement the initial algebra semantics faithfully. This generally slows down the implementation, since often an initial specification demands too much detail, as has been discussed by Baker-Finch [Bak84].

In [MG85] and [ST85] another implementation criterion for algebraic specifications is provided. They focus on observable sorts, while the present paper takes a functionally oriented point of view. Their approach is a special case of the approach presented here. More detail can be found in section 3.2.2.

There is a strong resemblance to *abstract data type* theory as practiced in the verification of correctness of programs (cf. Jones [Jon80]). After all, an algebraic specification is a nice way to describe a data type. While the specifications look similar, the point of view is different. Constructor functions (i.e. functions describing the data type) really construct the type in algebraic specifications, while they only serve as a description tool in [Jon80].

Techniques which use *term rewriting systems* have the advantage of allowing (semi-)automatic translation schemes, but pay the price with severe restrictions on the set of equations allowed. Perhaps the overhead of a completion procedure for generation of rewrite rules is needed, e.g. the Knuth-Bendix procedure (see [HO80] and [ODo85] for more detail). The technique presented here allows for faster implementations, but does not support automatic translation.

1.4. An outline of this paper

In section 2 brief introductions to both specification formalisms used (the algebraic specification formalism ASF and Hoare logic) are given. Section 3 begins with a description of certain disadvantages of the initial algebra approach to motivate the theoretical framework leading to an algebraic implementation notion in the second half. An example giving an implementation according to this notion follows in section 4, which may be read before section 3.2 to get the flavour, or in the order provided to convince oneself of the rigour of the approach. The functional implementation notion is described as an extension of the algebraic notion in section 5, preceded by an example to show the insufficient strength of the latter notion for our purpose. The example of section 4 is implemented in an imperative language in section 6 according to this notion. Finally some conclusions are formulated in section 7.

2. THE FORMALISMS INFORMALLY

2.1. Algebraic specifications

The algebraic specifications in this paper are presented in the specification formalism *ASF* (for Algebraic Specification Formalism), of which a complete treatment of syntax and semantics is given by Bergstra, Heering and Klint in [BHK87]. The choice of ASF is not essential to the paper, so there is no need to explain this formalism in great detail. Various features (e.g., renaming, infix operators) are not used in the paper and will not be discussed here at all.

A specification in ASF consists of a list of modules. Every module is named and contains the following (optional) sections:

- A *parameters* section, which contains a list of sorts and functions to be bound to fully define the module.
- An *exports* section, containing the sorts and (typed) functions *visible* to the outside world (which is an importing module).
- An *imports* section, containing a list of modules. The sorts and functions exported by the modules in the list are imported in the current list and exported again. Parameters can be bound in this section. The sorts and functions of this and the preceding section provide the visible signature in the corresponding formal treatment of the algebraic specification.
- A *sorts* section, and a *functions* section, providing the hidden signature of the algebraic specification. These two sections together are often informally dubbed the *hidden* section. Definitions here are local to the module.
- A *variables* section, which quantifies the list of typed variables universally over the equations presented in the
- *equations* section, containing positive conditional equations (i.e., equations of the form $A=B$ or $A=B$ **when** $P_1=Q_1 \wedge \cdots \wedge P_n=Q_n$). Terms in equations consist of open terms generated by all (also the hidden) functions.

The equations which hold in a module are all equations of the module itself and the equations of the (directly and indirectly) imported modules with proper renaming of hidden functions, sorts and variables from the imported modules.

A special place in ASF has the function `if`, which is predefined. This function has three arguments of which the first must be of type `BOOL` and the second and third of the same, but arbitrary, type. The term `if(bool,x,y)` (with variables `x`, `y` of the same sort) may be interpreted as *if* `bool` *then* `x` *else* `y`.

The semantics of a module is defined by the initial algebra over the export (visible) signature and the function `if`. This will be encountered in more detail in the remainder of the paper. Various ASF-specifications will appear in the sequel, to which one is referred for examples.

2.2. Hoare logic and abstract data types

Hoare logic is a well-known technique to describe the behaviour of programs in both imperative and functional languages. It has found its way into various text books, e.g. [LS84] and [Bac86]. Briefly, Hoare logic allows one to write {P} S {Q}, meaning that evaluation of program S in a state in which *precondition* P holds results in a state in which *postcondition* Q holds. These conditions describe the state vector, i.e., the variables and their contents, of the program. Various proof rules and proof techniques are available to verify such a program.

In the paper some functions specified in an algebraic way will be specified in an equivalent Hoare logic way by giving conditions on its input terms and its output. Such a specification is independent of the actual implementation program, which may be changed (and preferably optimized). Since Hoare logic techniques can be formulated for many languages the ultimate program could be written in any appropriate language, at a cost in interfacing. Hence a large degree of language independence for the implementation is achieved, allowing various kinds of optimization strategies.

One way to interpret an algebraic specification is as a high level specification of an *abstract data type*. Hence the implementation strategy for algebraic specifications presented here bears a more than casual resemblance to the theory of implementation of abstract data types. An abstract data type is some type together with a set of functions on the type. An implementation is a more concrete (i.e., closer to machine level) type with a corresponding set of functions which model the abstract type and functions. This is done by providing a translation back and forth between the abstract and concrete types, such that the abstract functions are simulated correctly by the combination of the translation to the concrete type, application of the concrete function and the translation back to the abstract type (cf. Jones [Jon80]).

The scheme in the paper basically relaxes the translation conditions for all terms in the initial model of the algebraic specification by demanding translations for specific terms only. This stems from the functional orientation: only the input terms need to be translated and only the output terms need to be translated back. Section 5 provides more detail.

3. ALGEBRAIC IMPLEMENTATION

3.1. Initial algebra semantics and reusability

The question we want to consider is the following. Suppose we have an algebraic specification and we want to provide an efficient implementation for further use by someone else, as in a library. What is the interaction between efficiency and semantics?

Initial algebra semantics have much in favour. They are characterized by 'no junk', i.e., it is clear which objects exist, and 'no confusion', i.e., closed terms (terms without variables) are only equal if they can be proved equal using equational logic. While these two characterizations are clearly desirable in many circumstances this is not always the case.

The 'no confusion' condition generates overspecification in the sense that terms might be distinguished from each other without necessity. If the writer of a specification does not care about whether two terms are equal or not (in the common case that their usage is identical), and hence does not specify their equality, they are unequal. This puts a burden on the implementor of the specification to provide this inequality, not allowing a possibly more efficient identification. If such an identification could be allowed the burden is shifted to the shoulders of the specifier, who has to provide additional equations. While the extra amount of work is undesirable it is also not clear in general what additional equations are necessary and whether a sufficient set can be found at all. For discussions see [Bak84], [Kam83] and [Wan79].

Apart from the question whether a satisfactory solution can be found in general this is contrary to the amount of detail one wants to specify algebraically. For this two important considerations can be given, one philosophical and one practical:

- Algebraic specification is a higher level programming formalism. While the formalism is powerful enough to express bit level if necessary, this is a waste of effort. There are more than enough lower level programming languages already.
- An algebraic specification (and indeed any specification) is made with a certain use in mind. This use is what has to be specified in detail, since that is what has to be implemented. Other details specified are peripheral in the sense that one might have chosen another description. The less detail is fixed by these peripheral specifications the more freedom an implementor has for optimizing it. The choice of models for implementation should not be restricted to one model (up to isomorphism), but rather be as broad as the class of all models. So demanding the implementation of initial algebra semantics is too restrictive.

For the remainder of the paper we distinguish three important subsets in the signature of an algebraic specification. The consequences of this tripartition for the theory are investigated in the next section. These subsets are:

- The **visible** signature which generates the terms existing in the specification for the outside world.
- The **hidden** signature, which is necessary to obtain finite initial algebra specifications on the one hand and useful for alternative data description on the other hand. The complete signature is the union of the visible and the hidden signature.
- The **observing** signature, which restricts the terms generated by the visible signature. It contains the functions through which visible terms may be used and the sorts with terms which may be used as observing terms. A term is an observing term if both the head function and its sort are in the observing signature. This signature is the subset of the visible signature, that one wants to be implemented as specified.

The choice of the functions and sorts in the observing signature depends on the goal one has in mind for the specification. Making this signature bigger enhances the possibilities for use but restricts the freedom of the implementor. So one can opt for a fast, but narrowly applicable implementation, or for a more generally usable, but slower implementation.

Of course, the speed of a certain function in an observable signature is not only dependent on the signature but also on the implementations of other (not necessarily observing) functions. One can for instance trade the speed of an insertion function for the speed of a retrieval function by gearing the underlying data structure (at this level of abstraction represented by the visible functions that are not observing and the hidden functions) to the other task.

3.2. A theory of algebraic implementation

This section is devoted to the development of a theory for the subsequently introduced notion of *algebraic implementation* with respect to an *observing signature*. Roughly speaking two algebraic specifications are algebraic implementations of each other when the behaviour of the observing functions is the same in both specifications. An annotated example is provided in section 4. The reader may wish to read the example first, referring back to notations and details in this section where needed.

3.2.1. Notations (algebraic specifications)

In the rest of the paper the following conventions are used:

a. A **signature** Σ is a tuple (S,F) in which S is a set of sorts and F a set of typed functions. (Note that there is no intrinsic relation between the sorts in S and F.) Often an element of F is denoted by its name only, providing typing when necessary. Two functions with the same name, but different typing are different functions.

b. A **complete signature** Σ = (S,F) is a signature in which for all $f: s_1 \times \cdots \times s_k \rightarrow s \in F$ holds that all sorts in the typing of f are available in S, so $s_1, \cdots, s_k, s \in S$.

c. For a signature Σ is $T(\Sigma)$ the **set of closed terms**; $T_s(\Sigma)$ is the subset of terms of sort s from $T(\Sigma)$.

d. Union, intersection and inclusion are defined for signatures Σ_1, Σ_2 ($\Sigma_i = (S_i, F_i)$), as:

$$\Sigma_1 \cup \Sigma_2 = (S_1 \cup S_2,\ F_1 \cup F_2),\quad \Sigma_1 \cap \Sigma_2 = (S_1 \cap S_2,\ F_1 \cap F_2),\quad \text{and}\quad \Sigma_1 \subseteq \Sigma_2 = S_1 \subseteq S_2 \wedge F_1 \subseteq F_2.$$

e. An **algebraic specification** is a tuple (Σ_V, Σ_H, E) with

- $\Sigma_V = (S_V, F_V)$ a complete signature (the **visible** signature),
- $\Sigma_H = (S_H, F_H)$ a signature (the **hidden** signature) such that $\Sigma_V \cup \Sigma_H$ (the **internal** signature) is a complete signature, and
- E a set of equations over $T(\Sigma_V \cup \Sigma_H)$.

f. Let (Σ_V, Σ_H, E) be an algebraic specification and let $t, t' \in T(\Sigma_V \cup \Sigma_H)$. For an equation $e \in E$, ***t* and *t'* are equal through direct substitution in equation** e (i.e., in one step) is written as $t =_e t'$.

***t* and *t'* are equationally equal**, i.e., equal through zero or more direct substitutions in one or more equations from E, is written as $t =_E t'$.

3.2.2. Definitions (Σ_O-observability and -equality)

Let (Σ_V, Σ_H, E) be an algebraic specification and $\Sigma_O = (S_O, F_O)$ (the **observing** signature) a signature such that $\Sigma_O \subseteq \Sigma_V$.

a. The **set of closed Σ_O-terms over Σ_V**, also called the **set of observing terms** is the set of terms in $T(\Sigma_V)$ of sort in S_O and head function symbol in F_O. It is defined as:

$$T(\Sigma_O, \Sigma_V) = \{t \in T(\Sigma_V) \mid \exists f{:}s_1 \times \cdots \times s_k \to s \in F_O,\ s \in S_O\ \exists u_1 \in T(\Sigma_V) \cdots \exists u_k \in T(\Sigma_V)\ [t \in T_s(\Sigma_V) \wedge t = f(u_1, \cdots, u_k)]\}.$$

The **set of closed Σ_O-terms over Σ_V of sort** s is written as $T_s(\Sigma_O, \Sigma_V)$.

Note that it is possible to have functions in F_O whose output sort is not in in S_O, or sorts in S_O which cannot be reached from F_O. This choice of notation is motivated by the function-oriented approach of this paper. By choosing a set of observing functions F_O and all visible sorts S_V for S_O all sorts in S_V which cannot be reached do not influence $T(\Sigma_O, \Sigma_V)$. For symmetry reasons the definition is formulated in such a way that one can also restrict the sorts and not the functions, as will be done in point e below. Alternatively, it is possible to define S_O as the set of sorts in the range of F_O without affecting the theory.

b. Where no confusion can arise the abbreviations $T_O = T(\Sigma_O, \Sigma_V)$, $T_V = T(\Sigma_V)$, $T_{s,O} = T_s(\Sigma_O, \Sigma_V)$, and $T_{s,V} = T_s(\Sigma_V)$ are used.

c. A **context** (for sort s) $T(\bullet_s)$ is a term with a missing subterm of sort s. The **empty context** (i.e., a context in which the top term is missing) is written as $\bullet_s$.

A term $t \in T_{s,V}$ is **Σ_O-observable** if and only if there exists a context $T(\bullet_s)$ such that $T(t) \in T_O$;

a Σ_O-observable term $t \in T_{s,V}$ is **directly Σ_O-observable** if and only if $t \in T_O$ (the empty context $T(\bullet_s) = \bullet_s$ satisfies $T(t) \in T_O$);

a Σ_O-observable term $t \in T_{s,V}$ is **indirectly Σ_O-observable** if and only if $t \notin T_O$ ($T(\bullet_s) = \bullet_s$ does not satisfy $T(t) \in T_O$).

d. **Σ_O-equality** (i.e., equality with respect to observations through terms in the observing signature Σ_O) is defined as follows for two terms $t,\ t' \in T_{s,V}$:

$$t \sim_{E,\Sigma_O} t' \Leftrightarrow \forall T(\bullet_s)\,[T(t), T(t') \in T_O \to T(t) =_E T(t')\,].$$

Where no confusion can arise $\sim_{E,\Sigma_O}$ is abbreviated to $\sim_O$.

e. Let $f \in F_V$. A term $t \in T(\Sigma_V)$ is **f-observable** if and only if t is (S_V, $\{f\}$)-observable;

two terms in $T(\Sigma_V)$ are **f-equal** if and only if they are (S_V, $\{f\}$)-equal.

Let $s \in S_V$. A term $t \in T(\Sigma_V)$ is **s-observable** if and only if t is ($\{s\}$, F_V)-observable;

two terms in $T(\Sigma_V)$ are **s-equal** if and only if they are ($\{s\}$, F_V)-equal.

Since the definition in case c ignores unreachable sorts and functions to unavailable sorts, only terms with head symbol f in the first two cases, and with range s in the last two, are relevant.

The notion of observability via a sort corresponds to the notion in [MG85], and is underlying the behavioural equivalence notion in [ST85]. In the latter paper, the observational equivalence notion is very general, since it is parameterized with the logic used to reason about observations. Thus Σ_O-equality corresponds to observational equivalence under conditional equational logic in the terms of [ST85]. By concentrating here on one logic more can be said about the implementation.

3.2.3. Some facts about Σ_O-observability and -equality

In final algebra semantics terms are equal unless they can be proved different, so in models with final semantics there is the maximum amount of 'confusion' consistent with the inequalities which must exist in the model. As such, Σ_O-equality is a notion from final algebra semantics. If you want to show that two closed terms are different you have to find a context for which these terms behave differently, thus proving their inequality. If no such context can be found the terms cannot be distinguished from each other. In initial semantics, on the contrary, they are distinguished unless they are equationally equal, in other words, unless they can be transformed into each other via equations from E, thus proving their equality.

Let (Σ_V, Σ_H, E) be an algebraic specification, $\Sigma_O \subseteq \Sigma_V$, and $t,\ t' \in T_{s,V}$, then the following facts hold:

a. $T(\Sigma_V, \Sigma_V) = T(\Sigma_V)$.

Observing through the visible signature gives all visible terms. This follows immediately from definition 3.2.2.a.

b. If $\Sigma'_O \subseteq \Sigma_O$ then $T(\Sigma'_O, \Sigma_V) \subseteq T(\Sigma_O, \Sigma_V)$.

A smaller observing signature results in less observing terms. Again this follows from definition 3.2.2.a.

c. If $\Sigma'_O \subseteq \Sigma_O$ then $t \sim_{E,\Sigma_O} t' \to t \sim_{E,\Sigma'_O} t'$.

This follows from the definition of Σ_O-equality and fact b, since there are less contexts in $T(\Sigma'_O, \Sigma_V)$ than in $T(\Sigma_O, \Sigma_V)$ to show the difference between t and t'.

d. If t and t' are not Σ_O-observable they are Σ_O-equal.

Since there is no context to show the difference between t and t' this follows from the definition.

e. If t is Σ_O-observable and t' is not then they are Σ_O-equal.

The argument for fact d holds here also.

f. It should be noted that in cases d and e both $t \sim_{E,\Sigma_V} t'$ and $\neg t \sim_{E,\Sigma_V} t'$ can be true. Take for example:

$$\Sigma_V = (\{s\},\ \{a,\ b\}) \text{ with } a,\ b \in s, \text{ and}$$

$$\Sigma_O = (\{s\},\ \{a\}) \text{ for case e, or } \Sigma_O = (\{s\},\ \emptyset) \text{ for case d.}$$

When E is empty $a \sim_{\emptyset,\Sigma_O} b$ and $\neg a \sim_{\emptyset,\Sigma_V} b$ hold; E = $\{a=b\}$ has as result that $a \sim_{\{a=b\},\Sigma_O} b$ and $a \sim_{\{a=b\},\Sigma_V} b$.

The following lemma states that the initial algebraic structure is retained on directly observable terms. So only indirectly observable and unobservable terms can lose their initial behaviour. It follows immediately (corollary 3.2.5) that no restriction on the observability (i.e., $\Sigma_O = \Sigma_V$) retains the initial algebraic structure.

3.2.4. Initial Algebra Lemma

For $t,\ t' \in T_s(\Sigma_O, \Sigma_V)$: $t \sim_{E,\Sigma_O} t' \iff t =_E t'$.

Proof direct from definition 3.2.2.d (omitted).

3.2.5. Corollary ($\Sigma_O = \Sigma_V$ preserves initial algebra semantics)

For $t,\ t' \in T_s(\Sigma_V)$: $t \sim_{E,\Sigma_V} t' \iff t =_E t'$.

3.2.6. Witness Existence Lemma

The following lemma formulates a nice fact for proofs with observable terms. Two terms are Σ_O-equal unless there is a context proving the opposite. Hence two terms are Σ_O-equal when there is no common context. So it is important to have at least one common context. In this lemma existence of a witness context is asserted for Σ_O-observable terms of the same sort.

Lemma: For two Σ_O-observable terms $t,\ t' \in T_{s,V}$ there exists a context $T(\bullet_s)$ such that $T(t),\ T(t') \in T_O$.

Proof (omitted).

3.2.7. Σ_O-equality as congruence: a problem with transitivity

We would have liked to use the notation of $=_O$ instead of $\sim_O$ since it should define a congruence similar to $=_E$. However, there are some problems connected with the final nature of $\sim_O$ and the initial nature of $=_E$. A congruence $\sim$ satisfies the laws of *symmetry* ($t \sim t$), *reflexivity* (if $t \sim t'$ then also $t' \sim t$), *transitivity* (if $t \sim t'$ and $t' \sim t''$, then also $t \sim t''$), and the *substitution property*, (if $t_1 \sim t_1' \wedge \cdots \wedge t_n \sim t_n'$ holds then also $f(t_1, \cdots, t_n) \sim f(t_1', \cdots, t_n')$ holds). For terms in $T(\Sigma_V)$ reflexivity, symmetry and the substitution property of $\sim_O$ follow immediately from the corresponding properties of $=_E$ and definition 3.2.2.d. However, in section 3.2.3 facts d and e show that transitivity is not guaranteed on $T(\Sigma_V)$. Since these facts deal with terms that are not observable, this is no real problem. However, $\sim_O$ is also not transitive on the subset of Σ_O-observable terms in $T(\Sigma_V)$. This is illustrated in the following example.

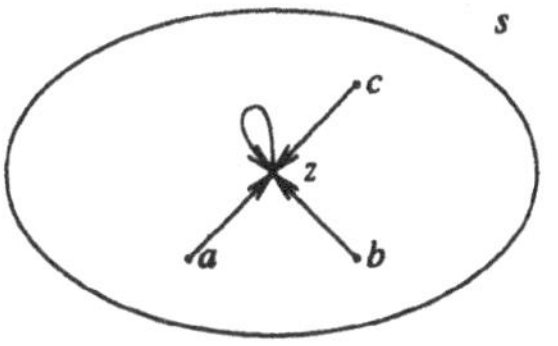

FIGURE 3.1

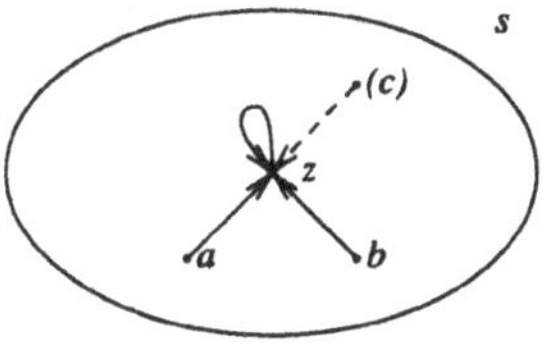

FIGURE 3.2

Let $\Sigma_V = (\{s\},\ \{a,\ b,\ c,\ z,\ f\})$ with $a,\ b,\ c,\ z \in s$ and $f : s \to s$, E consists of the equation $f(x) = z$ with x a variable of sort s, and $\Sigma_O = (\{s\},\ \{a,\ b,\ z,\ f\})$. This structure is shown in FIGURE 3.1. Then $a \sim_O c$, since $f(a) =_E f(c)$, $f(f(a)) =_E f(f(c))$, etc., and similarly $c \sim_O b$, though $\neg a \sim_O b$. Still, this is not unreasonable. If one only looks at Σ_O any relation involving c is irrelevant. The new structure is given in FIGURE 3.2, forgetting the dashed arrow. If later on one would want to add a new constant named c, then c could be a new name for an old constant like a, b, or z, or a completely new constant. So if c is observably not equal to one or more of the constants, this would rule out some of the possibilities. Hence, the freedom allowed when introducing c would be limited in an undesirable way.

The precise criteria conserving transitivity, and hence making $\sim_O$ a congruence are given in Theorem 3.2.8. Some important classes of observable signatures that are transitivity conserving are given in a corollary (3.2.9).

3.2.8. Transitivity Theorem

Let t, t', t'' be Σ_O-observable terms of sort s such that $t \sim_O t'$ and $t' \sim_O t''$, then

$$\neg t \sim_O t'' \Leftrightarrow t, t'' \in T_O \wedge t' \in T_V - T_O \wedge \forall T(\bullet_s)\, T(t), T(t'') \in T_O \rightarrow [\, T(t) \neq_E T(t'') \leftrightarrow T(\bullet_s) = \bullet_s \,]$$

Proof based on the fact that $\bullet_s$ is used to compare t with t'', but not t' with t or t'' (omitted).

3.2.9. Transitivity conserving constraints

The transitivity theorem states that two *directly* Σ_O-observable terms can be Σ_O-unequal, even though there is an *indirectly* Σ_O-observable term which is Σ_O-equal to both. This is the case in the example in 3.2.7. Hence Σ_O-inequality is stronger for directly observable terms than for indirectly observable terms.

The theorem above provides necessary and sufficient conditions for transitivity. This may be unwieldy to use in practice. However, it is conveniently possible to give criteria, that are important from the point of view of implementation, to check whether $\sim_O$ is an equivalence relation. Intuitively, the implementation of directly observable terms only has to follow the initial algebra semantics (Lemma 3.2.4), while indirectly observable and unobservable terms are less demanding for the implementation. Some criteria are formulated below:

Corollary:

Let T_s be the subset of Σ_O-observable terms from $T_{s,V}$. The relation $\sim_{E,\Sigma_O}$ is an equivalence relation on T_s if either of the following holds:

a. $T_{s,O} = \emptyset$, i.e., sort s is not directly observable. Consequently its internal representation may be changed without altering the directly observable sorts.

b. $T_{s,O} = T_s$, i.e., T_s has to be implemented with initial algebra semantics.

c. for all $t \in T_s$ there is precisely one $t' \in T_{s,O}$ such that $t' \sim_O t$, i.e., there is exactly one directly observable term Σ_O-equal to any term of T_s. This term plays the role of a canonical form and has to be implemented faithfully. All other terms may be implemented by their canonical equivalent.

d. $\Sigma_O = (S_O, F_V)$ for some $S_O \subseteq S_V$, i.e., if $s \in S_O$ then all constructor functions for terms of sort s are available, hence $T_s = T_{s,O}$ (case b), and, if $s \notin S_O$ then no constructor function for terms of sort s qualifies as outermost function in T_O, hence $T_{s,O} = \emptyset$ (case a).

This case states that for s-observability $\sim_O$ is a congruence for terms of any sort $s' \in S_V$, including s itself. Hence it is a rephrasing of the well-known fact that observability through a sort conserves the congruence (see [MG85]).

Generally $\sim_O$ will be a congruence. If that is the case it is usually written as $=_O$ in the sequel. Similarly $\sim_{E,\Sigma}$ becomes $=_{E,\Sigma}$.

3.2.10. Definition (Algebraic Implementation)

The following definition represents the central notion in this section, namely the notion of implementation for an algebraic specification relative to an observing signature. Intuitively, two specifications are algebraic implementations of each other when they have the same congruence on the observable terms. This is inherently an almost symmetric notion: if a small specification implements part of a large one then the large specification implements the same part of the small one (and more, but that is redundant) if the set of observable terms is the same. We provide the following *definition*:

- Let (Σ_V, Σ_H, E) and $(\Sigma'_V, \Sigma'_H, E')$ be algebraic specifications and Σ_O be a signature such that $\Sigma_O \subseteq \Sigma_V \cap \Sigma'_V$.

  $(\Sigma'_V, \Sigma'_H, E')$ is a **Σ_O-implementation of** (Σ_V, Σ_H, E) if and only if for all $s \in S_V$ and for all Σ_O-observable terms $t, t' \in T_s(\Sigma_V)$:

$$t \sim_{E,\Sigma_O} t' \Leftrightarrow t \sim_{E',\Sigma_O} t'.$$

3.2.11. Some facts about algebraic implementations

a. If $\Sigma_O \subseteq \Sigma_V$ then an algebraic specification (Σ_V, Σ_H, E) is a Σ_O-implementation of itself. As an even more trivial special case (Σ_V, Σ_H, E) is a Σ_V-implementation of itself.

b. If $(\Sigma'_V, \Sigma'_H, E')$ is a Σ_O-implementation of (Σ_V, Σ_H, E) and $\Sigma'_O \subseteq \Sigma_O$ then $(\Sigma'_V, \Sigma'_H, E')$ is also a Σ'_O-implementation of (Σ_V, Σ_H, E).

c. Σ_O-implementation is a symmetric relation on the class of algebraic specifications with the same set of Σ_O-observable terms.

d. Σ_O-implementation is also a transitive relation under the conditions of case c.

While the facts above provide some idea about the usefulness of the definition two important properties have to be proved. Of course we want to conserve the property in initial algebra semantics that the hidden signature and the set of equations may be changed as long as this does not affect the congruence on the visible signature. This is asserted in lemma 3.2.12.

Next, in the central theorem a functionally oriented criterion is given for an algebraic implementation. This serves as a starting point for section 5, in which a notion of functional implementation will be given.

3.2.12. Initial Algebra Implementation Lemma

Let $(\Sigma_V, \Sigma'_H, E')$ be a Σ_V-implementation of (Σ_V, Σ_H, E), then for all $s \in S_V$ and for all $t, t' \in T_{s,V}$: $t =_E t' \Leftrightarrow t =_{E'} t'$.
Proof follows from the fact that all terms in T_V are Σ_V-observable, and corollary 3.2.5 (omitted).

3.2.13. Algebraic Implementation Theorem

Let (Σ_V, Σ_H, E) and $(\Sigma'_V, \Sigma'_H, E')$ be algebraic specifications and $\Sigma_O \subseteq \Sigma_V \cap \Sigma'_V$.
If for all $f \in F_O$, $f: s_1 \times \cdots \times s_k \rightarrow s_0$, with $s_0 \in S_O$, for all $t \in T_{s_0}(\Sigma_V)$ and for all $(u_1, \cdots, u_k) \in (T(\Sigma_V))^k$ $f(u_1, \cdots, u_k) =_E t \Leftrightarrow f(u_1, \cdots, u_k) =_{E'} t$ holds, then $(\Sigma'_V, \Sigma'_H, E')$ is a Σ_O-implementation of (Σ_V, Σ_H, E).
Proof by unfolding all Σ_O-observable terms in $T(\Sigma_V)$ (omitted).
Note: this theorem is sufficiently strong to describe the behaviour of a function up to the congruence defined by $\sim_{E,\Sigma_o}$, if such a congruence exists. An example of the use of the theorem is given in the next section. A more restrictive definition of implementation, strong enough to describe functional implementation, is given in section 5.

4. An Example: Tables

In this section, two definitions of elementary data structures for objects of arbitrary sort ELEM are given. Both data structures support storage and retrieval with elements of an arbitrary sort KEY with equality function eq as selection criterion.

The first specification describes a sort TABLE. An element of this sort is a list of all entries with corresponding keys in the data structure. This data structure can be searched from the last entry to the first, in linear time. The second specification uses a hidden sort TREE to implement the same data in a search-tree. This is possible when we have a total ordering on sort KEY. In the example function lt, combined with eq, provides such an ordering.

The specifications below are parameterized with sorts KEY and ELEM at the specification level. To guide the intuition, one should think of two (perhaps equal) sorts which are already well-known, e.g. CHAR for ELEM and INT for KEY. ASF does not provide a semantics for unbound parameter sorts, since there is no mechanism to force restrictions on the actual parameter (like the total ordering in the example). In the paper restrictions are given in the commentary, so it will be clear what the semantics should be.

The remainder of this section is devoted to a proof sketch of the fact that the modules Tables and Tables-as-trees are algebraic implementations of each other when one observes through the retrieve function lookup only, in other words, with respect to lookup-equality. So we take for the observing signature ({BOOL, ELEM, KEY, TABLE}, {lookup}), or ({ELEM}, {lookup}), since ELEM is the range of lookup.

The simple specification is given below:

```
module Tables -- original specification
begin
  parameters Keys-and-Elements
    begin sorts KEY, ELEM
          functions eq: KEY # KEY -> BOOL -- equality
    end Keys-and-Elements
  exports
    begin sorts TABLE
          functions nulltable:                        -> TABLE
                    tableadd : KEY # ELEM # TABLE -> TABLE
                    lookup   : KEY # TABLE          -> ELEM
                    errorelem:                        -> ELEM
    end
  imports Booleans
  variables key, key1, key2: -> KEY
            elem           : -> ELEM
            table          : -> TABLE
equations
[1] lookup(key, nulltable) = errorelem
[2] lookup(key1, tableadd(key2,elem,table)) = if(eq(key1,key2),elem,
                                                  lookup(key1,table))
end Tables
```

This specification speaks for itself. Function tableadd is underspecified and hence the problems indicated in section 3.1 can arise. To avoid them we restrict the set of observing terms to those with function lookup as outermost symbol. Hence an implementor of this module can concentrate on the correct implementation of lookup.

To get an efficient implementation of lookup more detailed information about sort KEY is needed. If KEY is a small set something similar to a bounded array is feasible. If a hash function could be defined, a hash table might be used as implementation. Each of these structures can be algebraically specified as hidden structure, thus providing an algebraic specification which upon implementation gives an equivalent, but more efficient, implementation of `lookup`.

For this example it is assumed that a total ordering can be defined on the set `KEY` with the functions `eq` and `lt` (lower-than). The total ordering allows the definition of a binary search-tree. This is done in module `Tables-as-trees` below:

```
module Tables-as-trees
begin
  parameters Keys-and-Elements
    begin sorts KEY, ELEM
          functions eq: KEY # KEY -> BOOL -- equality
                    lt: KEY # KEY -> BOOL -- lower-than    -- new
                    -- eq and lt must provide a total ordering on sort KEY
    end Keys-and-Elements
  exports
    begin sorts TABLE
          functions nulltable:                    -> TABLE
                    tableadd : KEY # ELEM # TABLE -> TABLE
                    lookup   : KEY # TABLE        -> ELEM
                    errorelem:                    -> ELEM
    end
  imports Booleans
  -- hidden section
  sorts TREE                                                -- new
  functions tree      : TREE # KEY # ELEM # TREE ->  TREE  -- new
            niltree   :                          ->  TREE  -- new
            treeadd   : KEY # ELEM # TREE        ->  TREE  -- new
            lookuptr  : KEY # TREE               ->  ELEM  -- new
            tbltotree: TABLE                     ->  TREE  -- new
  variables key, key2   : -> KEY
            elem, elem2 : -> ELEM
            table       : -> TABLE
            tree1, tree2: -> TREE
 equations                                                    -- all new
 [h1] tbltotree(nulltable) = niltree
 [h2] tbltotree(tableadd(key,elem,table)) = treeadd(key,elem,tbltotree(table))
 [h3] treeadd(key,elem,niltree) = tree(niltree,key,elem,niltree)
 [h4] treeadd(key,elem,tree(tree1,key2,elem2,tree2))
                           = if(eq(key,key2),tree(tree1,key,elem,tree2),
                                if(lt(key,key2),
                                   tree(treeadd(key,elem,tree1),key2,elem2,tree2),
                                   tree(tree1,key2,elem2,treeadd(key,elem,tree2))))
 [h5] lookuptr(key,niltree) = errorelem
 [h6] lookuptr(key,tree(tree1,key2,elem,tree2))
                           = if(eq(key,key2),elem,
                                if(lt(key,key2),lookuptr(key,tree1),
                                   lookuptr(key,tree2)))
 [h7] lookup(key,table) = lookuptr(key,tbltotree(table))
 end Tables-as-trees
```

Note that all equations contain hidden sorts. Equation h7 defines `lookup` in terms of `lookuptr`, the retrieval function on trees, itself defined in h5 and h6. Equations h1 through h4 define the build-up of a tree from a table.

It is possible to declare all hidden sorts and functions visible rather than hidden. The effect would be that module `Tables-as-trees` would still be an implementation with respect to `lookup`-observability of module `Tables`, but not the other way around. The reason for the latter is the existence of observable terms containing constructor functions for `TREE` in module `Tables-as-trees`, terms which are not existent in module `Tables`.

The following proof sketch first defines a well-formedness predicate *searchtree* for terms of sort `TREE`, since not all constructible terms are search-trees. Then it is proved that the predicate *searchtree* is invariant over the insertion function `treeadd`, and that the retrieval function `lookuptr` is well-defined for single additions to a tree which satisfies this predicate. Finally the equivalence between the two specifications is proved with induction on the number of insertions.

4.1. Definition (well-formedness of searchtrees)

The predicate *searchtree*(`t`) for a term `t` of sort `TREE` describes the well-formedness of a tree as search-tree. It can be used in to derive properties about the behaviour of the data structure generated by function `treeadd`. This holds in particular for the behaviour observed through function `lookuptr`, which is needed to derive the behaviour of function `lookup`. The predicate is defined as follows (with `t1`, `t2` of sort `TREE`, `j`, `k`, `l` of sort `KEY`, and `e` of sort `ENTRY`):

- *searchtree*(`niltree`) = true;
- *searchtree*(`tree(t1,k,e,t2)`) = *searchtree*(`t1`) $\wedge \forall$ `j` $\in$ *set-of-keys*(`t1`) [`lt(j,k) = true`] $\wedge$ *searchtree*(`t2`) $\wedge \forall$ `l` $\in$ *set-of-keys*(`t2`) [`lt(k,l) = true`],

with *set-of-keys*(`t`) for terms `t` of sort `TREE` a set containing all keys in `t`.

4.2. Well-formedness lemma for trees

Let `k`, `k'` be of sort `KEY`, `e`, `e'` be of sort `ENTRY`, and `t` be of sort `TREE`, then we can formulate the following *Lemma*:

a. searchtree(`t`) $\rightarrow$ *searchtree*(`treeadd(k',e',t)`).

b. searchtree(`t`) $\rightarrow$ [`eq(k,k') = true` $\rightarrow$ `lookuptr(k,treeadd(k',e',t)) = e'`] $\wedge$
[`eq(k,k') = false` $\rightarrow$ `lookuptr(k,treeadd(k',e',t)) = lookuptr(k,t)`].

Proof by induction on the number of nodes in the tree (omitted).

4.3. Proof of `lookup`*-equality*

`Lookup`-equality can now be proved by induction with respect to the number of insertions using function `tableadd`. The well-formedness predicate *searchtree* makes the proof straightforward. If the equivalence defined by the equations from module `Tables` is called $=_{Tb}$ and from module `Tables-as-trees` $=_{Tr}$, then (Theorem 3.2.13) it is sufficient to prove for all pairs (`k`, `t`) $\in T_{KEY,V} \times T_{TABLE,V}$ and for all terms `e` $\in T_{ELEM,V}$

$$\texttt{lookup(k,t)} =_{Tb} \texttt{e} \Leftrightarrow \texttt{lookup(k,t)} =_{Tr} \texttt{e}.$$

The proof (subsequently omitted) proceeds by assuming that `e` does not contain the function `lookup`. Next, it can be extended to general terms `e` $\in T_{ELEM,V}$ by replacing such terms with equivalent terms not containing function `lookup`.

5. Functional implementation

5.1. The functional view

The implementation Theorem (3.2.13 in section 3.2) gives an algebraically clean criterion for implementation. However, it is not sufficient as a tool to fix implementations of functions in the classical sense: a function has a certain result value for every combination of input values. Of course the result value should depend on the input values, but it should not depend on the implementation.

The violation of this property is shown by taking $\Sigma_V = (\{s, t\}, \{a, b, p, q, f\})$ with $a,b \in s$, $p,q \in t$ and f: $s \rightarrow t$, $\Sigma_O = (\{s, t\}, \{a, b, f\})$, $\Sigma_H = \varnothing$, E = {f(a)=p, f(b)=p}, and E′ = {f(a)=q, f(b)=q}. The Σ_O-observable terms in T_V are a, b, f(a) and f(b). Obviously f(a) $=_{E,\Sigma_O}$ f(b) and f(a) $=_{E',\Sigma_O}$ f(b). Hence (Σ_V, $\varnothing$, E) and (Σ_V, $\varnothing$, E′) are Σ_O-implementations of each other. However, f clearly has different result values.

Additional restrictions are needed to be able to view a term in T_O as a function (the header function) defined on tuples in T_V and with range T_V. In initial algebra semantics the 'result' is the congruence class defined by the set of equations E. Hence any term in the congruence class will do, since it fixes (for specific E and Σ_V) the class. So we need a canonical form, which is a representative for every congruence class. In a confluent and terminating term rewriting system this canonical form is called 'normal form', and it is defined by the system itself.

The following three sets of terms within T_V are induced by Σ_O:

- the *directly* Σ_O-observable terms,
- the *indirectly* Σ_O-observable terms, and
- the terms *reachable* from T_O, i.e., terms not necessarily in T_O but in the congruence class of some term in T_O.

Note that the last two sets may overlap. The input values for functions in F_O with range in S_O form a subset of the union of the first two sets. Any element of the first and the third sets could be in the range of a function in F_O.

The directly Σ_O-observable terms do not necessarily contain a desired result value. For example, a specification of *string-of-characters* might contain a function *length* from strings to integers. The set of *length*-observable terms contains the *length* function applied to various strings, but it does not contain the integers, which is clearly the desired set of result values.

In the subsection below this idea is formalized for a specific observing function. The function has input terms, which should be well-typed, and an output term, depending on the input terms and the set of equations, which must be in a certain set of canonical terms. There is an obvious link with the theory of *abstract data types* (cf. Jones [Jon80]) here. The well-typedness of the input terms serves as precondition and the equations and a characterization of the set of canonical terms serve as postcondition.

In general one has more than one observing function, so some preliminary work has to be done to allow a decomposition of the observing set of functions into singletons.

5.2. A theory of functional implementation

5.2.1. Definitions (input-, reachable and canonical terms)

Let (Σ_V, Σ_H, E) be an algebraic specification and $\Sigma_O \subseteq \Sigma_V$. Then

a. the set $I(\Sigma_O, \Sigma_V)$ of Σ_O-**input terms over** Σ_V is defined as:
$I(\Sigma_O, \Sigma_V) = \{t \in T(\Sigma_V) \mid \exists f \in F_O\ f: s_1 \times \cdots \times s_k \to s,\ s \in S_O\ \exists i \leq k\ t \in T_{s_i}(\Sigma_V)\}$.

b. the set $R(\Sigma_O, \Sigma_V)$ of Σ_O-**reachable terms over** Σ_V is defined as: $R(\Sigma_O, \Sigma_V) = \{t \in T(\Sigma_V) \mid \exists t' \in T(\Sigma_O, \Sigma_V)\ t =_E t'\}$.
Note that terms containing hidden functions and sorts are not considered reachable.

c. A set $C(\Sigma_O, \Sigma_V) \subseteq R(\Sigma_O, \Sigma_V)$ is a **set of canonical terms** if and only if $\forall t, t' \in C(\Sigma_O, \Sigma_V)\ [t =_E t' \to t = t']$.

d. A set of canonical terms $C(\Sigma_O, \Sigma_V)$ is **complete** if and only if $\forall t \in T(\Sigma_O, \Sigma_V)\ \exists t' \in C(\Sigma_O, \Sigma_V)\ t =_E t'$.

e. A **reduction to canonical terms** $\twoheadrightarrow_{C(\Sigma_O, \Sigma_V)}$ (abbreviated $\twoheadrightarrow_C$ or even $\twoheadrightarrow$) is defined as follows:

$$t \twoheadrightarrow_{C(\Sigma_O, \Sigma_V)} t' \Leftrightarrow t \in R(\Sigma_O, \Sigma_V) \wedge t' \in C(\Sigma_O, \Sigma_V) \wedge t =_E t'.$$

f. Analogous to the definitions of T_O and $T_s(\Sigma_O, \Sigma_V)$ the following shorthand conventions are adopted:

$I_O = I(\Sigma_O, \Sigma_V)$, $R_O = R(\Sigma_O, \Sigma_V)$, $C_O = C(\Sigma_O, \Sigma_V)$,
$I_{s,O} = I_s(\Sigma_O, \Sigma_V) = I(\Sigma_O, \Sigma_V) \cap T_s(\Sigma_V)$, $R_{s,O} = R_s(\Sigma_O, \Sigma_V) = R(\Sigma_O, \Sigma_V) \cap T_s(\Sigma_V)$, $C_{s,O} = C_s(\Sigma_O, \Sigma_V) = C(\Sigma_O, \Sigma_V) \cap T_s(\Sigma_V)$.

5.2.2. Some facts

a. $R(\Sigma_O, \Sigma_V) \supseteq T(\Sigma_O, \Sigma_V)$.

b. Every term in $I(\Sigma_O, \Sigma_V)$ is Σ_O-observable.

c. The converse of fact b does not hold, i.e., not every Σ_O-observable term is a Σ_O-input term.

5.2.3. Lemma

Let $C(\Sigma_O, \Sigma_V)$ be a complete set of canonical terms. The terms in $C(\Sigma_O, \Sigma_V)$ with the (adapted) functions on $R(\Sigma_O, \Sigma_V)$ form a canonical term algebra if the operation of these functions on $R(\Sigma_O, \Sigma_V)$ is restricted to reach $C(\Sigma_O, \Sigma_V)$ by application of the reduction to canonical terms $\twoheadrightarrow_C$ after the normal application of the function in $R(\Sigma_O, \Sigma_V)$. Then $C(\Sigma_O, \Sigma_V)$ as a term algebra is isomorphic to $R(\Sigma_O, \Sigma_V)/{=_E}$.

Proof from the definition of $R(\Sigma_O, \Sigma_V)$ and $C(\Sigma_O, \Sigma_V)$ (omitted).

5.2.4. Functional decomposition of a reduction to canonical terms

Next we want to pursue a 'divide and conquer' strategy to provide an implementation of a reduction to canonical terms $\twoheadrightarrow_C$. The decomposition chosen is made on the typed head symbol (the "function") of the term to be reduced. This allows for a separate implementation for each function. The total implementation of $\twoheadrightarrow_C$ can be constructed from the union of these separate implementations.

It should be noted that a reduction to canonical terms $\twoheadrightarrow_C$ as a total map from R_O to C_O is fixed by C_O and the congruence $/{=_E}$. This follows from the definition of C_O, since for every term in R_O exactly one term in C_O is in the same congruence class. So it is possible to define the map $\twoheadrightarrow_C$ as a union of partial maps to the set of canonical terms.

It is also possible to define a complete set of canonical terms implicitly by defining a (possibly partial) map $\twoheadrightarrow$ from T_O to R_O for which the following holds:

1) $\forall t \in T_O, t' \in R_O\ [t \twoheadrightarrow t' \Leftrightarrow t =_E t']$,

2) $\forall t \in T_O\ card(\{t' \in R_O \mid \exists t'' \in T_O\ [t =_E t'' \wedge t'' \twoheadrightarrow t']\}) = 1$.

It can easily be seen that the range of $\twoheadrightarrow$ is a complete set of canonical terms. So a reduction to canonical terms can be described by its behaviour on terms in T_O. A well-known example of such an implicit definition is the set of normal forms defined by a confluent and terminating term rewriting system.

5.2.5. Definitions (functional implementation)

a. Let $\twoheadrightarrow_C$ be a reduction to canonical terms and let $\Sigma \subseteq \Sigma_O$. Then $\twoheadrightarrow_{\Sigma,C}$ is defined as the restriction of $\twoheadrightarrow_C$ to the domain $T(\Sigma, \Sigma_V)$.

b. Let (Σ_V, Σ_H, E) be an algebraic specification, Σ_O be a signature such that $\Sigma_O \subseteq \Sigma_V$, and C_O be a complete set of canonical terms. Then a map $\twoheadrightarrow$ is a **functional implementation** if and only if $\forall t \in T_O, t' \in C_O \; [t \twoheadrightarrow t' \leftrightarrow t =_E t']$.

5.2.6. Some facts about functional implementations

a. Let (Σ_V, Σ_H, E) be an algebraic specification, $\Sigma_O \subseteq \Sigma_V$, C_O a set of canonical terms, and $\twoheadrightarrow_C \restriction_{T_O}$ the restriction of reduction to canonical terms $\twoheadrightarrow_C$ to domain T_O. Then $\twoheadrightarrow_C \restriction_{T_O} = \bigcup_{f \in F_O} \twoheadrightarrow_{(S_O, \{f\}), C}$ holds.

Hence $\twoheadrightarrow_C \restriction_{T_O}$ (and according to section 5.2.4 thus by extension $\twoheadrightarrow_C$) can be defined for each function in Σ_O separately.

b. Let (Σ_V, Σ_H, E) and $(\Sigma'_V, \Sigma'_H, E')$ be Σ_O-implementations of each other (so $\Sigma_O \subseteq \Sigma_V \cap \Sigma'_V$). Then a functional implementation $\twoheadrightarrow_C \subseteq T_O \times C_O$ of $(\Sigma'_V, \Sigma'_H, E')$ is also a functional implementation of (Σ_V, Σ_H, E) if for all $t \in T_O, t' \in C_O$ $t =_E t' \leftrightarrow t =_{E'} t'$ holds.

c. If two algebraic specifications are Σ_O-implementations of each other and both have a functional implementation then these implementations are isomorphic.

5.2.7. Concrete representation

Eventually, we want to convert an algebraic specification into a working computer program. For this a representation function ι from the set of input terms I_O to the concrete representation of input terms is needed to be able to execute implemented functions. When confusion arises the restriction of ι to the domain $I_{s,O}$ will be written as ι_s. Additionally, a set of retrieval functions ρ_s from concrete representations of output terms to the set of canonical terms $C_{s,O}$ is needed.

This is formalized in the following *definitions*:

Let I be a set of data types for a programming language L. I is an **implementation in L of I_O and R_O** if there is a total function ι: $I_O \rightarrow$ I (**the implementation function**) and a set of (partial) functions $\{\rho_s: I \rightarrow I_{s,O} \cup R_{s,O} \mid s \in S_O\}$ (**the retrieval functions**) such that $\rho_s(\iota(t)) =_O t$ for all $t \in I_{s,O}$.

Generally, if $I_{s,O}$ is not empty then $\iota(I_{s,O})$ will correspond to a subset of a data type in L. It could very well happen that two different input types are implemented by the same data type, so differently named retrieval functions are needed for every sort. Only one name (ι) is needed for the implementation function, since the sort of the argument provides type information.

5.2.8. Implementation theorem

Let (Σ_V, Σ_H, E) be an algebraic specification, $\Sigma_O \subseteq \Sigma_V$, and C_O a set of canonical terms. Let I be an implementation in a programming language L of I_O and R_O with implementation function ι and retrieval functions $\{\rho_s \mid s \in S_O\}$, and $S(x_1, \cdots, x_n)$, storing its result in c, a program operating on I. Then the statement $S(x_1, \cdots, x_n)$, describes a functional implementation $\twoheadrightarrow_{(S_O, \{f\}), C}$ for $f: s_1 \times \cdots \times s_n \rightarrow s$, $s \in S_O$, if the following holds:

$\{c_1 \in s_1 \wedge \cdots \wedge c_n \in s_n \wedge k_1 = \iota(c_1) \wedge \cdots \wedge k_n = \iota(c_n)\}$

$S(k_1, \ldots, k_n)$

$\{\rho_s(c) \in C_{s,O} \wedge f(c_1, \ldots, c_n) =_E \rho_s(c)\}$.

Proof proceeds by looking at the function defined by S (omitted).

5.2.9. Decidability of the conditions

It is a pleasant property of Theorem 5.2.8 that in practice satisfaction of the precondition can be computed if the implementation function ι can be computed. Since the terms in I_O are typed, a typechecking algorithm provides the statements on membership of the input terms. Generally there are no extra restrictions to ensure computability, since obviously the implementation has to be computed anyway.

The decidability of the postcondition depends on the computability of the retrieval function ρ_s, the decidability of the check on membership of the set of canonical terms C_O, and the decidability of the congruence $=_E$. The first condition is necessarily fulfilled for the same reasons as the computability of the implementation function. The second depends on the definition of C_O, which will allow computation in practical cases (who wants a canonical form wild enough to be unrecognizable as such?). The decidability of $=_E$ is not ensured in general. So a separate proof may be needed. Of course, for many classes this congruence is decidable. For specifications where the congruence is undecidable, e.g. an algebraic specification of a programming language, an implementation will provide at least a partial decision procedure, even when it cannot be completed.

6. AN EXAMPLE: TABLES REVISITED

To illustrate the use of Theorem 5.2.8 an implementation of module `Tables` in an imperative language is given. Though the implementation again uses trees there is an important difference with the algebraic implementation in section 4 in the sense that recursion is eliminated.

The language Pascal (described in [JW78]) is chosen for the imperative implementation. This choice is motivated by its availability and by its convenient type system. Of course, any other imperative language would serve as well. It should be noted that a functional implementation is very well possible, even in Pascal, but we want to illustrate the possibility to give a correct implementation in a non-functional way.

Generally it is easier to derive a functional program from an ASF-specification, since writing an algebraic specification has strong similarities to functional programming. The specification of `Tables-as-trees`, for instance, is easily converted into a functional program for `lookup`. Thus a functional implementation has the advantage of being easily derived from the specification, and also of being faster in general than a term rewriting implementation.

The first step in the implementation is the choice of a data structure. This is provided for by the data type declarations *pointer* = ↑*tree*, and *tree* as a record with fields *l*, *r* (pointers to the left and right subtrees), *k* of type *key*, and *e* of type *elem*. In a concrete program it is necessary to bind the sorts *key* and *elem*. One could take, for instance, integers and characters; the only prerequisite is that an ordering must be established on the keys.

The values `niltree` and `errorelem` require different treatment in Pascal. For the first we can use the standard notion *nil*, the second has to be declared as variable and set to some unused value. The auxiliary functions on *key* pose no problems with the current choice, since integers are already ordered. For familiarity reasons the function names *eq* and *lt* are retained instead of the operators = and <.

Next the implementation function ι must be defined. The domain of ι is $T_{\mathrm{KEY},V} \cup T_{\mathrm{ELEM},V} \cup T_{\mathrm{TABLE},V}$ and its range is the union of the data types *key*, *elem* and *tree* (or rather *pointer* to *tree*) already indicated above. Since a specification of the terms of type `ELEM` and `KEY` has not been given in section 3 an identification with *elem* and *key* is assumed, so ι is 'defined' backwards by $\iota(t)=t$ for $t \in T_{\mathrm{KEY},V} \cup T_{\mathrm{ELEM},V}$. Hence also $\rho_{\mathrm{ELEM}}(t)=t$, the only retrieval function needed for the example. For $t \in T_{\mathrm{TABLE},V}$, ι can be defined by ι(`nulltable`) = *nil* and ι(`tableadd(key, elem, table)`) = *ptr* when *treeadd* (ι(`key`), ι(`elem`), *ptr*) is executed with *ptr* = ι(`table`).

This definition uses procedure *treeadd* defined below. It should be noted that function ι restricted to terms of type `TABLE` plays the same role as function `tbltotree` in section 4. Evidently, procedure *treeadd* below and function `treeadd` in section 4 are closely related also. A procedure with a variable parameter is a common way to handle data structures in a language like Pascal. A function definition would have the advantage of a more elegant definition of function ι, but the definition below shows that other programming styles can be handled too.

```
procedure treeadd (ky:key; el: elem; var root: pointer);
var cur, anc: pointer; inserted: boolean;
begin cur:= root; inserted:= false;
      while not inserted do
      begin if cur = nil
            then  begin new(cur); cur↑.l:= nil; cur↑.r:= nil; cur↑.k:= ky; cur↑.e:= el;
                         if root = nil then root:=cur
                         else if lt(ky, anc↑.k) then anc↑.l:=cur else anc↑.r:=cur;
                         inserted:= true
                  end
            else  begin if eq(ky,cur↑.k) then begin cur↑.e:= el; inserted:= true end
                         else  if lt(ky,cur↑.k) then begin anc:=cur; cur:=cur↑.l end
                               else begin anc:=cur; cur:=cur↑.r end
                  end
      end
end;
```

The proof of correctness of this implementation closely resembles the proof sketch in section 4. Following this lead we provide two well-formedness functions on structures of type *pointer* (to *tree*), again called *searchtree* and *set-of-keys*. They are defined in the obvious way. This allows us to state the well-formedness of implemented terms by providing the following parallel to Lemma 4.2.*a*:

6.1. Second well-formedness lemma for trees (part a)
Let *ptr* be of type *pointer* and `t` $\in T_{\mathrm{TABLE},V}$. Then *ptr* = ι(`t`) $\rightarrow$ *searchtree*(*ptr*).
Proof by induction on the number of nodes in the list (omitted).
Next we provide the function *lookuptr*:

```
function lookuptr (ky: key; root: pointer): elem;
var cur: pointer; searched: boolean;
begin cur:= root; searched:= false;
      while not searched do
      begin if cur = nil
```

```
                then begin lookuptr:= errorelem; searched:= true end
                else    begin if eq(ky,cur↑.k)
                                then begin lookuptr:= cur↑.e; searched:= true end
                                else if lt(ky,cur↑.k) then cur:= cur↑.l else cur:= cur↑.r
                        end
        end
    end;
```

Presently, a lemma similar to lemma 4.2.*b* can be formulated. It states that *lookuptr* is well-defined for single additions to a well-formed tree.

6.2. Second well-formedness lemma for trees (part b)

Let k, k′ be of sort KEY, e of sort ENTRY, and t of sort TREE, and let $ptr' = \iota(\texttt{treeadd(k', e, t)})$. Then

$ptr = \iota(\texttt{t}) \rightarrow [eq(\iota(\texttt{k}),\iota(\texttt{k}'))= true \rightarrow lookuptr(\iota(\texttt{k}), ptr') = \texttt{e}] \wedge$

$[eq(\iota(\texttt{k}),\iota(\texttt{k}')) = false \rightarrow lookuptr(\iota(\texttt{k}), ptr') = lookuptr(\iota(\texttt{k}), ptr)]$

Proof directly from the observation that $ptr' = \iota(\texttt{treeadd(k', e, t)})$ is defined in terms of $ptr = \iota(\texttt{t})$ (omitted).

According to Theorem 5.2.8 it is now sufficient to prove (E the set of equations from module Tables):

$\{\texttt{k} \in \texttt{KEY} \wedge \texttt{tbl} \in \texttt{TABLE} \wedge ky = \iota(\texttt{k}) \wedge root = \iota(\texttt{tbl})\}$

$elt := lookuptr(ky, root)$

$\{\rho_{ELEM}(elt) \in C_{ELEM,O} \wedge \texttt{lookup(k, tbl)} =_E \rho_{ELEM}(elt)\}$.

This follows immediately from lemma 6.2, and the definition of ρ_{ELEM}.

7. CONCLUSIONS

7.1. The results

The paper provides a functionally oriented (black box) approach to the implementation of modular algebraic specifications. The main advantages are listed below.

- It provides a theoretical background for the *separate implementation* of modules.
- The implementation above is based on the *initial* behaviour of certain functions, the observing functions. This provides an intuitively clear semantics.
- A correctness criterion for implementations is given in Hoare logic, allowing the application of *standard optimization techniques*. In algebraic terms this means that functions which are not observing may have more or less *final* semantics.
- The combination of separate implementation and (hence separate) optimization allows the construction of a *library* of (possibly optimized) modules.

The loss of the *initial algebra semantics* might instead be listed as a disadvantage. Terms are only judged different when they have different effects (**confusion** is allowed) and other invisible terms (**junk**) may be introduced. On the one hand, precisely these two "undesirable" effects allow the introduction of optimal implementations. On the other hand, they make the semantics of a module less clear to the user (i.e., someone writing a module importing the optimized module). This problem is minimized by the fact that the criteria for use of the module, allowing the set of observing terms only, are rather easy.

7.2. Further research

Both theoretical and practical extensions of the work in this paper are feasible. The former include:

- Investigation of the significance for *import semantics* in an algebraic specification formalism with initial algebra semantics, except for observable imports.
- The *combination* with an implementation as a *term rewriting system* of the importing module of an observable implementation has to be investigated to allow for automatic translation of modules built around an observable module.

Of more practical nature are:

- The design and implementation of a *module library*, containing efficient (e.g. built-in) implementations.
- The construction of an *implementation* of modules on top of the module library, using the normalization (i.e., elimination of imports, renamings and bindings by combining modules) semantics from ASF [BHK87] for the top level modules.

Acknowledgements

Discussions with P.R.H. Hendriks, P. Klint, and especially J. Heering greatly improved the content of this paper. They, J. Rekers, and the referees for ESOP '88 made useful comments on one or more earlier versions.

REFERENCES

[Bac86] R.C. BACKHOUSE (1986). *Program Construction and Verification*, Prentice-Hall.

[Bak84] C. BAKER-FINCH (1984). "Acceptable models of algebraic semantics," *Australian Computer Science Communications*, vol. 6, no. 1, pp. 5-1/10, Proceedings of the Seventh Australian Computer Science Conference, Adelaide, ed. C.J. Barter.

[BHK85] J.A. BERGSTRA, J. HEERING, and P. KLINT (1985). "Algebraic definition of a simple programming language," Report CS-R8504, Centre for Mathematics and Computer Science, Amsterdam.

[BHK86] J.A. BERGSTRA, J. HEERING, and P. KLINT (1986). "Module algebra," Report CS-R8617, Centre for Mathematics and Computer Science, Amsterdam.

[BHK87] J.A. BERGSTRA, J. HEERING, and P. KLINT (1987). "ASF - an algebraic specification formalism," Report CS-R8705, Centre for Mathematics and Computer Science, Amsterdam.

[BK86] J.A. BERGSTRA and J.W. KLOP (1986). "Conditional rewrite rules: confluence and termination," *Journal of Computer and System Sciences*, vol. 32, no. 3, pp. 323-362.

[BT82] J.A. BERGSTRA and J.V. TUCKER (1982). "The completeness of the algebraic specification methods for computable data types," *Information and Control*, vol. 54, no. 3, pp. 186-200.

[BT83] J.A. BERGSTRA and J.V. TUCKER (1983). "Initial and final algebra semantics for data type specifications: two characterization theorems," *SIAM Journal on Computing*, vol. 12, no. 2, pp. 366-387.

[BDMW81] M. BROY, W. DOSCH, B. MÖLLER, and M. WIRSING (1981). "GOTOs – a study in the algebraic specification of programming languages," in *GI – 11. Jahrestagung*, ed. W. Brauer, Informatik-Fachberichte, vol. 50, pp. 109-121, Springer-Verlag.

[Die86] N.W.P. VAN DIEPEN (1986). "A study in algebraic specification: a language with goto-statements," Report CS-R8627, Centre for Mathematics and Computer Science, Amsterdam.

[DE84] K. DROSTEN and H.-D. EHRICH (1984). "Translating algebraic specifications to Prolog programs," Informatik-Bericht Nr. 84-08, Technische Universität Braunschweig.

[FGJM85] K. FUTATSUGI, J.A. GOGUEN, J.-P. JOUANNAUD and J. MESEGUER (1985). "Principles of OBJ2", in *Conference Record of the Twelfth Annual ACM Symposium on Principles of Programming Languages*, pp. 52-66, ACM.

[GM82] J.A. GOGUEN and J. MESEGUER (1982). "Universal realization, persistent interconnection and implementation of abstract modules," in *Proceedings 9th International Conference on Automata, Languages and Programming*, eds. M. Nielsen & E.M. Schmidt, Lecture Notes in Computer Science, vol. 140, pp. 265-281, Springer-Verlag.

[GM84] J.A. GOGUEN and J. MESEGUER (1984). "Equality, types, modules, and (why not?) generics for logic programming," *Journal of Logic Programming*, vol. 2, pp. 179-210.

[GMP83] J.A. GOGUEN, J. MESEGUER and D. PLAISTED (1983). "Programming with parameterized abstract objects in OBJ", in *Theory and Practice of Software Technology*, eds. D. Ferrari, M. Bolognani & J.A. Goguen, pp. 163-193, North-Holland.

[HO80] G. HUET and D.C. OPPEN (1980). "Equations and rewrite rules: a survey," in *Formal Language Theory, Perspectives and Open Problems*, ed. R.V. Book, pp. 349-405, Academic Press.

[JW78] K. JENSEN and N. WIRTH (1978). *Pascal: User Manual and Report* (second edition), Springer-Verlag.

[Jon80] C.B. JONES (1980). *Software Development: a Rigorous Approach*, Prentice-Hall.

[Kam83] S. KAMIN (1983). "Final data types and their specification," *ACM Transactions on Programming Languages and Systems*, vol. 5, no. 1, pp. 97-123.

[LS84] J. LOECKX and K. SIEBER (1984). *The Foundation of Program Verification*, Wiley-Teubner.

[MG85] J. MESEGUER and J.A. GOGUEN (1985). "Initiality, induction, and computability," in *Algebraic Methods in Semantics*, eds. M. Nivat & J.C. Reynolds, pp. 459-541, Cambridge University Press.

[ODo85] M.J. O'DONNELL (1985). *Equational Logic as a Programming Language*, MIT Press.

[ST85] D. SANNELLA and A. TARLECKI (1985). "On observational equivalence and algebraic specification," in *Mathematical Foundations of Software Development. Proceedings International Joint Conference on Theory and Practice of Software Development, TAPSOFT '85*, eds. H. Ehrig, C. Floyd, M. Nivat & J. Thatcher, Lecture Notes in Computer Science, vol. 185, pp. 308-322, Springer-Verlag.

[Wan79] M. WAND (1979). "Final algebra semantics and data type extensions," *Journal of Computer and System Sciences*, vol. 19, pp. 27-44.

be statically type checked, even if they behave well at runtime. We extend the Mycroft/O'Keefe system to deal with subtypes, when information about the possible dataflow in a clause is available. This dataflow information can be provided by a mode system [Warren 77, Bruynooghe 82, Smolka 84, Dietrich 88], or by global analysis [Mellish 85].

Type checking can be performed completely at compile time, that is, type informations do not change but rather document the runtime behaviour of programs. Therefore a programmer is not forced to fully declare his program. A type-checker is able to derive missing type information to some extent, and it is also possible to develop programs in a rapid prototyping manner adding type specifications later in order to increase the programming security, documentation quality, and reusability of these programs. A somewhat different view of typing and type checking a Prolog program is taken in [Mishra 84] and [Zobel 87], where automatic type inference is used to detect goals which can never succeed.

The paper is organized as follows: After introducing some basic notions in section 2, we recall the type system of Mycroft/O'Keefe and discuss its advantages and disadvantages in section 3. In section 4 we show how it can be extended to deal with subtypes, and we give an outline of the type checking algorithm in section 5. Some conclusions and open problems are considered in section 6.

2. Formal Preliminaries

We assume familiarity of the reader with the basic notions of first order logic and the foundations of logic programming. In this section, we only recall some often used notions.

Programs. We assume the following sets to be given:

- **V**, a countable, infinite set of ***variables*** ($x,y,z,... \in \mathbf{V}$).
- **F**, a countable set of ***function symbols*** with arity ($f/n \in \mathbf{F}$).
- **P**, a countable set of ***predicate symbols*** with arity ($p/m \in \mathbf{P}$).

Based on these sets, ***terms, atomic formulae (atoms), literals*** and ***(Horn-) clauses*** are defined as usual in first order logic. Horn clauses may be ***facts*** ($H \leftarrow$), ***implications*** ($H \leftarrow B_1, \ldots, B_m$) and ***goals*** ($\leftarrow B_1, \ldots, B_m$). If S is a term, an atom, a clause or a set of those, $var(S)$ denotes the set of variables occurring in S. A ***program*** is a finite set of facts and implications. Because we restrict ourselves to *Horn* logic programming, throughout the paper a ***clause*** is always meant to be a *Horn clause.*

Substitutions. A *Substitutions* can be denoted by a finite set of variable replacements ($\theta = \{x_1 \leftarrow t_1, \ldots, x_n \leftarrow t_n\}$) Of a and b are terms or atoms, $mgu(a,b)$ denotes the set of most general unifiers for a and b, which may be empty or contains one element up to renaming of variables. "$\preceq$" denotes the ***subsumption ordering*** on terms: $s \preceq t$ iff a substitution θ exists such that $\theta s = t$. In this case we say that s is ***more general*** than t or t is an ***instance*** of s by θ. We say that s is a ***renaming*** of t ($s \simeq t$) iff $s \preceq t$ and $t \preceq s$. That is, s and t only differ in the names of their variables.

SLD-derivations and answer substitutions. Horn logic programs usually are interpreted using the resolution principle, especially linear resolution with selection function. This yields the notion of *SLD-derivations*, *SLD-refutations* (*SLD*-derivations of the empty clause) and ***answer substitutions.*** For a comprehensive presentation of these topics see [Lloyd 1984].

A Polymorphic Type System with Subtypes for Prolog*

Roland Dietrich, Frank Hagl

GMD Forschungsstelle an der Universität Karlsruhe
(German National Research Center for Computer Science)
Haid-und-Neu-Straße 7, D-7500 Karlsruhe

Abstract. From a software engineering point of view, logic programming lacks many properties allowing secure development of large programs by many programmers. In this paper we try to improve these properties by proposing a polymorphic type system for Prolog. Our type system is able to deal with subtype relations if information about dataflow within clauses is available. This information can be given by a mode system. We give an outline of a type checking algorithm for this type system and discuss several problems which do not arise in type systems without subtypes.

1. Introduction

Despite its good rapid prototyping quality, most logic programming systems lack certain properties which are essential when developing large programs by several programmers. Especially in Prolog, there is no possibility to formally specify what kind of arguments a predicate is intended to have, and the input/output behaviour cannot be specified although most predicates of a program are used with a fixed input/output mode (cf. [Drabent 87]). Such informations are useful for several reasons: They provide a good deal of documentation; in a module system they can be part of the interface description of a module; they make the discovery of many typing errors easier; and a Prolog compiler can use them for optimization purposes.

The notion of types has a long tradition in programming languages. Especially, polymorphic type systems have been broadly studied in the functional programming area (see [Cardelli, Wegener 85] for a survey). Imposing type structures to first order logic resulted in many sorted logic for which appropriate deduction mechanism have been developed, for example [Walther 83, Schmidt-Schauss 86]. This also enabled the use of logic as a typed programming language including subtype structures (order sorted logic). Examples are [Goguen, Meseguer 84] and [Smolka, Nutt 87]. In [Huber, Varsek 87] order sorted resolution is used instead of ordinary resolution as an execution model for logic programming including an adaptation of Warren's abstract Prolog machine [Warren 83] to this model. All these approaches to types in logic programming do not allow parametric polymorphism and the type information directly impacts the deduction mechanism which often results in a considerable restriction of the search space.

In contrast, our approach considers a purely static type discipline which leaves the operational semantics of logic programs completely unchanged. It is based on the type sytem of [Mycroft, O'Keefe 84] which itself is an adaptation of Milner's type system for ML to Prolog. This type system lacks the possibility to deal with subtype relations, which makes some programs impossible to

* This work has been done within a joint project of GMD and SFB 314 (artificial intelligence) at the University of Karlsruhe.

Occurrences. In order to refer precisely to subterms or atoms occurring in clauses, we recall the well-known notion of occurrences of terms and extend it to occurrences of atoms and clauses. Occurrences of terms are usually defined as sequences of natural numbers. Occurrences of atoms can be defined in the same way, because their syntactical structure is the same one. Occurrences of clauses can be obtained by prefixing occurrences of atoms with a number, indicating the position where the atom occurs in the clause[1]. That is, if c is a clause then $c/0$ denotes the clause head and c/i denotes the $i-th$ literal of the body for $i \geq 1$. For example, if $c = p(f(X),g(Y,X)) \leftarrow q(X),p(X,Y)$. then $c/0.1 = f(X)$, $c/0.2.1 = Y$ and $c/2.2 = Y$. For any syntactic object s $O(s)$ denotes the *set of occurrences* of s.

3. The Type System of Mycroft/O'Keefe

In this section we give an informal outline of the type system defined in [Mycroft, O'Keefe 84] by means of some examples, and we discuss its advantages and drawbacks. The type system is based on Milner's work on polymorphic types for functional programming languages [Milner 78]. A formal description can easily be extracted from the definition of its extension to deal with subtypes given in section 4.

A programmer can define *typings for function and predicate symbols* occurring in his program via *type declarations* and *predicate declarations*. Types itself are terms over a special alphabet disjoint from the program's alphabet. Types are *polymorphic*, if they contain type variables. Typings of n-ary function symbols are of the form $(\tau_1, \ldots, \tau_n \longrightarrow \tau)$, where τ and τ_i are types. τ_i are called *argument types* and τ *result type*. Typings for n-ary predicate symbols are of the form $(\tau_1, \ldots, \tau_n)$, where τ_i are types.

The following example for a general list type and natural numbers and the predicates *append/3*, *reverse/3*, *member/2*, and *length/2* shows a possible Prolog syntax for such declarations:[2]

```
:- type list(α) => nil, .(α,list(α)).
:- type nat => 0, s(nat).
:- pred append(list(α),list(α),list(α)).
:- pred length(list(α),nat).
```

If we denote typings of (function and predicate) symbols by superscribing the symbols with its type, these declarations induce the following typing

$$\{ \mathtt{nil}^{list(\alpha)},\ .^{\alpha, list(\alpha) \rightarrow list(\alpha)},\ \mathtt{0}^{nat},\ \mathtt{s}^{nat \rightarrow nat},\ \mathtt{append}^{list(\alpha), list(\alpha), list(\alpha)},\ \mathtt{length}^{list(\alpha), nat} \}$$

A *typing for a clause* associates a type with every occurrence of the clause, which means that the term at this occurrence is of the associated type. *Type checking* a clause consists in *deriving* a typing for a clause, such that every occurrence of the clause is associated with a type wich is compatible with the given typing of symbols. For example, from the above typing we can derive the

1 Interpreting a clause as a term with binary function symbols '$\leftarrow$' and ',' and using occurrences of terms would be quite unreadable.

2 We use the dot-notation to abbreviate the cons-operator. Type variables are denoted by greek letters. The may be replaced by ordinary Prolog variables in practice.

following typings for *append*-clauses:

$$\texttt{append(nil}^{list(\alpha)}\texttt{,L}^{list(\alpha)}\texttt{,L}^{list(\alpha)}\texttt{).}$$
$$\texttt{append(.(X}^{\alpha}\texttt{,L1}^{list(\alpha)}\texttt{)}^{list(\alpha)}\texttt{,L2}^{list(\alpha)}\texttt{,.(X}^{\alpha}\texttt{,L3}^{list(\alpha)}\texttt{)}^{list(\alpha)}\texttt{) :- append(L1}^{list(\alpha)}\texttt{,L2}^{list(\alpha)}\texttt{,L3}^{list(\alpha)}\texttt{).}$$

If for every occurrence a compatible type and, especially, for every variable (for which no typings must be defined) a ***unique*** type can be derived, the clause is said to be ***well-typed***. This is formally defined by ***well-typing rules*** in [Mycroft, O'Keefe 84]. If different types for the same variable are derived, these types must be ***unifiable*** in order to preserve well-typedness. This can effect instantiation of type variables in other parts of the clause, too. For example type checking the goal clause

```
:- length(nil,X), append(.(X,nil),L,LL).
```

the variable X is first associated with type ***nat*** (by the declaration of $lenght^{list(\alpha),\,nat}$) and then, by the declaration of $.^{\alpha,list(\alpha)}$, with type α, which yields the (type) substitution $\alpha \leftarrow nat$. This substitution expresses among others that ***append*** is used with type $(list(nat),list(nat),list(nat))$ in this clause.

If a program is well-typed, it is guaranteed that during runtime no type conflicts can happen. That is, every resolvent produced during a refutation of a goal is also well-typed, and every variable of the goal is instatiated according to its associated type by any answer substitution. This is paraphrased by "well-typed programs can't go wrong" in [Mycroft, O'Keefe 84].

The type system of Mycroft and O'Keefe has several advantages: The typing information describes very closely the intention of the programmer when defining predicates. This increases the documentation facilities of Prolog. The type-checker can detect a lot of typing errors. The polymorphism enables the programmer to use instantiations of previously defined types in predicate declarations. A type-checker can easily be implemented in Prolog (see [Mycroft, O'Keefe 1983] for details) and type checking is not expensive because it works locally on clauses.

However, there is a serious drawback: relations between types cannot be specified. Types can be defined neither as unions nor as subtypes of other types. For example, the following type declarations and the predicate declaration for a predicate ***diff*** specify the differentiation function for arithmetic expressions[1]:

```
:- type var => x, y, z,...
:- type integer => 0, -1, 1, -2, 2,...
:- type expr => x, y, z,... ,
                0, -1, 1, -2, 2,... ,
                - expr, expr + expr, expr * expr, ln(expr), sin(expr),...
:- pred diff(expr,var,expr).
```

Note that these type declarations make use of overloading (some functors may belong to more than one type), which can easily be built into Mycroft and O'Keefe's type system. The fact

```
diff(X,X,1).
```

1 In practice, of course, either the number of symbols belonging to a type must be finite or the type must be "built-in" as, for example, the type "integer".

cannot be well-typed, because the variable X occurs with type *var* and *expr* which are not unifiable. Alternatively, we can delcare

```
:- pred diff(expr,expr,expr).
```

which avoids type conflicts but reflects less precisely the intention of the programmer. It would be more appropriate to provide a possibility to declare subtype relations or union types, and to change the well-typing conditions for clauses. For example we can define subtype relations

```
:- subtype var < expr, integer < expr.
```

or, redefine the type *expr* as a *union* of other types. If the well-typing conditions allow different types of variables to be subtypes of each other, the fact

$\mathtt{diff}(\mathtt{X}^{expr}, \mathtt{X}^{var}, \mathtt{1}^{expr})$

is well-typed. But then the goal

$\mathtt{:-\ diff}(\mathtt{x{+}y}^{expr}, \mathtt{Y}^{var}, \mathtt{1}^{expr})$

is statically well-typed and yields a dynamic type conflict when applying the above fact with the substitution $\{Y \leftarrow x+y\}$. The reason for this conflict is the following: The second argument of the goal is used as an output argument, whereas the second argument of the diff predicate is intended for input. In other words, the goal causes a dataflow from the first into the second argument of the fact and, in parallel, a transition from a supertype to a subtype ($expr \longrightarrow var$).

These observations suggest that there is a close connection between data flow and type consistency when subtype relations are involved. In the next section, we extend the type system of Mycroft and O'Keefe to deal with subtypes and define a new notion of well-typedness based on dataflow informations.

4. A Polymorphic Type System with Subtypes

4.1 Modes and Dataflow

As stated in the previous section, in order to deal with subtypes information about the dataflow within a clause is needed. We suppose that this information is given by input/output modes of predicates. We distinguish three modes: input (I), output (O), and inout (IO).

Definition 1 (*modes*).
Let P be a program over $\mathbf{V} \cup \mathbf{F} \cup \mathbf{P}$. A set of modes for P is a set of functions $M = \{m_p \mid p \in \mathbf{P}\}$ such that $m_{p/n}: \{1, \ldots, n\} \longrightarrow \{I, O, IO\}$ for every $p/n \in \mathbf{P}$. P and a goal g are said to be *mode consistent with respect to* M iff for any goal $\leftarrow p(t_1, \ldots, t_n)$ which is produced during a refutation of g and for all $i \in \{1, \ldots, n\}$ the following conditions hold:

(1) If $m_p(i) = I$, then for every answer substitution θ it is $\theta t_i = t_i$.
(2) If $m_p(i) = O$, then t_i is a variable.

∎

In other words, input arguments of a goal are not further instantiated by execution of the goal and output arguments are free variables at call time (that is, they are not instantiated by answer substitutions for previously called goals). For inout arguments nothing is known about the degree of instantiation. Some mode systems additionally require input arguments to be ground at call time and output arguments to be ground at return time [Warren 77, Bruynooghe 82]. For a comprehensive discussion of different modes and mode systems see [Dietrich 88].

We suppose that modes can be assigned to predicates via *mode declarations* like

```
:- mode append(i,i,o), member(i,i), unify(io,io).
```

These mode declarations imply modes m_{append}, m_{member}, and m_{unify} such that

$m_{append}(1) = m_{append}(2) = I$, $m_{append}(3) = O$,
$m_{member}(1) = m_{member}(2) = I$, and
$m_{unify}(1) = m_{unify}(2) = IO$.

Another way to obtain mode information is to perform global analysis like [Mellish 85].

Given a set of modes for a program, a unique mode can be assigned to every *occurrence* of a clause. This especially aims at assigning modes to variable occurrences in clauses.

Definition 2. (*modes of occurrences of clauses*).
Let P be a program and M a set of modes for P. Let $c := A_0 \leftarrow A_1, \ldots, A_m \in P$ be a clause and $i.u \in O(c)$. The *mode of* c *at* $i.u$, $m(c,i.u) \in \{I,O,IO\}$ is defined as follows:

(1) $m(A_0 \leftarrow A_1, \ldots, A_n, i.u) = I$ iff $A_i = p(t_1, \ldots, t_k)$ and
$[\ i=0 \Rightarrow m_p(i)=I\ ]$ and $[\ i>0 \Rightarrow m_p(i)=O\ ]$.

(1) $m(A_0 \leftarrow A_1, \ldots, A_n, i.u) = O$ iff $A_i = p(t_1, \ldots, t_k)$ and
$[\ i=0 \Rightarrow m_p(i)=O\ ]$ and $[\ i>0 \Rightarrow m_p(i)=I\ ]$.

(3) $m(A_0 \leftarrow A_1, \ldots, A_n, i.u) = IO$ iff $A_i = p(t_1, \ldots, t_k)$ and $m_p(i)=IO$

■

Note that in the body of a clause the *mode of an occurrence* is converse to the *mode of the predicate* of that occurrence. If the mode of a body occurrence is I, values are passed from the head of an eventually applied clause into this occurrence. That is, the mode of the predicate must be O. If the mode of a body occurrence is O, values are passed from this occurrence into the head of an eventually applied clause, and therefore the mode of the predicate must be I.

Based on the notion of occurrences of clauses, we can now define a relation describing dataflow within a clause.

Definition 3. (*dataflow relation*).
Let P be a program and M a set of modes for P. The *dataflow relation* of P w.r.t. M $df^M(c) \subseteq O(c) \times O(c)$ is defined by

$$(u,v) \in df^M(c) \quad \text{iff} \quad c/u = c/v \in \mathbf{V} \text{ and } m(c,u) \in \{I,IO\} \text{ and } m(c,v) \in \{O,IO\}.$$

■

4.2 Types and Typings

We extend the alphabet given in section 2 with the following sets:

- **TV**, a countable, infinite set of *type variables* ($\alpha, \beta, \gamma, \cdots \in \mathbf{TV}$, $\mathbf{V} \cap \mathbf{TV} = \emptyset$),
- **TC**, a countable set of symbols with arity, the *type constructors* ($\mathbf{F} \cap \mathbf{TC} = \emptyset$).

Types are terms over **TC** and **TV** (*type terms*). We denote the set of all type terms over **TC** and **TV** by Σ ($\rho, \sigma, \tau \in \Sigma$). Ground type terms are called *monotypes*, others *polytypes*. *Extended types* are types or sequences of types, written $(\sigma_1, \ldots, \sigma_n)$ or $(\sigma_1, \ldots, \sigma_k \rightarrow \tau)$. We denote the set of extended types over Σ by Σ^*. *Type substitutions* are substitutions on type terms in the same sense as substitutions on ordinary terms.

We interpret types as sets of terms (subsets of the Herbrand universe). The *subtype relation* is a binary relation $\subseteq$ on type terms, which is interpreted as the subset relation on sets of terms. That is, $\sigma \subseteq \tau$ iff and only if the set of terms belonging to σ is a subset of the set of terms belonging to τ.

A *typing* of a set of (predicate, function, and variable) symbols associates extended types to every symbol. A typing of a clause, or atom, or term associates an extended type to every symbol occurring in the clause or atom or term.

Definition 4. (*Typings*)
Let $S \subseteq \mathbf{V} \cup \mathbf{F} \cup \mathbf{P}$. A *typing of* S is a relation $t_S \subseteq S \times \Sigma^*$ such that

(i) If $s \in \mathbf{V}$ and $(s, \sigma) \in t_S$ then $\sigma \in \Sigma$

(ii) If $s/k \in \mathbf{F}$ and $(s, \sigma) \in t_S$ then

- $\sigma = \sigma_1, \ldots, \sigma_k \rightarrow \sigma_0$, $\sigma_i \in \Sigma$, $\sigma_0 = c(\alpha_1, \ldots, \alpha_n)$, $c \in \mathbf{TC}$, $\alpha_i \in \mathbf{TV}$ and $var(\sigma_j) \subseteq var(\sigma_0)$ for $j > 0$,
- for all $\tau \in \Sigma^*$ with $(s, \tau) \in t_S$ $\tau = \tau_1, \ldots, \tau_k \rightarrow \tau_0$, $\tau_i \simeq \sigma_i$ for $i > 0$[1].

(iii) If $s/n \in \mathbf{P}$ and $(s, \sigma) \in t_S$ then

- $\sigma = \sigma_1, \ldots, \sigma_n$, $\sigma \in \Sigma$,
- for all $\tau \in \Sigma^*$ with $(s, \tau) \in t_S$ $\tau = \sigma$.

If $(\tau_1, \ldots, \tau_n \rightarrow \tau_0, f) \in t_S$, τ_i, $i \geq 1$ are called *argument types* of f and τ_0 is called *result type* of f.

■

As shown in section 3, we denote typings for clauses by superscribing the terms occurring in a clause with the corresponding types.

Given a typing of the function symbols, the types themselves can be interpreted as sets of terms as follows: If $\sigma = c(\alpha_1, \ldots, \alpha_n)$ and $(f, (\sigma_1, \ldots, \sigma_k \rightarrow \sigma)) \in t_S$ then $f(t_1, \ldots, t_k) \in \phi\sigma$ iff $t_i \in \phi\sigma_i$ for any type substitution ϕ and $i = 1, \ldots, k$.

4.3 Well-Typed Programs

The notion of well-typings expresses consistency between typed clauses and separately given typings of the symbols occurring in the clause. Well- typings for clauses can be derived by the following type inference rules which are taken from [Mycroft, O'Keefe 84] and extended to allow variables

1 If we admit $\tau_i \not\simeq \sigma_i$ this corresponds to overloading.

and function symbols to have more than one typing (i.e. typings are not functions, but relations).

Definition 5 (*type inference rules*).
Let $S \subseteq \mathbf{V} \cup \mathbf{F} \cup \mathbf{P}$ and $ts \subseteq S \times \Sigma^*$ a typing of S.

(TI1) $ts \vdash p(t_1^{\tau_1}, \ldots, t_k^{\tau_k}) \leftarrow A_1, \ldots, A_m$ if $p/k \in \mathbf{P}$ and
$(p,\rho) \in ts$ and $(\tau_1, \ldots, \tau_k) \simeq \rho$ and and $ts \vdash t_j^{\tau_j}$ for $j \in \{1, \ldots, k\}$ and
$ts \vdash A_i^{\tau_i}$ for $i \in \{0, \ldots, m\}$.

(TI2) $(ts,M) \vdash p(t_1^{\tau_1}, \ldots, t_k^{\tau_k})$ if $p/k \in \mathbf{P}$ and
$(p,\rho) \in ts$ and $(\tau_1, \ldots, \tau_k) \succeq \rho$ and and $ts \vdash t_j^{\tau_j}$ for $j \in \{1, \ldots, k\}$.

(TI3) $ts \vdash f(t_1^{\tau_1}, \ldots, t_n^{\tau_n})^\sigma$ if $f \in \mathbf{F}$ and
$(f,\rho) \in ts$ and $\tau_1, \ldots, \tau_n \rightarrow \sigma \succeq \rho$ and $ts \vdash t_i^{\tau_i}$ for $i \in \{1, \ldots, n\}$.

(TI4) $ts \vdash x^\sigma$ if $x \in \mathbf{V}$ and $(x,\sigma) \in ts$

■

As shown in section 3, the principle "well-typed programs can't go wrong" is not longer true, if variables can have different types. To re-establish this principle we have to introduce a new notion of well-typedness with respect to the dataflow in clauses given by modes.

Definition 6 (*well-typedness modulo a set of modes*).
Let c be a typed clause, $S \subseteq \mathbf{V} \cup \mathbf{F} \cup \mathbf{P}$ containing every symbol occurring in c, M a set of modes for the predicate symbols occurring in c and ts a typing for S. ts is called a *well-typing modulo M for c* ($ts \vdash_{\overline{M}} c$) iff $ts \vdash c$ and the following *variable typing condition* holds:

(VTC) For all $u,v \in O(c)$ such that $c/u = x_\sigma$ and $c/v = x_\tau$ and $x \in \mathbf{V}$:
$(u,v) \in df^M(c) \Rightarrow \sigma \subseteq \tau$ and $(v,u) \in df^M(c) \Rightarrow \tau \subseteq \sigma$.

■

The variable typing condition (VTC) guarantees that in well-typed clauses dataflow cannot happen from a supertype occurrence to a subtype occurrence. In the example shown in section 3

```
:- mode diff(i,o,i).
diff(X^expr,X^var,1^expr).
```

this condition obviously is hurt ($(0.1, 0.2) \in df^M(c)$), which results in a possible runtime type conflict.

The proof for our main theorem that well-typed clauses produce well-typed resolvents (modulo a set of modes) works along the lines shown in [Mycroft, O'Keefe 84]. We only have to pay special attention to multiple occurrences of variables with different types (which is always ill-typed in Mycroft/O'Keefe's system).

In the following, let P be a program, M a set of modes for P and ts a typing for every function and predicate symbol occurring in P. Lemma 7 states that most general unifiers computed when building resolvents from well-typed clauses instantiate variables according to their derived types up to instantiations of type variables.

Lemma 7. Let $c := B_0 \leftarrow B_1, \ldots, B_n \in P$, $g := \leftarrow A_1, \ldots, A_m$ a goal, and $\theta \in mgu(B_0,A_1)$. If P and g are mode consistent with respect to M, $ts \vdash_{\overline{M}} c$ and $ts \vdash_{\overline{M}} g$ then there is a type substitution ϕ such that

(a) If $x \in var(B_0)$ and $t_S \vdash x^\sigma$ then $t_S \vdash \theta x^{\phi\sigma}$,

(b) If $x \in var(A_1)$ and $t_S \vdash x^\tau$ then $t_S \vdash \theta x^\tau$.

Proof. We first show how the type substitution ϕ can be determined: Let $B_0 = p(s_1^{\sigma_1}, \ldots, s_k^{\sigma_k})$, $A_1 = p(t_1^{\tau_1}, \ldots, t_k^{\tau_k})$, and $(p, \rho) \in t_S$. Because c and g are well-typed modulo M we can infer from (TI1) and (TI2) that

(1) $\rho \simeq (\sigma_1, \ldots, \sigma_k)$ and $t_S \vdash s_i^{\sigma_i}$ for $i=1, \ldots, k$ and

(2) $\rho \preceq (\tau_1, \ldots, \tau_k)$ and $t_S \vdash t_i^{\tau_i}$for$i=1, \ldots, k$.

Defining $\phi := mgu((\sigma_1, \ldots, \sigma_k), (\tau_1, \ldots, \tau_k))$ we have

(3) $\phi(\sigma_1, \ldots, \sigma_k) = (\tau_1, \ldots, \tau_k)$.

If there is no variable occurring twice in B_0 or A_1 with different types, (a) and (b) follow directly from (1), (2) and (3). Otherwise (a) and (b) are guaranteed by (VTC). Suppose, for example, that there are $x \in \mathbf{V}$, $iu \in O(B_0)$ and $jv \in O(B_0)$ such that $m_p(i) = I$, $m_p(j) = O$, $B_0/iu = x^\sigma$ and $B_0/jv = x^\tau$. Then $(iu, jv) \in df^M(c)$ and $\sigma \subseteq \tau$ (VTC). Because $m_p(i) = I$ it is $\theta A_1/i = A_1/i$ and therefore $\theta x = A_1/iu$. Then from (2) and (3) follows that $t_S \vdash \theta B_0/iu^{\phi\sigma}$ and because $\sigma \subseteq \tau$ also $t_S \vdash \theta B_0/jv^{\phi\tau}$. All other cases can be proven by similar considerations.

■

Theorem 8. Let $c \in P$, g a goal such that P and g are mode consistent with respect to M. If $t_S \vdash_{\overline{M}} c$ and $t_S \vdash_{\overline{M}} g$ then $t_S \vdash_{\overline{M}} g'$ for any SLD-resolvent g' of g.

Proof. Let $c = B_0 \leftarrow B_1, \ldots, B_n$, $g = \leftarrow A_1, \ldots, A_m$ and $\theta \in mgu(B_0, A_1)$. Then $g' = \leftarrow \theta B_1, \ldots, \theta B_n, \theta A_2, \ldots, \theta A_m$. We show that

(*) $t_S \vdash \theta B_i^\phi$ for $i=1, \ldots, n$ and

(**) $t_S \vdash \theta A_i$ for $i=2, \ldots, m$

wehere ϕ is the type substitution determined by Lemma 7 and B_i^ϕ denotes the typed literal obtained from B_i by applying ϕ to all its associated types. Let $B_i = p(s_1^{\sigma_1}, \ldots, s_k^{\sigma_k})$ and $(p, rho) \in t_S$. Because $t_S \vdash_{\overline{M}} c$ it is $t_S \vdash B_i$ and (TI2) implies that

(1) $\rho \preceq (\sigma_1, \ldots, \sigma_k) \preceq \phi(\sigma_1, \ldots, \sigma_k)$ and

(2) $t_S \vdash s_j^{\sigma_j}$ for $j=1, \ldots, k$

and we can show

(3) $t_S \vdash \theta s_j^{\phi\sigma_j}$ for $j=1, \ldots, k$.

by induction on the structure of s_j:

- If s_j is a constant, then there is $\rho' \in \Sigma$ such that $(s_j, \rho') \in t_S$ and $\rho' \preceq \sigma_j \preceq \phi\sigma_j$ and (TI3) implies (3).
- If s_j is a variable not occurring in B_0 then $\theta s_j = s_j$ and (3) follows from (2). If $s_j \in var(B_0)$ then (3) is guaranteed by (VTC): If, for example, there is a dataflow from an occurrence s_j^τ in B_0 to $s_j^{\sigma_j}$ in B_i then $\tau \subseteq \sigma_j$ and $t_S \vdash \theta s_j^{\phi\tau}$ (Lemma 7 (a)) which implies (3).
- If $s_j = f(t_1^{\tau_1}, \ldots, t_l^{\tau_l})^\tau$ then there is $\rho' \in \Sigma$ such that $(f, \rho') \in t_S$ and $\rho' \preceq (\tau_1, \ldots, \tau_l \rightarrow \tau) \preceq \phi(\tau_1, \ldots, \tau_l \rightarrow \tau)$ and $t_S \vdash t_r^{\tau_r}$ for $r=1, \ldots, l$. By induction hypothesis it follows that $t_S \vdash \theta t_r^{\phi\tau_r}$ and (TI3) implies (3).

Now (1) and (3) imply (*) and (**) can be proven in a similar way from $t_S \vdash A_i$, $i=1, \ldots, m$, and Lemma 7 (b). It remains to show that (VTC) holds for g'. This can be deduced from the fact that (VTC) holds for c and g and that all variables are instantiated according to their types (Lemma 7). (Note that if variables of some θB_i, $i=1, \ldots, n$ also occur in one of θA_j, $j=2, \ldots, m$ there must have been a dataflow between A_1 and A_j and between B_0 and B_i).

■

Corollary 9. If P and a goal g are mode consistent with respect to M and $ts \vdash_{\overline{M}} c$ for all $c \in P \cup \{g\}$ then for every variable $x^r \in var(g)$ and every answer substitution θ for g with respect to P $ts \vdash\!\!- \theta x^r$.

Proof. Induction on the length of an SLD-refutation of g. The base case is given by Lemma 7 and Theorem 8.

■

5. Type Checking

In practice, a Prolog programmer only defines a typing for the predicate and function symbols (or only some of them) occurring in his program. Then a *type−checker* can automatically derive typings for the variables and undeclared functors of the program such that the given typing is a well-typing for any clause. If this is possible, the program is said to be well- typed. In this section we give an outline of this type checking and type derivation process and discuss some special problems which only occur in the presence of subtypes.

The type-checker processes the literals of a clause "top down" in the following way: From the (given) typing of a predicate symbol or a function symbol, type requirements for the arguments can be inferred by (TI1), (TI2), or (TI3), respectively: If $p(t_1, \ldots, t_n)$ is the processed literal and $((\tau_1, \ldots, \tau_n), p) \in ts$ the type of the arguments t_i must be an instance of τ_i (for the head literal, they must be identical up to renaming of variables). This leads to type requirements for the arguments which must be checked to be kept. If a term $t=f(s_1, \ldots, s_n)$ has a type requirement τ, there must be types $\tau_1, \ldots, \tau_n$ such that $((\tau_1, \ldots, \tau_n \rightarrow \tau), f) \in ts$, and then s_i must be checked against τ_i in the same way, until constants or variables are reached. The type of a constant must be of the reqired type. If an untyped variable is reached, the type of this variable occurrence becomes the required type.

If there is a (program) variable which has been assigned different types at different occurrences, the variable typing condition (VTC) must be verified. (VTC) can be enforced by instantiating type variables, if they are not part of the types in the clause head.[1] If this is not possible, the program is not well-typed.

The verification of (VTC) may be quite complicated. We demonstrate the steps which must be performed by some examples. Consider the following clause with type and mode declarations:

```
:- pred p(α,list(α)), q(nat,nat), r(β,list(β)).
:- mode p(i,o), q(i,o), r(i,o).
p(X,Y)  :-  q(X,Z)  ,  r(Z,Y).
```

1 In Mycroft/O'Keefe's type system this is performed by simply *unifying* the different type assignments.

The type checking process as outlined above leads to the following type assignments for variables (every column contains the assignments derived when processing one literal):

X: α	X: nat	Z: β
Y: list(α)	Z: nat	Y: list(β)

To ensure (VTC), these types must meet the following subtype relations:

(1) $\alpha \subseteq$ nat,
(2) list(α) $\subseteq$ list(β),
(3) nat $\subseteq \beta$.

The next problem is how to decide for two given types σ and τ, whether $\sigma \subseteq \tau$. Consider the following type declarations:

```
:- type nat => 0,1,2,3,...
:- type int => 0,1,-1,2,-2,...
:- type list(γ) => nil, .(γ,list(γ)).
:- type tree(γ) => empty, t(t(γ),γ,t(γ)).
:- type tl(α,β) = list(α) ; tree(β).
```

Obviously, we have that $nat \subseteq int$, because every term of type nat (which are only constants in this definition) is also of type *int*. Although the type $tl(\alpha,\beta)$ is the union of $list(\alpha)$ and $tree(\beta)$, we cannot generally say that $list(\gamma)$ or $tree(\gamma)$ are subtypes of $tl(\alpha,\beta)$. It depends on the (type) values which the type variables α, β and γ can take. But they are subtypes, if γ is a subtype of α or β, respectively. As a special case, $list(\alpha)$ and $tree(\beta)$ are subtypes of $tl(\alpha,\beta)$. Due to these properties of polymorphic types, we define the notion of a *conditional subtype relation*:

$$[\sigma \subseteq \tau \mid \alpha_1 \subseteq \beta_1, \ldots, \alpha_n \subseteq \beta_n]$$

where $\{\alpha_1, \ldots, \alpha_n\} \subseteq var(\sigma)$ and $\{\beta_1, \ldots, \beta_n\} \subseteq var(\tau)$. The '|' in the expression can be interpreted as "if". From the above declaratios we can infer the following conditional subtype relations:

```
nat ⊆ int.
list(α) ⊆ list(β) | α ⊆ β.
tree(α) ⊆ tree(β) | α ⊆ β.
tl(α1,β1) ⊆ tl(α2,β2) | α1 ⊆ α2 , β1 ⊆ β2.
list(α) ⊆ tl(β,γ) | α ⊆ β.
tree(α) ⊆ tl(β,γ) | α ⊆ γ.
```

The following definition determines how all conditional subtype relations of a typing can be computed.

Definition 10 (*conditional subtype relation*).
Let P be a program and t_S a typing of all symbols occurring in P. For $c/n \in TC$ let $F(c) := \{f/k \in \mathbf{F} \mid \exists \tau_1, \ldots, \tau_k \in \Sigma, \exists \alpha_1, \ldots, \alpha_n \in \mathbf{TV}: ((\tau_1, \ldots, \tau_n \rightarrow c(\alpha_1, \ldots, \alpha_n)), f) \in t_S\}$ the set of all function symbols with result type $c(\alpha_1, \ldots, \alpha_n)$. The *set of conditional subtype relations* $CSR(t_S)$ is defined by

$[c_1(\alpha_1, \ldots, \alpha_n) \subseteq c_2(\beta_1, \ldots, \beta_m) \mid \alpha'_1 \subseteq \beta'_1, \ldots, \alpha'_p \subseteq \beta'_p] \in CSR(t_S)$ iff

$c_1/n, c_2/m \in \mathbf{TC}$ and $F(c_1) \subseteq F(c_2)$ and

$\{\alpha'_1 \subseteq \beta'_1, \ldots, \alpha'_p \subseteq \beta'_p\}$ is the minimal (possibly empty) set such that

$(\tau_1, \ldots, \tau_k \to c_1(\alpha_1, \ldots, \alpha_n), f) \in t_S$ and $(\sigma_1, \ldots, \sigma_k \to c_2(\beta_1, \ldots, \beta_m), f) \in t_S$
and $\forall i \in \{1, \ldots, k\}: \phi\tau_i = \sigma_i$ and $\phi = \{\gamma_1 \leftarrow \gamma'_2, \ldots, \gamma_q \leftarrow \gamma'_q\}$
$\Rightarrow \{\gamma_1 \subseteq \gamma'_1, \ldots, \gamma_q \subseteq \gamma'_q\} \subseteq \{\alpha'_1 \subseteq \beta'_1, \ldots, \alpha'_p \subseteq \beta'_p\}$.

∎

Note that in the above definition it is

$\{\gamma_1, \ldots, \gamma_q\} \subseteq \{\alpha'_1, \ldots, \alpha'_q\} \subseteq \{\alpha_1, \ldots, \alpha_n\}$ and
$\{\gamma'_1, \ldots, \gamma'_q\} \subseteq \{\beta'_1, \ldots, \beta'_q\} \subseteq \{\beta_1, \ldots, \beta_n\}$.

The type substitution ϕ is the renaming substitution required for argument types of function symbols with more than one typing (cf. Definition 4 (ii)).

Deciding whether or not $\sigma \subseteq \tau$ for two type terms consists in "applying" the conditional subtype relations and evaluating the conditions. For example we have

list(nat) $\subseteq$ **list(int), list(int)** $\not\subseteq$ **list(nat).**

because

nat $\subseteq$ **int.**

Checking whether

tl(α,nat) $\subseteq$ **tl(int,α)**

leads to subtype relations

(4) nat $\subseteq$ α**,** α $\subseteq$ **int**

which cannot be further evaluated, but can be shown to be satisfiable because of the transitivity of the subtype relation. That is, *nat* and *int* can be seen as some kind of lower and upper bound for the (type) value of α, and we have $tl(\alpha, int) \subseteq tl(nat, \alpha)$ whenever $nat \subseteq \alpha \subseteq int$. Evaluating

tl(α,nat) $\subseteq$ **tl(nat,α)**

even yields that

(5) α **= nat**

which means that *nat* is a lower *and* upper bound for α.

That is, in general one cannot absolutely determine whether a subtype relation between two polytypes hold. It can only be said that the relation holds if the values of type variables range between some lower and upper bounds. These lower and upper bounds can be computed by means of the conditional subtype relations $CSR(t_S)$, as described by the following algorithm:

compute_buonds($\sigma, \tau, CSR, LB, UB$):
Input: σ, τ: type terms; *CSR*: a set of conditional subtype relations.

Output: *LB*, *UB*: The sets of lower and upper bounds for type variables occurring in σ and τ with respect to *CSR*. (If $(\alpha,\tau) \in LB$ then τ is a lower bound for α, if $(\alpha,\tau) \in UB$ then τ is an upper bound for α.) If the algorithm stops with failure then $\sigma \not\subseteq \tau$.

$LB := \emptyset$; $UB := \emptyset$; *compute_bounds1*(σ,τ);
if *compute_bounds1* has stopped with failure then stop with failure else stop with success.

compute_bounds1(σ,τ,*CSR*):
Input: σ, τ: type terms; *CSR*: a set of conditional subtype relations.
Global Variables: LB, UB.

1. If $\sigma \in \mathbf{TC}$ and $\tau \in \mathbf{TC}$
   then [if $[\sigma \subseteq \tau] \in CSR$ then stop with success else stop with failure];
2. If $\tau \in \mathbf{TV}$ then $LB := LB \cup \{(\tau,\sigma)\}$;
3. If $\sigma \in \mathbf{TV}$ then $UB := UB \cup \{(\sigma,\tau)\}$;
4. If there are $c_1, c_2 \in \mathbf{TC}$, $\alpha_1, \ldots, \alpha_n, \beta_1, \ldots, \beta_m \in \mathbf{TV}$ and a type substitution ϕ such that
   $\sigma = \phi c_1(\alpha_1, \ldots, \alpha_n)$ and $\tau = \phi c_2(\beta_1, \ldots, \beta_m)$ and
   $[c_1(\alpha_1, \ldots, \alpha_n) \subseteq c_2(\beta_1, \ldots, \beta_m) \mid \alpha'_1 \subseteq \beta'_1, \ldots, \alpha'_p \subseteq \beta'_p] \in CSR$
   then for $i = 1, \ldots, p$ execute *compute_bounds1*($\phi\alpha'_i$, $\phi\beta'_i$,*CSR*);
5. If one of the *compute_bounds1* executions in step 5. has stopped with failure then stop with failure else stop with success.

Coming back to our type checking example above which resulted in subtype relations (1) - (3), we can evaluate the relation (2) to

(6) $\alpha \subseteq \beta$

and from (1),(3) and (6) we obtain the following lower and upper bounds for α and β (α.*lb*, α.*ub*, β.*lb* and β.*ub*):

```
β.ub = { β }            β.lb = { α , nat }
α.ub = { nat , β }      α.lb = { α }
```

These upper and lower bounds among others restrict the kind of terms the predicate *p* can be called with without causing dynamic type conflicts (α must be a subtype of *nat*!). This information can be useful for the programmer (either he has specified the predicate too generally or there is a programming error).

Summarizing the type checking process, we can determine four main tasks:

(1) derive type requirements for pogram variables by means of (TI1),...,(TI4),
(2) from these derive subtype relations which must be kept by means of (VTC),
(3) determine lower and upper bounds for type variables by means of the conditional subtype relations (algorithm *compute_bounds*),
(4) determine whether the upper and lower bounds for every variable are consistent. That is, for any type variable every lower bound must be a subtype of every upper bound.

6. Conclusions

Trying to improve some software engineering qualities of logic programming, we have proposed a system of polymorphic types for Prolog. It extends the type system of [Mycroft, O'Keefe 84] to deal with subtypes. Static type checking is possible, if information about the dataflow within clauses is available. Among others, this information can be provided by a mode system. We have outlined the type checking process and discussed several problems which make type checking more sophisticated when subtype relations are involved. In general, it is not possible to decide whether or not a type is a subtype of another type if the types are polytypes. It depends on the values that type variables can be instantiated with. This led to the notion of conditional subtype relations.

Unification of type terms, which is a central operation in Mycroft/O'Keefe's type checking algorithm, must be replaced by showing a set of subtype relations among type terms to be satisfiable. It is a subject of further research to develop efficient algorithms for this problem and to characterize the typings for which it is decidable. This includes the question whether some of the restrictions imposed on typings (Definition 4) can be dropped without weakening our results.

Type and mode declarations do not have any influence on the execution of programs, therefore they can be seen as optional. A type checker can be part of a Prolog programming environment and implemented by preprocessing. The program itself can be interpreted or compiled without modifications as usual.

A Prolog implementation of a type checker for our type system is described in [Hagl 87].

Acknowledgements. We thank our colleagues from the KAP group (KArlsruhe Prolog project) A. Bockmayr, P. Kursawe and I. Varsek, for many fruitful discussions and their critical comments on earlier versions of this paper, and H. Lock for providing me with useful references about type systems in the functional programming area.

References

M. Bruynooghe, *Adding Redundancy to Obtain More Reliable and More Readable Prolog Programs*, 1st International Conference on Logic Programming, Marseille, 1982.

L. Cardelli, P. Wegner, *On understanding Types, Data Abstraction, and Polymorphism*, Computing Surveys, Vol. 17, No. 4, December 1985.

R. Dietrich, *Modes and Types for Prolog*, Arbeitspapiere der GMD Nr. 285, January 1988.

W. Drabent, *Do Logic Programs Resemble Programs in Conventional Languages?*, 4th IEEE Symposium on Logic Programming, San Francisco, 1987, 389-397.

J. A. Goguen, J. Meseguer, *Equality, Types, Modules, and Generics for Logic Programming*, Proc. 2nd International Conference on Logic Programming, Uppsala, Sweden, 1984, 115-126.

F. Hagl, *Statische Analyse von Prolog Programmen mit Datenfluß- und Typangaben*, Diplomarbeit, Universität Karlsruhe/GMD Karlsruhe, July 1987

M. Huber, I. Varsek, *Extended Prolog for Order-Sorted Resolution*, 4th IEEE Symposium on Logic Programming, San Francisco, 1987, 34-45

J. W. Lloyd, *Foundations of Logic Programming*, Springer, 1984 (2nd Edition 1987).

C. S.Mellish, *Some Global Optimizations for a Prolog Compiler*, J. Logic Programming 1985, No. 1, 43-66.

R. Milner, *A Theory of Type Polymorphism in Programming*, J. Computer System Science 17(3), 1978, 348-375.

P. Mishra, *Towards a Theory of Types in Prolog*, Proc. 1st IEEE International Symposium on Logic Programming, 1984, 289-298.

A. Mycroft, R. A. O'Keefe, *A Polymorphic Type System for Prolog*, DAI Research Paper 211, Dept. of Artificial Intelligence, Edinburgh University, 1983.

A. Mycroft, R. A. O'Keefe, *A Polymorphic Type System for Prolog*, Artificial Intelligence 23, 1984, 295-307.

M. Schmidt-Schauß, *Unification in a Many-Sorted Calculus with Declarations*, Proc. 8th Conference on Automated Deduction, Oxford, UK., July 1986, LNCS 230, 538-552.

G. Smolka, *Making Control and Data Flow in Logic Programs Explicit*, Proc. 1984 ACM Symposium on LISP and Functional Programming, Austin, Texas, August 1984.

G. Smolka, W. Nutt, *Order-Sorted Equational Computation*, Proc. CREAS, Austin, Texas, May 1987.

C. Walther, *A Many-Sorted Calculus Based on Resolution and Paramodulation*, Proc. 8th International Joint Conference on Artificial Intelligence, Karlsruhe, W. Germany, 1983, 882-891.

D. H. D. Warren, *Applied Logic - It's Use and Implementation as a Programming Tool*, PhD Thesis, University of Edinburgh, 1977. Available as: Technical Note 290, June 1983, SRI International.

D. H. D. Warren, *An Abstract Prolog Instruction Set*, Technical Note 309, Artificial Intelligence Center, SRI International, 1983.

J. Zobel, *Derivation of Polymorphic Types for Prolog Programs*, Proc. 4th International Conference on Logic Programming, Melbourne, Australia, May 1987, 817-838.

Type Inference with Subtypes

You-Chin Fuh Prateek Mishra
Department of Computer Science
The State University of New York at Stony Brook
Stony Brook, New York 11794-4400
CSNET: yfuh@sbcs, mishra@sbcs

Abstract

We extend polymorphic type inference to include subtypes. This paper describes the following results:

- We prove the existence of (i) principal type property and (ii) syntactic completeness of the type checker, for type inference with subtypes. This result is developed with only minimal assumptions on the underlying theory of subtypes.
- For a particular "structured" theory of subtypes, those engendered by coercions between type constants only, we prove that principal types are compactly expressible. This suggests that a practical type checker for the structured theory of subtypes is feasible.
- We develop efficient algorithms for such a type checker. There are two main algorithms: MATCH and CONSISTENT. The first can be thought of as an extension to the unification algorithm. The second, which has no analogue in conventional type inference, determines whether a set of coercions is consistent.

Thus, an extension of polymorphic type inference that incorporates the "structured" theory of subtypes is practical and yields greater polymorphic flexibility. We have begun work on an implementation.

1 Introduction

Polymorphic type inference, as embodied in the type-checker for Standard ML, has attracted widespread interest in the programming language community. The main results therein [DM82] [Lei83] [Wan87b] are (i) the principal type property: type correct programs possess multiple types all of which are substitution instances of a unique principal type, and (ii) syntactic completeness of the type checker, which always finds the principal type. This principal type may be instantiated, depending on the context of program use to yield an appropriate type. Thus, a program may be used in many different contexts, and yet be correctly type-checked. In addition, the type checker requires few type declarations, supports interactive programming and is efficiently implementable [Car85,Mal87].

In this work we extend type inference to include subtypes. This provides additional flexibility as a program with type t may be used wherever *any* supertype of type t is acceptable. Our subtype concept is based on type embedding or coercion: type t_1 is a subtype of type t_2, written $t_1 \rhd t_2$, if we have some way of mapping every value with type t_1 to a value of type t_2. Traditional subtype relationships are subsumed by this framework: $int \rhd real, char \rhd string$ etc. In addition, we accomodate subtype relationships between user-defined types. For example, the following natural relationship, which might arise when defining an interpreter or denotational semantics for a programming language, is expressible.

$$term \rhd expr, var \rhd term, const \rhd term, int \rhd expr, bool \rhd expr$$

Of course, in addition to indicating the relationship between types the user must also provide coercion functions that map values from the subtype to the supertype.

We have three main results:

- We prove the existence of (i) principal type property and (ii) syntactic completeness of the type checker, for type inference with subtypes. This result is developed with only minimal assumptions on the underlying theory of subtypes.
- For a particular "structured" theory of subtypes, those engendered by coercions between type constants only, we prove that principal types are compactly expressible. This suggests that a practical type checker for the structured theory of subtypes is feasible.
- We develop efficient algorithms for such a type checker. There are two main algorithms: MATCH and CONSISTENT. The first can be thought of as an extension to the unification algorithm. The second, which has no analogue in conventional type inference, determines whether a set of coercions is consistent.

Thus, an extension of polymorphic type inference that incorporates the "structured" theory of subtypes is practical and yields greater polymorphic flexibility. We have begun work on an implementation.

1.1 What's the problem?

What are the problems caused by adding subtypes into a polymorphic type inference system? Consider the term $I \equiv \lambda x.x$ with (conventional) principal type $\alpha \rightarrow \alpha$. Now, one type I possesses is $int \rightarrow real$, as $int \rhd real$. This type is not a substitution instance of $\alpha \rightarrow \alpha$. A first "solution" is to redefine the principal type property: type τ is a principal type of term t if any type τ' that

t possesses is either a instance of τ or *is a supertype of some instance of* τ. From the standard semantics for $\rightarrow$, we have:

$$int \rhd real \Rightarrow int \rightarrow int \rhd int \rightarrow real$$

Hence, with the new definition, it appears that $\alpha \rightarrow \alpha$ is the principal type for I. However, consider the term $twice \equiv \lambda f.\lambda x.f(f\ x)$ with principal type $\tau \equiv (\alpha \rightarrow \alpha) \rightarrow (\alpha \rightarrow \alpha)$. One type $twice$ possesses is $(real \rightarrow int) \rightarrow (real \rightarrow int)$. A simple case-analysis demonstrates that there is *no* substitution instance τ' of τ, such that

$$int \rhd real \Rightarrow \tau' \rhd (real \rightarrow int) \rightarrow (real \rightarrow int)$$

1.2 A General Solution

The example above demonstrates that in the presence of subtypes we cannot represent the set of all typings of a program by a type expression alone. Instead, types are represented by a *pair* consisting of a set of coercion statements $\{t_i \rhd t_j\}$ (called a coercion set) and a type expression. The idea is that any substitution that satisfies the coercion set can be applied to the type expression to yield an instance of the type. Given a program how do we compute such a type expression? Our first result, described in Section 3, states that it is enough to carry out type inference in the standard manner with the additional requirement that at each step during type inference we conclude we have inferred a supertype of the standard type. The collection of such conclusions yields the coercion set. Furthermore, with only minimal assumptions about the underlying structure of subtypes, we show that the resulting type is the principal type associated with the program. For example, we would compute the coercion set-type pair (C, γ) for the identity function I, where $C \equiv \{\alpha \rightarrow \beta \rhd \gamma, \alpha \rhd \beta\}$. Any substitution S that satisfies every coercion in C yields a typing $S(\gamma)$ for I.

1.3 A Structured Theory of Subtypes

While the results in Section 3 provide a general framework for type inference in the presence of subtypes, it should be clear that types of the form shown above for I are not practically useful.

In practice, we are interested in subtype theories with a great deal more "structure". One of the simplest such subtype theories is one in which *every* coercion is the consequence of coercions between type constants: $int \rhd real$, $term \rhd expr$ and so on. Any coercion between structured types, say $(t_1, t_2) \rhd (t_1', t_2')$, follows precisely from coercions between its components, $t_1 \rhd t_1', t_2 \rhd t_2'$. For such a subtype theory, in Section 5, we show that we can always transform the coercion set-type pair into a form where the coercion set consists only of *atomic* coercions: coercions between type constants and type variables. The typing for I would now take the form:

$$(\{\alpha \rhd \beta\}, \alpha \rightarrow \beta)$$

To build a type inference system based on this concept we need efficient implementations of two algorithms: MATCH and CONSISTENT. Both appear to be polynomial time algorithms and are described in Section 6.

1.4 Polymorphism

The framework described above does not deal with the problem of polymorphism: permitting user-defined names to possess multiple types. Our approach is to follow ML, and use the "let" syntax combined with a limited form of "bounded" type quantification. This provides precisely as much flexibility as in ML and avoids the complexities of type inference with general quantification [Lei83][Mit84b]. This system is described in section 7.

2 Related Work

Discussion on the semantics of subtypes in a very general category-theoretic setting has appeared in [Rey80]. In [Rey85] inference rules for type inference with subtypes are given. However, strong assumptions are made about the subtype structure: every pair of subtypes must possess a unique least supertype. In [Mit84a] it was first shown that types with a "structured" subtype theory can be represented using coercion sets consisting only of atomic types. A type inference procedure was also outlined therein (in particular, we follow Mitchell in using the term MATCH), but algorithms were omitted. In [MR85] type inference methods for a theory of types with a general "type union" operator were developed, but the issue of completeness of the type checker was not addressed.

In a different direction, Cardelli [Car84] has suggested that inheritance be modelled by subtyping through the use of record structures with named fields. Recently, Wand [Wan87a] has given a type inference algorithm that models a form of inheritance based on record structures. In contrast to our work, Wand's algorithm is based on an extension of unification. We plan to investigate the possibility of extending our system to include some form of record-based inheritance.

3 Preliminary Definitions

There are two basic components in any type inference system, the language of *value* expressions and the language of *type* expressions. Value and type expressions are defined by the following abstract syntax.

$N \in$ Value Expressions	$t \in$ Type Expressions
$x \in$ Value Variables	$\alpha \in$ Type Variables
$f^m \in$ Value Constructors	$g^n \in$ Type Constructors

$$N ::= x \mid f^m[\bar{x}](N_1, \ldots, N_m) \quad t ::= \alpha \mid g^n(t_1, \ldots, t_n)$$

As examples, consider value expressions

$$\lambda[x](N),\ ifthenelse[](N,N_1,N_2),\ \ \textbf{fix}\ [x](N),\ \ 7$$

and type expressions $int \rightarrow (\alpha \rightarrow bool)$, (int, α).

A coercion is an ordered pair of types written $t_1 \rhd t_2$. A coercion set $C = \{t_i \rhd r_i\}$ is a set of coercions. A type assumption A is a finite mapping from value variables to type expressions, often written $\bar{x} : \bar{t}$. Let Z be a set of value variables; by $A|_Z$ we mean A restricted to domain Z. A substitution S is a mapping from type variables to type expressions that is not equal to the identity function at only finitely many type variables. $[t_1/\alpha_1, \cdots, t_n/\alpha_n]$ is the substitution that maps α_i to t_i and is otherwise equal to the identity function. If t is a type expression, by $S(t)$ we mean the simultaneous replacement of every variable in t by its image under S. The meanings of $S(C)$ and $S(A)$ are defined in the standard fashion.

We will often consider some distinguished set of coercions as *valid* or *true* coercions. The only restriction we place on the set of valid coercions, is considered as a relation on *Type* $\times$ *Type* it should be (i) reflexive (ii) transitive and (iii) closed under substitution. Our intention here is that the set of valid coercions $\{t \rhd r\}$ consists of those pairs of types such that the first component may reasonably be transformed into the second. The three conditions on the set of valid coercions indicate that any type should be transformable to itself, that transformations between types be composable and that the transformation be unaffected by instantiation of type variables.

We say coercion $t \rhd r$ is *solvable* or *consistent* if there exists some substitution S such that $S(t) \rhd S(r)$ is valid. Define the relation $\Vdash$ on coercions by:

$$a \rhd b \Vdash c \rhd d \iff S(a) \rhd S(b) \text{ valid entails } S(c) \rhd S(d) \text{ valid}$$

We lift the relation $\Vdash$ to coercion sets by considering a coercion set to be a conjunction of all its coercions. Informally $C_1 \Vdash C_2$ should be read as saying that substitution S renders the coercions in C_2 valid, whenever it renders the coercions in C_1 valid. Observe that $\Vdash$ as a relation on coercion sets is (i) reflexive (ii) transitive and (iii) closed under substitution. Observe that $a \rhd b$ is valid iff $\emptyset \Vdash \{a \rhd b\}$.

3.1 Type Inference System

A type inference system is a system of rules that defines a relation, called a *typing*, over the four-tuple:

Coercion Set $\times$ Type Assumption $\times$ Value Expression $\times$ Type Expression

A *typing statement* is written $C, A \vdash M : t$. By $A\ ;\ \bar{x} : \bar{s}$ we mean a type assumption identical to A, except that it maps value variable x_i to type expression s_i. In the rules below, we would expect to have an instance of a FUN rule for each value constructor symbol f^m. FUN rules for zero-ary constants may have empty antecedents.

$$VAR \qquad C, A \vdash x : A(x)$$

$$FUN_{f^m} \qquad \frac{C, A\,;\, \bar{x} : \bar{s}^f \vdash N_1 : r_1^f, \ldots, N_m : r_m^f}{C, A \vdash f^m[\bar{x}](N_1, \ldots, N_m) : \alpha^f}$$

$$COERCE \quad \frac{C, A \vdash e : t, C \Vdash \{t \rhd p\}}{C, A \vdash e : p}$$

For some instances of FUN consider the following:

$$\frac{C, A\,;\, x : t_1 \vdash N : t_2}{C, A \vdash \lambda^1[x](N) : t_1 \rightarrow t_2}$$

$$\frac{C, A \vdash P : bool, M : t, N : t}{C, A \vdash \text{if } P \text{ then } M \text{ else } N \ : t}$$

$$C, A \vdash true : bool$$

$\boxed{C, A \vdash N : p}$ is a *typing* if

$\boxed{N \equiv x}$ and $C \Vdash \{A(x) \ \rhd p\}$.

$\boxed{N \equiv f^m[\bar{x}](N_1, \ldots, N_m)}$
and

(1) $(\bar{q}, v_i, u)$ is a substitution instance of $(\bar{s}^f, r_i^f, \alpha^f)$,
(2) $C, A\,;\, \bar{x} : \bar{q} \vdash N_i : v_i$ are typings,
(3) $C \Vdash \{u \ \rhd p\}$.

Observe that it is an immediate consequence of the transitivity of $\rhd$ that in any typing we need at most a single COERCE step after an application of a VAR or FUN step.

Definition 1 (Instance) *Typing statement $C', A' \vdash N : t'$ is an instance of typing statement $C, A \vdash N : t$, if there exists substitution S such that:*

1. $t' = S(t)$.
2. $A'|_{FV(N)} = S(A)|_{FV(N)}$.
3. $C' \Vdash S(C)$.

Lemma 1 *Typings are closed under the instance relation; i.e. if $C, A \vdash N : t$ is a typing then so is every instance $C', A' \vdash N : t'$.*

Proof: Proof is by induction on structure of term N. The main property required is that $C_1 \Vdash C_2 \Rightarrow S(C_1) \Vdash S(C_2)$. □

3.2 Algorithm TYPE

In this section, we describe an algorithm that constructs a distinguished representative of all typings for a term M, the *principal type* for M. We assume the existence of function *new* : $(Type\ Expression)^k \rightarrow (Type\ Expression)^k$, such that $new(t_1, \ldots, t_k)$ is obtained by consistently replacing all the type variables in types t_i by "new" type variables.

Algorithm TYPE:Type Assumption × Value Expression → Type Expression × Coercion Set

Input: (A_0, e_0), where $FV(e_0) \subseteq domain(A_0)$.

Initially:

$C = \emptyset$, $G = \{(A_0, e_0, \alpha_0)\}$, where α_0 is a new variable.

While G is not empty do:

Choose any g from G;

case g of:

$(A, f^m[\bar{x}](e_1, ..., e_n), t)$:

$$\begin{aligned} (\bar{q}, v_i, u) &= new(\bar{s}, r_i, \alpha); \\ C &\leftarrow C \cup \{u \rhd t\}; \\ G &\leftarrow (G - \{g\}) \cup \{(A[\bar{x} : \bar{q}], e_i, v_i)\}; \end{aligned}$$

(A, x, t) :

$$\begin{aligned} C &\leftarrow C \cup \{A(x) \rhd t\}; \\ G &\leftarrow G - \{g\}; \end{aligned}$$

end case;

Output: (α_0, C).

Example 1 *Let $N \equiv \lambda f.\lambda x.fx$ and $A = \emptyset$. Then*

$$TYPE(A, N) = (t_N, \left\{ \begin{array}{c} t_f \rightarrow t_{\lambda x.fx} \rhd t_N \\ t_f \rhd t_1 \rightarrow t_2 \\ t_x \rightarrow t_{fx} \rhd t_{\lambda x.fx} \\ t_2 \rhd t_{fx} \\ t_x \rhd t_1 \end{array} \right\})$$

It is interesting to compare our algorithm with that given by Mitchell [Mit84a]. Mitchell's algorithm works for a particular "structured" subtype theory and interleaves the generation of the constraint set with the process of simplifying it and checking it for consistency. In contrast, our algorithm is designed to work for a class of subtype theories and is concerned only with the generation of the relevant constraint set. In this way, we separate the "syntactic" aspects of type inference (traversal of the abstract syntax tree, generation of constraint set) from the details of processing the constraint set. One consequence is that we are able to give a general proof of soundness and syntactic completeness that makes use only of the assumptions about the relations: typing, $\triangleright$ and $\Vdash$, that we have presented above. Further, as our algorithm does not commit itself to any particular method for processing constraint sets, it can serve as the basis for algorithms that utilize a variety of different methods. This is of importance as details of constraint set processing depend critically on the particulars of the subtype theory as well as on the particular application area of interest.

Theorem 1 *TYPE is sound and (syntactically) complete.*

Proof: Proof is given below. □

3.3 TYPE is sound and complete

Our proof follows Wand's [Wan87b] concise proof of soundness and completeness of parametric type inference. One difference between his proof and ours is that we need to reason about coercion sets instead of sets of equations used in his work.

A tri-tuple (A, e, t) is a *goal* if A is a type assumption, e is a value expression, and t is a type expression. The pair of coercion set and substitution, (C, σ), solves the goal (A, e, t), denoted by $(C, \sigma) \models (A, e, t)$, if $C, \sigma(A) \vdash e : \sigma(t)$. Let G be a set of goals: $(C, \sigma) \models G$, if $\forall g \in G$, $(C, \sigma) \models g$. We also say that $(C, \sigma) \models C_0$ if $C \Vdash \sigma(C_0)$. We can extend the notion of solvability to pairs of coercion set and set of goals: $(C, \sigma) \models (C_0, G)$ if $(C, \sigma) \models C_0$ and $(C, \sigma) \models G$.

To prove soundness and completeness, it's sufficient to prove the following invariants:

TYPE is Sound: $(\forall(\bar{C}, \sigma))\,((\bar{C}, \sigma) \models (C, G) \implies \bar{C}, \sigma(A_0) \vdash e_0 : \sigma(\alpha_0))$

TYPE is Complete: $\bar{C}, \bar{A} \vdash e_0 : \bar{t} \wedge \exists\delta\ \bar{A}|_{FV(e_0)} = \delta(A_0)|_{FV(e_0)}$

$$\implies (\exists\sigma)((\bar{C}, \sigma) \models (C, G) \wedge \bar{A}|_{FV(e_0)} = \sigma(A_0)|_{FV(e_0)} \wedge \bar{t} = \sigma(\alpha_0))$$

proof: (TYPE is sound)

Basis: Since $G = \{(A_0, e_0, \alpha_0)\}$, by definition of $\models$, $\bar{C}, \sigma(A_0) \vdash e_0 : \sigma(\alpha_0)$.

step: (Let C_0 and G_0 denote the values of C and G before the iteration)

(A, x, t) :

$(\bar{C}, \sigma) \models (C, G)$

$\Longrightarrow$ $(\bar{C}, \sigma) \models \{A(x) \rhd t\}$

$\Longrightarrow$ $(\bar{C}, \sigma) \models (A, x, t)$ (by typing rule)

$\Longrightarrow$ $(\bar{C}, \sigma) \models (C_0, G_0)$

$\Longrightarrow$ $\bar{C}, \sigma(A_0) \vdash e_0 : \sigma(\alpha_0)$ (By hypothesis)

$(A, f^m[\bar{x}](e_1, ..., e_n), t)$:

$(\bar{C}, \sigma) \models (C, G)$

$\Longrightarrow$ $(\bar{C}, \sigma) \models \{u \rhd t\}$ and $(\bar{C}, \sigma) \models \{A[\bar{x} : \bar{q}], e_i, v_i\}$

$\Longrightarrow$ $\bar{C} \Vdash \sigma(\{u \rhd t\})$ and $\bar{C}, \sigma(A[\bar{x} : \bar{q}]) \vdash e_i : \sigma(v_i)$ (by definition of $\models$)

$\Longrightarrow$ $\bar{C}, \sigma(A) \vdash f^m[\bar{x}](e_1, ..., e_n) : \sigma(t)$ (By typing rule)

$\Longrightarrow$ $(\bar{C}, \sigma) \models (C_0, G_0)$

$\Longrightarrow$ $\bar{C}, \sigma(A_0) \vdash e_0 : \sigma(\alpha_0)$ (By hypothesis)

proof: (TYPE is complete)

Basis: $\bar{C}, \bar{A} \vdash e_0 : \bar{t}$. Since α_0 is a new variable and $\exists\delta\ \bar{A}|_{FV(e_0)} = \delta(A_0)|_{FV(e_0)}$, it's obvious that $\exists\sigma$ such that $\bar{A}|_{FV(e_0)} = \sigma(A_0)|_{FV(e_0)}$ and $\bar{t} = \sigma(\alpha_0)$.

step: (Let C_0 and G_0 denote the values of C and G before the iteration)

(A, x, t) :

$\bar{C}, \bar{A} \vdash e_0 : \bar{t}$

$\Longrightarrow$ $(\exists\sigma)\,((\bar{C}, \sigma) \models (C_0, G_0) \wedge \bar{A}|_{FV(e_0)} = \sigma(A_0)|_{FV(e_0)} \wedge \bar{t} = \sigma(\alpha_0))$ (By hypothesis)

$\Longrightarrow$ $\bar{C} \Vdash \sigma(\{A(x) \rhd t\})$ (By typing rule)

$\Longrightarrow$ $(\bar{C}, \sigma) \models \{A(x) \rhd t\}$ (by definition of $\models$)

$\Longrightarrow$ $(\bar{C}, \sigma) \models (C, G) \wedge \bar{A}|_{FV(e_0)} = \sigma(A_0)|_{FV(e_0)} \wedge \bar{t} = \sigma(\alpha_0)$

$(A, f^m[\bar{x}](e_1, ..., e_n), t)$:

$\bar{C}, \bar{A} \vdash e_0 : \bar{t}$

$\Longrightarrow$ $(\exists\sigma_0)\,((\bar{C}, \sigma_0) \models (C_0, G_0) \wedge \bar{A}|_{FV(e_0)} = \sigma_0(A_0)|_{FV(e_0)} \wedge \bar{t} = \sigma_0(\alpha_0))$ (By hypothesis)

$\Longrightarrow$ $\bar{C}, \sigma_0(A) \vdash f^m[\bar{x}](e_1, ..., e_n) : \sigma_0(t)$ (hence $(\bar{C}, \sigma_0) \models (A, f^m[\bar{x}](e_1, ..., e_n), t)$)

$\Longrightarrow$ $(\exists\gamma)(\bar{C}, (\sigma_0(A))[\bar{x} : \gamma(\bar{q})] \vdash e_i : \gamma(v_i) \wedge \bar{C} \Vdash \{\gamma(u) \rhd \sigma_0(t)\}$ (by typing rule)

$\Longrightarrow$ Since γ and σ_0 have disjoint domain, we can choose σ to be $\gamma \cup \sigma_0$

$\Longrightarrow$ $\bar{C}, \sigma(A[\bar{x} : \bar{q}]) \vdash e_i : \sigma(v_i) \wedge \bar{C} \Vdash \sigma(\{u \rhd t\}) \wedge \bar{A}|_{FV(e_0)} = \sigma(A_0)|_{FV(e_0)} \wedge \bar{t} = \sigma(\alpha_0)$

$\Longrightarrow$ $(\bar{C}, \sigma) \models (C, G) \wedge \bar{A}|_{FV(e_0)} = \sigma(A_0)|_{FV(e_0)} \wedge \bar{t} = \sigma(\alpha_0)$

□

4 Well-typings

A typing $C, A \vdash N : t$ should be viewed as standing for a set of all possible instances $C', A' \vdash N : t'$, where C' is valid. Informally, the set of all *valid instances* of a typing expresses the "information content" of a typing, in that it describes all possible "correct" ways of using a typing. For an example, all valid instances of $\{\alpha \rhd real\}, \emptyset \vdash N : \alpha$ are of the form $\{t' \rhd real\} \cup C, A \vdash N : t'$, provided the coercions in $\{t' \rhd real\} \cup C$ are valid.

Typings of the form $C, A \vdash N : t$ which possess no valid instances are of no interest to us. This is the case when C contains contradictory information; for an example take C to be $\{bool \rhd \alpha, int \rhd \alpha, \alpha \rhd real\}$. We cannot find any type t such that replacing α by t in C results in a valid coercion set.

Define a *well-typing* to be a typing $C, A \vdash N : t$, where C is consistent. Immediately, the question arises whether the theory developed in previous sections carries over to well-typings (instance, principal type property, algorithm TYPE). Lemma 1 holds with the following obvious modification: If $C, A \vdash N : t$ is a well-typing, then so is every instance $C', A' \vdash N : t'$, whenever C' is consistent.

How do we compute well-typings? We simply run algorithm TYPE and check the final coercion set for consistency. If it is consistent, we are done; otherwise, we fail and conclude that no well-typing exists. That this method is sound is obvious; its completeness is argued below:

WTYPE :Type Assumption $\times$ Value Expression $\rightarrow$ Well Typing $+\{fail\}$
let $(p, C) = TYPE(A, N)$ in
if C is consistent then $C, A \vdash N : p$
else fail

To see that algorithm WTYPE is complete, we need to consider two cases. For the first, we have that C is consistent. But then, the syntactic completeness of TYPE ensures the syntactic completeness of WTYPE. For the second case, let C be inconsistent. We will argue that no well-typing $C', A' \vdash N : p'$ exists. Assume otherwise; as TYPE is syntactically complete we can find substitution S with $C' \Vdash S(C)$. Now, since C' is consistent we must have that $S(C)$ is consistent. But then C must be consistent as well and we have arrived at a contradiction.

5 Structured Type Inclusion

In this section, we develop type inference methods for the case where the underlying theory of type inclusion is structured. We study the simplest such case: all inclusions are the consequences of inclusions between type constants.

The abstract syntax of types t, is given by:

$$t ::= g_c \mid t_1 \rightarrow t_2 \mid (t_1, t_2)$$

The type inference rules are given by:

$C, A \vdash x : A(x)$	$\dfrac{C, A \vdash N : t_1 \to t_2, M : t_1}{C, A \vdash NM : t_2}$
$\dfrac{C, A\,;\{x : t_1\} \vdash M : t_2}{C, A \vdash \lambda x.M : t_1 \to t_2}$	$\dfrac{C, A \vdash M : boolean, N : t, O : t}{C, A \vdash \text{if } M \text{ then } N \text{ else } O\ : t}$
$\dfrac{C, A\,;\{x : t_1\} \vdash M : t_1}{C, A \vdash \textbf{fix}\ x.M : t_1}$	$C, A \vdash c : g_c$
$\dfrac{C, A \vdash M : t_1, C \Vdash t_1 \rhd t_2}{C, A \vdash M : t_2}$	

The following rules define the relation $\Vdash$ for the theory of interest.

$[AXIOM]$	$M \cup \{t_1 \rhd t_2\} \Vdash t_1 \rhd t_2$	$[CONST]$	$M \Vdash g_{c_i} \rhd g_{c_k}$
$[TRANS]$	$\dfrac{M \Vdash t_1 \rhd t_2, t_2 \rhd t_3}{M \Vdash t_1 \rhd t_3}$	$[REFLEX]$	$M \Vdash t \rhd t$
$[ARROW-I]$	$\dfrac{M \Vdash t_1 \rhd t'_1, t'_2 \rhd t_2}{M \Vdash t'_1 \to t'_2 \rhd t_1 \to t_2}$	$[PROD-I]$	$\dfrac{M \Vdash t_1 \rhd t'_1, t_2 \rhd t'_2}{M \Vdash (t_1, t_2) \rhd (t'_1, t'_2)}$
$[ARROW-II]$	$\dfrac{M \Vdash t'_1 \to t'_2 \rhd t_1 \to t_2}{M \Vdash t_1 \rhd t'_1, t'_2 \rhd t_2}$	$[PROD-II]$	$\dfrac{M \Vdash (t_1, t_2) \rhd (t'_1, t'_2)}{M \Vdash t_1 \rhd t'_1, t_2 \rhd t'_2}$

Rule [CONST] is the only means of introducing "new" statements about type inclusion in the system. Such statements are restricted to be relationships between type constants. Rules [TRANS] and [REFLEX] indicate that the relation $\Vdash$ is transitive and reflexive. Rules [ARROW-I], [PROD-I], [ARROW-II] and [PROD-II] are "structural" rules that define coercions between structured types in terms of coercions between their components.

An *inclusion statement* is written $C \Vdash t_1 \rhd t_2$. A proof for $C \Vdash t_1 \rhd t_2$ is a sequence of inclusion statements $IS_1, \cdots, IS_k \equiv C \Vdash t_1 \rhd t_2$, where each IS_i is a substitution instance of (i) [AXIOM], [CONSTANT] or [REFLEX] rules or (ii) is derived by an application of a substitution instance of one of the remaining rules to some finite subset of $IS_1, \cdots, IS_{i-1}$. In such a case, we say that the statement $C \Vdash t_1 \rhd t_2$ is true. We say $C_1 \Vdash C_2$ if $C_1 \Vdash t_i \rhd t_j$ for each $\{t_i \rhd t_j\} \in C_2$. It is decidable whether $C_1 \Vdash C_2$, where C_1 and C_2 are finite sets of coercions.

The description of $\Vdash$ given above indicates that the inclusion relationship between types is much more "structured" than the very general notion of $\Vdash$ studied in section 3. As a consequence, we will show that we need only consider coercion sets restricted to be of the format $\{t_i \rhd t_j\}$ where each t_i, t_j is an *atomic* type: either a type variable or a type constant.

5.1 Instantiating Coercion Sets

In section 4 we have defined the information content of a typing to be set of its valid instances. This suggests that there may exist distinct typings with identical information content. One way this might occur is if well-typing $C, A \vdash N : t$ and some instantiation $C', A' \vdash N : t'$, have identical information content. Further, it seems reasonable to consider the second typing preferable to the first as it contains more "structural" information than the first and therefore reveals more information to the user.

Example 2 *Consider the typing $C, \emptyset \vdash N : \alpha$, where*

$$C = \{\alpha \rhd \beta \rightarrow \gamma\}$$

Every valid instance of C requires α to be instantiated to an "arrow" type; hence in place of the above typing we can use one of the form $C', \emptyset \vdash N : \delta \rightarrow \rho$ where

$$C' = \{\delta \rightarrow \rho \rhd \beta \rightarrow \gamma\}$$

Both typings have identical information content but the second has more explicit "structural" information.

The notion of information content is essential in defining the equivalence of typings under instantiation. It is not the case, in Example 2 above, that $C \equiv C'$. Neither $C \Vdash C'$ holds, nor is it the case that $C' \Vdash C$. Further, arbitrary instantiation of coercion sets does not preserve information content: for example, if we instantiate $\alpha \rhd \beta \rightarrow \gamma$ to $\delta \rightarrow (\sigma \rightarrow \tau) \rhd \rho \rightarrow (\psi \rightarrow \mu)$, we are missing out on the possibility that α can be instantiated to a type with a "single" arrow type in some valid instance of $\alpha \rhd \beta \rightarrow \gamma$.

To see the general form of information content preserving instantiations we first need to characterize the "shape" of valid coercion sets. Define the relation *Match* over pairs of type expression by:

$Match(t_1, t_2)$ is true, if both t_1, t_2 are atomic types.
$Match(t_1 \rightarrow t_2, t_1' \rightarrow t_2')$ whenever $Match(t_1, t_1'), Match(t_2, t_2')$.
$Match((t_1, t_2), (t_1', t_2'))$ whenever $Match(t_1, t_1'), Match(t_2, t_2')$.

We say C is a matching coercion set if every coercion $r \rhd s \in C$ is matching. Matching is a necessary condition for coercion sets to be valid; whenever coercion set C is valid every coercion contained in C must be matching. Proof is by induction on the number of proof steps needed to show $\emptyset \Vdash C$ and is straightforward.

Given that valid coercion sets are always matching, what kinds of instantiation preserve information content? If $t_1 \rhd t_2$ is a consistent coercion we will argue that we can always find a information-content preserving substitution S such that $S(t_1) \rhd S(t_2)$ is matching. Further, S is the least such substitution, in that any other matching instance of $t_1 \rhd t_2$ must also be an instance of $S(t_1) \rhd S(t_2)$.

Theorem 2 *Let $C, A \vdash N : t$ be a well-typing. There exists well-typing $C_*, A_* \vdash N : t_*$ with the property that:*

1. *$C_*, A_* \vdash N : t_*$ is a matching instance of $C, A \vdash N : t$.*
2. *$C_*, A_* \vdash N : t_*$ and $C, A \vdash N : t$ have identical information content.*
3. *If $C', A' \vdash N : t'$ is any other typing that satisfies property (1); then $C', A' \vdash N : t'$ is an instance of $C_*, A_* \vdash N : t_*$.*

Proof: See technical report # 87-25, SUNY Stony Brook. □

We will speak of $C_*, A_* \vdash N : t_*$ as the minimal matching instance of $C, A \vdash N : t$.

Example 3 *Let $N \equiv \lambda f.\lambda x.fx$, $A = \emptyset$ and let $TYPE(A, N) = (t_N, C)$ as in Example 1.*

$$C_* \equiv \left\{ \begin{array}{c} (\alpha_3 \to \alpha_4) \to (\alpha_1 \to \alpha_2) \rhd (\beta_3 \to \beta_4) \to (\beta_1 \to \beta_2) \\ \alpha_3 \to \alpha_4 \rhd t_1 \to t_2 \\ t_x \to t_{fx} \rhd \alpha_1 \to \alpha_2 \\ t_2 \rhd t_{fx} \\ t_x \rhd t_1 \end{array} \right\}, (t_N)_* \equiv (\beta_3 \to \beta_4) \to (\beta_1 \to \beta_2)$$

Finally, we need to ensure that representing a well-typing by its minimal matching instance does not perturb the most general type property. We need to show the following: let well-typing $C', A' \vdash N : t'$ be an instance of $C, A \vdash N : t$; then, we must have that $C'_*, A'_* \vdash N : t'_*$ is an instance of $C_*, A_* \vdash N : t_*$. To see this, observe that $C'_*, A'_* \vdash N : t'_*$ is a matching instance of $C, A \vdash N : t$; hence, it must be an instance of the minimal matching instance $C_*, A_* \vdash N : t_*$.

5.2 Simplifying Coercion Sets

Example 4

$$C_1 \equiv \{(\alpha \to \beta) \rhd (\delta \to \gamma)\}$$
$$C_2 \equiv \{\delta \rhd \alpha, \beta \rhd \gamma\}$$

C_1, C_2 are equivalent in that each entails the other: $C_1 \Vdash C_2$ and $C_2 \Vdash C_1$. As

$$C_1 \Vdash C_2 \Rightarrow S(C_1) \Vdash S(C_2)$$

both have identical information content. Finally, C_2 contains less redundant information and therefore seems preferable to C_1.

SIMPLIFY $C = C$, if all coercions in C are atomic
SIMPLIFY $C \cup \{t_1 \rightarrow t_2 \rhd r_1 \rightarrow r_2\}$ = SIMPLIFY $C \cup \{r_1 \rhd t_1, t_2 \rhd r_2\}$
SIMPLIFY $C \cup \{(t_1, t_2) \rhd (r_1, r_2)\}$ = SIMPLIFY $C \cup \{t_1 \rhd r_1, t_2 \rhd r_2\}$

Function SIMPLIFY maps matching coercion sets into the maximally simplified set of *atomic* coercions. It is trivially clear that $SIMPLIFY$ preserves information content; as $SIMPLIFY$ does not effect in any way the type variables contained in an coercion set it is also obvious that the most general well-typing property is also preserved.

Example 5 *Let C_* be as in Example 3 above.*

$SIMPLIFY(C_*) = \{\alpha_3 \rhd \beta_3,\ \beta_4 \rhd \alpha_4,\ \beta_1 \rhd \alpha_1,\ \alpha_2 \rhd \beta_2,\ \alpha_1 \rhd t_x,\ t_{fx} \rhd \alpha_2,\ t_1 \rhd \alpha_3,\ \alpha_4 \rhd t_2,\ t_2 \rhd t_{fx},\ t_x \rhd t_1\}$

In a practical implementation, we would only be concerned with $\{\beta_1 \rhd \beta_3, \beta_4 \rhd \beta_2\}$.

6 Algorithm WTYPE Revisited

WTYPE :Type Assumption $\times$ Value Expression $\rightarrow$ Well Typing $+\{fail\}$
let $(p, C) = TYPE(A, N)$ in
if C is consistent then
let $C_*, A_* \vdash N : p_*$ in
$SIMPLIFY(C_*), A_* \vdash N : p_*$ else fail

In practice, determining consistency is overlapped with computing the minimal matching instance for a typing. Instead of the "consistency check-instantiate-simplify" sequence given above, we use the following sequence of tests and reductions:

MATCH : Coercion Set $\rightarrow$ Substitution $+\{fail\}$
SIMPLIFY : Coercion Set $\rightarrow$ Atomic Coercion Set
CONSISTENT : Atomic Coercion Set $\rightarrow$ Boolean $+\{fail\}$

If $MATCH(C)$ succeeds and returns substitution S, then $S(C)$ is the minimal matching instance of C. If it fails, C is *structurally* inconsistent: it either entails a cyclic inclusion ($\alpha \rhd \alpha \rightarrow \beta$) or an inclusion where the type constructors differ at the top-level ($\alpha \rightarrow \beta \rhd (\gamma, \delta)$). $CONSISTENT(C)$ determines whether C is consistent: whether there exists some S such that $S(C)$ is valid.

6.1 Algorithm MATCH

It is useful to consider MATCH as a variation on the classical unification algorithm [MM82]. A unification algorithm can be modelled as the process of transforming a set of equations E into a substitution S, such that S unifies E. Similarly, MATCH should be viewed as transforming a coercion set C into a substitution S, such that S(C) is the minimal matching instance of C. In addition to S and C, MATCH maintains a third data-structure M which represents an equivalence relation over atomic types occurring in C and M. The main idea is that if atomic types a, a' belong to the same equivalence class in M, we must ensure that $S(a), S(a')$ are matching. Following the description of unification in [MM82] we describe MATCH in terms of three transformations on the tuple (C, S, M): (i) Decomposition (ii) Atomic Elimination and (iii) Expansion.

We write $\{(a, a') \mid \; a \; M \; a'\}$ for M. The following conventions are followed below: (1) v denotes type variables (2) a, a' denote atomic type expressions (3) α, β, α', and β' denote type expressions (4) t, t' denote non atomic type expressions. Let M be an equivalence relation defined as before, M_v is the equivalence relation obtained from M by deleting the equivalence class containing v and :

$$[a]_M \stackrel{\text{def}}{=} \{a' \mid (a, a') \in M\}$$
$$[t]^M \stackrel{\text{def}}{=} \{[a]_M \mid a \text{ occurs in } t\}$$

If A is a set of pairs of atomic types then A^* is the reflexive, symmetric, and transitive closure of the relation represented by A. $ALLNEW(t)$ is the type expression obtained from t by substituting "new" variables for every occurrence of variable or constant in t. $ALLNEW(v \rightarrow v * int) = \alpha \rightarrow \beta * \gamma$, where α, β, and γ are new variables.

$$PAIR(t, t') \stackrel{\text{def}}{=} \{(a, a') \mid \; a \text{ occurs in t at the same position as } a' \text{ occurs in } t'\}$$

Definition 2 Decomposition
$(C \cup \{t \rhd t'\}, S, M)$:

case $t \rhd t'$ of:

(1) $\alpha \rightarrow \beta \;\; \rhd \;\; \alpha' \rightarrow \beta'$:
Replace $C \cup \{t \rhd t'\}$ by $C \cup \{\alpha' \rhd \alpha, \; \beta \rhd \beta'\}$
(2) $\alpha * \beta \;\; \rhd \;\; \alpha' * \beta'$:
Replace $C \cup \{t \rhd t'\}$ by $C \cup \{\alpha \rhd \alpha', \; \beta \rhd \beta'\}$
(3) **else fail**

Definition 3 Atomic elimination
$(C \cup \{a \rhd a'\}, S, M)$:
Replace M *by* $(M \cup \{(a, a')\})^*$ *and delete the coercion* $a \rhd a'$ *from* C.

Definition 4 Expansion
$(C \cup \{e\}, S, M)$ where e is either $v \rhd t$ or $t \rhd v$.

if $[v]_M \in [t]^M \vee [v]_M$ contains type constant **then fail else**
for $x \in [v]_M$ **do**
begin
$t' \longleftarrow ALLNEW(t);$
$\delta \longleftarrow \{t'/x\};$
$(C, S, M) \longleftarrow (\delta(C), \delta \circ S, (M \cup PAIR(t, t'))^*);$
end
$M \longleftarrow M_v$

procedure $MATCH(\bar{C})$
begin
$(C, S, M) \longleftarrow (\bar{C}, Id, \{(a, a) \mid a \in \bar{C}\});$
while $C \neq \emptyset$ **do**
begin
choose any $e \in C$;
case e of:
(1) $t \rhd t'$: perform **Decomposition**
(2) $a \rhd a'$: perform **Atomic elimination**
(3) $v \rhd t \vee t \rhd v$: perform **Expansion**
end case
end
return S
end

Example 6 *Let* $\bar{C} = \{\alpha \rightarrow \beta \rhd int \rightarrow int * \gamma,\ int \rhd \gamma\}$.

C	S	M	Action
$\bar{C}$	Id	$\{\{\alpha\}, \{\beta\}, \{\gamma\}, \{int\}\}$	–
$\{int \rhd \alpha, \beta \rhd int * \gamma, int \rhd \gamma\}$	Id	$\{\{\alpha\}, \{\beta\}, \{\gamma\}, \{int\}\}$	*Decomposition*
$\{\beta \rhd int * \gamma, int \rhd \gamma\}$	Id	$\{\{\alpha, int\}, \{\beta\}, \{\gamma\}\}$	*AtomicElim.*
$\{\beta \rhd int * \gamma\}$	Id	$\{\{\alpha, int, \gamma\}, \{\beta\}\}$	*AtomicElim.*
$\emptyset$	$\{\beta' * \beta''/\beta\}$	$\{\{\alpha, int, \beta', \beta'', \gamma\}$	*Expansion*

As expected, $\{\beta' * \beta''/\beta\}$ *is the minimal matching substitution for* $\bar{C}$.

Example 7 *Let* $\bar{C} = \{v \rhd \alpha \rightarrow \beta, v \rhd \alpha\}$, *the coercion set associated with the expressio*
$\lambda\, x.\ x\ x.$

C	S	M	Action
$\bar{C}$	Id	$\{\{\alpha\}, \{\beta\}, \{v\}\}$	–
$\{v' \rightarrow v'' \rhd \alpha\}$	$\{v' \rightarrow v''/v\}$	$\{\{\alpha, v'\}, \{\beta, v''\}\}$	*Expansion*

Now let $e \equiv v' \to v'' \;\; \triangleright \alpha$. *As* $[\alpha]_M = \{\alpha, v'\}$ *and* $[v' \to v'']^M = \{\{\alpha, v'\}, \{\beta, v''\}\}$, *Therefore the Expansion step fails, causing MATCH to fail and indicating that the coercion set* $\bar{C}$ *is inconsistent.*

The correctness of MATCH is proved below.

6.2 MATCH is correct

We first introduce the concept of "**approximation**" to model our algorithm. Let C be a coercion set, S be a substitution, and M be an equivalence relation on atomic types occurring in C or S. The tri-tuple (C, S, M) is an **approximation** to a coercion set $\bar{C}$ iff the following conditions hold:

1. $\forall \lambda, \;\; \lambda(C)$ is matching $\wedge$ λ respects $M \;\; \supset \;\; (\lambda \circ S)(\bar{C})$ is matching.
2. $\forall \theta, \;\; \theta(\bar{C})$ is matching $\;\supset\;\; \exists \lambda$ such that:
   - $\theta = \lambda \circ S$
   - $\lambda(C)$ is matching
   - λ respects M

where λ respects M iff $\forall a, \;\; a \; M \; a', \;\; \Rightarrow \lambda(a)$ matches $\lambda(a')$. Intutively, the first condition should be read as: if substitution λ "solves" C and M then we can solve $\bar{C}$ by $\lambda \circ S$. The second condition should be read as: any solution to $\bar{C}$ can be obtained from S by composing it with some solution to C and M. Therefore, S is the partial solution of $\bar{C}$ and C and M correspond to the unsolved part of $\bar{C}$. In particular, let $M = \{(a, a')\}$ iff $a = a' \;\; \in \;\; \bar{C}$, $C = \bar{C}$, and $S = Id$ then $A_0 \stackrel{\text{def}}{=} (C, S, M)$ is an **approximation** to $\bar{C}$ and further any substitution that makes $\bar{C}$ match must make C match and respect M. Moreover, if there exists an **approximation** $(\emptyset, S, M)$ to $\bar{C}$ then, by choosing λ to be the identity substitution Id in (2) above, we can show that S is the most general matching substitution for C. As shown above, MATCH starting from A_0, generates a sequence of **approximations** $A_0, A_1, \ldots$ by nondeterministically executing Decomposition, Atomic Elimination and Expansion. If $\bar{C}$ is matchable the algorithm terminates with $A_n = (\emptyset, S_n, M_n)$. Otherwise it fails.

Lemma 2 Let $(C \cup \{t \;\triangleright t'\}, S, M)$ be an **approximation** to $\bar{C}$. If **Decomposition** fails then $\bar{C}$ is not matchable else the resulting (C, S, M) is still an **approximation** to $\bar{C}$.

proof: Trivial. □

Lemma 3 Let $(C \cup \{a \triangleright a'\}, S, M)$ be an **approximation** to $\bar{C}$. The result of applying **Atomic elimination** is still an **approximation** to $\bar{C}$.

proof: Trivial. □

Lemma 4 Let $(C \cup \{e\}, S, M)$ be an **approximation** to $\bar{C}$, where e is either $v \rhd t$ or $t \rhd v$. If **Expansion** fails then $\bar{C}$ is not matchable else the resulting tri-tuple is still an **approximation** to $\bar{C}$.

proof: By the fact that $[v]_M$ is finite and left unchanged during the execution of the loop, the for loop must terminate. The rest of the proof is by induction on the number of times the for loop is executed. □

We now prove the termination of this algorithm. Let $|M|$ be the number of equivalent classes in M and $|C|$ be the number of occurrences of symbols in C. We define the lexicographic order $<$ between pairs of M and C in the natural way. More precisely, $(M_1, C_1) < (M_2, C_2)$ iff either $| M_1 | < | M_2 |$ or $| M_1 | = | M_2 |$ and $| C_1 | < | C_2 |$. Obviously, the set of M, C pairs is well founded under $<$. In the following Lemma, we show that "$MATCH$" always terminates.

Lemma 5 "$MATCH$" always terminates.

proof: Let M_1, C_1 and M_2, C_2 denote the values of M, C before and after any pass of the while loop. No matter what transformation is made, we have $(M_2, C_2) < (M_1, C_1)$. By the well-founded property, the algorithm must terminate. □

Theorem 3 (Correctness of $MATCH$)
If $\bar{C}$ is not matchable then $MATCH$ fails else S is returned where $S(C)$ is the minimal matching instance of $\bar{C}$.

proof: By previous lemmas.

6.3 Algorithm CONSISTENT

Let C be an atomic coercion set. C is consistent if we can find some substitution S, mapping type variables in C to type constants, such that $\emptyset \Vdash S(C)$. As we are not interested in any details of the substitution S, CONSISTENT determines whether there is anyway C can be consistent.

Let T be a finite set of type constants, $T\uparrow = \{t \mid \exists t' \in T, \; \Vdash t' \rhd t\}$ and $T\downarrow = \{t \mid \exists t' \in T, \; \Vdash t \rhd t'\}$. With each $a \in C$ we associate I_a to stand for the set of types that a can be instantiated to. We set $I_a = \{*\}$ to indicate there are no constraints on a. Let a be an atomic type expression, $var(a)$ is $True$, if a is a variable, $False$, otherwise. Let T_1 and T_2 be finite sets of type constants.

$$COMPRESS(T_1, T2) \stackrel{\text{def}}{=} \text{if } T_1 \cap T_2 = \emptyset \text{ then } fail$$
$$\text{else if } T_1 \cap T_2 = T_1 \text{ then } (True, T_1) \text{ else } (False, T_1 \cap T_2)$$

procedure CONSISTENT(C);
begin
    for each $a \in C$ **do**
        if $var(a)$ **then** $I_a \longleftarrow \{*\}$ **else** $I_a \longleftarrow \{a\}$;

```
    do
        stable ← True;
        for a ▷ a' ∈ C do
            begin
                (stable, I_a') ← let (flag, I) = COMPRESS(I_a', I_a ↑) in (stable ∧ flag, I);
                (stable, I_a) ← let (flag, I) = COMPRESS(I_a, I_a' ↓) in (stable ∧ flag, I);
            end
    until stable
    return True
end;
```

In CONSISTENT, we start by initializing I_a to $\{*\}$, if $var(a)$, $\{a\}$, otherwise. During each pass of the loop, if some I_a converges to $\emptyset$ then C is obviously inconsistent and the algorithm fails. Otherwise either all I_a's are left unchanged, causing the algorithm to terminate and return *True*, or at least one of them is decreased, causing the do loop to be executed again. Since there are only finitely many type constants and the assignment to I_a is finite therefore the algorithm must terminate. Moreover, when the algorithm terminates successfully, the following condition holds:

$$\forall a \in C,\ I_a = (\textstyle\bigcap_{a' \in above(a)} I_{a'} \downarrow) \cap (\bigcap_{a'' \in below(a)} I_{a''} \uparrow)$$

where $above(a) = \{a' \mid a \rhd a' \in C\}$ and $below(a) = \{a'' \mid a'' \rhd a \in C\}$. We conjecture that this condition guarantees the consistency of C. However, how to prove this is still an open question.

Example 8 *Let posint $\rhd$ int, int $\rhd$ real be the valid atomic coercions and let* $C = \{int \rhd v_1,\ v_1 \rhd v_2,\ v_2 \rhd v_3,\ v_3 \rhd int\}$.

iteration	*edge*	I_{int}	I_{v_1}	I_{v_2}	I_{v_3}
0		$\{int\}$	$\{*\}$	$\{*\}$	$\{*\}$
1	$int \rhd v_1$	$\{int\}$	$\{int, real\}$	$\{*\}$	$\{*\}$
1	$v_1 \rhd v_2$	$\{int\}$	$\{int, real\}$	$\{int, real\}$	$\{*\}$
1	$v_2 \rhd v_3$	$\{int\}$	$\{int, real\}$	$\{int, real\}$	$\{int, real\}$
1	$v_3 \rhd int$	$\{int\}$	$\{int, real\}$	$\{int, real\}$	$\{int\}$
2	$int \rhd v_1$	$\{int\}$	$\{int, real\}$	$\{int, real\}$	$\{int\}$
2	$v_1 \rhd v_2$	$\{int\}$	$\{int, real\}$	$\{int, real\}$	$\{int\}$
2	$v_2 \rhd v_3$	$\{int\}$	$\{int, real\}$	$\{int\}$	$\{int\}$
2	$v_3 \rhd int$	$\{int\}$	$\{int, real\}$	$\{int\}$	$\{int\}$
3	$int \rhd v_1$	$\{int\}$	$\{int, real\}$	$\{int\}$	$\{int\}$
3	$v_1 \rhd v_2$	$\{int\}$	$\{int\}$	$\{int\}$	$\{int\}$

The last change occurs in the third iteration; the algorithm will go through a fourth step and find that no I assignment has changed.

Example 9 Let $C = \{int \rhd v_1,\ v_2 \rhd v_1,\ v_2 \rhd bool\}$. Let the valid atomic coercions be as before.

iteration	edge	I_{int}	I_{v_1}	I_{v_2}	I_{bool}
0	-	{ int }	{*}	{*}	$\{bool\}$
1	$int \rhd v_1$	{ int }	{ int,real }	{*}	$\{bool\}$
1	$v_2 \rhd v_1$	{ int }	{ int,real }	$\{int, real\}$	$\{bool\}$
1	$v_2 \rhd bool$	{ int }	{ int,real }	$\emptyset$	$\{bool\}$

In the first iteration we find that there is no consistent assignment to type variable v_2.

7 Polymorphism

A major practical goal in type inference systems is to permit programmer-defined names to possess multiple types. This phenomenon has been given the name *polymorphism*. In the system described above, expressions may possess multiple typings but in any individual typing programmer-defined names can only behave monomorphically – possess single types.

In ML this problem is resolved by the use of syntactic device: the *let* expression. Names defined using "let" are permitted to possess type-schemes (quantified types) instead of a type. Names defined in lambda-expression continue to behave monomorphically, and may only possess types. Quantified type is suitably instantiated in different contexts to permit the let-bound name to behave polymorphically.

We take a similar approach in our system. We distinguish between types, written τ, and type-schemes, written σ. In contrast to ML the notion of a simple quantified type, as in $\forall\alpha.\sigma$, is *not* adequate for our purposes. Instead, the relevant concept is that of a *conditionally* quantified type $\forall\alpha|_C.\sigma$. The quantified variable α is conditioned by the constraints appearing in C.

$$\sigma \ ::= \tau \mid \forall\alpha|_C.\sigma$$

By a generic instance of a type scheme $\forall\alpha|_C.\sigma$ we mean the pair $(C', \sigma') = [t/\alpha](C, \sigma)$, provided no capture of free variables in t occurs. We also write $(C', \sigma') \in geninst(\forall\alpha|_C.\sigma)$.

$$C \downarrow \alpha = C', \text{ where } (\alpha \text{ subterm of } t_i \text{ or } t_j \ \wedge\ C \Vdash t_i \rhd t_j) \implies C' \Vdash t_i \rhd t_j$$

$$\frac{C, A \vdash N : \forall\alpha|_{C_1}.\sigma, (C_1', \sigma') \in geninst(\forall\alpha|_{C_1}.\sigma), C \Vdash C_1'}{C, A \vdash N : \sigma'}$$

$$\frac{C, A \vdash N : \sigma, \alpha \notin FV(A)}{C, A \vdash N : \forall\alpha|_{C\downarrow\alpha}.\sigma}$$

$$\frac{C, A \vdash N : \sigma, \quad C, A\,;\, x : \sigma \vdash M : \tau}{C, A \vdash \mathbf{let\ x = N\ in\ M} : \tau}$$

References

[Car84] L Cardelli. A semantics of multiple inheritance. In *Semantics of Data Types: LNCS 173*, 1984.

[Car85] L Cardelli. Basic polymorphic typechecking. 1985. Manuscript.

[DM82] L Damas and R. Milner. Principal type schemes for functional programs. In *POPL IX*, 1982.

[Lei83] D Leivant. Polymorphic type inference. In *POPL X*, 1983.

[Mal87] J Malhotra. *Implementation Issues for Standard ML*. Master's thesis, SUNY at Stony Brook, August 1987.

[Mit84a] J. C. Mitchell. Coercion and type inference. In *POPL XI*, 1984.

[Mit84b] J. C. Mitchell. Type inference and type containment. In *Semantics of Data Types: LNCS 173*, 1984.

[MM82] A Martelli and U Montanari. An efficient unification algorithm. *TOPLAS*, 4(2), 1982.

[MR85] P Mishra and U.S Reddy. Declaration-free type inference. In *POPL XII*, 1985.

[Rey70] J. C. Reynolds. Transformational systems and the algebraic structure of atomic formulas. In *Machine Intelligence 5*, 1970.

[Rey80] J. C. Reynolds. Using category theory to design implicit conversions and generic operators. In *Semantics-Directed Compiler Generation: LNCS 94*, 1980.

[Rey85] J. C. Reynolds. Three approaches to type structure. In *TAPSOFT 1985: LNCS 186*, 1985.

[Wan87a] M. Wand. Complete type inference for simple objects. In *LICS II*, 1987.

[Wan87b] M Wand. A simple algorithm and proof for type inference. 1987. Manuscript.

A THEORY OF SOFTWARE REUSABILITY

M.C. GAUDEL[1] and Th. MOINEAU[1,2]

(1) Laboratoire de Recherche en Informatique
Unité associée au CNRS UA 410
Bât. 490, Université Paris-Sud
91405 ORSAY CEDEX
FRANCE

(2) SEMA-METRA
16 Rue Barbès
92126 MONTROUGE
FRANCE

Abstract : Software reusability is a topic of first practical importance. Most of the current approaches are based on empirical methods and there is no general approach to this problem. This paper suggests a definition for software reusability based on algebraic specifications and modularity. This criterion is not completely constructive, but it provides a guideline to find out reusable software components and prove their reuse. Moreover, we state how to exploit reusability in hierarchical specifications.

Key-words : reuse, abstract data types, formal specifications, modularity, PLUSS.

Introduction

Software reusability is a topic of first practical importance. Most of the current approaches are based on empirical methods such as key words or descriptions in natural language. For some specific fields there exist good libraries of software components, and the description of the component is given in the terminology of the application area (mathematics, management, ...). However, there is no general approach to this problem.

To reuse a piece of software is only possible if **what** this piece of software does is precisely stated. It means that a specification of this software component is available. In this paper, we consider the case of software components which are formally specified using algebraic specifications. We deal with the following problem : given a specification SP' to be implemented, and a specification SP of an already implemented software component, is this component reusable for the implementation of SP' ? Thus we are not considering reusability of software design, or reusability of specification (which are also important problems) but reusability of code. A software component library should, at least, contain couples of the form <*formal specification, piece of code*>. Our claim is that the use of formal and structured specifications is fundamental for reusability. We define rigorously, in the case of algebraic structured specifications, the relations "is reusable for" and "is efficiently reusable for" between two specifications, the first one being already implemented. Moreover, it turns out that these definitions fit well with the primitives of our specification language.

We consider partial algebraic data types [GH 78,BW 82] and hierarchical specifications [WPPDB 83]. The specification language we use for our examples is PLUSS [Gau 85,Bid 87] which is based on the ASL primitives [Wir 83]. The first part of the paper is a short presentation of these basic concepts. In part 2 we define, following [Bid 87], the semantics of the use of predefined specifications. Part 3 is an informal introduction of our definitions of reusability. Part 4 states precisely these definitions. Part 5 explores the relationship between reusability and hierarchy : several theorems are given which show that our definitions are compatible both with the classical definitions of hierarchical specifications and with the practical aspects of software reusability.

Thus this paper suggests a criterion for software reusability which is theoretically founded. This criterion is not completely constructive, but it provides a guideline to find out reusable software components and prove their reuse. Moreover, the theorems of part 5 state how to exploit reusability in hierarchical specifications.

1 Basic definitions

A **signature** $\Sigma = (S, F)$ consists of a set S of sort names and a set F of operation symbols, for each of which a profile $s_1 \dots s_n \longrightarrow s_{n+1}$ with $s_i \in S$ is given.

A **Σ-algebra** A is a family $(s^A)_{s \in S}$ of carrier sets together with a family of *partial* functions $(f^A)_{f \in F}$, such that the profiles of the operation names $f \in F$ coincide with the profiles of the functions f^A.

A (total) **Σ-morphism** ϕ from A to B is a family $(\phi_s)_{s \in S}$ of (total) applications $\phi_s : s^A \longrightarrow s^B$, such that for all operation name $(f : s_1 \dots s_n \longrightarrow s) \in F$ and all objects $a_1 \in s_1^A, \dots, a_n \in s_n^A$ the following holds : if $f^A(a_1, \dots, a_n)$ is defined then $\phi_s(f^A(a_1, \dots, a_n)) = f^B(\phi_{s_1}(a_1), \dots, \phi_{s_n}(a_n))$. Two Σ-algebra A and B are isomorphic, written $A \simeq B$, iff there is an isomorphism (bijective Σ-morphism) between them.

T_Σ is the well-known **term-algebra**. The interpretation t^A of a term t in a Σ-algebra A is specified by :

- if $t = c \in F$, then $t^A =_{def} c^A$.
- if $t = ft_1 \dots t_n$, then $t^A =_{def} f^A(t_1^A, \dots, t_n^A)$ provided that all the interpretations t_i^A and $f(t_1^A, \dots, t_n^A)$ are defined; otherwise t^A is undefined.

$T_{\Sigma \cup V}$ is the free Σ-algebra of terms with variables in V.

$PALG(\Sigma)$ is the category of the partial Σ-algebras with Σ-morphisms, $PGEN(\Sigma)$ is the category of finitely generated Σ-algebras (i.e. all elements of the carrier sets can be obtained by the interpretation t^A of a term $t \in T_\Sigma$).

A **specification** $SP = (\Sigma, E)$ consists of a signature Σ and a set E of *positive conditional axioms* on Σ : $\Phi_1 \wedge \dots \wedge \Phi_n \Longrightarrow \Phi_{n+1}$, where Φ_i are either equations $(t_1 = t_2)$ or definedness predicates $D(t)$ where t_1, t_2 and t are terms of $T_{\Sigma \cup V}$ (a Σ-algebra A satisfies $D(t)$ iff t^A is defined for all assignments of its variables).

$PALG(SP)$ is the category of all the models of SP (the Σ-algebras satisfying all axioms of E). $PGEN(SP)$ is those of finitely generated models. T_{SP} is the initial model of $PALG(SP)$ and $PGEN(SP)$. If $A \in PALG(SP)$, I_A is the unique Σ-morphism $I_A : T_{SP} \longrightarrow A$.

We use the abbreviation $SP_0 \subseteq SP$ for $\Sigma_0 \subseteq \Sigma$ ($S_0 \subseteq S$ and $F_0 \subseteq F$) and $E_0 \subseteq E$. We write $SP = SP_0 \cup \Delta SP$ for $\Sigma = \Sigma_0 \cup \Delta\Sigma$ ($S = S_0 \cup \Delta S$ and $F = F_0 \cup \Delta F$) and $E = E_0 \cup \Delta E$. ΔSP is called an **enrichment**. Note that these definitions are purely syntactic (union of presentations).

If $SP_0 \subseteq SP$, we note $U : PALG(\Sigma) \longrightarrow PALG(\Sigma_0)$ the **forgetful functor** defined by : $s^{U(A)} = s^A$ for $s \in S_0$ and $f^{U(A)} = f^A$ for $f \in F_0$. $U(A)$ corresponds to the Σ_0-reduct of A as defined in [WPPDB 83].

As mentioned in the introduction, we will deal with hierarchical specifications denoted by $SP = SP_0 + \Delta SP$ (this corresponds to the ENRICH construct of ASL).

2 Hierarchical models, implementations, realizations

2.1 Hierarchical models

As a preliminary to any study of reusability, it is necessary to define what is a correct implementation of a specification. This definition is dependent on the semantics considered for the specifications, i.e. the models associated with the specification. There are several approaches :

1. the models are those isomorphic to T_{SP}; such a semantics is called **initial semantics**.
2. the models are those isomorphic to the terminal algebra; such a semantics is called **terminal semantics**.
3. the models are all the models in $PALG(SP)$, such a semantics is called **"loose" semantics**.
4. a loose semantics may consider only finitely generated models, those in $PGEN(SP)$ [WPPDB 83].

Loose semantics makes it possible to give a simple definition of implementations [SW 82] : an algebra is an implementation of a specification SP, if, via some forgetting, restriction and identification, it is a model of SP.

However, loose semantics without hierarchy introduces trivial algebras among the models : the solution is to start from some basic specifications (such as booleans, naturals) with initial semantics, and to consider enrichments of specifications with hierarchical constraints.

Most of the time, it is convenient to consider finitely generated models : all the values are denotable by a term and thus are computable in a finite number of steps. Non finitely generated models are sometimes useful, but as we are concerned with reusability, it seems sound to choose finitely generated models : it means that the specification of a software component is supposed to mention all the functions of this components.

Thus we consider that the semantics of a specification SP is a subclass of $PGEN(SP)$ noted $HMOD(SP)$ of hierarchical finitely generated models, where the hierarchical constraints ensure that any model (implementation) of $SP = SP_0 + \Delta SP$ restricts into a model of SP_0. More precisely the forgetful functor from SP into SP_0 applied to a hierarchical model of SP gives a hierarchical model of SP_0.

Definition 2.1 *The class of the* **hierarchical models** *of a specification is :*

- $HMOD(SP_0) = \{T_{SP_0}\}$ *if* SP_0 *is a basic specification* (Σ_0, E_0).
- $HMOD(SP) = \{A \in PGEN(SP) | \ U(A) \in HMOD(SP_0)\}$ *if* SP *is a hierarchical specification :* $SP = SP_0 + \Delta SP$ *(*U *is the forgetful functor from* $PALG(\Sigma)$ *into* $PALG(\Sigma_0)$*).*

$HMOD(SP)$ is a full sub-category of $PGEN(SP)$. The existence of initial or terminal model is not ensured (T_{SP} is not always a hierarchical model [Ber 87]).

Of course, the class of models of a specification depends of its hierarchy; for instance :

$$HMOD((SP_0 + \Delta SP_1) + \Delta SP_2) \subseteq HMOD(SP_0 + (\Delta SP_1 \cup \Delta SP_2))$$

But the reverse is not always true. This will turn out to be quite important for reusability aspects.

We do not restrict the class of models to minimally defined ones [BW 82]. It means that an operation can be implemented in such a way that it is more defined than what is specified. This seems interesting in the framework of reusability.

2.2 Realization

As stated in introduction, we consider couples <*specification, program*>, where the program is correct with respect to the specification. In the algebraic specification framework [EKMP 80,SW 82,BBC 86] it means that the program is a model of the specification modulo some forgettings, restrictions and identifications.

However, as soon as software is modular, we are concerned mainly with pieces of software which use other pieces of software. For instance, a module implementing a specification of the sets of integers includes some code for the operations insert and is-a-member, and uses some already existing implementation of the operations on integers. Thus, given a structured specification $SP = SP_0 + \Delta SP$ we call a "realization" of ΔSP a piece of software such that when coupling it with a hierarchical model (implementation) of SP_0, one gets a hierarchical model of SP. In order to be reusable, a realization of ΔSP must accept any model of SP_0 : no assumptions can be made on the implementation of SP_0. This property is not only important for reusability, but also in large software projects where several programmers are working concurrently on various modules.

These considerations lead to the following definition :

Definition 2.2 *A* **realization** *of enrichment ΔSP of SP_0 is a functor Δ from $HMOD(SP_0)$ into $HMOD(SP_0 + \Delta SP)$ such that : $\forall A_0 \in HMOD(SP_0)$, $U(\Delta(A_0)) \simeq A_0$.*

The class of realizations of ΔSP on the top of SP_0 is noted $REAL_{SP_0}(\Delta SP)$.

As stated above, this functor must be conservative. For instance, if SP_0 is an implementation of the integers by 8 bits strings, Δ will provide an implementation of SP where integers are implemented by 8 bits strings, not by 16 bits strings : there is no recoding of the integers by the realization of, for instance, the sets of integers.

Composition of realizations works well :

Theorem 2.1 *Let $SP_1 = SP_0 + \Delta SP_1$, $SP_2 = SP_1 + \Delta SP_2$ and $\Delta SP_3 = \Delta SP_1 \cup \Delta SP_2$.*
If $\Delta_1 \in REAL_{SP_0}(\Delta SP_1)$ and $\Delta_2 \in REAL_{SP_1}(\Delta SP_2)$, then $\Delta_2 \circ \Delta_1 \in REAL_{SP_0}(\Delta SP_3)$.

Proof : The forgetful functor U_3 from $ALG(SP_3)$ into $ALG(SP_0)$ is equal to $U_1 \circ U_2$ where U_1 et U_2 are the forgetful functors from $ALG(SP_1)$ into $ALG(SP_0)$ and from $ALG(SP_2)$ into $ALG(SP_1)$. Thus $\forall A_0 \in HMOD(SP_0)$: $U_3(\Delta_2 \circ \Delta_1(A_0)) = U_1 \circ (U_2 \circ \Delta_2) \circ \Delta_1(A_0) \simeq U_1 \circ \Delta_1(A_0) \simeq A_0$. □

It is important to note that there does not always exist a realization for a ΔSP. If ΔSP removes some models from $HMOD(SP_0)$, assuming for instance some implementation choices of SP_0, there exist no realization. However $SP = SP_0 + \Delta SP$ may have hierarchical models, thus global implementations. The existence of a realization means that the implementation choices in ΔSP and in SP_0 are completely independent.

3 What is reusability ?

3.1 Intuitive introduction

This part is an intuitive introduction to the formal definitions which are given in part 4.

Let us consider an example : suppose we have in a software components library a program corresponding to the specification INT of figure 1; we want to develop a program corresponding

```
SPEC : NAT
    USE : BOOL
    SORT : Nat
    OP : 0, s
        +, *, fact, ≤
    AXIOMS :
        0 + y = y
        s(x) + y = s(x + y)
        0 * y = 0
        s(x) * y = (x * y) + y
        fact(0) = s(0)
        fact(s(x)) = s(x) * fact(x)
        0 ≤ 0 = true
        s(x) ≤ 0 = false
        0 ≤ s(x) = true
        s(x) ≤ s(y) = x ≤ y
    WHERE :
        x, y : Nat
```

```
SPEC : INT
    USE : BOOL
    SORT : Int
    OP : zero, succ, pred
        +, −, ≤
    AXIOMS :
        succ(pred(x)) = x
        pred(succ(x)) = x
        x + zero = x
        x + succ(y) = succ(x + y)
        x + pred(y) = pred(x + y)
        x − zero = x
        x − succ(y) = pred(x − y)
        x − pred(y) = succ(x − y)
        x ≤ x = true
        zero ≤ pred(zero) = false
        zero ≤ x = true
            ⟹ zero ≤ succ(x) = true
        zero ≤ x = false
            ⟹ zero ≤ pred(x) = false
        succ(x) ≤ y = x ≤ pred(y)
        pred(x) ≤ y = x ≤ succ(y)
    WHERE :
        x, y : Int
```

Figure 1: NAT and INT specifications

to the specification NAT of figure 1. Following our intuition and our experience of programming, it is obvious that the code of INT is reusable for implementing NAT. More precisely, BOOL, Nat, 0, s and $\leq$ can be implemented by reusing INT.

In this example, we notice that :

- a renaming is needed between INT and NAT;
- the axioms of INT and NAT are different;
- INT provides functions which are not required by NAT;
- some functions required by NAT are missing in INT.

These remarks lead to the scheme of figure 2 which shows that reusability of SP for SP' w.r.t. a subsignature Σ'_r of Σ' implies the existence of two specifications SP_1 and SP'_1 such that :

1. SP_1 is an extension of SP : the missing functions (and possibly some hidden functions) are added to SP : $SP_1 = SP + \Delta SP_1$. Practically speaking, a realization of ΔSP_1 must be developed, since the reused program is only known by its specification SP.
2. SP'_1 is an enrichment of SP' which is equivalent, modulo a renaming, to SP_1. This equivalence states the validity of the reuse of SP for SP' and makes it possible to have different axioms in SP and SP', as in example of figure 1. A more (and too) restrictive definition of reusability could consider only syntactic renaming from SP_1 to SP'_1.
3. Any model of SP'_1 can be *restricted* via the forgetful functor to a model of SP' : unnecessary

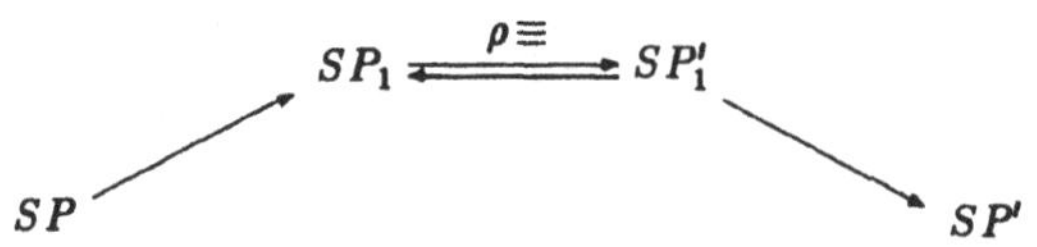

Figure 2: Scheme of reuse.

functions of SP, and hidden functions are forgotten :

$$\forall A_1' \in HMOD(SP_1'),\ U'(A_1') \in HMOD(SP')$$

4. In order to ensure that sorts and operations of Σ_r' are actually reused from SP, Σ_r' must be a renaming of a subsignature of Σ.

However condition 3 is too restrictive in some cases : if we consider the example of figure 1, implementing NAT by reuse of INT, the result of the forgetful functor is not a (hierarchical) finitely generated model of NAT, since the negative integers are kept. Thus we need a "stronger" forgetful functor than the classical one : by the way, it is a forget-restrict functor in the sense of [EKMP 80,SW 82]. Other problems arise if some functions are more defined in SP than in SP'. Part 4 gives the corresponding definitions.

3.2 Reusability vs abstract implementation

Reuse is a special, simpler case of abstract implementation of algebraic data types [EKMP 80,SW 82,BBC 86]. In this paper we are concerned by direct reuse. It means that the "abstraction functions" of [BBC 86] or the "copy functions" of [EKMP 80] are just identities, and that the "identify function" is no more necessary to get a model of SP'.

4 Reusability : definitions

As mentioned above, we have a reusability definition in three steps : extension, equivalence modulo a renaming, and forget-restricting. We study each of them successively.

4.1 Extension

The extension phase consists in giving an enrichment ΔSP_1 on the top of SP, which must be realizable :

Definition 4.1 ΔSP_1 *is* **realizable** *on the top of* SP_0 *iff* $REAL_{SP_0}(\Delta SP) \neq \emptyset$.

This property is noted $SP_0 \longrightarrow SP$ or $SP = SP_0 \oplus \Delta SP$.

Remark.

$REAL_{SP_0}(\Delta SP)$ is the semantics of the USE construct of the PLUSS specification language [Bid 87]. PLUSS makes a distinction between the USE construct, which corresponds to the modular structure of the software, and the ENRICH construct which expresses the incremental development of specifications and which has the same semantics as in ASL.

$SP = SP_0 \oplus \Delta SP$ corresponds to the following construct in PLUSS :

```
SPEC : SP
     USE : SP0
     ΔSP
```

Realizability is a transitive relation :

Theorem 4.1 *If* $SP_1 = SP_0 \oplus \Delta SP_1$ *and* $SP_2 = SP_1 \oplus \Delta SP_2$ *then* $SP_3 = SP_0 \oplus (\Delta SP_1 \cup \Delta SP_2)$.

Proof : Let $\Delta SP_3 = \Delta SP_1 \cup \Delta SP_2$. One can take $\Delta_1 \in REAL_{SP_0}(\Delta SP_1)$ and $\Delta_2 \in REAL_{SP_1}(\Delta SP_2)$. From theorem 2.1, $\Delta_2 \circ \Delta_1 \in REAL_{SP_0}(\Delta SP_3)$, and thus $REAL_{SP_0}(\Delta SP_3) \neq \emptyset$. □

Note that $HMOD(SP_3)$ is generally different from $HMOD(SP_2)$. SP_2 and SP_3 are equal if they are considered as non hierarchical specifications, but are different as hierarchical ones.

The definitions above does not cope with parameterization : Δ may perfectly take into account some properties of the specification SP_0. It must not take into account properties of the implementation of SP_0. Parameterized specifications and generic modules introduce additional difficulties and are not considered in this paper.

4.2 Equivalence of hierarchical specifications modulo a renaming

A renaming between two signatures Σ_1 and Σ_2 is a signature isomorphism $\rho : \Sigma_1 \longrightarrow \Sigma_2$ [EM 85]. Some authors define renamings as injective signature morphisms [Pro 82]. Since we are interested in equivalence of specifications, we consider bijective renamings. Signature renamings easily extend into term renamings, algebra renamings, and (hierarchical) specification renamings.

The classical notion of specification equivalence is that SP and SP' are equivalent iff $\Sigma = \Sigma'$ and $T_{SP} \simeq T_{SP'}$. For hierarchical specifications, the definition is :

Definition 4.2 : hierarchical equivalence.

Two basic specifications SP_0 *and* SP'_0 *are hierarchically equivalent iff* $\Sigma_0 = \Sigma'_0$ *and* $T_{SP_0} \simeq T_{SP'_0}$.

Two hierarchical specifications $SP = SP_0 + \Delta SP$ *and* $SP' = SP'_0 + \Delta SP'$ *are hierarchically equivalent iff :*

- SP_0 *and* SP'_0 *are hierarchically equivalent*
- $\Delta\Sigma = \Delta\Sigma'$.
- $HMOD(SP) = HMOD(SP')$.

Hierarchical equivalence is denoted by $SP \equiv SP'$. It means that two hierarchical specifications are hierarchically equivalent iff they have the same (unfolded) signature, the same hierarchy, the same hierarchical models. Only the axioms can differ.

Proposition 4.2 *Let* $SP = SP_0 + \Delta SP$ *and* $SP' = SP'_0 + \Delta SP'$. *If* $SP_0 \equiv SP'_0$, $\Delta\Sigma = \Delta\Sigma'$ *and* $T_{SP_0} \simeq T_{SP'_0}$, *then* $HMOD(SP_0 + \Delta SP) = HMOD(SP'_0 + \Delta SP')$ *and thus* $SP \equiv SP'$.

Proof : by induction on the hierarchy. □

From the definitions above, it comes :

Definition 4.3 *Two hierarchical specifications* SP *and* SP' *are* **hierarchically equivalent modulo a renaming** ρ *(*$SP \ \rho\!\equiv SP'$*) iff* $\rho(SP) \equiv SP'$.

4.3 Forget-restrict functor

As noted above, we need a forget-restrict functor in order to get finitely generated models of SP' (see fig. 2).

Definition 4.4 *Let $SP' \subseteq SP'_1$ two specifications.*
The **forget-restrict functor** $V : PALG(SP'_1) \longrightarrow PGEN(SP')$ *is defined by :*

- $\forall A \in PALG(SP'_1)$,
  - $\forall s \in S'$, $s^{V(A)} = [I_{U(A)}]_s(s^{T_{SP'}})$.
  - $\forall (f : s_1 \ldots s_n \longrightarrow s) \in F'$,

$$f^{V(A)}(a_1, \ldots a_n) = \begin{cases} f^{U(A)}(a_1, \ldots, a_n) & \textit{if } f^{U(A)}(a_1, \ldots, a_n) \in s^{V(A)} \\ \textit{undefined} & \textit{otherwise} \end{cases}$$

- $\forall \phi : A \longrightarrow B$, *$V(\phi)$ is the restriction of $U(\phi)$ to $V(A)$.*

As defined above, $I_{U(A)}$ is the unique morphism from $T_{SP'}$ into $U(A)$.

V(A) is the finitely generated part of $U(A)$ with respect to Σ' ($s^{V(A)} = \{a \in s^A | \exists t \in T_{SP'}, a = t^A\}$). By the way, the sorts of SP' are subsorts of those of SP'_1 [FGJM 85]. It's easy to prove that V is a functor from $PALG(SP'_1)$ into $PGEN(SP')$, and that composition of forget-restrict functors works well : if V_2 is the forget-restrict functor from SP_2 to SP_1 and V_1 is the forget-restrict functor from SP_1 to SP_0 then $V_1 \circ V_2$ is the forget-restrict functor from SP_2 to SP_0.

Besides, by definition, the forget-restrict functor restricts the domain of functions in such a way that only finitely generated objects can be got as result.

4.4 Reusability

We now put together the three steps and define reusability.

Definition 4.5 *SP is* **reusable for SP' w.r.t. a signature Σ'_r modulo a renaming ρ** *($SP\ \rho\hookrightarrow SP'[\Sigma'_r]$) iff there exist two specifications SP_1 and SP'_1 such that :*

[R1] $SP_1 = SP \oplus \Delta SP_1$.

[R2] $SP_1\ \rho\!\equiv SP'_1$.

[R3] $SP' \subseteq SP'_1$.

[R4a] $\forall A'_1 \in HMOD(SP'_1)$, $V'(A'_1) \in HMOD(SP')$.

[R5] $\Sigma'_r \subseteq \Sigma'$ *and* $\rho^{-1}(\Sigma'_r) \subseteq \Sigma$.

where V' is the forget-restrict functor from $PALG(SP'_1)$ into $PGEN(SP')$.

Note that in A'_1, some functions can be more defined than what is required by SP'. It does not matter since $HMOD(SP')$ is not limited to minimally defined models (as defined in [BW 82]).

Definition 4.6 *SP is* **efficiently reusable for SP' w.r.t. a signature Σ'_r modulo a renaming ρ** *($SP\ \rho\leadsto SP'[\Sigma'_r]$) iff there exist two specifications SP_1 and SP'_1 such that :*

[R1] $SP_1 = SP \oplus \Delta SP_1$.

[R2] $SP_1\ \rho\!\equiv SP'_1$.

[R3] $SP' \subseteq SP_1'$.

[R4b] $\forall A_1' \in HMOD(SP_1'),\ U(A_1') \in HMOD(SP')$.

[R5] $\Sigma_r' \subseteq \Sigma'$ *and* $\rho^{-1}(\Sigma_r') \subseteq \Sigma$.

where U' *is the forgetful functor from* $PALG(SP_1')$ *into* $PALG(SP')$.

The intuitive notion behind efficient reusability is that the carriers of SP are finitely generated with respect to SP' : there are no useless values.

At the practical level, our definition of reusability in three steps will result in specifications of the form :

```
SPEC : X FORGET ...
    (USE : SP
      ΔSP1) RENAMING ... INTO ...
END X
```

Note that X is an abstract implementation of SP' : $HMOD(X) \subseteq HMOD(SP')$.

The second step (equivalence modulo a renaming) can be skipped : SP_1 and SP_1' can be embedded in an unique but more complex specification SP_2 :

Theorem 4.3 *SP is reusable (resp. efficiently reusable) for SP' w.r.t. Σ_r' modulo a renaming ρ iff there exists a specification SP_2 such that :*

[1] $SP_2 = SP \oplus \Delta SP_2$.

[2] $SP' \subseteq \rho(SP_2)$.

[3] $\forall A_2 \in HMOD(SP_2),\ V'(\rho(A_2)) \in HMOD(SP')$ *(resp.* $U'(\rho(A_2)) \in HMOD(SP')$*)*.

[4] $\Sigma_r' \subseteq \Sigma'$ *and* $\rho^{-1}(\Sigma_r') \subseteq \Sigma$.

Proof : $\Longleftarrow$ Take $SP_1 = SP_2$ and $SP_1' = \rho(SP_2)$.
$\Longrightarrow$ Take $SP_2 = (\Sigma_1, E_1 \cup \rho^{-1}(E_1'))$. Since $SP_1\ \rho\!\equiv SP_1'$ the axioms of SP_1' (renamed by ρ^{-1}) do not change the hierarchical models of SP_1. □

This approach is less close to reality, but easier to deal with theoretically. Consequently, in the rest of this paper we will consider reuses in two steps. Besides, we ignore renaming, since it is only a matter of syntactic sugar. However, the results still hold in the case of reuse with a renaming. Reusability and efficient reusability without renaming are noted $\hookrightarrow$ and $\rightsquigarrow$. We will denote a specific reuse of SP for SP' by the scheme : $SP \longrightarrow SP_1 \searrow^{V} SP'[\Sigma_r']$, and an efficient reuse by $SP \longrightarrow SP_1 \searrow^{U} SP'[\Sigma_r']$.

Properties.

- if SP is efficiently reusable for SP' w.r.t. Σ_r' then SP is reusable for SP' w.r.t. Σ_r'.
- if $SP \longrightarrow SP'$ then SP is efficiently reusable for SP' w.r.t. Σ.

Example.

The following example illustrates these definitions. We consider four specifications and look at the relations of reusability between them.

SPEC : NAT1	SPEC : NAT2	SPEC : INT1	SPEC : INT2
USE : BOOL	USE : BOOL	USE : BOOL	USE : BOOL
SORT : Int	SORT : Int	SORT : Int	SORT : Int
OP : 0, s, + , *	OP : 0, s, $\leq$	OP : 0, s, p	OP : 0, s, p, $\leq$
AX : ...	AX : ...	AX : ...	AX : ...

The axioms are the classical ones and are omitted. The hierarchical models are :

- $HMOD(\text{NAT1}) = \{N\} \cup \{Z/nZ \mid n \in N\}$
- $HMOD(\text{NAT2}) = \{N\}$
- $HMOD(\text{INT1}) = \{Z\} \cup \{Z/nZ \mid n \in N\}$
- $HMOD(\text{INT2}) = \{Z\}$

Thus :

- NAT2 is efficiently reusable for NAT1 w.r.t. $\Sigma_{BOOL} \cup \langle\{Int\}, \{0, s\}\rangle$.
- INT1 is reusable for NAT1 w.r.t. $\Sigma_{BOOL} \cup \langle\{Int\}, \{0, s\}\rangle$.
- INT2 is reusable for NAT2 w.r.t. $\Sigma_{BOOL} \cup \langle\{Int\}, \{0, s, \leq\}\rangle$.

But :

- NAT1 is not reusable for NAT2 w.r.t. $\Sigma_{BOOL} \cup \langle\{Int\}, \{0, s\}\rangle$. Since $Z/2Z$ is a NAT1 model for which there is no extension into N, and N is the only model of NAT2.
- NAT1 is not reusable for INT1 w.r.t. $\Sigma_{BOOL} \cup \langle\{Int\}, \{0, s\}\rangle$.
- NAT2 is not reusable for INT2 w.r.t. $\Sigma_{BOOL} \cup \langle\{Int\}, \{0, s, \leq\}\rangle$.

□

The reusability and efficient reusability relations are not symmetric (see NAT1 and INT1 above). This is not surprising as soon as we want integers to be reusable for the naturals but not the reverse. The transitivity of these relations is discussed below.

5 Reusability, reuse and hierarchy

Our formal definition of reusability is applicable only if it is compatible with the primitives of most of the specification languages. This part of the paper discusses the relationship between reusability, reuse and hierarchy.

5.1 What about primitives specifications ?

The first result we give is negative :

Fact 5.1 *There exist specifications SP and SP' such that $SP = SP_0 \oplus \Delta SP$ and $SP \hookrightarrow SP'[\Sigma_r]$ (resp. $SP \leadsto SP'[\Sigma_r]$) but $SP_0 \not\hookrightarrow SP'[\Sigma_r \cap \Sigma_0]$ (resp. $SP_0 \not\leadsto SP'[\Sigma_r \cap \Sigma_0]$) .*

Counter-example : Consider the specifications (here SP_0 is the specification BOOL) :

```
SP
SPEC : NAT
    USE : BOOL
    SORT : Int
    OP : 0, succ,
         ≤
    AX : ...
```

```
SP'
SPEC : LIST
    USE : NAT
    SORT : List
    OP : nil, cons, car
         error
    AX :
         car (cons(n,l)) = n
         car (nil) = error
```

```
SP1
SPEC : SP1
    USE : BOOL
    SORT : Nat, List
    OP : 0, succ, error
         nil, cons, car
    AX :
         car (cons(n,l)) = n
         car (nil) = error
```

SP is reusable for SP' w.r.t. Σ_{NAT}, but SP_0 is not reusable for SP' w.r.t. Σ_{BOOL} via SP_1. For the Σ_1-algebra A_1 such that $Int^{A_1} = N \cup \{error\}$ and $(error \leq n) = true$ is a hierarchical model of SP_1. But A_1 is not a hierarchical model of SP' since $U'(A_1)$ is not finitely generated with respect to Σ_{NAT} (cf. *error*). □

This result seems surprising : if SP is reusable for SP', it seems tempting to reuse a primitive part of SP for SP'. It is well known that as soon as we consider hierarchical specifications, hierarchy is of first importance. This result exemplifies this importance : one may not modify the hierarchy, or ignore it, without care.

It is clear that, if it is possible to flatten the specifications without modification of the hierarchical models, there is no problem. However, fact 5.1 points out that reusability is not generally transitive. Fortunately we will see in part 5.2 that reuse is nevertheless compatible with hierarchy.

Our second result is a kind of symmetric one :

Theorem 5.2 *If $SP \hookrightarrow SP'[\Sigma_r]$ (resp. $SP \rightsquigarrow SP'[\Sigma_r]$) and $SP' = SP'_0 \oplus \Delta SP'$, then $SP \hookrightarrow SP'_0[\Sigma_r \cap \Sigma'_0]$ (resp. $SP \rightsquigarrow SP'_0[\Sigma_r \cap \Sigma'_0]$).*

Proof : straightforward □

5.2 What about enrichment (efficient case)

Let us consider now the case when SP is efficiently reusable for SP' via SP_1. What can be done for implementing $SP'' = SP' \oplus \Delta SP''$.

Theorem 5.3 *Reusability of enrichment.*

$$\begin{array}{ccc} HMOD(SP_2) & \xrightarrow{U_2''} & HMOD(SP'') \\ \uparrow \overline{\Delta} & & \uparrow \Delta \\ HMOD(SP_1) & \xrightarrow{U_1'} & HMOD(SP') \end{array}$$

Let SP, SP_1 and SP' be specifications such that $SP \longrightarrow SP_1 \searrow^{U} SP'$ (SP is efficiently reusable for SP' w.r.t. some Σ'_r), and SP'' a specification which use SP' : $SP'' = SP' \oplus \Delta SP''$.

If $\Sigma_1 \cap \Delta\Sigma'' = \emptyset$, then $SP_2 = SP_1 \oplus \Delta SP''$ and for all realization Δ of $\Delta SP''$ on top of SP', there exists a realization $\overline{\Delta}$ of $\Delta SP''$ on top of SP_1, such that the above diagram commute, i.e. :

$$\forall A_1 \in HMOD(SP_1),\ U_2'' \circ \overline{\Delta}(A_1) \simeq \Delta \circ U_1'(A_1)$$

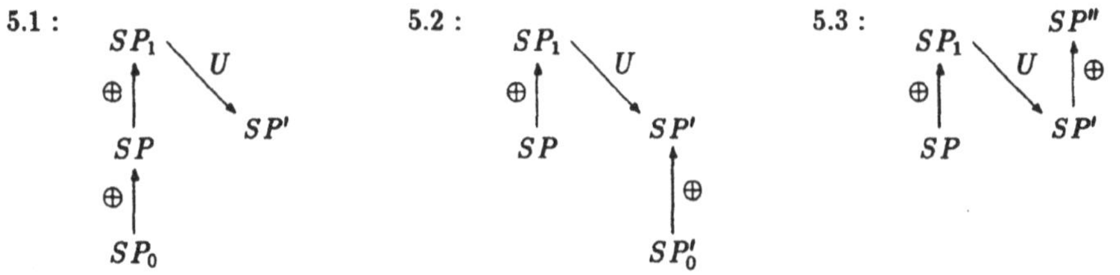

Figure 3: Situations of fact 5.1 and theorems 5.2 and 5.3

Proof : See [GM 87]. □

As noted by a referee, this theorem is a generalization of the extension lemma given in [EM 85] for equational specifications and total, initial algebras.

Figure 3 shows the difference between the situations studied in fact 5.1 and theorem 5.3. By the way theorem 5.3 deals with another kind of reusability : those of the realization of $\Delta SP''$. Moreover it shows that $\Delta SP''$ can be realized independently of the reuse done for SP'.

The proof of the theorem 5.3 is constructive : it shows how to get a realization of $\Delta SP''$ on the top of SP_1 given a realization of $\Delta SP''$ on the top of SP' : just putting together the carriers and the operations of A_1 (which is an implementation of SP_1) and of A''. Practically it corresponds to putting together type declarations and code of operations.

This result is important : it allows to consider a program as a set of pieces, the bodies of which can be replaced or developed in an independent way. For instance, let us suppose that we have to develop the components below :

```
SPEC : L_NAT
     USE : NAT
     SORT : List
     OP : nil, cons, ...
     AX : ...
```

```
SPEC : NAT
     USE : BOOL
     SORT : Nat
     OP : 0, succ, +, *, ≤
     AX : ...
```

and we already have programs implementing :

```
SPEC : L_NAT1
     USE : NAT1
     SORT : List
     OP : nil, cons, ...
     AX : ...
```

```
SPEC : NAT1
     USE : BOOL
     SORT : Nat
     OP : 0, succ, ≤
     AX : ...
```

```
SPEC : NAT2
     USE : BOOL
     SORT : Nat
     OP : 0, succ, +, *, ≤
     AX : ...
```

We know, from theorem 5.3, that it is possible to replace the NAT1 component by the NAT2 component in L_NAT1, and to use L_NAT1 (with NAT2) to implement L_NAT. This avoids to implement addition and multiplication on naturals.

Remark. The condition $\Sigma_1 \cap \Delta\Sigma'' = \emptyset$ is essential; it is not a problem to satisfy it using appropriate renaming of what is forgotten from SP_1 to SP'. □

SPEC : SET
USE : NAT
SORT : Set
OP : empty, insert, is-in
AX :
(1) is-in(x,empty) = false
(2) x = y ⇒ is-in(x,insert(y,s)) = true
(3) x ≠ y ⇒ is-in(x,insert(y,s)) = is-in(x,s)
(4) is-in(x,s) = true ⇒ insert(x,s) = s
(5) (is-in(x,s) = false) ∧ (x ≤ 0 = true)
⇒ insert(x,s) = insert(0,s)

```
(defun empty ()
      '())
(defun is-in (n set)
      (member n set))
(defun insert (n set)
      (if (is-in n set)
          set
          (if (<= n 0)
              (insert 0 set)
              (cons n set))))
```

Figure 4: A specification and a (strange) realization of sets of naturals numbers.

5.3 What about enrichment (non efficient case)

It would be nice to extend the previous results to the non efficient reusability, unfortunately the previous theorem is no more valid. For instance, let us consider the specifications NAT and INT of figure 1 and the specification SET of the figure 4 (the last axiom looks strange, but it is on purpose).

INT is not efficiently reusable for NAT; SET = NAT⊕ΔSET, but INT+ΔSET has no hierarchical models since :

$$\begin{array}{rcll} \text{true} & = & \text{is-in(-1,insert(-1,empty))} & \text{from (2)} \\ & = & \text{is-in(-1,insert(0,empty))} & \text{from (5)} \\ & = & \text{is-in(-1,empty))} & \text{from (3)} \\ & = & \text{false} & \text{from (1)} \end{array}$$

By the way, the problem is more fundamental than it seems : suppose now that the strange axiom (5) is removed. The LISP program of figure 4 is a correct (but strange) realization of sets of natural numbers. However, it is no more the case if naturals are replaced by relatives. Then, the only way to get such a realization is to define a predicate is-a-nat and to add a check of this predicate in front of each function. Unfortunately, the introduction of such predicates (i.e. subsorts) makes the reuse process much more complicated.

Definition 5.1 *Let $SP_0 \subseteq SP$ two specifications which use a specification BOOL of booleans. A* **discriminant predicate** *between SP and SP_0, for $s \in S_0$, is an operation $(p_s : s \longrightarrow Bool) \in F$ such that :*

$$\forall A \in PGEN(SP),\ \forall a \in s^A,\ p_s^A(a) = \begin{cases} true & \text{if } a \in s^{V(A)} \\ false & \text{otherwise} \end{cases}$$

If $s \in S \backslash S_0$, by convention, $p_s^A(a) = false, \forall a \in s^A$.

Remark.

A discriminant predicate is the characteristic function of the finitely generated part of $s^{V(A)}$. If SP and SP_0 have free generators C and C_0 ($C_0 \subseteq C$), the definition of the p_s predicates is straightforward :

- $p_s(c_0) = true$ for all constant $(c_0 :\longrightarrow s) \in C_0$.
- $p_{s_1}(x_1) = true \wedge \ldots \wedge p_{s_n}(x_n) = true \Longleftrightarrow p_s(f_0(x_1 \ldots x_n)) = true$ for all $(f_0 : s_1 \ldots s_n \longrightarrow s) \in C_0$.
- $p_s(c) = false$ for all constant $(c :\longrightarrow s) \in C \backslash C_0$.
- $p_s(f(x_1 \ldots x_n)) = false$ for all $(f : s_1 \ldots s_n \longrightarrow s) \in C \backslash C_0$.

If it is not the case, the definition of these predicates is highly dependent on the rest of the specification.

□

Definition 5.2 : extended enrichment.

Let $SP_0 \subseteq SP_1$ be two specifications, ΔSP an enrichment of SP_0, such that $\Sigma_1 \cap \Delta\Sigma = \emptyset$, and $(p_s)_{s \in S_1}$ the discrimant predicates between SP_0 and SP_1.

An extended enrichment of ΔSP from SP_0 to SP_1, is the enrichment $\overline{\Delta SP} = (\Delta\Sigma, \widehat{\Delta E} \cup P_{\Delta\Sigma})$ where :

- *$P_{\Delta\Sigma}$ is the set of axioms : $D(f(x_1, \ldots, x_i, \ldots, x_n)) \Longrightarrow p_{s_i}(x_i) = true$, where $(f : s_1 \ldots s_n \longrightarrow s) \in \Delta F$ and $s_i \in S_0$.*
- *$\widehat{\Delta E}$ is obtained from ΔE by the following transformations :*
  - *If an axiom is of the form : $D(\theta_1) \wedge \ldots \wedge D(\theta_m) \wedge (t_1 = t'_1) \wedge \ldots \wedge (t_n = t'_n) \Longrightarrow (t = t')$, it becomes : $\Phi \wedge D(\theta_1) \wedge \ldots \wedge D(\theta_m) \wedge (t_1 = t'_1) \wedge \ldots \wedge (t_n = t'_n) \Longrightarrow (t = t')$ where :*
    $\Phi = \bigwedge_i [p_{s_i}(\theta_i) = true] \wedge \bigwedge_j [p_{s'_j}(t_j) = true \wedge p_{s'_j}(t'_j) = true] \wedge [p_s(t) = true \wedge p_s(t') = true]$
    (s_i is the sort of θ_i, s'_j is the sort of t_j et t'_j, s is the sort of t and t'. Moreover, in order to simplify the transformation, we define, for $s \in \Delta S$, $p_s(x) = true$, $\forall x$; these predicates are useless but for the transformation.)
  - *If an axiom is of the form :*
    $D(\theta_1) \wedge \ldots \wedge D(\theta_m) \wedge (t_1 = t'_1) \wedge \ldots \wedge (t_n = t'_n) \Longrightarrow D(f(t''_1, \ldots, t''_p))$, *it becomes :*
    $\Phi \wedge D(\theta_1) \wedge \ldots \wedge D(\theta_m) \wedge (t_1 = t'_1) \wedge \ldots \wedge (t_n = t'_n) \Longrightarrow D(f(t''_1, \ldots, t''_p))$ *where :*
    $\Phi = \bigwedge_i [p_{s_i}(\theta_i) = true] \wedge \bigwedge_j [p_{s'_j}(t_j) = true \wedge p_{s'_j}(t'_j) = true] \wedge \bigwedge_k [p_{s''_k}(t''_k) = true]$
    (with the same conventions as above, and s''_k is the sort of t''_k)

The $P_{\Delta\Sigma}$ axioms express that the operations of ΔSP, when SP_1 is used instead of SP_0, must be restricted to the parts of the sorts of SP_1 which are finitely generated by Σ_0. Similarly, the Φ premisses added to the axioms ΔE express that these axioms are valid on these parts of the sorts. Examples of this transformation can be found in [GM 87].

We have a theorem similar to theorem 5.3 :

Theorem 5.4 *Reusability of enrichment.*

$$\begin{array}{ccc} HMOD(SP_2) & \xrightarrow{V''_2} & HMOD(SP'') \\ \uparrow \overline{\Delta} & & \uparrow \Delta \\ HMOD(SP_1) & \xrightarrow{V'_1} & HMOD(SP') \end{array}$$

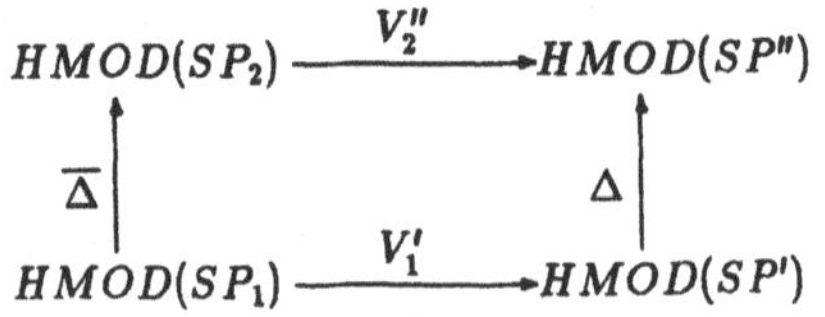

Let SP, SP_1 et SP' be specifications such that $SP \longrightarrow SP_1 \searrow^V SP'$ (SP is reusable for SP' w.r.t. some Σ'_r), and $SP'' = SP' \oplus \Delta SP''$, with $\Sigma_1 \cap \Delta\Sigma'' = \emptyset$.

Then $SP_2 = SP_1 \oplus \overline{\Delta SP''}$, and for all realization $\Delta \in REAL_{SP'}(\Delta SP'')$, there is a realization $\overline{\Delta} \in REAL_{SP_1}(\overline{\Delta SP''})$, such that the diagram above commutes, i.e. :

$$\forall A_1 \in HMOD(SP_1),\ V''_2 \circ \overline{\Delta}(A_1) \simeq \Delta \circ V'_1(A_1)$$

Proof : See [GM 87]. □

Conclusions and further researches

We have given a criterion for "efficient" software reusability, and proved that this notion of reusability fits well for hierarchical specifications. We have introduced "non efficient reusability" (such as integer for naturals) in order to be more permissive. However, the results on this kind of reusability are slightly disappointing since they seem rather complex to apply.

It is interesting to note that non efficient reusability is not exactly what we have called "direct reusability", and is a step forward implementation. These results enforce our opinion that the kind of reusability we are studying, i.e. code reusability using its specification, should be done on as-it-is bases whenever possible. This is quite coherent with practice.

This study was devoted to structured specification and modular programs. It is clear that it must be extended to parameterized specifications and generic programs.

Acknowledgements

Our thanks to Michel Bidoit and Gilles Bernot for numerous fruitful discussions and friendly encouragements.

This work is partially funded by ESPRIT (Meteor Project) and by the PRC-Greco "Programmation et outils pour l'intelligence artificielle". Th. Moineau's grant is funded by Sema-Metra.

References

[BBC 86] G. Bernot, M. Bidoit and C. Choppy, "Abstract implementation and correctness proofs", in *Proc. 3rd STACS*, Jan. 1986, Springer-Verlag LNCS 210, Jan. 1986.

[Ber 87] G. Bernot, "Good functors ... are those preserving philosophy !", in *Proc. 2nd Summer Conference on Cotegory Theory and Computer Science*, Edinburgh, Sept. 1987.
also *LRI report* No. 354, June 1987.

[Bid 87] M. Bidoit, "The stratified loose approach : A generalization of initial and loose semantics", to appear.

[BW 82] M. Broy and M. Wirsing, "Partial abstract types", *Acta Informatica*, No. 18, 1982.

[EKMP 80] H. Ehrig, H. Kreowski, B. Mahr and P. Padawitz, "Algebraic implementation of abstract data types", *Theoretical Computer Science*, Oct. 1980.

[EM 85] H. Ehrig and B. Mahr, "Fundamentals of algebraic specification", Springer Verlag, Berlin-Heidelberg-New York-Tokyo, 1985.

[FGJM 85] K. Futatsugi, J.A. Goguen, J-P. Jouannaud and J. Meseguer, "Principles of OBJ2", in *proc. 12th ACM Symposium on Principles of Programming Languages*, Jan. 1985.

[Gau 85] M.C. Gaudel, "Towards structured algebraic specifications", *ESPRIT'85 - Status Report*, Part I, pp. 493–510, North Holland, 1986.

[GM 87] M.C. Gaudel and Th. Moineau, "A theory of software reusability", *LRI report* No. 380, Oct. 1987.

[GH 78] J.V. Guttag and J.J. Horning, "The algebraic specification of abstract data types." *Acta Informatica*, No. 10, 1978.

[Pro 82] K. Proch, "ORSEC : Un Outil de Recherche de Spécifications Equivalentes par Comparaison d'exemple", Thèse de 3eme cycle, Nancy I, Dec. 1982.

[SW 82] D. Sanella and M. Wirsing, "Implementation of parametrized specifications", *Report CSR-102-82*, Department of Computer Science, University of Edinburgh.

[Wir 83] M. Wirsing, "Structured algebraic specifications : a kernel language", Habilitation Thesis, Technische Universität München, Sept. 1983.

[WPPDB 83] M. Wirsing, P. Pepper, H. Partsch, W. Dosch and M. Broy, "On hierarchy of abstract data types", *Acta Informatica*, No. 20, 1983.

Parametric Overloading in Polymorphic Programming Languages

Stefan Kaes

Fachbereich Informatik

Technische Hochschule Darmstadt

Magdalenenstr. 11c, D-6100 Darmstadt

BITNET: xlp2fgpl@ddathd21

Abstract

The introduction of unrestricted overloading in languagues with type systems based on implicit parametric polymorphism generally destroys the principal type property: namely that the type of every expression can uniformly be represented by a single type expression over some set of type variables. As a consequence, type inference in the presence of unrestricted overloading can become a NP-complete problem. In this paper we define the concept of parametric overloading as a restricted form of overloading which is easily combined with parametric polymorphism. Parametric overloading preserves the principal type property, thereby allowing the design of efficient type inference algorithms. We present sound type deduction systems, both for predefined and programmer defined overloading. Finally we state that parametric overloading can be resolved either statically, at compile time, or dynamically, during program execution.

1 Introduction

Over the last decade, a considerable number of (functional) programming languages with type disciplines based on the concept of parametric polymorphism [Milner78] have been developed. Among the better known are ML [Milner84], HOPE [BMQS80] and Miranda [Turner85]. The success of parametric polymorphism is largely due to the following facts.

Security: Programs are forced to be statically type correct, enabling the detection of a large number of programming errors at compile time.

Flexibility: Parametric polymorphism provides the programmer with a type system which allows the reuse of functions for arguments of various types, provided the meaning of the function does not depend on a particular type.

Efficiency: Since all type checking is done at compile time, expensive runtime type checks can be eliminated, thus increasing the efficiency of functional language implementations.

At a closer look, however, one can observe that the type systems employed in these languages are not as secure and flexible as they should be. For example, let us consider some predefined operators in the context of a type system containing integers, reals, booleans, lists of homogenous element type and functions.

A typical example for a parametrically polymorphic function is the function *len*, which determines the length of lists of arbitrary element type *t*. In a parametrically polymorphic type system the type of *len* could be expressed using the type expression $\forall t.\ list(t) \rightarrow int$, where *t* stands for an arbitrary type.

In regard to flexibility, we would certainly like to have an operator +, to denote both integer- and real addition at the same time. Thus, we require + to be *overloaded*. In a parametrically polymorphic type system, this can only be described by assigning a set of type expressions, (equivalent to the conjunctive types of [Coppo80]) as the type of +, namely: $\{\ int \times int \rightarrow int\ ,\ real \times real \rightarrow real\ \}$.
This presents no conceptual problems for type inference, since it is well known how to deal with this kind of overloading (see [BaSne86] for a possible approach). However, in the presence of arbitrary sets of types and undeclared identifiers, the problem becomes computationally hard to solve, in fact, it can be shown to be NP-complete [ASU86]. It appears as if this problem has led the designers of HOPE, Miranda and ML(at least in the original version) to the decision of collapsing types integer and real into a single data type of numbers. Nonetheless, we feel that the distinction of integer and real numbers is essential and should therefore be reflected in the type system of any programming laguage.

Note that there is also a semantical difference between overloading and polymorphism: In the case of the overloaded + operator, we would expect different code to be executed for integer and real addition respectively, whereas we expect the code of *len* to be usable for lists of any type. This distinction has led to the name "adhoc polymorphism" [Str67]. At a second glance it is somewhat superficial: we could easily imagine a built-in addition instruction, which tests the type of the operands and then performs either integer or real addition.

As a striking example for the insecurity of pure parametric polymorphism, let us assume that = , the equality operator, is applicable to two values of the same type, provided there is no comparison between functional values involved.

The reason for this restriction is rather obvious: since equality of functions is in general undecidable, we would like the type system to prohibit any attempt to do so. Using type expressions over some set of ordinary type variables, one can only assign $\forall t.\ t \times t \rightarrow bool$ as a polymorphic type to =. This type expression can be interpreted as: for any type t, = maps two values of type t to a boolean value. Since any type is admissible, this implies that even two functions of identical type, say $int \rightarrow int$, are comparable.

Now this example has a flavor not found in the first one: if we were to represent the overloaded type of = by a set of type expressions, we would be forced to use an infinite number of types:

$$\{\ int \times int \rightarrow bool, \ldots,\ list(int) \times list(int) \rightarrow bool, \ldots,\ list(list(int)) \times list(list(int)) \rightarrow bool, \ldots\ \}$$

We conclude therefore that it is necessary to introduce a finite representation for such sets, especially since these sets arise frequently, some examples being the sets of types of =, ≤, etc. . Such a representation is possible, if we restrict ourselves to *parametric overloading*. The difference between the various kinds of polymorphism can roughly be summarized by the following comparison:

Parametric polymorphism: One semantic object can have different types at each usage, all being instances of a single type expression over variables.

Overloading ("adhoc polymorphism"): A single name can be used to denote different semantic objects, the types of these objects being completely unrelated.

Parametric overloading: A single name can be used to denote several objects, the types of these objects being instances of a single type expression over some extended set of type variables.

The remainder of this paper is devoted to the development of a theory of parametric overloading. It is organized in the following way: First, we recapitulate the theoretical foundations of the notion of parametric polymorphism in the context of a simple expression language. We present a denotational semantics for this language, define syntax and semantics of types, give a deduction system for inferring well typed programs, and state that our type system is sound w.r.t. the semantics of expressions and types. Second, we give a formal definition of parametric overloading, based on the concept of overloading assumptions and sorted type variables, restricting ourselves to the case of predefined overloaded function symbols. We then proceed to show that a unification algorithm for the modified set of type expressions exists, and that, by simply replacing robinsons algorithm used in Milner's type inference algorithm W with this new algorithm, we obtain an algorithm to compute principal well typings in presence of parametrically overloaded functions. In Chapter 4 we extend our base language to include user definable overloading, and give a deduction system for well typings. Finally we discuss two alternative semantics for the extended language: the first one is given by mapping overloaded expressions back to expressions of the original language, resolving overloading statically, the second one is given by changing the semantic equations to resolve overloading dynamically, during program execution.

2 Parametric Polymorphism

2.1 Syntax and Semantics of Expressions

Assuming that x ranges over a countable set of variables, the expressions of our example language **Expr** are generated by the grammar

$$M ::= x \mid \lambda x.M \mid M_1\ M_2 \mid \mathbf{let}\ x = M_1\ \mathbf{in}\ M_2$$

In order to assign meaning to expressions we postulate the existence of a domain of denotable values **V** as a solution to the recursive domain equation

$$\mathbf{V} = \mathbf{W} \oplus \left(\oplus\ S_c(\mathbf{V}^{a(c)}) \right)$$

where $\oplus$ denotes disjoint union and

(1) **W** = { · } is the domain of the value · , used to model runtime type errors, where ·, as a member of **V** will be denoted by *wrong*.

(2) C is a finite set of type constructors with arity a(c); e.g. {int, real, ×, →, ... }

(3) $S_c(D_1,...,D_{a(c)})$ is a domain corresponding to type constructor $c \in C$; e.g.:

S_{int}	- the flat cpo of integers
S_{real}	- likewise for real numbers
$S_{\times}(A,B)$	- cartesian product space
$S_{\to}(A,B)$	- space of continous function from A to B

The meaning of any expression M is given in terms of a function $\mathcal{E}[\![M]\!]$, mapping environments $\eta \in$ **Env** = **Id** $\Rightarrow$ **V** to denotable values:

$\mathcal{E}$: **Expr** → **Env** → **V**

$\mathcal{E}[\![x]\!]\eta = \eta(x)$

$\mathcal{E}[\![\lambda x.M]\!]\eta = (\lambda v.\ \mathcal{E}[\![M]\!]\eta\ \{v/x\})$

$\mathcal{E}[\![M_1\ M_2]\!]\eta =$ *if* f ε F *then* (f | F) v *else wrong* , where $f = \mathcal{E}[\![M_1]\!]\eta$, $v = \mathcal{E}[\![M_2]\!]\eta$

$\mathcal{E}[\![\mathbf{let}\ x = M_1\ \mathbf{in}\ M_2]\!]\eta = \mathcal{E}[\![M_1]\!]\ \eta\{\ \mathcal{E}[\![M_2]\!]\eta/x\ \}$

where F denotes the function space $S_{\rightarrow}(V,V)$ and $\eta\{\ v/x\ \} \equiv \lambda y.$ *if* x=y *then* v *else* $\eta(y)$.

Note that the only possible type error apparent from the equations above, is the application of non-functions to argument values. However, we may assume that application of functions in η to arguments outside their domain can cause type errors as well.

2.2 Syntax and Semantics of Type Expressions

Let **Tvars** = {α,β,...} be a countable set of *type variables* and c range over C. The syntax of *types* τ and *type-schemes* σ is defined by

$$\tau ::= \alpha \mid c(\tau_1,\ldots,\tau_n) \qquad \text{and} \qquad \sigma ::= \tau \mid \forall\alpha.\sigma$$

The variables $\alpha_1,\ldots,\alpha_n$ in type-scheme $\forall\alpha_1,\ldots,\alpha_n.\tau$ (an abbreviation of $\forall\alpha_1. \ldots \forall\alpha_n.\ \tau$) are called *generic*, whereas any type variable free in τ is called *specific*. *Monotypes* t are types not containing type variables. Substitutions S ε **Subst** = **Tvars** $\rightharpoonup$ **Types** are finite mappings of type variables to types. If σ is a type-scheme, $S = [\tau_i/\alpha_i]$ ε **Subst**, then $S(\sigma)$ is the type-scheme obtained by instantiating each free occurence of α_i in σ to τ_i, where bound variables in σ may be renamed to avoid name clashes (cf. α-conversion). A type scheme $\sigma' = \forall\beta_1,\ldots,\beta_n.\tau'$ is called *generic instance* of σ (written $\sigma' < \sigma$), if $\sigma = \forall\alpha_1,\ldots,\alpha_n.\tau$ and $\tau' = [\tau_1/\alpha_1,\ldots,\tau_n/\alpha_n]\tau$ and no β_i is free in τ.

Following [MQPS84] types can be interpreted as elements in the lattice of *weak ideals* $\mathbf{I}(\mathbf{V})$. Ideals $\mathbf{I} \subseteq \mathbf{V}$ do not contain *wrong* , are non-empty, downward closed and limit closed. Moreover, $\mathbf{I}(\mathbf{V})$ is closed under union and intersection. For any c ε C of arity n, let $\iota(c)(\mathbf{I}_1,\ldots,\mathbf{I}_n)$ denote the image of $S_c(\mathbf{I}_1,\ldots,\mathbf{I}_n)$ in **V**. For example, let $\iota(\mathrm{int}) = S_{\mathrm{int}}$, $\iota(\mathrm{real}) = S_{\mathrm{real}}$, $\iota(\times)(\mathbf{I},\mathbf{J}) = \{\ \langle a,b\rangle \mid a \in A,\ b \in B\ \}$ and $\iota(\rightarrow)(\mathbf{I},\mathbf{J}) = \{\ f \in V \rightarrow V \mid x \in \mathbf{I} \Rightarrow f(x) \in \mathbf{J}\ \}$.

Let φ ε **Tenv** = **Tvars** $\rightharpoonup$ **I**(**V**), then function $\mathcal{T}$ below maps type schemes σ to ideals under an assignment φ of ideals to type variables free in σ:

$$\mathcal{T}[\![\alpha]\!]\varphi = \varphi(\alpha)$$

$$\mathcal{T}[\![c(\tau_1,\ldots,\tau_n)]\!]\varphi = \iota(c)(\mathcal{T}[\![\tau_1]\!]\varphi,\ldots,\mathcal{T}[\![\tau_n]\!]\varphi)$$

$$\mathcal{T}[\![\forall\alpha.\sigma]\!]\varphi = \bigcap_{t \in \mathbf{Types}} \mathcal{T}[\![\sigma]\!]\ \varphi\{\ \mathcal{T}[\![t]\!]\varphi/\alpha\ \}$$

2.3 Well-typed Expressions

A *typing* is a statement of the form $A \vdash M : \tau$, where A, a finite set of pairs x:σ, is called *type assumption*, assigning types to variables occuring free in M. If A is a type assumption, then A. x:σ denotes A ∪ {x:σ} and A_x denotes A, except that x does not occurr in A_x. $\overline{A\tau}$, the closure of τ with respect to A is defined as $\overline{A\tau} =_{def} \forall\alpha_1,\ldots,\alpha_n.\tau$, where $\{\alpha_1,\ldots,\alpha_n\}$ is the largest set of type variables which occur free in τ, but not in A.

Typing $A \vdash M : \tau$ is said to be a *well-typing* if it can be derived using the following axioms and inference rules:

$$[\text{VAR}] \quad A_x.\ x{:}\ \sigma \vdash x : \tau \qquad \text{if } \tau < \sigma$$

$$[\text{ABS}] \quad \frac{A_x.\ x : \tau_a \vdash M : \tau_r}{A \vdash \lambda x.M : \tau_a \rightarrow \tau_r}$$

$$[\text{APP}] \quad \frac{A \vdash M_1 : \tau_a \rightarrow \tau_r\ ,\ A \vdash M_2 : \tau_a}{A \vdash M_1\ M_2 : \tau_r}$$

$$[\text{LET}] \quad \frac{A \vdash M_1 : \tau_1\ ,\ A_x.\ x{:}\ \overline{A\tau_1} \vdash M_2 : \tau_2}{A \vdash \textbf{let } x = M_1 \textbf{ in } M_2 : \tau_2}$$

Note that this system differs from the one given in [DaMi82] in two aspects: instantiation of type schemes ($<$) is restricted to variable usage and generalisation of types ($\overline{A\tau}$) is restricted to let-introduced identifiers. The system was first used in [CDDK86], where it was shown to be equivalent to the system of [DaMi82] in the following sense: Every well-typing derivable in the system above is also derivable in the system of [DaMi82]. Conversely, if $A \vdash M : \sigma$ is derivable in the system of [DaMi82], then there exists a well-typing $A \vdash M : \tau$, derivable in the above system, such that $\sigma < \overline{A\tau}$.

The following two theorems state the key properties of well-typings, namely, that well-typed expressions do not produce runtime type errors and that type inference can be used to compute principal types:

Theorem1 (Milner): *soundness of type inference*

If $A \vdash M : \tau$ is a well-typing and $x{:}\sigma \in A \Rightarrow \eta(x) \in \mathcal{T}[\![\sigma]\!]\varphi$ then $\mathcal{E}[\![M]\!]\eta \in \mathcal{T}[\![\overline{A\tau}]\!]\varphi$.

Theorem2 (Hindley-Damas-Milner): *principal well-typings*

Let A be a type assumption, A' an instance of A and FV(M) be the variables free in M.
If $A' \vdash M : \tau'$ is a well-typing, then there exists a principal well-typing $A \vdash M : \tau$, such that there exists a substitution S satisfying $A'|_{FV(M)} = S(A|_{FV(M)})$ and $\overline{A'\tau'} < \overline{SAS\tau}$.
Moreover, there exists an algorithm (Algorithm W) to compute $A \vdash M : \tau$.

3 Parametric Overloading

3.1 Overloading Schemes and Overloading Assumptions

In this chapter we will to introduce the concept of parametric overloading, which can be characterised by a set of restrictions on ordinary overloading:

- overloading is restricted to function symbols (identifiers)
- the result type of a function application f(x,...,z) is uniquely determined by the outermost type constructor of the argument types

Moreover, in order to make type inference feasible, we require that the set of types of an overloaded function can always be represented by a pair consisting of a designated type expression called *overloading scheme* and a set of instantiation rules both of which together are called *overloading assumption.*

Definition: *overloading scheme*

Let \$ be a special symbol not found in $C \cup$ Tvars, then ω is called an overloading scheme **iff** $\omega = \omega_0 \times \ldots \times \omega_{n-1} \rightarrow \omega_n$ where for all $i \in 0..n$, ω_i is either a type τ, or the special symbol \$, and $\omega_{n-1} = \$ \Rightarrow \exists\ i \in 0..n-1$ such that $\omega_i = \$$.

In any overloading scheme $ designates the argument positions which may be overloaded.

Examples of overloading schemes are:

$\$ \to int$	a discrete measure
$\$ \to real$	a continuous measure
$\$ \to \$$	succ, pred
$\$ \times \$ \to bool$	=, ≠, ≤, ≥, <, >
$\$ \times \$ \to \$$	+, *, −, ∧, ∨

Let ω be an overloading scheme and τ some type expression, then:

τ overloads ω with τ' **iff** $\tau = [\tau'/\$]\omega$ and τ' is of the form $c(\alpha_1,...,\alpha_n)$ for some $c \in C$.

In this case we also say that τ' is an overloading for ω. The restriction on the form of τ' is due to the fact that we want to resolve overloading by looking at outermost type constructors only.

Definition: *overloading assumption*

An overloading assumption O is a finite set of pairs $x{:}\langle\omega,s\rangle$, where each x occurs only once in O, ω is an overloading scheme and s is a set of overloadings for ω, such that no type constructor occurs twice in s.

Using this definition we could now define the set of valid overloadings of $x{:}\langle\omega,s\rangle$ to be the set of types t such that $t = [t'/\$]\omega$ where t' is an instance of some type constructor $c \in s$.

The overloading assumption $\{ +{:} \langle\$ \times \$ \to \$, \{ int, real \} \}$ would then specify the type set $\{ int \times int \to int, real \times real \to real \}$. However, if we try to define the possible overloadings of the predefined equality operator using the assumption

$\{ ={:} \langle\$ \times \$ \to \$, \{ int, real, list(\alpha) \}\rangle\}$,

we still get too large a set: although we have effectively excluded functions from appearing as arguments of =, we still allow lists of functions to be compared. In order to remedy this situation, we refine our notion of type variables: type variables come equipped with a set of operator names X, where intuitively, α_X stands for the set of all types that can appear at an overloaded argument position of every operator $x \in X$. The overloading assumption

$\{ ={:} \langle\$ \times \$ \to \$, \{ int, real, list(\alpha_{\{=\}}) \} \rangle\}$,

would then restrict the type of arguments for = to all types constructed from the type constructors int, real and list.

Definition: *$x \triangleright \tau$, $X \triangleright \tau$, valid overloadings*

Let O be an overloading assumption. If α is a type variable marked with a set of operator names, then let ops(α) denote that set. Type τ can appear at an overloaded argument position of operator x (written $x \triangleright \tau$) **iff** either $\tau \in Tvars \wedge x \in ops(\tau)$ or $\tau = c(\tau_1,...,\tau_n) \wedge O = O_X.\ x{:}\langle\omega,\{...\ c(\alpha_1,...,\alpha_n)\ ...\}\rangle \wedge \forall\ i=1..n{:}\ \forall y \in ops(\alpha_i){:}\ y \triangleright \tau_i$.

If X is a set of operators, then $X \triangleright \tau \equiv \forall x \in X.\ x \triangleright \tau$. The set of valid overloadings of x is given by $\{ [t/\$]\omega \mid x \triangleright t \}$.

Example: Suppose we want to impose the following restrictions on the set of valid overloadings of the operators +, = and ≤ : equality is defined for integers, reals, lists and sets, provided set and list elements can be compared. + is overloaded with integer and real addition, and set union, whereas ≤ is used to denote the arithmetic ≤-relation, the sublist- and subset relation. These restrictions are correctly specified by the overloading assumption

$+ \; : \langle \$ \times \$ \rightarrow \$ \;,\; \{ \text{int, real, set}(\alpha_{\{=\}}) \} \rangle$

$= \; : \langle \$ \times \$ \rightarrow \text{bool}, \{ \text{int, real, list}(\alpha_{\{=\}}), \text{set}(\alpha_{\{=\}}) \} \rangle$

$\leq \; : \langle \$ \times \$ \rightarrow \text{bool}, \{ \text{int, real, list}(\alpha_{\{=\}}), \text{set}(\alpha_{\{=\}}) \} \rangle$

3.2 Well-typed Expressions

Let A be a type assumption and O be an overloading assumption. We say that A agrees with O **iff** whenever $x:\langle\omega,s\rangle \in O$ and $x:\sigma \in A$ then $\sigma = [\alpha_{\{x\}}/\$]\omega$. Let $<_O$ be the generic instance relation respecting $\triangleright$ and let us assume that predefined operators cannot be redeclared. The following deduction system can be used to infer valid typings in the presence of a fixed overloading assumption:

$$[\text{VAR}] \quad A_x.\, x:\sigma \vdash^{O} x:\tau \qquad \text{if } \tau <_O \sigma$$

$$[\text{ABS}] \quad \frac{A_x.\, x:\tau_a \vdash^{O} M:\tau_r}{A \vdash^{O} \lambda x.M : \tau_a \rightarrow \tau_r} \qquad \text{if not } x \in O$$

$$[\text{APP}] \quad \frac{A \vdash^{O} M_1 : \tau_a \rightarrow \tau_r \;,\; A \vdash^{O} M_2 : \tau_a}{A \vdash^{O} M_1\, M_2 : \tau_r}$$

$$[\text{LET}] \quad \frac{A \vdash^{O} M_1 : \tau_1 \;,\; A_x.\, x: \overline{A\tau_1} \vdash^{O} M_2 : \tau_2}{A \vdash^{O} \textbf{let } x = M_1 \textbf{ in } M_2 : \tau_2} \qquad \text{if not } x \in O$$

Note that the main difference between this system and the one given for nonoverloaded expressions is the restriction that generic instantiation has to respect $\triangleright$.

Example: Using the system above one can deduce, that given type assumption

$A = \{ +: \forall\alpha_{\{+\}}.\ \alpha_{\{+\}} \times \alpha_{\{+\}} \rightarrow \alpha_{\{+\}},\ *: \forall\alpha_{\{*\}}.\ \alpha_{\{*\}} \times \alpha_{\{*\}} \rightarrow \alpha_{\{*\}} \},$

and overloading assumption

$O = \{ +: \langle \$ \times \$ \rightarrow \$, \{ \text{int, real} \} \rangle,\ *: \langle \$ \times \$ \rightarrow \$, \{ \text{int, real} \} \rangle \}$

the typing

$A \vdash^{O} \textbf{let } f = \lambda x.\ x + x * x \textbf{ in } (f\ 5) : \text{int}$

is a well typing. Note that the declaration of f causes the type-scheme assigned to f to be

$\forall\alpha.\alpha_{\{+,*\}} \times \alpha_{\{+,*\}} \rightarrow \alpha_{\{+,*\}}$

which says that f is a overloaded function applicable to values to which both + and * are applicable simultaneously. The type of f in the application (f 5) is then instantiated to int x int → int, since int is a valid instantiation for $\alpha_{\{+,*\}}$.

Proving a soundness theorem for the modified deduction system requires an adjustment to the semantic function $\mathcal{T}$, taking into account that variables are sorted w.r.t. operator names. For a fixed overloading assumption O and $\varphi \in$ **Tenv**, such that $\alpha_s \in \text{dom}\ \varphi \Rightarrow \exists t.\, s \triangleright t \wedge \varphi(\alpha_s) = \mathcal{T}_O[\![t]\!]\emptyset$, we define $\mathcal{T}_O$ as:

$$\mathcal{T}_O[\![\alpha_s]\!]\varphi = \varphi(\alpha_s)$$

$$\mathcal{T}_O[\![c(\tau_1,\ldots,\tau_n)]\!]\varphi = \iota(c)(\mathcal{T}_O[\![\tau_1]\!]\varphi,\ldots,\mathcal{T}_O[\![\tau_n]\!]\varphi)$$

$$\mathcal{T}_O[\![\forall\alpha_s.\sigma]\!]\varphi = \bigcap_{\substack{t \in \textbf{Types} \\ s \triangleright t}} \mathcal{T}_O[\![\sigma]\!]\ \varphi\{ \mathcal{T}_O[\![t]\!]\varphi/\alpha \}.$$

In order for $\mathcal{T}_O$ to be well defined we have to request that for every set of operator names s, the set $\{ t \mid s \triangleright t \}$ is always nonempty. This can be achieved simply by adding a nonsense type contructor ? of zero arity to C, such that $x \triangleright ?$ holds for every operator x. Additionally, the domain of denotable values is extended by the single valued domain $S_? = \{ ? \}$. Note that the value ? can never be denoted by expressions. This construction is only necessary in order to simplify the statement and proof of soundness theorems to follow.

Theorem: *soundness of type inference in the presence of predefined overloaded operators:*

If $A \vdash^{\mathcal{O}} M : \tau$ is a well-typing, A agrees with O and $x{:}\sigma \in A \Rightarrow \eta(x) \in \mathcal{T}_O[\![\sigma]\!]\varphi$ then $\mathcal{E}[\![M]\!]\eta \in \mathcal{T}_O[\![\overline{A\tau}]\!]\varphi$.

(Note: the proof of this and all other theorems in this paper can be found in [Kaes87].)

3.3 Type Inference in the Presence of a Fixed Overloading Assumption

In order to develop a type inference algorithm which computes principal typings for our modified deduction system, all we need to do is, find an unification algorithm for type expressions over variables marked with operator names, replace it for the Robinson algorithm in Milner's algorithm W and we are done ! We will therefore concentrate on the presentation of the new unification algorithm.

For sake of simplicity, for the rest of the paragraph we assume that O is a fixed over loading assumption. Then, let the functions $m: C \to 2^{Id}$ and $d: C \times Nat \times 2^{Id} \to 2^{Id}$ be defined in the following way:

$$m(c) =_{def} \{ x \mid x: \langle \omega, \{\ldots c(\ldots) \ldots\} \rangle \in O \}$$

$$d_c(i, X) =_{def} \bigcup_{x \in X} \{ ops(\alpha_i) \mid x: \langle \{\ldots c(\alpha_1,\ldots,\alpha_n) \ldots\} \rangle \in O \}$$

m(c) maps type names to the set of operators, where such a type name may possibly occur at an overloaded argument position. $d_c(i,X)$ maps sets of type names to the set Y_i, such that if $Y_i \models \tau_i$ holds for i=1..n and $X \subseteq m(c)$ then $X \models c(\tau_1,\ldots,\tau_n)$ holds as well.

Let S be a substitution. We say that S respects variable sorts if $\alpha \in dom\ S \Rightarrow ops(\alpha) \models S(\alpha)$. Let τ_1 and τ_2 be types. τ_2 is a valid instance of τ_1 ($\tau_1 \geq \tau_2$), if there exists a substitution S, respecting variable sorts, such that $\tau_2 = S\tau_1$. If S_1 and S_2 are substitutions, S_1 is more general than S_2 ($S_1 \geq S_2$), if $dom\ S_1 \subseteq dom\ S_2$ and $\alpha \in dom\ S_1 \Rightarrow S_1(\alpha) \geq S_2(\alpha)$.

Lemma: *most general substitutions*

Let τ be a type and X be a set of operator names. Then there exists either no substitution satisfying $X \models \tau$ or a most general one. Moreover, the algorithm cs given below can be used to compute such a substition.

$cs(X, \alpha) = [\beta/\alpha]$ — β a new type variable, $ops(\beta) = s \cup ops(\alpha)$

$cs(X, c(\tau_1,\ldots,\tau_n)) = S_n$ — if $X \subseteq m(c) \wedge \exists\ S_0 \ldots S_n$ such that
$\forall\ i=1..n{:}\ S_i = cs(d_c(i,X), S_{i-1}(\tau_i)) \cdot S_{i-1}$

cs fails in all other cases.

Proof: By computational induction one can show that (i) if cs succeeds, it will return a substitution S which respects variable sorts and (ii) for any other substitution R which satisfies (i) one can find a substition S' such that $R = S' \cdot S$.

As an immediate consequence of the existence of most general substitutions respecting variable sorts we get the following

Theorem: *most general unifiers*

Given types τ_1 and τ_2 there exists either no unifier S, such that $S(\tau_1) = S(\tau_2)$, or a most general one. Moerover, if a mgu of τ_1 and τ_2 exists, it can be computed by the unification algorithm $\mathcal{U}$ below:

$\mathcal{U}(\tau, \tau) = [\,]$

$\mathcal{U}(\tau, \alpha) = \mathcal{U}(\alpha, \tau)$ if not $\tau \in$ Tvars

$\mathcal{U}(\alpha, \tau) = [S(\tau)/\alpha] \cdot S$ if $S = cs(ops(\alpha), \tau)$ exists and not $\alpha \in vars(\tau)$

$\mathcal{U}(c(\tau_1,\dots,\tau_n), c(\tau_1',\dots,\tau_n')) = S_n$ if $\exists\, S_0,\dots,S_n.\ S_0 = [\,] \wedge \forall\, i=1..n$:

$$S_i = \mathcal{U}(S_{i-1}(\tau_i), S_{i-1}(\tau_i')) \cdot S_{i-1}$$

$\mathcal{U}(\tau, \tau')$ fails in all other cases.

Proof: Computational induction using the lemma above.

Observe that the algorithms cs and $\mathcal{U}$ are quite independend of the actual semantics behind the functions m and d and are therefore more general than appears at first sight. For example, given appropriate definitions of d and m, one can obtain an unfication algorithm for *order sorted algebras* from $\mathcal{U}$ and cs (cf. the algorithm in [BaSne86]). Details of the construction may be found in [Kaes87].

4 User Definable Parametric Overloading

4.1 Syntax and Type Deduction

In this paragraph we investigate the effect of extending our base language to enable programmers to define their own overloaded function symbols. We add two clauses:

M ::= x | λx.M | M_1 M_2 | **let** x = M_1 **in** M_2
  | **letop** x: ω **in** M
  | M_1 : σ **extends** x **in** M_2

The letop-clause declares x as an identifier with overloading scheme ω, overloadable in M, whereas the extend-clause overloads x with the meaning of M_1 in M_2, provided σ is a valid overloading of overloadable operator x.

As an example, the following program defines the usual overloading of multiplication under the assumption that pair: $\forall\alpha,\beta.\alpha\to\beta\to(\alpha,\beta)$ contructs pairs, fst:$\forall\alpha,\beta.(\alpha,\beta)\to\alpha$ and snd:$\forall\alpha,\beta.(\alpha,\beta)\to\beta$ select the first resp. second components of pairs:

letop *: \$ × \$ → \$ **in**
intmult: int × int → int **extends** * **in**
realmult: real × real → real **extends** * **in**
let addsquares = λp. fst(p)*fst(p)+snd(p)*snd(p) **in**
addsquares (pair 3 5)

It is not very surprising that we can adapt our type deduction system to the new situation, by moving the overloading assumption, under which we infer valid types, to the assumption part of our typings. Therefore $A \overset{O}{\vdash} M : \tau$ now becomes $\langle O,A\rangle \vdash M : \tau$, which can be read as: under overloading assumption O and type assumption A for identifiers free in M we can derive that τ is a valid type for M. This leads to the following deduction system:

[VAR] $\langle O, A_x.\ x{:}\ \sigma \rangle \vdash x : \tau$ if $\tau <_O \sigma$

$$[\text{ABS}]\quad \frac{\langle O_x, A_x.\ x: \tau_a \rangle \vdash M : \tau_r}{\langle O, A \rangle \vdash \lambda x.M : \tau_a \to \tau_r}$$

$$[\text{APP}]\quad \frac{\langle O, A \rangle \vdash M_1 : \tau_a \to \tau_r\ ,\ \langle O, A \rangle \vdash M_2 : \tau_a}{\langle O, A \rangle \vdash M_1\ M_2 : \tau_r}$$

$$[\text{LET}]\quad \frac{\langle O, A \rangle \vdash M_1 : \tau_1\ ,\ \langle O_x, A_x.\ x: \overline{A\tau_1} \rangle \vdash M_2 : \tau_2}{\langle O, A \rangle \vdash \textbf{let}\ x = M_1\ \textbf{in}\ M_2 : \tau_2}$$

$$[\text{OP}]\quad \frac{\langle O_x.\ x: \langle\omega,\{?\}\rangle,\ A_x.\ x: \forall\alpha_{\{x\}}.[\alpha_{\{x\}}/\$]\omega \rangle \vdash M : \tau}{\langle O, A \rangle \vdash \textbf{letop}\ x: \omega\ \textbf{in}\ M : \tau} \qquad \text{if } \beta_s \in \text{vars}(\tau) \Rightarrow x \notin s$$

$$[\text{OV}]\quad \frac{\begin{array}{l}\langle O_x.\ x:\langle\omega, d\rangle,\ A \rangle \vdash M_1 : \sigma \\ \langle O_x.\ x:\langle\omega, d \cup \{\tau\}\rangle,\ A \rangle \vdash M_2 : \tau'\end{array}}{\langle O_x.\ x:\langle\omega, d\rangle,\ A \rangle \vdash M_1: \sigma\ \textbf{extends}\ x\ \textbf{in}\ M_2 : \tau'} \qquad \begin{array}{l}\text{if } \sigma \text{ overloads } \omega \text{ with } \tau, \\ \tau = c(\alpha_1,\ldots,\alpha_n) \wedge \text{not } c \in d\end{array}$$

The condition $\beta_s \in \text{vars}(\tau) \Rightarrow x \notin s$ in the OP-rule ensures, that no overloading can be exported out of its scope, whereas the condition in OV guarantees, that no type constructor can appear twice in any overloading set.

Theorem: *principal well-typings in the presence of user definable overloading*

If $\langle O,A' \rangle \vdash \tau'$ is a well typing in the system above and A' an instance of A, then there exists a principal well-typing $\langle O,A \rangle \vdash M : \tau$ such that there exists a substitution S satisfying $A'|_{FV(M)} = S(A|_{FV(M)})$ and $\overline{A'\tau'} <_O \overline{SAS\tau}$. Moreover, there exists an algorithm (Algorithm Z) to compute $\langle O,A \rangle \vdash M : \tau$.

Algorithm Z is a rather straightforward extension of algorithm W, obtained by adding the overloading assumption as an extra parameter and including some functions to manipulate it in the appropriate way. For details the reader is again referred to [Kaes87].

Although type inference remains relatively simple, the semantics of expressions gets rather complicated. We can try two approaches: Static overloading resolution, through removal of every occurrence of letop- or extend clauses from our expessions, or a more direct semantics, extending semantic domains and equations, thus enabling dynamic overloading resolution.

4.2 Static Overloading Resolution

Static overloading resolution aims at execution efficiency by avoiding any type checking necessary for overloading resolution at runtime. It does not come for free though, complicating compilation through the need of (possibly costly) compile time program transformations. In this paragraph we present a overloading resolution function $\mathcal{R}$, mapping well typed overloaded expressions back to expressions of our original language.

Let $\langle O,A \rangle \vdash M : \tau$ be a well typing and M^τ be the well typed expression M where all its sub-expressions are annotated with their type. Let $\rho \in$ **Renv** = **TypedId** → **Expr** be an overloading resolution environment and let $\rho\backslash x$ denote ρ with all occurences of x removed, then function $\mathcal{R}$: **Expr** → **Renv** → **Expr** removes any user defined overloading from M:

$$\mathcal{R}[\![x^\tau]\!]\ \rho = \textit{if}\ \exists\ x^\sigma \in \text{dom}\ \rho.\ \sigma = \forall\alpha_i.\tau'\ ,\ \tau = S(\tau'),\ S \text{ overloading resolving}$$
$$\qquad \textit{then}\ \mathcal{R}[\![S(\rho(x^\sigma))]\!]\ \rho\ \textit{else}\ x^\tau$$

$\mathcal{R}[\![(M_1\ M_2)^\tau]\!]\ \rho = (\mathcal{R}[\![M_1]\!]\rho\ \ \mathcal{R}[\![M_2]\!]\rho\ )^\tau$

$\mathcal{R}[\![(\lambda x.M)^\tau]\!]\ \rho = (\ \lambda x.\mathcal{R}[\![M]\!]\ \rho\backslash x\ )^\tau$

$\mathcal{R}[\![(\mathbf{let}\ x^\sigma = M_1\ \mathbf{in}\ M_2)^\tau]\!]\ \rho =$ *if* σ is overloaded *then* $\mathcal{R}[\![M_2]\!]\ \rho\{\ \mathcal{R}[\![M_1]\!]\rho\ /x^\sigma\ \}$
else $(\ \mathbf{let}\ x^\sigma = (\ \mathcal{R}[\![M_1]\!]\rho\ )\ \mathbf{in}\ (\ \mathcal{R}[\![M_2]\!]\ \rho\backslash x\ )\ )^\tau$

$\mathcal{R}[\![\mathbf{letop}\ x\!:\ \omega\ \mathbf{in}\ M]\!]\ \rho =\ \ \mathcal{R}[\![M]\!]\ \rho$

$\mathcal{R}[\![M_1\!:\ \sigma\ \mathbf{extends}\ x\ \mathbf{in}\ M_2]\!]\ \rho = \mathcal{R}[\![M_2]\!]\ \rho\{\ \mathcal{R}[\![M_1]\!]\rho\ /x^\sigma\ \}$

$\mathcal{R}[\![M]\!]$ traverses the expression M, recursively expanding instances of overloaded operators until every letop- and extend-clause has been removed. Upon encountering $M_1 : \forall\alpha_i.\tau$ **extends** x **in** M_2, the resolution environment ρ is enhanced by the association $x^{\forall\alpha_i.\tau} \rightarrow \mathcal{R}[\![M_1{}^\tau]\!]\rho$. If, during the resolution of overloadings in M_2, some instance of this particular overloading of x is found, say $x^{S(\tau)}$, where S instantiates some overloaded type variable in τ to a type c(...), then x will be replaced by the result of resolving all overloadings in $S(\mathcal{R}[\![M_1]\!]\rho)$. let-clauses are also removed from M, if they introduce overloaded definitions. This corresponds to the view, that overloaded function definitions are not functions in the usual sense, but macros which are expanded according to an implicit type parameter.

Note, that for any well-typing $\langle O,A\rangle \vdash M : \tau$, $\mathcal{R}[\![M^\tau]\!]\ \rho$ is well defined if $x{:}\sigma \in A \Rightarrow \mathcal{R}[\![x^{\tau'}]\!]\rho$ well defined for every generic instance $\tau' <_O \sigma$.

Theorem: *semantic soundness of $\mathcal{R}$:*

Let $\langle O,A\rangle \vdash M : \tau$ be a well-typing, $\eta \in$ **Env**, $\varphi \in$ **Tenv**, $\rho \in$ **Renv** and $M' = \mathcal{R}[\![M^\tau]\!]\rho$.
If $x{:}\sigma \in A \Rightarrow \mathcal{E}[\![\ \mathcal{R}[\![x^{\tau'}]\!]\rho\ ]\!]\eta \in \mathcal{T}_O[\![\tau']\!]\varphi$ for every $\tau' <_O \sigma$ then $\mathcal{E}[\![M']\!]\eta \in \mathcal{T}_O[\![\ \overline{A\tau}\ ]\!]\varphi$.

4.3 Runtime Overloading Resolution

As an alternative to static overloading resolution we present a semantics for dynamic, i.e. runtime overloading resolution. The key idea behind this scheme is, that given a well-typed application of an overloaded operator, one can determine the particular overloading instance that is needed to compute the result by just looking at the summands of arguments.

Speaking in operational terms this implies, that arguments of overloaded operators have to be evaluated before applying the operator, thereby making it strict in its overloaded argument positions! An additional semantic complication is due to the fact, that the meaning of overloaded operators cannot be fixed statically in the declaring scope: Suppose we define an overloading for set-equality to be used in M, reducing equality on sets to equality on set elements. Suppose further, that we define a list comparison overloading inside M to be used in some yet deeper nested expression M'. Then we would certainly expect sets of lists of integers to be comparable in M'. However, having fixed the meaning of set equality to overloadings visible in M we can only compare lists of sets.

A similar observation can be made in the simpler case of let-introduced overloaded functions, which leads us to the introduction of a runtime equivalent of the static overloading resolution environment called operator environment.

$\mathbf{Openv} = \mathbf{Id} \rightharpoonup \mathbf{C} \rightharpoonup \mathbf{Openv} \rightarrow \mathbf{V}$

Intuitively, $\vartheta \in$ **Openv** maps operator identifiers to functions which, when given the outermost type constructor (or summand) of the arguments of an operator application, will return a function mapping an operator environment to a real function (seen as an element of **V**).

Moreover, let-introduced identifiers will be treated as elements of the domain **Openv** → **V**, requiring a change to the static environment domain.

$$\mathbf{Env'} = \mathbf{Id} \nrightarrow (\, \mathbf{V} \oplus (\mathbf{Openv} \to \mathbf{V})\,)$$

Finally, the semantics is given by the function $\mathcal{E}'$: **Expr** → **Env'** → **Openv** → **V**, assuming that identifiers introduced in let- and extend clauses have been annotated with their type rsp. overloading scheme by the type inference algorithm:

$$\mathcal{E}'[\![x]\!]\ \eta\ \vartheta = \mathit{if}\ \eta(x) \in \mathbf{Openv} \to \mathbf{V}\ \ \mathit{then}\ \ \eta(x)\ \vartheta\ \ \mathit{elsif}\ \eta(x) \in \mathbf{V}\ \ \mathit{then}\ \eta(x)\ \ \mathit{else}\ \ \mathit{wrong}$$

$$\mathcal{E}'[\![\lambda x.M]\!]\ \eta\ \vartheta = (\lambda v.\ \mathcal{E}'[\![M]\!]\ \eta\{\, v/x \,\}\ \vartheta)$$

$$\mathcal{E}'[\![M_1\ M_2]\!]\ \eta\ \vartheta = \mathit{if}\ f \in F\ \ \mathit{then}\ \ (f|F)\ v\ \ \mathit{else}\ \ \mathit{wrong}\ ,\ \ \text{where } f = \mathcal{E}'[\![M_1]\!]\eta\vartheta\ ,\ v = \mathcal{E}'[\![M_2]\!]\eta\vartheta$$

$$\mathcal{E}'[\![\mathbf{let}\ x^{\sigma} = M_1\ \mathbf{in}\ M_2]\!]\ \eta\ \vartheta = \mathit{if}\ \sigma \text{ is overloaded }\ \mathit{then}\ \mathcal{E}'[\![M_2]\!]\ \eta\{\, \mathcal{E}'[\![M_1]\!]\eta\ /x \,\}\ \vartheta$$
$$\mathit{else}\ \ \mathcal{E}'[\![M_2]\!]\ \eta\{\, \mathcal{E}'[\![M_1]\!]\eta\ /x \,\}\ \vartheta$$

$$\mathcal{E}'[\![\mathbf{letop}\ x\!:\ \omega\ \mathbf{in}\ M]\!]\ \eta\ \vartheta = \mathcal{E}'[\![M]\!]\ \eta\{\, \mathrm{resolve}(x,\omega)/x \,\}\ \vartheta\{\, \lambda c.\lambda\vartheta'.\bot\ /x \,\}$$

$$\mathcal{E}'[\![M_1\!:\ \sigma\ \mathbf{extends}\ x^{\omega}\ \mathbf{in}\ M_2]\!]\ \eta\ \vartheta =$$
$$\mathit{if}\ \ \eta(x)\ \mathbf{Openv} \to \mathbf{V} \text{ and } \sigma \text{ overloads } \omega \text{ with } c(\ldots)$$
$$\mathit{then}\ \ \mathcal{E}'[\![M_2]\!]\ \eta\ \vartheta\{\ (\ (\vartheta\ x)\{\, \mathcal{E}'[\![M_1]\!]\eta\ /x \,\}\ )\ /\ x\ \}\ \ \mathit{else}\ \ \mathit{wrong}$$

$$\mathrm{resolve}\!:\ (\mathbf{O},\ \mathbf{Id}) \to\ \ \mathbf{Openv} \to \mathbf{V}$$

$$\mathrm{resolve}\ (\omega_1 \times \ldots \times \omega_n \to \omega_r\ ,\ x)\ \ \vartheta =$$
$$\lambda(v_1,\ldots,v_n).\ \mathit{if}\ \exists\ c \in C.\ \omega_i = \$ \Rightarrow v_i \in S_c(\mathbf{V}^{a(c)})$$
$$\mathit{then}\ (\ (\vartheta\ x)\ c\ \vartheta)\ \ (v_1,\ldots,v_n)$$
$$\mathit{else}\ \ \mathit{wrong}$$

Rather than delving into the details of this denotational semantics, we give a theorem stating the relationship between compile time and runtime overloading resolution, namely that runtime overloading resolution delivers the same results, apart from possibly introducing nontermination.

Theorem: $\mathcal{E}'$ *weakly implements* $\mathcal{E} \cdot \mathcal{R}$

Let $\langle O,A \rangle \vdash M^{\tau}$ be a well typing , $\eta' \in$ **Env'**, $\vartheta \in$ **Openv**, $\eta \in$ **Env** and $\rho \in$ **Renv**.

If $x : \sigma \in A \Rightarrow\ \mathcal{E}'[\![x]\!]\eta'\ \vartheta \sqsubseteq \mathcal{E}[\![\ \mathcal{R}[\![x^{\tau'}]\!]\rho\ ]\!]\eta$ for every $\tau' <_o \sigma$

then $\mathcal{E}'[\![M]\!]\eta'\ \vartheta \sqsubseteq \mathcal{E}[\![\ \mathcal{R}[\![\ M^{\tau}]\!]\ ]\!]\ \eta$.

5 Final Remarks

We have shown that the restriction to parametric overloading results in rather simple and efficient tpye-inference algorithms, while still allowing the specification of many useful overloaded functions. Moreover, it turns out, that overloading resolution is possible either statically, thus yielding no runtime overhead at all, or dynamically (at runtime), which is particularly advantagous in the context of a language incorporating a module concept. Indeed, any sensible mixture of the two strategies can be used in a specific implementation.

On the other hand, one may object that the restriction imposed on the set of possible overloadings is to severe, disallowing some useful overloaded operations. Although we do not share this opinion, we suppose that it is possible to integrate unrestricted with parametric overloading, using the framework of *context relations* described in [BaSne86].

We have successfully used parametric overloading in developing the predefined operations of the functional programming language SAMPLE (see [JGK87] for some details of the type system). Having used the SAMPLE environment for over a year in a number of projects, our personal experience shows that the inclusion of parametric overloading has significantly improved the usability and type security of SAMPLE. Our next step will therefore be the integration of user definable overloading for operations on abstract data types, along the lines outlined in chapter 4.2 and 4.3.

A number of possible extensions to parametric overloading have not been discussed here, partly due to space limitations, partly because their inclusion would have over complicated the presentation. First, it is possible to combine parametric overloading with the subtyping displicines of [Mitchell84], [Letsch86] and [FuhMi87] (we have actually implemented a type inference algorithm handling both concepts for the SAMPLE language). Second, the set of possible overloading schemes can be extended to cope with overloadings such as $\forall\alpha.\ \alpha \times \$(\alpha) \rightarrow$ bool, where \$ can appear as a typeconstructor. A main application of this kind of overloading is the member function, with the typeset { $\forall\alpha.\alpha \times$ list(α) $\rightarrow$ bool, $\forall\alpha.\alpha \times$ set(α) $\rightarrow$ bool, ... }. Third, one can devise a scheme which removes the strictness restriction from runtime overloading resolution by implicitly adding type parameters to overloaded functions.

References:

[ASU86] A.V. Aho, R. Sethi and J.D. Ullman: *Compilers: Principles, Techniques, and Tools*, p384, 1986.

[BaSne86] R. Bahlke and G. Snelting: *The PSG-System: From Formal Language Definitions to Interactive Programming Environments*, TOPLAS 8,4, p547-576, October 1986.

[BMQS80] R. Burstall, D.B. MacQueen and D. Sanella: *HOPE: An Experimental Applicative Language*, 1st International LISP Conference, Stanford 1986.

[Coppo80] M. Coppo: *An Extended Polymorphic Type System for Applicative Languages*, LNCS 88, p194-204, September 1980.

[DaMi82] L. Damas and R.Milner: *Principal Type Schemes for Functional Programs*, IX POPL, p207, January 1982.

[CDDK86] D. Clement, J. Despeyroux, T. Despeyroux and G. Kahn: *A simple applicative language: Mini-ML*, 1986 ACM Symposium on LISP and Functional Programming, p13-27, 1986.

[FuhMi87] Y. Fuh and P. Mishra: *Type Inference With Subtypes*, Manuscript, SUNY at Stony Brook, July 1987.

[JGK87] M. Jäger, M. Gloger and S. Kaes: *SAMPLE - A Functional Language*, Report PI-R5/87, TH-Darmstadt, Fachbereich Informatik.

[Kaes87] S. Kaes: *Parametric Overloading in Polymorphic Programming Languages*, Report PI-R7/87, TH-Darmstadt, Fachbereich Informatik.

[Letsch86] T. Letschert: *Typinferenzsysteme*, Doctoral Thesis, TH Darmstadt, Fachbereich Informatik, 1986.

[Milner78] R. Milner: *A Theory of Type Polymorphism in Programming*, JCCS 17,3, p348-375, 1978.

[Milner84] R. Milner: *A Proposal for Standard ML*, 1984 ACM Symposium on LISP and Functional Programming, p184-197, Austin, August 1984.

[Mitchell84] J.C. Mitchell: *Coercion and Type Inference*, XI POPL, p175-185, 1984.

[MQPS84] D.B. MacQueen, G.D. Plotkin and R. Sethi: *An Ideal Model for Recursive Polymorphic Types*, XI POPL, p165-174, 1984.

[Str67] C. Strachey: *Fundamental Concepts in Programming Languages*, International Summer School in Computer Programming, Kopenhagen 1967.

[Turner85] D.A. Turner: *Miranda: A non-strict Functional Language with Polymorphic Types*, LNCS 201, September 1985.

PROGRAMMING WITH PROOFS: A SECOND ORDER TYPE THEORY

Michel PARIGOT
Equipe de Logique, CNRS UA 753
Université Paris 7, UFR de Mathématiques,
2 place Jussieu, 75251 PARIS Cedex 05

Abstract

We discuss the possibility to construct a programming language in which we can program by proofs, in order to ensure program correctness. The logical framework we use is presented in [13].

The main objection to that kind of approach to programming being the inefficiency of the program produced by proofs, the greater part of the paper is devoted to investigate how to define data types and how to construct programs for combining proofs and efficiency. Several solutions are proposed using recursive data types which lead, in particular, to new representations of natural numbers in lambda-calculus.

Introduction: proofs as programs.

We know that in mathematics the problem of the correctness has been solved for a long time: the correctness of a (detailed) proof is easy to verify, even automatically. We also know that a constructive proof of a theorem has an algorithmic content. Putting these two facts together, we are tempted to consider **(formalized) mathematics as a programming language**. This would mean that writing a program satisfying some specifications becomes writing a proof of a statement expressing these specifications.

The theoretical basis of this approach exists: it can be found in the works of logicians on intuitionistic logic, essentially HEYTING, MARTIN-LOF and GIRARD. The **Heyting semantics** for intuitionistic logic explains proofs in terms of programs, and if we invert the perspective it gives a foundation for a programming language where programs are proofs (the essential point in this semantics is that a proof of $A \to B$ is an algorithm which transform each proof of A into a proof of B.).

There has been a lot of works using this principle, mainly N.G. deBRUIJN [2], R.L. CONSTABLE [5], J.C. REYNOLDS [19], T. COQUAND [3]. We will discuss here an other approach presented in [11] and [13], based on second order intuitionistic logic, which allows to write in a natural way exact specifications and correct programs.

The paper is organized as follows. In §1 we recall the general theory:

syntactic and semantic notions of type; definition of data types by second order formulas and extraction by proof of a representation of the data from the definition; expression of the specifications of a program and extraction by proof of a program which meets these specifications. In §2 we discuss the problem of efficiency and conclude to the necessity of new representations of data. In §3 we presents two kind of solutions using recursive definition of data types, which leads to new representations of the data allowing to write efficient programs: in particular we obtain new representations of natural numbers in lambda-calculus for which there exists a program computing the predecessor in one step. Finally we present in §4 a way of programming by proofs with these recursive data types.

1. INTUITIONISTIC SECOND ORDER LOGIC AS A PROGRAMMING LANGUAGE

1.1 Lambda-calculus as a machine language

To really become programs, proofs which naturally appear as trees, have to be linearly coded as terms of lambda-calculus.

The **terms** of lambda-calculus are obtained from variables x,y,z... by a finite number of applications of the following rules:

(a) if t and u are terms, then (t u) is a term - which represents the application of the function t to the argument u.

(b) if x is a variable and t is a term, then $\lambda x.t$ is a term - which represents the function $x \mapsto t$.

The notion of **computation** for terms is the reduction: a reduction in the term t is the replacement of the leftmost subterm of the form $(\lambda x.u\ v)$ by $u[v/x]$ (i.e the result of substituting v to the occurrences of x in u). We say that a term t is reducible to a term t' (and note $t \Rightarrow t'$) if t' is obtained from t by a finite number of reductions. A term is normal if it does not contain a subterm of the form $(\lambda x.u\ v)$. In order to compute a function t on an argument u we reduce the term (t u); there are two possibilities: either we obtain, after a finite number of reductions, a normal term which is called the result of the computation, or there is an infinite number of possible reductions and the computation does not terminate. Using this notion of computation, all the recursive functions are representable by terms of the lambda-calculus.

It is possible to transform lambda-calculus in a programming language using an implementation of reduction. In fact it can be considered as a real machine language, where the symbols of lambda-calculus (,λ,x are interpreted as elementary instructions. Such an implementation has been realized by J.L. KRIVINE.

1.2. The logical framework

The logical language contains logical symbols, fixed parameters, and additional parameters depending of the data types we consider. The logical symbols are: the connective $\rightarrow$, the quantifier $\forall$, individual variables: x, y, z ..., predicate variables of arbitrary arity: X,Y,Z... . The fixed parameters are: a binary function constant **Ap** (application) and two individual constants **K**,**S** (combinators). Additional parameters contains predicate constants of arbitrary arity (predicate constants of arity 0 are called propositional constants), and function constants of arbitrary arity (function constants of arity 0 are called individual constants).

The individual terms and the (second order) formulas are defined in the usual way using this logical language. Note that in second order (intuitionistic) logic, the logical symbols $\bot,\wedge,\vee,\neg$ and $\exists$, as well as the identity relation $=$, are definable from $\rightarrow$ and $\forall$: for instance $A \wedge B$ is defined by $\forall X[[A \rightarrow [B \rightarrow X]] \rightarrow X]$.

The intended model $\mathcal{M}$, representing the programs from a denotational point of view, is the following. The universe is the set Λ of terms of lambda-calculus modulo reduction (more precisely modulo $\beta\eta$-reduction). The function **Ap** is interpreted by the function $u,v \longmapsto (u\ v)$. The constants **K** and **S** are interpreted by $\lambda x.\lambda y.x$ and $\lambda x.\lambda y.\lambda z.((x\ z)\ (y\ z))$ respectively. This model is in fact the usual way of coding lambda-calculus into a logical structure used in Combinatory Logic; it will be enriched by interpretations of the additional parameters. In the sequel term will also mean term modulo reduction.

The rules of proof for second order logic are the following (A, B denotes formulas and Γ sequences of formulas):

R1 $A \vdash A$. (axiom)

R2 if $\Gamma, A \vdash B$, then $\Gamma \vdash A \rightarrow B$. (abstraction)

R3 if $\Gamma \vdash A \rightarrow B$ and $\Gamma \vdash A$, then $\Gamma \vdash B$. (application)

R4 if $\Gamma \vdash A$ and x is an individual variable which does not occur free in Γ, then $\Gamma \vdash \forall xA$. (generalisation)

R5 if $\Gamma \vdash \forall xA$ and b is an individual term, then $\Gamma \vdash A[b/x]$. (specialization)

R6 if $\Gamma \vdash A$ and X is a predicate variable which does not occur free in Γ, then $\Gamma \vdash \forall XA$. (generalisation)

R7 if $\Gamma \vdash \forall XA$ and B is a formula, then $\Gamma \vdash A[B/X]$. (specialization)

R8 if $\Gamma \vdash A$, and Δ is obtained from Γ by permutation, contraction or extension, then $\Delta \vdash A$. (this rule will be omitted in formal derivations)

R9 if $\Gamma \vdash \neg\neg A$, then $\Gamma \vdash A$ (RA)

The rules R1 to R8 are the rules for intuitionistic second order logic.

1.3 The syntactic notion of type.

From the point of view of Heyting semantics the rules of proof for intuitionistic logic can be considered as construction rules for programs (terms). Instead of handling formulas we handle expressions like t : A (read **t is a term of type A**), the hypothesis being replaced by variables declarations x : A. The rules become:

R1 $x : A \vdash x : A$.

R2 if Γ, $x : A \vdash t : B$, then $\Gamma \vdash \lambda x.t : A \to B$.

R3 if $\Gamma \vdash t : A \to B$ and $\Gamma \vdash u : A$, then $\Gamma \vdash (t\ u) : B$.

R4 if $\Gamma \vdash t : A$ and x is an individual variable which does not occur free in Γ, then $\Gamma \vdash t : \forall xA$.

R5 if $\Gamma \vdash t : \forall xA$ and b is an individual term, then $\Gamma \vdash t : A[b/x]$.

R6 if $\Gamma \vdash t : A$ and X is a predicate variable which does not occur free in Γ, then $\Gamma \vdash t : \forall XA$.

R7 if $\Gamma \vdash t : \forall XA$ and B is a formula, then $\Gamma \vdash t : A[B/X]$.

R8 if $\Gamma \vdash t : A$, and Δ is a sequence obtained from Γ by permutation, contraction or extension, then $\Delta \vdash t : A$.

From a programming point of view the expression "t is of type A", which relies a term to a formula, has to be read **"the program t realizes the specification A"**. Terms of lambda-calculus represent programs in machine language, whereas formu-las represent specifications expressed in a high level language. It remains to explain the relation between the program and the specification.

There are two well-known properties of terms obtained by proofs : **type preservation** and **termination**. The first one, which says that if a term t reduces to a term t' and t is of type A then t' is of type A, is essentially evident. The second one is much deeper: whereas the terms of lambda-calculus allow to represent all algorithms, including those which do not terminate, the terms obtained from proofs represent algorithm which always terminate. More precisely, each time we derive an expression "t : A" we are sure that t reduces to a normal term. This property becomes more and more difficult to prove when the expressive power of the logic increase (the proof for second order logic is due to GIRARD [7]).

There is one more essential property: second order intuitionistic logic can be considered as a programming language allowing to write **exact specifications and correct programs**. We will detail this point using a semantic notion of type.

1.4 The semantic notion of type.

The expression t : A (t is of type A) has been defined syntactically using the deduction rules for intuitionistic second order logic. But we can view a type A as a set, namely the set of terms of type A (or propositional traces of proofs of A). Doing so we can define a kind of intuitionistic semantic in the style of LAUCHLI [14]: a statement being interpreted by a subset of Λ (instead of a boolean value), a unary predicate by a function from Λ into $\mathcal{P}(\Lambda)$ (or equivalently by a binary relation on Λ),.... It can be defined using the classical semantic of formulas in the model Λ in the following way: we associate to each n-ary predicate variable X (resp. n-ary predicate constant P) a (n+1)-ary predicate variable X' (resp. (n+1)-ary predicate constant P'), and define inductively, for each formula A and variable y, a formula y ∈ A as follows

$$y \in \Pi x_1 \ldots x_n := \Pi' x_1 \ldots x_n y \quad \text{(for } \Pi' \text{ predicate variable or constant)}$$
$$y \in A \to B \quad := \forall z[z \in A \to (y\ z) \in B]$$
$$y \in \forall xA \quad := \forall x[y \in A]$$
$$y \in \forall XA \quad := \forall X'[y \in A]$$

Now we have a semantic notion of type t ∈ A ("t is in the type A") - meaning that the statement t ∈ A is true in the intended model. The following lemma shows that the semantic notion of type extends the syntactic one in the sense that all the programs typable from the syntactical point of view are also typable with the same type from the semantical point of view.

Conservation lemma: Let A be a statement. If t : A, then t ∈ A.

The equality between types, A = B, is defined as $\forall y[y \in A \leftrightarrow y \in B]$.

1.5 Definition of data types.

The second order formalism allows natural definitions for all the data types usually defined by induction: integers, lists, trees .... For instance, the set of natural numbers can be defined as "the smallest set containing zero and closed by the successor operation". Formally we introduce parameters for the constructors of the type: an individual constant $\underline{0}$ (for zero) and a function constant $\underline{s}$ (for the successor operation), and consider the formula Ix saying "x is a natural number"

$$\forall X[\forall y[Xy \to X\underline{s}y],\ X\underline{0} \to Xx].$$

(we use A, B → C as an abbreviation for A → [B → C])

A representation of the constructor $\underline{0}$ in lambda-calculus is given by a term in the type $I\underline{0}$; it can be obtain by a formal derivation of $I\underline{0}$

$$f : \forall y[Xy \to X\underline{s}y],\ a : X\underline{0} \vdash a : X\underline{0} \qquad \text{(by R1)}$$
$$f : \forall y[Xy \to X\underline{s}y],\ \vdash \lambda a.a : X\underline{0} \to X\underline{0} \qquad \text{(by R2)}$$
$$\vdash \lambda f.\lambda a.a : \forall y[Xy \to X\underline{s}y],\ X\underline{0} \to X\underline{0} \qquad \text{(by R2)}$$
$$\vdash \lambda f.\lambda a.a : \forall X[\forall y[Xy \to X\underline{s}y],\ X\underline{0} \to X\underline{0}] \qquad \text{(by R6)}$$

We obtain the representation $0 = \lambda f.\lambda x.x$ for the constructor $\underline{0}$, which is precisely the Church numeral 0.

A representation of the constructor $\underline{s}$ in lambda-calculus is given by a term in the type $\forall x[Ix \to I\underline{s}x]$; it can be obtained by a formal derivation of $\forall x[Ix \to I\underline{s}x]$.

Let ν : Ix. We look for a term of type $I\underline{s}x$, i.e. $\forall X[\forall y[Xy \to X\underline{s}y], X\underline{0} \to X\underline{s}x]$. Let f : $\forall y[Xy \to X\underline{s}y]$, and a : $X\underline{0}$. In this context we have ν : $\forall y[Xy \to X\underline{s}y], X\underline{0} \to Xx$ and therefore (ν f a) : Xx; because f : $\forall y[Xy \to X\underline{s}y]$, we have also (f ($\nu$ f a)) : $X\underline{s}x$. Finally $\lambda\nu.\lambda f.\lambda x.(f\ (\nu\ f\ a))$: $\forall x[Ix \to I\underline{s}x]$.

We obtain the representation $s = \lambda\nu.\lambda f.\lambda x.(f\ (\nu\ f\ a))$ for the constructor $\underline{s}$, which is precisely a term for the successor function on the Church numerals.

Now we can complete our intended model by interpreting $\underline{0}$ by 0 and $\underline{s}$ by the function generated by s. The crucial property is that the Church numeral $(s^n\ 0)$ is the unique term of type $I\underline{s}^n\underline{0}$. More precisely we define a **formal data type** as a formula A[x] such that there is an interpretation of individual and function constants such that the following holds in the model:

$$y \in A[x] \leftrightarrow y = x \wedge A[x].$$

It is readily seen that Ix is a formal data type. In fact all the usual data types can be defined by formal data types.

1.6 Logic as a high level programming language.

In order to program a function between data types (say the predecessor function from I to I), we have to

(a) introduce a function constant $\underline{p}$.

(b) find a set of equations which uniquely determine $\underline{p}$ on I, for example $\underline{p}\underline{0} = \underline{0}$ and $\underline{p}\underline{s}x = x$, and interpret $\underline{p}$ by a function satisfying these equations.

(c) derive a term of type $\forall x(Ix \to I\underline{p}x)$ using the previous set of equations.

Why do we obtain in that way a program for the predecessor function? Consider a term t of type $\forall x(Ix \to I\underline{p}x)$ and a term u satisfying Ix; because Ix is a formal data type, we have (t u) = p[u]; therefore t is a program for the function p on I and thus for the predecessor function.

This programming method extends to all the usual data types. The correctness of the programs is ensured by the way we derive them (we just have to verify that the deduction rules are well applied, and this can be checked automatically).

Example: a program for the addition

We introduce a binary function constant $\oplus$, and the usual equations defining addition: $x \oplus \underline{0} = x$, $x \oplus \underline{s}y = \underline{s}[x \oplus y]$. Then we look for a term t of type $\forall x \forall y[Ix, Iy \to I[x \oplus y]]$.

Let ν : Ix, μ : Iy, f : $\forall y[Xy \to X\underline{s}y]$, and a : $X\underline{0}$; we have to find a term of type $X[x \oplus y]$ in this context; we proceed by induction i.e. we look for terms of

type $X[x \oplus 0]$ and $\forall z[X[x \oplus z] \to X[x \oplus \underline{s}z]]$.
Clearly (ν f x) is of type Xx and thus of type $X[x \oplus \underline{0}]$ (by the first equation). By R5 and R4, f is of type $\forall z[X[x \oplus z] \to X\underline{s}[x \oplus z]]$ and by the second equation of type $\forall z[X[x \oplus z] \to X[x \oplus \underline{s}z]]$. By R7, with $B = X[x \oplus .]$, μ is of type $\forall z[X[x \oplus z] \to X[x \oplus \underline{s}z]], X[x \oplus \underline{0}] \to X[x \oplus y]$.
Therefore (μ f (ν f x)) is of type $X[x \oplus y]$. Finally $\lambda\nu.\lambda\mu.\lambda f.\lambda x.(\mu\ f\ (\nu\ f\ x))$ is of type $\forall x\forall y[Ix, Iy \to I[x \oplus y]]$ and thus a program for addition.

2. THE QUESTION OF EFFICIENCY

Intuitionistic logic certainly provides a programming language allowing to write exact specifications and correct programs. But doing so, correctness has a counterpart: programs are often not efficient. There is first a practical reason: programming being reduced to the search of proofs, one can write programs without thinking at "how the program works". But in fact, inefficiency is the main objection to the "programming by proof" approach: we can distinguish three theoretical sources of inefficiency:

(i) the better proofs from a conceptual point of view are not necessary the better ones from an algorithmic point of view.

(ii) the efficient algorithms of pure lambda-calculus do not always come from proofs, even in second order intuitionistic logic.

(iii) the efficient algorithms are not always expressible in pure lambda-calculus.

The order in which these problems are enumerated indicates the increasing difficulties to find remedies for them. The first one does not call our approach in question: it just says that we must learn what are the best proofs from an algorithmic point of view (for instance, an immoderate use of proofs by induction can lead to disastrous algorithms). The second one objects to the choice of the high level language: the crude version of second order intuitionistic logic does not provide a real programming language, and we must at least construct more elaborate versions. The third one is a priori more worrying: our machine language seems too weak; fortunatly there is another possible diagnosis: the existence of some algorithms depends on the coding of the data in lambda-calculus. Let us give simple examples for the last two problems.
In order to program the inf of two natural numbers we have to deduce the statement "if x and y are natural numbers, then inf[x,y] is a natural number" from the set of equations defining the inf; doing this we must choose x or y as base of the induction; if for instance we choose x, then the resulting program will need at least 512 steps to compute inf[512,0]! In fact there exists a program in lambda-calculus

which computes inf[x,y] in inf[x,y] steps, but it doesn't come from a proof (thisresult is proved in J.L. KRIVINE [12]).
The situation get worse if we try to construct a program computing the predecessor of a natural number. The classical definition of natural numbers by induction gives the Church numerals (which are of the form $\lambda f.\lambda x.(f^n\ x)$); whereas the program for the successor function is obtained by a direct proof, all the programs for the predecessor function require a proof by induction, which means from an algorithmic point of view that the computation of the predecessor of 512 uses at least 512 steps! Moreover, the proof by induction which gives a "bad" algorithm is essentially the only possible one, and even in pure lambda-calculus no better algorithm exists.The same phenomena appears for all the usual data types: we are in the situation of a LISP language without direct access to the **cdr** of the lists (each time we need to recalculate the entire list). Such a situation become disastrous when we execute complicated programs such as sorting programs where the call to the **cdr** is iterated.

How to solve these basic difficulties without destroying the essential, i.e. programming with proofs in order to obtain correct programs? There are at least two ways that give enought new algorithms: we can either extend lambda-calculus, or change the definition of the data types. Here we will take the second way and present a solution based on the semantic notion of type. Because of lack of space, we only investigate the example of the predecessor.

3. RECURSIVE DATA TYPES

We look for definitions of data types satisfying the following requirements:

(a) the definition must be a formal data type in order to obtain correct programs.

(b) the representation of data must allow efficient programming (in particular direct access to **cdr**).

(c) the formula defining the data type must remain closely related to our intuition of the data type.

Two kinds of solutions have a particular interest: we will present them for the type of natural numbers, but they easely extend to all usual data types. They are based on a deep use of the semantic notion of type: instead of considering a type as a formula, we will consider a type as predicate defined by axioms.

3.1 The type Number

We introduce a unary predicate constant **N** and two constructors $\underline{0}$ (for zero) and $\underline{\sigma}$ (for the successor function). We define the intuitionistic interpretation $y \in \mathbf{N}x$ of the type Number $\mathbf{N}$ as the minimal solution K of the equation

$$Kx = \forall X[\forall y[Ky, Xy \to X\underline{\sigma}y], X\underline{0} \to Xx]$$

Note that because K occurs positively in $\forall X[\forall y[Ky, Xy \to X\underline{\sigma}y], X\underline{0} \to Xx]$,this solution exists.

One possible motivation for this recursive definition of the type Number is the following: the equation $\mathbf{N}x = \forall X[\forall y[\mathbf{N}y, Xy \to X\underline{\sigma}y], X\underline{0} \to Xx]$ is a possible formulation of induction where the induction step is not formulated for arbitrary elements but just for natural numbers.

<u>Representation of the constructors</u>.

A representation 0 of the constructor $\underline{0}$ in lambda-calculus is given by a term in the type $\mathbf{N}\underline{0}$, i.e. in the type $\forall X[\forall y[\mathbf{N}y, Xy \to X\underline{\sigma}y], X\underline{0} \to X\underline{0}]$. Clearly $\lambda f.\lambda a.a$ is in this type, and we have the same representation as for the type Iterator.

A representation σ of the constructor $\underline{\sigma}$ in lambda-calculus is given by a term in $\forall x[\mathbf{N}x \to \mathbf{N}\underline{\sigma}x]$. Let $\nu \in \mathbf{N}x$, $f \in \forall y[\mathbf{N}y, Xy \to X\underline{\sigma}y]$ and $a \in X\underline{0}$; then $(\nu\ f\ a) \in Xx$ and $(f\ \nu) \in Xx \to X\underline{\sigma}x$; therefore $((f\ \nu)\ (\nu\ f\ a)) \in X\underline{\sigma}x$ and finally $\lambda\nu.\lambda f.\lambda a.((f\ \nu)\ (\nu\ f\ a)) \in \forall x[\mathbf{N}x \to \mathbf{N}\underline{\sigma}x]$.

We complete our intended model by interpreting $\underline{0}$ by 0 and $\underline{\sigma}$ by the function generated by σ. Because we have a predicate instead of a formula we must also define the classical interpretation $\mathbf{N}x$ of the type Number $\mathbf{N}$. Of course, we take "the smallest set containing 0 and closed by the function generated by σ"; this mean that the following holds in the model: $\mathbf{N}x \leftrightarrow \forall X[\forall y[Xy \to X\underline{s}y], X\underline{0} \to Xx]$. It is easy to see that with this interpretation $\mathbf{N}x$ is a formal data type.

<u>An equivalent definition of the type Number</u>.

We can give an inductive definition of the type Number using a universal formal data type $\mathbf{U}$ defined as follows: the intuitionistic interpretation is defined in the model by $\forall x \forall y[x \in \mathbf{U}y \leftrightarrow x = y]$, and the classical one is just Λ (note that this type is not syntactically definable). The new definition of the type Number $\mathbf{N}x$ is just $\forall X[\forall y[\mathbf{U}y, Xy \to X\underline{\sigma}y], X\underline{0} \to Xx]$.

This definition gives a new intuition of the type Number: take the definition Ix of the type of iterators but replace the trivial interpretation of the universal quantification by the traditional constructivist one: a proof of $\forall xA$ is a function which associates to each element u of the domain a proof of $A[u/x]$.

<u>Example</u>: a program for the predecessor

The type Number has an essential property which is due to its recursive definition: there exists a program which <u>compute the predecessor in one step</u> (to be more precise: by five elementary reductions). We introduce a new function constant $\underline{q}$ and two axioms which define $\underline{q}$ semantically

$\underline{q}\underline{0} = \underline{0}$

$\underline{q}\underline{\sigma}x = x$

We have to find a term t ∈ ∀x[Nx → N$\underline{q}$x]. Let ν ∈ Nx; by specialization to N$\underline{q}$., we obtain ν ∈ [∀y[Ny, N$\underline{q}$y → N$\underline{q}\underline{\sigma}$y], N$\underline{q}\underline{0}$ → N$\underline{q}$x], and by the equations

ν ∈ [∀y[Ny, N$\underline{q}$y → Ny], N$\underline{0}$ → N$\underline{q}$x].

Clearly λx.λy.x ∈ ∀y[Ny, N$\underline{q}$y → Ny] and λx.λy.y ∈ N$\underline{0}$;

therefore (ν λx.λy.x λx.λy.y) ∈ N$\underline{q}$x and λν.(ν λx.λy.x λx.λy.y) ∈ ∀x(Nx → N$\underline{q}$x).

Example: inductive programming on the type number.

Though the type Number has a recursive definition it allows to program using proofs by induction. As an example we will construct a program which translates numbers into iterators. We introduce an unary function constant $\underline{h}$ and axioms semantically defining $\underline{h}$

$\underline{h}\underline{0} = \underline{0}$

$\underline{h}\underline{\sigma}x = \underline{s}\underline{h}x$

We have to find a term t ∈ ∀x(Nx → I$\underline{h}$x). Let ν ∈ Nx. By specialization to I$\underline{h}$., we obtain ν ∈ [∀y[Ny, I$\underline{h}$y → I$\underline{h}\underline{\sigma}$y], I$\underline{h}\underline{0}$ → I$\underline{h}$x] and using the equations ν ∈ [∀y[Ny, I$\underline{h}$y → I$\underline{s}\underline{h}$y], I$\underline{0}$ → I$\underline{h}$x]. We have λu.λv.(s v) ∈ ∀y[Ny, I$\underline{h}$y → I$\underline{s}\underline{h}$y] and λf.λx.x ∈ I$\underline{0}$. Therefore (ν λu.λv.(s v) λf.λx.x) ∈ I$\underline{h}$x and λν.(ν λu.λv.(s v) λf.λx.x) is the term we looked for.

A comparison.

There is an interesting formal analogy between this new representation of the natural numbers and the Von Neumann's representation of natural numbers in Set Theory:

n+1 in Lambda-calculus λf.λx.(f n (n f x))

n+1 in Set Theory {n} ∪ n

In the first part of the representation of n+1, we have n as a complete entity, whereas in the second part n is executed: it is precisely the first part of the representation which allows to compute directly the predecessor.

From a computational point of view, this representation has an apparent inconvenient from the programming point of vue: as for the Von Neumann's representation, the developed form of the natural number n has lenght 2^n. We will see later that this is no real problem; however, it would be nice to have a type for natural numbers with direct access to the predecessor and a developed representation of n of lenght n. This is in fact possible: in the same way the iterators are obtained from the numbers by just keeping the second part of the representation, we can obtain other natural numbers (called "stacks"), which will have the required properties, by just keeping the first part of the representation.

3.2 The type Stack

We introduce a unary predicate constant S and two constructors $\underline{0}$ (for zero) and $\underline{\tau}$ (for the successor function). We define the intuitionistic interpretation $y \in Sx$ of the type Stack S as the minimal solution K of the equation

$$Kx = \forall X[\forall y[Ky \to X\underline{\tau}y],\ X\underline{0} \to Xx]$$

Note that the definitions of the types Iterator and Stack are both obtained from that of the type Number by removing a part of the definition: either Ky or Xy.

Representation of the constructors.

The representation of the constructors of the type Stack is obtained as for the type Number: the representations of $\underline{0}$ and $\underline{\tau}$ are respectively $0 = \lambda f.\lambda a.a$ and $\tau = \lambda\nu.\lambda f.\lambda a.(f\ \nu)$. We interpret $\underline{0}$ by 0 and $\underline{\tau}$ by the function generated by τ, and define the classical interpretation Sx of the type Stack in the model by: $Sx \leftrightarrow \forall X[\forall y[Xy \to X\underline{\tau}y],\ X\underline{0} \to Xx]$. With this interpretation, Sx is a formal data type.

Example: a program for the predecessor

We introduce a new function constant $\underline{r}$ and two axioms which define $\underline{r}$ semantically: $\underline{r0} = \underline{0}$ and $\underline{r\tau}x = x$.

We have to find a term $t \in \forall x[Sx \to S\underline{\tau}x]$. Let $\nu \in Sx$; by specialization to $S\underline{r}$. we obtain $\nu \in [\forall y[Sy \to S\underline{r\tau}y],\ S\underline{r0} \to S\underline{r}x]$, and by the equations

$$\nu \in [\forall y[Sy \to Sy],\ S\underline{0} \to S\underline{r}x].$$

Clearly $\lambda x.x \in [\forall y[Sy \to Sy]$ and $\lambda x.\lambda y.y \in S\underline{0}$;

therefore $(\nu\ \lambda x.x\ \lambda y.\lambda x.y) \in S\underline{r}x$ and $\lambda\nu.(\nu\ \lambda x.x\ \lambda y.\lambda x.y) \in \forall x(Sx \to S\underline{r}x)$.

In the case of stacks we again obtain a program which compute the predecessor in one step, and this time we have a representation of lenght n for the natural number n. There is however an apparent problem: how can we make proofs by induction with this purely recursive definition of the type?

4. PROGRAMMING USING RECURSIVE DATA TYPES

In the case where a type is defined by induction, like the type Iterator, we obtain directly a term for the proofs by induction. For instance the term $ind = \lambda x.\lambda f.\lambda\nu.(\nu\ f\ x)$ is in the type $\forall X[X0,\ \forall y[Xy \to X\underline{s}y] \to \forall x[Ix \to Xx]]$, and comes directly from a proof of this statement. But for types having a purely recursive definition, we have to construct such a term using a metareasoning.

Induction on the type Stack

We look for a term rec in the type $\forall X[X0,\ \forall y[Xy \to X\underline{\tau}y] \to \forall x[Sx \to Xx]]$;

assuming $\alpha \in X0$ et $\beta \in \forall y[Xy \to X\underline{r}y]$, we have to find a term γ in the type $\forall x[Sx \to Xx]$.

<u>lemma</u>: if γ satisfies the equations

$$(\gamma\ 0) = \alpha$$
$$(\gamma\ \underline{r}y) = (\beta\ (\gamma\ y)),$$

then $\gamma \in \forall x[Sx \to Xx]$.

<u>proof</u>. We have to prove that $(\gamma\ y) \in Xx$ follows from the hypothesis $y \in Sx$; because Sx is a formal data type, it suffices to prove that $(\gamma\ x) \in Xx$ follows from the hypothesis Sx, or equivalently from the hypothesis $\forall X[\forall y[Xy \to X\underline{r}y], X\underline{0} \to Xx]$. We proceed by induction (formally this means that we specialize the previous formula to $(\gamma\ .) \in X.$): for $x = 0$, the first equation gives the result; now assume that $(\gamma\ y) \in Xy$; because $\beta \in \forall y[Xy \to X\underline{r}y]$ we have $(\beta\ (\gamma\ y)) \in X\underline{r}y$ and by the second equation $(\gamma\ \underline{r}y) \in X\underline{r}y$.

It remains to find γ satisfying the equations of the lemma. Because elements of the type Stack are binary functions, we look for a term γ of the form $\lambda x.t[(x\ \rho\ \iota)]$ where t,ρ,ι are unknown (intuitively, ι is the initial condition and ρ the recursive one). It follows

$$(\gamma\ \underline{0}) = t[(\underline{0}\ \rho\ \iota)] = t[\iota]$$
$$(\gamma\ \underline{r}y) = t[(\underline{r}y\ \rho\ \iota)] = t[(\rho\ y)]$$

and the equations become

$$t[\iota] = \alpha$$
$$t[(\rho\ y)] = (\beta\ t[(y\ \rho\ \iota)]).$$

Because ρ appears in the second part of the equation, we will have a recursive call of ρ. The simplest possible form for t is $t[z] = (z\ \rho)$. In this case the equations are

$$(\iota\ \rho) = \alpha$$
$$(\rho\ y\ \rho) = (\beta\ (y\ \rho\ \iota\ \rho)).$$

We can take

$$\iota = \lambda d.\alpha$$
$$\rho = \lambda y.\lambda r.(\beta\ (y\ r\ \iota\ r)).$$

Finally we have $\gamma = \lambda x.(x\ \rho\ \iota\ \rho)$, with the previous values for ρ and ι.

<u>Example</u>.

Having the possibility of reasoning by induction on stacks, we are able to construct all the programs we want using the general method presented for the type iterator. As an example we give a program translating stacks into iterators. Consider a unary function constant f and the following set of equations which semantically define the translation

$f\underline{0} = \underline{0}$

$f\underline{\tau}x = \underline{s}fx$.

We have to find a term t in $\forall x[Sx \rightarrow Ifx]$. It follows directly from the equations that

$0 \in If\underline{0}$

$s \in \forall y[Ify \rightarrow If\underline{\tau}y]$.

(recall that 0 and s are the programs for the constructors of the type I)

Therefore $\lambda x.(x\ \rho\ 0\ \rho)$ with $\rho = \lambda y.\lambda r.(s\ (y\ r\ 0\ r)$ is in the type $\forall x[Sx \rightarrow Ifx]$.

Two kinds of induction on the type Number.

In the case of the type **N**, we have two terms for proofs by induction, which gives two completely different programming methods. The first one, which is the analogue of the term ind for the type I, follows the inductive definition of the type **N**: a direct proof shows that $\lambda x.\lambda f.\lambda \nu.(\nu\ \lambda d.f\ x)$ is in the type $\forall X[X\underline{0}, \forall y[Xy \rightarrow X\underline{\tau}y] \rightarrow \forall x[Ix \rightarrow Xx]]$. The second one is obtained using the same reasoning as in the case of the term rec for the type **S**, and has the same recursive nature: this term is $\lambda x.\lambda f.\lambda \nu.(\nu\ \rho\ \iota\ \rho)$, with $\iota = \lambda d.x$ and $\rho = \lambda y.\lambda z.\lambda r.(f\ (y\ r\ \iota\ r))$.

Therefore, for the type number we can choose, depending of the function we want to compute, either an inductive programming method or a recursive one or even mix them together, and this flexibility increases our ability to write efficient programs.

We will now briefly explain why the fact that the number n has a normal representation of lenght 2^n is not an objection for programming. We have to distinguish between execution (which is not a rewriting for the implementation we have in mind) and output storage. For input and output, we can choose a representation of lenght n for the number n, for instance $(\sigma^n\ 0)$. During the execution the developped form of n, which is a binary tree of height n, never appears: execution corresponds to a run along a branch of the tree (the two programming methods correspond to runs along the left-most branch and the right-most branch).

A TEMPORARY CONCLUSION

In the case of inductively defined data types, it is possible to program just using proofs. But doing so we are condemned to write inefficient programs. On the other hand with recursive data types, we have to construct preliminary tools using a different method; but then we can write efficient programs just using proofs (and thus ensuring correctness).

Once we have found the term rec, we can give an alternative presentation of the type **S** in the style of P. MARTIN-LOF [16]:

S-introduction

$$0 \in S\underline{0} \qquad\qquad \frac{y \in Sx}{(\tau\ y) \in S\underline{\tau}y}$$

S-elimination

$$\frac{c \in Sx \qquad \alpha \in X\underline{0} \qquad \dfrac{u \in Xy}{(\beta\ u) \in X\underline{\tau}y}}{(\mathrm{rec}\ \alpha\ \beta\ c) \in Xx}$$

An essential difference with MARTIN-LOF's approach is that **the definition of the type S gives the implementation of 0, τ and rec**.

The point which seems to be a difficulty for programming with recursive data types in comparison with inductive data types, namely the fact that for each data type we have to construct preliminary tools like rec, can be overcome using an other programming method based on the universal data type **U** and a fixed point operator (see [18]).

BIBLIOGRAPHIE

[1] H.P. BARENDREGT, *The Lambda Calculus*, Studies in Logic, North-Holland, 1981.

[2] N. DE BRUIJN, *A survey of the project Automath*, to H.B. CURRY: essays on combinatory logic, λ-calculus and formalism, Seldin/Hindley (eds), pp 579-606, Academic Press, 1980.

[3] T. COQUAND, *Une théorie des constructions*, Thèse de 3eme cycle, Université Paris 7, 1985.

[4] T. COQUAND, G. HUET, *Constructions: a higher order proof system for mechanizing mathematics*, Proc. EUROCAL 85, LNCS 203.

[5] R.L. CONSTABLE et. al., *Implementing Mathematics with the Nuprl Proof Development System*, Prentice-Hall, 1986.

[6] G. COUSINEAU, P.L. CURIEN, M. MAUNY, *The categorical abstract machine*, LNCS 201, 1985.

[7] J.Y. GIRARD, *Une extension de l'interprétation de Gödel à l'analyse, et son application àl'élimination des coupures dans l'analyse et dans la théorie des types*, Proc. 2nd Scandinavian Logic Symp., pp 63-92, North-Holland, 1970.

[8] J.Y. GIRARD, *Interprétation fonctionnelle et élimination des coupures de l'arithmétique d'ordre supérieur*, Thèse d'état, Université Paris 7, 1972.

[9] J.Y. GIRARD, *The System F of variable types, fifteen years later*, Theoretical Computer Science, 1987.

[10] W.A. HOWARD, *The formulae as types notion of construction*, manuscript, 1969 (published in Seldin/Hindley (eds), To H.B. CURRY: essays on combinatory logic, λ-calculus and formalism, pp 479-490, Academic Press, 1980).

[11] J.L. KRIVINE, *Programmation en Arithmetique Fonctionnelle du Second Ordre*, manuscript.

[12] J.L. KRIVINE, *Un algorithme non typable dans le système F*, CRAS, 1987.

[13] J.L. KRIVINE, M. PARIGOT, *Programming with proofs*, preprint, presented at 6th Symposium on Computation Theory, Wendisch-Rietz, November 1987.

[14] H. LAUCHLI, *An abstract notion of realizability for which intuitionistic predicate calculus is complete*, in Kino/Myhill/vesley (eds), Intuitionism and proof theory, pp 227-234, North-Holland, 1970.

[15] P. MARTIN-LOF, *Constructive Mathematics and Computer programming*, Proc. 6th Cong. Logic, Methodology and Philosophy of Science, pp 153-175, North-Holland, 1982.

[16] P. MARTIN-LOF, *Intuitionistic type theory*, Bibliopolis, 1984.

[17] M. PARIGOT, *Preuves et programmes: les mathématiques comme langage de programmation*, *Images des Mathématiques*, Courrier du CNRS (à paraître).

[18] M. PARIGOT, *Recursive programming with proofs*, preprint, december 1987.

[19] J.R. REYNOLDS,*Three approaches to type structure*, LNCS 185, 1985, pp 97-138.

An Exception Handling Construct for Functional Languages

Manfred Bretz, Jürgen Ebert
EWH Koblenz, Informatik
D-5400 Koblenz/West Germany

1. Introduction and Overview

Exception handling is a way of dealing with situations at program runtime, which could affect program reliability. Exception handling covers error handling and error recovery, as well as programming techniques for dealing with legal but presumably rare, thus "exceptional", situations.

Even for conventional (von Neumann-) languages there are relatively few workable approaches to this problem, compared to the overwhelming number of papers on other program constructs. Only a few languages have a construct for exception handling, the most important being PL/I [19], ADA [16] and CLU [15]. Basic conceptual work on exception handling has been done by Cristian [4,5], Goodenough [9] and Yemini&Berry [21,22].

The so-called replacement model of Yemini and Berry seems to be the most powerful approach, since it allows a variety of handling options, like resuming the interrupted operation, retrying the interrupted operation in a changed state, or terminating the interrupted operation in a defined way. The model adopts an expression-oriented von Neumann view, using ALGOL 68 as the host language to carry the proposed constructs.

If a language is conformant to the paradigm of functional programming, there are some additional basic problems, when an exception handling construct is to be introduced:

a) There is a fundamental conflict between parallel/nondeterministic function evaluation on one hand and sequential/deterministic evaluation on the other hand (independent of which evaluation strategy is followed). If there are (e.g.) two exceptional points inside a given function the result of a corresponding parallel function application could be different, depending on which signal operation is executed first (e.g. using the language described below, the function

def f := λx.(**signal** I 3) + (**signal** I 5)

signals I;

in an application like

f(1) **handle** I:= λx.x **terminate**

could yield *3* or *5* as its result).

b) Exception handling might cause side effects in expression evaluation and hence might violate the property of referential transparency. Anything done by a handler to remove an exception occurrence within an expression is a side effect, since it depends on the environment in which the exception is evaluated instead of where it is defined.

c) Since there may be higher order functions, which yield functions as their results, an unrestricted use of exceptions may lead to situations where knowledge of which exceptions might be signalled inside a given expression might be lost.

Because of these difficulties today's functional programming languages do not have strong exception handling facilities, the only major exception being ML [18] where there is a raise/handle construct. But ML allows only for termination as the single handler response.

In this paper, we show how the approach of Yemini and Berry can be brought into the context of functional programming, thus allowing resume, retry and terminate as handler responses. While problem a) is intrinsic to exception handling (thus, ML has a sequential semantics, too), we solve problem b) by introducing handlers (to a certain extent) as additional function parameters where exceptions can only explicitly be transferred into a different environment, and deal with problem c) by using a strong but polymorphic typing approach to restrict the use of exception handling to those cases, where security can be achieved.

In section 2, we define a language construct for exception handling, by introducing a sample ISWIM-like [12] language, called ALEX, as the basis of the discussion. We give some examples to show the usefulness of the approach and to explain informally the meaning and intentions of the construct. In section 3, we give the concrete semantics of ALEX using the operational SECD approach of [11]. Section 4 contains the type inference rules, which are an extension of the usual (polymorphic) type system for functional languages by an additional exception type and its consistency conditions. We finish the paper with a detailed example.

ALEX has been implemented on a UNIX-based system using graph technology according to [8]. The translator, which translates a given ALEX program into an internal graph representation, is built using the compiler tools LEX and YACC [13,10]. The representation is a directed, attributed and ordered graph which represents the abstract syntax as well as the dataflow of the given functional program, also being the internal code on which the evaluator operates [6]. Type inference, derived from the rules below, is done by building an additional type subgraph to the functional graph using the same approach. The (functional) graph is taken as an input for a SECD-like graph interpreter which attributes values to its vertices according to [7].

ALEX, as described in the paper, is kept as simple as possible, since it is only used as a vehicle for describing the fundamental concepts and its formal background. Thus, the focus is not on pragmatics which are somewhat verbose for clarity's sake. But several practical extensions to ALEX are quite easy, some of which like

- multiple handlers
- default exception clauses
- unparameterized exceptions

have also been sucessfully added to the prototype implementation.

2. ALEX - An Applicative Language with a Language Construct for Exception Handling

This paper uses the applicative language ISWIM [12] to carry its exception handling proposal. The sample language is called ALEX. We present a decorated abstract syntax of ALEX, summarize the essentials of the exception handling construct and give three examples involving the construct.

2.1 Syntax

The language of ALEX expressions *expr* is given by the following decorated abstract syntax. The comments should help the reader to understand the intended meaning of the rules.

expr =

(a1) c
/* constant */

(a2) | id
/* identifier */

(a3) | "if" $expr_1$ "then" $expr_2$ "else" $expr_3$
/* conditional */

(a4) | $expr_1$ $expr_2$
/* application */

(a5) | expr_1 expr_2 "handle" handler
/* application with handler; associated with $expr_1$ may be an exception id in which case there must be a handler for id. */

(a6) | "λ" id "." expr
/* abstraction */

(a7) | "λ" id_1 "." expr "signals" id_2
/* abstraction with exception; the specified function may signal the exception id_2 i.e. may be a signaller. */

(a8) | "fix" id "." expr
/* fixpoint */

(a9) | "signal" id expr
/* signal; the exception id is signalled and $expr$ is the parameter of the signalled exception */

handler =

id_1 ":=" "λ" id_2 "." expr stat
/* $\lambda id_2.expr$ denotes the λ-expression (handler body) which is the paramerterized handler for the exception id_1 */

stat =

"resume"
| "retry"
| "terminate"

Remark:
We extend our notation by adding the ability to name ALEX-expressions. The syntax for definitions is: *"def" id ":=" expr ";"*. The definition facility is only introduced for abbrevation (and not for the definition of recursive functions).

2.2 Essentials of Exception Handling

The essential characteristics of the ALEX exception handling mechanism are [8,15,21]:

- Exceptions must be declared within the functions' interfaces.
- Handlers are statically bound to exceptions.
- The immediate invoker of a function is considered responsible to handle that function's exceptions.

- Exceptions can be propagated explicitly along the dynamic invocation chain.
- Resume, retry and terminate are the possible handler responses.
- Exceptions can be parameterized.

2.3 Examples

As an introduction to the exception handling mechanism we consider the following simple function abstraction:

```
def f := λx.if  x<0  then (signal I  x)>1
                     else true fi
          signals I;
```

Then, the function applications (a)-(c) yield the following results

(a) f(-5) **handle** I := λx.x+4 **resume**
The handler value *(λx.x+4)(-5) = -1* is calculated, and then the function f is resumed where it left off . Hence the result is *false*.

(b) f(-5) **handle** I := λx.x+4 **retry**
The handler value *(λx.x+4)(-5) = -1* is calculated, and then the function f is invoked again with -1 as new argument. This again leads to a signalling. Finally the result is *true* where two retries are done.

(c) f(-5) **handle** I := λx.false **terminate**
The handler value *(λx.false)(-5) = false* is calculated and is used as the value of the function application. Hence the result is *false*.

As a second, more instructive example the well-known curried while-functional

```
def while:= fix while.λp.λf.λx.if p(x) then (while p f) (f x)
                                 else x fi
```

may also be rewritten as a (functional) expression using the exception handling constructs:

```
def while1:= λp.(λx.if p(x) then (signal I x)
                        else x fi
                      signals I);
```

Assume that *pa* denotes an arbitrary predicate and *fa* an arbitrary function. Then, for all arguments *x* the evaluation of the expression

```
(while pa fa) (x)
```

yields the same result as the evaluation of the expression

```
(while1 pa) (x) handle I:= fa retry
```

As a third, more practical example, we develop a recursive ALEX function which converts a given sequence of integer numbers into a sequence of ASCII-characters [21,22]. The function takes as its input a list of integer numbers. For every list element the function tests whether there exists a corresponding ASCII-character. If the test yields *true* then the number's character representation is appended to the result list; otherwise the exception *Bad_code* is signalled:

```
def Convert :=
   fix Convert.
      λl.if null(l)  then <>  /*empty list */
         else
            if  (0≤head(l))  and  (head(l)≤127)
               then chr(head(l)) /* chr is the transfer function in ALEX */
               else (signal Bad_code head(l))
            fi :: Convert(tail(l)) handle Bad_code := λy.(signal Bad_code y) resume
         fi
      signals Bad_code;
```

Since for a function with a *signals-clause* a handler has to be given for every application of that function in this prototype language, at least a "dummy" handler for propagating the exception *Bad_code* has to be added in *Convert's* body. (This is forced by the typing rules, see section 4.)

To complete this example *Convert* is applied to a list *ll* twice.

- Convert(ll) **handle** Bad_code := λi.**if** i<0 **then** '-' **else** '+' **fi** **resume**
  The handler for *Bad_code* specifies that negative numbers are represented as '-' and numbers greater then 127 as '+'.

- Convert(ll) **handle** Bad_code := λi.<> **terminate**
  The handler for *Bad_code* specifies that the result of the application is the empty list.

3. Operational Semantics for ALEX

An operational semantics specifies a language by defining an interpreter for the abstract syntax of the language. For ALEX we develop a variant of the SECD machine proposed by Peter J. Landin in 1964 [11] as an interpreter for its abstract syntax. Our SECD machine supports lazy evaluation since our ALEX implementation is lazy. But that is not essential. Here only those parts concerning exception handling are described. A full description of the interpreter is given in [1]. If the function *NEXT_STATE* yields no longer a new state, then *head(S)* is the result.

```
def NEXT_STATE:=
  λ[S,E,C,D].
      if is_empty (C) and not is_empty (D) then
      /* an intermediate evaluation has been terminated */
          let S == res::S0 and
              D == [S1, E1, C1]::D1 in
          if is_su(res) then
              let res == [su, expr, E2] in
              [<>,E2,<expr>,D]
          elsif is_sr(res) then
              let res == [sr, closure, [su, rand, E2]] in
              [<[su, rand, E2],  closure>,<>,<ap>,D]
          else
              [res::S1, E1, C1, D1]
          fi
      elsif not is_empty (C) then
          let C == X::C1 in
      (s1) if is_constant (X) or is_su (X) or is_sr (X) then
              [X::S, E, C1, D]
      (s2) elsif is_identifier (X) then
              [value(X, E)::S, E, C1, D]
          ...
      (s5) elsif is_application_with_handler (X) then
              letrec X == rator rand "handle" handler and
                  handler == exc_id ":="  "λ"bv"."body  stat in
              [<>, E1,<rator,   [su, rand, E], ap>, D1]
              whererec D1 == [S, E, C1]::D and
                  E1 == (exc_id ← [stat,[cl,bv,body,E], D1, rator])::E
          ...
      (s7) elsif is_abstraction_with_exception (X) then
              let X ==  "λ"bv"."body  "signals" exc_id in
              [[cl, bv, body, E]::S, E, C1, D]
          ...
      (s9) elsif is_signal (X) then
              letrec X == "signal" exc_id rand and
                  [stat, closure, D1, rator] == value(exc_id, E) and
                  D1 == [S0, E0, C0]::D0 in
              if stat == "resume" then /* resumption */
                  [<[su, rand, E],  closure>,  E, ap::C1, D]
              elsif stat == "retry" then /* retrying */
                  [<>,  E1, <rator,[sr, closure, [su, rand, E]],  ap>,  D1]
                  where E1 == (exc_id ← [stat, closure, D1, rator])::E0
              else /* termination */
                  [<[su, rand, E],  closure>,<>,<ap>,D1]
              fi
          ...
          fi
      else
          /* no new state */
      fi
```

The following explanations point out how the SECD machine processes the exception handling constructs. The exception handling mechanism leads to two different kinds of activities at run time:

case (s5):

When an application with a handler is executed, the handler body has to be bound to the exception identifier together with the information needed to compute associated signal-expressions appropriately. Thus, execution continues with an enlarged environment. Since for the terminate- and retry-actions the computation has to continue from the current state, we associate the state in the form of a dump *D1* with the identifier. Retry-actions also need the current operator *rator*. Thus, we decided to associate also this information to *exc_id*.

case (s7):

An abstraction with exception does not lead to additional actions at execution time. The signals-clause is only used for type inference.

case (s9):

When an exception *exc_id* is signalled, different actions have to be done depending on the handler's status *stat*:

(s9a) resume means: the handler body should be applied and with that result execution continues.

(s9b) retry means: the handler body should be applied, but then execution should continue with the handler's application using the new result value as the new rand.

(s9c) terminate means: the handler body should be applied and the execution should continue with that result as the result of the handler's application.

Note also, that to make the re-application at retry really lazy we need a structure to suspend cl/su-pairs. This is done by a new intermediate result, a sr-suspension, in the implementation.

As another example, note that the overall discipline of the SECD machine could be described using the exception handling constructs of ALEX, as well.

```
SECD_MACHINE:=
    λexpr.  NEXT_STATE1([<>,<>,<expr>,<>])
                  handle finish:=  λ[S,E,C,D].head(S)  terminate
```

In this case the state-transition function *NEXT_STATE1* should call itself recursively and signal an exception *finish*, if there is no successor state.

```
def NEXT_STATE1:=
    fix NEXT_STATE1.
        λ[S,E,C,D].
            NEXT_STATE1(
                        if is_empty (C) and not is_empty (D) then
                            /* an intermediate evaluation has been terminated */
                            ...
                        elsif not is_empty (C) then
                            ...
                        else
                            /* no new state */
                            signal finish [S,E,C,D]
                        fi)
            handle finish:= λx.(signal finish x) resume
        signals finish;
```

4. Type Inference in ALEX

Since there are higher order functions in functional languages, in an expression ($expr_1$ $expr_2$) the operator $expr_1$ can itself be an application expression whose evaluation yields a function which can signal an exception *exc_id* (cf. example 2 above). In this case there must a handler definition for *exc_id* be attached to the expression ($expr_1$ $expr_2$) because for our language construct we have required that the immediate invoker of a function handles that function's exceptions. We propose to check this by a polymorphic typechecking algorithm [3,14,17]. The type system of ALEX is formalized as a type deduction system [2] that prescribes how to establish the type of an expression from the types of its subexpressions. The following is a list of the inference rules ordered to parallel the abstract syntax of ALEX.

Let e be an expression and let π be a type assignment (i.e. a mapping from the identifiers occurring free in e into type expressions). The notation $\pi \vdash e : \tau$ means that given π we can deduce that e has type τ. The horizontal bar reads as "implies"; # is the overwrite operator for mappings. To force the correct use of the exception handling constructs, all neccessary information is collected in an exception type, which is constructed from

1) the exception identifier *exc_id*
2) the resume-handler type
3) the retry-handler type
4) the terminate-handler type

by using the type constructor *exc*.

Since exceptions are associated with abstractions, we also use a type constructor to model functions of the type "from τ_1 to τ_2 with an exception type τ_3" and write in mixfix notation "$\tau_1 \otimes \tau_3 \rightarrow \tau_2$".

Typing rules:

(r1) /* constant; *c* is a constant of type *b* */

$$\pi \vdash c : b$$

(r2) /* identifier */

$$\pi \vdash id : \pi(id)$$

(r3) /* conditional */

$$\frac{\pi \vdash e_1 : bool, \quad \pi \vdash e_2 : \tau, \quad \pi \vdash e_3 : \tau}{\pi \vdash \text{“if”}\ e_1\ \text{“then”}\ e_2\ \text{“else”}\ e_3 : \tau}$$

(r4) /* application */

$$\frac{\pi \vdash e_1 : \tau_1 \rightarrow \tau_2, \quad \pi \vdash e_2 : \tau_1}{\pi \vdash e_1\, e_2 : \tau_2}$$

(r5a) /* application with handler */

$$\frac{\pi \vdash e_1 : \tau_1 \otimes exc(\{id_1\},\tau_3,\tau_4,\tau_5) \rightarrow \tau_2 \qquad \pi \vdash e_2 : \tau_2, \quad \pi \vdash \text{“}\lambda\text{”}\ id_2\ \text{“.”}\ e_3 : \tau_3}{\pi \vdash e_1\, e_2\ \text{“handle”}\ id_1\ \text{“:=”}\ \text{“}\lambda\text{”}\ id_2\ \text{“.”}\ e_3\ \text{“resume”} : \tau_2}$$

(r5b)

$$\frac{\pi \vdash e_1 : \tau_1 \otimes exc(\{id_1\},\tau_3,\tau_4,\tau_5) \rightarrow \tau_2 \qquad \pi \vdash e_2 : \tau_2, \quad \pi \vdash \text{“}\lambda\text{”}\ id_2\ \text{“.”}\ e_3 : \tau_4}{\pi \vdash e_1\, e_2\ \text{“handle”}\ id_1\ \text{“:=”}\ \text{“}\lambda\text{”}\ id_2\ \text{“.”}\ e_3\ \text{“retry”} : \tau_2}$$

(r5c)

$$\frac{\pi \vdash e_1 : \tau_1 \otimes exc(\{id_1\},\tau_3,\tau_4,\tau_5) \rightarrow \tau_2 \qquad \pi \vdash e_2 : \tau_2, \quad \pi \vdash \text{“}\lambda\text{”}\ id_2\ \text{“.”}\ e_3 : \tau_5}{\pi \vdash e_1\, e_2\ \text{“handle”}\ id_1\ \text{“:=”}\ \text{“}\lambda\text{”}\ id_2\ \text{“.”}\ e_3\ \text{“terminate”} : \tau_2}$$

(r6) /* abstraction */

$$\frac{\pi\ \#\ [id:\tau_1] \vdash e : \tau_2}{\pi \vdash \text{“}\lambda\text{”}\ id\ \text{“.”}\ e : \tau_1 \rightarrow \tau_2}$$

(r7) /* abstraction with exception */

$$\frac{\pi\ \#\ [id_1:\tau_1,\ id_2:exc(\{id_2\},\tau_3,\ \tau_4 \rightarrow \tau_1, \tau_4 \rightarrow \tau_2)] \vdash e : \tau_2}{\pi \vdash \text{“}\lambda\text{”}\ id_1\ \text{“.”}\ e\ \text{“signals”}\ id_2 : \tau_1 \otimes exc(\{id_2\},\tau_3,\ \tau_4 \rightarrow \tau_1,\tau_4 \rightarrow \tau_2) \rightarrow \tau_2}$$

(r8) /* recursive functions */

$$\frac{\pi\ \#\ [id:\tau] \vdash e : \tau}{\pi \vdash \text{“fix”}\ id\ \text{“.”}\ e : \tau}$$

(r9) /* signal */

$$\frac{\pi \vdash \text{id} : \text{exc}(\{\text{id}\},\ \tau_1 \to \tau_2, \tau_1 \to \tau_3,\ \tau_1 \to \tau_4) \qquad \pi \vdash \text{e} :\ \tau_1}{\pi \vdash \text{"signal" id e} :\ \tau_2}$$

A bottom-up typing algorithm can be extracted from the rules in a straightforward way [2].

5. A Detailed Example

Suppose l is a sorted list. We develop a recursive function which inserts an element x into l in case that x is not already a member of l; otherwise the exception *Multiple* is signalled. (The reader might excuse that we use multi-argument functions without introducing them formally, too.):

```
def Insert:=
    fix Insert.
        λ[x,l].
            if null(l) then <x>
            else
                if  x<head(l)  then x :: l
                elsif x=head(l) then (signal Multiple (x, head(l)))  ||  l
                else
                    head(l) :: Insert(x, tail(l))
                                handle Multiple:= λ[x,y].(signal Multiple(x,y)) resume
                fi
            fi
        signals Multiple;
```

We proceed as follows: first we focus on the bottom-up derivation of the type of *Insert* (or more correctly of the type of the ALEX-expression which we have named *Insert*); second we present some reasonable applications of *Insert*.

The bottom-up derivation of the type of *Insert* can be understood by looking at the following principal snapshots of the derivation, where an a priori typing of the list handling operations is assumed:

1. The type of the else-part of the inner conditional is derived using the typing rules (r5a) and (r9), together with some other rules. The resulting type of it is

   "αlist"

   and the type assignment π contains the following types for the free identifiers:

x: α'
l: αlist
Multiple: exc({*Multiple*}, $\beta\times\beta'\rightarrow\gamma$, $\beta\times\beta'\rightarrow\delta$, $\beta\times\beta'\rightarrow\zeta$)
Insert: ($\alpha\times\alpha$list) $\otimes$ exc({*Multiple*}, $\beta\times\beta'\rightarrow\gamma$, κ, ι) $\rightarrow$ αlist

2. Next, we type the body of the abstraction with exception by using the rules (r3) and (r9) especially. Thus,

"αlist"

is also the type of the abstraction's body and the free identifiers have types as follows:

x: α
l: αlist
Multiple: exc({*Multiple*}, $\alpha\times\alpha\rightarrow\alpha$list, $\alpha\times\alpha\rightarrow\delta$, $\alpha\times\alpha\rightarrow\zeta$)
Insert: ($\alpha\times\alpha$list) $\otimes$ exc({*Multiple*}, $\beta\times\beta'\rightarrow\gamma$, κ, ι) $\rightarrow$ αlist

3. According to rule (r7), then the abstraction with exception has type

"($\alpha\times\alpha$list)$\otimes$exc({*Multiple*}, $\alpha\times\alpha\rightarrow\alpha$list, $\alpha\times\alpha\rightarrow\alpha\times\alpha$list, $\alpha\times\alpha\rightarrow\alpha$list) $\rightarrow\alpha$list"

where π contains for *Insert* the type

Insert: ($\alpha\times\alpha$list) $\otimes$ exc({*Multiple*}, $\beta\times\beta'\rightarrow\gamma$, κ, ι) $\rightarrow$ αlist

4. Finally, the rule for recursive function definitions (r8) yields for the whole expression the type

"($\alpha\times\alpha$list)$\otimes$exc({*Multiple*}, $\alpha\times\alpha\rightarrow\alpha$list, $\alpha\times\alpha\rightarrow\alpha\times\alpha$list, $\alpha\times\alpha\rightarrow\alpha$list) $\rightarrow\alpha$list"

where the type assignment π is empty.

There are several possibilities for handlers for an application of *Insert*. Assume, *nl* is a sorted list and *n* is a new entry. The following applications with handler are only some significant examples out of a variety of possibilities:

(1) Insert(n,nl) **handle** Multiple:= λ[new,old].<new> **resume**
    /* replaces old entry by new entry */
(2) Insert(n,nl) **handle** Multiple:= λ[new,old].<old> **resume**
    /* keeps old entry only */

(3) Insert(n,nl) **handle** Multiple:= λ[new,old].<new,old> **resume**

/* stores new entry in front of old one */

(4) Insert(n,nl) **handle** Multiple:= λ[new,old].<> **resume**

/* deletes both entries */

(5) Insert(n,nl) **handle** Multiple:= λ[new,old].nl **terminate**

/* same as case (2) */

(6) Insert(n,nl) **handle** Multiple:= λ[new,old].[modify(new),nl] **retry**

/* tries to insert a modified entry into nl */

Conclusion

An exception handling proposal for applicative languages which seems quite powerful and conceptually simple has been presented. The appropriate language construct was defined by introducing an ISWIM-like language, called ALEX. Its abstract syntax and its operational semantics were specified, for the latter using a variant of the SECD maschine. A type system for ALEX has been developed to restrict the use of the exception handling constructs, whereby security can be achieved.

Finally, a brief comparison between the ML exception handling mechanism [18] and our mechanism may show the benefits of our proposal:

(a) ML only supports the handler response "terminate the signaller". The signalling expression is terminated and the handler's result replaces the result of the (signalling) expression. ALEX supports with resume, retry and terminate three different possible handler responses.

(b) In ML exceptions are propagated automatically along the dynamic invocation chain as long as no handler is found. As was pointed out in [15] multilevel mechanisms are in contrast to the hierachical program design methodology. In ALEX exceptions must be propagated explicitly along the dynamic invocation chain and handlers are bound statically to exceptions.

(c) In both, ML and ALEX, exceptions can be parameterized.

On the other hand, the algorithmic language Scheme [20] provides the possibility to program with continuations, which allows management of control in a general and powerful manner. Scheme's "call-with-current-continuation" feature is useful for implementing a wide variety of control structures, including exception handling. To us this possibility seems to general whereas the proposal in this paper was meant to be specific to exception handling. We hope, it could become a practical and versatile help for programming.

References:

[1] **Bretz, M.:**
Exception Handling in Functional Programs,
in: W.-M. Lippe (Hrsg.),
"4. Workshop - Alternative Konzepte für Sprachen und Rechner",
Universität Münster, Schriftenreihe "Angewandte Mathematik und Informatik", Band 2/87-I

[2] **Bretz, M.; Ebert, J.:**
Type Inference for Exception Handling,
Internal Report, EWH Koblenz, 1987

[3] **Cardelli, L.:**
Basic Polymorphic Typechecking,
Science of Computer Programming, 8(1987), pp. 147-172

[4] **Cristian, F.:**
Robust Data Types,
Acta Informatica, 17(1982), pp.365-397

[5] **Cristian, F.:**
Dependable Programs: Concepts and Terminology,
IBM Research Laboratory, San Jose, CA, 1986 (Technical Report)

[6] **Ebert, J.:**
Graph Implementation of a Functional Language,
in: H. Noltemeier (ed.),
Proceedings of the WG' 85,
Trauner, Linz, 1985, pp. 73-84

[7] **Ebert, J.:**
Ein SECD-artiger Graphenauswerter,
in: W.-M. Lippe (Hrsg.),
"4. Workshop - Alternative Konzepte für Sprachen und Rechner",
Universität Münster, Schriftenreihe "Angewandte Mathematik und Informatik", Band 2/87-I

[8] **Ebert, J.:**
A Versatile Data Structure for Edge-Oriented Graph Algorithms,
Comm. ACM, 30(6, 1987) (June 1987), pp. 513-519

[9] **Goodenough, J.B.:**
Exception Handling: Issues and a Proposed Notation,
Comm. ACM, 18(12, 1975), (Dec. 1975), pp. 683-696

[10] **Johnson, S.C.:**
YACC - Yet Another Compiler Compiler,
Bell Laboratories, Murray Hill, NJ, 1975 (CSTR 32)

[11] **Landin, P.J.:**
The Mechanical Evaluation of Expressions,
Computer Journal 6, 1964, pp. 308-320

[12] **Landin, P.J.:**
The Next 700 Programming Languages,
Comm. ACM, 9(3, 1966) (March 1966), pp. 157-166

[13] **Lesk, M.E.; Schmidt E.:**
LEX - A Lexical Analyzer Generator,
Bell Laboratories, Murray Hill, NJ, 1975 (CSTR 39)

[14] **Letschert, T.:**
Type Inference in the Presence of Overloading, Polymorphism and Coercions,
in: Tagungsband der 8ten Fachtagung "Programmiersprachen und Programmentwicklung", Zürich 1984, pp. 58-70

[15] **Liskov, B.H.; Snyder, A.:**
Exception Handling in CLU,
IEEE Trans. on Soft. Eng., 5(6, 1979) (Nov. 1979), pp. 546-558

[16] **Luckham, D.C.; Polak W.:**
Ada Exception Handling - An Axiomatic Approach,
ACM Trans. on Prog. Lang. Syst., 2(2, 1980) (April 1980), pp. 225-233

[17] **Milner, R:**
A Theory of Type Polymorphism in Programming,
Journal of Computer and System Sciences, 17(1978), pp. 348-375

[18] **Milner, R.:**
A Proposal for Standard ML,
ACM Conf. Record of the 1984 Symposium on Lisp and Functional Programming, 1984, pp. 184-197

[19] OS and DOS PL/I Language Reference Manual,
IBM Corporation, 1981

[20] **Rees, J.; Clinger W. et. al.:**
Revised Report on the Algorithmic Language Scheme,
SIGPLAN Notices, 21(12, 1986) (Dec. 1986), pp. 37-79

[21] **Yemini, S.; Berry, D.M.:**
A Modular Verifiable Exception Handling Mechanism,
ACM Trans. on Prog. Lang. Syst., 7(2, 1985) (April 1985), pp. 214-243

[22] **Yemini, S.; Berry, D.M.:**
An Axiomatic Treatment of Exception Handling in an Expression-Oriented Language,
ACM Trans. on Prog. Lang. Syst., 9(3, 1987) (July 1987), pp. 390-407

A Functional Language for the Specification of Complex Tree Transformations

Reinhold Heckmann

FB 10 - Informatik
Universität des Saarlandes
6600 Saarbrücken
Bundesrepublik Deutschland

email: heckmann%sbsvax.uucp@germany.csnet

ABSTRACT

Transformations of trees and rewriting of terms can be found in various settings e.g. transformations of abstract syntax trees in compiler construction and program synthesis.

A language is proposed combining features of a general purpose functional language with special means to specify tree transformations. Atomic transformations are considered first order functions and described by pattern matching. The pattern specification language allows for partitioning trees by arbitrary vertical and horizontal cuts. This goes beyond what is possible in similar languages [2,13,14]. High order functions and functional combinators are used to express strategies for the controlled application of transformations.

1. Introduction

The PROSPECTRA project (PROgram development by SPECification and TRAnsformation) aims to provide a rigorous methodology for developing correct software [10]. It integrates program construction and verification, and is based on previous work in the CIP project [3].

A formal specification is gradually transformed into an optimized executable program by stepwise application of transformation rules. These are carried out by the system, with interactive guidance by the implementor, or automatically by transformation tools.

Each transition from one program version to another is done by application of an individual transformation rule or a transformation script invoking rules systematically. The language to express such transformation scripts as well as individual rules is designed in functional style since transformations are functions in some tree domain, and scripts may be build up by calling high order functions parametrized by transformations.

Starting points for the transformation language 'TrafoLa' were the functional languages HOPE [2], ML [13], and Miranda [14] which are quite similar with respect to their functional kernel. They all use a very restricted form of pattern matching for trees that only allows for the specification of some fixed region near the root of the tree and for selecting subtrees adjacent to

This research was partially supported by the Commission of the European Communities under Esprit Project Ref. No. 390 (PROSPECTRA) and by Sonderforschungsbereich 124 - VLSI Design Methods and Parallelism

this region. Thus, it is neither possible to specify a region or to refer to a subtree whose root is far from the root of the whole tree, nor to bind the context of such a subtree to a variable.

In these languages, sequences are represented as trees, and thus, their treatment is always biased to their leftmost item. Patterns only allow for selecting a fixed number of items at the left end of the sequence and its remainder. It is impossible to access some infix or the last item of a sequence directly.

A completely different approach was given by Huet [9]. His second order patterns allow for the specification and selection of arbitrary subtrees of a given subject tree. The patterns are used to express powerful transformations, but they are not embedded into a functional language. Pattern matches usually result in more than one solution, but there is no means to control sets of solutions by 'Boolean' pattern operators. In fact, Huet's patterns contain only a few pattern operators, and one – the inverse application – is extremely complex. The generality of this operator is often not needed, and consequently, TrafoLa provides other, less complex operators for usual purposes.

TrafoLa was developed by increasing the power of patterns of Hope [2], ML [13], and Miranda [14] towards the power of Huet's patterns [9] – or in other words, by embedding Huet's patterns into a nice functional language. Non-determinism is used to ease the description – the user only needs to specify the shape of the subtree he/she wants to select, not where or how such a subtree is to be found (nevertheless, this is also possible). The resulting set of solutions is handled following Prolog [4] – by enumerating the elements by means of backtracking or by cutting it down to one element.

We shall first consider the structure of the objects to be transformed. Then we shall define patterns and raise their power step by step. At last, they will allow for partitioning trees by arbitrary vertical and horizontal cuts. We shall introduce functions describing transformations and functional combinators. Finally, we shall give an example of a complex transformation. We do not treat the development or correctness of transformations; this is done in [12].

2. Objects of the transformation language

The objects of the transformation language called 'values' are trees and sequences of trees – the objects to be transformed – and also functions – these are transformations and strategies.

The domain of values is recursively defined as follows:

1) Constants such as 'true' and '0' are values.
2) There is a special constant '@' indicating the place where a subtree was cut out of some bigger tree.
3) Any sequence '[v_1, ... , v_n]' of values is a value. A special case of this is the empty sequence '[]'. We do not distinguish between tuples and sequences.
4) Each tree is a value. A tree 'op v' consists of a root operator 'op' and some value 'v' standing for the children list of the tree.
5) Functions mapping values into values (or sets of values) are functional values.

Examples of values: 0 [] [1, 2, 3]
ife [eq [i1, i2], add [i1, 1], sub [i1, i2]]

where '0', '1', '2', '3', 'i1', and 'i2' are constants, and 'ife', 'eq', 'add', and 'sub' are operators.

Values may be checked for equality and inequality. For functional values, this is realized by some approximation e.g. syntactic comparison, guaranteeing that different functions are never claimed to be equal – whereas equal functions may be claimed to be different.

We adopted the following conventions in TrafoLa:

1) Square brackets [] are used as tuple and sequence delimiters. Parentheses () will be used in patterns and expressions of TrafoLa only to solve syntactic ambiguities.
2) Constant and operator names start with a lower case letter or are numbers.
3) Variable names (they did not yet occur) start with upper case letters.
4) Type names are printed in *italics*, and keywords of TrafoLa in **bold face**.

Subsets of values may be specified by data type definitions. We give an example describing the abstract syntax of a tiny imperative programming language. The generated trees will also be the objects of our example transformations.

type	*Program*	=	*Proc-dec*
and	*Proc-dec*	=	procedure [*Id*, *Id**, *Decl**, *Stm**]
and	*Func-dec*	=	function [*Id*, *Id**, *Decl**, *Stm**]
and	*Decl*	=	*Proc-dec* ∣ *Func-dec*
and	*Stm*	=	noop ∣ assign [*Id*, *Exp*] ∣ pcall [*Id*, *Exp**] ∣ ifs [*Exp*, *Stm**, *Stm**] ∣ while [*Exp*, *Stm**]
and	*Exp*	=	false ∣ true ∣ *Num* ∣ *Id* ∣ *Unop* [*Exp*] ∣ *Binop* [*Exp*, *Exp*] ∣ ife [*Exp*, *Exp*, *Exp*] ∣ *Fcall*
and	*Fcall*	=	fcall [*Id*, *Exp**]
and	*Num*	=	0 ∣ 1 ∣ 2 ∣ etc.
and	*Id*	=	... (identifiers)
and	*Unop*	=	sign ∣ not
and	*Binop*	=	eq ∣ lt ∣ add ∣ sub ∣ mul ∣ etc.

The construct '*T**' denotes the type of all sequences of items of type '*T*'.

Later, it will turn out that the type expressions at the right hand sides of the type definitions are nothing else than patterns, i.e. data type definitions may be viewed as recursive patterns.

Example of a value with type '*Stm*':

```
while [ lt [i, n] , [ assign [s, add [s, i]], assign [i, add [i, 1]] ] ]
/* while i < n do s := s + i; i := i + 1 od */
```

3. Patterns

3.1. Informal semantics of patterns

The following transformations seem to be useful:

```
dec If-true      = { ife [true, T, E]  => T }
dec If-false     = { ife [false, T, E] => E }
dec While-false  = { while [false, S]  => noop }
```

These are declarations binding functional values – denoted by the construct '{ pattern => expression }' – to the variables 'If-true' etc.

What is the semantics of the function '{p => e}' applied to some value *v*?

If *p* does not match *v*, the rule fails, otherwise the variable names occurring in *p* are bound to values (subterms of *v*). Thus *p* matched against *v* returns an environment *r*. Then the expression e is evaluated in this environment to a new value *v'*. The transformation '{p => e}' thus describes a partial mapping of values. 'If-true', for instance, is undefined for 'while' statements, even when a matching 'if' expression occurs in its condition or body.

Later, we shall consider non-deterministic patterns that may match in different ways thus returning a set *s* of environments when matched against a value *v*. The failure case fits well with this view, the pattern then returns the empty set of environments. The expression *e* will be evaluated in *s*, and thus eventually produce a set of results. Later, we shall present different methods how to handle this non-determinism.

3.2. Formal semantics of patterns

The formal semantics of patterns is described by means of a semantic function

$$P: \text{Pattern} \rightarrow \text{Env} \rightarrow \text{Value} \rightarrow 2^{\text{Env}}$$

matching a pattern against a value in some environment and producing a set of environments. An environment is a mapping from variables to values or 'unbound'. We shall denote environments by

$$<A_1 \rightarrow v_1; \ldots ; A_n \rightarrow v_n>$$

were A_i are distinct variables and v_i values (not 'unbound').

Notice that we shall abstract from error cases when we shall present parts of the definition of P.

3.3. Atomic patterns

Atomic patterns are constructors, variables, syntactic types, and wild cards.

A constructor (constant or operator) *c* (or @) matches just itself:

$$P\,(c)\;r\;v \;=\; \text{if } v = c \text{ then } \{<>\} \text{ else } \emptyset$$

If the value equals *c*, the match succeeds returning just one environment, namely <> i.e. the empty environment mapping all variables to 'unbound'. Otherwise, the match fails returning Ø, the empty set of environments.

Variables may be used in two ways: either to bind subvalues or to import values into a match.

Binding variables (called 'open' in [1]) match any value and create a new environment where they are bound to this value:

$$P\,(A)\;r\;v \;=\; \{<A \rightarrow v>\}$$

Importing variables (called 'closed' in [1]) match just the value they are bound to in the environment of the match:

$$P\,(\%\,A)\;r\;v \;=\; \text{if } v = r\,(A) \text{ then } \{<>\} \text{ else } \emptyset$$

When a type name such as '*Stm*' is encountered in a pattern, its meaning is looked up in the environment of the match. The meaning will be a predicate on values.

$$P\,(T)\;r\;v \;=\; \text{if } r\,(T)\;v \text{ then } \{<>\} \text{ else } \emptyset$$

The wild card ' _ ' matches any value: $P(\_)\ r\ v \;=\; \{<>\}$

Constructors, binding variables, and the wild card also occur in Hope, ML, and Miranda, but importing variables and types don't.

3.4. Structural patterns

Structural patterns specify the structure of the matched value. They consist of subpatterns to match designated subvalues, and the resulting sets of environments are combined into one.

Sequence enumeration

The pattern '$[p_1, \dots, p_n]$' matches values of shape '$[v_1, \dots, v_n]$':

$$P([p_1, \dots, p_n])\ r\ v \;=\; \text{if } v = [v_1, \dots, v_n] \text{ then } P(p_1)\ r\ v_1 \oplus \dots \oplus P(p_n)\ r\ v_n \text{ else } \emptyset$$

If n = 0, this becomes to $P([])\ r\ v \;=\; \text{if } v = [] \text{ then } \{<>\} \text{ else } \emptyset$

The combination ' ⊕ ' will be defined in the next but one section. As first approximation assume that it superposes all environments in its first argument with all in its second one.

Uniform sequence

The pattern 'p^*' matches sequences of arbitrary length whose items are all matched by *p*, and '$p+$' matches the same sequences except the empty one '[]'.

$$P(p^*)\ r\ v \;=\; \text{if } v = [v_1, \dots, v_n],\ n > 0 \text{ then } P(p)\ r\ v_1 \oplus \dots \oplus P(p)\ r\ v_n \text{ else if } v = [] \text{ then } \{<>\} \text{ else } \emptyset$$

$$P(p+)\ r\ v \;=\; \text{if } v = [v_1, \dots, v_n],\ n > 0 \text{ then } P(p)\ r\ v_1 \oplus \dots \oplus P(p)\ r\ v_n \text{ else } \emptyset$$

Tree pattern

Pattern 'p q' matches trees whose operator is matched by *p* and whose children list is matched by *q*.

$$P(p\ q)\ r\ v \;=\; \text{if } v = op\ w \text{ then } P(p)\ r\ op \oplus P(q)\ r\ w \text{ else } \emptyset$$

Note that *p* is not necessarily an operator name; this goes beyond what is possible in Hope, ML, and Miranda.

Examples

'ife [true, T, E]' matches 'if' expressions with condition 'true' and binds T and E to 'then' resp. 'else' part.

'ife A' matches any 'if' expression and binds A to its children list, i.e. A is bound to a value of type *[Exp, Exp, Exp]*.

'O A' matches any tree and binds O to the operator and A to the children list.

'T' matches any value and binds T to it.

If we don't want to bind a subvalue to a name, we may use the symbol ' _ ' or the name of a syntactic sort such as '*Stm*'.

'ifs [C, *Stm*, *Stm*]' is equivalent to 'ifs [C, _ , _]' due to the structure of the language. Both patterns match 'if' statements and bind the condition to C.

3.5. Non-linear patterns

A pattern is non-linear if a variable occurs more than once in it or occurs inside an iterated subpattern 'p*' or 'p+'.

Let p = add [E, E] be a typical example for a non-linear pattern. *p* matches the value 'add [a, b]' iff the subvalues *a* and *b* are equal, *E* is then bound to *a*.

Examples:

Pattern	Value	Result
add [E, E]	add [1, 1]	{<E → 1>}
add [E, E]	add [1, 2]	∅
A+	[1, 1, 2]	∅
A+	[1, 1, 1]	{<A → 1>}

Non-linear patterns are allowed in Miranda, Prolog, and Huet's language, but forbidden in Hope and ML.

3.6. Combination of sets of environments

Now, we shall define the combination 's ⊕ t' of two sets of environments *s* and *t*. The result is the set of all pairwise superpositions of environments where the case of inconsistent bindings of variables must be excluded in order to achieve the desired semantics of non-linear patterns:

Definition:

s ⊕ t = { a + b | a in s, b in t, a and b are consistent }

a + b = λN. if b (N) = unbound then a (N) else b (N)

a and b are consistent iff

for all variables N, a (N) = unbound or b (N) = unbound or a (N) = b (N)

Examples: Remember P ([p, q]) r [u, v] = P (p) r u ⊕ P (q) r v

Pattern	Value	Result	
[A, B]	[1, 2]	{<A → 1>} ⊕ {<B → 2>}	= {<A → 1; B → 2>}
[A, 2]	[1, 2]	{<A → 1>} ⊕ {<>}	= {<A → 1>}
[A, 1]	[1, 2]	{<A → 1>} ⊕ {}	= {}
[A, A]	[1, 1]	{<A → 1>} ⊕ {<A → 1>}	= {<A → 1>}
[A, A]	[1, 2]	{<A → 1>} ⊕ {<A → 2>}	= {}

The superposition of environments ' + ' is not commutative – the second operand dominates the first one – , but associative, and has a neutral element, namely the empty environment '<>'. Since a + b = b + a holds iff a and b are consistent, the combination ' ⊕ ' is commutative, associative, and has neutral element {<>}. In addition, it distributes over set union and satisfies s ⊕ ∅ = s. Unfortunately, it is not idempotent, e.g.

{<A → 1>, <B → 2>} ⊕ {<A → 1>, <B → 2>} =
{ <A → 1>, <B → 2>, <A → 1; B → 2> }

But if the environments contained in *s* are 'uniform' i.e. each environment binds the same set of variables, then s ⊕ s = s holds.

The algebraic properties mentioned here are stated and proved in [7] together with some additional ones.

3.7. Correspondence between TrafoLa patterns and TrafoLa expressions

Some pattern operators directly correspond to operators in TrafoLa expressions. There are expressions being constants denoting themselves, and being variables denoting the value the variable is bound to, and there are expressions '[e_1, ... , e_n]' for sequences and expressions 'e e'' for trees.

The meanings of the pattern '[A, B]' and the expression '[A, B]' are inverse: the pattern '[A, B]' matches pairs, decomposes them into their two components, and binds A to the first one and B to the second one. The expression '[A, B]' composes the values bound to the variables A resp. B to a new pair.

The operators denoting concatenation and insertion - introduced below - will behave analogously.

3.8. Concatenation and its inverse operation

Assume we want to delete superfluous 'noop' statements in statement lists. Then we need a rule

{ (L1 . [noop] . L2) => (L1 . L2) }

where the dot stands for concatenation and its inverse operation. The pattern partitions the sequence of statements into three subsequences such that the second one is '[noop]', and binds L1 to the first one and L2 to the third one. The expression concatenates L1 and L2 to a new sequence of statements.

By abstracting from 'noop', we obtain an example for importing variables:

{ X => { L1 . [% X] . L2 => L1 . L2 } }

This is a function of second order. Given an argument x, it returns a function that removes an occurrence of x from a sequence.

Examples for patterns with concatenation:

'L1 . [while [C, B]] . L3'	matches lists of arbitrary length containing a 'while' statement.
'[S, noop] . L'	matches lists whose second element is 'noop'.

The dot operator is a potential source of non-determinism:

L1 . [noop] . L2 matched against [a1, noop, a2, noop]

where the subvalues ai are statements other than 'noop', yields a set of two environments:

$<$L1 → [a1]; L2 → [a2, noop]$>$ and $<$L1 → [a1, noop, a2]; L2 → []$>$

Formally, the semantics of the dot operator is defined by a union over all possible partitions:

$$P\,(p\,.\,q)\;r\;v \;=\; \bigcup_{u.w=v} P\,(p)\;r\;u \oplus P\,(q)\;r\;w$$

This operator allows for selecting arbitrary subsequences, and is not contained in any of Hope, ML, and Miranda.

3.9. Tree fragments, insertion and horizontal cuts

The dot operator for patterns allows for partitioning values by vertical cuts into a left and a right hand side since it inverts concatenation. Now we want to introduce an operation - also not contained in Hope, ML, and Miranda - performing horizontal cuts to obtain an upper and a lower part. The upper part is not a complete tree; it contains a hole '@' denoting the place where the lower part was cut out.

In TrafoLa expressions, the operator '^' denotes insertion of a value into the hole of a tree fragment:

ife [c, @, e]	^ t	=	ife [c, t, e]
add @	^ [a, b]	=	add [a, b]
ifs [c, @, []]	^ [s1, s2]	=	ifs [c, [s1, s2], []]
[s1, @, s4]	^ [s2, s3]	=	[s1, [s2, s3], s4]

The pattern operator '^' inverts insertion as the dot operator inverts concatenation. When a pattern 'p ^ q' is matched against a value *v*, *v* is separated in all possible ways into two values *u* and *w* such that *u* contains exactly one hole and *v* = *u* ^ *w* holds. Then *p* is matched against *u* and *q* against *w*:

$$\mathrm{P}\ (\mathrm{p} \wedge \mathrm{q})\ \mathrm{r}\ \mathrm{v} \quad = \quad \bigcup_{u \wedge w = v} \mathrm{P}\ (\mathrm{p})\ \mathrm{r}\ \mathrm{u} \oplus \mathrm{P}\ (\mathrm{q})\ \mathrm{r}\ \mathrm{w}$$

Examples:

Let v = mul [add [a, b], add [c, d]].

add [A, B] does not match v

U ^ add [A, B] matches v in two ways:

<U → mul [@, add [c, d]]; A → a; B → b> and
<U → mul [add [a, b], @]; A → c; B → d>.

U ^ mul [@, A] ^ B matched against v gives one solution only:

<U → @; A → add [c, d]; B → add [a, b]>

Both '.' and '^' are associative such that no parentheses are needed in the last example.

3.10. 'Boolean' pattern operators

The following pattern operators don't have a direct correspondent in the world of expressions. They serve to extend or restrict the set of environments produced by pattern matches.

Intersection

The pattern 'p & q' is used to specify that a value to be matched must satisfy both the requirements imposed by pattern *p* and by pattern *q*. If the pattern *p* is simply a variable – this is an important special case – we write 'V: q' instead of 'V & q' due to aesthetic reasons. Hope and ML contain only the special case ('&' in Hope, 'as' in ML) whereas Miranda contains nothing of this feature.

Example: S: (L1 . [W: while _] . L2) & *Stm**

matches any sequence of statements containing a 'while' statement. The 'while' statement is bound to W, its left context to L1, and its right context to L2, whereas the whole sequence is bound to S.

Formal definition: P (p & q) r v = P (p) r v ⊕ P (q) r v

Union

The pattern 'p | q' matches all values matched by *p* or by *q* or by both *p* and *q*. The sets of environments produced by *p* and by *q* are simply joined together:

$$P\,(p \mid q)\; r\; v \;=\; P\,(p)\; r\; v \;\cup\; P\,(q)\; r\; v$$

Example: matching sums or products: A: (add [*Exp, Exp*] | mul [*Exp, Exp*])

The '|' operator is also a potential source of non-determinism. There are some problems with variables explained in the next section.

Complement

If *p* is a pattern matching some values, then '!p' is a pattern matching all but those values.

$$P\,(!p)\; r\; v \;=\; \text{if } P\,(p)\; r\; v = \emptyset \text{ then } \{<>\} \text{ else } \emptyset$$

Note that the pattern '!p' does not bind variables since there are no subvalues they could be bound to when '!p' matches i.e. *p* does not match. Thus, the pattern '!!p' is not equivalent to *p* – it matches the same values but does not bind variables. This is similar to Prolog's 'not' predicate [4].

Examples

Pattern	Value	Result
add [A, B] & ! add [E, E]	add [1, 2]	{<A → 1; B → 2>}
add [A, B] & ! add [E, E]	add [1, 1]	∅

Deterministic 'noop' elimination rule:

{ (L1: (*Stm* & !noop)*) . [noop] . (L2: *Stm**) => L1 . L2 }

The sequence bound to L1 must not contain 'noop' statements such that the rule eliminates the first occurrence of 'noop'. Later, we shall give examples for functions deleting all occurrences.

Assume we want to select a function call in an assignment:

assign [V, E] ^ F: *Fcall*

The additional constraint that the function call is not the whole expression may be expressed as

assign [V, E & !@] ^ F: *Fcall*

3.11. Binding variables in patterns

Let V(p) denote the set of variables that are eventually bound by *p*. It is defined recursively:

$$V\,(c) = V\,(\_) = V\,(T) = V\,(\%\,A) = V\,(!p) = \emptyset$$
$$V\,(A) = \{A\}$$
$$V\,(p\;q) = V\,(p\,.\,q) = V\,(p\,\hat{}\,q) = V\,(p\,\&\,q) = V\,(p \mid q) = V\,(p) \cup V\,(q)$$
$$V\,([p_1, \ldots, p_n]) = V\,(p_1) \cup \ldots \cup V\,(p_n) \qquad V\,([\,]) = \emptyset$$
$$V\,(p^*) = V\,(p+) = V\,(p)$$

Alternatives 'p | q' must be considered a little bit closer. Their components independently try to match and bind only the variables contained in themselves.

For instance, the (strange) pattern 'A | B' matches any value v and produces a set of two environments {<A → v>, <B → v>}. Such strange patterns are forbidden; both operands of an '|' operator must bind the same set of variables. A similar problem arises with 'p*' when matching the empty sequence.

Adopting these restrictions, the sets of environments produced by a pattern will be uniform:

Theorem:

Let p be a normal pattern i.e. satisfying two restrictions:
1) For all subpatterns $q_1 \mid q_2$ of p, $V(q_1) = V(q_2)$ holds.
2) For all subpatterns q^* of p, $V(q) = \emptyset$ holds.
Then for all environments r_0, all values v and all environments r in $P(p)\, r_0\, v$, the set of variables bound in r is just $V(p)$

The restriction to normality excludes some awkward transformations, and implies the equivalence of 'p & p' with *p* for all patterns *p* due to the idempotence of '$\oplus$' for uniform sets of environments.

3.12. Other operators

There are a few other pattern operators already integrated in TrafoLa (see [8]), but the generality of Huet's inverse application is not yet reached. Its full integration will be investigated soon.

4. Expressions and definitions

Besides patterns, TrafoLa contains two other basic syntactic sorts: expressions and definitions. Patterns serve to analyze values, whereas expressions are used to synthesize values. Definitions occur at the top level of TrafoLa and in 'let' and 'letrec' constructs and bind variables to values.

The partners of the PROSPECTRA project did not yet agree upon the handling of non-determinism introduced by the pattern operators '.', '^', and '|'. There are two variants of TrafoLa: a deterministic one (D-TrafoLa [8]) where each function returns exactly one value, and a non-deterministic one (N-TrafoLa [5]) where each function returns a set of values that is enumerated by backtracking as in Prolog [4]. Accordingly, the semantic function for expressions has different type:

D-TrafoLa: E: Expression $\rightarrow$ Env $\rightarrow$ Value
N-TrafoLa: E: Expression $\rightarrow$ Env $\rightarrow$ 2^{Value}

4.1. Unfunctional expressions

These expressions are quite straightforward and only enumerated here:

Constructors:	c
Variables:	A
Sequences:	$[e_1, \ldots, e_n]$
Application:	e e'
Concatenation:	e . e'
Insertion:	e ^ e'
Comparison:	e = e' resp. e != e'
'let' expressions:	**let** d **in** e **end** resp. **letrec** d **in** e **end** where 'd' is a definition (see below)

Application also comprises tree construction e.g. 'add [1, 2]'. The present evaluation strategy is call by value since the complex patterns – especially '^' – exclude lazy evaluation, and abstract syntax trees to be transformed are usually finite.

In N-TrafoLa, non-determinism is accumulated by these operations: if 'e' denotes n values and 'e'' denotes m values, then 'e . e'' will denote up to $n \cdot m$ values.

4.2. Functional expressions

Functional expressions are abstraction by a pattern and superposition of functions. The abstraction has syntax '{ p => e }' where p is a pattern and e an expression. Its meaning depends on the handling of non-determinism:

N-TrafoLa: $E\,(\{p => e\})\,r = \lambda x. \bigcup_{r' \text{ in } P(p)\, r\, x} E\,(e)\,(r + r')$

If p does not match the argument x, the function returns $\emptyset$.

D-TrafoLa:

Here, abstraction contains an implicit 'cut' operator as known from Prolog:

Let select: $2^{Env} \rightarrow Env$ be some mapping with select $s \in s$ if $s \neq \emptyset$

Then $E\,(\{p => e\})\,r = \lambda x.$ if $s = \emptyset$ then fail else $E\,(e)\,(r + \text{select } s)$
where $s = P\,(p)\,r\,x$

'fail' is a special value indicating that the pattern p failed to match the argument value x. All expressions except the '|' construct below are assumed to be strict with respect to 'fail' i.e. if one operand evaluates to 'fail' then the whole expression will also.

The superposition of (partial) functions is denoted by '|'. This is a common operator in functional languages, but in Hope, ML, and Miranda, it is allowed in the context $(p_1 => e_1 \mid \ldots \mid p_n => e_n)$ only.

In D-TrafoLa, '|' is only applicable to functions, and the first operand dominates:

$$E\,(f \mid g)\,r = \lambda x. \text{ if } E\,(f)\,r\,x = \text{fail then } E\,(g)\,r\,x \text{ else } E\,(f)\,r\,x$$

In N-TrafoLa, it may be applied to all TrafoLa expressions:

$$E\,(e \mid e')\,r = E\,(e)\,r \cup E\,(e')\,r$$

Both variants of TrafoLa might contain the facility to collect the set of solutions into one sequence. In D-TrafoLa, this is done by a second abstraction mechanism '{ p => all e }'.

4.3. Definitions and top level declarations

Definitions have syntax $A_1 = e_1$ and ... and $A_n = e_n$

Instead of 'A = {p => e}', we may write 'A p = e'.

Top level declarations are written 'dec d' if they shall not be recursive, and 'rec d' otherwise.

4.4. Some syntactic sugar:

Original form:	Alternative syntax:
$(\{p_1 => e_1\} \mid .. \mid \{p_n => e_n\})\ e$	**case** e **of** $\{p_1 => e_1\} \mid .. \mid \{p_n => e_n\}$ **end**
$(\{\text{true} => e_1\} \mid \{\text{false} => e_2\})\ e$	**if** e **then** e_1 **else** e_2 **end**
$\{X => g\,(f\,X)\}$	f; g

4.5. Examples

All examples are given for D-TrafoLa.

Function to simplify 'if' expressions:

```
dec Sim-if = { ife [true, T, _] => T } | { ife [false, _, E] => E }
```

Identity:	dec I X	= X /* alternatively for dec I = {X => X} */
Totalization by identity:	dec Total F	= (F | I)
Repetition:	rec Repeat F	= (F; Repeat F) | I

'Total f v' computes 'f v'. If it is defined, it is the result, otherwise the result is the original argument *v*. 'Repeat f' repeatedly applies *f* until it is no longer possible.

Functionals for sequences

```
rec Map F     = { [] => [] } | { [H] . T  =>  [F H] . Map F T }
rec Extend F  = { [] => [] } | { [H] . T  =>  F H . Extend F T }
```

Note the difference: 'Map' applies a function item by item to a list, whereas 'Extend' performs a homomorphic extension of its argument function from items to lists.

With	dec Double X = [X, X]
we obtain	Double [a1, a2, a3] = [[a1, a2, a3], [a1, a2, a3]]
	Map Double [a1, a2, a3] = [[a1, a1], [a2, a2], [a3, a3]]
and	Extend Double [a1, a2, a3] = [a1, a1, a2, a2, a3, a3]

Other classical functionals:

```
rec Fold F X0 = { [] => X0 } | { [H] . T => (F H (Fold F X0 T)) }
```

where F is a binary function and X0 typically is its neutral element.

Example: Fold (*) 1 [1, 2, 3, 4, 5] = 120.

```
rec Filter P = { [] => [] } | { [H] . T => if P H then [H] else [] end . Filter P T }
```

'Filter' removes all list items not satisfying the predicate P.

Three functions deleting all 'noop' statements from sequences of statements:

```
Repeat {S1 . [noop] . S2  =>  S1 . S2}
Extend ({noop => []}  |  {X => [X]})
Filter  {X  =>  X != noop}
```

Flat insertion

Remember that insertion '^' treats its second argument as a unit:

```
[1, @, 4] ^ [2, 3]  =  [1, [2, 3], 4]
```

But it is not difficult to define a function 'flat-insert' splicing its second argument into the hole of the first:

```
dec Flat-insert  =  { U ^ (L . [@] . R)  => { X  =>  U ^ (L . X . R) } }
```

This is a curried function with two arguments. The first argument is partitioned by the pattern 'U ^ (L . [@] . R)' into an upper context U, a left context L, and a right context R of the hole. The second argument is bound to X.

Flat-insert (ifs [c, [s1, @], []]) []	=	ifs [c, [s1], []]	(U = ifs [c, @, []] L = [s1] R = [])
Flat-insert [1, @, 4] [2, 3]	=	[1, 2, 3, 4]	(U = @ L = [1] R = [4])
Flat-insert (add @) [1, 2]	=	fail	(pattern match fails)
Flat-insert [1, @, 3] 2	=	error	(L . X . R = [1] . 2. [3] = error)

5. A complex transformation: removal of function calls

5.1. The problem

At last, we shall give a larger example of program transformation. The problem is to replace function calls in a Pascal like language by procedure calls; it is first described in [11], and also presented in [12].

5.2. How to get a new identifier

We shall first define some functions relying on an implementation of identifiers as numbers. All functions except these will be independent from this specific implementation.

```
type Id = id Num
dec Leastid = id 0                                              /* Id */
dec Max (id A) (id B) = if A < B then id B else id A end        /* Id → Id → Id */
dec Nextid (id A) = id (A + 1)                                  /* Id → Id */
```

'Leastid' is the least identifier that may occur in a program. Naturally, we must be sure that this is guaranteed by the tools generating the actual program.

When given a program, we may construct a new identifier not occurring in it by looking for the maximal identifier in the program and then building a greater one by 'Nextid'.

```
dec Maxid = { _ ^ X: Id => all X } ;             Fold Max Leastid
            /* computes list of all identifiers */ /* determines maximum of list */
dec Newid = Maxid; Nextid
```

5.3. Subtasks to be done

Our task is to transform function calls in a Pascal like programming language into procedure calls by adding a new parameter exporting the result. To do so, we must first achieve that all function calls occur as right hand side of assignments only. In a second step, these assignments are transformed into procedure calls, and function declarations into procedure declarations.

```
/* Func-to-proc: Program → Program */
dec Func-to-proc = Unnest-all; Transform-all
```

5.4. Unnesting of function calls

The transformation 'Unnest-all' will transform the program such that it subsequently contains only calls 'V := F (...)'.

```
/* Unnest-all: Program → Program */
dec Unnest-all = Repeat { P: Program => Unnest-1 (Newid P) P }
```

'Unnest-all' repeatedly calls the function 'Unnest-1' until it is no more defined. 'Unnest-1' unnests just one function call and uses the new identifier 'Newid P'.

A type name such as '*Exp*' only matches complete values i.e. values without holes. We use '*Exp@*' to match upper fragments of expressions. The unnesting of function calls already having the desired form 'v := f(...)', is avoided by the pattern 'assign [*Id*, *Exp@* & !@]'.

```
/* Unnest-1: Id → Program → Program */
dec Unnest-1 NEW =
    { U ^ S: assign [Id, Exp@ & !@] ^ F: Fcall
        => Flat-insert U [assign [NEW, F], S ^ NEW] } |
```

```
   /* v := ... f (...) ...    => NEW := f (...); v := ...NEW... */
   { U ^ S: pcall _ ^ F: Fcall
        => Flat-insert U [assign [NEW, F], S ^ NEW] } |
   /* p (... f (...) ...)   => NEW := f (...); p (...NEW...) */
   { U ^ S: ifs [Exp@, Stm*, Stm*] ^ F: Fcall
        => Flat-insert U [assign [NEW, F], S ^ NEW] } |
   /* if .. f (..) .. then .. else .. fi   => NEW := f (..); if ..NEW.. then .. else .. fi */
   { U ^ while [E: Exp@, SL: Stm*] ^ F: Fcall
        => Flat-insert U [assign [NEW, F], while [E ^ NEW, SL . [assign [NEW, F]]]] }
   /* while .. f (..) .. do .. od
        => NEW := f (..); while ..NEW.. do .. ; NEW := f (..) od */
```

Note that we replace one statement by two; thus, we need the 'Flat-insert' function to avoid the building of nested subsequences.

The function 'Unnest-1' may be made a little bit more readable (hopefully) by introducing a bigger upper context 'BU' and a name for the new assignment.

```
/* Unnest-1: Id → Program → Program */
dec Unnest-1 NEW =
{ (BU: Program@ & ! (_ ^ assign [Id, @])) ^ F: Fcall =>
     let AS = assign [NEW, F] in
          case BU of  { U ^ S: (assign _ | pcall _ | ifs [Exp@, Stm*, Stm*])
                             => Flat-insert U [AS, S ^ NEW] } |
                      { U ^ while [E: Exp@, SL: Stm*]
                             => Flat-insert U [AS, while [E ^ NEW, SL . [AS]]] }
          end
     end
}
```

5.5. The real transformation

We define the function 'Transform-all' by repetition of a simpler function transforming functions with some specific name only:

```
/* Transform-all: Program → Program */
dec Transform-all = Repeat { P: (_ ^ function [FN, _, _, _])
                                    => Transform-1 FN (Newid P) P }
```

'Transform-1 FN PN' transforms all functions named FN into procedures named PN. The function name is added as an additional formal parameter such that the assignment to the function name in the body will export the result of the call.

```
/* Transform-1: Id → Id → Program → Program */
dec Transform-1 FN PN =
     Repeat ( { U ^ function [% FN, PL, D, B] => U ^ procedure [PN, PL . [FN], D, B] } |
              /* fun FN (...) => proc PN (... , FN) */
              { U ^ assign [V, fcall [% FN, EL]] => U ^ pcall [PN, EL . [V]] }
              /* V := FN (...) => PN (... , V) */
            )
```

Here, we don't need the function 'Flat-insert' since we replace one by one: one function declaration by one procedure declaration, and one assignment with function call by one procedure call.

5.6. Optimization of the transformation

Each call to 'Newid' always computes the maximal identifier in the program from scratch, but we know that it is always the previous new one. Thus, we store the actual maximal identifier at the root of the program tree.

```
/* Func-to-proc': Program → Program */
dec Func-to-proc' =   {P: Program => [Maxid P, P]} ;
                      Unnest-all' ; Transform-all' ;
                      {[_, P] => P}
```

We compute the maximum identifier once and store it at the root, then we transform, and omit it at the end.

```
/* Unnest-all', Transform-all': [Id, Program] → [Id, Program] */
dec Unnest-all' = Repeat { [MI, P] => let NI = Nextid MI in [NI, Unnest-1 NI P] end }
dec Transform-all' =
    Repeat { [MI, P: (_ ^ function [FN, _, _, _])]
               => let NI = Nextid MI in [NI, Transform-1 FN NI P] end }
```

The mappings 'Unnest-1' and 'Transform-1' may still be used, such that this optimization can be done with little effort.

6. Conclusion and future research

The ability to specify patterns partitioning trees by arbitrary vertical and horizontal cuts allows for the definition of powerful transformation rules. Usual features of functional languages may be used to combine individual rules to transformation programs. A polymorphic type discipline has to be developed including both high order functions and tree grammar like data types.

The most significant element of our language is the powerful patterns. Many algebraic properties concerning the semantic equivalence of patterns hold e.g. the associativity of the pattern operators '|', '&', '.', and '^' (see [7]). An abstract pattern matching machine has been designed having many degrees of freedom such that there will be a flexible trade-off between the amount of precomputation by analyzing the pattern and the efficiency of matching it against concrete values. A prototype implementation of D-TrafoLa is available in ML [13]; it was created by translating the semantic clauses of TrafoLa into ML and does not yet include data type definitions and occurrences of data type names in patterns.

Acknowledgement

I wish to thank B. Gersdorf, B. Krieg-Brückner, U. Möncke, and R. Wilhelm for many discussions of TrafoLa, and H. G. Oberhauser and the ESOP '88 referees for comments on earlier drafts of this paper.

References

[1] Bobrow, D. G., Raphael, B.: New Programming Languages for Artificial Intelligence Research, ACM Comp. Sur. 6, 153 – 174, (1974)

[2] Burstall, R., MacQueen, D., Sannella, D.: HOPE: An Experimental Applicative Language, Report CSR - 62 - 80, Computer Science Dept., Edinburgh, (1980)

[3] CIP Language Group: The Munich Project CIP. Volume I: The wide spectrum language CIP - L, Springer, LNCS 183, (1985)

[4] Clocksin, F. W., Mellish, C. S.: Programming in Prolog, Springer (1981)

[5] Gersdorf, B.: A Functional Language for Term Manipulation, PROSPECTRA M.3.1.S1 - SN - 2.0, (1987)

[6] Heckmann, R.: A Proposal for the Syntactic Part of the PROSPECTRA Transformation Language, PROSPECTRA S.1.6 - SN - 6.0, (1987)

[7] Heckmann, R.: Semantics of Patterns, PROSPECTRA S.1.6 - SN - 8.0, (1987)

[8] Heckmann, R.: Syntax and Semantics of TrafoLa, PROSPECTRA S.1.6 - SN - 10.0, (1987)

[9] Huet, G., Lang., B.: Proving and Applying Program Transformations Expressed with Second Order Patterns, Acta Inf. 11, 31 - 55, (1978)

[10] Krieg-Brückner, B.: Informal Specification of the PROSPECTRA System, PROSPECTRA M.1.1.S1 - R - 9.1, (1986)

[11] Krieg-Brückner, B.: Systematic Transformation of Interface Specifications, in: Partsch, H. (ed.): Program Specification and Transformation, Proc. IFIP TC2 Working Conf. (Tölz '86), North Holland, (1987)

[12] Krieg-Brückner, B.: Algebraic Formalisation of Program Development by Transformation, Springer, this volume, (1988)

[13] Milner, R.: The Standard ML Core Language, In: Polymorphism, Vol. II, Number 2, (Oct. 1985)

[14] Turner, D. A.: Miranda: a non-strict Functional Language with Polymorphic Types, Springer, LNCS 201, (1985)

Garp : Graph Abstractions for Concurrent Programming

Simon M. Kaplan*
University of Illinois
Department of Computer Science
Urbana, IL 61081

Gail E. Kaiser†
Columbia University
Department of Computer Science
New York, NY 10027

Abstract: Several research projects are investigating parallel processing languages where dynamic process topologies can be constructed. Failure to impose abstractions on interprocess connection patterns can result in arbitrary interconnection topologies that are difficult to understand. We propose the use of a graph-grammar based formalism to control the complexities arising from trying to program such dynamic networks.

keywords: abstraction, actors, concurrency, distributed system, graph grammar, message passing, object-oriented system, parallel processing

There is a growing need for effective ways to organize ... distributed programs [14].

1 Introduction

Languages with the ability to generate arbitrary networks of processes are increasingly a focus of research. Little effort has been directed, however, towards abstractions of the resulting topologies; failure to support such abstractions can lead to chaotic programs that are difficult to understand and maintain. We propose graph grammar-based abstractions as a means for imposing structure on topologies. This paper introduces GARP (Graph Abstractions for Concurrent Programming), a notation based on graph grammars [11] for describing dynamic interconnection topologies.

Graph grammars are similar to string grammars, except that (1) the body of a production is a graph and (2) the rewriting action is the replacement of a vertex by a graph.

---

*Netmail: kaplan@a.cs.uiuc.edu. Supported in part by a grant from the AT&T Corporation.

†Netmail: kaiser@cs.columbia.edu. Supported in part by grants from the AT&T Foundation, Siemens Research and Technology Laboratories, and New York State Center for Advanced Technology — Computer & Information Systems, and in part by a Digital Equipment Corporation Faculty Award.

The purpose of GARP is to replace arbitrary dynamic communication patterns with abstractions in the same sense that Dijkstra [6] replaced goto-ridden spaghetti code with structured control constructs. There is a cost to this, of course. Just as there are some sequential programs that are difficult to write in a programming language without gotos, there are topologies that are difficult if not impossible to specify using GARP. There is, however, a major difference between the graph grammar approach taken in GARP and the adding of structured programming constructs to sequential programming languages: In the latter case, a fixed set of constructs are always used, while in the former we know that we *need* abstractions, but not what specific patterns to provide. So in GARP the grammar is used to give a set of patterns for a particular program, not for all programs.

GARP uses graph grammars as follows. For a graph generated from a graph grammar, each vertex is interpreted as a process (which we call an *agent*). Agents have *ports* through which they can send and receive messages. Edges in the graph provide asynchronous communications paths between ports. Rewriting of an agent by a production corresponds to the spawning of a graph of new processes as defined in the body of the production, and connecting these into the process topology to replace the agent being rewritten using a connection strategy specified in the production. The agents perform all computation (including the initiation of rewrites on the graph) while the graph grammar acts as an abstraction structure that describes the legal process topologies.

To illustrate the use of the GARP framework we adopt a model in which GARP agents are Scheme [19] programs augmented with port operations (definable in terms of core scheme and a *bag* data type) and operations to control rewriting (defined in terms of graph grammar theory). We emphasize that this model of agents is not central to our use of graph grammars to control process topology complexities; our ideas are equally applicable to other proposals for process models, including Actors [2], Cantor [4], NIL [20] and Argus [14].

Section 2 defines the agents component of GARP, section 3 defines graph grammars and section 4 shows how graph grammars are adapted into the GARP programming formalism. Section 5 discusses the Scheme implementation of our ideas and illustrates GARP with two examples. Section 6 summarizes GARP in the light of the examples. Section 7 compares GARP to related work, especially Actor systems and other applications of graph grammars to distributed systems.

let m = a message (contents are irrelevant)
    b = a bag. The internal representation for the Message Handler.
    [] = an empty bag
operations
    `(M-receive b m)` ⇒ `b` ← `(⊙ m b)`
    `(M-empty b)` ⇒ `(if (= b []) ` *true false*`)`
    `(M-send b)` ⇒ `(choice b)` and `b` ← `(rest b)`
end

Figure 1: Semantics for Message Handlers

2 Message Handlers, Ports and Agents

Computation in GARP is performed by groups of *agents*. Agents communicate among themselves by writing messages to or reading messages from *ports*. Messages written on ports are stored by a *message handler* until read by another agent.

A message handler represents the pool of messages that have been sent to it, but not yet delivered to any agent, as a *bag*. If `a` is an item that can be inserted into a bag and `b` and `c` are bags, the operations on bags are: `(⊙ a b)` (insertion), `(∈ a b)` (membership), `(= b c)` (equality), `(choice b)`, (which nondeterministically chooses an element of `b`) and `(rest b)` (which returns the remainder of the bag after a `choose`). Manna and Waldinger [15] give a theory of bags.

Message handlers are an abstraction built on top of bags. The operations on message handlers, together with their semantics, are given in figure 1. These operations are atomic. An additional level of detail is needed if sending a message to a port is to be a *broadcast* operation; this is a simple extension and the details are omitted.

Agents communicate by reading from and writing to ports. They can be implemented in any language, but must support the following minimal set of porthandling constructs (with behaviour in terms of the message handling commands in figure 1:

- `(send port message)` is interpreted as `(M-recieve port message)`.
- `(msg? port)` is interpreted as `(not (M-empty port))`.
- `(on port body)` is interpreted as wait until `(msg? port)` is true, then apply `body` to the result of `(M-send port)`.

With these operations, more sophisticated operations can be defined, such as:

- (on-and portlist body). Wait until each port in the portlist has a message, and then apply the body to the message(s).
- (on-or ({(port body)}*)). Nondeterministically choose a port with a message, and apply the corresponding body to the message.
- Looping versions of on, on-or and on-and.

An agent can be thought of as a closure whose parameters include the ports through which it will communicate with other agents, and is similar to a process in CSP [10] or NIL, an actor in Actor Systems, an object in Cantor, a guardian in Argus or a task in Ada[1] [1]. As in Actor Systems, Cantor and NIL, communication among agents is asynchronous, and the arrival order of messages at a port is nondeterministic. By *asynchronous* we mean that the sending process does not know the state of the intended reciever, as opposed to a *synchronous* communication, in which the reciever must be ready and willing to recieve a message before the sender can transmit it.

The interconnections among agents are determined using the graph grammar formalism described in the following section.

3 Graph Grammars

Graph grammars are similar in structure to string grammars. There is an alphabet of symbols, divided into three (disjoint) sets called the terminals, nonterminals and portsymbols. Productions have a nonterminal symbol as the goal (the same nonterminal may be the goal of many productions), and the right-hand side of the production has two parts: a graph (called the bodygraph) and an embedding rule. Each vertex in the bodygraph is labeled by a terminal or nonterminal symbol, and has associated with it a set of portsymbols. Any portsymbol may be associated with many terminals or nonterminals.

The rewriting action on a graph (the host graph) is the *replacement* of a vertex labeled with a nonterminal by the bodygraph of a production for which that nonterminal is the goal, and the *embedding* of the bodygraph into the host graph. This embedding process involves connecting (ports associated with) vertices in the bodygraph to (ports associated with) vertices in the host graph. The embedding process is restricted so that when a vertex v is rewritten, only vertices that are in the *neighborhood* of v—those connected to v by a path of unit length—can be connected to the vertices in the bodygraph that replaces v.

[1] Ada is a trademark of the United States Government, Ada Joint Program Office.

Because we use these graph grammars as an abstraction construct for concurrent programming, we call them concurrent abstraction grammars (CAGs).

Each symbol in the alphabet of terminals and nonterminals has associated with it a set of symbols called ***portsymbols***. The same portsymbol may be associated with several terminals or nonterminals. We denote terminals and nonterminals by uppercase characters $X, Y, \cdots$ and portnames by Greek characters $\alpha, \beta, \cdots$. Vertices are denoted $v, w, \cdots$ and the symbol labeling a vertex v is identified by Lab_v. PS_X denotes the set of portsymbols associated with the (terminal or nonterminal) symbol X.

For any graph G, let V_G denote the vertices in G and E_G the edges of G. Each vertex v can be qualified by the portsymbols in PS_{Lab_v} to form a *port-identifier*. Edges are denoted by pairs of port-identifiers, for example $(v.\alpha, w.\beta)$. For any vertex v in a graph G, the neighborhood of v, $\mathcal{N}_v$, is $\{w \mid (v, w) \in E_G\}$.

Definition 1 *A concurrent abstraction graph grammar is a tuple $CAG = (N, T, S, P, Z)$, where N is a finite set of symbols called the nonterminals of the grammar, T is a finite set of symbols called the terminals of the grammar and S is a finite set of symbols called the portsymbols of the grammar such that $T \cap N = N \cap S = T \cap S = \emptyset$; P is a set of productions, where productions are defined in definition 2 below; and Z is a unique distinguished nonterminal known as the axiom of the grammar.*

The axiom Z is the goal of exactly one production and may not appear in any bodygraph. This requirement is not a restriction in practice as one can always augment a grammar with a distinguished production that satisfies this requirement.

Definition 2 *A production in a CAG is defined as: $p : L_p \rightarrow B_p, F_p$ where p is a unique label; $L_p \in N$ is called the goal of the production; B_p is an arbitrary graph (called the bodygraph of the production), where each vertex is labeled by an element of $T \cup N$; and F_p is the embedding rule of the production: a set of pairs $(X.\alpha, L_p.\gamma)$ or $[X.\alpha, Y.\beta]$, where X labels a vertex in $B_p, \alpha \in PS_X, \beta \in PS_Y, \gamma \in PS_{L_p}$.*

The same symbol may appear several times in a bodygraph; this is resolved by subscripting the symbol with an index value to allow them to be distinguished [22].

Definition 3 *The rewriting (or refinement) of a vertex v in a graph G constructed from a CAG by a production p for which Lab_v is the goal is performed in the following steps:*

- *The neighborhood $\mathcal{N}_v$ is identified.*
- *The vertex v and all edges incident on it are removed from G.*
- *The bodygraph B_p is instantiated to form a daughter-graph, which is inserted into G.*

- *The daughter graph is embedded as follows. For each pair in F_p of the form $(X.\alpha, L_p.\gamma)$ an edge is placed from the α port of each vertex in the daughter-graph labeled by X to whatever $v.\gamma$ was connected to before the start of the rewriting. For each pair in F_p of the form $[X.\alpha, Y.\beta]$ an edge is placed from the α port of each vertex in the daughter-graph labeled by X to the β port of each vertex in the set $\{w \mid w \in \mathcal{N}_v$ and $Lab_w = Y\}$.*

Note there are two ways to specify an embedding pair, using () or [] notation. The former is often more convenient, but more restrictive as it gives no way to take a port-identifier with several inputs and split those over the vertices in the bodygraph when rewriting.

The most important property that CAGs should have is *confluence*. Such a property would mean that any vertices in the graph can be rewritten in parallel. Unfortunately, we will prove that two vertices that are in one another's neighborhoods cannot be rewritten in parallel (although the graphs are otherwise confluent). This important result means that the rewriting action must be atomic. We approach the proof of this result in two steps: first we prove an intermediate result about the restriction of the extent of embeddings; the limited confluence result follows.

Definition 4 *By* recursive rewriting *of a vertex v we mean possibly rewriting v to some graph—the instantiation of the bodygraph B_p of some rule p for which v is the goal—and then rewriting recursively the vertices in that graph.*

Definition 5 *For any vertex v in a graph G, let $\mathcal{N}_v^*$ denote the universe of possible neighbourhoods of v that could arise by rewriting (recursively) the vertices of $\mathcal{N}_v$; G_v^* denote the universe of graphs obtainable by all possible recursive rewritings of v; and let $S_v^* = G_v^* - (G - \{v\})$,*[2] i.e., *$S_v^*$ is just the set of subgraphs constructable from v in the recursive rewriting.*

Lemma 6 *Given a vertex v in a graph G, any (recursive) rewriting of v will not introduce edges from the vertices of the daughter graph of v (or any daughter graph recursively introduced into that daughter graph) to any vertex that is not in $\mathcal{N}_v^* \cup S_v^*$.*

Proof: By induction on the rewriting strategy.

Basis: Consider a graph G with a nonterminal vertex v. Refine v by a production p for which Lab_v is the goal. By definition of CAGs, all the vertices in G to which the vertices of the daughter-graph may be connected are in N_v. Therefore the base case does not contradict the theorem.

Inductive Step: Consider now the graph G' with a vertex v', where G' has been formed from G by a

[2]Note this is set difference so the "-" does not distribute.

series of refinements (starting with a vertex v), and v' has been introduced into the graph by one of these refinements. $N_{v'}$ will include only vertices introduced into G by the refinement(s) from v to v', and vertices in N_v^*. Now rewrite v'. Only vertices in $N_{v'}$ can receive edges as the result of embedding the new daughter-graph, so the statement of the theorem remains true under the effect of the rewriting. This completes the proof.

□

Theorem 7 *Two vertices v and w in each other's neighbourhood (i.e. $v \in \mathcal{N}_w$ and $w \in \mathcal{N}_v$) may not be rewritten in parallel.*

Proof: Suppose that it were possible to rewrite the two vertices in parallel and that any rewrite of w would introduce a new vertex x such that $Lab_w = Lab_x$, that would connect to v by the embedding rule, and *vice versa*. Suppose further that once the daughter-graph replacing w hs been instantiated, but before the edge to v has been placed, the rewriting of v begins by removing v from the graph. Clearly at this point there is no vertex v to which to perform the embedding. Therefore it cannot be possible to rewrite two vertices that are in one another's neighbourhoods in parallel.

□

Corollary 8 *Given a graph G constructed from a CAG, the vertices in G may be rewritten in any order.*

Proof: Follows from previous theorem and lemma.

□

4 Relating Graph Grammars and Agents

A GARP program has two parts: a CAG and code for each agent. Vertices in the graph grammar represent agents. Each agent name is either a terminal or nonterminal symbol of the grammar. We extend the reportoire of the agents to include a `rewrite` operation with form:

```
(rewrite name exp ...)
```

where `name` is the label of a production that has the name of the agent about to be rewritten as goal and the `exp ...` are parameters to the production. The interpretation of this operation is the definition of rewriting given in section 3. The `rewrite` action must be the agent's last, because the model of rewriting requires that the agent be replaced by the agents in the bodygraph of the production used in the rewriting.

We extend the production labels of graph grammars to have a list of formal parameters. Each element of the list is a pair `<agent, parameter>`, which identifies the agent in the bodygraph of the production to which the parameter must be passed, and the specific formal parameter for that agent that should be used. When rewriting, the agents specified in the parameter list are passed the appropriate actual parameter when they are created. This ability to pass arguments from an agent to the agents that replace it provides a way to pass the state of the agent to its replacements. This feature is not unique to our agent system and can be found in Actors and Cantor.

5 Examples

This section of the paper illustrates the use of GARP with two examples written in GARP/Scheme, a version of GARP that uses Scheme as the underlying language for agents. In this system, agents and productions are implemented as first-class scheme objects; we can therefore experiment with parallel programming and our ideas on process struture while retaining all the advantages of a small but extremely powerful programming language[3]. All the features of a programming language required for GARP agents have been implemented in Scheme using that language's powerful macro facilities to provide rewrite rules into core Scheme. There is nothing about the implementation that is unique to Scheme, however; another implementation using the object-oriented language MELD [13] as an underlying framework is under development.

The first example gives a GARP program for quicksort as a tutorial: this is not the most efficient way to sort a stream of numbers, but the GARP program is easy to understand. The second example demonstrates a systems application: this GARP program takes as input an encoding of a dataflow program, generates a dataflow machine tailored for it, and then executes it. This could be useful in allocating processors in a large MIMD machine to dataflow tasks.

The graph grammar for the quicksort example is found in figure 2, and the code for the agents in figure 3. There are two further agents, not shown, modeling standard input and output. This program takes a stream of numbers from standard input, sorts them using divide and conquer, and then passes the result to standard output. The program executes recursively: When the `sort-abs` agent receives a message that is not the end-of-file object, it rewrites itself to a `sort-body` bodygraph, passing the message just read as a seed value to the `split` vertex introduced in the rewrite. This `split` vertex passes all values received by it that are greater than the seed through the `hi` port, all other values through the `lo` port, and the seed itself through the `seedport`. The `join` agent waits for messages on its `lo`, `hi` and `seed` ports and passes the concatenation of these three messages to its `out` port. The `lo` and `hi` ports are connected to `sort-abs` agents, which in turn rewrite themselves to `sort-body` graphs on receipt of an appropriate message. When end-of-file is

[3]A copy of this implementation is available from the first author.

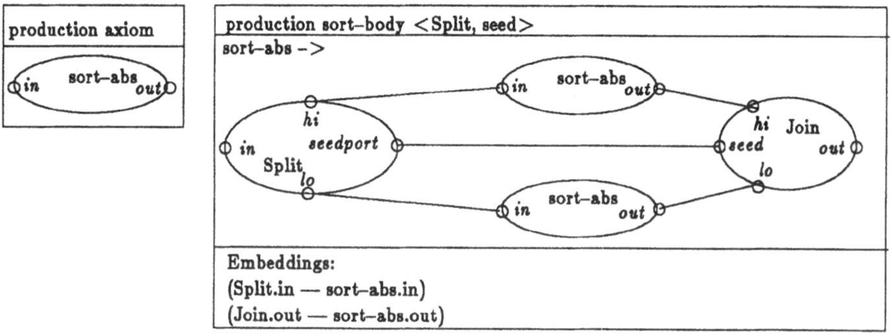

Figure 2: Sort Example - Graph Grammar

encountered, it is propagated through the graph and the `sort-abs` agents left in the graph send the empty list as a "result" value. The `axiom` production starts the program running.

The graph grammar for the dataflow example is given in figure 4 (the agent code is omitted due to space restrictions). In this system, the `controller` agent reads dataflow programs as input messages, and passes them to the `prog` node, which immediately rewrites itself to a new `prog`, an `out-handler` and a `df` agent. The new `prog` waits for another dataflow program, while the `df` node rewrites itself to a dataflow machine (using the `arithmetic`, `identity` and `if-statement` productions, and the `out-handler` waits for the output from the dataflow machine. At each stage of this construction process the `df` agent looks at its `program` parameter, decides what sort of construct to rewrite to, breaks up the `program` accordingly, and passes the components to the new agents via the parameters of the production used in the rewriting. For example, when an arithmetic operation is identified, the `program` can be broken up into the operation, a "left" program fragment and a "right" program fragment. The `df` agent recognizes these components and rewrites itself using the `arithmetic` production, passing the operation to the `arithop` agent and the "left" and "right" program fragments to the appropriate new agents. Leaf values, such as constants, are handled internally by the `df` agent (and therefore are in no production explicitly).

Only a simple dataflow language is supported in this example; extension to more complex constructs is not difficult. Once the dataflow machine has been built, it executes the program for which it was constructed and then passes the results to the `out-handler` agent.

GARP is also particularly well suited to the large class of *adaptive grid* programs, such as linear differential equation solvers[21]. In such a program, a grid is constructed and the function solved at each point in the

```
(agent sort-abst
       (ports inport outport)
       (on inport (lambda  (message)
                    (if (eq? message eof-object)
                        (send outport '())
                        (rewrite sort-body message)))))

(agent split
       (args seed)
       (ports in hi seedport lo)
       (send seedport seed)
       (loop in (lambda (in)
                  (if (not (eq? in eof-object))
                      (begin
                        (if (< in seed)
                            (send lo in)
                            (send hi in)))
                      (begin
                        (send hi eof-object)
                        (send lo eof-object)
                        (break))))))

(agent join
       (ports hi seed lo out)
       (on-and (his seed lo)
               (lambda (hi seed lo)
                 (send out (append lo (list seed) hi)))))
```

Figure 3: Sort Example – Agent Code

grid. Grid points in each other's neighborhood then transmit their solutions to one another. If there is too large a discontinuity between results at any point, that point is rewritten to a finer grid and the process repeated. Solutions to such problems find natural expression in GARP.

6 Graphs and Abstractions

We can now summarize how CAGs help control network topologies. Rather than allowing agents to connect to other agents in arbitrary ways, the interconnections are taken care of by the CAG. We see several advantages to this approach. First, it forces grouping of agents (via productions) that will cooperate together to perform some aspect of the computation. It is easy to see which agents will work together; one just has to look at the CAG. Second, interconnection topologies are determined at the level of the CAG, not at the level of individual agents. This means that setting up topologies becomes the province of the designer rather than of the programmers implementing the agents, as good software engineering practice dictates.

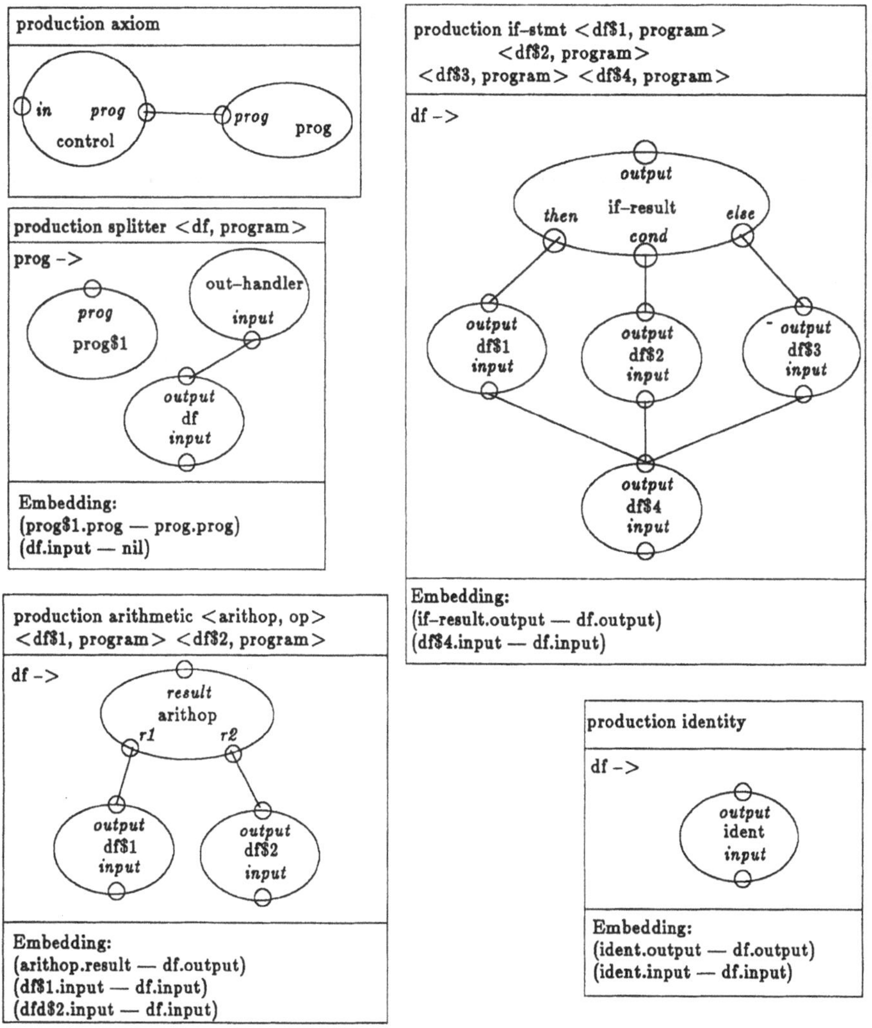

Figure 4: Dataflow Example - Graph Grammar

7 Related Work

There is a large body of literature on graph grammars (see, for example, [7]). Some researchers have developed very powerful formalisms where graphs can be rewritten to graphs rather than just rewriting vertices [8] [17]. This work is quite attractive on the surface, but would be almost impossible to implement: identifying the graph to be rewritten is NP-hard, and it is not clear how to synchronize the mutual rewriting of the vertices in the graphs. The primary focus of these researchers has been on theoretical issues such as the confluence of various classes of graph grammars and the hardness of the recognizability problem. We have instead based CAGs on a more limited form of graph grammar, Node Label Controlled (NLC) grammars [11]. The basic difference between CAG and NLC grammars is each CAG production has its own embedding rule. Our "semi-confluence" theorem does not, to our knowledge, appear in the literature. GARP can be viewed as an extension of NLC grammar research into a more practical domain.

Kahn and MacQueen [12] have investigated a parallel programming model in which individual processes are replaced by networks; while our work is similar, the major difference is that we have a formal way of modelling the network topologies that are created.

Degano and Montanari [5] have used a graph grammar formalism similar to CAG as the vehicle for modeling distributed systems. Although their work differs from ours in several respects—a more restricted model of embedding is used, there is no model of communication among processes, graphs in their formalism carry history information, and the grammars are used to model programs rather than as a programming formalism in their own right—it is still an interesting complement to our work, and we believe that many of their results will be transferable.

GARP is most similar to Actors[4] [3] [9]. An important difference is that in GARP communications patterns are defined in the grammar, whereas in actors they are set up by passing of addresses among Actors. We believe that this lack of structure is potentially dangerous, as it relies on the goodwill and cooperation of the programmers building the system. As long as the programmers continue to cooperate successfully, the system will work; but the smallest error in propagation of Actor addresses could lead to chaos. Experience with large software systems written in sequential programming languages strongly suggests that lack of suitable structuring constructs for the network will cause serious software engineering problems. An attempt to address this problem using *receptionists* allows the programmer to break up the Actors into groups by convention only; a mischevious programmer may still break the system by passing "internal" Actor addresses out to other Actors. In GARP this cannot happen.

[4]Space dictates that we assume the reader is familiar with Actor systems

The distinction between the process spawning supported by Actors and by GARP is analogous to the replacement of conditional and unconditional branches in sequential programming languages with structured control constructs. The distinction between the communication patterns is analogous to the distinction between dynamic and lexical scoping.

Two other ways of describing parallel networks—CCS [16] and Petri Nets [18]—are also related to our work. With CCS we share the concept of ports and the idea of a network of processes; however, we use asynchronous communication where CCS is synchronous and needs no notion of global time. It also seems that the application of CCS is limited to fixed topology networks. Petri nets use asynchronous communication, but are also limited to fixed topology.

There are several other approaches to concurrent programming that we have cited in the text: Ada focuses on providing a good language model for a process, and all but ignores interprocess topology issues; Cantor is interested in parallel object-oriented programming and gives the same support for topology control as does Actor Systems; and Argus focuses on issues of atomicity and robustness. These issues are orthagonal to those addressed in this paper.

8 Conclusions

MIMD computer systems make inevitable the development of large parallel programs. At present there are no adaquate ways to specify the interconnections among processes in these programs. We believe that this will lead to a situation in which programs can generate completely arbitrary process topologies. Such programs will be difficult to debug, verify, or maintain. This problem is analogous to the "goto problem" of the 1960's, and we propose an analogous solution: rather than being able to construct arbitrary networks, abstractions should be imposed that control network structure. However, unlike the "goto problem", we do not believe that it will be possible to derive a set of standard form similar to the "if" and "do" forms used in sequential programming; rather, we believe that for each parallel program, the designer should identify a set of interconnection topology templates and use those as the abstractions for that program.

Graph grammars provide an excellent medium in which to encode these templates, and in the GARP system we have shown that a mechanical interpretation of a subclass of graph grammars – CAG grammars – does indeed allow the specification of interprocess connections and their automatic use in a parallel programming system.

Acknowledgements

Thanks to Roy Campbell and Steve Goering for frequent discussions on the GARP system and the theory underlying it, as well as their comments on earlier drafts of this paper.

References

[1] *Reference Manual for the Ada Programming Language.* Technical Report MIL-STD 1815, United States Department of Defense.

[2] Gul Agha. *ACTORS: A Model of Concurrent Computation in Distributed Systems.* M.I.T. Press, Cambridge, Mass., 1986.

[3] Gul Agha. Semantic considerations in the actor paradigm of concurrent computation. In A. W. Roscoe S. D. Brookes and G. Winskel, editors, *Seminar on Concurrency, LNCS 197*, pages 151–179, Springer-Verlag, New York, 1985.

[4] W. C. Athas and C. L. Seitz. *Cantor User Report.* Technical Report 5232:TR:86, California Institute of Technology, January 1987.

[5] Pierpaolo Degano and Ugo Montenari. A model for distributed systems based on graph rewriting. *J. ACM*, 34(2):411–449, April 1987.

[6] Edsger W. Dijkstra. *A Discipline of Programming.* Prentice-Hall, Englewood Cliffs, NJ, 1976.

[7] Hartmut Ehrig, Manfred Nagl, and Grzegorz Rozenberg (eds). *Graph Grammars and their Application to Computer Science, Lecture Notes in Computer Science 153.* Springer-Verlag, 1984.

[8] Hartmut Erhig. Introduction to the algebraic theory of graph grammars. In Hartmut Erhig Volker Claus and Grzegorz Rozenberg, editors, *Graph Grammars and their Application to Computer Science and Biology*, pages 1–69, Springer-Verlag, Heidelberg, 1979.

[9] C. Hewitt, T. Reinhart, G. Agha, and G Attardi. Linguistic support of receptionists for shared resources. In A. W. Roscoe S. D. Brookes and G. Winskel, editors, *Seminar on Concurrency, LNCS 197*, pages 151–179, Springer-Verlag, New York, 1985.

[10] C. A. R. Hoare. Communicating sequential processes. *Communications of the ACM*, 21(8):666–677, August 1978.

EXTENDING FUNCTIONAL PROGRAMMING TOWARDS RELATIONS

Remi Legrand
LITP - CNRS UA 248, Université P. et M. Curie - Paris 6
2 place Jussieu, 75252 Paris Cedex 5, FRANCE
uucp : ....!mcvax!inria!litp!rl

Abstract : This article describes the relational programming paradigm. Because a function is a particular case of relation, we can consider the computation of points-to-set processes (relations) instead of points-to-point processes (functions). Relations are useful for parallel, non-deterministic or multi-valued algorithms. The first section presents the main features of the proposed language and it is shown how relations make programs more flexible and natural. Then, we present an efficient implementation of the language on a classical architecture.

1 - INTRODUCTION

In this section, the main principles of the relational programming concept are developed.

Functions and Relations : A computable function is a points-to-point process since it associates at most one value to its arguments. A n-ary function f can be defined by the n+1-ary relation R such that :

$$R = \{(x1,x2,....xn,y) \ / \ y=f(x1,...xn)\}$$

Relations are a generalization of functions in the sense that they associate a possibly infinite set of values to their arguments [Nguyen 85, Eilenberg 70]. For instance, the n+1-ary relation R(x1,..,xn,y) defines the points-to-set function f such that : $f(x1,..,xn) = \{y \ / \ R(x1,..,xn,y)\}$

Computable Relations : The automatic treatment of all mathematical relations is impossible so we must deal only with computable relations [Cutland 80]. The relations that we consider are defined by computable programs written in the language GREL given in the next section. The programs in GREL are constructed by combining smaller programs until we reach some primitives which are ordinary functions. Special operators are designed in order to turn several functions into a single relation with a finite number of results. And recursivity allows to construct relations with an infinite but nevertheless semi-computable set of results.

Relations and Continuations : The result of a relational program is a finite or infinite set of values. These values are returned one at a time and are used by the continuation of the relation which can be any kind of process, a function or an other relation. The overall program consisting of a relation followed by its continuation acts as a pipe where the relation provides input values and the continuation processes them. A special set of control operators allows to break the pipe or capture values.

[11] Dirk Janssens and Grzegorz Rozenberg. Graph grammars with node-label control and rewriting. In Hartmut Ehrig, Manfred Nagl, and Grzegorz Rozenberg, editors, *Proceedings of the second International Workshop on Graph Grammars and their Application to Computer Science, LNCS 153*, pages 186–205, Springer-Verlag, 1982.

[12] G. Kahn and D. MacQueen. Coroutines and networks of parallel processes. In *Information Processing 77*, pages 993–998, Academic Press, 1978.

[13] Gail E. Kaiser and David Garlan. Melding data flow and object-oriented programming. In *Conference on Object Oriented Programming Systems, Languages, and Applications*, Kissimmee, FL, October 1987.

[14] Barbara Liskov and Robert Scheifler. Guardians and actions: linguistic support for robust, distributed programs. *ACM TOPLAS*, 5(3):381–404, July 1983.

[15] Zohar Manna and Richard Waldinger. *The Logical Basis for Computer Programming, Volume 1.* Addison-Wesley, Reading, Mass., 1985.

[16] R. Milner. A calculus of communicating systems. In *Lecture Notes in Computer Science volume 92*, Springer-Verlag, Berlin, 1980.

[17] Manfred Nagl. A tutorial and bibliographical survey on graph grammars. In Hartmut Erhig Volker Claus and Grzegorz Rozenberg, editors, *Graph Grammars and their Application to Computer Science and Biology*, pages 70–126, Springer-Verlag, Heidelberg, 1979.

[18] C. A. Petri. Concurrency. In *Net Theory and Applications, LNCS 84*, Springer-Verlag, Berlin, 1980.

[19] J. Rees and W. Clinger (Editors). Revised (3) report on the algorithmic language scheme. *Sigplan Notices*, 21(12):37–79, December 1986.

[20] Robert E. Strom and Shaula Yemini. The nil distributed systems programming language: a status report. In S. D. Brookes, A. W. Roscoe, and G. Winskel, editors, *Seminar On Concurrency, LNCS 197*, pages 512–523, Springer-Verlag, New York, 1985.

[21] J. F. Thompson, Z.U.A Warsi, and C. W. Mastin. *Numerical Grid Generation: Foundations and Applications*. North-Holland, New York, 1985.

[22] William M. Waite and Gerhard Goos. *Compiler Construction*. Springer-Verlag, New York, 1984.

Multisets of Results : The same value may occur many times in a relation. Because a value is transmitted to the continuation as soon as it is computed, no trace is kept of it and it is not possible to remove its further occurrences. Although this case is rare and issued from computation organization, it is better to talk about points-to-multiset relations than points-to-set relations. Moreover, the elements of these multisets are computed sequentially and we must consider that they are ordered by their times of appearance.

Control of Relations : Therefore, a relation applied to some arguments becomes a value generator which can be controlled and used with appropriate tools provided by the language. For instance, the programmer can choose between different strategies which determine the order of appearance of the values.

Running vs. Suspended : As in most functional languages where programs are objects, the result of applying a relation can be considered as an object of the language as soon as it is created and captured. The object relation can be treated as any other object and looks like a suspended process. For instance, we can duplicate it, kill it or activate it in order to get the next value. Thus a relation may have two states, running or suspended. A running relation partakes of the current process whereas a suspended relation may be temporarily runned as an oracle providing values.

Use of Relation : The usefulness of relations in the design of algorithms appears when programs are non deterministic, parallel or multi-valued. For instance we can construct a class of values by giving parallel inductive rules of construction which can be applied non-deterministicaly. The class of numbers $P(x,y) = \{ x^p * y^q , p,q \in N\}$ can be defined by :

$$P(x,y) = \{1\} \cup \{x * k, k \in P(x,y)\} \cup \{y * k, k \in P(x,y)\}$$

Relations can also be used for streams generation because a stream is a particular case of relation where any value is given by a function of its predecessor. Finally, it will be shown that relations are efficiently and flexibly usable in programs where functions have multiple results.

Host Language for Relations : Since early 60's, a lot of functional languages have been designed but none of them have been extended so as to support the computation of relations. The main reason seems to be the presence of variables since almost all these languages are lambda-languages. As a matter of fact, variables compel the implementation to do a very complex environment management which seems unrealistic in the general case of relations. That is why the variableless programming language GRAAL [Bellot 86a, Bellot 86b] has been chosen as the host language for the relational calculus.

Principle of Implementation : It is important to see that a relation will not only be a kind of function with multi-values. In order to accept all recursive relations with eventualy an infinite set of results, partial results must be immediately transmitted and not "put in wait". It is implemented by a *pipe-oriented* mecanism. Because all resulting values of a relation are transmitted to its continuation, the same computation occurs as many times as there are such values. That is to say that the unfoldings of these computations in the stack are done every time although they are roughly identical one to each other. The main principle of the implementation is to preserve the first unfolding in the stack so that it can be used without being constructed by further computations. This is realized through an original system of caches onto the reduction stack. With this method of implementation, the average loss of GREL compared to GRAAL is only 10% so that Relational GRAAL is still among the fastest applicative languages.

The plan of the article is the following. The first section is a brief introduction to the programming language GRAAL and its principles. The second section describes the new operators required in order to support the relational concept. The third section shows how relations can be used in the design of algorithms. Finally, the last section describes the implementation of relations as an extension to the GRAAL reduction machine described in [Bellot 86a].

2 - GRAAL, the Host Language

We present a short digest of the language GRAAL. A complete presentation of GRAAL and its issues is in [Bellot 86b], and its theorical support is given in [Bellot 87]. GRAAL is a functional programming language without variable. It is based on the notions of functional forms and uncurryfied combinators. The functions are polyadic. The application of a function **f** to the arguments **a1,...,an** is denoted **(f : a1...an)**. Applications are reduced using call-by-value. The notation E ➨ F stands for "E reduces (or evaluates) to F". The objects are numbers, symbols,lists or functional forms. Lists, used as data, are denoted by brackets instead of parenthesis. Examples : <>, < a b < 1 c 2 > >.

The primitive functions are issued from Lisp systems [Chailloux 84]. Semantic of functions is described by reduction rules. Examples :

car : < a . b > ➨ a	car : <> ➨ <>
cdr : < a . b > ➨ b	cdr : <> ➨ <>
cons : a b ➨ < a . b >	
null : <> ➨ true	null : a ➨ <> if a ≠ <>
add : 2 3 ➨ 5	sub1 : 5 ➨ 4
true : a1...an ➨ true	false : a1...an ➨ <>
eq : a b ➨ true if a = b	id : a ➨ a

Arguments of a function are implicitly numbered starting from one. If **k > 0**, **#k** applied to n arguments with **k ≤ n**, reduces to the argument whose rank is **k**. Example :

#3 : a b c d e f ➨ c   #5 : a b c ➨ error

The reader in acquaintance with functional programming may complete by himself the set of primitive functions and their reduction rules.

More complex functions are built with functional forms which are combinations of functions. A functional form realizes a functional operation occurring frequently in programs. The primary syntax is **(opf p1 ...pn)** where **opf** is the name and **p1,p2,...pn** are the parameters. Despite of appearance, **(opf p1 ...pn)** is not a list. Functional behaviour of forms is described by reduction rules. The set of functional forms is not fixed. Only a few of them will be considered in this article.

<u>Composition</u> : the name of the composition form is **comp**. It accepts any number of parameters greater than two. Its reduction rule is :

$$\frac{gi : a1 \ldots an \Rightarrow bi, \quad 1 \le i \le p}{(\text{comp } f\ g1 \ldots\ldots gp) : a1 \ldots an \Rightarrow f : b1 \ldots bp}$$

For sake of readibility, the syntactic analyser of GRAAL will recognize the following notations :

1) f o g stands for (comp f g)
2) {f g1...gn} stands for (comp f g1...gn)
3) (f g1...gn) stands for (comp f g1...gn) if **f** is not a combinator but is defined.

Conditional : the name of this form is **if** and it accepts three parameters. Its rules of reduction are:

$$\frac{p : a1 \ldots an \Rightarrow \langle\rangle}{(\text{if } p\ f\ g) : a1 \ldots an \Rightarrow g : a1 \ldots an} \qquad \frac{p : a1 \ldots an \Rightarrow x\ ,\ x \neq \langle\rangle}{(\text{if } p\ f\ g) : a1 \ldots an \Rightarrow f : a1 \ldots an}$$

Constant : in order to program a constant function, we must use the one-parameter form whose name is **cste**. Its reduction rule is : (cste c) : a1 ...an ➡ c
The syntactic analyser of GRAAL recognizes the notation **'c** for **(cste c)**.

Examples of defined functions : the definition of a function **f** is given by the evaluation of the expression **(de : f b)**, where **f** is a symbol (the name) and **b** is a function (the body). So, we have the examples :

```
(de : caddr   car o cdr o cdr)

(de : last  (if   null o cdr   car   last o cdr))

(de : append
     (if   null o #1
           #2
           {cons  car o #1  {append  cdr o #1  #2}} ))
```

The reader may find a lot of programming examples in [Bellot 86b] and the scheme of implementation is given in [Bellot 86a].

3 - RELATIONAL GRAAL

The relational GRAAL is also called GREL (acronym of Graal RELationnel). It is a development of GRAAL towards the relations. All the primitive functions and forms in GRAAL are still used in GREL. The evaluation of a function is almost the same. But, in GREL we add special forms and functions in order to built "non-functional" relations.

Notation : when the application of a relation **f** to the arguments **a1,...an** gives a multiset of results **b1,b2,...** , we denote the reduction (evaluation) by : (f : a1...an) ➡ b1 b2 b3...

3.1 - Union form

The most important form used for the construction of relations is **union**. No restrictions of use are made for this form. For instance, recursivity and an infinite number of results are allowed. In case of an infinite number of results, there are computed one at a time, and are given at once to the continuation of the relation. In a first step, we do not consider the order of the results given by the evaluation of a relation. It will be studied in the next section. The union form is defined by the reduction rule :

$$\frac{\text{fi : a1...an} \Rightarrow \text{yi1.....yip}_i \quad , \quad 1 \leq i \leq n}{\text{(union f1 ...fn) : a1...an} \Rightarrow \text{y11.... y1p}_1 \ \text{y21....y2p}_2\text{....ynp}_n}$$

Examples :

```
(de foo : (union      (union add1 sub1)
                      (union id '3 '4 )))
(foo : 45) ➡ 46 44 45 3 4

(de : integer (union   '0    add1 o integer))
(integer : ) ➡ 0 1 2 3 ....

(de : even {mul '2 integer})
(even : ) ➡ 0 2 4 6 ...
```

3.2 - Order of computations results

A relation gives the results in a specific order which is described as follows. The choice of the order is very important in case of infinite results or infinite loops. In a first step, we describe how to define the order of results in a relation. Then, we explain the variable strategies which order all the relational computations.

a) Union tree

The order of results is defined from the **union tree** joined to each relation applied to the arguments. Each leaf corresponds to a result of the application, and each node corresponds to a union. The union tree joined to the application **(f : a1...an)** is recursively defined by :

1) If f is a primitive function, then the tree is only reduced to the leaf labelled by the value obtained by the reduction of the application **(f : a1...an)**.
2) If **f = (union f1 ...fp)**, then the union tree of **(f : a1...an)** is a tree with **p** subtrees constitued of the union tree of all the **(fi : a1...an)** :

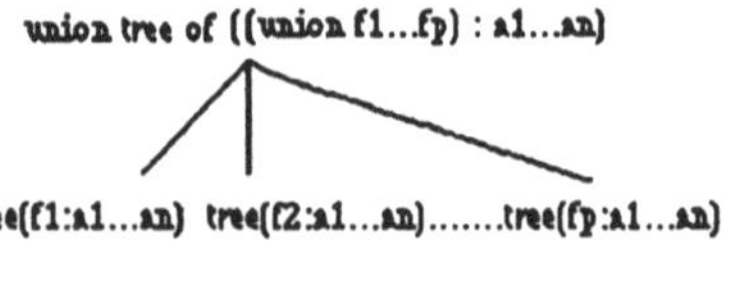

3) If **f = (cste x)**, then case 1 applies.
4) If **f = g o h**, then the union tree of **(f : a1...an)** is the union tree of **(h : a1...an)** in which each leaf **y** is replaced by the union tree of **(g : y)**. Example :

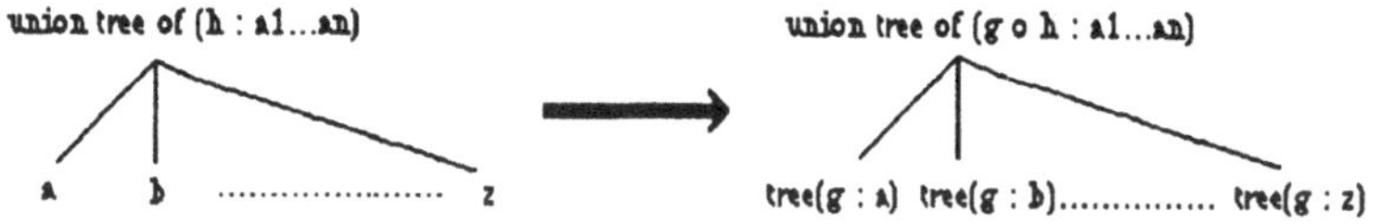

5) If **f = (if p q r)**, then the tree of **(f : a1...an)** is the union tree of **(p : a1...an)** in which each leaf **y** is replaced by :

i) The union tree of **(q : a1...an)** if **y** ≠ **<>**

ii) The union tree of **(r : a1...an)** else.

6) All other cases could be translated in one of the precedent cases, because all the considered forms may be only defined with the four forms union, cste, if and binary comp. The reader may also complete by himself the similar cases corresponding to the other forms.

Examples :

1) The union tree joined to the application **(foo : 45)** is :

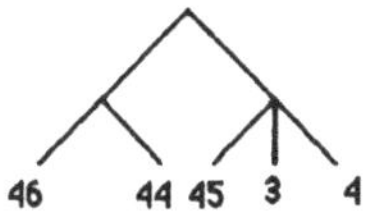

2) The union tree joined to the application **(integer :)** is :

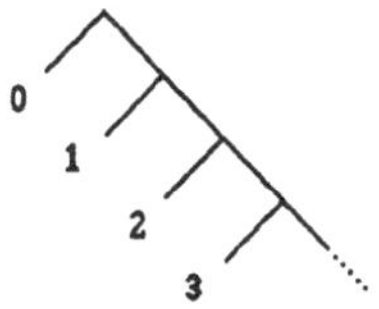

b) The control of relations

The order of results is characterized by the route (or strategy) chosen through the union tree. The reduction machine of the relational GRAAL contains a basic route used for all the relations. This route, called **limited-depth-first,** is complete (each result is find in a finite time) with no multi-computation of same partial results, which is not the case with the "Depth-First Iterative-Deepening" in [Korf 85].

Depth-first route : The rule bound to this strategy is to choose the subtree of a node before the other subtrees of last node encountered. The depth-first route of the union tree is the most efficient and easily implemented strategy. Nevertheless, it is not a complete strategy : some of the results are possibly not computed if there exists a infinite sub-tree. Therefore, we have used a **limited-depth-first** strategy which is complete and may be almost as efficient as depth-first strategy. This strategy is described as follows :

Limited-depth-first route : It is a depth first route whose depth is limited by a given value. At the beginning, the considered node is the root and we go over the tree with respect to the depth-first route, memorizing all the encountered nodes in which all the subtrees have not been go over. When we reach the maximal depth, we suspend and restart the route from the memorized node which is the nearest to the root. The route stops when there is no more memorized subtree.

It is a complete strategy because the maximal difference between two memorized nodes is lower than the maximal depth. Moreover, it is a efficient strategy when we choose a great maximal depth, because it will be almost a depth first strategy. The accessible parameter for the user is the maximal depth. In case of depth limited to one, it is a breadth first strategy. In case of infinite limit, it is a depth first strategy. Therefore limited depth strategy is a generalization of these two classical strategies.

So far, we know how to construct relation, that is to say that we are able to generate an infinite number of results using the union form. Now, we are faced to the problem of managing these results.

3.3 - Management of results

In some cases, we do not want to find or compute all the results of a relation but only a few of them. Thus, we define a lot of functions or forms which stop or do not execute the computations of unwanted results.

a) The cut

According to the portion of unwanted results, we use different "cut" as for example :

1) The function **culdesac** only cuts the current subtree of the union tree. Example :

((union '1 '2 o culdesac '3) :) ➡ 1 3

2) The function **stop** cuts all the subtrees of the union tree joined to the relation. Example :

((union '1 '2 o stop '3) :) ➡ 1

4) The form **exit** included in the form **tag** (with the same joined function) only cuts the subtrees appeared in the form **tag**.The second parameter of the form **exit** gives the last result of the form **tag**. Example :

((union '1 (tag end (union '2 '3 o (exit end '4) '5)) '6) ➡ 1 2 4 6

b) The first form

In order to obtain only the **n** first results of a relation, we use the **first** form. The reduction rules are :

$$\frac{f : a1...ap \Rightarrow r1 ...rq \,,\; q \le n}{(\text{first } n\ f) : a1...ap \Rightarrow r1 ...rq} \qquad \frac{f : a1...ap \Rightarrow r1 ...rq... \,,\; n \le q}{(\text{first } n\ f) : a1...ap \Rightarrow r1 ...rn}$$

Example : ((first 10 integer) :) ➡ 0 1 2 3 4 5 6 7 8 9

c) The set form

Results of a relation do not make a set because the same value may occur many times. With the set form, we built a set of values instead of a multiset. The form **set** is a filter which captures the results already computed and memorized in a list. This form is defined by the reduction rule :

$$\frac{(f : a1 \ldots an) \Rightarrow r1\ r2 \ldots rp \ , \ \bigcup_{1 \le i \le p} \{ri\} = \{s1, s2, \ldots sq\}}{(\text{set } f) : a1 \ldots an \Rightarrow s1\ s2 \ldots sq}$$

3.4 - Processes

The computation of results requires particular mecanisms which look like the control of processes in a parallel language. So, we can easily use the relations as processes without the need of a modification of the GREL reduction (evaluation) machine. A relation, seen as a process is an object, which can be handle with appropriate functions. A process is self modified each time it is activated, in order to give a new result of the relation at each new activation. Processes are useful to control the stream of computations results. They may be include in a relation or in an other process.

Creation : A relation is constructed as a process with the **create** function. Its reduction rule is :

create : f x1...xn ➨ (process f x1...xn)

The form (process f x1...xn) is a GREL object, which is interpreted as a suspended process, corresponding to the application of the relation **f** to **x1....xn.**

Activation : The activation of this process is given by the function **next**. This function computes the next result of the relation.

1) If **(f : x1...xn)** ➨ **y1 y2 ...** , then we have **(next : (process f x1...xn))** ➨ **y1**, and the process self modifies to a process (**process g z1...zm**) such that we have the reduction

(g: z1...zn) ➨ **y2 y3 ...**

2) If **(f : x1...xn)** has no result, then **(next : (process f x1...xn))** ➨ **error**.

With this form, we can compute all the results of a relation by repeating the function **next**. Example :

(de : foo (union next foo))

(foo o create : f x1 ...xn) ➨ y1 y2 ....

Peek : It is not possible to know if there exists other results without activating the process. But we can know if no more activations of the process may be done. The **peek** function applied to a process reduces to **true** if other activations are possible, else reduces to **nil.**

kill : In order to relieve the memory and the stack management, the **kill** function applied to a process deletes it, and frees memory space.

Duplicate : A process may be duplicated in order to compute the same results of a relation several times. Since GREL is a pure relational language, no partial memory copying is required. The **duplicate** function, applied to a process, does not copy the process but only keeps a continuation address.

4 - EXAMPLES

Because GREL is an extension of GRAAL, all functional problems may be very efficiently written in GREL. But, this language is particularly interesting when many results are required. In that case, it shows its full efficiency and flexibility. We give three examples of such programs.

4.1 - The powers of two and three

We want to compute all the numbers of the set $P(2,3) = \{ 2^p * 3^q , p,q \in N\}$. In order to have a constructive definition of P(2,3), we transform the definition in :

$$P(2,3) = \{1\} \cup \{2 * k, k \in P(2,3)\} \cup \{3 * k, k \in P(2,3)\}$$

So, the definition of the relation **pui23** which gives all the powers of **2** and **3** is :

```
(de : pui23
     (union    '1
               {mul '2 pui23}
               {mul '3 pui23} ))
```

In accordance with the strategy, the reduction of ((**set pui23**) **:**) gives powers of two and three in different orders :

1) If the limited depth is one
   ((set pui23):) ➨ 1 2 3 4 6 9 8 12.....
2) If limited depth is three
   ((set pui23) :) ➨ 1 2 4 8 16 12 24.....
3) If limited depth is infinite (i.e. a very large number)
   ((set pui23) :) ➨ 1 2 4 8 16 32 ....

But, we can also compute the subset of P(2,3) given by :

$$P^{n,m}(2,3) = \{ 2^p * 3^q ,\ 0 \le p \le n , 0 \le q \le m \}$$

We define the relation **pui23l** computing the elements of this set. The two arguments of **pui23l** are respectively the number of power of **2** and **3** allowed.

```
(de : pui23l
     (union    '1
               (if   {eq '0 #1}
                     culdesac
                     {mul '2 {pui23l sub1 o #1 #2}} )
               (if   {eq '0 #2}
                     culdesac
                     {mul '3 {pui23l #1 sub1 o #2}} ) ))
```

With a limited depth equal to one, we have the reductions :

((set pui23l) : 2 1) ➨ 1 2 3 4 6 12
((set pui23l) : 3 2) ➨ 1 2 3 4 6 9 8 12 18 24 36 72

4.2 - Subsets management

The subsets of a set : All the subsets are easily given by the relation (set are implemented as lists) :

```
(de : subsets
    (if   null
          nil
          (union    {cons car subsets o cdr}
                    subsets o cdr )))
(subsets : < 1 2 3 > ) ➡ <1 2 3> <1 2> <1 3> <1> <2 3> <2> <3> <>
```

The partitions : The partitions of a set are defined by the relation **partition** :

```
(de : partition
    (if   null
          nil
          {partition1 car partition o cdr}
```

The reduction rule of **partition1** is :

```
(partition1 : x < l1 l2 ....>) ➡ < <x . l1> l2...> <l1 <x . l2> ...> .....
```

The relation **partition1** is defined by :

```
(de : partition1
    (if   null o #2
          {cons     {cons #1 nil} nil}
          (union    {cons     {cons #1 car o #2}
                              cdr o #2}
                    {cons     car o #2
                              {partition1 #1 cdr o #2} })))
```

Remark : In case of an infinite limited depth, these two relations need a space in the stack and in the memory proportional to the number of elements in the set. In case of a pure functional programming of these two relations, the space is exponential in the number of elements in the set.

4.3 - Same fringe

With the relations used as processes, we are able to solve the **same fringe** problem defined in [Durieux 81]. The required algorithm must compare the leaves of two trees. The bad method is to linearize the two trees before to compare them. The difference may appear at the first leaf, and the two leaves lists would have been useless. The good solution which we describe here, is to compare the leaves streams of the two trees.

Representation of a tree : We only consider the binary trees with nodes labelled by a symbol. So, a tree is a atom (i.e. a leaf) or a list of three elements which are the symbol of the node and the two subtrees. Examples : <n1 <n2 a b> c>   c   <n d e>

The tree fringe : The fringe of a tree is the ordered list of its leaves. We define the relation **fringe** which computes the leaves. If the relation is evaluated with a infinite limited depth, then the order of results will be correct for the relation :

```
(de : fringe
        (if    atomp
               id
               (union      fringe o cadr
                           fringe o caddr)))
(fringe : <n1 <n2 a b> <n3 <n4 c d> e>>) ➡ a b c d e
```

Sentinel add : In order to mark the end of the fringe, we add two sentinels :

```
(de : fringe_s      (union fringe 'end1 (exit end2 true) ))
```

Same fringe relation : The relation **same_fringe** reduces to **true** if its two arguments have the same fringe, else it reduces to <>.

```
(de : same_fringe
        (tag  end2       {same_fringe1   {create 'fringe_s #1}
                                         {create 'fringe_s #2} }))
(de : same_fringe1
        (if   {eq   next o #1   next o #2}
              {same_fringe1 #1  #2}
              nil ))
(same_fringe : <n1 <n2 a b> <n3 <n4 c d> e>> <n a  <n b <n c <n d e>>>>) ➡ true
(same_fringe : <n1 a b > <n  b  <n c >) ➡ <>
```

5 - IMPLEMENTATION

The GREL system has been implemented on a VAX 11/780 at the LITP (Laboratoire d'Informatique Théorique et Programmation). It is based on a execution mecanism called **graph reduction machine** [Turner 79]. This machine runs on a classical Von Neumann machine. It is a extension of the reduction machine of GRAAL, which is described in [Bellot 86b]. We explain the GREL machine and the dynamic representation of graphs.

5.1 - GREL machine

The GREL machine reduces graphs describing expressions of the language, until the obtention of an irreducible expression, which is the result. We suppose that relations are monoadic in order to simplify the writing. So, we have to describe the graphs bound to GREL expressions, their reduction, and the strategy of reduction used.

Graph : Since a relation has a class of results, the graph considers classes of element corresponding to GREL expressions. A graph is represented by :

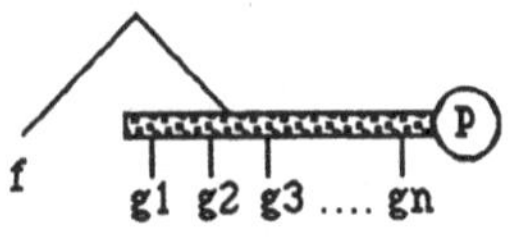

or

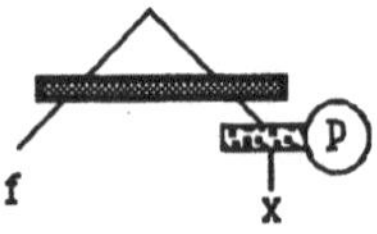

with **g1,...gn** graphs, **f** a relation, **x** a GREL object, and **p** an integer called the current depth, which will indicate when the limited depth is reached. In the first graph, **f** will have to be applied to the reduction of each graph **gi**. In the second graph, **f** will have to be applied to **x**. The grey bar indicates that the reduction have to be delayed. Moreover, this second graph (issued from the form union) is called "delayed node".

Initially, the graph representing the expression (f : x) is :

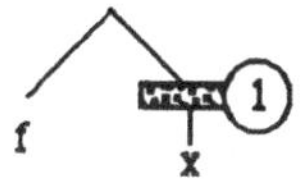

Reduction rules : They transform the graphs describing an expression from the initial representing until an irreducible graph. The reduction rules are classified in four groups.

1) Management results rules :

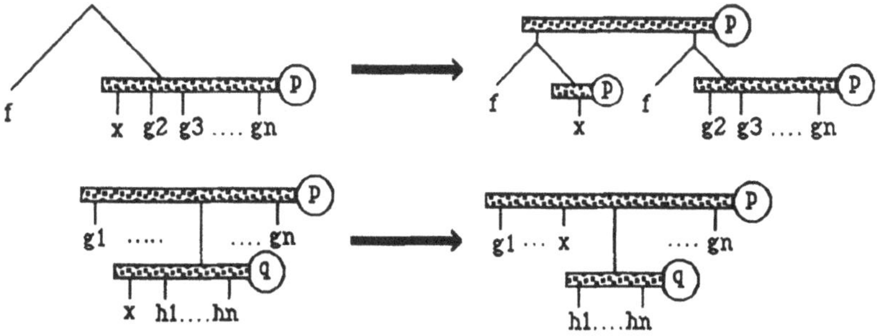

2) Primitive rules : Each primitive function behaviour is described with a reduction rule. These rules are intuitive but are not really graph reduction rules. Example :

3) Functional forms rules : We bind to each form a reduction rule. For instance the binary composition is bound to the rule :

4) Union rules : The form union is bind to a rule which is applicable only if **p** is smaller than the limited depth. This rule is :

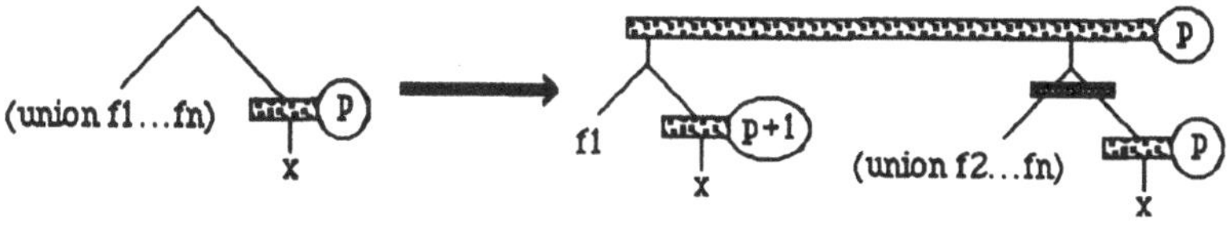

If **p** is equal to the limited depth, the reduction rule is :

Strategy of reduction : The call-by-value and the limited-depth-first route indicate in which order the reductions are done. Graphs Reductions are deterministic (at each step, only one reduction is allowed). The reductions must correspond to the call-by-value used in GREL. Thus, the reductions previously described are only allowed when **x** is a GREL object and not a graph. The limited-depth-first strategy corresponds to the two principles (the first must be tried before the second) :

1 - Between all the delayed nodes appeared in the graph, since the last reduction with the rule applied in next case (or since the beginning), we select the left most and depth most node in the graph. Thus, if the graph is irreducible, we apply the rule to this node:

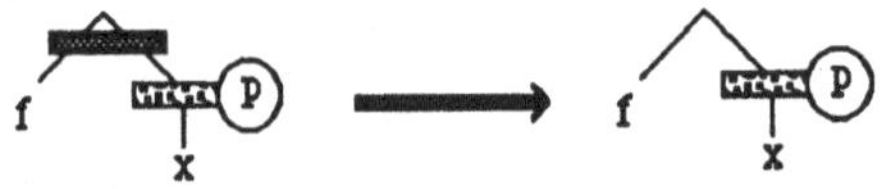

2 - If the graph is still irreducible, then we apply to the delayed node, which contains the smallest **p** in all the graph, the rule :

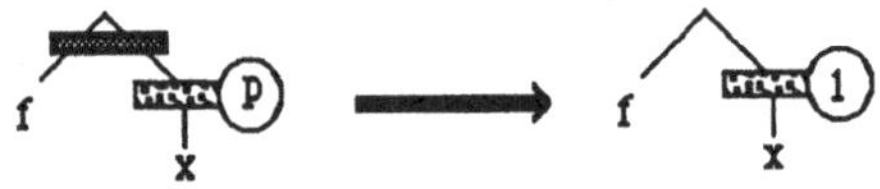

5.2 - Dynamic representation of graphs

This section describes how the graphs are represented in the memory. We do not entirely examine it, because it is a generalization of the GRAAL system which is explained in [Bellot 86b]. We just specify what is modified. In this way, there are two new developments to do : the memorization of delayed nodes, and the activation of delayed nodes. These two notions appear in the stack management.

Memorization : Only the form union creates delayed nodes in the reduction graph. The delayed nodes are memorized in the stack, but hiden to the rest of the stack. The correspondence between the graph and the stack is :

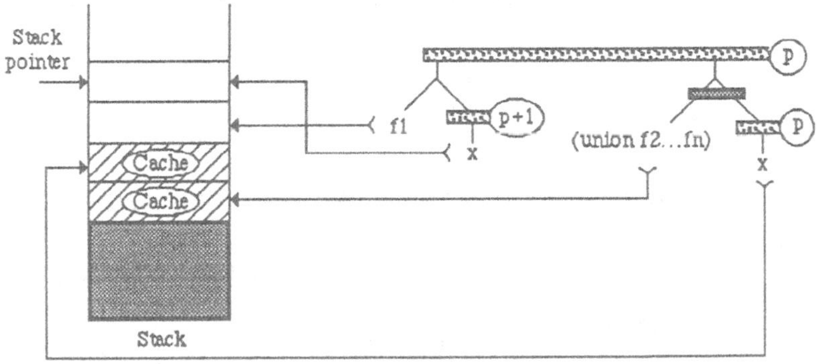

Remark : The creation of a delayed node is very simple : we just have to push in the stack the address of the form **(union f2...fn)** and the argument **x**. This is why GREL is implemented in a functional language and not in an applicative language. The applicative languages, as the Lisp system, require a **safeguard-restoration** mecanism to variables management. This is really unefficient, whereas the functional languages do not need it.

Activation : The caches are activated when the second principle is used. The correspondence between graphs, reductions and the stack is :

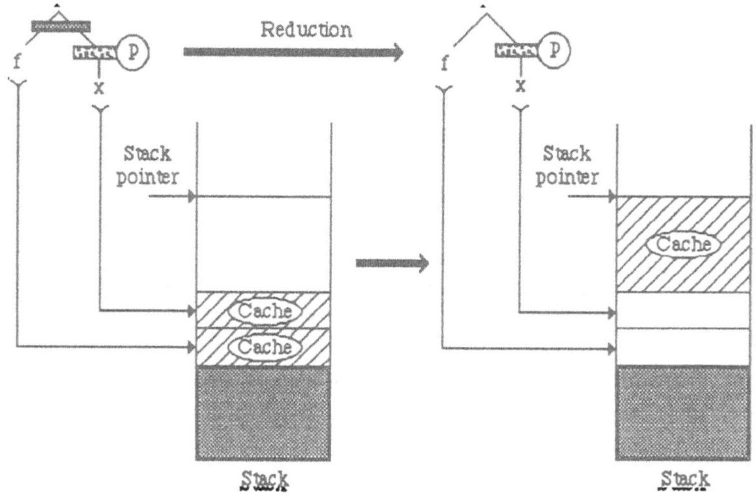

6 - CONCLUSIONS

This work describes a relational programming language without variable, issued from GRAAL system. This language is as efficient as a functional language and gives more flexibility.

The appearance of relations in programming almost preserves the same efficiency that the functional language, when they are implemented in a language without variable. This is another element on account of functional language better than applicative language.

As only functional languages have been developed until now, almost all the classical examples are functional. But, the class of "multi-results" problems is as important as the class of functional problems. In point of fact, the "multi-results" problems are implemented in functional languages, using side effects. They can not be efficiently written in a pure functional language, like the algorithm giving all the partitions of a set. So, relations avoid inappropriate programming, and allow more flexibility in programs writing.

One of the most important applications of Relational GRAAL is given by the programming in logic. The logic languages are declarative one. Relation appears as the procedure corresponding to the translation of a declarative Horn clause used in logic. Thus, relation is nearest computation than clauses, and consequently is more efficient. Therefore, logic languages can be naturally implemented in a relational language. Moreover, We have realized [Legrand 87] a programming language in logic from GREL . This kind of approach gives an easy and efficient implementation, because the bactracking used in logic programming is already implemented in the Relational Language. The limited-depth-first is even a generalization of the PROLOG strategy, and the relations as processes allow implementation of coroutines and predicate "freeze".

The programmers used to functional or applicative languages do not have to try to adapt when they use the relational programming. Relations give flexibility and efficiency to the functional languages without compensations.

Acknowledgement : I am thankful to P. Bellot and V. Jay for their generous contribution to this paper. I also thank O. Danvy, A. Belkhir, D. Sarni and C.T. Lieu for interesting discussions. This work has been supported by the Gréco de Programmation (Bordeaux) under project SPLA.

References

[Bellot 86a] P. Bellot, Graal : a functional programming system with uncurryfied combinators and its reduction machine, European Symposium on Programming, (ESOP 86), LNCS 213, Saarbrücken, mars 1986

[Bellot 86b] P. Bellot, Sur les sentiers du Graal, étude, conception et réalisation d'un langage de programmation sans variable, Thèse d'état, Rapport LITP 86-62, Paris, octobre 1986

[Bellot 87] P. Bellot, V.Jay, A theory for Natural Modelisation and Implementation of Functions with Variable Arity, to appear in LNCS, Portland, septembre 1987

[Chailloux 84] J. Chailloux, M. Devin, J.M. Hullot, LE_LISP, a portable and efficient LISP System, Conference Record of the 1984 ACM Symposium on LISP and functional Programming, p113-123, Austin, Texas, 1984

[Cutland 80] N.J. Cutland, An introduction to recursive function theory,

[Durieux 81] J.L Durieux, Sémantique des liaisons nom-valeur : application à l'implémentation des lambda-langages, Thèse d'état, Université Paul Sabatier, Toulouse, 1981

[Eilenberg 70] S. Eilenberg, C.C. Elgot, Recursiveness, Academic press, New york, 1970

[Korf 85] R.E. Korf, Depth-First Iterative-Deepening: An Optimal Admissible Tree Search, Artificial Intelligencc, Vol 27, p 97-109, 1985

[Legrand 87a] R. Legrand, Le calcul relationnel au service de l'implantation d'un langage de programmation en logique, Séminaire de programmation en logique, CNET Lannion, Ed M.Dincbas, p 333-346, Trégastel, 1987

[Legrand 87b] R. Legrand, Calcul Relationnel et Programmation en Logique, Thèse de l'Université Paris VI, 1987

[Turner 79] D.A. Turner, Another Implementation Technic for applicative Language, Software Practice and Experience, Vol. 9, 1979

[Nguyen 85] T.T. Nguyen, Algebraic theory of predicate transformers for relational programming, Research Report No RR 85-12, Louvain, 1985

Perfect Pipelining:
A New Loop Parallelization Technique*

Alexander Aiken
Alexandru Nicolau
Computer Science Department
Cornell University
Ithaca, New York 14853 USA

Abstract

Parallelizing compilers do not handle loops in a satisfactory manner. Fine-grain transformations capture irregular parallelism inside a loop body not amenable to coarser approaches but have limited ability to exploit parallelism across iterations. Coarse methods sacrifice irregular forms of parallelism in favor of pipelining (overlapping) iterations. In this paper we present a new transformation, *Perfect Pipelining*, that bridges the gap between these fine- and coarse-grain transformations while retaining the desirable features of both. This is accomplished even in the presence of conditional branches and resource constraints. To make our claims rigorous, we develop a formalism for parallelization. The formalism can also be used to compare transformations across computational models. As an illustration, we show that *Doacross*, a transformation intended for synchronous and asynchronous multiprocessors, can be expressed as a restriction of Perfect Pipelining.

1 Introduction

A significant amount of research has been done on parallelization, the extraction of parallelism from sequential programs. The extraction of *fine-grain parallelism*—parallelism at the level of individual instructions—using code compaction has emerged as an important sub-field. The model of computation for compaction-based parallelization is generally some form of shared-memory parallel computer consisting of many synchronous, statically-scheduled functional units with a single flow of control. Programs for these machines may be depicted as program graphs where nodes can contain multiple operations. Transformations on these programs rearrange operations to shorten—compact—the paths through the program graph. Numerous commercial machines (including Multiflow's Trace series, CHOPP, Cydrome, the FPS series, horizontal microengines, and RISC machines) use compaction techniques to exploit parallelism.

The standard approach to extracting parallelism from a loop through compaction is to compact the loop body. This yields some performance improvement, but does not exploit parallelism that may be present between separate iterations of a loop. To alleviate this problem, most systems *unroll* (replicate) the loop body a number of times before compacting. If a loop is unrolled k times, parallelism can be exploited inside this unrolled loop body, but the new loop still imposes sequentiality between every group of k iterations. We present a new loop parallelization technique, *Perfect Pipelining*, that overcomes this problem by achieving the effect of unbounded unrolling and compaction of a loop.

The program graph in Figure 1a illustrates the importance of Perfect Pipelining. (We have simplified the loop control code for clarity: the induction variable i is incremented implicitly on the backedge, as in a Fortran DO loop.) The running time of this loop is $4n$ steps, where n is the number of iterations executed. Multiple iterations of this loop may be overlapped subject to the constraint that the first operation of an iteration is dependent on the result of the first operation of the previous iteration. Figure 1b shows a schedule after the loop has been unwound three times and compacted. (Two additional memory locations are allocated to each array to handle the extra references generated when $i = n$.) Operation labels have been substituted for the operations; subscripts indicate the increment to the induction variable. Multiple operations within a node are evaluated concurrently. The running time of this loop is $2n$ steps. Figure 1c shows the loop unwound five times and compacted; in this case the running time is $\frac{8}{5}n$ steps. Note the low parallelism at the beginning and end of the loop body in both of these examples.

Additional unrolling and compaction will improve the running time further, although this becomes expensive very rapidly. Existing compaction transformations can achieve the schedules in Figures 1b

*This work was supported in part by NSF grant DCR-8502884 and the Cornell NSF Supercomputing Center.

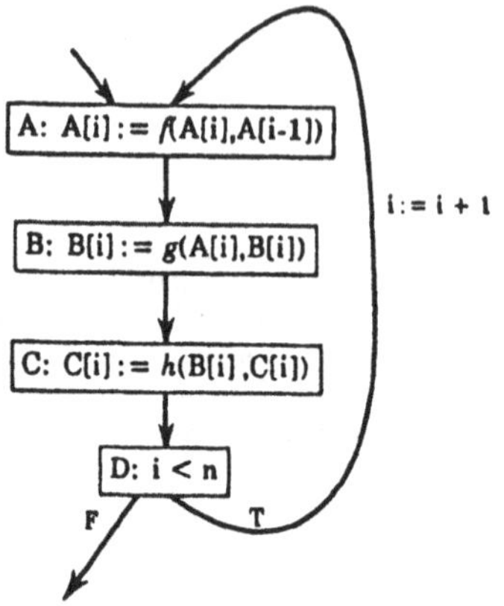

(a) Original loop.

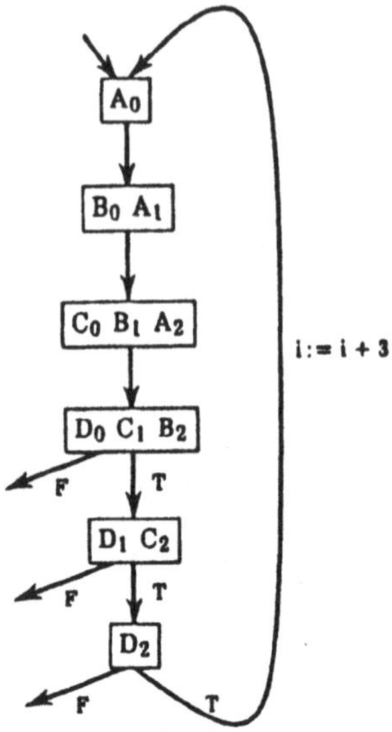

(b) Unwound three times and compacted.

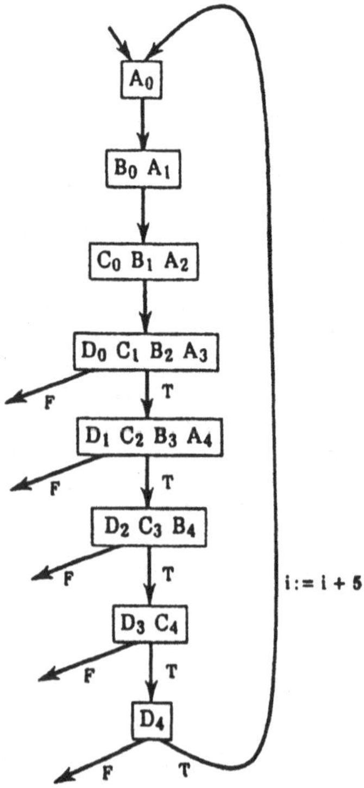

(c) Unwound five times and compacted.

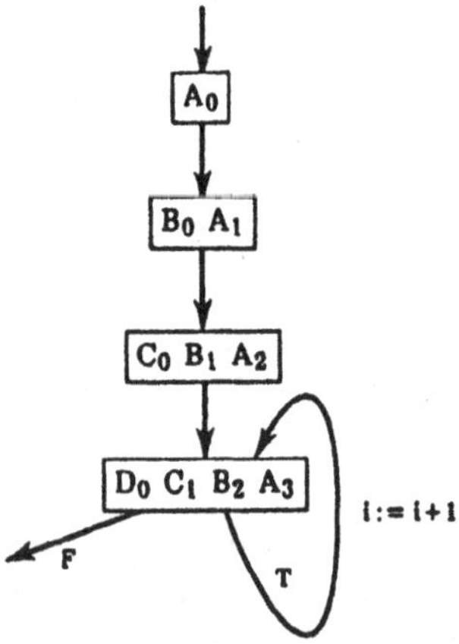

(d) Loop after pipelining.

Figure 1: A Perfect Pipelining example.

and 1c. Perfect Pipelining derives the program shown in Figure 1d. Intuitively, the transformation accomplishes this by noticing that the fourth and fifth nodes of Figure 1c execute the same operations from different iterations, and that further unrolling and compaction creates more nodes of the same type. The transformation achieves continuous (or perfect) pipelining of the loop iterations. The running time for this loop is $n + 3$ steps.

In the example, the pattern detected by Perfect Pipelining is very simple because there are no branches (other than exits) in the loop body. A surprising property of Perfect Pipelining is that it finds such a pattern on all paths given arbitrary flow of control within the loop body. This is a substantial improvement over previous techniques, which rely on heuristics to estimate the runtime flow of control [Fis81] or ignore branches altogether. Another important property of Perfect Pipelining is that the transformation applies even in the presence of resource constraints. We prove that the transformation finds a pattern given arbitrary resources and provide an example illustrating its performance when the loop has unpredictable flow of control and machine resources are a limiting factor.

Perfect Pipelining is defined using the primitive transformations of *Percolation Scheduling* [Nic85b] and loop unrolling. To make our claims precise, we develop a formal account of our transformations. We define the language to which the transformations apply and provide an operational semantics. A binary relation $\leq_p$ is defined on programs using the operational semantics; $\leq_p$ measures when one program is "more parallel" than another. We use $\leq_p$ to prove that Perfect Pipelining is better than any finite unrolling with compaction.

The resulting formalism is powerful enough to capture the intuitive notion of program improvement used informally throughout the literature on parallelization. Thus, we can use $\leq_p$ to compare seemingly unrelated transformations in a meaningful way. As an example, we show that *Doacross* [Cyt86] can be derived as a restriction of Perfect Pipelining. Since Doacross is a loop pipelining transformation intended for synchronous or asynchronous (loosely-coupled) multiprocessors, this result suggests that our formalism is generally applicable across the various models of computation and transformations proposed in the field of program parallelization.

2 A Simple Language

In this section we give an informal description of SPL, a Simple Parallel Language. In the next section we develop a formal definition of the language and an operational semantics. We have minimized the details of language design while keeping the language rich enough to allow discussion of the important problems. SPL is not so much a "real" programming language as a tool convenient for discussing parallelizing transformations.

SPL is graphical; programs are represented by a control flow graph as in Figure 1a. Each node in the graph contains zero or more primitive operations. These operations are divided into two categories: assignments and tests. The evaluation of an assignment updates the store, while tests affect the flow of control. Execution begins at the start node and proceeds sequentially from node to node. When control reaches a particular node, all operations in that node are evaluated concurrently; the assignments update the store and the tests return the next node in the execution sequence (see discussion below). Operations evaluated in parallel perform all reads before any assignment performs a write. Write conflicts within a node are not permitted.

Care must be taken to define how multiple tests are evaluated in parallel. The set of tests within a node is given as a directed acyclic graph (*dag*). Each test in the dag has two successors corresponding to its true and false branches. A successor of a test is either another test or a *name*; a name is a pointer to a program node. We require that the dag of tests be *rooted*—that it have a single element with no predecessors. To evaluate a dag in a state, select the (unique) path from the root to a name such that the branches on the path correspond to the value (true or false) of the corresponding test in the state. Evaluation of the dag returns the node name that terminates this path. On a real machine the evaluation of multiple tests can be very sophisticated to exploit parallelism. A hardware mechanism that efficiently implements general dags of tests is described in [KN85]; less general multiway jump mechanisms are used in many horizontal microengines and the Multiflow architecture.

SPL is powerful enough to model execution of a tightly-coupled parallel machine at the instruction level. It is at this level that our transformational system extracts parallelism from programs. A sample

Bool	=	tt + ff
Loc	=	$\mathcal{Z}$
Store	=	Loc → Val
Assign	=	Store → Loc × Val
Test	=	Store → Bool

(a) Basic domains.

succ: Node → $\mathcal{P}$(Node)
$succ(n) = H$ where $n = \langle A, \langle B, select, r, H\rangle\rangle$

pred: Node → $\mathcal{P}$(Node)
$pred(n) = \{n' | n \in succ(n')\}$

op: Node → $\mathcal{P}$(Assign + Test)
$op(n) = A \oplus B$ where $n = \langle A, \langle B, select, r, H\rangle\rangle$

node: Assign + Test → Node
$node(x) = n$ where $x \in op(n)$

(b) Useful functions.

Figure 2: Some definitions.

SPL program is shown in Figure 1a. Note that this program has only one operation per node; such a program is *sequential*. Another, more parallel version of the same program is given in Figure 1b.

3 Language Definition and Operational Semantics

The formal definition of SPL and its operational semantics provide a framework for proving properties of program transformations. In subsequent sections we develop a formalism for our transformations; this formalism uses the operational semantics of SPL to define when one program is more parallel than another. The operational semantics of SPL closely follows the structural style advocated by Plotkin [Plo].

Figure 2a lists the basic domains of SPL. Val is a domain of basic values—integers, floating-point numbers, etc. An assignment, a function of type Assign, deviates from the standard approach in that it does not return an updated store. Instead, an assignment returns a pair $\langle l, v\rangle$, where v is the new value of location l. This allows us to define the parallel execution of several assignments as the parallel binding of the new values to the updated locations. A *program* is a tuple $\langle N, n_0, F\rangle$ where:

N is a finite set of *nodes*
$n_0 \in N$ is the start node
$F \subseteq N$ is the set of final nodes

A node is a pair $\langle A, C\rangle$ where:

A is a set of *assignments*
C is a *dag*; a four-tuple $\langle B, select, r, H\rangle$ where:
B is a set of *tests*
$select : B \times \text{Bool} \rightarrow B + H$ is an edge function
r is the root test or a node name
H is a set of node names

In what follows, s and s' range over stores; variants of v, l, a, and t range over values, locations, assignments, and tests respectively. We assume that assignments and tests are total atomic actions of type Assign or Test. We use n for both the name of a node and the node itself; the meaning is clear from the context.

The transformations we define require knowledge of the locations that are read and written by the primitive operations to model *dependency analysis*. Dependency analysis determines when two program statements may refer to the same memory location. The analysis is used to determine when it is safe to perform instructions in parallel. We define $write(a, s)$ to be the location written by assignment a in store s; $read(a, s)$ is the set of locations read by assignment (or test) a in store s.

In Section 2, we discussed well-formedness conditions and semantic constraints on programs that are not implemented by the above description. We omit the formal definition of these requirements; the details can be found in [AN87b]. The constraints ensure that the dag of tests is well-formed and that two assignments in a node cannot write the same location. In addition, the start node should have no predecessors and a final node should have no successors. A final node contains a distinguished operation, *result*, that reads and returns the result of the computation. For the purposes of this paper, we assume that *result* returns the entire final store.

$$\frac{C = \langle B, select, r, H\rangle,\ t \in B,\ select(t, t(s)) = t'}{\langle C, s, t\rangle \rightsquigarrow \langle C, s, t'\rangle}$$

$$\frac{C = \langle B, select, r, H\rangle,\ n' \in H}{\langle C, s, n'\rangle \rightsquigarrow n'}$$

$$\frac{A = \{a_i\}, a_i(s) = \langle l_i, v_i\rangle,\ s[\ldots, l_i \leftarrow v_i, \ldots] = s'}{\langle A, s\rangle \rightsquigarrow s'}$$

$$\frac{n = \langle A, C\rangle, C = \langle B, select, r, H\rangle,\ n \notin F,\ \langle C, s, r\rangle \overset{*}{\rightsquigarrow} n',\ \langle A, s\rangle \rightsquigarrow s'}{\langle n, s\rangle \rightarrow \langle n', s'\rangle}$$

Figure 3: Operational semantics of SPL.

Figure 3 gives an operational semantics for SPL. The semantics consists of a set of rewriting rules in the style of inference rules of formal logic. There are two types of transitions: $\rightsquigarrow$, which defines transitions within a node, and $\rightarrow$, which defines transitions between nodes. Rules are read as stating that the assertion below the line holds if the assertions above the line hold. The first two rules deal with the evaluation of a dag of tests; the third rule describes the parallel evaluation of assignments. The fourth rule defines the execution of a node in terms of the evaluation of the node's test dag and assignments.

A rewriting sequence is an execution history of one computation of a program. For our purposes, a complete sequence contains much irrelevant detail; in particular, we are rarely interested in the internal evaluation of a node (the $\rightsquigarrow$ transitions). The following definition puts a rewriting sequence at the right level of abstraction for viewing execution as transitions from nodes to nodes:

Definition 3.1 The *execution trace* of program P in initial store s, written $T(P, s)$, is the sequence $\langle n_0, s_0\rangle \rightarrow \langle n_1, s_1\rangle \rightarrow \langle n_2, s_2\rangle \rightarrow \ldots \rightarrow \langle n_k, s_k\rangle$ where $s_0 = s$, n_0 is the start node of P, and $n_k \in F$. Traces are defined only for terminating computations.

4 The Core Transformations

The core transformations are the building blocks of Perfect Pipelining. These primitive transformations are local, involving only adjacent nodes of the program graph. Though simple, the core transformations can be used to express very powerful code motions [AN88].

Definition 4.1 The result $R(P, s)$ of a computation is the final store of $T(P, s)$. Two programs P and P' are ***strongly equivalent*** if $\forall s\ R(P, s) = s' \Leftrightarrow R(P', s) = s'$.

If T is a program transformation, then T is *correct* if $T(P)$ is strongly equivalent to P for all P. We require that transformations be correct; this guarantees that any sequence of transformations is strongly equivalent to the original program. The formal definitions of the transformations and proofs of correctness can be found in [AN87b]. In this paper, we briefly describe and illustrate each transformation.

Figure 2b lists some useful functions. *Succ* returns the immediate successors of a node; when it is convenient we refer to an edge (m, n) instead of writing $n \in succ(m)$. *Pred* returns the immediate predecessors of a node. The function *op* returns the operations in a node. *Node*(x) is the node containing operation x (we assume there is some way of distinguishing between multiple copies of the same operation).

The *Delete* transformation removes a node from the program graph if it is empty (contains no operations) or unreachable. A node may become empty or unreachable as a result of other transformations. Figure 4a gives a picture. Only the relevant portion of the program graph is shown; incoming edges are denoted by I_j and exiting edges by E_j. Note that an empty node has exactly one successor.

The *Unify* transformation moves a single copy x of identical assignments from a set of nodes $\{n_j\}$ to a common predecessor node m. This is done if no dependency exists between x and the operations of m and x does not kill any value live at m. Care must be taken not to affect the computation of paths passing through n but not through m. To ensure this, the original node n is preserved on all other paths. An illustration is given in Figure 4b.

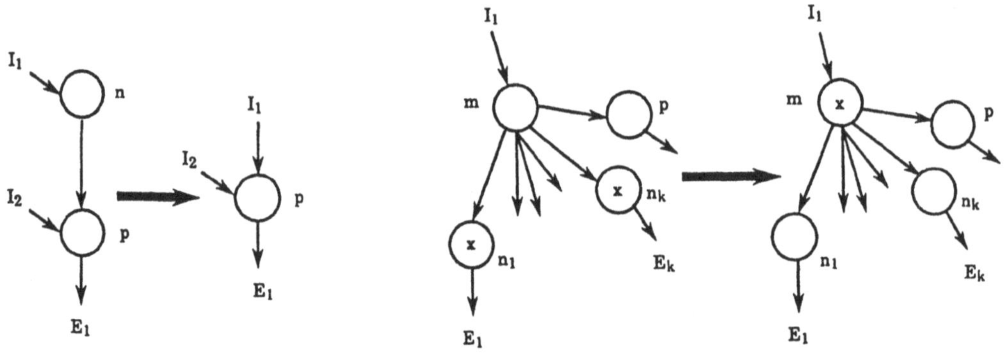

(a) The delete transformation.

(b) The unify transformation.

Figure 4: Primitive transformations.

The *Move-test* transformation moves a test x from a node n to a node m through an edge (m, n) provided that no dependency exists between x and the operations of m. Paths passing through n but not through m must not be affected; n is preserved on the other paths. Because we allow an arbitrary rooted dag of tests in a node and the test being moved may come from an arbitrary point in that dag, n is split into n_t and n_f, where n_t and n_f correspond to the true and false branches of x. An illustration of the transformation is given in Figure 5. In the illustration, a represents the dag of tests (in n) not reached by x, b represents the dag of tests reached on x's true branch, and c the dag of tests reached on x's false branch.

Loop *unrolling* (or unwinding) is a standard non-local transformation. When a loop is unrolled, the loop body is replicated to create a new loop. Loop unrolling helps exploit fine-grain parallelism by providing a large number of operations (the unrolled loop body) for scheduling. The operations in the unwound loop body come from previously separate iterations and are thus freer of the order imposed by the original loop. Recent work has focused on the correct unwinding of multiple nested loops [Nic85a,AN87a,CCK87]. The shorthand $u^i L$ denotes the loop where i copies of the loop body of L are unrolled.

5 A Formalization of Parallelism

In this section we develop a formal account of our transformations. This allows us to make precise claims about the effect of Perfect Pipelining and to compare Perfect Pipelining with other transformations. We restrict the development to transformations that exploit only control and dependency information; this is a natural and large class of transformations (including our transformations) dominating the literature on parallelization. Examples of transformations in this class include: vectorization, the hyper-plane method [Lam74], loop distribution [Kuc76], loop interchange [AK84], trace scheduling [FERN84], and Doacross [Cyt86].

We introduce a preorder on programs, "sim" (for similarity), that captures when one program approximates the control and dependency structure of another. We then introduce a relation $\leq_p$ that is a restriction of sim. If $P \leq_p P'$, then P' is a more parallel program than P.

Informally, a program P is sim to P' if P' executes the same operations as P in an order compatible with the data and control dependencies present in P. P' may, however, have additional operations on some paths that do not affect the output of the program. The sample program in Figure 1b has more operations on some paths than the program in Figure 1a, but the two programs compute the same function. The purpose of sim is to establish a dependency-preserving mapping between operations in traces of P and operations in traces of P'.

Definition 5.1 We say that y *depends on* x in trace $T(P, s)$, written $x \prec y$, if y reads a value written by x. Formally, let $\langle n_0, s_0\rangle \stackrel{*}{\rightarrow} \langle n_i, s_i\rangle \stackrel{*}{\rightarrow} \langle n_j, s_j\rangle$. Then $x \prec y$ if $x \in op(n_i)$, $y \in op(n_j)$, $write(x, s_i) \subseteq read(y, s_j)$, and there is no operation z in n_k for $i < k < j$ such that $write(x, s_i) = write(z, s_k)$.

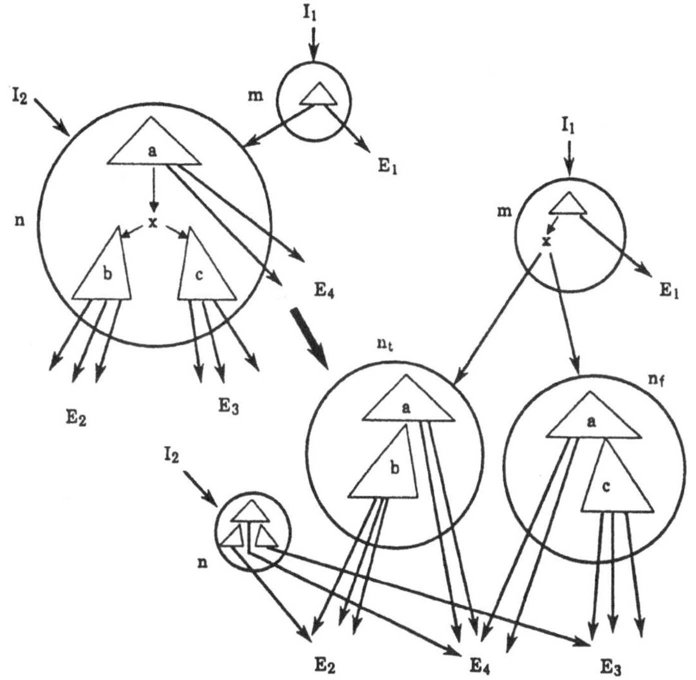

Figure 5: The move-test transformation.

The relation $\prec$ models *true* dependencies [Kuc76], which correspond to actual definitions and uses of values during execution. This is not conservative dependency analysis—the relation $\prec$ precisely captures the flow of values through an execution of a program. This is all that is required to define the relation **sim**.

Definition 5.2 (Similarity) P **sim** P' if and only if there exists a function f satisfying:

$$\begin{aligned} \forall s \quad & x \prec y \text{ in } T(P,s) \Rightarrow f(x) \prec f(y) \text{ in } T(P',s) \wedge \\ & f(x) \prec y' \text{ in } T(P',s) \Rightarrow x \prec f^{-1}(y') \text{ in } T(P,s) \end{aligned}$$

where f is 1-to-1 from operations in $T(P,s)$ to operations in $T(P',s)$ and $f(x)$ is an occurrence of x.

The function f provides a mapping demonstrating that P' preserves the dependency structure of P. It can be shown that P is strongly equivalent to P' if P **sim** P'. We now introduce the relation $\leq_p$. If $P \leq_p P'$, then all operations in P' are executed at least as early in the trace as corresponding operations in P. We use $\leq_p$ to prove that some improvement results from the application of the core transformations.

Definition 5.3 Let $x \in op(n_i)$ in $T(P,s)$. The position of x, written $pos(x)$, is i.

$$P \leq_p P' \Leftrightarrow P \textbf{ sim } P' \wedge \forall s \; pos(x) \text{ in } T(P,s) \geq pos(f(x)) \text{ in } T(P',s)$$

Theorem 5.4 Let T be any core transformation or unrolling. Then for all P, $P \leq_p T(P)$.

Proof: [sketch] The transformations preserve dependencies and do not remove an operation from any path on which it occurs—thus P **sim** $T(P)$. For each core transformation, if it succeeds, at least one operation appears earlier on at least one path, so $P \leq_p T(P)$. □

6 Pipelining Loop Iterations

Existing compaction systems all use the same technique to exploit parallelism across iterations of a loop. The loop is unwound a number of times and the new loop body is compacted. If there are no dependencies between the unwound iterations, then for a fixed size machine there is an unwinding that yields near optimal resource utilization after compaction.

If there are dependencies between the unwound iterations the result can be much worse. Typically, the compacted loop has nodes containing many operations near the beginning of the loop, but towards the end of the loop body operations "thin out" because of dependency chains between unwound iterations. Thus the code becomes increasingly sequential towards the end of the compacted loop body. The problem can be somewhat alleviated by additional unwinding and compaction; however, this becomes computationally expensive rapidly and there will still be a "tail" of sequential code at the end of the loop body.

We apply the results of the previous sections to develop a new loop transformation, *Perfect Pipelining*, that has the effect of unbounded unwinding and compaction. This transformation cannot be achieved directly using the core transformations. For this reason, the relation $\leq_p$ is crucial to proving properties of Perfect Pipelining.

6.1 The Problem

For simplicity, we disregard the particular strategy for compacting a loop and assume only that we are given a deterministic compaction operator C built on the core transformations. We assume that a program is a simple (innermost) loop of the type discussed in the section on unrolling. Nested loops can be handled using techniques for unrolling multiple loops [AN87a].

Consider the sequence $CuL, Cu^2L, Cu^3L, \ldots$. If $\forall i\ Cu^iL \leq_p Cu^{i+1}L$, then C is *well-behaved.* We give a method, for a class of programs and well-behaved compaction operators, to compute a program $Cu^\infty L$ satisfying

$$\forall i\ Cu^iL \leq_p Cu^\infty L$$

6.2 The Programs

A loop u^iL consists of unwound iterations $L_1, \ldots, L_i$. A *loop carried dependency* [AK84] is a dependency between separate iterations of a loop. In this context we are referring to the approximate dependency graphs a compiler computes using conservative dependency analysis, rather than the precise trace dependency graphs used to define $\leq_p$. We consider simple loops satisfying the following property for any unwinding:

Constraint 6.1 Assume there is a loop carried dependency between operations x and y in L. Then in u^iL, there is a dependency between operations x of L_j and y of L_{j+1} for all j.

Virtually all loops encountered in practice can be mechanically rewritten to satisfy this constraint [MS87]. In essence, the requirement is that the dependencies present in a loop unwound i times are a good predictor of the dependencies in the loop unwound $i+1$ times. In practice, these conditions can be checked by inspection of the loop without resorting to computation of the dependency graph.

7 Compaction Operators

We are interested in the class of *bounded* compaction operators. The key characteristic of these operators is that on any path of Cu^iL the distance between the first and last scheduled operations of L_j is bounded by a constant. The fact that any iteration L_j cannot be "stretched" too much allows us to compute $Cu^\infty L$. We present the simplest bounded operator, the simple rule. More powerful bounded operators are discussed in [AN87b]. Initially we assume that computational resources are unlimited; in Section 9 we discuss Perfect Pipelining when resources are bounded.

7.1 The Simple Rule

To simplify the algorithms, we combine the primitives Unify and Move-test into one operation *Move* (see Figure 6a). The simple rule moves an iteration L_j as far "up" in the program graph on as many paths as possible. Operations in the iteration remain in adjacent nodes and the iteration keeps its "shape"—operations appear in the order of the original loop body. These restrictions are not great; the original loop body L could have been compacted prior to application of unrolling and the simple rule, in which case the operations in an unwound L_j are actually nodes containing multiple operations.

One step of the simple rule moves each operation in one copy of an iteration up one node in the program graph. An algorithm that accomplishes this is given in Figure 6b. We assume that operations are identified with their L_j. A **fail** command causes the entire recursive computation to terminate and restores the original program graph.

The simple rule is given in Figure 7. The algorithm guarantees that all possible unifications are performed, thus minimizing code explosion. As iterations move through the program graph, copies of operations—forming distinct copies of the iteration—are generated where paths split. The top-level algorithm refers to the first operation in each copy of the iteration; the other operations are handled by Move_iteration. Let C stand for the simple rule. An important property of C is that it is maximal—for any C' using Move_iteration and for all programs P and unrollings i, $Cu^iP \not<_p C'u^iP$. The simple rule is well-behaved. Figure 1c shows a loop unwound and compacted using C. The only loop carried dependency is between the first operation of consecutive iterations; after application of C the iterations overlap, staggered by one node.

8 Perfect Pipelining

In this section, we require that loop carried dependencies satisfy Constraint 6.1 and that there be enough such dependencies that C cannot completely overlap unwound iterations on any path. In Section 9 we remove this stronger condition. The following two properties of the simple rule are required for Perfect Pipelining. Proofs of lemmas not included in this paper may be found in [AN87b].

Definition 8.1 Two nodes n and n' are *equivalent* if they have the same operations (from different iterations) and dag structure and there is a k such that if operation $x \in op(n)$ is from iteration L_j, then $x \in op(n')$ is from iteration L_{j+k}.

Lemma 8.2 (Property 1) Let n and n' be nodes in Cu^iL. Assume i is large enough that the successors of n and n' are unaffected by larger unwindings and applications of C—the stronger dependency assumption guarantees the existence of i. If n and n' are equivalent, then corresponding successors of n and n' are equivalent.

Lemma 8.3 (Property 2) There is a constant c, dependent only on L, satisfying

$$\forall i\ n \in Cu^iL \Rightarrow |op(n)| < c$$

Theorem 8.4 (Convergence) For a sufficiently large unwinding i, on every path in Cu^iL there exists a node n such that there is another node n' (not necessarily on the same path) equivalent to n.

Proof: Property 2 assures the existence of n and n', as every node can have operations from some fixed range of iterations and there are no more than c operations per node, implying that there are only finitely many distinct classes of equivalent nodes. □

This theorem combined with Property 1 shows that a loop repeatedly unwound and compacted using C eventually falls into a repeating pattern. The pattern itself may be very complex, but it is sufficient to find two equivalent nodes to detect when it repeats. For the simple rule, it is sufficient to unwind $k+1$ copies of L to find the pattern on every path, where k is the length of the longest path in the loop body. The Perfect Pipelining transformation is given in Figure 8. The algorithm finds equivalent nodes n and n' in the compacted program graph, deletes n', and adds backedges from the predecessors of n' to n. For the simple rule, it can be shown that the first node on any path without an operation from the first iteration is repeated.

```
move(x, n, m)
if x is an assignment
    then P ← unify(P, x, n, m)
    else P ← move-test(P, x, n, m)
if no change in P
    then return (False)
    else return (True)
```

(a) The Move operator.

```
move_iteration(x, n, m)
if x ∈ op(n)
    then
        if ¬move(x, n, m) then fail;
(*next_op_in_it(x, n, p) is next operation
in the iteration after x on edge (n, p). *)
for each ⟨p, y⟩ such that
    p ∈ succ(n) ∧ next_op_in_it(x, n, p) = y
    do move_iteration(y, p, n);
Delete all empty nodes;
```

(b) Moving an iteration.

Figure 6: Higher-level transformations.

```
(* Let P = u^i L *)
for each iteration L_1, ..., L_i do
    X ← {x} where x is the first operation in L_j
    repeat
        (* we assume that X always contains all copies of operation x *)
        1. while ∃y ∈ X s.t. pred(node(y)) = {p} and y's iteration can move
             do move_iteration(y, node(y), p)

        2. if ∃y ∈ X s.t. y can move to node p ∈ pred(node(y))
             and the rest of the iteration can move accordingly then
                 select y s.t. the depth of node(y) in the program graph is maximized;
                 move_iteration(y, node(y), p)
    until 2 fails.
    Delete all empty nodes.
```

Figure 7: The simple rule.

```
let k = length of longest path in the loop body L;
P ← Cu^(k+1) L;
for each path p through P do
    let n be the first node on p s.t. no operation
            in n is from iteration L_1.
        Find n' equivalent to n;
        Replace edges (m, n') by (m, n);
        Delete n' and any other unreachable nodes;
```

Figure 8: Perfect Pipelining.

Lemma 8.5 Let $Cu^{\infty}L$ be the result of the application of Perfect Pipelining. For sufficiently large unwindings i, $T(Cu^{\infty}L, s)$ is identical to $T(Cu^{i}L, s)$ for the first $i/2$ steps.

Theorem 8.6 For all i and L satisfying the dependency constraint, $Cu^{i}L \leq_p Cu^{\infty}L$.

Proof: Let k be the length of $T(Cu^{i}L, s)$. Consider a program $Cu^{j}L$ where $j \gg \mathbf{max}(i, k)$. By the previous lemma, $T(Cu^{j}L, s) = T(Cu^{\infty}L, s)$. Because C is well-behaved, $Cu^{i}L \leq_p Cu^{j}L$. We conclude that $Cu^{i}L \leq_p Cu^{\infty}L$. □

This shows that Perfect Pipelining is as good as full unwinding and compaction on all paths. The transformation computes a closed form of the pattern generated by repeated unwinding and compaction using C. Refer again to the loop in Figure 1a. The result of applying Perfect Pipelining to this loop is shown in Figure 1d. The length of the loop body of the original loop is four; in Figure 1c the loop has been unwound five times and compacted using C. The fourth and fifth nodes are equivalent. The transformation deletes the fifth node and all succeeding nodes and adds an edge from the fourth node to itself with an induction variable increment of one (the increment is the number k in Definition 8.1).

9 Pipelining with Limited Resources

Thus far we have assumed that our machine has unlimited resources. In practice, compilers must consider the fact that parallel computers have restrictions on the number of operations of a particular type that can be executed simultaneously. In our program graph representation, a node may not contain more than a fixed number of operations of a given type. The modification to Perfect Pipelining is made in the Move transformation (Figure 6). The change is simple: an operation may not move into a node if the node then violates the resource constraints.

Resource constraints guarantee Property 2 (Lemma 8.3) by imposing a fixed upper bound on the size of program nodes. Thus, the simple rule applies to all loops satisfying Constraint 6.1 without the stronger condition used in Section 8. A proof that Property 1 (Lemma 8.2) holds in the presence of resource constraints may be found in [AN87b].

Figure 9 shows a simple loop L. The loop searches an array of elements, saving the position of all elements that match a key in order on a list. As before, we have left the details of the loop control code implicit. There is also no exit test; we stress that this is only for simplicity. We assume that the target machine can execute up to three tests in parallel.

This particular loop highlights the problem that unpredictable flow of control presents in parallelization. Note that while the path corresponding to the true branches has tight dependencies preventing speedup, the path corresponding to the false branches has no dependencies whatsoever. Other paths (some true branches, some false branches) have intermediate parallelism.

Existing restructuring transformations for multiprocessors can do very little with such a loop. Doacross is a transformation that assigns the iterations of a loop to the processors of a synchronous or asynchronous multiprocessor [Cyt86]. Doacross computes a delay that must be observed between the start of a loop iteration L_i and the start of L_{i+1} on each path of L_i. For this loop, the computed delay is one on both paths; i.e., iteration $i+1$ may begin after iteration i has executed its first statement. The dynamic execution of this loop using Doacross is shown in Figure 10a. An equivalent static SPL schedule is shown in Figure 10b.

We now show how Perfect Pipelining applies to this loop. Figure 11 shows the original loop unwound seven times. The operations have been replaced by labels with subscripts indicating the increment to the induction variable. The result of applying the simple rule is shown in Figure 12. The dag of tests within each node is arranged as a chain with the false branches pointing to the next test and the true branches exiting the node; the lowest numbered test is the root of the dag.

The first four nodes in the left column of Figure 12 are equivalent and the start node is equivalent to the first two nodes in the right column. Figure 13 shows the result of applying Perfect Pipelining—only the first two nodes remain. In this program, three tests are performed in parallel. If T_j is the lowest numbered test that evaluates to true, then the induction variable i is incremented by j and control passes to the node with the append operation. If none of the tests is true, control transfers to the first node. The second node performs an append and evaluates the next three tests.

The pipelined loop executes three tests at every step, achieving optimal use of the critical resource. The final code can run on the Multiflow machine, a commercial tightly-coupled parallel architecture that supports multiway jumps. The running time of Perfect Pipelining with resource constraints is dependent on the size (number of resources) of the machine as well as the original loop.

10 Comparison with Doacross

As suggested in the previous section, loops transformed by Doacross can be represented in our formalism. In fact, a restriction on the pipelining transformation corresponds exactly to Doacross for single loops on synchronous multiprocessors. Another, more restrictive version corresponds to Doacross for asynchronous multiprocessors. Thus a family of transformations aimed at different machine models can be directly formulated and compared in our framework.

The basic algorithm for Doacross analyzes a loop body and decides where, on each path, it is safe to begin the next iteration. A communication instruction is added to the loop at those points. During execution, when a processor executing iteration i encounters a communication instruction, it sends a message signaling another processor that execution of iteration $i+1$ can begin.

Let $\mathcal{D}_{synch}$ be the compaction operator implementing Doacross for synchronous multiprocessors. The restriction to the pipelining algorithm is made in Move (see Figure 14). The new requirement is that if an iteration moves above a test, then it must move above that test on all paths. This restriction is necessary for Doacross because the various processors have independent flow of control—once an iteration is started on a processor it must be able to proceed regardless of the path taken by any other processor. It is easily shown that for $\mathcal{D}_{synch}L$, the first operation of iteration $i+1$ overlaps iteration i exactly where the communications are introduced by Doacross. The asynchronous case ($\mathcal{D}_{asynch}$) is similar and can also be written as a restriction on the pipelining transformation. The following theorem summarizes the relationship between the three transformations.

Theorem 10.1 For all loops L, $\mathcal{D}_{asynch}L \leq_p \mathcal{D}_{synch}L \leq_p \mathcal{C}u^{\infty}L$.

11 Efficiency

There are loops satisfying Constraint 6.1 for which Perfect Pipelining requires exponential time. In particular, if there are no loop carried dependencies at all—iterations are completely independent—then the running time is exponential in the unwinding if there is at least one test in the loop body. However, this can be detected after unrolling only once, because the iterations completely overlap after applying $\mathcal{C}$. In this case, the loop is completely vectorizable and generating good code is relatively easy.

It is also possible to construct examples with some loop carried dependencies for which Perfect Pipelining requires exponential time. However, several conditions must be simultaneously satisfied for this to happen. We believe that these conditions do not commonly arise in practice. In fact, for every program we have examined (including the examples in this paper and all of the Livermore Loops) the pipelining algorithm runs in low-order polynomial time and requires at most quadratic space. Convergence often occurs on many or all paths for unrollings much smaller than the worst case bound; thus interleaving unwinding, compaction, and the test for equivalent nodes substantially improves the efficiency of the algorithm. Using simple data structures, the check for equivalent nodes can be done very quickly.

12 Conclusion

We have presented a new technique, Perfect Pipelining, that allows full fine-grain parallelization of loops. Perfect Pipelining is currently being integrated into ESP, an Environment for Scientific Programming under development at Cornell. The environment already includes Percolation Scheduling and other transformations. We believe that Perfect Pipelining will greatly enhance the power of our environment by subsuming the effects of a class of coarse-grain transformations in a uniform, integrated fashion compatible with our fine-grain approach.

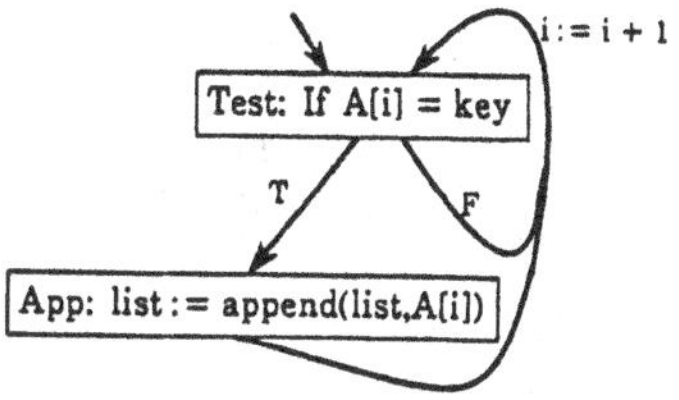

Figure 9: A simple loop L.

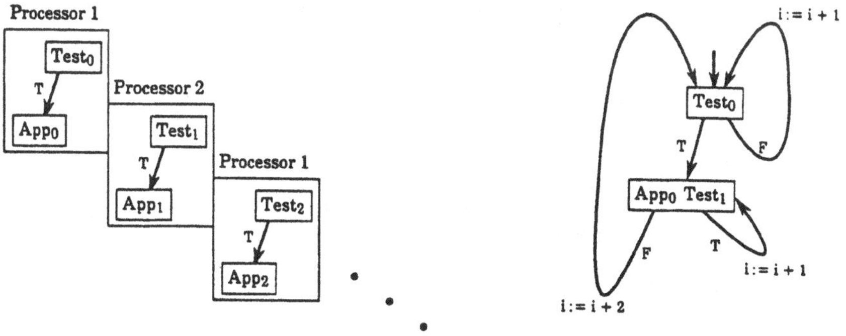

(a) Dynamic schedule.

(b) Static SPL program.

Figure 10: Doacross applied to L.

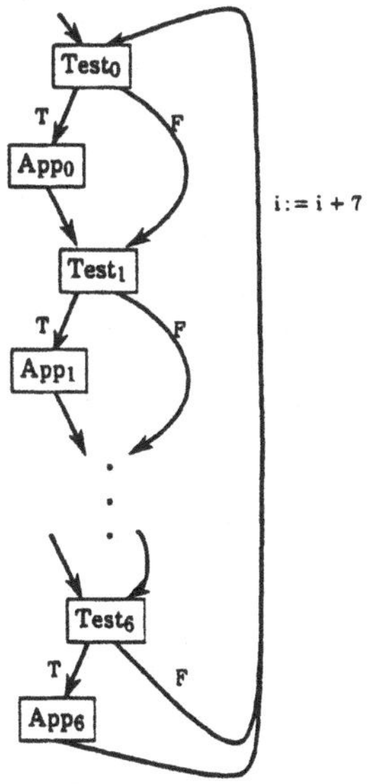

Figure 11: L unwound seven times.

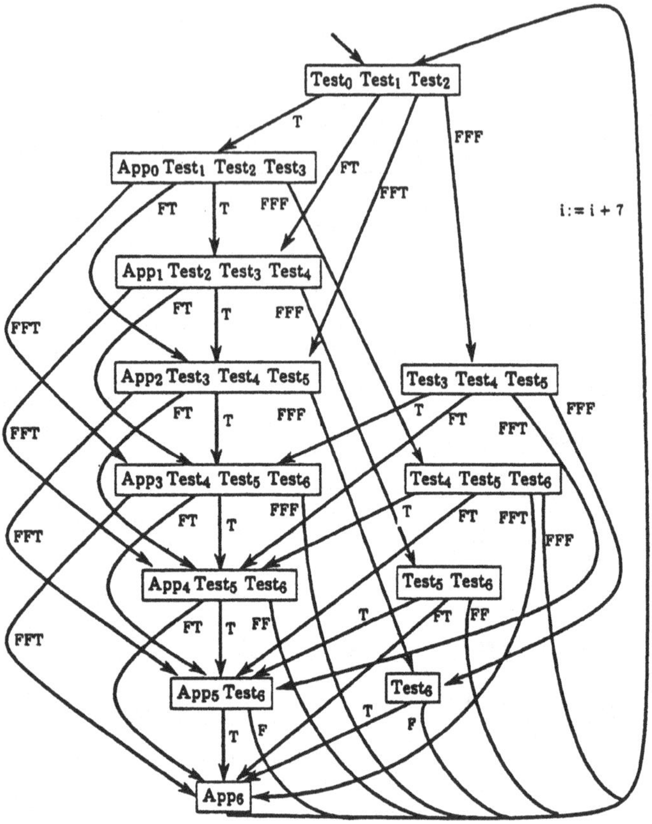

Figure 12: *L* unwound seven times and compacted.

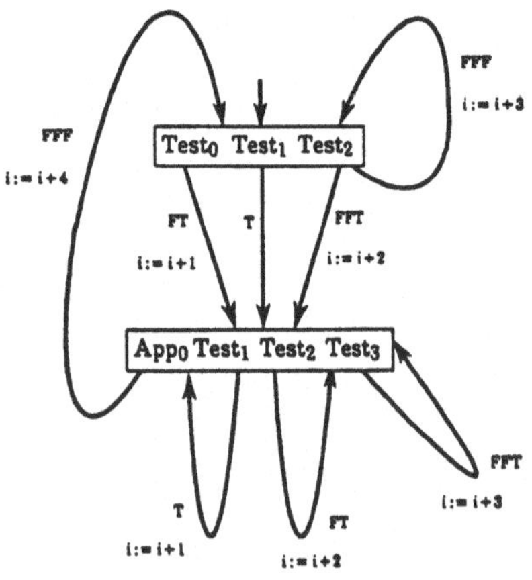

Figure 13: The same loop after pipelining.

move(x, n, m)
if x is an assignment
    then if $x \in op(s)$ for all $s \in succ(n)$
        $P \leftarrow unify(P, x, n, m)$
    else $P \leftarrow$ *move-test*(P, x, n, m)
if no change in P
    then return (*False*)
    else return (*True*)

Figure 14: The Move operator for $\mathcal{D}_{synch}$.

13 Acknowledgements

Anne Neirynck and Prakash Panangaden provided a great deal of helpful advice on many aspects of this work. Laurie Hendren, Prakash Panangaden, and Jennifer Widom criticized drafts of this paper and contributed greatly to its final form.

References

[AK84] J. R. Allen and K. Kennedy. Automatic loop interchange. In *Proceedings of the 1984 SIGPLAN Symposium on Compiler Construction*, pages 233–246, June 1984.

[AN87a] A. Aiken and A. Nicolau. *Loop Quantization: an Analysis and Algorithm*. Technical Report 87-821, Cornell University, 1987.

[AN87b] A. Aiken and A. Nicolau. *Perfect Pipelining: A New Loop Parallelization Technique*. Technical Report 87-873, Cornell University, 1987.

[AN88] A. Aiken and A. Nicolau. A development environment for horizontal microcode. *IEEE Transactions on Software Engineering*, To Appear March 1988. Also available as Cornell Technical Report TR 86-785.

[CCK87] D. Callahan, J. Cocke, and K. Kennedy. Estimating interlock and improving balance for pipelined architectures. In *Proceedings of the 1987 International Conference on Parallel Processing*, pages 297–304, August 1987.

[Cyt86] R. Cytron. Doacross: beyond vectorisation for multiprocessors. In *Proceedings of the 1986 International Conference on Parallel Processing*, pages 836–844, August 1986.

[FERN84] J. A. Fisher, J. R. Ellis, J. C. Ruttenberg, and A. Nicolau. Parallel processing: a smart compiler and a dumb machine. In *Proceedings of the 1984 SIGPLAN Symposium on Compiler Construction*, pages 37–47, June 1984.

[Fis81] J. A. Fisher. Trace Scheduling: a technique for global microcode compaction. *IEEE Transactions on Computers*, C-30(7):478–90, July 1981.

[KN85] K. Karplus and A. Nicolau. Efficient hardware for multi-way jumps and pre-fetches. In *Proceedings of the 18th Annual Workshop on Microprogramming*, pages 11–18, December 1985.

[Kuc76] D. Kuck. Parallel processing of ordinary programs. In *Advances in Computers*, pages 119–179, Academic Press, New York, 1976.

[Lam74] L. Lamport. The parallel execution of DO loops. *Communications of the ACM*, 17(2):83–93, February 1974.

[MS87] A. Munshi and B. Simons. *Scheduling Sequential Loops on Parallel Processors*. Technical Report 5546, IBM, 1987.

[Nic85a] A. Nicolau. *Loop Quantization, or Unwinding Done Right*. Technical Report 85-709, Cornell University, 1985.

[Nic85b] A. Nicolau. Uniform parallelism exploitation in ordinary programs. In *Proceedings of the 1985 International Conference on Parallel Processing*, pages 614–618, August 1985.

[Plo] G. D. Plotkin. A structural approach to operational semantics. Text prepared at University of Aarhus.

New Insights into Partial Evaluation: the SCHISM Experiment

Charles CONSEL

LITP – Université Paris 6
(Couloir 45–55, 2ème étage)
4 place Jussieu, 75252 Paris CEDEX 05, FRANCE
uucp : ... !mcvax!inria!litp!chac

Université Paris 8
2 rue de la Liberté, 93526 Saint Denis, FRANCE

Abstract

This article describes SCHISM: a self-applicable partial evaluator for a first order subset of Scheme. SCHISM takes place in the framework of mixed computation, and is situated along the line of the MIX project at the University of Copenhagen. The goal is automatically to generate compilers from interpreters by self-application and we have done this with an extensible and directly executable first order subset of Scheme.

SCHISM is an open-ended partial evaluator with a syntactic extension mechanism (macro-functions written in full Scheme). Furthermore, the set of primitives is extensible without any modification of the system.

Partial evaluation of functional languages relies on the treatment of function calls. We have chosen to use annotations for driving SCHISM to eliminate a call (unfold it) or to keep it residual (specialize it). They are local to each function rather than to each function call. This solves the problem of multiple calls to the same function with different patterns of static and dynamic arguments. Usually two pitfalls are possible in such a case: either to make all of these calls residual and specialize the function exponentially; or to eliminate the calls systematically and possibly start an infinite unfolding. Both are avoided by the use of a filter expression attached to functions. These filters drive SCHISM.

In this article we first describe our first order Scheme both with its abstract syntax and informally. Then we analyze the possibilities raised by keeping annotations local to each function. Finally we propose a partial solution to the open problem of reusing the store: the idea is to distinguish compile time and run time in the interpreter itself. In the end some conclusions and issues are proposed.

Keywords

Program transformation, applicative languages, partial evaluation, Scheme, SCHISM, mixed computation, program generation, specialization, unfolding, compiler generation.

Introduction

Partial evaluation [Futamura 82] is a general technique of program transformation. It is based on Kleene's S-m-n theorem [Kleene 52] and in essence consists of the specialization of a program with respect to some known data. To some extent, this encourages to view these known data as static and the unknown data as dynamic. The point is that all the parts in the program which manipulate static data can be processed statically. What remains then is a residual program ready to operate on the dynamic data or to be specialized further.

The idea of specializing programs is first used in [Lombardi 67] to perform incremental compilation. Applied to the triplet

$$< Interpreter, Program, Data >$$

it expresses that specializing an interpreter with respect to a program leads to compiling this program. [Futamura 71] generalizes that application by specializing the partial evaluator itself. This leads to producing a compiler from a partial evaluator and an interpreter, and to producing a compiler generator by specializing the partial evaluator with respect to itself. These applications are now known as the *Futamura projections* and require the partial evaluator to be self-applicable, that is an *autoprojector* [Ershov 82].

Mix [Jones *et al.* 85] was the first actual self-applicable partial evaluator. It is able to generate stand-alone compilers as well as a compiler generator.

This article presents our self-applicable partial evaluator SCHISM[1]: it is homogeneously specified in Scheme [Rees & Clinger 86] [Consel *et al.* 86] and offers some new insights in the domain of partial evaluation.

SCHISM is built on top of Scheme and written in Schismer: a first order[2] subset of Scheme. Schismer, as the language of an autoprojector, is self-interpretable. It offers a syntactic extension mechanism [Kohlbecker 86] to use high level constructs rather than only a language which sometimes reveals to be a bit too low level. These syntactic extensions are built in full Scheme and they generate Schismer code. We have also built SCHISM to be extensible: one can enrich the initial set of primitives with user defined Scheme functions.

[1] We have called it SCHISM because it operates on data which have been separated into static and dynamic parts.

[2] We have made Schismer first order because it still is an open problem to treat higher order languages, although we hope to offer here a new insight towards that direction.

SCHISM processing consists of specializing a Schismer program: it folds and unfolds function calls, eliminates them or keeps them residual. Annotations are the mean to drive partial evaluation during these transformations by specifying what is static and what is dynamic, that is: what to unfold, what to keep residual, what to specialize. We have taken the choice of keeping annotations local to Schismer functions.

This article is organized as follows. The first section presents the abstract syntax of Schismer and its informal description. The second section describes the partial evaluator; we show an example of a Schismer program in concrete syntax and the residual program produced by SCHISM. Section 3 makes a comparison of our strategy for handling function calls with the Mix approach and illustrates it with some examples. Section 4 describes how residual programs at run time may use data structures other than those available in a partial evaluator.

1 The language Schismer

Schismer is a first order subset of Scheme. Its surface syntax is almost familiar: it is the one from Scheme, enriched with filters. Filters are situated before the body of named functions and lambda-expressions. A Schismer program is basically a set of recursive, statically scoped equations.

Schismer has been conceived to be well-suited for a self-applicable partial evaluator: as shown in the abstract syntax below, the language is simple. However, we wanted to provide a language rich enough to express both a non-trivial autoprojector and a wide variety of interpreters. The idea has been to offer syntactic extensions (macros): they make a program more expressive and concise. Presently, one can either use already existing syntactic extensions or write his own ones in Scheme and with the full power of Scheme. Furthermore, the initial set of primitives is extensible with Scheme user defined functions.

1.1 Abstract syntax

K ∈ Con	constants, including quotations
I ∈ Ide	variables
E ∈ Exp	expressions
F ∈ Fun	functional objects
L ∈ Lam	λ-expressions
D ∈ Def	named definitions
P ∈ Prg	Schismer program

P⟶ `(program (I*) (D+) I)`

D⟶ (define (I$^+$) (filter E_0 E_1) E_2)

L⟶ (lambda (I*) (filter E_0 E_1) E_2)

F⟶ L | I

E ⟶ K | I | (F E*)
  | (if E_0 E_1 E_2)
  | (external I E*)

Figure 4 in section 2 displays a complete Schismer program, performing the catenation of two lists.

1.2 Informal description of Schismer

The constants are the integers, the boolean values **#!true** and **#!false**, the null object **()**, the quoted pairs and the quoted symbols.

A program is divided into three parts:

- A list of syntactic extensions files. They are loaded by the system and used to produce a pure Schismer source program. One can include the system files as well as his own files.
- A list of user defined functions. Named definitions cannot be embedded for the sake of simplicity.
- A variable that is the name of the main function of the program, *i.e.*, the function which starts the application.

A named definition has three parts. The first part is a list of variables, whose head is the function name and whose rest is the parameters list. The second part is the annotation (*filter*) which drives the partial evaluator for treating the function call. The last part is the body of the function.

A λ-expression also has three parts. The first part is the parameters list. The second part is the *filter*. The last part is the body of the λ-expression. It is the body which is partially evaluated.

The if construct is a ternary operator. The first part is evaluated. If it yields a true value then the second part is evaluated and its value is returned. Otherwise, the third part is evaluated and its value is returned.

```
(defschismer-macro (nth n l)
    (list 'car
          (let loop ((n n))
              (if (eq? n 0) l
                  `(cdr ,(loop (-1+ n)))))))
```

Figure 1: A syntactic extension written in Scheme: nth

The external construct allows one to include functions that produce side effects in his programs (this is analogous to the **x-functions** in Mix [Diku 87]).

1.3 Syntactic extensions

The syntactic extension facility provides a powerful language tool for building high level constructs by macro-generation of Schismer code. Using this mechanism, we have implemented a subset of the Common Lisp *structures* [Steele 84]. The syntactic extension defining a given structure generates a set of new syntactic extensions to create the object; to access each field; and to test whether an object is an instance of the given structure. This has proven useful.

Figure 1 displays the syntactic extension **nth** taking as arguments an integer (a constant) and an expression and generating the right combination of **car** and **cdr** to access the nth element of a list.

The syntactic extension mechanism could be viewed as a redundant feature together with a partial evaluator which sometimes performs the same task. However, it yields to constructs that may generate a complex combination of Schismer forms, uneasy to write by hand, such as **cond** and **case**. Moreover, a simple preprocessing phase is more reasonable than using the partial evaluator for what is after all a trivial program manipulation.

1.4 The environment

The initial environment used by SCHISM is built with two sets of functional objects. The *low environment* is the first set; it consists of all the primitives used by the interpreter. The *high environment* is the second set; it consists of all the user defined functions (named definitions).

The low environment is extensible. It is interesting to put unary functions in the low environment rather than defining them. Specializing a unary function with an unknown argument generally behaves like the identity. Conversely, with known argument the primitive will be directly called rather than symbolically processed: its execution time is much faster.

2 SCHISM: the partial evaluator

SCHISM is written in Schismer to be self-applicable. As in Scheme, the integers, the boolean values and the null object do not need any quotation since SCHISM considers the program and the partial evaluation environment as distinct domains. This makes programs more readable. This section focuses on the key point of our system: the treatment of function calls.

2.1 Function calls

For each function call, SCHISM determines whether the operator is a primitive, an **external**, a λ-expression or a named definition. This section presents the way SCHISM treats each of them.

2.1.1 A primitive

Since primitives are written in Scheme, they can be compiled for efficiency (and they are of course). If all the arguments of the primitive are known, the Scheme function is directly called and executed. The return value is used by SCHISM to continue processing. If some of the arguments are unknown, SCHISM substitutes all the known expressions by their values and makes the function call residual.

2.1.2 A λ-expression

Since Schismer offers only one side-effecting construct (**external**), it may be interesting to make an almost systematic β-reduction. However, this approach may generate programs where the same expressions are recomputed several times. It is better to make a selective reduction that avoids recomputation, as described in [Steele 78].

To make a selective β-reduction, a λ-expression includes a filter which drives the SCHISM treatment. Section 2.2 shows that filters for λ-expressions can be generated automatically.

The filter of a λ-expression consists of two expressions. When SCHISM encounters a redex, it evaluates the first expression of the filter (which is a Schismer expression) with the known or unknown

```
(define (fun a)
    ((lambda (x y)
          (filter #!false
                (list (known? x) (known? y)))
          (cons (f1 x) (f2 y)))
     a 11))
```

Figure 2: An simple example of λ-expression involving a filter

```
(define (fun a)
    ((lambda (x) (cons (f1 x) (f2 11))) a))
```

Figure 3: The effect of the filter to partially evaluate a λ-expression

value[3] of the arguments. This expression returns the truth value **#!true** if the requirements are fulfilled to β-reduce the λ-expression, *i.e.*, to substitute the parameters by the arguments and eliminate the λ-expression. If the requirements are not fulfilled the first expression returns the truth value **#!false** and SCHISM activates the second expression. As the first one, this expression receives the arguments of the application and returns a list of boolean values by mapping the list of arguments. For each **#!true** value the corresponding parameter is eliminated and the argument is substituted. For each **#!false** value, the parameter and its corresponding argument are kept residual. This treatment gives to SCHISM a particular piece of information for each parameter of the λ-expression.

Figure 2 illustrates with a simple example the use of a λ-expression (the filter of the function has been intentionally omitted). The first expression of this filter is **#!false**. It indicates to SCHISM that this λ-expression should never be β-reduced. The second expression builds a list where the first element is **#!true** if the parameter **x** has a known value. Otherwise, it is **#!false**. The value of the second element of the list (parameter **y**) is determined similarly. A value **#!true** in this list indicates to SCHISM that the corresponding parameter should be eliminated and the argument substituted in the λ-expression body. A value **#!false** keeps the corresponding parameter and argument residual. Figure 3 is the residual program generated by SCHISM if **a** is dynamic.

[3] A value is known when it is a list whose first element is **quote**. Otherwise the expression is unknown.

```
(program
   (user-syntactic-extensions.h)
   (
       (define (fun l)
           (filter #!false (list l))
           (append '(1 2 3) l))

       (define (append l1 l2)
           (filter (known? l1) '(l1 l2))
           (if (null? l1) l2
               (cons (car l1)
                     (append (cdr l1) l2))))
   )
   fun)
```

Figure 4: A program with filters in named definitions

```
(define (fun-0 l)
    (cons (quote 1)
          (cons (quote 2)
                (cons (quote 3) l))))
```

Figure 5: A residual program where SCHISM has unfolded the function append

2.1.3 A named definition

One generally names a function to call it recursively. For this reason, SCHISM carefully treats named function calls in order to avoid infinite unfolding or infinite specialization. Furthermore, as for λ-expressions, unfolding may generate inefficient code where expressions are recomputed several times.

Figure 4 shows two named functions: they contain a filter consisting of two expressions. As for λ-expressions, for each named function call, the first expression of the filter is evaluated with the values (known or unknown) of the arguments in the application. According to the values received, the first expression returns **#!true** if it wants SCHISM to unfold the call. If the first expression returns **#!false**, the second expression will be activated with the arguments. This second expression specifies how the function has to be specialized, *i.e.*, what are the parameters to be eliminated. A list of values containing a decision for each parameter (as above) is then returned. If a value is known, this constant will replace the corresponding parameter in the function body and the parameter will disappear.

Figure 5 displays the residual program of figure 4. The function **fun** has been renamed **fun-0** to distinguish it from the original version. According to the filter, unfolding has been performed to treat the call to the function **append**, as the induction variable is known.

2.2 Automatic generation of annotations

Experience in writing Schismer programs has shown that a number of program schematas have "obvious" annotations (traversing a list tail-recursively, *etc.*). As a first attempt to automatically generate annotations, we have defined some of them as syntactic extensions. For example we supply a syntactic extension **let** that macro-expands to the corresponding application of a λ-expression: a standard annotation is provided if none is specified. This generic filter produces code that allows SCHISM to eliminate a parameter if it is known or if it is unknown but bound to another variable. Similarly for the named functions, if the filter is not included in the definition, a systematic unfolding filter is inserted. Other cases may be treated. For instance we are currently developing the automatic generation of annotations for self recursive functions by providing some simple syntactic extensions implementing loop structures.

2.3 Reductions

Partial evaluation is based on constant propagation and reduction of expressions. This propagation may be stopped when one or several known data are combined with one or several unknown data. A simple example is **(car (cons 1 (f a)))**: this expression cannot be reduced if the partial evaluator does not know the semantics of **car**. To solve this problem we have enhanced SCHISM with some rules:

(car (cons E_0 E_1**))** $\rightarrow$ E_0
(cdr (cons E_0 E_1**))** $\rightarrow$ E_1
(null? (cons E_0 E_1**))** $\rightarrow$ **#!false**

Similarly, the conditional construct **if** is reduced by SCHISM according to the following rules:

(if E_0 E_1 E_1**)** $\rightarrow$ E_1
(if E_0 **#!true #!false)** $\rightarrow$ E_0
(if (equal? E_0 **#!false)** E_1 E_2**)**
    $\rightarrow$ **(if** E_0 E_2 E_1**)**
(if (equal? #!false E_0**)** E_1 E_2**)**
    $\rightarrow$ **(if** E_0 E_2 E_1**)**

These rules may appear trivial, and they certainly are. The point here is that a partial evaluator acts as a program specializer and uses some very general program transformation techniques. These simplification rules are not surprising in themselves. What is interesting is to know that they are present in a partial evaluator and intervene here in SCHISM.

Figure 6 displays a source program where an association list is used to represent an environment. This program could be the beginning of an interpreter. The function **make-env** builds the association list with a list of variables and a list of values. The function `lookup` calls the function `assoc` with the association list to find the value of the variable `var`.

Figure 7 shows the residual program when SCHISM knows that `var` is bound to `'c` and that `var*` is bound to `'(a b c d e)`. We can see that the access to the value of the variable c has been totally determined. Program specialization subsumes program simplification.

3 Why keeping the annotations local to the function?

This section compares our approach together with the approach taken in Mix [Jones *et al.* 87]. The goal is to decide for a function call whether it has to be unfolded or suspended.

Mix makes the decision about this for each function call encountered in a program. This implies that the annotation of a function call is made static. Figure 8 points out when this approach could be too conservative. It shows a classical function called twice with two different patterns of static and dynamic arguments. The Mix annotations [Jones *et al.* 85] [Sestoft 86] for the function calls are used: a function call marked `call` will always be unfolded (eliminated); a function call marked `callr` will be residual (specialized).

In figure 8, the function **append** has an induction variable `l1` [Aho *et al.* 86]. If `l1` is known, unfolding can be performed safely. If this variable is unknown, unfolding cannot take place and the only possible operation is specializing this function with respect to `l2`. A problem occurs if the function **append** is called once with the known induction variable, and a second time with the unknown induction variable. Since the recursive call in **append** is annotated to be residual both cases cannot be treated in an optimal way and the result is far too conservative.

```
(program
   (user-syntactic-extensions.h)
   (
      (define (lookup var var* val*)
         (filter #!false
                 (list var var* val*))
         (cdr (assoc var
                     (make-env var* val*))))

      (define (make-env var* val*)
         (filter (known? var*) 'void)
         (if (null? var*)
             '()
             (cons
                 (cons (car var*) (car val*))
                 (make-env (cdr var*)
                           (cdr val*)))))

      (define (assoc key alist)
         (filter (known? alist) 'void)
         (cond
            ((null? alist)
                #!false)
            ((equal? (car (car alist))
                     key)
                (car alist))
            (else
                (assoc key (cdr alist)))))
   )
   lookup)
```

Figure 6: A program representing an environment with an association list

```
(define (lookup-0 val*)
   (car (cdr (cdr val*))))
```

Figure 7: Effects of reduction rules

One may annotate the function **append** to make a systematic specialization: this is safe, but the residual program is huge, as each recursive call to **append** produces a residual function.

On the other hand, a strategy based on a systematic unfolding produces infinite loops at partial evaluation time. If in figure 8 the recursive call to **append** is annotated to be unfolded when the induction variable is unknown, the function will be unfolded infinitely.

In figure 9 (the Schismer version), the function **fun** is (locally) annotated to be always unfolded[4].

[4] Since **fun** is never to be specialized, the second part of the

```
(define (fun l)
    (cons (call append l '(1 2 3))
          (call append '(a b c) l)))

(define (append l1 l2)
    (if (null? l1)
        l2
        (cons (car l1)
              (callr append (cdr l1) l2))))
```

Figure 8: A too conservative annotation using MIX notations

```
(define (fun l)
    (filter #!true 'void)
    (cons (append l '(x y z))
          (append '(a b c) l)))

(define (append l1 l2)
    (filter (known? l1) (list 'l1 l2))
    (if (null? l1)
        l2
        (cons (car l1)
              (append (cdr l1) l2))))
```

Figure 9: The equivalent program in Schismer

The filter of **append** makes a call unfolded when its first argument is known. If not, the second part of the filter drives the specialization of the call with respect to l2.

Our strategy allows the annotations to drive SCHISM according to quantitative criteria, which is strictly more powerful than a boolean annotation. Figure 10 presents the same function **append** as figure 4 but with a new filter. It indicates that a call to **append** should be unfolded first if the parameter l1 is known *and* second when the length of the list is not greater than 20. Otherwise, a call to **append** is kept residual and *only* specialized with respect to l2 (if known). This last example shows that keeping annotations local to each function makes it possible to tune SCHISM precisely.

---

filter will not be activated. We note it as **void** for readability because this second part is to be ignored.

```
(define (append l1 l2)
    (filter
        (and (known? l1)
             (<= (length l1) 20))
        (list 'l1 l2))
    (if (null? l1)
        l2
        (cons (car l1)
              (append (cdr l1) l2))))
```

Figure 10: The equivalent program in Schismer

4 Extra data structures in residual programs

To be self-applicable a partial evaluator must be expressed with the same objects that it treats. Presently they are lists: one represents objects such as the environment in an interpreter with lists. In particular, an assignment in the interpreted language is commonly implemented by rebuilding the environment. The reason is that the interpreter is written without assignment. This is a problem because the naive specialization of an interpreter with respect to a target program with assignments leads to a program that rebuilds entire pieces of the interpretation environment. Then it may happen that the specialized program is not as efficient as could be expected.

We propose an approach for designing interpreters that makes it possible to generate residual programs where only the allocations of the program remain and *not* the allocations required by the interpreter.

This approach is based on splitting the bindings of identifiers to values [Jones *et al.* 87]. We use the same strategy as in denotational semantics, where the values of some variables are not given until run time. This creates frozen expressions [Gordon 79] [Schmidt 86]. The primitives that manipulate the store are changed according to the data type used to implement the store. Then compilation phase and run time phase are totally separated. As an example (see Appendix A) we have adapted the MP interpreter described in [Sestoft 85]. Unlike the residual program produced by Mix with respect to the **reverse** program, SCHISM has generated a residual program (see Appendix B) where the primitive **cons** is only used where it is needed in the program and not because it is needed in the interpreter (see figure 11). This is a first contribution to the open problem of reusing the store.

```
;;; variable l = offset 1
;;; variable res = offset 0

(define (execute-mp-0 input store)
    (store-ref
        (mp-while-1
            (store-set! store (quote 1) input))
        (quote 0)))

(define (mp-while-1 store)
    (if (null? (store-ref store (quote 1)))
        store
        (mp-while-1
            (mp-block-2
                (store-set!
                    store
                    (quote 0)
                    (cons
                        (car (store-ref
                                store
                                (quote 1)))
                        (store-ref
                            store
                            (quote 0)))))))))

(define (mp-block-2 store)
    (store-set!
        store
        (quote 1)
        (cdr (store-ref store (quote 1)))))
```

Figure 11: A residual program reusing the store

5 Conclusions and Issues

We have built a partial evaluator operating homogeneously on a first order subset of Scheme. We believe that it offers some new insights into partial evaluation engineering: the whole system is open-ended; annotations can partly be generated automatically; the set of primitives is extensible; local annotations allow to drive SCHISM with a high precision.

After this article has been written, we have achieved complete self-application. SCHISM generates small sized and readable compilers, and is currently experimented both at LITP and at DIKU.

Next stage in our work is to process a fully imperative language with SCHISM. We are now elaborating a new methodology that describes an imperative language together with its interpreter. The idea is to make the interpreter ready to be specialized. The variety of concepts is already raising problems and this experience is already enriching SCHISM.

Acknowledgements

Thanks to Anders Bondorf, Neil Jones, Torben Mogensen and Peter Sestoft for their welcome at DIKU and their close interaction during the workshop on Partial Evaluation and Mixed Computation. Special thanks to Olivier Danvy for many suggestions and discussions about my work and this paper.

Bibliography

Aho, A. V., Sethi, R. and Ullman J. D.
Compilers: Principles, Techniques and Tools,
Addison-Wesley [1986]

Bondorf A.
Towards a Self-Applicable Partial Evaluator for Term Rewriting Systems,
North Holland Publ. proceedings of the Workshop on Partial Evaluation and Mixed Computation, Denmark [1987]

Consel C., Deutsch A., Dumeur R. and Fekete J-D.
Skim Reference Manual,
Rapport Technique 86/09 Université de Paris 8, France [1986]

Diku, University of Copenhagen
The Mix System User's Guide Version 3.0
Diku internal report, University of Copenhagen, Denmark [1987]

Ershov, A. P.
Mixed Computation: Potential Applications and Problems for Study,
Theoretical Computer Science 18 (41-67) [1982]

Emanuelson, P. and Haraldsson A.
On Compiling Embedded Languages in Lisp,
Lisp Conference, Standford, California, (208-215) [1980]

Futamura, Y.
Partial Evaluation of Computation Process - an Approach to a Compiler-Compiler,
Systems, Computers, Controls 2, 5 (45-50) [1971]

Futamura, Y.
Partial Computation of Programs,
In E. Goto et al (eds.): RIMS Symposia on Software Science and Engineering, Kyoto, Japan.
Lecture Notes in Computer Science 147, 1983, (1-35) [1982]

Gordon, M. J. C.
The Denotational Description of Programming Languages,
Springer-Verlag [1979]

Jones, N. D., P. Sestoft, and H. Søndergaard
An Experiment in Partial Evaluation: the Generation of a Compiler Generator,
Rewriting Techniques and Applications, Dijon, France.
Lecture Notes in Computer Science 202, (124-140) Springer-Verlag [1985]

Jones, N. D., P. Sestoft, and H. Søndergaard
Mix: a Self-Applicable Partial Evaluator for Experiments in Compiler Generation,
Diku Report 87/08, University of Copenhagen, Denmark [1987]

Kleene, S. C.
Introduction to Metamathematics,
Van Nostrand [1952]

Kohlbecker, E. E.
Syntactic Extensions in the Programming Language Lisp,
PH. D. thesis, Technical Report No 199, Indiana University, Bloomington, Indiana [1986]

Lombardi, L. A.
Incremental Computation,
Advances in Computers 8 (ed. F. L. Alt and Rubinoff), Academic Press, (247-333) [1967]

Rees, J. and W. Clinger (eds.)
Revised^3 Report on the Algorithmic Language Scheme,
SIGPLAN Notices 21, 12, (37-79) [1986]

Schmidt, D. A.
Denotational Semantics: a Methodology for Language Development,
Allyn and Bacon, Inc. [1986]

Sestoft, P.
The Structure of a Self-Applicable Partial Evaluator,
Diku report 85/11, University of Copenhagen, Denmark. [1985].

Steele G. L. Jr.
Rabbit: a Compiler for Scheme,
MIT AIL TR 474, Cambridge, Mass. [1978]

Steele G. L. Jr.
Common Lisp,
Digital Press [1984]

Appendix A: The MP Interpreter in Schismer

```
;;; This MP-int is almost the same as the Mix version
;;; Activation: (program parameter locals block)

(program
    (mp.h)
    (
        (define (execute-mp program input store)
            (filter #!false (list program input))
            (let ((var-env (make-var-env (nth 2 program) (nth 1 program))))
                (let ((newstore (update-env (car (nth 1 program)) input var-env store)))
                    (filter #!false (list (known? newstore)))
                    (mp-block (nth 3 program) var-env newstore))))

        (define (make-var-env local-name* par-name*)
            (filter #!true 'void)
            (if (null? local-name*)
                par-name*
                (cons (car local-name*)
                      (make-var-env (cdr local-name*) par-name*))))

        (define (run-mp expr var-env store)
            (filter #!true 'void)
            (cond
                ((and (pair? expr)
                      (or (equal? (car expr) ':=)
                          (equal? (car expr) 'while)))
                    (run-command expr var-env store))
                (else
                    (run-expression expr var-env store))))

        (define (run-command expr var-env store)
            (filter #!true 'void)
            (case (car expr)
                ((:=)
                    (update-env (nth 1 expr)
                                (run-mp (nth 2 expr) var-env store)
                                var-env
                                store))
                (else
                    (mp-while (nth 1 expr) (nth 2 expr) var-env store))))

        (define (run-expression expr var-env store)
            (filter #!true 'void)
            (cond
                ((not (pair? expr))
                    (fetch expr var-env store))
                (else
                    (case (car expr)
                        ((cons)
                            (cons (run-mp (nth 1 expr) var-env store)
                                  (run-mp (nth 2 expr) var-env store)))
                        ((car)
                            (car (run-mp (nth 1 expr) var-env store)))
                        ((cdr)
                            (cdr (run-mp (nth 1 expr) var-env store)))
```

```
                ((equal?)
                    (equal? (run-mp (nth 1 expr) var-env store)
                            (run-mp (nth 2 expr) var-env store)))
                ((quote)
                    (nth 1 expr))
                ((if)
                    (if (not (null? (run-mp (nth 1 expr) var-env store)))
                        (run-mp (nth 2 expr) var-env store)
                        (run-mp (nth 3 expr) var-env store)))
                (else
                    '|unknown form|)))))

    (define (mp-block expr* var-env store)
        (filter #!true 'void)
        (if (null? (cdr expr*))
            (run-mp (car expr*) var-env store)
            (mp-block (cdr expr*) var-env (run-mp (car expr*) var-env store))))

    (define (mp-while condition body var-env store)
        (filter #!false (list condition body var-env 'store))
        (if (not (null? (run-mp condition var-env store)))
            (mp-while condition body var-env (mp-block body var-env store))
            store))

    (define (fetch var var-env store)
        (filter #!true 'void)
        (store-ref store (give-offset var var-env)))

    (define (update-env var val var-env store)
        (filter #!true 'void)
        (external store-set! store (give-offset var var-env) val))

    (define (give-offset var var-env)
        (filter #!true 'void)
        (cond
            ((null? var-env)
                '|undefined variable|)
            ((equal? var (car var-env))
                0)
            (else
                (+ 1 (give-offset var (cdr var-env))))))
)
execute-mp)
```

Appendix B: reverse written in MP

```
(program
    (l)
    (res)
    (
        (while l (
            (:= res (cons (car l) res))
            (:= l (cdr l)) ) )
        res
    ) )
```

Code Selection Techniques:
Pattern Matching, Tree Parsing, and Inversion of Derivors

Robert Giegerich
Karl Schmal

FB Informatik - Lehrstuhl V
Universität Dortmund
Postfach 500500
D-4600 Dortmund

1. Pattern Matching Approaches to Code Selection

1.1 Summary

Significant progress in the area of formal tools to support the construction of code generators in recent years has come along with a severe terminological confusion. Closely related techniques appear in different styles, further obscured by ad-hoc extensions. We try to alleviate this situation by suggesting that the code selection task should be understood as the problem of inversion of a hierarchic derivor. This understanding leads to several interesting generalizations. More expressive formalisms - heterogeneous tree languages, regular tree languages, derivor images -, can be used to define the code selectors input language. In all cases, we retain the ability to decide the completeness of the code selector specification as a side-effect of code selector generation. The extension to nonlinear matching, in combination with matching relative to a subsignature M with a nontrivial equational theory, allows to express the non-syntactic conditions formerly associated with a production in a Graham-Glanville style code generator description. Due to space restrictions, such extensions can only be sketched here, while the emphasis of this paper lies on motivating and demonstrating our reformulation of the classical pattern matching approach to code generation.

1.2 A Short Review of Recent Approaches to Code Selection

Initiated by the work of Graham and Glanville [GrGl77], many approaches to retargetable code generation have been presented in recent years. Commonly and correctly, they are subsumed under the phrase "pattern matching techniques". Some form of pattern matching is used to guide code selection, while other subtasks of code generation, such as register allocation, cost comparison of different coding alternatives, or evaluation ordering must be organized in some way along with the matching process. Henry [Henr84] has carefully and extensively demonstrated the limitations inherent in the original Graham-Glanville approach, which used LR-parsing techniques for pattern matching. We are particularly concerned here with work that attempts to overcome these limitations. While Graham and Glanville had demonstrated how the syntax-directed translation paradigm could be beneficially applied to code selection, it became clear that two kinds of improvements were desirable: using a more flexible kind of pattern matching for the "syntactic" aspects, and new techniques to describe other subtasks of code generation that have to be performed along with and are directed by the matching process. Several related suggestions have been made with respect to the first task, while the second has received less systematic treatment. As most workers in this area have observed, off-the-shelf tree pattern matching in the "classical" sense of [Kron75] or [HoOD82] is close to providing a solution, but is not quite expressive enough to serve as an adequate technique for code selection. Unfortunately, all approaches developed their own terminology and extensions, and the concepts used to formulate the individual pattern matching techniques have not been adequately separated from their particular application to the code generation task. As a result, the relative virtues of the different approaches can hardly be evaluated, as a comparison can only be made at a most technical or empirical level. Let us give a short discussion of the approaches we are referring to.

First variations of the Graham-Glanville approach still used string parsing techniques, e.g. [Henr84] and [CHK85]. [Turn86] uses a technique called up-down parsing, and actually parses trees, but sees his grammars still as string grammars. [Gieg84] and [Benk85] use parsing with (regular) tree grammars, resorting to classical terminology from formal language theory. [HaCh86], [WeWi86] and [AhGa85],[AGT87] use the name pattern matching, but with different meanings. Recent approaches, yet to be worked out further, try to embed code generation in a formalism of algebraic equational specifications and term rewrite systems [Gieg85], [MRSD86].

Let us further exemplify the terminological inhomogenity by a look at corresponding notions in different approaches. Maybe the best-understood terminology is that of nonterminals, terminals and productions of a tree grammar, as everyone can understand a tree grammar as a context free grammar where the righthand sides of productions are trees. (This view is used frequently, but it does have a pitfall, which we will address later.) [Turn86] is closest to this terminology, speaking of nonterminals, operators and prefix (string) expressions. [AGT87], [WeWi86] and [HaCh86] use "patterns" for productions. [AGT87] uses "labels" and "operators" for nonterminals and terminals, while [WeWi86] uses "labels" for both concepts. [HaCh86] calls terminals "node-type", and it seems at the first glance, that nonterminals show up here as "renaming symbols". But in fact, the correct counterpart of nonterminals is an index into some table, which may either be a "renaming symbol" or some proper sub-pattern. [Chas87], contributing a significant improvement of the classical pattern matching algorithm of [HoOH82], also discusses extensions necessary for code selection applications. He uses the most creative naming, calling nonterminals "introduced wildcards". Finally, with algebraically oriented approaches, we know (e.g. from [ADJ78]) that nonterminals correspond to the sorts of some signature, with terminals denoting the operators.

Of course, if this was only an inconsistency of namings, it would not be worth bothering about. But to the extent that formal language terminology is abandoned, the concept of a derivation disappears - and this concept is in fact a very useful one in the given context - although not quite sufficient. In spite of all similarities, it does make an important difference for the expressive power of an approach, whether it uses "trees over a ranked alphabet" or "terms from a given signature" as its basic concept. It is one of our goals in this paper to explicate these differences, which are often considered negligible.

We conclude this little survey by another observation with a similar lesson. Glanville [Glan77] originally addressed the problem of completeness of the code generator description (the "machine grammar"), partly ensuring it by imposing the condition of "uniformity". Much later work has been designed to remove this restriction. Interestingly, the more these approaches deviate from formal language terminology, the less inclined they are to address the completeness aspect.

2. A Sketch of an Algebraic Model of Code Generation

The overall goal of this work is not to suggest *another* pattern-directed technique for code selection. Our goal is a reformulation of such techniques, in a way suitable to handle code generation as well as other applications, combining the virtues of three areas:

- Efficiency and known generative techniques from classical pattern matching [Kron75], [HoOD82], [Chas87];
- clean concepts and decidability results from formal language theory [Brai69], [Benk85], together with a modest gain in expressive power;
- powerful specification, implementation and proof techniques available in equational algebraic specifications [ADJ78], [HuOp80], [HuHu80].

In order to show how this can be achieved, we must first sketch our understanding of code generation. This subsection is an excerpt of a more substantial investigation in the theory of code generation (unpublished at this point). A predecessor of the model sketched here can be found in [Gie85]. The goals of this work are shared by the approach of [MRSD86], which describes work on the design of a code generation tool based on term rewriting techniques.

To arrive at a model of code generation with the desired properties, we must break with two paradigms prevalent in previous approaches to code generation. The first is the "code emission paradigm". Typically, in code generator descriptions there are "actions" or parameterized code strings associated with the patterns, which, upon a match of the template, trigger the emission of target machine or assembly code to some file. The problem with this is that when code is emitted right away, it has to be perfect from the beginning. This leads to a tendency to overfreight the pattern matching with other tasks such as register allocation or peephole optimization, which should preferably be described separately, at least on the conceptual level. Instead, the code we generate will be machine code in abstract syntax, and we disregard the task of writing a linearization of it to some file.

The second paradigm we abandon is that "machine description" and "code generator description" have traditionally been treated as synonyms. It turns out to be very important to formally distinguish these two notions. The machine description says what (abstract) target programs are, the code generator specification says how they are related to source programs. We will now discuss approaches to code generation as if they had always been using our conceptual model. We focus on the central task of instruction selection for arithmetic and addressing calculations.

Let Q and Z be many-sorted signatures. Source (= intermediate) and target (= machine) language programs are terms in the term algebras T(Q) and T(Z), respectively. Code generation requires (among other tasks) to specify and implement a code selection morphism γ: T(Q) --> T(Z).

Two ways have been used to obtain γ. In handcrafted compilers, as well in systematic approaches striving for retargetability like [ACK83], one considers all relevant operator/ operand combinations in T(Q), and specifies for each some term from T(Z) as its target code. If good code is desired, the necessary analysis of special cases becomes intricate and error-prone. It was an important observation of [GrGl77], [Catt78], [Ripk77], that it may be more convenient to describe the target machine instructions in terms of the intermediate language, rather that vice versa. Hence, for each Z-operator (typically representing a machine instruction), one specifies some semantically equivalent term from T(Q). Let us call this description δ. With some right, it could be called a machine description rather than a code generator description. It specifies a homomorphism δ: T(Z) --> T(Q). (But traditionally it has not been understood this way, due to the two paradigms discussed above.) Algebraically, δ is a derivor [ADJ78] from Z to Q. Now the arrow goes the "wrong" way, but to obtain γ from δ, pattern matching techniques can be used. So, the gains of this approach are twofold - descriptive ease, and generative support for an efficient and correct implementation of the required case analysis. (Ignoring this aspect leads to the argument in [Hors87] that Graham-Glanville style code generation goes the "wrong way".)

A third advantage of the latter approach is the following. Inherent in the task of code generation there is some freedom of choice, usually exploited to optimize target code quality. The specification δ preserves this freedom. Correspondingly, to obtain the desired γ, one must not only invert δ, but also supply a choice function ξ wherever for some $q \in T(Q)$, there are several $z \in T(Z)$ with $\delta(z)=q$. For example, dynamic programming accoording to [AhJo76] has been used to implement this choice. On the conceptual level, we would like to have the functionality T(Q) --δ^{-1}--> $2^{T(Z)}$ --ξ--> T(Z), while on the technical level, we want to interleave ξ with the construction of δ^{-1}.

The same holds for other subtasks of code generation, such as register allocation, evaluation ordering, or machine specific data type coercions. In current approaches, these tasks have not found a formal specification. In our algebraic framework, they are described along with Q, Z, and δ by equational specifications for a so-called semantic subsignature M of Q and Z. ([Gieg85] provides an example of such a specification.) The main concern of our framework is that *all* aspects of code generation can be described formally and in a modular way, thus allowing proofs of completeness and correctness. But for the moment, this is still an open promise, and not the subject of the current paper.

With formal definitions still postponed, we illustrate the above by a small example.

Example 1

"semantic" subsignature M =

```
    sorts         Number  Type

    operators     word:        --> Type
                  long:        --> Type
                  0, 1, 2, ...:  --> Number
                  scale: Type  --> Number

    equations     scale(word) = 2
                  scale(long) = 4.
```

"source" signature Q = M +

```
    sorts         E

    operators     const: Number        --> E
                  +, *: E  E           --> E
                  mem: Type E          --> E
                  reg: Type  Number    --> E.
```

"target" signature Z = M +

```
    sorts         Exp Adr

    operators     ADD: Exp Exp                  --> Exp
                  ADDI, MULI: Exp Number        --> Exp

                  R: Type Number                --> Exp
                  M: Type Adr                   --> Exp

                  mk_adr: Exp                   --> Adr
                  bdx: Type Type Number Number Number --> Adr.
```

◊

The above target signature is a little contrived, in order to demonstrate both nonlinearity and the use of nontrivial semantic subterms. Z-operator bdx denotes the addressing mode "base-displacement-addressing with index", where the first argument indicates the word length to be used in the address calculation, while the second indicates the word length of the addressed memory cell, used to determine an automatic scaling factor. The other arguments are base and index register number, and the displacement.

We can now explain the role of M. It serves a threefold purpose.

i) Usually there are several variants of instructions or addressing modes like our bdx - depending on the available choices of operation, address and operand length. In Graham-Glanville style descriptions, this led to a phenomenon called "type crossing" [Henr84]: The size of the machine description is (essentially) multiplied by the number of machine data types, leading to extremely large descriptions. At least for the sake of readability, parameterization of the description is called for (which may be expanded automatically). In our approach, we just use machine data types as extra arguments to Z-operators, keeping the description concise without extra parametrization mechanisms, and avoiding expansion.

ii) From the beginning in [GrGl77], patterns have been augmented by semantic attributes, which were instantiated by concrete register numbers or constant values, and used to test semantic restrictions on the applicability of a pattern. Again, we need no special attribute concept for this purpose - the register number is just another argument (with a sort from S_M) of the reg operator.

iii) Functions calculating and predicates testing semantic attribute values in Graham- Glanville style descriptions are defined outside the formal specification. Here, they are defined as operators of OP_M by equations in E. "Testing a semantic predicate" is thus elegantly subsumed in the notion of matching modulo $=_E$.

This is further demonstrated by the second part of Example 1, the derivor specification. Note that the equation for bdx is nonlinear in t - our target machine uses word or longword addresses, but both base address and index must be of the same length. The M-subterm scale(tt) will match the numbers 2 or 4, but no others - according to the equations specified with M.

Example 1 - continued

hierarchic derivor δ*:Z --> Q*

(By definition, δ is the identity on M, and hence this part of δ is not shown.)

sort map δ: Exp --> E
Adr --> E

operator implementation equations -- using infix notation for + and * --

δ(M(t, a)) = mem(t, a)

δ(R(t,i)) = reg(t, i)

δ(ADD(e, f)) = e+f

δ(ADDI(e,n)) = e+const(n)

δ(MULI(e, n)) = e*const(n)

δ(bdx(t, tt, i, j, n)) = (reg(t, i) + const(n)) + reg(t, j) * const(scale(tt))

δ(mk_adr(e)) = e

◊

Example 2

q =

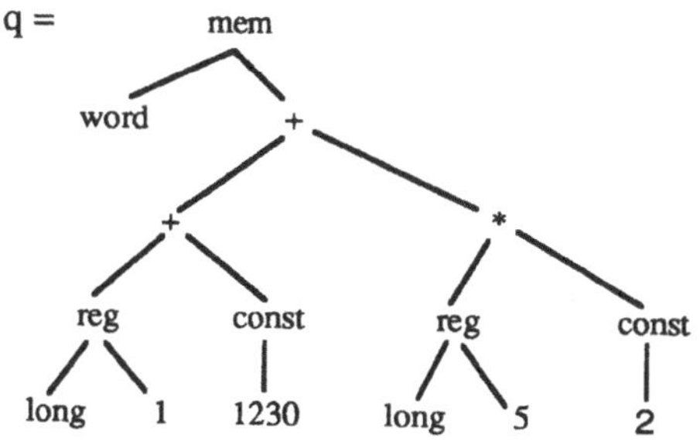

z =

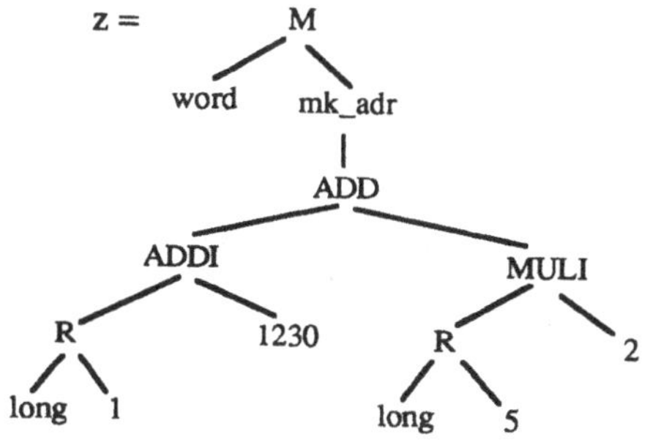

z´ =

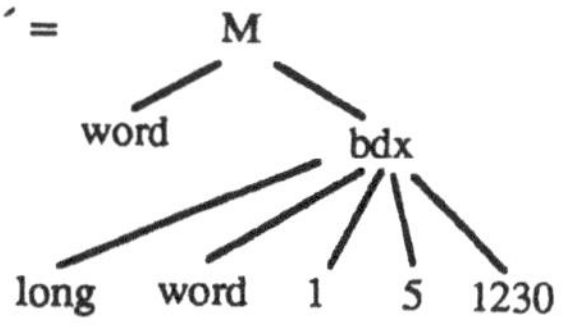

Example 2 shows z, z′ such that $\delta(z) =_E q$ and $\delta(z') =_E q$, which can be verified formally from the definition of δ. The terms describe a memory word addressed via base, displacement and scaled index, which could be written (in a VAX-like notation) either as operand 1230(R1.L)[R5.L] in a word instruction, or as operand (R1) preceded by the code sequence ADDI.L R1, 1230; MULI.L R5, 2; ADD.L R1, R5.

The reader is invited to attempt to construct z or z′ from q by performing the appropriate pattern matching, for the moment on an intuitive basis. Note also that if we replace the constant 2 in q by (say) another register, there is no target term for the modified q. The specification is incomplete.

3. Homogeneous Tree Languages, Heterogeneous Term Algebras, and Regular Tree Languages

This chapter introduces familiar concepts and notes some straightforward correspondencies and differences.

3.1 Homogeneous Tree Languages

Definition 1: Ranked Alphabet, Homogeneous Tree Languages

A ranked alphabet is a finite set A of symbols, together with a function rank, such that

- $rank(a) \geq 0$ for each $a \in A$.

The homogeneous tree language trees(A), also called the set of trees over the ranked alphabet A , is defined by

- $a \in trees(A)$, if $rank(a)=0$,
- $a(t_1, ..., t_n) \in trees(A)$, if $t_i \in trees(A)$ for $1 \leq i \leq n$, $a \in A$, and $rank(a)=n$.

◊

Example 3

Let A1 be the alphabet {0, 1, cons, nil}, with ranks 0, 0, 2, 0, respectively. Elements of trees(A1) are, for example: 0, nil, cons(nil, 1), cons(cons(0, 1), cons(nil, nil)).

◊

We shall also depict trees in graphical form, as in Example 2.

Observation 1

Consider the subset lists(A1) of trees(A1) containing the constants 0 and 1, plus all linear lists of binary digits, such as nil or cons(1, cons(0, nil)). It cannot be described as a homogeneous tree language trees(A) for any A.

◊

3.2 Regular Tree Languages

Definition 2: Regular Tree Grammars and Regular Tree Languages

A regular tree grammar G is a triple (N, A, P), where

- N is a finite set of nonterminal symbols,
- A is a ranked alphabet of terminal symbols, $A \cap N = \emptyset$,
- P is a finite set of productions of the form X --> t, with $X \in N$ and $t \in trees(A \cup N)$, with nonterminals given rank 0.

For t, $t' \in trees(A \cup N)$, t immediately derives t′, written t -> t′, if there is a $p \in P$, say X->t′′, such that t′ results from t by replacing a leaf labelled X by t′′. Where relevant, we indicate the p used in the derivation step, writing $->_p$. The relations $->^+$ and $->^*$ are the transitive and the transitive and reflexive closure of ->.

$L(X) := \{t \mid t \in trees(A) \text{ and } X \text{-->}^* t\}$, and
$L(G) := \{t \mid t \in L(X) \text{ for some } X \in N\}$ is the language of G.
◊

In our context, we are not interested in a particular root symbol, and so it was omitted from Definition 2.

Example 4

Let G1 be the regular tree grammar ({D, R}, A1, P1} with A1 as before, and
P1 = { R --> nil
R -->cons(D, R)
D -->0
D -->1}.
Clearly, L(G1) = lists(A1) of Observation 1.
◊

We call these grammars *regular* (following [Brai69]), since in their formal properties, they are a generalization of regular string grammars, rather than of context free string grammars. The usual view of Graham-Glanville style machine descriptions as *context free* grammars, with *prefix expressions* on the righthand sides of productions, does not adequately express how strong the restriction to "prefix expressions" really is. For example, language containment is undecidable for context free string grammars, but decidable for regular string grammars.We note:

Observation 2

For regular tree grammars G_1 and G_2, $L(G_1) \subseteq L(G_2)$ is decidable.
◊

A proof of this fact is given in [Benk85], although this result is probably much older. We will see a very important application of this result later. In the sequel, we shall need a few more technical notions:

Definition 3

A production of the form X -->Y, with X, Y ∈ N is a chain rule. Other productions are called structural rules.

A derivation containing a subderivation of the form $X \text{-->}^+ X$ (using chain rules only) is called a circular derivation.

A sentential form of G (for X) is a tree $t \in trees(A \cup N)$ such that $X \text{-->}^* t$.
◊

Observation 3

$t \in L(G)$ has infinitely many derivations iff it has a circular derivation.
◊

Of course, regular tree grammars may be ambigous, but observation 3 tells us, that if we restrict our attention to noncircular derivations, there will be only finitely many such derivations for any $t \in L(G)$.

3.3 Heterogeneous Term Algebras

For the standard terminology we need from algebraic specifications, we do not give full formal definitions (see [HuOp80] for that matter), but only explain the notation we are going to use.

Definition 4: Signatures, Specifications

For a signature $\Sigma = (S, OP)$, $T(\Sigma)$ denotes the set of terms over Σ, while the set of terms of a particular sort s is denoted T(Σ):s. T(Σ, V) is the set of Σ-terms over an S-sorted set V of variables. A specification (Σ, E) is a signature Σ together with a set E of equations of form t = t´, with t, t´∈T(S,V). It induces the equality relation $=_E$ on T(Σ,V).

Substitutions are mappings σ:V --> T(Σ, V), the application of σ to t is denoted by tσ.

The replacement of a subterm t´ in t by t´´ is written t[t´ <-- t´´].

◊

Example 5

Let Σ1 be the signature with sorts {D, R} and operators

{0: --> D, 1: --> D, cons: D R -->R, nil: -->R}.

Clearly, T(Σ1) is isomorphic to L(G1), and T(Σ1, V), when restricted to a single variable for each sort, is isomorphic to the sentential forms of G1.

◊

In the sequel, we will mainly be concerned with syntactic aspects - recognizing terms for which $=_E$ is the syntactic identity relation. However, we set the stage for a convenient generalization, allowing a subsignature for which nontrivial equations may hold. The idea is that equality relation of this subsignature can be implemented by some other means, for example by providing a canonical term rewrite system for it. The concept of a hierarchic signature here is the same as in algebraic compiler specifications with attribute coupled grammars [GaGi84]. There, the subsignature is called the "semantic" subsignature, while its complement is called "syntax". In this terminology, terms can be seen as syntactic trees with semantic terms at their leaves.

Definition 5: Hierarchic Signature

A signature Σ is hierarchic, if it contains a subsignature Σ´ such that all operators of Σ with result sorts from Σ´ are from Σ´.

◊

We shall restrict our attention to specifications where equations may only be given between terms of those sorts which belong to the subsignature Σ´. The particular significance of the subsignature M and its equational theory in the application to code generation was explained following Example 1 in section 2.

3.4 Simple Correspondencies

Let η be the grammar morphism that merges all nonterminals into a single one, modifying productions accordingly.

Observation 4

L(G) ⊆ L(η(G)) ⊆ trees(A).

◊

In general, the inclusion is proper. This is illustrated by Example 6.

Example 6

Let grammar G2 =({D, R}, A1, P2} with

P2= { R --> nil
R --> cons(0, R)
R --> cons(1, R)
D --> 0
D --> 1}.

We have L(G2) = L(G1). We have L(G2) ⊂ L(η(G2)) ⊂ trees(A1), proved by considering cons(0, 0) and cons(cons(0, 0), nil). Although L(G2) = L(G1), the second inclusion is not proper in the case of G1.
◊

Observation 5

For any A, trees(A) = L(G) for a regular tree grammar G in the following restricted form:
(RF1) G =({X}, A, P}, with
P = {X--> a(X, ..., X) | for a∈A and according to rank(a)}.
◊

Now we denote by η the signature morphism that identifies all sorts, yielding one-sorted signatures.

Observation 6

T(Σ) ⊆ T(η(Σ)) = trees(OP)
◊

To see that the above inclusion is proper, consider cons(0, 0) ∈ T(η(Σ1)) \ T(Σ1). More precisely, the inclusion above would have to be expressed as T(Σ) being isomorphic to a subset of T(η(Σ)), and the equality as isomorphism. Besides this, the equality in Observation 6 is justified below.

Observation 7

Any T(Σ) for Σ=(S, OP) is isomorphic to L(G) of a regular tree grammar G in the restricted special form
(RF2) G = (S, OP, P) with
P = {X_0 --> a(X_1, ..., X_n), for any a: X_1 ... X_n --> X_0 ∈ OP}.
◊

In G, we simply use sort symbols as nonterminals. If G has only one nonterminal, RF2 and RF1 coincide. Hence, the grammar corresponding to η(Σ) is in RF1, which proves T(η(Σ)) = trees(OP) of Observation 6.

According to the isomorphisms stated here, heterogeneous term algebras are rightfully called heterogeneous tree languages, and we will consider terms as trees and trees as terms, as convenient. For example, we will speak of a Σ-derivation of t as a way to sucessively construct some t∈T(Σ) from Σ-operators.

Summing up, we shortly address the question of what concept to use when designing an intermediate language. Expressive power is an important issue here. It is undesirable to specify an intermediate language which is a superset of what will actually occur, and then base subsequent compiler phases on assumptions on "that subset of the intermediate language actually produced by the front-end". (An interesting lesson is to be learned here from Henry´s experience with the portable C-Compiler [Henr84].) Summing up our observations, homogeneous tree languages are less powerful than heterogeneous tree languages, i.e. term algebras, which are in turn less powerful than regular tree languages. However, in section 4 we shall add another concept from algebraic data type specifications, which makes many-sorted term algebras more expressive than regular tree grammars.

3.5 Tree Parsing

Let G = (N, A, P) be a regular tree grammar. We now define what a G-parse for some t∈trees(A) is. Permitting t∈trees(A) rather than t∈L(G) means of course that a G-parse does not necessarily exist. Since in general, G is ambiguous, we define the notion of a parse such that it comprises all possible derivations of the given tree.

Definition 6

Let $t \in trees(A)$, $G = (N, A, P)$.

The G-semi-parse of t is the function ϕ' associating with each subtree t' of t the set of all productions p of form $X \to t''$ such that $X \to_p t'' \to^* t'$.

The G-parse of t is the function ϕ associating with each subtree t' of t the set of all productions p of form $X \to t''$ such that for any p: $X \to t'' \in \phi(t')$, there is some derivation $X' \to^* t[t' \leftarrow X] \to_p t[t' \leftarrow t''] \to^* t$.

◊

Usually, the grammar G of concern will be clear from the context, and we speak just of semi-parses and parses. Clearly, a semi-parse may associate productions with some subtree that cannot be part of a derivation of the overall tree.

Observation 8

Let ϕ be the parse, and ϕ' the semi-parse of t.

i) ϕ and ϕ' coincide at the root: $\phi(t) = \phi'(t)$.

ii) $t \in L(G)$ iff $\phi(t) \neq \emptyset$.

iii) If $\phi(t') = \emptyset$ for some proper subtree t', this does not imply $t \notin L(G)$.

◊

In case iii), the root of subtree t' may still be derived as an inner node of the righthand side of some production.

Given $\phi(t)$, we can enumerate all derivations for t. If G is noncircular, or if we restrict our interest to noncircular derivations, their number is finite, and a simple backtracking traversal of t is sufficient to

enumerate them. But generally, although ϕ can clearly be represented in space linear in the size of t, there may be exponentially many noncircular derivations, and a complete enumeration or explicit representation is not what one is interested in. We shall return to the problem of what to do with a parse in chapter 8.

4. Derivors and Their Inversion

Derivors [ADJ78] are an implementation concept in algebraic data type specifications: By a derivor $\delta: Q \to Z$, the operators of some signature Q are implemented by composite operators in some other signature Z, which are specified as terms of T(Z, V). Sometimes a derivor in the opposite direction, $\delta: Z \to Q$, is used to (partially) specify a morphism γ: $T(Q) \to T(Z)$, which one is interested in. For $q \in T(Q)$, we require $\gamma(q)$:= some $z \in T(Z)$ such that $\delta(z) =_E q$. The task, then, is to construct in some way an inverse of δ. Code selection is an important and natural example for this phenomenon when understood in the way outlined in section 2).

4.1 Derivors and Linearity

Definition 7

A derivor δ: $Z \to Q$ is specified by

- a sort implementation map δ: $S_Z \to S_Q$,
- an operator implementation map δ: $OP_Z \to T(Q, V)$, specified for each operator

$a{:}s_1 \ldots s_n \dashrightarrow s_0 \in OP_Z$ by operator implementation equations of the form

$\delta(a(v_1{:}s_1, \ldots, v_n{:}s_n){:}s_0) = t_a(v_1{:}\delta(s_1), \ldots, v_n{:}\delta(s_n)){:}\delta(s_0)$.

(Not all variables of the lefthand side must actually occur in t_a.)

A derivor is linear, if for all $a \in OP_Z$, none of the variables v_i occurs more than once in the term t_a.

When Q and Z are hierarchic signatures (cf. Definition 5) over the same subsignature Σ', we call δ hierarchic if it is the identity on Σ'.

◊

On the righthand side of these equations, the variable v_i of the Q-sort $\delta(s_i)$ denotes the δ-image of the i-th argument (whose sort is s_i) of operator a. For an example, return to Example 1 in section 2.

The terms t_a are called derived operators in Q, and forgetting the original operators of Q turns T(Q) into a Z-algebra. The Z-homomorphism defined by δ is readily implemented by reading the operator implementation equations left to right as rewrite rules over $T(Q \cup Z)$, where the elements of T(Q) are the normal forms. As there is, by definition, one equation for each Z-operator, there are no critical pairs, and the rules trivially form a canonical rewrite system.

However, while δ translates target into intermediate language programs, our interest goes in the opposite direction. Simply orienting the equations right to left to obtain a rewrite system for γ, an inverse of δ, will generally fail for two reasons:

(1) If δ is not injective, the rewrite system so obtained will not be confluent.

(2) If δ is not surjective, some $t \in T(Q)$ will have normal forms that are not in T(Z).

Injectivity of δ cannot be enforced (- at least when a certain freedom of choice in γ is inherent in the problem under consideration -), so standard rewrite techniques cannot be used for implementing γ. Surjectivity (modulo $=_E$) of δ will be required - as δ should specify γ for any input term -, and for practical matters we need a way to verify this requirement.

Definition 8

Let there be given a derivor δ: Z --> Q, specifying (as outlined in section 1.3) some inverse mapping γ: T(Q) --> T(Z). We call this δ complete, if δ is surjective modulo $=_E$, i.e.

for all $q \in T(Q)$, there is some $z \in T(Z)$ such that $q =_E \delta(z)$.

◊

4.2 Derivor Inversion by Tree Parsing

Observation 9

If δ is linear, $\delta(T(Z)) \subseteq T(Q)$ can be described by a regular tree grammar Δ_δ of the following form:

$\Delta_\delta = (S_Z, OP_Q, \{s_0 \dashrightarrow t_a(s_1, \ldots, s_n)$ for each operator implementation equation

$\delta(a(v_1{:}s_1, \ldots, v_n{:}s_n){:}s_0) = t_a(v_1{:}\delta(s_1), \ldots, v_n{:}\delta(s_n)){:}\delta(s_0)$ of $\delta\})$.

◊

Where δ is clear from the context, we just write Δ for Δ_δ. Note that Δ constructs terminal trees over OP_Q, using as nonterminals the sorts of S_Z. Single variables on righthand sides of operator implementation equations give rise to chain productions in Δ, while proper terms yield structural productions. Equations with the same righthand sides and the same result sort s_0 give rise to the same production in Δ, in spite of the fact that they implement different Z-operators.

As one easily verifies, for a linear δ, L(s) as defined by Δ is the set of δ-images of T(Z):s. This means that, for a linear δ, the problem of constructing γ, the inverse of δ, is solved by constructing Δ-parses. The reader is invited to construct Δ_δ for δ as given in Example 1, (ignoring its nonlinearity for the moment), to construct the Δ_δ-parse of q, and to obtain from it z and z´ as shown in Example 2.

Theorem 1

Let E = Ø. If γ is specified to be an inverse of a linear derivor δ, then
i) completeness of the specification is decidable,
ii) any choice for $\gamma(q)$ can be obtained from a Δ-parse of $q \in T(Q)$.

Proof:
i) follows from Observations 2, 7 and 9: Completeness now means verifying that, with Q seen as a grammar according to Observation 7, $L(Q) \subseteq L(\Delta)$.
ii) We construct a Z-derivation of z´ "in parallel" to a Δ-derivation of $\delta(z') = q$: For each application of $s_0 \dashrightarrow t_a(s_1, ..., s_n)$ in a Δ-derivation of q , apply $s_0 \dashrightarrow a(s_1, ..., s_n)$ for some $a \in OP_Z$ with $\delta(a(v_1{:}s_1, ..., v_n{:}s_n){:}s_0) = t_a(v_1{:}\delta(s_1), ..., v_n{:}\delta(s_n)){:}\delta(s_0)$ being an operator implementation equation, thus obtaining a Z-derivation of $z' \in T(Z, S_Z)$. Obtain z from z´ by substituting different variables for all occurences of sort-symbols in z´. For any substitution σ, $\delta(z\sigma) = q$.

◊

Note that several terms z can be constructed from the same Δ-derivation of t according to the above proof. One reason is that there is a choice of a, if several operators with the same result sort s_0 have implementation equations with the same righthand side t_a. The other reason is that if there are equations where some variable of the lefthand side does not occur on the righthand side, the corresponding Z-subterm is "forgotten" by δ, and hence may be chosen arbitrarily by σ.

4.3 Expressive Power Revisited

We now remark that many-sorted signatures together with the concept of linear derivors have the same expressive power as regular tree languages. Observation 9 showed that they do not have more expressive power, as every linear derivor image can be generated by a regular tree grammar. It is easy to see that the reverse also holds:

Observation 10

Let Q be a many-sorted signature. For any regular tree grammar G with $L(G) \subseteq T(Q)$, there exist a signature Z and a linear derivor δ such that $L(G) = \delta(T(Z))$.

Proof:

1. For any G with L(G)⊆T(Q), there exists a G´ such that for all nonterminals X of G´, there is a unique Q-sort s such that for all t∈L(X), sort(t)=s. We construct this G´ as follows: Let X $-->_p$ t:s, X $-->_{p'}$ t´:s´ with s≠s´, and both p and p´ be structural productions. X cannot occur on the righthand side of any structural production, as this would violate L(G)⊆T(Q) by generating a non-wellsorted term. We replace X by a new nonterminal symbol X´ in p´, and add for each chain rule Y->X a further chain rule Y->X´. The same argument applies to Y with Y -->X, Y -->X´, and X $-->_p$ t:s, X´ $-->_{p'}$ t´:s´ with s≠s´. Successive application of this step yields the desired G´, with L(G´)=L(G).

2. Now w.l.o.g. let G be such that for all nonterminals X of G, there is a unique Q-sort s such that for all t∈L(X), sort(t)=s. Let us denote this s as sort(X). We define Z and δ as follows:

$S_Z = N_G$. OP_Z has an operator $p:X_1...X_n$ --> X_0 for each production p: X_0--> $t_p(X_1...X_n) \in P_G$.

The derivor δ is given by the sort map

$$\delta(X) = sort(X),$$

and the operator implementation equations

$$\delta(p(v_1, ..., v_n)) = t_p(v_1, ..., v_n).$$

◊

Note that the derivor constructed in Observation 10 is linear. Hence, regular sub-languages of a term algebra can be seen as homomorphic images of some other term algebra, specified by a linear derivor. Images of nonlinear derivors can define sub-languages that cannot be specified by regular tree grammars.

5. Two Notions of Matching

While "matching" (between terms) has a precise and uniform meaning in the field of term rewrite systems (cf. Definition 4), the phrase "pattern matching" is sometimes used more vaguely - for matching a single pattern against a tree, for determining all matches of a pattern set in a given tree, or sometimes for purposes that would more rightfully be called parsing of trees. This section clarifies the correspondencies by describing parsing as a slightly generalized form of matching between terms.

Definition 9

Let R be some subset of T(Σ, V). A substitution σ is a substitution from R, or an R-substitution for short, if vσ≠v implies σ(v)∈R.

◊

In the application we have in mind, R will be described by a grammar, but for Definitions 9 and 10, this is irrelevant.

Definition 10

Let (Σ, E) be a specification, let p, t∈T(Σ,V), R⊆T(Σ,V).

- p matches t, if there exists a substitution σ such that $p\sigma =_E t$.
- p R-matches t, if there exists an R-substitution σ such that $p\sigma =_E t$.

◊

Note that if p R-matches t, this does not imply t∈R!

Theorem 2

Given Σ, let G be such that $L(G) \subseteq T(\Sigma)$, and $t{:}s \in T(\Sigma){:}s$, $v{:}s \in V$. Then we have:

$t \in L(G)$ iff v L(G)-matches t.

◊

This is in fact the trivial case of Definition 10, with p being a single variable. The point is that we can formulate it in a more constructive way by separating out the "topmost production" of t:

Corollary

$t \in L(G)$ iff, for some production p of form X-->t′, with $t' \in T(\Sigma, V)$, t′ L(G)-matches t.

◊

Matching a term p against t (in the sense of Definition 10) is a local task - only the non-variable part of p must be compared against the outermost portion of t. The required substitution is determined automatically by associating subterms of t to variables of p in corresponding positions. (If p is nonlinear, subtree comparison must also be performed, but we ignore nonlinearity for the moment.) The expensive part of this, if any, is testing the equality relation $=_E$ underlying the comparison. In tree pattern matching, as in [Kron75], [HoOD82], no equality other than syntactic equality is considered, and matching a single pattern against a tree is still a local task. But in typical applications, one is interested in all matches of a set of patterns at all subtrees of t, and this is the reason why the matching algorithms studied there perform a complete top-down or bottom-up traversal of t.

With matching relative to L(G), this is different: In order to determine a single match of p, say at the root of t, we must not only compare p and the appropriate portion of t, but also ensure that the substitution so obtained is an L(G)-substitution. This in turn requires L(G)-matching the variables of p to the corresponding subtrees of t, and so forth. So in any case, a complete analysis of t is required.

6. Algorithms for Derivor Inversion

We formulate algorithms for derivor inversion, retaining the classical pattern matching algorithm as a special case.

6.1 Problem Statement and Outline of Solution

Given:

- Two hierarchic signatures $Q=(S_Q, OP_Q)$ and $Z=(S_Z, OP_Z)$ over a common subsignature $M=(S_M, OP_M)$.
- A set E of equations of form m=m′, with $m, m' \in T(M, V)$, defining the relation $=_E$ (equality modulo E) on T(M, V), T(Q, V) and T(Z, V), such that unification, equality and matching in T(M,V) (and hence T(Q, V) and T(Z, V)) modulo E are decidable (and presumably efficiently implementable).
- δ:Z --> Q, a hierarchic derivor.

Desired:

- For $q \in T(Q)$, some representation of the set $\delta^{-1}(q) := \{z \in T(Z) \mid \delta(z) =_E q\}$.
- A criterion for "specification completeness", i.e. for $T(Q) \subseteq_E \delta(T(Z))$.

Special cases:

For space reasons, we can consider here in detail only the case where M is empty and δ is linear. For $|S_Z| = |S_Q| = 1$ this is the case of classical pattern matching according to [HoOD82] or [Kron75]. In this section we will generalize the notion of matching sets appropriately to handle the heterogeneous case, and shortly comment on the other generalizations.

Outline of the solution:
Let $\Delta=(N^{\Delta}, OP^{Q}, P^{\Delta})$ be the regular tree grammar for δ, constructed according to Observation 9. $L(\Delta)$ describes $\delta(T(Z))$, if δ is linear, and else a superset of $\delta(T(Z))$. For $X \in N^{\Delta}$, $sort(X) \in S_Q$ is uniquely defined as in Observation 10, which follows from the way in which Δ is constructed.

Definition 11: Pattern, Pattern Forest, Matching Sets

- Let $P \subseteq T(Z, V)$ be the set of terms occuring on the righthand sides of the operator implementation equations of δ. P is called the set of "patterns".

- Let $PF = \{p' \mid p'$ is a subterm of some $p \in P\}$, the "pattern forest". (Note that $P \subseteq PF$.)

- For $q \in T(Q)$, let the "matching set" of q be
  $MS(q) = \{p \in PF \mid p\ \delta(T(Z))$-matches $q\}$.

- Let $MSs = \{M \mid M = M(q)$ for some $q \in T(Q)\}$.

◊

These notions are analogous to those used in pattern matching in homogeneous tree languages, but significantly more general. Basing the definitions on $\delta(T(Z))$-relative matching of terms (with variables) accomodates heterogenity, nonlinearity, and a nontrivial equational theory of M.

Definition 12: Algorithm Building Blocks

build$_a$: For $m_1, ..., m_n \subseteq PF$, $a \in OP_Q \backslash OP_M$,
$build_a(m_1, ..., m_n) = \{p \in PF \mid p = a(p_1, ..., p_n), p_i \in m_i\}$.

prod: For $p \in P$ with $p = t(v_1{:}\delta(s_n), ..., v_n{:}\delta(s_n))$, $prod(p) = t(s_1, ..., s_n)$.
(Remember: $N^{\Delta} = S_Z$.)

nonlin$_q$: For any $q \in T(Q)$, $m \subseteq PF$,
$nonlin_q(m) = \{p \in m \mid p = t(v_1{:}s_1, ..., v_n{:}s_n)$ such that
i) $prod(p) \rightarrow^{*} q'$ for some $q \in T(Q)$ with $q' =_E q$.
Let q_i' be the subtree derived from s_i in the derivation of q'.
ii) ($v_i = v_j$ implies $q_i' =_E q_j'$ for any $i, j \in 1..n$)$\}$.

chain: Let $N' \subseteq N^{\Delta}$, and $closure(N') := \{X \in N^{\Delta} \mid X \rightarrow^{*} Y, Y \in N'\}$.
For $R \subseteq prod(PF)$, $chain(R) = closure(\{X \in N^{\Delta} \mid (X \rightarrow t) \in P^{\Delta}, t \in R\})$.

vars: For $X \in N^{\Delta}$, $vars(X) = \{v \in PF \cap V \mid sort(v) = sort(X)\}$.

prod and vars are extended to sets element-wise.
◊

$build_a$ just constructs the set of patterns rooted by a, given choices of subpatterns for the $n \geq 0$ arguments of a. chain determines nonterminals from which certain righthand sides can be derived by (possibly empty) chains, ending in a structural production whose righthand side is in R. prod and vars are used to translate between the algebraic-view and the grammar-view of δ. For $p \in P$, prod(p) is the righthand side of the corresponding Δ-production(s). Ignoring $=_E$ for the moment, if δ is linear, the notions of derivation and L(Δ)-relative matching coincide. In this sense, prod(p) can also be thought of as a rewritten pattern p with variables renamed to make it linear. δ(T(Z))-relative matching of p against some q can thus be separated into two "parts": derivation of q from prod(p) with $q_i \in \delta(T(Z))$, and verifying the nonlinearity condition. $nonlin_q$ checks nonlinearity of patterns p which - if they were linear - would match at the root of q. (In an implementation, one uses the functionality nonlin(p, q) instead of $nonlin_q(p)$.)

Algorithms calculating matching sets will be composed from these functions. MS(q) and the matching sets for all subterms of q will be the desired representation of $\delta^{-1}(q)$. The following theorem shows that matching sets are an extension of the notion of a semi-parse φ′.

Theorem 3:

Let M be empty and δ linear. We have the following correspondence between the matching sets and a semi-parse φ′ of q ∈ T(Q) (and for all subterms of q):

$$\phi'(q) = \{X \text{ --> } prod(p) \in P^{\Delta} \mid p \in MS(q) \cap P\}.$$

◊

We now have to show - for the general case - that MS(q) in fact represents $\delta^{-1}(q)$ in a precise way. The following two definitions are mutually recursive:

Definition 13a

For p ∈ P, let Z-op(p) = $\{f(v_1, ..., v_n) \mid f \in OP_Z$ and $\delta(f(v_1, ..., v_n)) = p$ is an operation implementation equation of δ}.

For q ∈ T(Q), define Z-terms(q) ⊆ T(Z,V) as follows:

i) for q ∈ T(M): Z-terms(q) = $\{t \in T(M) \mid t =_E q\}$.

ii) for q ∈ T(Q) \ T(M):

Z-terms(q) = {fρ | f ∈ Z-op(p) for some p ∈ MS(q) ∩ P, and ρ a matching substitution for p over q}.

◊

Case i) comes from the fact that δ by definition is the identity on T(M). One may choose to represent Z-terms(q) by q in this case. Case ii) constructs a Z-term rooted by f, taking as its arguments Z-terms from the corresponding variable positions in p, as matched against q. This correspondence is defined formally as the notion of a "matching substitution", which substitutes Z-terms for variables, and hence applies to $f(v_1, ..., v_n)$ rather than p.

Definition 13b

For p∈MS(q), we say that ρ: V->T(Z, V) is a matching substitution for p over q, iff one of the following applies:

i) p = v (a single variable) and vρ ∈ Z-terms(q);

ii) p∈T(M,V) and pρ∈Z-Terms(q);

iii) v does not occur in p and vρ is a new unique variable;

iv) $p = a(p_1, ..., p_k)$, $a \in OP_Q \backslash OP_M$, $p_i \in T(Q,V)$, (and hence $q = a(q_1, ..., q_k)$), and ρ is a matching substitution for p_i over q_i for $1 \le i \le k$.

◊

If p is nontrivial, case iv) applies and takes us down to the positions in q that correspond to the variables in p. It ensures that variables occuring in several leaf positions are consistently substituted. Cases ii) and iii) should be clear, but case i) contains a subtlety that needs further explanation.

On the one hand, case i) is just the terminating case in the parallel structural induction over p and q as specified by case iv). However, considering the situation where the pattern p considered in case ii) of Definition 13a is a single variable, Definitions 13a and 13b seem circular. When $\delta(f(v))=v$, and $v \in MS(q)$, they say that $f(t) \in$ Z-Terms(q) if $t \in$ Z-Terms(q). When t and f(t) happen to be of the same sort, this even implies $f^i(t) \in$ Z-Terms(q) for $i \geq 0$. This is exactly what we need here: it models the situation where δ plainly forgets Z-structure, which is recovered by finding (potentially circular) derivations using the chain productions in Δ that stem from operation implementation equations of the form $\delta(f(v_1, ..., v_n) = v_i$.

Note that Z-terms(q) may contain terms of different sorts. They contain variables for subterms "forgotten" by δ. Finally, we observe:

Theorem 4

$\delta^{-1}(q) = \{t\sigma \mid t \in$ Z-terms(q) and σ a ground substitution$\}$.

◊

Now we are left with the task of efficiently calculating MS(q) for a given $q \in T(Q)$.

6.2 The Basic Dynamic Algorithm

With the functions of Definition 12, it is straightforward to describe our basic algorithm for determining matching sets for a given input term q. Subsequently, we shall derive table driven versions from this Algorithm 1.

Algorithm 1:

Input: $r \in T(Q)$, PF.

Output: For each subterm q of r (including r itself): MS(q).

(1) for all subterms q of r with sort(q) $\in S_M$ *)
do MS(q)= $\{p \in$ PF$\mid$ p matches m (modulo E)$\}$ od;
(2) i:= 1;
(3) while $i \leq$ height(r)
(4) do for all subterms $q = a(q_1, ..., q_n)$, $n \geq 0$, of r with height(q) = i and sort(q) $\notin S_M$
(4a) do MS(q) := let $\underline{m} = (MS(q_1), ..., MS(q_n))$ in
$(nonlin_q \circ build_a)(\underline{m}) \cup (vars \circ chain \circ prod \circ nonlin_q \circ build_a)(\underline{m})$
od;
(4b) i:= i+1;
od

◊

*) Actually it suffices to compute the matching sets of "semantic" subterms m (i.e. sort(m)$\in S_M$),which are not subterms of a semantic subterm themselves, because on the one hand $\delta^{-1}(m) = m$, and on the other hand we need the matching sets of such "complete" subterms m, in order to be able to compute the matching sets of the "syntactic" superterms q´ (i.e. sort(q´) $\notin S_M$) containing them.

6.3 Table-Driven Algorithm for M empty and δ linear

For this section, we let M be empty and δ linear. In step 4a) of Algorithm 1, all functions except $nonlin_q$ are independent of the actual input term q. When δ is linear, $nonlin_q$ is the identity on pattern sets, for any q. Hence, the matching set of a term $q = a(q_1, ..., q_n)$ is computed (only) from the operator "a" and the matching sets of the subterms $q_1, ..., q_n$.

As noted earlier, the set of all matching sets, MSs, is finite. These facts gave rise to the idea (in the treatment of the homogeneous case in [Kron75] and [HoOD82]) to precompute the information which is dynamically computed in step 4 of Algorithm 1. This information is represented by tabulating the following functions f_a, for each $a \in OP_Q$:

$$f_a(\underline{m}) = build_a(\underline{m}) \cup (vars \circ chain \circ prod \circ build_a)(\underline{m}).$$

The functionality of f_a could be seen as f_a: $(MSs)^{rank(a)}$ ---> MSs, but this would be excessively expensive in table size and generation time. Instead, f_a should only be tabulated for those combinations of arguments that can actually occur. A restriction of the possible combinations is observed by exploiting the heterogenity of the input language: All patterns matching a term q must have the same sort as q. We may partition MSs according to S_Q:

$$MSs = \cup \; N\text{-}MSs, \text{ for } N \in S_Q, \quad \text{with } MS(q) \in N\text{-}MSs \text{ iff } sort(q)=N.$$

It suffices to precompute the following (generally smaller) tables:

For $(a: N_1...N_n \text{ --> } N_0) \in OP_Q$: $f_a: N_1\text{-}MSs \times ... \times N_n\text{-}MSs \text{ ---> } N_0\text{-}MSs$.

(As observed in [Kron75] for the one-sorted case, the N-MSs as carriers and f_a as functions form a Q-algebra. Another such algebra could be defined over the carriers $C_N = 2^{\{p \in PF \mid sort(p)=N\}}$, with f_a extended accordingly. This algebra is the worst case of our approach with respect to size of the precomputed tables. Work on the homogeneous case has shown that the tables for f_a as defined above are significantly smaller in many practical applications.)

Provided that we have precomputed f_a for all $a \in OP_Q$, we get the following table driven version of Algorithm 1:

Algorithm 2:

Input: $r \in T(Q)$; for all $a \in OP_Q$: f_a
Output: as Algorithm 1

```
(1)   -- step 1 is omitted as we assume M to be empty --
(2)   i:= 1;
(3)        while i ≤ height(r)
(4)        do    for all subterms q = a(q1,...,qn), n≤0, of r with height(q) = i
(4a)             do   MS(q):= f_a (MS(q1),...,MS(qn)) od;
(4b)             i:= i+1
           od
◊
```

Obviously, this matching algorithm is linear in the size of r, as it consists of a single table-lookup per node of the input term r.

The principle idea in the following table generating algorithm is to compute successively the matching sets of all terms from T(Q) of height 0,1,2, etc. until MSs, the set of all matching sets, converges. Terms are not enumerated explicitely. Rather, a term of height i is represented by its top operator and the possible matching sets for its arguments. The first iteration (for nullary a) is taken out of the repeat loop, as its repeated calculation cannot yield further matching sets.

Algorithm 3:

Input: PF, OP_Q, S_Q.

Output: for all $a \in OP_Q$: f_a.

for all $N \in S_Q$ do $N\text{-}MSs^0 := \emptyset$ od;

for all $(a : \text{-->} N) \in OP_Q$

do tabulate f_a;

$N\text{-}MSs^0 := N\text{-}MSs^0 \cup f_a$

od;

i:=1;

repeat for all $(a : N_1 \ldots N_n \text{-->} N) \in OP_Q$, $n \geq 1$,

do for all $N \in S_Q$ do $N\text{-}MSs^i := \emptyset$ od;

for all $(R_1,\ldots,R_n) \in N_1\text{-}MSs^{i-1} \times \ldots \times N_n\text{-}MSs^{i-1}$ *)

do tabulate $f_a(R_1,\ldots,R_n)$;

$N\text{-}MSs^i := N\text{-}MSs^i \cup f_a(R_1,\ldots,R_n)$

od

od;

for all $N \in S_Q$ do $N\text{-}MSs^i := N\text{-}MSs^i \cup N\text{-}MSs^{i-1}$ od;

i:= i+1

until for all $N \in S_Q$, $N\text{-}MSs^{i-1} = N\text{-}MSs^{i-2}$

◊

*) Here we can demand at least one R_j to be computed in the last iteration step of the repeat-loop, in order to ensure that there will be computed matching sets of terms of height i indeed.

Observation 12:

The specification is complete, i.e. $T(Q) = L(\Delta)$ $(= \delta(T(Z)))$, iff for all table-entries $f_a(R_1,\ldots,R_n) = R$ holds: $R \cap P \neq \emptyset$.

◊

6.4 Extensions

Space does not allow to explicate the extension of the generator algorithm to the cases where M is non-empty, and the derivor may be non-linear. This will be done in an extended version of this paper, planned to appear elsewhere. We only sketch here the particular problems to be solved for each of these, and one further extension.

Extension to non-empty M

A particular initial step is needed to calculate the s-MSs for $s \in S_M$. Generally, not all subsets of $2^{PF:s}$ can occur, since some patterns in PF:s may not be independent, as for example the patterns car(cons(1, v)) and 1 in the presence of the usual axioms. Here we need the prerequisite of our problem statement that unification modulo E be decidable.

Extension to nonlinear δ

Consider Algorithm 1. In the linear case, $nonlin_q$ is the identity, and the composite effect of step 4a) can be precomputed. $nonlin_q$, however, can only be evaluated dynamically, and so we have to generate separate tables representing $build_a$ and $f(\underline{m}) := \underline{m} \cup (vars \circ chain \circ prod)(\underline{m})$. Now the central step (4a) in Algorithm 2 becomes

$$MS(q) := \text{let } m' = nonlin_q \circ build_a(MS(q_1), \ldots, MS(q_n)) \text{ in } m' \cup f(m'),$$

where $build_a$ and f are tabulated. $nonlin_q$ introduces twofold complications: In order to know for which arguments $build_a$ and f must be precomputed, we must anticipate the effect of $nonlin_q$. Furthermore, for applying $nonlin_q$ dynamically, information about matching substitutions must be calculated along with the matching sets.

Extension to More Refined Input Languages

Let IL be the input language to our pattern matcher. So far, we have assumed that it is a term algebra, IL=T(Q) for some Q. But an actual IL may be some subset of T(Q), being the output of earlier compiler phases. IL may be L(G) $\subseteq$ T(Q) for some regular tree grammar G, or it may be ρ(T(P)) for some other signature P and a (possibly nonlinear) derivor ρ: P --> Q. In these cases, the table driven algorithm with tables generated as if IL = T(Q) will still work correctly, but the tables may contain matching sets that cannot actually occur for the more restricted IL. Besides tables being larger than necessary, our completeness criterion is only a sufficient, but no longer a necessary condition. But in both cases, our generative algorithms can be adapted to generate the precise matching sets for the given IL. There is no need to study further generalization to input languages such as

IL = $(\rho_2 \circ \rho_1)$(T(P)), as derivors are closed under composition.

7. Table Size and Generation Effort

Measuring space and time efficiency in terms of the size of the given pattern set P, it is known from work on the homogeneous case [HoOD82], that there is an exponential worst case behaviour. Fortunately, it has also been experienced that this behaviour does not occur for many practical situations, in particular when the compacting technique of [Chas87] is used. As our algorithms include the homogeneous case when $|S_Q|$ (= $|S_Z|$) = 1, these worst case observations are still valid. On the other hand, one can construct a specification with $|S_Q|$ = 1 and $|S_Z|$ >1 that yields a linear number of matching sets, but turns into the worst-case example of [Chas87] when applying the sort-identifying morphism of section 3.4 to the target signature Z.

The generator algorithm (Alg. 3) is a 360-line PROLOG program. It uses the compacting generation technique of [Chas87], and some care was given to the way in which PROLOG's backtracking is used. The largest example it has been run with is a fairly complete description for the MC68000 processor, containing 37 sorts and 92 operators in the target signature. The (compiled) generator produces 76 matching sets in about 32 seconds on a SUN-3 (25MHz) workstation, and the generated tables (in the form of PROLOG facts) occupy 53K bytes of storage. (Without Chase's compacting technique, generation time is about 2 hours!) With the present data, it seems that space and time requirements of the code selector and its generator will no longer be a problem. But experiments comparable to those of [Henr84] have not yet been performed.

8. Conclusion and Future Work

We expect that more general machine specific aspects or code generation subtasks such as register allocation, that were previously treated in an ad-hoc manner, can be expressed by extending the target signature Z by equational specifications. Such code generator specifications may look rather different from the ones in most of the approaches discussed here (with the exception of [MRSD86]), but the underlying implementation technique will still be pattern matching as developed here. The long-term goal of this work is to make code generator specifications more formal and complete, such that proof methods from the area of term rewrite systems [HuOp80], [HuHu80], [RKKL85] can be used to verify the correctness of code generators.

The recent approaches we have discussed shortly in the introduction should be evaluated in terms of the formalism presented here. Besides by peculiarities in their pattern matching mechanisms, they are characterized by the way in which the evaluation of the "choice function" ξ is interleaved with the construction of δ^{-1}. Both ideas which have been used - dynamic programming at matching time, and reduction of generated tables at generation time according to cost criteria - can be incorporated with our approach. Most interesting may be an hybrid scheme, using table reduction where it retains completeness and optimality, and matching-time cost comparison otherwise.

Finally, a conceptually interesting and technically demanding problem spared out in this paper is the following: Having implicitly represented $\delta^{-1}(q)$ in a compact way (cf. Theorem 4), how do we extract from it an interesting subset according to cost minimality or other well-formedness criteria that express machine properties not covered by δ itself? Some progress has been achieved [Weis87] by work subsequent to [WeWi86], but an eventual solution to this problem also depends on what further subtasks of code generation are to be integrated into the overall approach.

References

[ACK83] *A. Tanenbaum, H. van Staveren, E. Keizer, J. Stevenson:* A Practical tool Kit for making Portable Compilers. CACM 26 (9), pp. 654-660, 1983]

[ADJ78] *J.A. Goguen, J.W. Thatcher, E.G. Wagner:* An initial algebra approach to the specification, correctness and implementation of abstract data types. In R. Yeh (ed.): Current trends in programming methodology, Vol. IV, Prentice Hall, 1978.

[AhGa85] *A.V. Aho, M. Ganapathi:* Efficient tree pattern matching: an aid to code generation. Proceedings POPL 12, pp.334-340, 1985.

[AGT86] *A.V. Aho, M. Ganapathi, S.W.K. Tjiang:* Code Generation Using Tree Matching and Dynamic Programming. Report , Bell Laboratories, Murray Hill, 1986.

[AhJo76] *A.V. Aho, S.C. Johnson:* Optimal Code Generation for Expression Trees. JACM 23(3), pp. 488-501, 1976.

[Benk85] *M. Benk:* Tree grammars as a pattern matching mechanism for code generation. Report TUM-I8524, Technical University München, 1985.

[Brai69] *W.S.Brainerd:* Tree generating regular systems. Information and Control 14, pp. 217-231, 1969.

[Catt77] *R.G.G. Cattell:* Formalization and Automatic Derivation of Code Generators. Dissertation, Report CMU-CS-78-117, Carnegie-Mellon-University, Pittsburgh 1978.

[Chas87] *D.R. Chase:* An improvement to bottom-up tree pattern matching. Proceedings POPL 14, 1987.

[CHK84] *Th.W. Christopher, Ph.J. Hatcher, R.C. Kukuk:* Using dynamic programming to generate optimized code in a Graham-Glanville style code generator. Proceedings SIGPLAN ´84 Symposium on Compiler Construction, SIGPLAN Notices 19, 6, 1984.

[GaGi84] *H. Ganzinger, R. Giegerich:* Attribute coupled grammars. Proceedings 2nd SIGPLAN Symposium on Compiler Construction, SIGPLAN Notices 19 (6), pp.70-80, 1984.

[Gieg84] *R. Giegerich:* Code generation phase models based on abstract machine descriptions. Report TUM-I8412, Technical University München, 1984.

[Gieg85] *R. Giegerich:* Logic specification of code generation techniques. In: H. Ganzinger, N.D. Jones (Eds.): Programs as data objects. LNCS 217, Springer Verlag, 1985.

[Glan77] *R.S. Glanville:* A Machine Independent Algorithm for Code Generation and its Use in Retargetable Compilers. Dissertation, Report UCB-CS-78-01, University of California, Berkeley 1977.

[GrGl77] *R.S. Glanville, S.L. Graham:* A new method for compiler code generation. Proceedings 5th ACM Symposium on Principles of Programming Languages, pp. 231-240, 1977.

[HaCh86] *Ph. J. Hatcher, Th. W. Christopher:* High quality code generation via bottom-up tree pattern matching. Proceedings SIGPLAN '86 Symposium on Compiler Construction, SIGPLAN Notices 21, 6, 1986.

[Henr84] *R.R. Henry:* Graham-Glanville code generators. Dissertation, Report UCB-CSD-84-184, Berkeley 1984.

[HoOD82] *Ch. Hoffman, M. O'Donnell:* Pattern matching in trees. JACM , pp.68-95, 1982.

[Hors87] *N. Horspool:* An alternative to the Graham-Glanville code-generation method. IEEE Software, pp. 33-39, May 1987.

[HuHu80] *G. Huet, J.-M. Hullot:* Proofs by induction in equational theories with constructors. Proceedings 21st SFCS, Lake Placid, pp 96-107, 1980.

[HuOp80] *G. Huet, D.C. Oppen:* Equations and rewrite rules: A survey. In R. Book (ed.): Formal language theory: Perspectives and open problems. Academic Press, 1980.

[Kron75] *H. Kron:* Tree templates and subtree transformational grammars. Dissertation, UC Santa Cruz, 1975.

[MRSD86] *M. Mazaud, R. Rakatozafy, A. Szumachowski-Despland:* Code Generation Based on Template-Driven Target Term Rewriting; Rapport de Recherche, INRIA, 1986.

[Ripk77] *K. Ripken:* Formale Beschreibung von Maschinen, Implementierungen und optimierender Maschinencodeerzeugung aus attributuerten Programmgraphen. Dissertation, TUM-INFO-7731, Institut für Informatik, TU München, 1977.

[RKKL85] *P. Rety, C. Kirchner, H. Kirchner, P. Lescanne:* NARROWER: a new algorithm for unification and its application to logic programming. Proc. 1st Conference on Rewriting Techniques and Applications, LNCS 202, Springer Verlag, pp. 141-157, 1985.

[Turn86] *P.K. Turner:* Up-down parsing with prefix grammars. SIGPLAN Notices 21, (12), 1986.

[Weis87] *B. Weisgerber:* Private communication.

[WeWi86] *B. Weisgerber, R. Wilhelm:* Two tree pattern matchers for code generation. Internal Report, University Saarbrücken, 1986.

Adding Relational Query Facilities to Software Development Environments

SUSAN HORWITZ
University of Wisconsin–Madison

Software development environments should include query handlers. Query handlers based on the relational database model are attractive because the model provides a uniform, non-procedural approach to query writing. There are two drawbacks to using the relational model to support query handlers in software development systems: (1) Standard relational database systems require that all information be stored in relations; however, the data structures used by existing software development environments are generally non-relational, and it is impractical to replace them with relations. (2) The standard relational operators are not powerful enough to express certain important classes of queries.

In [10] we proposed a model of editing environments, based on the use of relationally-attributed grammars, that supports a relational query facility. We introduced a new kind of relations, *implicit relations*, and a new approach to query evaluation to handle queries that use implicit relations.

In this paper we illustrate the utility of implicit relations in contexts other than relationally-attributed grammars. We extend the definition of implicit relations and show how they can be used to support relational query facilities in software development environments without giving up the use of non-relational data structures. Implicit relations can also be used to provide non-standard relational operations such as transitive closure.

1. INTRODUCTION

It is easy to see the benefits of including query facilities in components of software development environments, such as language-based editors, debuggers, and version-control managers. However, existing systems that provide query facilities generally do so in a limited way; the user is restricted to a pre-defined set of queries, and query answers cannot be used as inputs to further queries. This is because the query facilities are implemented in an *ad hoc* manner. A better approach would be to take advantage of current database technology, basing the query facility on the *relational database model* [4]. Under this model, arbitrary queries can be written by

---

This work was supported in part by the National Science Foundation under grant DCR-8603356.

Author's address: Computer Sciences Department, University of Wisconsin – Madison, 1210 W. Dayton St., Madison, WI 53706.

applying a standard set of operators to a set of relations. Query answers are themselves relations, thus are available as inputs to further queries. An advantage of the relational model over the hierarchical and network database models is that the relational model provides a *uniform, non-procedural* approach to query writing.

Two systems that provide query facilities based on the relational database model are Omega [12] and Masterscope [15]. Omega is a language-based programming environment in which all program information is represented using relations. This representation has the advantage of allowing queries about program structure to be written; unfortunately, some traditional editing operations became unacceptably slow when performed using the relational representation. For example, using the standard INGRES relational database management system [19], the display of a ten-line procedure body required forty seconds of elapsed time. Even using a version of INGRES specially tuned for this task, the display required seven seconds. By contrast, display of such procedures by language-based editors that use more traditional tree data structures is virtually instantaneous.

Masterscope, which provides a query handler to users of the Interlisp system [20], takes a different approach. Some information is maintained explicitly in relations; other information is computed as needed, either from existing relations or from Interlisp data structures.

Our goal has been to generalize the approach taken in Masterscope so that a relational query facility can be added to any existing software-development environment, without requiring that fundamental data structures be replaced with relations. Our general model for relational query facilities relies on the use of *implicit relations*, introduced in [10] and extended herein. From the query-writer's point of view, an implicit relation is indistinguishable from any other relation; however, implicit relations are not stored as sets of tuples, instead the informational content of an implicit relation is computed as needed during query evaluation from stored relations, from non-relational data structures, or using pure mathematical functions.

The key to the use of implicit relations is the definition of a query-evaluation method that treats uniformly both implicit and "normal" (henceforth called *explicit*) relations [10]. This query-evaluation method uses three functions, a membership-test, a selective-retrieval, and a relation-producing function, to access *all* relations, both implicit and explicit, used in the query.

The remainder of the paper is organized as follows: Section 2 describes how membership-test, selective-retrieval, and relation-producing functions can be used to provide a query-evaluation method that handles queries with both implicit and explicit relations. Section 3 uses a hypothetical program-development environment that includes an interpreter to clarify the concept of implicit relations. The three approaches to defining implicit relations are illustrated; implicit relations are defined (1) using operations on a non-relational data structure, (2) using non-relational operations on a stored relation, and (3) using pure mathematical functions. Queries that use these implicit relations are defined, and their evaluation using the method outlined in Section 2 is discussed. Section 4 compares the ideas presented in this paper with previous work.

2. QUERY-EVALUATION USING ACCESS FUNCTIONS

The query-evaluation method presented in this section relies on queries being represented as expression trees (examples appear in Figures 1 and 2). Each node of a tree represents a relation: leaf nodes represent implicit or explicit relations, and internal nodes represent intermediate relations. The key to the evaluation method is the use of three access functions, *membership test*, *selective retrieval*, and *relation producing* functions:

Definition:

(1) The membership-test function for relation R, given tuple t, returns **true** if t is in R, and otherwise returns **false**.

(2) The selective-retrieval function for relation R, given list of fields $f_1, f_2, \ldots f_n$, and list of values $v_1, v_2, \ldots v_n$, returns the set of tuples in R that have value v_i in field f_i for all i.

(3) The relation-producing function for relation R returns the set of tuples in relation R.

Every node of the query tree has a membership-test, a selective-retrieval, and a relation-producing function associated with it. Access functions for implicit relations are provided as part of their definition; examples are given in Section 3. Access functions for explicit relations are also determined when the relations are defined, and depend on the specified storage and access methods. Access functions for internal nodes of the query tree are built as part of query evaluation; a function at node n can call any of the functions associated with the children of n in the tree.

A query is evaluated by calling the relation-producing function associated with the root node of the query tree. The success of the query-evaluation method depends on the use of membership-test and selective-retrieval functions to avoid materializing both implicit and intermediate relations. For example, the intersection and set difference operators can use an operand relation's membership-test function in place of an explicit representation of the operand relation. Given an explicit representation of relation R1, and a membership-test function for relation R2, one can implement (R1 $\cap$ R2) or (R1 $-$ R2) as follows: a single scan is made through R1 considering each tuple t in turn; t is in (R1 $\cap$ R2) if it is a member of R2; t is in (R1 $-$ R2) if it is *not* a member of R2.

Similarly, equi-join can be implemented using one explicit operand relation and the other operand relation's selective-retrieval function. A single scan is made through the explicit operand relation; for each tuple t, the selective-retrieval function of the other operand relation is called with the number of the join field and the appropriate value from t. All returned tuples are joined with t and added to the result relation.

The use of a membership-test function to implement intersection or set difference, or of a selective-retrieval function to implement equi-join is essentially equivalent to the use of an index when the relation being accessed is a materialized relation. The important innovation introduced by our technique is that this relation need not be materialized; it can be an implicit relation, or can represent an arbitrary relational computation. Membership-test and selective-retrieval functions for intermediate relation R can often be implemented so that neither R itself nor any of the intermediate relations involved in its computation need to be built. Instead, the membership-test or selective-retrieval functions associated with the nodes of the subtree rooted at the node representing relation R are called. These calls propagate down the query tree until the membership-test or selective-retrieval functions provided for the implicit and/or explicit relations named at the leaves of the tree are called.

Figure 1 illustrates an example query with an intersection operator at its root. As discussed above, the relation-producing function associated with the intersection node can call either of its children's relation-producing functions and then, for each tuple t in the result, call the other child's membership-test function. The select node's membership-test function can be implemented as follows: given tuple t, return true if and only if t satisfies the selection predicate and t is in relation R3 (determined by calling the membership-test function of the select node's child – the root of the subtree that defines R3). Similarly, the union node's membership-test function can be implemented by calling its children's membership-test functions; tuple t is in the relation represented by the union node if it is in either R1 or R2.

Further examples of query trees and of their evaluation using membership-test and selective-retrieval functions are given in Section 3. Details of the evaluation method can be found in [9] and [10].

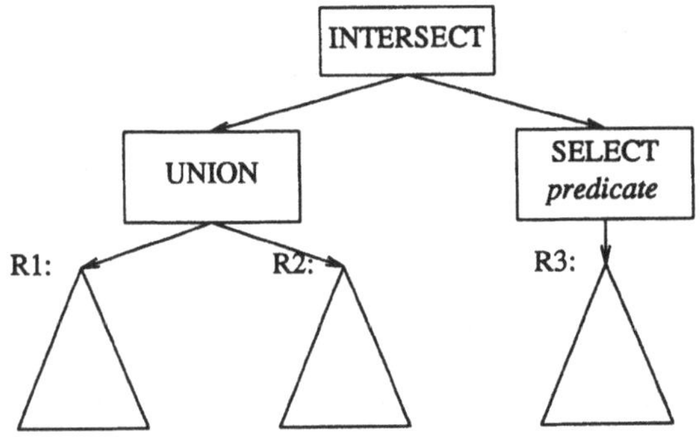

Figure 1. Example query tree. Relations R1, R2, and R3 are intermediate relations whose actual definitions are omitted.

3. IMPLICIT RELATIONS: EXAMPLES FROM PROGRAM-DEVELOPMENT ENVIRONMENTS

In this section we illustrate the three ways that implicit relations can be defined: using arbitrary operations on non-relational data structures, using arbitrary operations on stored relations, and using pure mathematical functions. In each case we consider how the three access functions – membership-test, selective-retrieval, and relation-producing functions – would be defined. We define queries that use our example implicit relations, and discuss how the queries would be evaluated using the technique outlined in Section 2. A program-development environment that includes an interpreter is used as the basis for our examples.

3.1. Defining implicit relations using non-relational data structures

Providing a query facility as part of an interpreter allows a programmer to ask questions about a program as it executes. An important class of questions are those that deal with the current state of the runtime stack. For example, assuming that access to non-local variables is handled using links maintained in the stack, a query that uses information from the stack is: "What are the current values of all global variables used by the currently active procedure?". Answering this question requires information about the current global environment as well as information about which variables are used but not declared in each procedure.

As discussed in Section 1, it is probably impractical to replace the traditional runtime stack representation with a relational representation (*cf* [5]). While it may be reasonable to store in an explicit relation information about the set of global variables used by each procedure (since this information does not change as the program executes), it is probably *not* reasonable to maintain an explicit relational representation of the current global environment. Instead, the global environment can be defined as an *implicit* relation whose schema is:

GlobalEnv(variable name, current value).

The information that is *conceptually* stored in the GlobalEnv relation is *actually* stored in the runtime stack. Membership-test, selective-retrieval, and relation-producing functions are provided as part of the definition of the GlobalEnv relation. These access functions all involve traversals of the stack, following access links. The membership-test function, given a variable name and a value, follows links backward in the stack, searching for a local data field labeled with the given name. The function returns true if and only if such a field is found and the stored value matches the given value. Similarly, the selective-retrieval function, given a variable name, searches for a local data field labeled with that name, and returns the corresponding value. Given a value, the selective-retrieval function searches back through the entire stack, building up a relation containing the names of all visible variables that have the given value. The relation-producing function must also traverse the entire stack, building the complete GlobalEnv relation.

The question "What are the current values of all global variables used by the currently active procedure?", can be formulated as a relational query using the implicit GlobalEnv relation and an *explicit* relation containing information about global variable usage:

GlobalsUsed(procedure name, variable name).

Figure 2 shows the example query in tree form.

Figure 3 shows an example program (consisting of three procedures: main, DeclaresXUsesY, and UsesXY), the corresponding GlobalsUsed relation, the runtime stack as it would appear after the call to UsesXY from DeclaresXUsesY, and the relation produced by evaluating the query of Figure 2 for the given program and runtime stack. For simplicity, we assume that the programming language in use uses dynamic scoping, and our illustration of the runtime stack includes only control-link and local data fields.

To evaluate this example query using the method outlined in Section 2, membership-test, selective-retrieval, and relation-producing functions are built for each internal node of the query

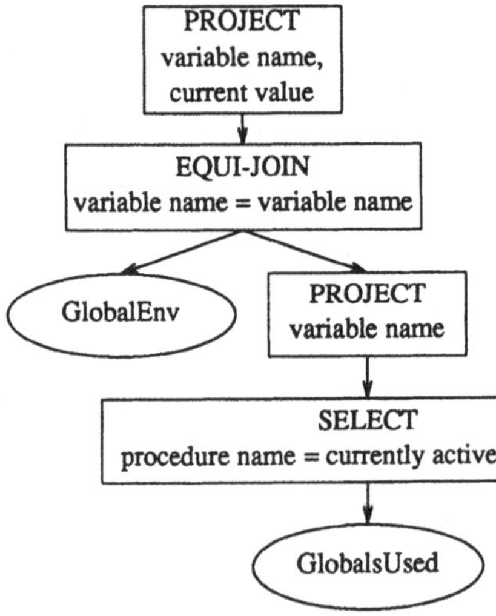

Figure 2. Example query tree: "What are the current values of the global variables of the currently-active procedure?".

```
procedure main
var x,y,z: integer;
begin
   x := 20;
   y := 20;
   z := 20;
   DeclaresXUsesY;
   UsesXY
end
```

```
procedure DeclaresXUsesY
var x: integer;
begin
   x := y * 2;
   UsesXY
end
```

```
procedure UsesXY
begin
   x := x + y
end
```

GlobalsUsed

procedure name	variable name
DeclaresXUsesY	y
UsesXY	x
UsesXY	y

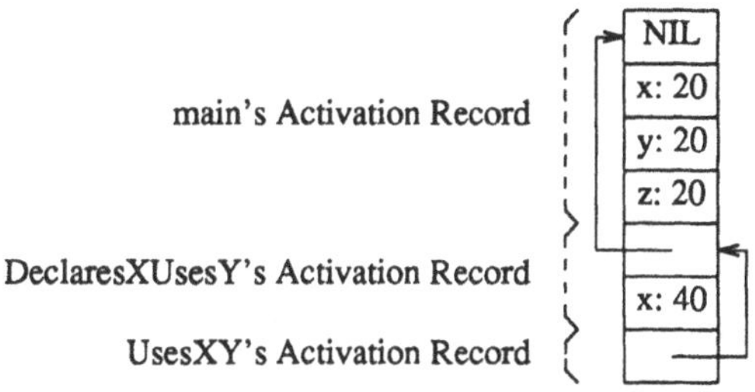

Result

variable name	current value
x	40
y	20

Figure 3. Example program, corresponding GlobalsUsed relation, the runtime stack after DeclaresX-UsesY calls UsesXY, and the answer to the query "What are the current values of the global variables of the currently-active procedure?". Each activation record on the stack includes a control link field and a field for each local variable.

tree, and the relation-producing function of the root node is called. This function calls the relation-producing function associated with the equi-join node, which may perform any of the following actions:

(1) Call the relation-producing functions associated with each of the children of the equi-join node, and join the results.

(2) Call the relation-producing function associated with the GlobalEnv implicit relation; for each tuple t in the result, call the selective-retrieval function associated with the project node, and join t with the result of this call.

(3) Call the relation-producing function associated with the project node; for each tuple t in the result, call the selective-retrieval function associated with the GlobalEnv implicit relation, and join t with the result of this call.

For the trivial example illustrated in Figure 3, any of these three possibilities will do. However, the cost of calling GlobalEnv's relation-producing function is proportional to the depth of the runtime stack; thus, the third approach, which uses GlobalEnv's selective-retrieval function in place of its relation-producing function, will be advantageous given a deep stack.

3.2. Defining implicit relations using non-relational operations on explicit relations

One disadvantage of the relational model is the limited power of the standard relational operators; certain computations of interest cannot be formulated as relational queries [3]. In this section we illustrate how implicit relations defined using non-relational operations on explicit relations can help to overcome this problem.

The query we wish to express is: "Which procedures, called transitively from the current procedure, set the value of variable x?".

As shown in Figure 4, this query can be expressed using two relations, one containing information about transitive calls:

CallsTransitively(calling procedure, called procedure)

and one containing information about which variables are set by each procedure:

AssignsTo(procedure name, variable name).

While it would be possible to maintain a CallsTransitively relation, it may be preferable to maintain only the unclosed Calls relation, and to define CallsTransitively as an implicit relation. CallsTransitively can be defined in terms of Calls using the following rules:

(1) CallsTransitively(p, q) **if** Calls(p, q).

(2) CallsTransitively(p, q) **if** Calls(p, r) **and** CallsTransitively(r, q).

The definition of an implicit relation must include definitions of the relation's three access functions. The access functions for CallsTransitively are most easily defined as logic programs using the two rules given above.

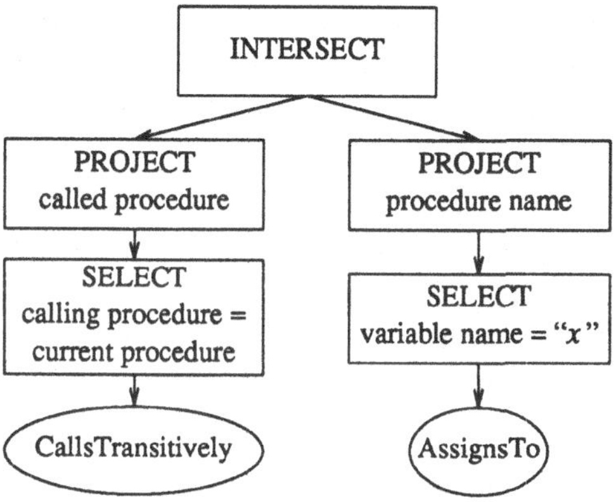

Figure 4. Example query tree: "Which procedures, called transitively from the current procedure, set the value of variable x?".

The AssignsTo relation could be an explicit relation; alternatively, if the program-development environment maintains a tree representation of programs, the AssignsTo relation could be an implicit relation defined in terms of operations on the program tree.

The query shown in Figure 4 could be evaluated in a number of ways including the following:

(1) For every tuple t in the intermediate relation represented by the right subtree of the query, the membership-test function of the left subtree of the query is called. This leads to a sequence of calls to CallsTransitively's membership-test function.

(2) Alternatively, CallsTransitively's selective-retrieval function could be called to compute the set of procedures called transitively from the current procedure; these procedure names would then be passed to the membership-test function of the right subtree of the query, leading to a sequence of calls to AssignsTo's membership-test function.

When AssignsTo is an explicit relation, the choice of evaluation method depends on its size and access methods. When AssignsTo is an implicit relation defined in terms of the program tree, the first alternative requires a traversal of the entire tree; thus, the second alternative is probably preferable.

3.3. Defining implicit relations using mathematical functions

An example of an implicit relation with associated access functions defined using arithmetic operations is the (infinite) Plus relation: Plus(value1, value2, sum). Membership testing for

Plus is trivial, as is selective retrieval as long as at least two fields are specified. How to handle selective retrieval when given only one field, and how to implement a relation-producing function is not obvious, and would depend on the context in which Plus is used. One possibility is to consider erroneous a query whose evaluation requires a call to Plus's relation-producing function or to Plus's selective-retrieval function with just one specified field. Another possibility is to produce one tuple at a time until some cut-off signal is given.

Although arithmetic operations like addition are supplied as aggregate functions in "real" database systems, they are not expressible using the standard relational operators. Defining Plus as an implicit relation provides a way to extend the power of the standard relational operators without requiring the use of aggregates. For example, given relation R with two integer fields: R(intvalue1, intvalue2), it is possible to use the Plus relation to write a query that sums the fields of each tuple in R. This query is shown in Figure 5.

The join operation in this query is performed by calling Plus's selective-retrieval function once for every tuple in relation R. Because two fields are passed to the selective-retrieval function, the result is a single value, computed by adding the two given field values. Thus, the overall time required to evaluate the query is proportional to the size of R.

4. RELATION TO PREVIOUS WORK

In this paper, we have extended the definition of implicit relations introduced in [10]. In so doing, we provide the foundation for adding relational query facilities to software-development environments, in which it is impractical to store all information in relations. Related work falls

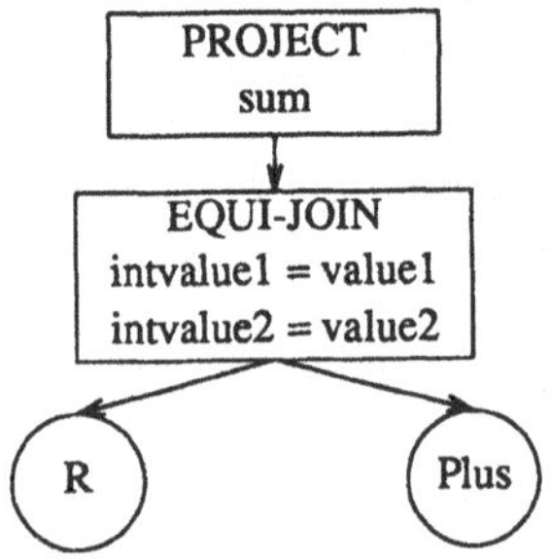

Figure 5. Example query: Sum the two fields of each tuple of relation R.

in three categories: (1) Other approaches to providing query facilities in development environments, (2) Concepts similar to implicit relations, and (3) Techniques similar to the query-evaluation method described here.

4.1. Software-development systems with query facilities

The most relevant previous work in this area [12], and [15] was discussed in Section 1. [11] describes another approach to providing a query facility during program development. Komorowski's approach is similar to Linton's, except that he stores program information in a Prolog database rather than in a relational database. Because Prolog's operators are inherently more powerful than the relational operators (for example, transitive closure can be expressed in Prolog but not using the standard relational operators), Komorowski's system can handle some queries that Linton's system cannot. The major weakness of Komorowski's system is that the database is not maintained incrementally; instead, programs are translated from a textual representation to Prolog form to allow interrogation of the database. An interesting area for future work would be to investigate the practicality of performing editing operations directly on the Prolog representation of the program.

4.2. Implicit relations

The concept of implicit relations has some similarities with the concept of *views* [21]. In both cases, the user of a database is given access to relations that are not actually stored as sets of tuples. View relations and implicit relations differ in how they can be defined, and in their intended use.

A view relation is defined by a query; conceptually, the query is re-evaluated after every modification to the database, and the view relation is the result of the most recent evaluation. View definitions are limited to relational operators applied to explicit or view relations.

By contrast, implicit relations are defined by three access functions: membership-test, selective-retrieval, and relation-producing functions. These access functions can be defined by applying *arbitrary operators* to *arbitrary data structures*; thus, implicit relations can be viewed as a generalization of view relations.

Implicit relations defined using non-relational operations on explicit relations have strong ties to logic programming. As noted in Section 3.2, logic programs may be the best way to define access functions for this class of implicit relations. While implicit relations provide a uniform approach to query writing and evaluation, the three access functions provided as part of the definition of an implicit relation can, in general, be implemented in an *ad hoc* fashion. The use of logic programming to implement these access functions provides a uniform approach at this level as well.

Logic programming does not, however, address the question of extracting information from non-relational data structures. Thus, implicit relations can be viewed as a more general concept, with logic programming providing a very important foundation for the definition of one class of implicit relations.

4.3. Query evaluation using access functions

The goals of our query-evaluation method are to avoid materializing both implicit and intermediate relations whenever possible. Having just considered the similarities between view relations and implicit relations, one is led to ask whether there is an analog to our first goal, avoiding the materialization of implicit relations, in the context of queries that use view relations. The answer is that query-evaluators do try to avoid the materialization of view relations used in queries. Because view relations are defined as relational operations on explicit relations, the mechanism for avoiding the materialization of view relations is straightforward: the view definition is inserted into the query in place of the view relation, and the entire query is optimized [18].

Of course, this approach will not work when an implicit relation is used in a query because implicit relations may not be defined in terms of relational operations on explicit relations. Thus, while the goal of avoiding the materialization of implicit relations is similar to the goal of avoiding the materialization of view relations, the methods used to achieve that goal must differ. Our approach to avoiding the materialization of implicit relations is to use the membership-test and selective-retrieval functions provided for these relations in place of the relations themselves.

Membership-test and selective-retrieval functions are also used to achieve our second goal, avoiding the materialization of *intermediate* relations. This can be viewed as a combination and generalization of the methods of [22] and [13].

Our use of selective-retrieval functions to evaluate joins corresponds to "tuple substitution" as presented in [22]. Our method can be considered to be a generalization of theirs because we are able to do lookups on non-materialized operand relations and because we allow the operands of joins to be defined using set operators, while they only consider queries defined using selection, projection, and join.

[13] proposes the use of membership tests for the evaluation of some set operators. However, because Liu was concerned with optimizing the execution of set-oriented programming languages, he considers *only* the set operators, and not selection, projection, or join. While it is rather trivial to build membership-test functions for all nodes of a query tree that contains only set operators, it is not obvious how to do so for a query tree that includes selection, projection, and join. Some of the subtleties that arise in the latter case are mentioned in [10]; a complete treatment appears in [9].

Other approaches to query optimization that seek to avoid building intermediate relations are the use of pipelining [14, 17, 23] and of tree transformations [8, 17]. When pipelining is used, a tuple in the result of one operation can be used as input to another operation as soon as it is produced, rather than waiting until an entire intermediate relation is formed. Pipelining is thus similar to our query-evaluation method in that intermediate relations are not materialized. It is dissimilar in that, when pipelining is used, the tuples of intermediate relations are all computed, whereas our method seeks to avoid or reduce the computation (as well as the materialization) of intermediate values. To understand this difference, consider the following query:

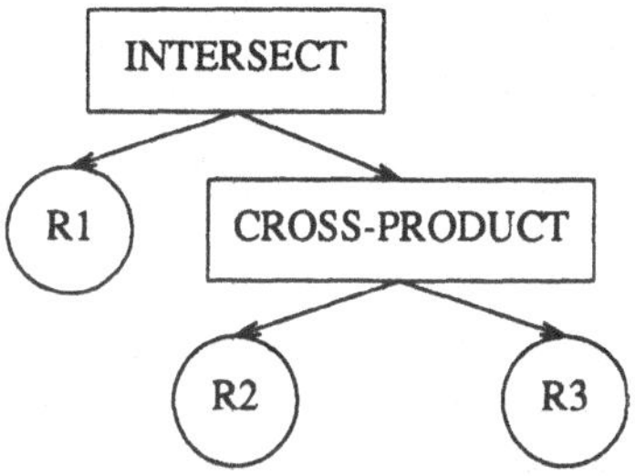

One way to evaluate this query without materializing the temporary relation represented by the CROSS-PRODUCT node is to use an index on relation R1 and to pipeline the result of the cross product. The cross product is computed a tuple-at-a-time, and for each tuple a lookup is done in R1's index; the tuple is in the result relation if it is in R1. While no temporary relation is materialized using this approach, all tuples of the cross product are computed.

By contrast, given indexes on relations R2 and R3, the query can be evaluated using our method without materializing the temporary relation, and without computing any of the tuples of the cross product: Relation R1 is scanned, each tuple t is divided into two tuples, t_1 and t_2, according to the arities of R2 and R3, and lookups are done on t_1 and t_2 in the index for R2 and R3 respectively. Tuple t is in the result relation if t_1 is in R2 and t_2 is in R3.

Of course, factors like the sizes of the three relations will determine which of the two methods is actually best; this example is merely meant to illustrate the philosophical difference between our approach and pipelining, and to indicate the potential advantages of our method. Further, the two approaches are not incompatible; pipelining can be incorporated into our approach by having selective-retrieval and relation-producing functions use pipelining rather than returning entire relations.

Tree transformations such as combining sequences of projections into a single projection and combining sequences of selections into a single selection, can reduce the number of intermediate relations represented by the internal nodes of the query tree; moving selection operators ahead of construction operators can reduce the sizes of these intermediate relations. These techniques do not, however, address the question of whether one can avoid building some of the intermediate relations of the transformed tree.

As with pipelining, incorporating tree transformations into our method will be important to its success. A query can often be represented using a number of different trees, and a different relation-producing function will be built for the root node of each such tree. It is important that transformations be used to produce trees in which the cost of the root node's relation-producing function is minimized.

Similarly, other optimization techniques could be used to produce more efficient membership-test, selective-retrieval, and relation-producing functions. Exploiting idempotency and unsatisfiability to simplify *conditions* [6,8] can lead to more efficient membership-test and relation-producing functions; using the methods of [1,2,16,23] for access path selection, the methods of [17] for choosing sort orders, and the methods of [7,22] for calculating join orders can all lead to more efficient relation-producing functions.

5. SUMMARY

Software development environments can include relational query facilities without giving up traditional, non-relational data structures, through the use of *implicit relations*. Information contained in non-relational data structures is *conceptually* stored as sets of tuples, and can be accessed by using implicit relations in queries. Implicit relations can also be defined using non-relational operations on stored relations and using pure mathematical functions, thus indirectly extending the class of queries that can be expressed using the standard relational operators.

REFERENCES

1. Astrahan, M. M. and D. D. Chamberlin, "Implementation of a structured English query language," *Communications of the ACM* **18**(10) pp. 580-588 (Oct. 1975).

2. Blasgen, M. W. and K. P. Eswaran, "Storage and access in relational databases," *IBM Systems Journal* **16**(4) pp. 363-377 (1977).

3. Chandra, A., "Programming primitives for database languages.," *Conference Record of the 8th ACM Symposium on Principles of Programming Languages*, pp. 50-62 (Jan. 1981).

4. Codd, E. F., "A relational model of data for large shared data banks," *Communications of the ACM* **13**(6) pp. 377-387 (June 1970).

5. Deutsch, L. P. and A. M. Schiffman, "Efficient implementation of the Smalltalk-80 system," *Conference Record of the 11th ACM Symposium on Principles of Programming Languages*, pp. 297-302 (Jan. 1984).

6. Eswaran, K. P., J. N. Gray, R. A. Lorie, and I. L. Traiger, "The notions of consistency and predicate locks in a database system," *Communications of the ACM* **19**(11) pp. 624-633 (1976).

7. Gotlieb, L. R., "Computing joins of relations," *ACM SIGMOD International Conference on Management of Data*, pp. 55-63 (May 1975).

8. Hall, P. A. V., "Optimization of single expressions in a relational data base system," *IBM J. Res. Develop.* **20** pp. 244-237 (May 1976).

9.
Horwitz, S., "Generating language-based editors: A relationally-attributed approach," TR 85-696 (Ph.D. thesis), Department of Computer Science, Cornell University (Aug. 1985).

10.
Horwitz, S. and T. Teitelbaum, "Generating editing environments based on relations and attributes," *ACM Transactions on Programming Languages and Systems* **8**(4) pp. 577-608 (Oct. 1986).

11.
Komorowski, H. J., "Rapid software development in a database framework - A case study," *IEEE 1984 Proceedings of the International Conference on Data Engineering*, (1984).

12.
Linton, M.A., "Implementing relational views of programs," *Proceedings of the ACM SIGSOFT/SIGPLAN Software Engineering Symposium on Practical Software Development Environments*, pp. 132-140 (Apr. 23-25, 1984).

13.
Liu, L., "Essential uses of expressions in set-oriented expressions," Ph.D. Thesis, Department of Computer Science, Cornell University (May 1979).

14.
Lu, H. and M. J. Carey, "Some experimental results on distributed join algorithms in a local network," *Proceedings of VLDB*, pp. 292-304 (1985).

15.
Masinter, L., "Global program analysis in an interactive environment," Ph.D. Thesis, Stanford University, Stanford, CA (Jan., 1980).

16.
Selinger, P. G., M. M. Astrahan, D. D. Chamberlin, R. A. Lorie, and T. G. Price, "Access path selection in a relational database management system," *ACM SIGMOD International Conference on Management of Data*, pp. 23-34 (May-June, 1979).

17.
Smith, J. M. and P. Chang, "Optimizing the performance of a relational algebra database interface," *Communications of the ACM* **18**(10) pp. 568-579 (Oct. 1975).

18.
Stonebraker, M., "Implementation of integrity constraints and views by query modification," *ACM SIGMOD International Conference on Management of Data*, pp. 65-78 (May 1975).

19.
Stonebraker, M., E. Wong, P. Kreps, and G. Held, "The design and implementation of INGRES," *ACM Transactions on Database Systems* **1**(3) pp. 189-222 (Sept. 1976).

20.
Teitelman, W., *Interlisp Reference Manual*, Xerox PARC (Dec. 1978). (as cited in [Masinter 80])

21.
Ullman, J., *Principles of Database Systems*, Computer Science Press, Potomac, MD (1980).

22.
Wong, E. and K. Youssefi, "Decomposition - a strategy for query processing," *ACM Transactions on Database Systems* **1**(3) pp. 223-241 (Sept. 1976).

23.
Yao, S. B., "Optimization of query evaluation algorithms," *ACM Transactions on Database Systems* **4**(2) pp. 133-155 (1979).

Compilation of Logic Programs for Restricted And-Parallelism

Dean Jacobs and Anno Langen
Computer Science Department, University of Southern California
Los Angeles, California 90089-0782

1. Introduction

A variety of different techniques for executing logic programs in parallel have been proposed. One common approach is to provide new language constructs for explicitly controlling the order in which goals execute. Languages containing such constructs include Concurrent Prolog[Shapiro 86], Parlog[Clark 86], and Epilog[Wise 82, Wise 86]. An alternative approach is to have the implementation schedule goals automatically. Conery [Conery 81, Conery 87] has developed mechanisms for monitoring program variables and scheduling goals at run-time. This approach provides a great deal of parallelism, however, it can incur considerable overhead. Chang[Chang 85a, Chang 85b] schedules goals on the basis of a static analysis of the program at compile-time. This approach reduces run-time support, however, it may miss important opportunities for parallelism.

DeGroot [DeGroot84] has developed the *Restricted And-Parallelism* (RAP) execution model for logic programming which combines compile-time analysis with run-time monitoring. In this model, programs are compiled into special control expressions, called *Execution Graph Expressions* (EGEs), which initiate goals on the basis of tests on program variables. The RAP model is easier to implement than a general graph-based scheme such as Conery's because EGEs have a linear form; goals are collected into groups for scheduling. This permits simple "fork/join"-style synchronization mechanisms. In general, this linear form restricts the amount of parallelism that can be achieved because initiation of a goal cannot be made dependent upon the completion of an arbitrary collection of other goals. DeGroot argues that RAP can still achieve more than enough parallelism to keep a moderately-sized multiprocessor computer busy. Recent empirical evidence [Carlton 88] lends support to these arguments.

Research on the RAP model has focused primarily on the problem of implementing EGEs efficiently on multiprocessor computers. Hermenegildo [Hermenegildo 87] has extended Warren's Abstract Machine for Prolog [Warren 83] to support RAP. The complementary problem of compiling clauses into EGEs has been addressed only briefly [DeGroot 87a]. This problem is difficult for two reasons. First, determining whether an EGE is correct for a clause may entail considerable reasoning about tests and goals. Second, choosing from among various correct alternatives may require a rather subjective assessment of their benefits. This is because different EGEs may achieve more parallelism in different circumstances. Moreover, an EGE which achieves a great deal of parallelism may be unacceptably large.

In this paper, we introduce a novel approach to generating correct EGEs and choosing between them. In our approach, a clause is first converted into a graph-based computational form, called a *Conditional Dependency Graph* (CDG), which achieves *Maximal And-Parallelism* (MAP). MAP is the maximal and-parallelism possible while maintaining correctness. This CDG is then gradually transformed into an EGE, potentially at a loss of parallelism, using two rewrite rules operating on hybrid expressions. Since these rules are sound, in the sense that they always produce correct results from correct sources, correct EGEs are always produced. Compilation algorithms are defined within this framework by giving heuristics for choosing where and how rules should be applied. We briefly discuss initial work on the design of such heuristics.

This paper is organized as follows. In section 2, we introduce the RAP model, define EGEs, and motivate the compilation problem. In section 3, we define correctness and MAP. In section 4, we define CDGs and prove that a clause can be converted into a CDG which achieves MAP. In section 5, we introduce our compilation framework, define the rules for transforming CDGs into EGEs, and prove their soundness. In section 6, we develop certain algorithms for reasoning about CDGs. In section 7, we summarize this work and discuss our current research.

2. Restricted And-Parallelism

There are two basic kinds of parallelism available in a logic program: and-parallelism, in which independent parts of the same solution are pursued simultaneously, and or-parallelism, in which different solutions are pursued simultaneously. In general, it can be difficult to exploit or-parallelism effectively since the pursuit of alternatives which are not used can waste considerable resources. Many implementations therefore limited the amount of or-parallelism which can occur.

The RAP model was designed to exploit only and-parallelism. Or-parallelism occurs whenever concurrently executing goals produce different values for a shared variable. The RAP model avoids or-parallelism by ensuring that goals are scheduled for concurrent execution only if they do not share variables. This is accomplished by compiling clauses into special control expressions, called Execution Graph Expressions, which initiate goals on the basis of dependency tests.

2.1 Execution Graph Expressions

We use the following terminology in discussing EGEs. *Variable identifiers* appear textually within goals, e.g., x and y appear in $A(x,y)$, and are bound to terms when a program executes. *Variables* are unnamed objects which appear inside terms and may be unified with other terms. Let variable identifiers x and y be bound to terms t and u respectively. x becomes *further instantiated* when a variable in t becomes unified with a term. x is *grounded* if t contains no variables. x and y are *dependent* if t and u contain a common variable, otherwise they are *independent*. Two goals are *dependent* if there is a variable identifier of the first goal and a variable identifier of the second goal which are dependent, otherwise they are *independent*.

EGEs are defined inductively as follows. Every goal is an EGE and for EGEs E_1 and E_2 the following are EGEs.

$(PAR\ \ E_1\,E_2)$
$(SEQ\ \ E_1\,E_2)$
$(IF\ P\ \ E_1\,E_2)$
$(CPAR\ P\ \ E_1\,E_2)$

Execution of an EGE proceeds from the outermost expression inwards. A *PAR* expression executes the subexpressions concurrently. A *SEQ* expression executes the subexpressions sequentially from left to right. An *IF* expression executes E_1 or E_2 depending on whether the condition P is true or false. A *CPAR* expression may be viewed as an abbreviation for

```
(IF P (PAR  E1 E2)
      (SEQ  E1 E2))
```

A condition P is a conjunction of basic tests on variable identifiers and is used to determine whether goals are independent. Two kinds of basic tests are provided: Ixy holds iff x and y are independent and Gx holds iff x is grounded.

We now give several examples of EGEs. The clause $H(x,y)$:- $A(x)$, $B(y)$ can be compiled into the EGE $(CPAR\ Ixy\ \ A(x)\ B(y))$ since $A(x)$ and $B(y)$ can execute in parallel as long as x and y are independent. Similarly, the clause $H(x)$:- $A(x)$, $B(x)$ can be compiled into the EGE $(CPAR\ Gx\ \ A(x)\ B(x))$ since $A(x)$ and $B(x)$ can execute in parallel as long as x is grounded. The clause $H(x,y)$:- $A(x)$, $B(y)$, $C(x,y)$ can be compiled into the EGE

```
(IF Gx (PAR A(x) (CPAR Gy B(y) C(x,y)))
       (IF Gy (PAR B(y) (SEQ A(x) C(x,y)))
              (IF Ixy (SEQ (PAR A(x) B(y)) C(x,y))
                      (SEQ A(x) (SEQ B(y) C(x,y))))))
```

which executes one of four sub-EGEs depending on x and y.

2.2 The Compilation Problem

In this section, we motivate our compilation techniques by way of several examples. These examples show that a compiler must be able to

- reason about independence of goals to ensure correctness,
- accurately determine when losses of parallelism occur, and
- choose between different alternatives when losses of parallelism occur or when the "perfect" expression is unacceptably large.

To determine whether an EGE is correct, a compiler must be able to infer that, whenever two goals might execute in parallel, the sequence of tests that lead to that point were sufficient to ensure that the goals were independent. As an example, consider the first branch of the last EGE in the previous section. Since x is grounded on this branch, we know x and y are independent so $A(x)$ can execute in parallel with the other goals. In addition, $B(y)$ and $C(x,y)$ can execute in parallel if y is grounded. Similar arguments show that the other branches are correct. In general, the inferencing necessary to determine whether an EGE is correct can be quite complex. For example, in the EGE (*IF* *Ixy* (*SEQ* E_1 E_2) E_3) it may be necessary to analyze E_1 to determine if *Ixy* still holds when E_2 starts executing.

The following example demonstrates that the linear form of EGEs restricts the amount of and-parallelism that can be achieved. In this example, and throughout this paper, we consider only those EGEs which lead to dependent goals executing in the same order as they appear in the original clause. This restriction is in the spirit of Prolog; we rely on the programmer to determine the best order in which to execute dependent goals. The limitations of EGEs are still present if goal reordering is permitted.

Consider the clause $H(x,y)$:- $A(x)$, $B(x)$, $C(y)$, $D(x,y)$. An EGE of the form

(*IF* *Gx* E_1 (*IF* *Gy* E_2 (*IF* *Ixy* E_3 E_4)))

tests all relevant initial cases for this clause and therefore can achieve the maximal possible parallelism. Now consider the third branch, where x and y are independent but neither is grounded. Suppose we decide to construct E_3 using the subexpression (*PAR* (*SEQ* $A(x)$ $B(x)$) $C(y)$) for which there is no loss of parallelism. Under no condition can $D(x,y)$ be initiated in parallel with this subexpression since $D(x,y)$ cannot start until after $A(x)$ finishes. We must therefore compose $D(x,y)$ sequentially after this subexpression. But if $A(x)$ grounds x and $C(y)$ finishes before $B(x)$, then $D(x,y)$ will needlessly wait for $B(x)$ to finish. As an alternative, if we try starting with (*PAR* $A(x)$ $C(y)$) then $B(x)$ will end up needlessly waiting for $C(y)$ to finish. Finally, if we let $A(x)$ execute on its own, then $C(y)$ will end up needlessly waiting for $A(x)$ to finish. Thus, every possible EGE for E_3 leads to losses in parallelism. This is because initiation of a goal cannot be made dependent on the completion of an arbitrary collection of other goals. Note that none of these expressions is clearly the best with respect to parallelism alone, since for each of them there are circumstances where it does better than the others.

We conclude this section with a discussion of certain implementation details of the RAP model and the way in which these details affect compilation. In general, evaluation of a test such as *Ixy* requires scanning the terms bound to x and y at run-time. Since such terms can be arbitrarily large and may have to be scanned quite frequently, testing can introduce considerable overhead. An important part of the RAP model is an algorithm which efficiently computes an *approximation* to these tests. This algorithm is safe in the sense that it never allows a test to succeed when it should have failed. Thus, independent goals may be viewed as being dependent but not the converse.

It is our view that the inexactness of tests should not directly affect the compilation process; the same strategy for deriving EGEs should be used regardless of whether tests are exact or inexact. However, the inexactness of tests should *indirectly* affect compilation. Consider the EGE (*IF* *Ixy* (*SEQ* E_1 E_2) E_3) introduced earlier. Suppose analysis of E_1 shows that *Ixy* still holds when E_2 starts executing. If the tests were exact, we would be at liberty to retry *Ixy* in E_2 anyway; at worst we would be performing a redundant test. However, since the tests are inexact, if we retry *Ixy* in E_2 it may fail, thereby reducing the amount of parallelism achieved. Thus, it is important to avoid redundant testing as much as possible.

3 Maximal And-Parallelism

In this section, we present a formal notion of correctness and define MAP to be the maximal and-parallelism possible while maintaining correctness.

Execution of a clause begun in some initial state is correct if the following two restrictions are observed.

- Dependent goals never execute concurrently.
- Dependent goals never execute out of order.

The second restriction is in the spirit of Prolog; we rely on the programmer to determine the best order in which to execute dependent goals. These restrictions are characterized by the following constraint on scheduling.

Definition: Constraint on Scheduling

(*) A goal should not be initiated while there is a dependent goal to its left which has not finished executing. ∇

Theorem: (*) Characterizes the Correctness of Execution

Dependent goals never execute concurrently or out of order if and only if (*) is observed.

Proof Outline:

Only if: Suppose (*) is not observed.

At the point (*) is violated, a goal B is initiated while there is a dependent goal A to its left which has not finished executing. If A is currently executing, then two dependent goals are executing concurrently, violating the first restriction. If A is not executing, then A and B are executing out of order, violating the second restriction.

If: Suppose (*) is observed.

First, we show that concurrently executing goals A and B, A left of B, must be independent. Under (*), A and B must be independent at the time B is initiated. We can show that they will remain independent as long as B is executing since no goal can get access to variables of both A and B. Second, we show that dependent goals A and B, A left of B, cannot execute out of order. Under (*), B cannot be initiated until A has finished. ∇

MAP is the maximal and-parallelism possible while maintaining correctness.

Definition: Scheduling Discipline for MAP

(**) A goal should be initiated *as soon as* all dependent goals to its left have finished executing. ∇

Definition: Correctness and MAP

Let E be the representation of a clause in some computational formalism such as EGEs. E is *correct* if execution of E begun in any initial state observes (*). E *achieves MAP* if execution of E begun in any initial state implements (**). ∇

4 Conditional Dependency Graphs

In this section, we introduce CDGs and prove that a clause can be converted into a CDG which achieves MAP.

A CDG is a directed acyclic graph where the vertices are goals and each edge is labeled by a condition. The CDG $\Theta(L)$ associated with a clause L has a vertex for each goal of L and an edge from goal A to goal B if A is left of B. The condition labeling edge $<A,B>$ is *indep*(A,B), defined as follows.

Definition: indep

The condition *indep*(A,B) is the conjunction of the following tests: Gx for every variable identifier x occurring in both A and B, and Ixy for every variable identifier x occurring in A but not B and variable identifier y occurring in B but not A. ▽

It is easy to show that goals A and B are independent if and only if the condition *indep*(A,B) holds. Note that there is no need to test whether a variable identifier occurring in both goals is independent from other variable identifiers since we require that it be grounded.

As an example, the clause $H(x,y)$:- $A(x)$, $B(y)$, $C(x,y)$. given in section 2.1 is associated with the following CDG.

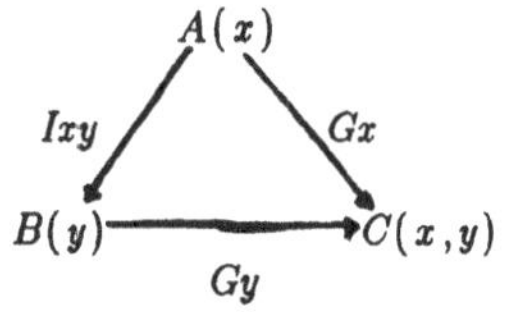

The CDG execution model is as follows.

Definition: CDG Execution Model

Perform the following two step execution cycle repeatedly. A cycle should start as soon as a goal finishes or a variable identifier is further instantiated.

1) Edge Removal: Remove every edge whose origin has finished executing. If the conditions hold on all edges going into a goal, then remove those edges.

2) Goal Initiation: Initiate all goals with no incoming edges. ▽

The following theorem shows that $\Theta(L)$ achieves MAP.

Theorem: $\Theta(L)$ achieves MAP

Execution of $\Theta(L)$ begun in any initial state implements (**).

Proof:

We must show that a goal B is initiated during execution of $\Theta(L)$ as soon as all dependent goals to its left have finished executing. Consider the change which results in all goals left of B being either finished or independent of B for the first time. A CDG execution cycle will start as soon as this change occurs. Since all edges going into B come from goals on its left, all such edges will be removed after the first step of this cycle. Thus, B will be initiated in the second step of this cycle. It remains to be shown that B could not have been initiated in a previous cycle. During every previous cycle, there was some dependent goal A to B's left which had not finished executing. The edge $<A,B>$ initially in $\Theta(L)$ could not have been removed after step one in any of these cycles. Thus, there was always an edge going into B and B could not have been initiated in step two. ▽

5 A Compilation Framework

In this section we introduce our framework for compiling clauses into EGEs. In our approach, a clause L is first converted into the CDG $\Theta(L)$ which achieves MAP. This CDG is then gradually transformed into an EGE, potentially at a loss of parallelism, using two rewrite rules operating on hybrid expressions. We show the rules are sound in the sense that they always transform correct hybrids into correct hybrids. This ensures that any EGE derived from $\Theta(L)$ will be correct since $\Theta(L)$ is correct.

The hybrid expressions consist of EGEs with CDGs as well as goals as elementary components. The rewrite rules replace a CDG within a hybrid by an EGE containing more refined sub-CDGs. When an *IF* expression is introduced, facts about dependencies between variable identifiers become known. Such facts are used to simplify conditions on the edges of sub-CDGs -- edges whose conditions have been simplified to true are removed. This embodies the process of reasoning about sequences of tests. In general, facts can become invalidated during execution and inferencing is necessary to determine where they can be applied. Such inferencing can be complex since the question of whether a particular goal can invalidate a particular fact depends on what other facts are known.

To facilitate simplification, we introduce the notion of an *Extended CDG* (ECDG) $<\Gamma,C>$ consisting of a CDG Γ together with a set of facts C referred to as its *context*. Hybrid expressions consist of EGEs with ECDGs as well as goals as elementary components. We arrange it so that, roughly speaking, each fact in the context of an ECDG holds before its first goal is initiated. We use two functions for manipulating contexts which are defined in the next section. The first, $post(C,\Gamma)$, returns the set of facts in context C which are maintained by execution of CDG Γ. The second, $simplify(\Gamma,C)$, returns the CDG Γ simplified under the context C.

Our first rewrite rule, called the Split Rule, introduces *PAR*, *SEQ*, and *CPAR* expressions.

Definition: The Split Rule

Input to the Split Rule consists of a ECDG $<\Gamma,C>$ and a partitioning of Γ into two sub-CDGs α and β. The Split Rule may be applied only if there are no edges from β to α. If there are no edges at all between α and β, then the result of the Split Rule is $(PAR\ \ <\alpha,C>\ <\beta,C>)$. Otherwise, let $CG_{\alpha\beta}$ be the conjunction of the conditions on edges from α to β. If $CG_{\alpha\beta}$ is equivalent to *false*, then the result is $(SEQ\ <\alpha,C>\ <\beta,post(C,\alpha)>)$ otherwise the result is $(CPAR\ CG_{\alpha\beta}\ <\alpha,C>\ <\beta,post(C,\alpha)>)$. ∇

Our second rewrite rule, called the If Rule, introduces *IF* expressions.

Definition: The If Rule

Input to the If Rule consists of a ECDG $<\Gamma,C>$ and a condition P. Let $C_T = C \cup P$ and $C_F = C \cup \neg P$ where $C \cup X$ denotes the context C extended with all facts derivable from X. The result of the If Rule is $(IF\ P\ \ <simplify(\Gamma,C_T),C_T>\ <simplify(\Gamma,C_F),C_F>)$. ∇

As an example, we use the two rewrite rules to derive the EGE

$$\begin{array}{l}(IF\ Gx\ \ (PAR\ \ A(x)\ (CPAR\ \ Gy\ \ B(y)\ C(x,y)))\\ \qquad\quad (IF\ Gy\ \ (PAR\ \ B(y)\ (SEQ\ \ A(x)\ C(x,y)))\\ \qquad\qquad\qquad (IF\ Ixy\ \ (SEQ\ \ (PAR\ \ A(x)\ B(y))\ C(x,y))\\ \qquad\qquad\qquad\qquad\qquad (SEQ\ \ A(x)\ (SEQ\ \ B(y)\ C(x,y))))))\end{array}$$

given for the clause $H(x,y)$:- $A(x)$, $B(y)$, $C(x,y)$. in section 2.1. The CDG associated with this clause was given in section 3. We first apply the If Rule with the condition Gx. When the "then" branch is simplified, both edges coming out of $A(x)$ are removed, since Gx implies Ixy. Applying the Split Rule to separate $A(x)$ from the other goals results in the PAR expression with a sub-CDG in the second half. Splitting this sub-CDG results in the CPAR for $B(y)$ and $C(x,y)$.

When the "else" branch is simplified, the condition on the edge from $A(x)$ to $C(x,y)$ is replaced by *false*. We now apply the If Rule with the condition Gy to this CDG. When the "then" branch is simplified, the edges from $A(x)$ to $B(y)$ and $B(y)$ to $C(x,y)$ are both removed. Applying the Split Rule to separate $B(y)$ from the other goals results in the PAR expression with a sub-CDG in the second half. Splitting this sub-CDG results in the SEQ for $A(x)$ and $C(x,y)$. The other two branches are derived in an analogous manner.

We now prove the soundness of the rewrite rules. To accomplish this we define an execution model for hybrid expressions which is a straight-forward combination of the EGE and CDG execution models. At the outermost level, hybrids execute according to the EGE model. The CDG in an ECDG occurring in place of a goal is initiated at the point that goal would be initiated, executes according to the CDG model, and finishes as soon as all its goals have finished. Using this execution model, we define a notion of correctness for hybrids.

Definition: Correctness of Hybrids

A hybrid H is *correct under some context* if during execution of H begun in any initial state satisfying that context

1) goals are scheduled correctly and

2) for each ECDG $<\Gamma,C>$ in H, every fact in C which is *relevant* to Γ holds before the first goal in Γ is initiated. ∇

The relevant facts for Γ are those facts which can affect its simplification, as described in the next section.

Theorem: Soundness of the Split Rule

If the Split Rule is applied to an ECDG $<\Gamma,C>$ in a source hybrid which is correct under some context, then the result hybrid will also be correct under that context.

Proof Outline:

First, we argue that goals in the result hybrid will be scheduled correctly. It is always correct when α and β execute concurrently in the result hybrid since they would have executed concurrently in the source hybrid. It is always correct when α executes sequentially before β in the result hybrid since there are no edges from β to α.

Second, we argue that appropriate contexts are introduced. If α and β execute concurrently in the result hybrid, then there are no dependencies between them and it follows from results in the next section that neither can invalidate relevant facts for the other. If α executes sequentially before β

then all facts in C will hold before α executes and, by the correctness of *post*, all facts in *post*(C,α) will hold before β executes. ∇

Theorem: Soundness of the If Rule

If the If Rule is applied to an ECDG $<\Gamma, C>$ in a source hybrid which is correct in some context, then the result hybrid will also be correct in that context.

Proof:

It is clear that appropriate contexts are introduced. The fact that goals will be scheduled correctly follows directly from the above statement and the correctness of *simplify*. ∇

We now argue that every EGE derived in our framework is correct. The initial context $\Omega(L)$ for a clause L is derived using the fact that the first occurrence of a "local" variable identifier is guaranteed to be independent from all other variable identifiers. For example, the initial context for the clause $H(x)$:- $A(x)$, $B(y)$, $C(x,y)$ consists of the fact Ixy. Note that input mode information about the arguments of a procedure, e.g., that some argument is always grounded, can be easily incorporated into the initial context. Such information may be derived from global program analysis[Chang 85b] or programmer annotations[Shapiro 87].

Compilation begins with the initial hybrid $<$*simplify*($\Theta(L)$,$\Omega(L)$),$\Omega(L)>$. The correctness of $\Theta(L)$ and *simplify* ensures that the initial hybrid is correct under $\Omega(L)$. By the soundness of the rewrite rules, every EGE derived from the initial hybrid will be correct under $\Omega(L)$.

6 Simplification Algorithms

In this section, we develop algorithms for maintaining contexts and simplifying CDGs. We define the following two functions which appear in the previous section.

post(C,Γ) returns the set of facts in context C which are maintained by execution of CDG Γ.

simplify(Γ , C) returns the CDG Γ simplified under the context C.

In our framework, the fact that variable identifiers x and y are independent is denoted Ixy and the fact that they are dependent is denoted Dxy. The fact that variable identifier x is grounded is denoted Ixx and the fact that it is not grounded is denoted Dxx. We write Fxy when we want to discuss a fact independently of whether it is of the form Ixy or Dxy.

Definition: Contexts

A *context* C is a set of facts which satisfies the following properties.

$Ixy \in C$ iff $Iyx \in C$
$Dxy \in C$ iff $Dyx \in C$
$Ixy \in C \Rightarrow Dxy \notin C$
$Dxy \in C \Rightarrow Ixy \notin C$
$Ixx \in C \Rightarrow Ixy \in C$ for all relevant y ∇

As a first step in computing *post*, we define the function $MF(C, G\vec{v})$ which determines the set of facts in context C which are maintained by execution of a single goal $G\vec{v}$ with variable identifiers v_i. We assume a fact Fxy is maintained iff, according to C, the v_i are either independent from x or independent from y. Note that output mode information about the arguments of a procedure, e.g., that some argument always becomes grounded, can be incorporated into the function MF to allow more facts to be maintained. Such information may be derived from global program analysis[Chang85b] or programmer annotations[Shapiro87]. In the following definition, we write $I\vec{v}x \in C$ to denote $\forall i(Iv_i x \in C)$.

Definition: Maintained Facts

$MF(C,G\vec{v}) = \{Fxy \in C \mid I\vec{v}x \in C \vee I\vec{v}y \in C\}$ ∇

The following theorem shows that MF is correct and complete.

Theorem: Correctness and Completeness of MF

$Fxy \in MF(C,G\vec{v})$ iff $Fxy \in C$ and Fxy holds after execution of $G\vec{v}$ begun in any state satisfying C.

Proof:

To invalidate Ixy, x and y must be further instantiated so that the terms they are bound to share a common variable; variables must be unified with terms containing this common variable. To invalidate Dxy, x and y must be further instantiated so that the terms they are bound to no longer share common variables; all common variables must be unified with ground terms. A goal may perform such actions iff it has access to a variable in the term bound to x and a variable in the term bound to y. $G\vec{v}$ has access only to variables in the terms bound to the v_i. Thus, $G\vec{v}$ can invalidate Fxy iff $I\vec{v}x \in C \vee I\vec{v}y \in C$ does not hold. ∇

As a second step in computing *post*, we define the function *propagate*(C,S) which returns the set of facts in context C which are still valid after a *sequence* of goals S has finished executing. We write $< >$ to denote the empty sequence and $G.S$ to denote the sequence S with the goal G appended to the front.

Definition: propagate

propagate$(C,< >)=C$

propagate$(C,G.S)=$*propagate*$(MF(C,G)\ ,\ S)$ ∇

The correctness and completeness of *propagate* follows directly from the correctness and completeness of MF.

Intuitively, *post*(C,Γ) should be the intersection of *propagate*(C,S) over all possible sequences of goals S from Γ. We now prove certain properties of MF which show that it is not necessary to consider all such sequences. The following theorem characterizes the propagation of a context across two goals. We write $I\vec{v}\vec{w} \in C$ to denote $\forall i,j(Iv_i w_j \in C)$.

Theorem: Propagation Across Two Goals

$Fxy \in MF(MF(C,G\vec{v})\ ,\ H\vec{w})$ iff $Fxy \in C$ and at least one of the following conditions hold.

1) $I\vec{v}x \in C \wedge I\vec{w}x \in C$
2) $I\vec{v}x \in C \wedge I\vec{w}y \in C \wedge I\vec{v}\vec{w} \in C$
3) $I\vec{v}y \in C \wedge I\vec{w}y \in C$
4) $I\vec{v}y \in C \wedge I\vec{w}x \in C \wedge I\vec{v}\vec{w} \in C$

Proof:

First, we show that these conditions are sufficient. In the first case, $I\vec{v}x \in C$ guarantees $Fxy \in MF(C,G\vec{v})$ and $I\vec{w}x \in MF(C,G\vec{v})$, since $I\vec{w}x \in C$. Together, these facts imply

$Fxy \in MF(MF(C,G\vec{v}), H\vec{w})$. In the second case, $I\vec{v}x \in C$ guarantees $Fxy \in MF(C,G\vec{v})$ and $I\vec{v}\vec{w}$ guarantees $I\vec{w}y \in MF(C,G\vec{v})$, since $I\vec{w}y \in C$. Together, these facts imply $Fxy \in MF(MF(C,G\vec{v}), H\vec{w})$. The consideration is symmetric for the third and fourth cases.
Second, we show that these conditions are necessary. Suppose neither $I\vec{v}x$ nor $I\vec{v}y$ holds, then $Fxy \notin MF(C,G\vec{v})$ and therefore $Fxy \notin MF(MF(C,G\vec{v}), H\vec{w})$. Suppose only $I\vec{v}x$ holds; the consideration is symmetric if only $I\vec{v}y$ holds and leads to the third and fourth cases. If $Fxy \in MF(MF(C,G\vec{v}), H\vec{w})$ is to hold, then either $I\vec{w}x \in MF(C,G\vec{v})$ or $I\vec{w}y \in MF(C,G\vec{v})$ must hold. The first of these is possible only if $I\vec{w}x \in C$; this is the first case. The second of these is possible only if $I\vec{w}y \in C \wedge I\vec{v}\vec{w} \in C$; this is the second case. ∇

The previous theorem has an important corollary: the set of facts which result when a context is propagated across a sequence of goals is independent of the order in which the goals appear in the sequence.

Corollary: Commutativity of *MF*

$MF(MF(C,G), H) = MF(MF(C,H), G)$

Proof:

The characterization of the propagation of a context across two goals is symmetric in those goals. Note this relies on the property $Ixy \in C$ iff $Iyx \in C$, since the characterization contains the condition $I\vec{v}\vec{w} \in C$. ∇

Corollary: Permuting Sequences

Let $\hat{S}$ be any permutation of a sequence S of goals, then $\textit{propagate}(C,S) = \textit{propagate}(C,\hat{S})$.

Proof:

By commutativity of *MF*. ∇

As stated earlier, $\textit{post}(C,\Gamma)$ should be the intersection of $\textit{propagate}(C,S)$ over all possible sequences of goals S from Γ. The corollary above shows that it suffices to consider any one sequence. In the following definition, we use $\textit{nat}(\Gamma)$, the sequence of goals of Γ in their "natural" left-to-right order with respect to the original clause.

Definition: post

$\textit{post}(C,\Gamma) = \textit{propagate}(C,\textit{nat}(\Gamma))$ ∇

The correctness and completeness of *post* follows directly from the above corollary and the correctness and completeness of *propagate*.

We now develop an algorithm to compute $\textit{simplify}(\Gamma,C)$, the CDG Γ simplified under the context C. Simplification consists of reducing conditions on edges and removing edges whose conditions have been reduced to true. To modify edges going out of a goal G, we compute the set of facts which hold before G is initiated; this set is called the initiation context for G.

We might define the initiation context for G to be $\textit{propagate}(C,S)$, where S is a sequence of all the goals in Γ which could execute before G. This would be too pessimistic, however, since a goal right of G in the original clause can execute before G only if the goals are independent. More facts can be maintained by taking into account the independence of G and goals to its right. The following theorem shows that, in fact, goals right of G need not even be included in S because they cannot affect facts which are *relevant* to G. A fact is relevant to G iff it appears in a condition labeling an edge going out of G. Thus, it suffices if $S = nat(\Gamma, G)$, the sequence of all goals in Γ which are left of G in their natural order.

Definition: Relevant Facts

A fact Fxy is *relevant* to G iff x or y is a variable identifier of G. ∇

Theorem Ignoring Goals to the Right

Suppose $Fxy \in C$ and Fxy is relevant to G. $Fxy \in propagate(C, nat(\Gamma, G))$ iff Fxy holds when G is initiated during execution of Γ begun in any initial state satisfying C.

Proof Outline:

Only if: Suppose Fxy holds whenever G is initiated. Since it is possible that all goals left of G finish execution before G is initiated, $Fxy \in propagate(C, nat(\Gamma, G))$ by the completeness of *propagate*.

If: Suppose $Fxy \in propagate(C, nat(\Gamma\ , G))$ but Fxy does not hold when G is initiated during execution of Γ begun in some initial state satisfying C. By the correctness of *propagate*, some goal $R\overline{v}$ right of G must have executed before G and caused Fxy not to hold. Consider the facts in C that $R\overline{v}$ might have invalidated to do this. Such facts include Fxy itself and every fact necessary to maintain Fxy through the goals initiated after $R\overline{v}$ and before G. Let SS be the set of goals initiated after $R\overline{v}$ and before G. We assume SS does not contain any goals right of G; an inductive generalization of our argument covers this case. Every fact of interest must have a variable identifier w in common with G or a goal in SS. In order for $R\overline{v}$ to invalidate such a fact, $Dv_i w$ for some i must have held when $R\overline{v}$ was initiated. But then (*) was violated since $R\overline{v}$ is right of G and every goal in SS. ∇

The theorem above shows that we can define the initiation context for G to be $propagate(C, nat(\Gamma\ , G))$. This suggests an efficient algorithm for computing $simplify(\Gamma\ , C)$: compute $propagate(C, nat(\Gamma))$ and, along the way, reduce edges coming out of each goal as it is encountered. The correctness and completeness of *simplify* with respect to relevant facts follows directly from the above theorem and the correctness and completeness of *propagate*.

7 Summary and Current Research

In this paper, we have presented a framework for compiling clauses into EGEs. We showed how a clause can be converted into a Conditional Dependency Graph which achieves Maximal And-Parallelism, and then gradually transformed into an EGE, potentially at a loss of parallelism, using two rewrite rules. The problem of reasoning about the correctness of EGEs within this framework was solved by developing algorithms for maintaining sets of facts about test results and simplifying sub-CDGs.

A primary focus of our current research is the development of heuristics for determining where and how rules should be applied. We base such heuristics on two important insights. First, the Split Rule divides its source CDG into smaller pieces while the If Rule duplicates its source CDG. Thus, compilation should be driven by attempts to apply the Split Rule. Second, there is a loss of parallelism associated with the Split Rule but not with the If Rule. This means that the Split Rule cannot be applied blindly; an attempt must be made to apply it in circumstances where the least amount of parallelism is lost. The If Rule should be used to set up such circumstances, but not to the extent that it makes the resulting EGE too large.

We are exploring ways of quantifying the loss of parallelism associated with applications of the Split Rule to facilitate choosing between different places to split. In the result of the Split Rule, ($CPAR\ CG_{\alpha\beta}\ \alpha\ \beta$), the goals in α and β have been collected into groups for scheduling. Thus, a goal in β can run concurrently with a goal in α only if *all* goals in β can run concurrently with *all* goals in α. Losses of parallelism occur when goals in β have to wait unnecessarily for goals in α to finish. We are also exploring ways of quantifying the usefulness of particular conditions in applications of the If Rule. Such conditions are useful to the extent that simplification of the "then" and "else" branches leads to subsequent low-cost splits. It remains to be seen whether a single sequence of transformations can produce acceptable EGEs or whether backtracking will be required.

There are several other important issues which we plan to address. First, we plan to characterize the set of EGEs which can be derived in our framework. We will show that the rules are complete for the set of all EGEs that might be "reasonably" produced by a compiler. Second, we plan to investigate ways of taking advantage of mode information about the arguments of procedures, which might be derived from global program analysis[Chang 85] or programmer annotations[Shapiro 87]. Input mode information can be added to the initial context for a clause and output mode information can be used in *MF* to maintain more facts. Third, we plan to investigate ways of handling the extra-logical features of Prolog such as *assert*, *retract*, *read*, *write*, and *cut*. The simplest way of doing this is to introduce artificial dependencies between every side-effect goal and the goals before and after it. While this produces the correct semantics for Prolog, it unnecessarily restricts the amount of parallelism that can be achieved. DeGroot has dealt with this problem by incorporating special synchronization constructs into the RAP model[DeGroot 87b]. We plan to extend our techniques to deal with these constructs. Finally, we plan to extend our framework to allow goal reordering.

References

[Carlton 88] Carlton,M. and Van Roy,P., A distributed Prolog system with and-parallelism, Dept. of EECS, Univ. of Cal. at Berkeley, Submitted to *1988 Hawaii International Conference on System Sciences*, (1988).

[Chang 85a] Chang, J.-H., High Performance Execution of Prolog Programs Based on a Static Data Dependency Analysis, Ph.D. thesis in Dept. of EECS, Univ. of Cal. at Berkeley, Report No. UCB/CSD 86/263, (1985).

[Chang 85b] Chang, J.-H., Despain, A., and DeGroot, D., AND-parallelism of logic programs based on a static dependency analysis, *Proc. Spring Compcon*, IEEE, (1985), 218-225.

[Clark 86] Clark, K.L., and Gregory, S., PARLOG: Parallel programming in logic, *ACM TOPLAS* 8,1 (1986), 1-49.

[Conery 81] Conery, J., and Kibler, D., Parallel interpretation of logic programs, *Proc. Conf. on Func. Prog. Lang. and Comp. Arch.*, ACM (1981), 163-170.

[Conery 87] Conery, J., *Parallel Execution of Logic Programs*, Kluwer Academic Publishers, (1987).

[DeGroot 84] DeGroot, D., Restricted and-parallelism, *Proc. Int. Conf. Fifth Gen. Comp. Sys.*, ICOT, (1984), 471-478.

[DeGroot 87a] DeGroot, D., A technique for compiling execution graph expressions for restricted and-parallelism in logic programs, *Proc. Int. Supercomputing Conf.* Athens, Greece (1987).

[DeGroot 87b] DeGroot, D., Restricted and-parallelism and side-effects, *Proc. Symp. Log. Prog.*, IEEE, San Francisco, (1987).

[Hermenegildo 87] Hermenegildo, M., *A Restricted And-Parallel Execution Model and Abstract Machine for Prolog Programs*, Kluwer Academic Press, (1987).

[Shapiro 86] Shapiro, E., Concurrent Prolog: a progress report, *IEEE Computer* 19, 8 (1986), 44-58.

[Warren 83] Warren, D.H.D., An abstract Prolog instruction set, Tech. Note 309, SRI International, Oct. (1983).

[Wise 82] Wise, M.J., A parallel Prolog: the construction of a data driven model, *Proc. Conf. LISP and Func. Prog.*, ACM, (1982).

[Wise 86] Wise, M.J., *Prolog Multiprocessors*, Prentice-Hall International, (1986).

Implementation of Lazy Pattern Matching Algorithms

Alain Laville
I.N.R.I.A. (Projet FORMEL)
B.P. 105   78150 Le Chesnay CEDEX   France
and Université de Reims
B.P. 347   51062 Reims CEDEX   France

1 Introduction

Several of the recently developped functional programming languages include a function definition capability that uses a "pattern matching" mechanism. These languages handle structured values which may be given as argument to the functions. The calculation to perform in order to get the result of the function call is choosen according to the structure of the argument. One may find this feature in such languages as HOPE ([3]), MIRANDA ([13]) or ML ([1], [10], [12]). Pattern matching, and algorithms to perform it, has been widely studied in the theory of "Term Rewriting Systems". It is here used in a more or less restricted way (linearity of patterns, patterns without function symbols ... for example in ML).

Although pattern matching comes from "Term Rewriting Systems" theory, languages using it often add a complementary mechanism that does not belong to this theory. One generally asks computations to be deterministic, which is not the case if a value may match several patterns (this is called ambiguity). Such a trouble may be avoided using unambiguous sets of patterns. But, since such a constraint leads to tedious work from the programmer, ambiguity is allowed between the patterns, and a "meta-rule" is added to choose between ambiguous patterns. Various priority rules have been suggested, the two most frequently used are the following :

- when a value matches several patterns, choose the first one in the list (ordered as given by the programmer).
- when a value matches several patterns, choose the most defined one.

We only shall address in this paper the first case of priority rule, which is the one used in ML.

There is also a growing interest in "lazy" evaluation (see [11] for precise definition). This essentially means that a value is effectively computed only when it is needed to produce the result, and, for a structured value, that only the needed parts are evaluated. This ensures that the language is *safe*, i.e. if computation fails there was no way to avoid this failure. This moreover gives to the language the ability of handling infinite data structures as long as only finite parts of them are used in calculations. MIRANDA and at least two implementations of ML include this feature : Lazy CAML at INRIA (see [8] or [9]) and LML the implementation of Gõteborg (see [1]).

However there are problems when using pattern matching in a lazy language. The question is : "How to find which pattern is matched by a given value, without doing useless computations ?". It is connected with other troubles such as expression evaluations which succeed or fail depending on the order of the arguments in the function definition.

Example Define the two functions :

```
let f1 = function (true, false) -> true
                | (false, x)    -> false;;

let f2 = function (false, true) -> true
                | (x, false)    -> false;;
```

and denote by $\perp$ an infinite computation. One would expect, in a lazy system that both `f1 (false, ⊥)` and `f2 (⊥, false)` evaluate to `false`. This is not the case in existing functional languages : since they use explicit top-down and left-to-right scanning of the patterns they succeed evaluating `f1 (false, ⊥)` to `false` and loop evaluating `f2 (⊥, false)` (see for example the pattern matching compilations described in [2] or [14]). The algorithms we give here provide a compilation of pattern matching with which the two function calls return `false`.

This leads to the question of the existence of a lazy pattern matching algorithm (and of its effective building). The answer was known when no ambiguity exists between patterns since the work of G. Huet and J.J. Lévy (see [5]). In [6], we extended this result to the case of ambiguity with priority meta-rule. However, the results established in this work are essentially theoretical ones and do not give a practical implementation tool (for example, compilation of real pattern matching definitions, using algorithms of [6] may need up to several hours of CPU time).

We present here improved algorithms of practical use, together with an efficiency study of a compiler which incorporates them. This study was done with the CAML system (see [12]), a version of ML using the Categorical Abstract Machine (CAM, see [4]) currently implemented at I.N.R.I.A.

A very detailed version of both the theoretical and the implementation aspects may be found in the author's thesis ([7]).

2 Theoretical Results

We first recall those of the theoretical results of [6] which are useful to state our practical algorithms.

2.1 Notations and definitions

Definition 1 A *pattern* is a term built from the pairing operator, some constructors of (already defined) concrete data types and the special symbol Ω. The meaning of Ω is that one doesn't care, during the pattern matching process, about what may appear at the place where it is used. It replaces both the variables and the "don't care" symbol.

A value of CAML is said to be an *instance* of a pattern if it can be obtained from the pattern by replacing all the Ω's by any values.

With a list of patterns [$p_1, \ldots, p_n$], we shall say that a value v of CAML *matches* the pattern p_i if p_i is the *first* pattern in the list, of which v is an instance.

We shall say that a function is *defined by pattern* if

1. Its definition consists of an ordered list of pairs (pattern, expression)
2. Its value when applied to an argument v is obtained in the following way : first find the first pattern, say p, in the list such that v is an instance of p and then evaluate the result of the corresponding expression.

Assume now that we want to compile the definition by pattern of a function :

$$\Pi = \begin{cases} function & p_1 & \rightarrow & exp_1 \\ \mid & p_2 & \rightarrow & exp_2 \\ \cdots & \cdots & \cdots & \cdots \\ \mid & p_n & \rightarrow & exp_n \end{cases}$$

Here the p_i's are the patterns to be matched against the argument of the function call (if the function has arity greater than 1, the patterns p_i's are t-uples).

We define a signature Σ containing all the constructors of the types used in the patterns $p_1, \ldots, p_n$ and two other symbols : Ω, which will denote the "unknown" or "undefined", and otherwise which will be used to group many cases into a single one (see section 4).

Definition 2 Since such terms will often denote partially known, or partially evaluated values, we shall call *partial term* every term built over Σ. We shall only use *term* to denote a partial term in which there is no symbol Ω (but we do not forbid to use "partial term" even in this case).

Partial terms provide us with a formalism suited for patterns (which are partially undefined terms) as well as for lazy values (which may be thought of as partially unknown since they are not completely evaluated).

Definition 3 We define a partial ordering (denoted by $\leq$) over the set of all partial terms as follows :

- For each partial term $M : \Omega \leq M$
- $F(M_1, \ldots, M_n) \leq F(N_1, \ldots, N_n)$ if and only if $M_i \leq N_i$ $(1 \leq i \leq n)$

The ordering $\leq$ is a kind of prefix ordering with the meaning that a partial term is less than another if it is less defined (or less known).

We shall use the following notations :

- $M \uparrow N$ means that M and N have a common upper bound (and we shall say that M and N are compatible)
- $M \sharp N$ means that they don't have one (and we shall say that M and N are incompatible)
- $\vee$ and $\wedge$ will respectively denote the l.u.b. (when it exists) and the g.l.b. of two partial terms
- $[M, N[$ will denote the set of partiel terms t verifying $M \leq t$ and $t < N$.

Definition 4 When seeing partial terms as trees, we shall say that M_i is the ith *son* of the partial term $F(M_1, \ldots, M_n)$. We call *occurrence* an integer list which designates a subterm of a given partial term. For example, the occurrence [2; 3] points to the third son of the second son of the full partial term. The prefix ordering of occurrences will be denoted by $\leq$. For a given partial term M, we shall denote $\mathcal{O}(M)$ the set of all occurrences in M, $\overline{\mathcal{O}}(M)$ the set of occurrences in M where the symbol is not Ω and $\mathcal{O}_\Omega(M)$ the set of occurrences in M where the symbol is Ω. The symbol in M at occurrence u will be denoted by $M(u)$.

We shall now define some predicates over the set of partial terms (i.e. functions with values in the set {tt, ff} of the truth values).

Definition 5 For each $i \in \{1, \ldots, n\}$, the predicate $match_i$ is defined by $match_i(M) = \text{tt}$ if and only if the following two conditions hold :

1. $p_i \leq M$
2. $\forall j < i \quad p_j \sharp M$

We then define the predicate $match_\Pi$:
$match_\Pi(M) = \text{tt}$ if and only if $match_i(M) = \text{tt}$ for some $i \in \{1, \ldots, n\}$.

The meaning of these predicates is the following :

$match_i(M) = \text{tt}$ iff M is sufficiently defined to know that every value better defined than M is an instance of p_i and not one of a pattern with higher priority than p_i (i.e. a pattern p_j with $j < i$).

$match_\Pi(M) = \text{tt}$ iff M is sufficiently defined to decide which pattern will be matched by any value better defined than M.

Lemma 1 *If we order the set of truth values by defining ff < tt, all these predicates are monotonically increasing functions from the partial terms into the truth values.*

2.2 Lazyness Results

Definition 6 We shall call *minimally extended pattern* (associated with Π) any partial term t verifying the following two properties :

1. $match_{\Pi}(t) = \text{tt}$
2. $\forall t' < t,\ match_{\Pi}(t') = \text{ff}$

We shall denote the set of all minimally extended patterns by MEP_{Π}.

Definition 7 Let *match* be one of the predicates $match_i$ or $match_{\Pi}$ and M be a given partial term. Let $u \in O_{\Omega}(M)$ be such that $\forall N \geq M\ match(N) = \text{tt}$ implies $N(u) \neq \Omega$. We shall say that such an occurrence is an *index of match in M.*

We shall say that *match* is *sequential at M* if and only if the two conditions $match(M) = \text{ff}$ and there exists $N \geq M$ such that $match(N) = \text{tt}$ imply together that there exists an index of *match* in M.

Definition 8 We call *pattern matching algorithm* any deterministic algorithm which will match any partial term against Π (i.e. which finds the first $p_i \in \Pi$ of which the partial term is an instance).

We say that a pattern matching algorithm is *lazy* if it never does useless work (as partial terms are trees and a pattern is a prefix of any partial term that matches it, this process has to work in a top-down way). We may express this constraint in the following way : Assume we want to match a value v against Π and let U be the set of all occurrences in v where the symbol was evaluated during the pattern matching process. Denote v_{Ω} the partial term which coincides with v along U and is completed with Ω's according to the arities of the symbols used. Then we ask v_{Ω} to be less than or equal to (for the ordering of partial terms) every prefix of the full value v which is sufficient to choose the right hand side.

Example Consider the two classical function definitions :

```
let AND = function (true, true)   -> true
                 | (x, y)         -> false;;


let XOR = function (true, false) -> true
                 | (false, true) -> true
                 | (x, y)        -> false;;
```

it is easy to see that any pattern matching algorithm is lazy in the case of XOR (both parts of the pair are always needed), and none is lazy in the case of AND (each part of the pair is useless if the other is `false`).

We may now present the main results that were established in [6].

Theorem 1 *1. If the signature Σ is finite the set* MEP_Π *is finite and computable from the list of patterns* Π.

2. Given a function defined by pattern, there exists an associated lazy pattern matching algorithm if and only if the predicate $match_\Pi$ is sequential at any partial term.

3. If two members of MEP_Π *are compatible then there exists no lazy pattern matching algorithm.*

4. If all the elements of MEP_Π *are pairwise incompatible, the existence of a lazy pattern matching algorithm is decidable. Moreover, if such an algorithm exists, one may mechanically be built from the initial list of patterns.*

We only look at these parts of the proof that are useful to present the algorithms of the next sections, and particularly to the effective building of the lazy pattern matching algorithm.

When all the minimally extended patterns are pairwise incompatible, the predicate $match_\Pi$ is the ordinary matching predicate against the set of patterns MEP_Π. Hence its sequentiality is easily decided using already known methods. One only has to check if this predicate is sequential at every partial term which is a prefix of an element of MEP_Π. Moreover, one can exhibit a lazy pattern matching algorithm when the checking succeeds. These two goals are achieved by trying to build a "matching tree" (see for details Huet and Lévy [5] where this method is introduced). A matching tree is a tree of which each node contains a partial term M with an index u of $match_\Pi$ in M, and the branches issued from a node $< M, u >$ are labelled with the symbols that may be placed at u in M in order to get a match. Leaves contain elements of MEP_Π which mean a success in the matching process. The root of the tree contains the partial term Ω with the trivial index of $match_\Pi$ at this partial term.

Given the matching tree and a value v to be matched, the lazy pattern matching algorithm is as follows : start at the root of the tree and when reaching a node take the symbol in v at the occurrence contained in the node ; if there is a branch labelled with this symbol starting from the node then follow it, else the matching process fails ; when reaching a leave one ensures that v is greater than the element, say p, of MEP_Π contained in the leave. Hence the value matches the unique initial pattern p_i such that $match_i(p) = \mathrm{tt}$.

The proof of computability of MEP_Π only consists of the following remark : The set of occurrences in any member of MEP_Π may be bounded by $\bigcup_{i=1}^{n} \overline{\mathcal{O}}(p_i)$ and the signature Σ is finite. Such a characterisation leads to practically useless algorithms because of the exponential growth of the number of partial terms to compute, when the number of patterns or the number of constructors grow. We shall now give pratical algorithms.

3 Building of the Matching Tree

We shall address now the question of efficiently building the matching tree defined in the preceding section[1]. This process asks for finding (at least) an index in each partial term one has to place in the tree. If one has previously generated the set of all the minimally extended patterns, it is easy to find an index in a partial term M less defined than some of the extended patterns. One only has to check if there exists an occurrence $u \in \mathcal{O}_\Omega(M)$ such that u belongs to $\overline{\mathcal{O}}(p)$ for all minimally extended pattern p greater than M.

However, generating all the minimally extended patterns is a very costly process. Hence we shall try to build the tree without using the minimally extended patterns. We shall show that in many cases one can find some index in a partial term without knowing the minimally extended patterns that are greater (see section 3.1). Unfortunately this method may fail to give any index in partial terms where such indexes exist. In such cases we shall have to compute the minimally extended patterns, but only from a restricted set of initial patterns. Once we have generated these patterns we may use them to find indexes in subsequent partial terms.

In the following we only shall deal with partial terms that appear in the matching tree. Hence, we state here two properties of such partial terms which will be used in some of the proofs of the following sections.

Notations : We shall denote $M[u \leftarrow N]$ the partial term obtained by replacing in M the subterm at occurrence u by the partial term N. $F(\vec{\Omega})$ will denote the partial term whose top symbol is F and all the sons (according with arity of F) are Ω.

Proposition 1 *Let M be a partial term appearing in some non terminal node of the matching tree. One has the two following properties :*

1. *There exists a minimally extended pattern p such that $M < p$.*
2. *M has been built by filling indexes, i.e. there exists a sequence $M_0, \ldots, M_q$ of partial terms and a sequence $u_0, \ldots, u_{q-1}$ of occurrences such that :*
   - *(a)* $M_0 = \Omega$
   - *(b)* $M_q = M$
   - *(c) for all* $i \in \{0, \ldots, q-1\}$, *u_i is an index of* $match_\Omega$ *in* M_i
   - *(d)* $\forall i \in \{0, \ldots, q-1\}\ \exists F_i \in \Sigma \quad (M_{i+1} = M_i[u_i \leftarrow F_i(\vec{\Omega})])$

Proof : Both properties are obvious consequences of the definition of a matching tree. ■

Definition 9 We shall call *accessible from* a partial term M, each initial pattern p_i such that $match_i(N) = tt$ for some partial term $N \geq M$.

[1] I would like to thanks one of the referees of this paper for his careful reading and very useful comments. They led to great improvement in the presentation of this section.

3.1 Easy indexes

We shall give here a way of finding an index in a partial term M that is already present in some non terminal node of the matching tree without using the set of all the minimally extended patterns. Looking for efficiency in the compilation process, we do not try to generate *all* the indexes, only to give one as soon as possible.

We first remark that the set of indexes of $match_\Pi$ in M is the intersection of the sets of indexes in M of all the predicates $match_i$ for those i such that p_i is accessible from M. This fact follows obviously from the definition of $match_\Pi$.

Let p_i be accessible from M. What are the indexes of $match_i$ in M ?

First, it is clear that all the occurrences in $\overline{\mathcal{O}}(p_i) \cap \mathcal{O}_\Omega(M)$ are such indexes. Moreover, if we assume that p_i is incompatible with any pattern p_j with $j < i$, then we got here all the indexes of $match_i$ in M.

Assume now that p_i is ambiguous with some patterns of higher priority, denoted here $q_1, \ldots, q_n$, and that $M \uparrow q_j$ for all $j \in \{1, \ldots, n\}$. Since we assumed that there exists a partial term on which $match_i$ returns tt, the set of occurrences $\overline{\mathcal{O}}(q_j) \setminus \overline{\mathcal{O}}(p_i)$ is nonempty for all $j \in \{1, \ldots, n\}$ (it contains the occurrences where one may exclude q_j in order to recognize p_i). We shall denote by U_j the set of occurrences in $\mathcal{O}_\Omega(M)$ which are a prefix of at least one element of $\overline{\mathcal{O}}(q_j) \setminus \overline{\mathcal{O}}(p_i)$.

Consider a partial term N such that $N \geq M$ and $match_i(N) = $ tt. There must exist an occurrence $u_j \in U_j$ such that $N(u_j) \neq \Omega$. If the set U_j only has one element, we may thus ensure that this unique element is an index of $match_i$ in M. Repeating this for all j, we show that the union of those U_j which are singletons is contained in the set of the indexes of $match_i$ in M.

Remark 1 The condition on U_j to be a singleton, although sufficient, is not a necessary one. Suppose, for example, that we deal with this definition of an "Exclusive Or" function :

```
let XOR = function (true, false) -> true
                 | (false, true) -> true
                 | (x, y)        -> false;;
```

It is associated with the list of initial patterns Π = [(true,false) ; (false,true) ; (Ω,Ω)]. Here pattern p_3 is ambiguous with both p_1 and p_2. If we deal with the partial term $M = (\Omega,\Omega)$ and search for indexes of $match_3$ in M, we get $U_1 = U_2 = \{[1],[2]\}$. Hence the preceding method does not give any index for $match_3$ in M.

On the other hand, the set of all the minimally extended patterns is here :

$$\{(true, false), (false, true), (true, true), (false, false)\}$$

so that, in M, both occurrences [1] and [2] are indexes of $match_\Pi$ (and of course of $match_3$ too).

Remark 2 It is not easy to check if a given pattern p_i is accessible from a partial term M. However one may ensure that if p_i is accessible from M then one has $M \uparrow p_i$. Hence we shall use the preceding result with *all* the initial patterns compatible with M rather than with the accessible ones. It is obvious that this does not produce wrong indexes.

3.2 Restricting the Set of Initial Patterns

We are now faced with the problem of finding an index (if it is possible) in a partial term M where the method of the preceding section has failed. From the properties of the partial terms in the matching tree, we know that it suffices to compute the minimally extended patterns greater than M. Moreover these patterns will give us an easy way to find indexes in all the partial terms appearing in nodes of the matching tree below the node of M.

Using the fact that M was built by filling indexes (see proposition 1), we may give the following characterisation of those minimally extended patterns which are greater than M. It essentially means that one may built them starting from M and discarding all the initial patterns not accessible from M. Denoting Π' the list of patterns accessible from M, the sets $\{t \geq M\ ;\ match_{\Pi}(t) = \text{tt}\ \}$ and $\{t \geq M\ ;\ match_{\Pi'}(t) = \text{tt}\ \}$ have the same minimal elements.

Proposition 2 *Let $\{p_{i_1}, \ldots, p_{i_n}\}$ be a subset of the initial patterns list, containing all the initial patterns accessible from M (we assume that $i_j < i_k$ whenever $j < k$). Let t be a partial term greater than M. Then t is a minimally extended pattern if and only if it satisfies the two following conditions :*

1. $\exists k\ (t \geq p_{i_k}$ *and* $\forall j < k\ (t \sharp p_{i_j}))$
2. $\forall t' \in [M, t[\ \forall k\ (t' \wedge p_{i_k} < p_{i_k}$ *or* $\exists j < k\ (t' \uparrow p_{i_j}))$

Proof : Assume that t is a minimally extended pattern. Since $t \geq M$ and $match_{\Pi}(t) = \text{tt}$, using definition of the subscripts i_k, we can find some k such that $match_{i_k}(t) = \text{tt}$. This means that $t \geq p_{i_k}$ and for all $j < i_k$, we get $t \sharp p_j$. This implies that if $j < k$ (and hence $i_j < i_k$) we have $t \sharp p_{i_j}$: t satisfies the first condition.

In order to get the second condition, let t' be a partial term such that $t' < t$. Since t is a minimally extended pattern, one has $match_{\Pi}(t') = \text{ff}$, and then for all k, either $t' \wedge p_{i_k} < p_{i_k}$, or there exists $j < i_k$ such that $t' \uparrow p_j$. If for all k, $t' \wedge p_{i_k} < p_{i_k}$ holds, we get the desired result. Assume now that for some k, this condition does not hold, then we have to show that there exists $l < k$ such that $t' \uparrow p_{i_l}$. Due to assumption above we know that there exists $j < i_k$ such that $t' \uparrow p_j$. Thus it suffices to show that this subscript j is one of the subscripts i_m. Since moreover t' is greater than or equal to M we have $t' \vee p_j \geq M$ and $match_j(t' \vee p_j) = \text{tt}$. Hence p_j is one of the patterns p_{i_m}, we proved that t satisfies the second condition.

Conversely, let t be a partial term greater than M and satisfying the two conditions given above. Since $t \geq M$, if $j \notin \{i_1, \ldots, i_n\}$ we have $match_j(t) = \text{ff}$. Combining this result with the first condition we get :

$$\exists k\ (t \geq p_{i_k} \text{ and } \forall j < i_k\ (match_j(t) = \text{ff}))$$

which implies that $match_{i_k}(t) = \mathrm{tt}$, hence $match_\Pi(t) = \mathrm{tt}$.

It remains to show that such a t is minimal. To get this result, assume that there exists a partial term $t' < t$ such that $match_\Pi(t') = \mathrm{tt}$. We shall prove that this leads to a contradiction. From the monotonicity of the predicates $match_i$ (see lemma 1), one has $match_{i_k}(t') = \mathrm{tt}$ for the same k as t. If we assumed that t' is greater than or equal to M (i.e. $t' \in [M, t[$) then the second condition would imply that $match_{i_k}(t') = \mathrm{ff}$. This contradiction ensures that t' is not greater than or equal to M. Hence we can find an occurrence v such that $t'(v) = \Omega$ and $M(v) \neq \Omega$. There exists a subscript j_0 such that $M_{j_0+1} = M_{j_0}[v \leftarrow F_{j_0}(\vec{\Omega})]$ and v is an index of $match_\Pi$ in M_{j_0}. This implies $M_{j_0}(v) = \Omega$. Now look at the partial term $t' \vee M_{j_0}$: it is greater than or equal to M_{j_0}, by monotonicity it satisfies $match_\Pi(t' \vee M_{j_0}) = \mathrm{tt}$. Since it has a symbol Ω at occurrence v this contradicts the assumption that v is an index of $match_\Pi$ in M_{j_0}.

In all cases we get a contradiction when we assume that $match_\Pi(t') = \mathrm{tt}$. Hence, t is a minimally extended pattern associated with the initial list of patterns. ■

Remark 3 We shall use this proposition with the list of patterns *compatible* with M since we do not have an easy way to compute the list of patterns *accessible* from M.

3.3 Generating the Useful Extended Patterns

According to the results of section 3.2, we shall give an algorithm generating all the minimally extended patterns, greater than a given partial term. This set will be built incrementally using two different steps.

In the following we assume given a partial term M and we shall denote by $\{p_1, \ldots, p_n\}$ a subset of the initial patterns list containing at least all those initial patterns which are accessible from M. We assume moreover that the ordering on the patterns has not been removed, i.e. if $i < j$ then p_i has higher priority than p_j. We shall give a construct of the set of all the minimally extended patterns that are greater than M. According to proposition 2, this set may be defined as :

$$\begin{aligned} EM = \{\, t; \;\; & 1) \;\; t \geq M \\ & 2) \;\; \exists k \; (t \geq p_k \text{ and } \forall j < k \; (t \not\uparrow p_j)) \\ & 3) \;\; \forall t' \in [M, \; t[\;\; \forall i \; (t' \wedge p_i < p_i \text{ or } \exists j < i \; (t' \uparrow p_j)) \,\} \end{aligned}$$

EM is the set of minimal elements of $\{t \geq M \; ; \; match_\Pi(t) = \mathrm{tt}\,\}$ (the third condition meaning $match_i(t) = \mathrm{ff}$).

Proposition 3 *The set EM is the union, for all the subscripts $k \in \{1, \ldots, n\}$, of the disjoint sets, denoted by EM_k, of the minimal partial terms greater than M verifying $match_k$. EM_k may be defined as follows :*

$$EM_k = \{\, t;\ \ 1)\ \ t \geq M \vee p_k$$
$$2)\ \ \forall j < k\ (t \not\uparrow p_j)$$
$$3)\ \ \forall t' \in [M \vee p_k,\ t[\ \forall i \leq k$$
$$(t' \wedge p_i < p_i \text{ or } \exists j < i\ (t' \uparrow p_j))\ \}$$

Proof : We first remark that each $t \in EM_k$ satisfies the two conditions : $t \uparrow p_k$ and $\forall j < k\ (t \not\uparrow p_j)$. This ensures that t does not belong to EM_i for $i \neq k$.

Now let $t \in EM$, and let k be the subscript for which t satisfies the second condition in the definition of EM. Then $t \in EM_k$.

Conversely, let $t \in EM_k$ for some k. It is obvious that t satisfies the first two conditions in the definition of EM. To establish the third one, let t' be a partial term in the interval $[M,\ t[$. Since $t' < t$ and $t \uparrow p_k$, we get $t' \uparrow p_k$. Hence t' is compatible with a pattern (p_k) with higher priority than each p_i for $i > k$: for these i the third condition is satisfied.

Assume now that $i < k$ and denote by t'' the partial term $t' \vee p_k$. Since $t \geq p_k$, one has $t'' \in [M \vee p_k,\ t[$. It follows that :

- either $t'' \wedge p_i < p_i$ and hence (since $t' \leq t''$) $t' \wedge p_i < p_i$,
- or one can find $j < i$ such that $t'' \uparrow p_j$ and $t' \uparrow p_j$. ■

We shall give a method to build stepwise the sets EM_k. Each step of the building will let grow the partial term p_k in order to make it incompatible with one of the patterns with higher priority.

Proposition 4 *Let $k \in \{1, \ldots, n\}$. We recursively define the sets $EM_k^1, \ldots, EM_k^k$, in the following way :*

1. *EM_k^1 is the singleton $\{M \vee p_k\}$*
2. *We assume EM_k^i to be built, for some $i \in \{1, \ldots, k-1\}$. We define EM_k^{i+1} as the union, for all $t \in EM_k^i$, of the following sets E_t :*
   - *if $t \not\uparrow p_{k-i}$ then $E_t = \{t\}$*
   - *else $E_t = \{t' \geq t$; there exists a unique occurrence where the symbols in t' and p_{k-i} are distinct (and are not Ω) and $\overline{\mathcal{O}}(t') \subseteq \overline{\mathcal{O}}(t) \cup \overline{\mathcal{O}}(p_{k-i})\}$.*

Then EM_k is the set of all the elements of EM_k^k that are minimal according to the ordering over the partial terms.

Proof :

We shall establish, using induction on i, the following three properties of the sets EM_k^i :

1. $\forall t \in EM_k^i \; t \geq M \vee p_k$

2. $\forall t \in EM_k^i \; t \sharp p_j \; (j = k-i+1, \ldots, k-1)$

3. If a partial term t satisfies

$$t \geq M \vee p_k \text{ et } t \sharp p_j \;\; (j = k-i+1, \ldots, k-1)$$

then there exists $t_0 \in EM_k^i$ such that $t \geq t_0$

The three properties hold obviously for $i = 1$. Assume they hold for some i and look at EM_k^{i+1}.

1. Since the elements of EM_k^{i+1} are greater than or equal to those of EM_k^i the first property remains true.

2. Let $t \in EM_k^{i+1}$. There exists $t_0 \in EM_k^i$ such that $t \in E_{t_0}$. Since $t \geq t_0$ and $t_0 \sharp p_j$ $(j = k-i+1, \ldots, k-1)$ (from the induction hypothesis), we have the following property : $t \sharp p_j$ $(j = k-i+1, \ldots, k-1)$. From the definition of E_{t_0}, we know that t is incompatible with all the partial terms p_{k-i}. We get so the second property.

3. Let $t \geq M \vee p_k$ satisfying $t \sharp p_j$ $(j = k-i, \ldots, k-1)$, we shall exhibit an element t_0 of EM_k^{i+1} less than or equal to t. From the induction hypothesis, we know that there exists an element t_1 of EM_k^i less than or equal to t. If this element is not compatible with p_{k-i}, it is a member of EM_k^{i+1} and we may take $t_0 = t_1$. If it is compatible, let u_0 be an occurrence, minimal for the prefix ordering on occurrences, where the symbols in t and p_{k-i} are different and not equal to Ω. Such an occurrence exists from the hypothesis on t. We may then define t_0 by the conditions $\overline{\mathcal{O}}(t_0) = \overline{\mathcal{O}}(t_1) \cup \{u; u \leq u_0\}$ and $t_0 \leq t$. These two conditions may hold together since $\overline{\mathcal{O}}(t_1) \cup \{u; u \leq u_0\} \subseteq \overline{\mathcal{O}}(t)$.

   Moreover, t_0 and p_{k-i} only differ at occurrence u_0 and $t_1 < t_0$. We get $t_0 \in E_{t_1}$, and hence the result. ∎

Remark 4 In the preceding construct, we may replace each set E_t (see proposition 4) by the set of its minimal elements (for the ordering over the partial terms). The first two properties of the sets EM_k remain since we only reduce the size of these sets. The third one remains since we keep all the minimal elements.

We have now to give a method to build the sets which we called E_t in the proposition 4. This building may be done in an obvious way : given the partial terms t and p_j, E_t is the set of all the partial terms we get by replacing in $t \vee p_j$ the subterm at an occurrence u in $\overline{\mathcal{O}}(p_j) \setminus \overline{\mathcal{O}}(t)$ by $F(\vec{\Omega})$, where F is any constructor other than $p_j(u)$.

There are at least two reasons for inefficiency in this method. First, it does not use the fact that one is not allowed to place any constructor at a given occurrence in a partial term : ML's typing constraints only allow a constructor of the same type than $p_j(u)$ to appear at occurrence u in p_j. The second reason is that it does not use remark 4, building many partial terms that are to be discarded. We shall not address here the question of using only useful symbols when generating the set of all the minimally extended patterns. It essentially relies on looking at which symbols appear in still accessible patterns when one tries to extend a partial term toward a minimally extended pattern ; we shall discuss it in a section dealing with properties which depend on ML specificities (see below section 4).

In order to use remark 4 in the construct given in proposition 4, replacing E_t by its minimal elements, we have to characterize these minimal elements of a set E_t. This is done in the following lemma.

Lemma 2 *With the notations of the proposition 4, assume given $t \in EM_k^i$ such that $t \uparrow p_{k-i+1}$. Let $t' \in E_t$ and denote by u_0 the occurrence where t' is incompatible with p_{k-i+1}. Then t' is minimal in E_t if and only if $\overline{\mathcal{O}}(t') = \overline{\mathcal{O}}(t) \cup \{u; u \leq u_0\}$.*

Proof : To get a partial term less than t', we have to replace in t the subterm at an occurrence $u \in \overline{\mathcal{O}}(t')$ by Ω. If we want that the result remains greater than or equal to t, we must choose $u \notin \overline{\mathcal{O}}(t)$. If u is a prefix of u_0, the resulting partial term is compatible with p_{k-i+1}. If u is not a prefix of u_0, the result is still an element of E_t. ∎

4 Restricting the Set of Constructors

We present in this section a way of improving the pattern matching compilation by restricting the set of symbols one has to place in an extended pattern at a given occurrence.

As was previously stated, only the symbols that appear in the initial patterns accessible from a partial term M, are useful when building the minimally extended patterns greater than M : if we find, during the pattern matching process, another constructor in the value to be matched, it only excludes from the accessible patterns all those which have not an Ω at the occurrence we just looked at. This does not depend on the symbol we found, only on the fact that it does not appear at this occurrence in the patterns accessible from the prefix we have already scanned.

This point relies on using infinite data types in patterns, such as `Integer` or `String`. In such a case one cannot assume that the signature is finite, an assumption that we used when proving that the set EMP_Π is computable. However, the preceding remark gives the answer : When dealing with infinite data types we collect all the values that appear in the initial patterns and group the other values as a single one (denoted "`otherwise`" in Σ). In such a way we get a finite signature. The same method gives us a restriction on the set of useful constructors : Rather than using all the constructors in the types that appear in the initial patterns, we only deal with the constructors that are present in the patterns which are accessible from the already scanned prefix. Of course we have to add the "`otherwise`" cases each time that not all the constructors of a type appear in the patterns list : the other ones may be present in the values which will be given to the pattern matching algorithm.

The way to restrict the set of constructors we just described has a disadvantage : one has to handle some bookkeeping of the accessible patterns all along the building of the minimally extended patterns. This may be avoided, using weaker restrictions over the sets of constructors to be tested. We give here two restrictions which may be set only looking at the set of initial patterns. They may be combined, but the resulting constraint remains weaker than it could be done.

Using typing information

The type constraints of the ML system require that the patterns of a pattern matching definition have a common most general (polymorphic) type. This implies that every prefix of one of these patterns has a type more general than this one. Moreover, the typechecker of the ML system ensures that when we have looked at a prefix M of some ML value v, we may find the type of each constructor that may appear in v at an occurrence u belonging to $\mathcal{O}_\Omega(M)$. It is the (common) type of all the constructors that appear at occurrence u in the initial patterns accessible from M. Hence, we don't have to worry about constructors belonging to other types.

Using occurrences information

A simple way to restrict the set of constructors to deal with, is building an A-list which associates each occurrence with the set of all the constructors appearing at that occurrence in at least one of the initial patterns. There is of course no reason to consider any other constructor to fill an occurrence when building the extended patterns (assuming the use of an "`otherwise`" case which groups all other constructors).

Remark 5 Even combining the last two restrictions does not eliminate all useless extended pattern as shows the following example. Of course these useless patterns do not affect lazyness ; moreover, cases where there arise, are rather uncommon. One has here to make a choice between compile-time and run-time efficiency.

Example The following pattern matching is part of a function (see page 15) which performs some optimizations over the CAM code generated by the CAML compiler ("::" is the infix notation CAML uses for the CONS function) :

```
function (Push :: Car :: Swap :: _)     -> 1
       | (Push :: Quote _ :: App :: _) -> 2
       | c                              -> 3;;
```

If we try to generate the minimally extended patterns greater than (`Push :: Car :: Ω :: Ω`) we have to replace the first Ω. Typing constraints give here no restriction, since all the patterns are lists of instructions. Using occurrence's information restricts the set of constructors to {Swap, App} (and "otherwise"). It is a real improvement (the type "instruction" has about 15 constructors, 5 of them appearing in the patterns list). However it could be sufficient to consider Swap and "otherwise".

5 Efficiency results

5.1 Compile time

Efficiency's assessment has been done by using various examples of pattern matching definition. These examples have been taken from the CAML system itself (this system is written in CAML and bootstrapped, see [12]). Using definitions that were written before our implementation work, we ensure that these examples are not biased toward or against our algorithms[2].

The bigger example is the following one (there are 74 cases but we do not explicitly state all of them) :

```
function []                                         -> 1
       | (Push::Quote O::Swap::CC)                  -> 2
       | (Push::Quote <<'()>>::Branch(_,Pop::F)::CC) -> 3
       | (Push::Quote _::Branch(Pop::T,_)::CC)      -> 4
       | (Push::Quote O::App::CC)                   -> 5
       | (Push::Quote O::Call(2,fn)::CC)            -> 6
       | (Push::Quote <<(quote ^OO . ^Z)>>::CCO)    -> 7
       | (Push::Car::Swap::CC)                      -> 8
       | (Push::Cdr::Swap::CC)                      -> 9
       | (Push::Acc O::Swap::CC)                    -> 10
       | (Push::Rest 1::Swap::CC)                   -> 11
       | (Push::Swap::CC)                           -> 12
       | (Push::Cons::CC)                           -> 13
       | (Push::Rplac1 O::Pop::CC)                  -> 14
       | (Push::Pop::CC)                            -> 15
       | (Push::CC)                                 -> 16
........................................................
       | (Push_trap(xl,C1)::_ as CC)                -> 74;;
```

It is a function that performs some optimizations over the CAM code generated by the CAML compiler. Hence, the patterns are lists of CAM instructions representing various code structures. In order to only study the pattern-matching process, we replaced the right hand side expressions by integer constants representing the rule number.

[2] at least not intentionnally

We did not try to evaluate the improvement due to the restrictions over the set of constructors to deal with : it may be very important, but is easy to implement and is obviously an improvement.

However this improvement is not sufficient to get an effective implementation. For example, we generated the set of minimally extended patterns, using only the theoretical existence algorithm and the restrictions on the constructors, for the above function definition. The generation used more than two hours of C.P.U. time on a Vax 11-780 !!

In order to study the effect of the other improvements given in this paper, we compare compilation time of some parts of this same function.

First, we give results of compiling the complete function. If we generate all the minimally extended patterns, using the incremental building method given in section 3.3 but without the restriction of the set of initial patterns given in section 3.2, the compilation took 373 seconds on a Vax 11-780 (of which about 230 seconds are G.C. time). Including the restriction, the compilation took only 160 seconds (with about 90 seconds of G.C. time).

In order to see the effect of the restriction method, we compiled with and without it, some parts of the function above. Keeping only rules 3, 4 and 7 we get an highly ambiguous pattern matching in which the method of section 3.2 does not reject any rule before looking at a set of extended patterns. In fact the two compilations need comparable time (40 seconds vs. 37 seconds), with a slight gain since in the second case the generation process does not start from Ω but from a more precise partial term (corresponding to `(Push :: Quote _ :: _)`).

Keeping now the following pattern matching :

```
function []                                         -> 1
       | (Push::Quote 0::Swap::CC)                  -> 2
       | (Push::Quote <<'()>>::Branch(_,Pop::F)::CC) -> 3
       | (Push::Quote _::Branch(Pop::T,_)::CC)      -> 4
       | (Push::Quote 0::Call(2,fn)::CC)            -> 6
       | (Push::Quote <<(quote ^00 . ^Z)>>::CC0)    -> 7
       | (Push::Car::Swap::CC)                      -> 8
       | (Push::Acc 0::Swap::CC)                    -> 10
       | (Push::Swap::CC)                           -> 12
       | (Push::Rplac1 0::Pop::CC)                  -> 14
       | (Push::CC)                                 -> 16;;
```

the difference between the two compilation times is 101 seconds vs. 49 seconds. The second method needs generating six sets of minimally extended patterns, one from four of the initial patterns, the other five from only two of the original patterns.

The experiments we made with other pattern matching definitions lead to results of the same order of magnitude.

We tried to compare the compilation times needed by our algorithms with those needed by the compiler of the CAML system. These comparisons are made using various pattern matching definitions from the CAML system itself. They are not perfectly precise since the work of the CAML compiler has to be distinguished from the typechecking, and these two processes are somewhat interleaved in the present system.

Depending on the kind of pattern matching (numerous ambiguity cases or not, number of constructors, size of the patterns ...), our compilation needs from 2/3 of the time used by the present compiler up to three times this time. It is not clear which are the most important features in these differences between the various cases. However, the comparisons with the present CAML compiler are essentially intended to ensure that our algorithms run fast enough to be incorporated in a future version of the system, which is now the case.

5.2 Run time

The same comparisons as in the testing of compile time efficiency, have been run. We looked at two kinds of measurement : size of the generated code, and the time needed to recognize which rule has to be applied.

Concerning the second point, precise comparison would need to define some kind of *average* value to be matched. We did not try to do such a work. However, with various attempts, the two codes do the pattern matching using about the same amount of time.

Concerning the size of the generated code, we estimate it by the number of instructions in the generated CAM code. This is a machine independent value, and it does not depend on other parts of the CAML system. The number of CAM instructions, in the code given by our algorithms, is about two third of the number of CAM instructions in the code generated by the present compiler. The gain comes from more efficient access to parts of the value, and from a less number of testing instructions to provide. The gain on the number of testing instructions is about 20 % in all the cases we tried. For example, in the case of the function given page 15 our compiler gives a code with 1011 CAM instructions and 203 test versus 1490 instructions and 242 tests with the present system.

However, the values we give here are only approximate ones. One may build specific ML pattern matching and values which do not fit with these estimates. This is the main reason why we used pattern matching of the CAML system in order to make our comparisons. Thus, since we did not use ad hoc examples, we mean that the values we give here are a rather correct estimate of the efficiency one may expect from our algorithms.

6 Conclusion

The compiler we used all along this paper is not actually implemented in the CAML system. There are two main reasons for this fact. The first one is that we want to do more experiments on some features of this compiler (it may be modified to use its data structures in the binding of the patterns' variables, it could be useful to implement some heuristics to deal with cases where no index exists in a partial term ...). The second one is that we have to provide an interface with the whole compiler and the typechecker and it is likely that these processes will have to be somewhat adapted according to which features we eventually retain in our pattern matching compiler.

However, the work we present in this paper shows that it is effectively possible to use lazy pattern matching in a functional language. This is a needed feature in a lazy system. We show that this may be a useful one even in a strict version : it gives a more compact object code without loss of run-time performance and with a quite acceptable compile-time performance. This is an incitement to further study the possible uses of this kind of mechanism.

References

[1] L. Augustsson "A Compiler for Lazy ML", A.C.M. Conference on Lisp and Functional Programming, Austin 1984, pp 218-225

[2] L. Augustsson "A Pattern Matching Compiler", Conf. on Functional Programming Languages and Computer Architecture, Nancy, 1985 (LNCS 217)

[3] R. Burstall D. MacQueen D. Sannella "HOPE : An Experimental Applicative Language", A.C.M. Conference on Lisp and Functional Programming, Stanford 1980, pp 136-143

[4] G. Cousineau P.L. Curien M. Mauny "The Categorical Abstract Machine", in J.P. Jouannaud ed. Functional Programming Languages and Computer Architecture, L.N.C.S. 201, Springer Verlag 1985

[5] G. Huet J.J. Lévy "Call by Need Computations in Non Ambiguous Linear Term Rewriting Systems", Rapport IRIA Laboria 359, August 1979

[6] A. Laville "Lazy Pattern Matching in the ML Language", Proceedings of the 7th Conference on Foundations of Software Technology and Theoretical Computer Science, Pune (India), December 1987, L.N.C.S.

[7] A. Laville "Filtrage et Evaluation paresseuse", Thèse de Doctorat, Université Paris 7, to appear

[8] M. Mauny "Compilation des Langages Fonctionnels dans les Combinateurs Catégoriques, Application au langage ML", Thèse de 3ème cycle, Université Paris 7, 1985

[9] M. Mauny A. Suarez "Implementing Functional Languages in the Categorical Abstract Machine", A.C.M. Conference on Lisp and Functional Programming, Cambridge 1986, pp 266-278

[10] R. Milner "A Proposal for Standard ML", A.C.M. Conference on Lisp and Functional Programming, Austin 1984, pp 184-197

[11] G. Plotkin "Call-by-need, Call-by-value and the Lambda Calculus", T.C.S. Vol 1, pp 125-159, 1975

[12] A. Suarez "Une Implémentation de ML en ML", Thèse, Université Paris 7, to appear

[13] D. Turner "Miranda a Non Strict Functional Language with Polymorphic Types", in J.P. Jouannaud ed. Functional Programming Languages and Computer Architecture, L.N.C.S. 201, Springer Verlag 1985

[14] P. Wadler, "Efficient Compilation of Pattern Matching", in S. Peyton Jones *The Implementation of Functional Programming Languages*, Prentice-Hall Series in Computer Science, 1987

ENHANCING PROLOG TO SUPPORT PROLOG PROGRAMMING ENVIRONMENTS

A.Martelli and G.F.Rossi

Dipartimento di Informatica - Università di Torino
C.so Svizzera 185 - 10149 Torino (ITALY)
uucp: ...!mcvax!i2unix!leonardo!mrt

Abstract

This paper describes the basic ideas we followed in the development of PROSE, a Prolog programming support environment we are implementing at our Department. We claim that standard Prolog must be adequately enhanced to be well suited to support the construction of an efficient programming environment. For this purpose, some new facilities are supplied by our Prolog (called Env_Prolog) which are mainly intended to allow the language:
- to handle programs as data and to partition the program database into disjoint sets of clauses;
- to support "editing" of clauses in the program database and the controlled execution of Prolog programs. Env_Prolog has been implemented by developing a new interpreter written in the C language. The paper will concentrate mainly on the interpreter and the support it offers to other tools of the environment.

1. Introduction

Programming environment tools for traditional programming languages are very often written in the same language which they are intended to support. This usually requires user programs to be converted into an *internal representation* which can be handled as a data structure of the language itself by all the tools of the environment.
The generation of the internal representation of a program is usually done by a syntax-based editor and has the form of a tree which reproduces the syntactic structure of a program as far as its abstract syntax is concerned.

On the contrary, using a programming language like LISP it is possible to directly view programs as data of the language itself. In this way tools written in LISP can handle user programs directly, without having to resort to any intermediate representation. Advantages of this approach are greater interactivity and expansibility of the environment and simplification of its development process.
Existing LISP environments are usually highly appreciated and demonstrate the effectiveness of this approach.

Prolog shares with LISP many valuable features for the construction of programming environments, such as symbolic manipulation capabilities, dynamic bindings, etc. However standard Prolog does not entirely satisfy the requirement of being able to handle programs as data. Indeed there are several built-in predicates to handle clauses and terms (e.g. *clauses, functor,...*) but clauses or programs (= finite set of clauses) cannot be handled as data.

Moreover, standard Prolog [4] does not supply the user with any facility to split a complex program into separate subcomponents ("modules"). Nevertheless this is an important requirement for a programming environment where many distinct programs (i.e. tools and user programs) must cohabit and cooperate. Some Prolog dialects let the language to have such capabilities by extending Prolog with various syntactic structures.

Unlike LISP, only few experiences have been done with the construction of Prolog programming support environments so far. One of the first effort to built such an environment is reported in [5]. Here an internal representation of Prolog is used to face the above problems. It serves also as a way to enrich the program with those informations which are necessary to the environment tools (in particular to the editor and debugger). Unfortunately in this way some of the potential advantages of Prolog with respect to traditional programming languages are missed.

The approach we have taken in the development of PROSE (=Prolog Support Environment) [10,13] is quite different from this one. Our goal has been to allow the whole environment to be written in Prolog without using any internal intermediate representation of programs; at the same time, neither the interpreter should be burdened too much nor Prolog should be extended too much.
The solution we have adopted consists in:

- giving the language the capability to handle programs as data and to partition the program d.b. into disjoint sets of clauses (in the basic form of *theories* as suggested in [2]);
- inserting into the interpreter all the facilities which are required for the development of the environment basic tools and which are very hard or highly inefficient to directly implement in Prolog. This requires the definition of a number of *new built_in* predicates which allow the user to exploit these new facilities.

Selecting which facilities must be supplied by the interpreter and which on the contrary must be implemented within the tools is a critical point. Our criteria has been to reduce as much as possible the number of new facilities that the interpreter must directly support so that its additional burden can be limited and good flexibility is assured in the development of tools.

At present, PROSE consists of three main components:
- **I_Prose**: interpreter for an extended Prolog (called **Env_Prolog**);
- **E_Prose**: Env_Prolog oriented editor;
- **D_Prose**: debugger.

The interpreter is written in C language, while other tools are all written in Env_Prolog. Our purpose is absolutely not that of building a complete and competitive programming environment. Our primary motivations to develop PROSE are rather the following ones:

- experimenting with usual interpreter implementation techniques in the special case of Prolog implementations;
- finding out possible extensions to standard Prolog which allows the language to better support the construction of programming environments (mainly in the direction of enhancing *metaprogramming* capabilities of Prolog);
- testing whether and how much techniques usually employed in the development of advanced tools for traditional programming languages are well suited to the special case of Prolog and, on the other hand, how Prolog special features influence and can be adequately exploited in the development of these tools.

2. An overview of I_Prose

I_Prose is the interpreter of the PROSE environment and its main component upon which all the other tools are based. The language implemented in I_Prose, named Env_Prolog, extends Prolog with new features which are mainly devoted to the support of the programming environment. More precisely, Env_Prolog extends the de-facto standard C_Prolog [15] with the following features:

- *infinite terms* [3];
- clauses and *programs as data,* and, as a consequence, the capability to have different programs in the program database at the same time;
- a number of *built-in* (meta-)predicates to handle terms and clauses;
- some mechanisms and built-in's for the *control of program execution.*

All these features will be discussed in more details in the next sections.

As regard to the implementation of I_Prose, we can mention the following features as the most distinguishing ones:
- a particular *unification algorithm* ;
- *uniform internal representation* of all terms and clauses of a program;
- derivation of the interpreter implementation by stepwise refinements of abstract formal specifications of an operational semantics of Prolog [11].

The unification algorithm used in I_Prose is an implementation of the algorithm proposed in [9] which in turn is a variation of the well-known algorithm by Martelli and Montanari [8], adapted to deal with infinite rational terms. This algorithm is based on the notion of *multiequation*, as a means to group together terms and variables which must be unified without having to perform any explicit substitution, and on some basic transformations on sets of multiequations which transform sets into equivalent ones [8,9].

Introduction of infinite terms is motivated firstly by interpreter's performance considerations (it is possible to suppress the occur-check operation still maintaining correctness) and, secondly, by the increased expressiveness of the language (cyclic data structures, e.g. graphs, circular lists, can be represented in a natural way). As an example, the program

```
eq(X,X).
?- eq(X,f(X)),eq(Y,f(Y)),eq(X,Y).
```

in Env_Prolog, has the solution:

```
{X,Y} = f(X)
```

whereas an implementation of Prolog with a standard unification algorithm loops forever trying to unify the infinite terms which are obtained from the first two subgoals in the given query (the result in the above example is a multiequation which expresses the fact that X and Y are equivalent and they are both bound to f(X)).

In the actual implementation of the unification algorithm, sets of multiequations are represented as *graph* data structures, which can be easily implemented in conventional imperative languages like C, by means of dynamic structures with pointers. Each multiequation corresponds to a different node in the graph (intermediate variables are introduced to have all terms with depth 1) and equivalent variables are linked together, with only the last one possibly bound to a non-variable term. (At this level our algorithm is very similar to the one proposed by Fages in [17]). For more details on the implementation of the unification algorithm see [16].

The use of this unification algorithm, in addition to the way I_Prose has been derived, that is by stressing similarities between interpreters for conventional programming languages and Prolog interpreters [11], has led to the choice of *"copying"* rather then *"structure sharing"* [12] to represent terms which are being unified.

On the other hand, the internal representation of source terms (i.e. not copied terms) has been designed in such a way to allow a *uniform view* of all internal data structures, without giving up the requirement of good execution efficiency and memory usage.

3. Programs as data

As we have already noted, the capability of a language to handle programs as data is a very valuable property in the construction of a programming environment. Standard Prolog implementations do not completely satisfy this requirement.

On the contrary, everything is considered as a term in Env_Prolog and can therefore be dealt with as data. In particular, a clause is a term with (infix) principal functor ":-", so that it is possible to write, for example:

```
        a :- b,c,d.
    ?- X :- Y,Z.
```

and have the answer:

```
        {X} = a
        {Y} = b
        {Z} = c,d
```

where the given clause is considered as a fact rather than a conditional rule to be executed. In C_Prolog, on the contrary, the special built-in predicate *clause(H,B)* is required to deal with clauses as data and some limitations are imposed on the way its arguments can be instantiated (namely, H cannot be a uninstantiated variable) due to the ad-hoc internal representation of clauses.

Moreover, in I_Prose, also a whole *program* (that is a finite set of clauses) is considered as a term, with (infix) principal functor "|". For example, the program:

```
p.
p :- q.     corresponds to the term:
q :- r.                  |
r.                      / \
                 p:-true   |
                          / \
                      p:-q   |
                            / \
                        q:-r   |
                              / \
                        r:-true  {}
```

A special *syntactic notation* has been defined to represent a program in a more concise form (like with lists in standard Prolog)

{c1.c2. ... .cn}

where c1, c2, .. are clauses and {} denotes the empty program.
The internal data structures that represent programs as terms are exactly the same as those used for other terms. Therefore it is possible to work uniformly on programs as well as on other terms, without loosing any efficiency in accessing inner subterms. The interpreter is able to distinguish between programs and other terms and to build suitable data structures (e.g. indexes, ...) which facilitate an efficient execution of the program itself.

All predicate names in a program are local to that program and the interpreter keeps different indexes for different programs. The set of clauses in the program database can be partitioned into smaller separate subsets. To allow a program to refer to a different one, meta-predicates of standard Prolog (namely, call, clause, assert and retract) have been modified in such a way they can explicitly specify the program they work on, as an additional argument. For example we can have

1. ?- **ecall**(p(X),{p(X):-q(X). q(a)}).
   {X} = a

2. try(X) :- Y = {p. p:-q. q:-r. r}, **eclause**(q,X,Y).

```
?- try(X).
{X} = r.
```

The built-in predicate *ecall* allows a goal to be solved into any program which is visible from it. Notice that the standard built-in *call* is still used whenever the goal has to be proved in the current program. Predicates *eclause, eassert* and *eretract* are defined in a way similar to the corresponding C_Prolog built-in predicates. In particular, *eassert* and *eretract* operate by side-effects on the program they receive as argument.

Several programs can be simultaneously present in the program database and it is easy to associate a different symbolic name to each of them. For example, the following definitions

```
alfa mod {p. p:-q. q:-r. r}.
beta mod {r(X):-s(X),p. p. s(a)}.
```

where *mod* is a *user-defined* infix operator, can be interpreted as the definition of two programs named *alfa* and *beta* respectively (we'll refer to them also as *"module"* definitions). Thus it is possible to solve a goal like:

```
?- alfa mod X.
```

getting as its result that X is bound to the program named *alfa*.

Names can be used in combination with metapredicates which operate on programs, as in the following example:

```
modcall(G,N) :- N mod P, ecall(G,P).

?- modcall(p(X),alfa).
{X} = a.
```

The *mod* operator is user-defined and can be changed as one wishes. The only built-in which is aware of this operator is the modified version of predicate **consult**. It has the form

```
consult(prog_file,prog_name)
```

and the Prolog program in *prog_file* is loaded into the main memory with the assertion:

```
prog_name mod {"program in prog_file"}.
```

The program can be now referred using *prog_name* in the way seen above. If *prog_name* is omitted the name *user* is used as a default.

Modules has been widely used in the construction of PROSE. E_Prose, D_Prose and user programs are distinct modules. Programs to handle graphical output on the screen or to manage files within the environment are defined as inner modules.
Modules can be nested at any depth, since they are terms. A program can use any predicate belonging to any module defined within it, but it can not use predicates belonging to modules defined at the same or outer level. To allow a module *alfa* to be visible to another module *beta*, an outer program must explicitly pass *alfa* to *beta*, like for example in the following program

```
alfa mod { ... }.
beta mod { ... }.
export :- alfa mod X,
          beta mod Y,
          eassert( (alfa mod X), Y).
```

After *export* has been called, program *beta* is modified in such a way it contains a definition of the module *alfa* and it can now refer to any predicate in *alfa* through one of the above metapredicates.

Programs can be used also as a way to collect clauses defining some data structure so that it can be managed as any other term (e.g. passed to a procedure as a parameter) maintaining all the advantages of the clausal representation (e.g. access by pattern-matching). For example, the following two clauses define a general program to find out a path between two nodes X and Y in a graph G:

```
p(X,Y,G) :- ecall(a(X,Y),G).
p(X,Y,G) :- ecall(a(X,Z),G), p(Z,Y,G).
```

where G is represented as a set of assertions (i.e. a program) like for instance in the goal:

```
?- p(a,d,{a(a,b).a(a,c).a(b,c).a(b,d).a(c,d)}.
```

Like with modules, it is also possible to associate a name to a graph. For example

```
g1 graph {a(a,b).a(a,c). a(b,c). a(b,d).a(c,d)}.
```

and thus the above goal could be rewritten as

```
?- g1 graph G, p(a,d,G).
```

Notice that the notion of *module* in Env_Prolog is similar to Bowen and Kowalski's notion of *theory* [2]., with *ecall* corresponding to the *demo* predicate. On the contrary, our approach is quite different from those proposals, like for instance M_Prolog [1], where modules are special syntactic entities which allow the programmer to specify visibility rules of names within them.

The *copying* based technique used in I_Prose would require that when solving a goal like ?-alfa mod X a new copy of the whole program bound to X is made if the program contains any variable. To avoid this heavy operation, we assume that a program is always considered as a "ground" term. I_Prose can recognize a ground term and avoid to make any copy of it when the term has to be unified. More complex operations on programs as data (like for instance appending two programs) are still being investigated at present.

4. Interpreter and programming environment

As we have pointed out in the first section, implementation of the environment tools requires that the implementation language supplies a number of facilities which are usually not available in standard Prolog implementations.

In the project described in [5] these Prolog deficiences have been overcome by using an *internal representation* of programs in the form of Prolog assertions which are accessible to all the tools of the environment.
We also have followed this approach in the development of a first prototypical implementation of an Editor and a Debugger for the PROSE environment, both written in C_Prolog. The internal representation of programs we have used is illustrated by the following example:

```
p(X) :- q(X,Y),r(a).
   ⇓
iclause(Cr,Pr,Nr,p(_1),[q(_1,_2),r(a)],[v(_1,'X'),v(_2,'Y')]).
```

where the first three arguments are used by the Editor to move from one clause to another (Cr, Pr, Nr = current, previous, next clause reference, respectively). The last argument allows the interpreter to maintain the association between the internal name and the corresponding external one for each variable in a clause (since C_Prolog does not provide this facility).
A program is transformed into its internal representation by the Editor.

An advantage of using this intermediate representation is the separation between predicate names of user programs (represented as *iclauses*) and predicate names of tools (anyway separation among tools is still a problem).
The major drawback of this solution is the necessity to introduce a translation step which of course limits environment interactivity.

Another drawback of this solution is the difficulty and/or inefficiency to implement some operations of the environment in standard Prolog, especially if compared to the relative simplicity they could be directly implemented within the interpreter. For example the Editor in PROSE should perform lexical and syntactic analysis being a language oriented editor. Implementation of these operations in Prolog is quite cumbersome and inefficient. On the other hand the interpreter already executes such operations internaly and it seems reasonable them to be exploited.
In the same way, such operations as storing the symbolic name of variables or traversing clauses could be done directly by the interpreter with only a negligible overhead.
As regard to the Debugger, it can be written in Prolog as a *metainterpreter* which is able to execute the *iclause* internal representation of a program. However to have a really significant tool, such a metainterpreter must simulate most of the execution process of the interpreter, resulting in a complex tool, which causes a program under debugging to be executed very slowly.
Again if the user could access to some of the information the interpreter uses internally to control the execution of a program, implementation of the Debugger would be strongly simplified.

The approach we have followed in PROSE assumes that the interpreter (I_Prose) maintains informations which are useful for the construction of the basic tools of the environment, letting these informations be accessible to the user through some new built_in predicates. We'll briefly describe these new facilities in the next two sections.

5. Editor support

In this section we briefly describe the most important new built-in predicates which Env_Prolog supplies and which are mainly used in the development of the editing facilities of the PROSE environment. Usually they define operations which are difficult or highly inefficient to implement directly in Prolog.

Syntactic analysis and term construction

- **mkterm**(L,T,N).
  L is a list containing the ASCII representation of the term T. If the representation in L is not syntactically correct, N is an integer indicating the position in L where the first error has been found.
  Identifiers with capital initials are considered as constants in T.

- **mkvars**(T1,T2).
  T1 and T2 are the same term except for identifiers with capital initials which are considered as constants in T1 and as variables in T2.

Example:

```
?- mkterm([102,40,97,44,103,40,97,41,41],T1,_),
   mkvars(T1,T2).

   {T1} = f('X',g(a))
   {T2} = f(X,g(a)).
```

These two new predicates allow the Editor input phase to be strongly simplified. Syntactic analysis is performed by the *mkterm* predicate and can be applied to single predicates or to a clause as a whole. A clause can be built incrementally, adding new predicates or modifying existing ones. Predicate *mkvars* allows equal variable identifiers to denote the same variables within a clause when the clause is stored

in the program database even if it is constructed incrementally.
Having these predicates as built-in does not limit the operations the Editor can still perform. For example, automatic balancing of parenthesis, removing superfluous blanks in the input stream, error diagnostic messages and many other editing operations are all charged to the editor.

Clauses handling

Some new built-in predicates are defined in Env_Prolog to exploit the physical ordering of clauses. Clauses are identified by an internal unique identifier (Clause Reference) whose value has no meaning for the user. The interpreter keeps clauses ordered using the same data structures it uses for the internal representation of a program (that is a tree of "|" operators) without having to add any new structure.

- **assertp**(Cl,ClRef).
  Clause *Cl* is stored in the program database just before the clause identified by ClRef. Insertion is made in such a way to guarantee that clauses belonging to the same procedure are all necessarily contiguous.

- **adj**(ClRef1,ClRef2).
  ClRef1 and ClRef2 are references to two adjacent consecutive clauses. If ClRef2 (ClRef1) is the reference to a clause and ClRef1 (CLRef2) is bound to a variable, then *adj* can be used to obtain the previous (next) clause of the given one. The program d.b. begins and ends with two fictitious clauses with ClRef=0 and ClRef=-1, respectively. Thus *adj* can be also used to find the first and the last clause in a program.
  The following is an example which shows a typical use of *adj*.

  Example: *go to* the n-th clause.

```
goto(N,Ref) :- first(FCl),go(N,1,FCl,Ref).
go(X,X,R,R).
go(N,I,R,NewR) :- adj(R,Next),
                  I is I +1,
                  go(N,I,Next,NewR).
first(ClRef) :- adj(0,ClRef).
```

Symbolic variable names

For each variable in a term I_Prose preserves the user defined name in the internal representation of the term itself. The built-in predicates **write**(X) prints a term (including clauses and programs) with non-instantiated variables represented by their original symbolic names, contrary to what is done by usual C_Prolog implementations. It is evident the utility of this facility both to the Editor and the Debugger.

A problem arises with *renaming* of variables which is done by the interpreter whenever a predicate is unified with the head of some clause. I_Prose faces this problem by appending a univocal index to the name of renamed variables. For example, given the program

```
p(f(X),Y) :- q(Y).
q(f(X)).
?-p(X,Y).
```

we get the result:

```
{X} = f(X_1)
{Y} = f(X_2).
```

6. Debugger support

In C_Prolog and in many other Prolog implementations the Debugger is completely embedded within the interpreter. This solution assures good efficiency but no flexibility at all as regard to debugging policies. At the opposite extreme is the solution based on metainterpretation, we have already cited in Section 4.

The approach we followed to develop the PROSE Debugger (D_Prose) can be considered as intermediate between these two extremes. Indeed, D_Prose is written in Env_Prolog but execution of the program under debugging is completely carried on at the object level. What the user can do in Env_Prolog is to force the interpreter to call a user-defined procedure whenever a goal has to be solved, and to control its execution through a number of special built-in predicates.

More precisely. When user requests the activation of debugging mode (through the execution of the built-in predicate **dbgon**) the interpreter transforms the execution of each goal G into the execution of the user defined procedure **dbgenter**(G). This procedure completely defines the Debugger. Within this procedure the debugger designer can use two new built-in predicates to control the execution of the given goal G:

- **select**(G,ClRef)
- **exec**(G,ClRef).

Predicate *select* gets the reference of the first clause in the (current) program whose head unifies with the given goal G. If no such clause is found, *select* fails. Upon backtracking, *select* gets the reference of the next clause, if it exists. Predicate *exec* solves goal G using the clause specified by *ClRef.*
If G is a built-in predicate, *select* does nothing more than to bind *ClRef* to the constant *builtin* and *exec* performs a *call(G)* .
Notice that procedure *dbgenter* can be composed of different alternative clauses like any other Prolog procedure and backtracking applies as usual to them.

Selection of these two primitives is the result of a careful tradeoff between efficiency and flexibility. Their implementation is done in such a way to avoid execution overhead as much as possible. In particular, substitutions computed during the execution of *select* are stored into an ad-hoc internal data structure so that they have not to be recomputed when the corresponding *exec* is called successively (this structure is automatically removed on exiting from the *dbgenter* predicate).

Of course *select* and *exec* must be used with the due care. In particular, the argument *ClRef* of *exec* must be the reference of a clause previously selected by a *select* predicate on the same goal G (actually G has been inserted in *exec* just to report the new variable substitutions that are possibly created by the execution of clause ClRef).

The current substitutions (created by *select* and *exec*) can be obtained if necessary at any time, through the special built-in **curr_substs**(G,ClRef,S1,S2), where S1 and S2 are two lists of pairs of the form:

[s(x1, t1),..., s(xn,tn)]

which represent current variable substitutions for G and ClRef respectively (G is always instantiated by *curr-substs* to its initial value, the one specified in the *select* call).

Another interesting new mechanism supplied by I_Prose which has been used in D_Prose is the one provided by the **do- undo** built-in predicates. It is mainly intended to support the implementation of an undo facility of the debugger but it can also be seen as a generalized cut, whose effect is not limited

to the procedure in which it appears. More precisely, the execution of the built-in predicate *undo*, causes the present computation to fail, and backtracking to be activated. All possible alternatives between *undo* and the immediately preceding *do* are rejected. Backtracking stops at the first possible alternative (if it exists) preceeding the *do* predicate.
For example, given

```
    p:-q,r,do,s.
    q.
    q:- qbody.
    r.
    s:-t,undo.
    s.
    t:- ... .
?-p.
```

after executing *undo*, control is passed to the second clause of the procedure *q*.
Predicate *qbody* can be defined for example as:

```
qbody :- undoing,q.
```

where *undoing* is another new built-in which is true iff an *undo* has been executed but a subsequent *do* has not yet (it allows normal backtracking to be distinguished from backtracking due to an *undo*). In this case the final result is re-executing the piece of program between *do* and *undo* in the very same way.
Predicate qbody could contain also another *undo*. Nesting of *undo* allows a whole computation to be redone backward.

The *do-undo* mechanism has been used in D_Prose to implement an undo facility which allows the user to undo any previous request to the debugger, redoing the computation again if needed.

With these facilities and with few other primitive mechanisms it is possible to build powerful debugging tools directly in Env_Prolog, in the way one likes more, without having to relay upon decisions already made and frozen within the interpreter. At present, D_Prose provides only facilities for tracing program execution like those provided by the C_Prolog debugger, but more sophisticated facilities and user interfaces are planned for the future and should be easily implemented in Env_Prolog.

7. Future work

The implementation of I_Prose has been completed at present and it needs to be extensively tested. It runs on VAX 780 and SUN under Unix 4.2 and its performance is almost the same as that of (interpreted) C_Prolog. For the near future we have planned to build also a compiler for Env_Prolog based on the WAM. The main purpose of this should not be to obtain better performance than with the interpreter, rather to experiment with the implementation of the new facilities Env_Prolog supplies in the framework of the now standard WAM.

The implementation of E_Prose and D_Prose using Env_Prolog has to be completed in few weeks (at present only simplified prototypical implementations are available). Some other tools to be integrated in the PROSE environment are under development at present. Namely, a partial evaluator, a type checker and a user interface.

PROSE will be used also to host the tools for the construction of knowledge based systems we are developing in a parallel project [14].

Another interesting problem we have planned to face in PROSE is the support of the notion of *program library*. It requires to tackle problems like those of visibility and protection of predicates, efficient loading and restoring of library procedures, etc. (see for example [6] and [7] p. 161). The notion of "module" of Env_Prolog should be used advantageously to face these problems.

Acknowledgments

We wish to thank all people who have contributed to the development of PROSE and in particular L.Arcostanzo, W.Manassero and G.Schmitz for their effective contribution to the implementation of I_Prose.
This work has been partially supported by MPI 40% project ASSI.

References

[1] J.Bendl, P.Koves, P.Szeredi: The MProlog System; in Proc. of the Logic Programming Workshop, (S-A.Tarlund ed.) Hungary, July 1980.
[2] K.A. Bowen and R.A. Kowalski: Amalgamating language and meta- language in logic programming; in Logic Programming, (K.L.Clark and S-A.Tarlund, Eds), Academic Press, 1982, 153-172.
[3] A.Colmerauer: Prolog and Infinite Trees; in Logic Programming, (K.L.Clark and S-A.Tarlund, Eds), Academic Press, 1982.
[4] W.F.Clocksin and C.S.Mellish: Programming in Prolog, Springer Verlag, Berlin 1981.
[5] N.Francez et al.: An Environment for Logic Programming; in Proc. of the ACM Sigplan Symp. on Languages Issues in Programming Environments; Seattle, June 1985, 179-190.
[6] A.Feuer: Building Libraries in Prolog; AAAI-83, August 1983, pp. 550-552.
[7] Kluzniak, Swpakozicw: Prolog for programmers; Academic Press, 1985.
[8] A.Martelli and U.Montanari: An Efficient Unification Algorithm; ACM TOPLAS, 4,2, April 1982.
[9] A.Martelli and G.F.Rossi: Efficient Unification with Infinite Terms in Logic Programming; in Proc. of FGCS84: International Conf. on Fifth Generation Computer Systems, Japan, 1984.
[10] A.Martelli and G.F.Rossi: Toward a Prolog Programming Support Environment (in italian); Proc. of the First National Conference on Logic Programming, Genova, March 1986.
[11] A.Martelli and G.F.Rossi: On the Semantics of Logic Programming Languages; in Proc of the 3rd Conf. on Logic Programming, London, July 1981.
[12] C.S.Mellish: An Alternative to Structure Sharing in the Implementation of a Prolog Interpreter; in Logic Programming, (K.L.Clark and S-A.Tarlund, Eds), Academic Press, 1982, 99-106.
[13] A.Martelli and G.F.Rossi: PROSE: a Prolog Support Environment (in italian); Proc. of the Second National Conference on Logic Programming, Turin, May 1987.
[14] L.Console and G.F.Rossi: FROG: a Prolog-based system for Prolog-based knowledge representation; in Artificial Intelligence and Information-Control Systems of Robots-87, (I.Plander, ed.), North-Holland, 1987,179-183.
[15] C-Prolog User's Manual - Version 1.5; edited by F.Pereira, Technical Rept. 82/11, Edinburgh Computer Aided Architectural Design, Univ. of Edinburgh, February 1984.
[16] A.Martelli and G.F.Rossi: An implementation of unification with infinite terms and its application to logic programming languages; Technical Rept., Dipartimento di Informatica, Univ. di Torino, 1987.
[17] F.Fages: Formes canoniques dans les algebres booleennes et applcations a la demonstration automatique; These de 3eme Cycle, Universite Paris VI, June 1983.

2-level λ-lifting

Flemming Nielson * Hanne R. Nielson †

Abstract

The process of λ-lifting (or bracket abstraction) translates expressions in a typed λ-calculus into expressions in a typed combinator language. This is of interest because it shows that the λ-calculus and the combinator language are equally expressive (as the translation from combinators to λ-expressions is rather trivial). This paper studies the similar problems for 2-level λ-calculi and 2-level combinator languages. The 2-level nature of the type system enforces a formal distinction between binding times, e.g. between computations at compile-time and computations at run-time. In this setting the natural formulations of 2-level λ-calculi and 2-level combinator languages turn out *not* to be equally expressive. The translation into 2-level λ-calculus is straight-forward but the 2-level λ-calculus is too powerful for λ-lifting to succeed. We then develop a restriction of the 2-level λ-calculus for which λ-lifting succeeds and that is as expressive as the 2-level combinator language.

1 Introduction

Modern functional languages are often built as enrichments of the λ-calculus. In the implementation of these languages various forms of combinators are useful, e.g. [15,16,3]. The success of this is due to the process of λ-lifting (or bracket abstraction) that allows to eliminate variables of a λ-expression thereby turning it into a combinator expression. The techniques used build on results developed by [13,2] and a recent exposition of the ideas may be found in [1]. The approach is equally applicable to typed and untyped languages and in this paper we shall only study the typed case. Following [1] we shall consider a type system with types t given by

$$t ::= A_i \mid t \times t \mid t \rightarrow t$$

where the A_i (for $i \in I$) are certain base types, $t \times t$ is the product type and $t \rightarrow t$ is the function type. It is possible also to add sum types and recursive types but for lack of space we shall not do so.

The distinction between compile-time and run-time is important for the efficient implementation of programming languages. In our previous work [10,11] we have made this distinction explicit by imposing a 2-level structure on the typed λ-calculus. The types tt will then be given by

$$tt ::= \overline{A}_i \mid \underline{A}_i \mid tt \mathbin{\overline{\times}} tt \mid tt \mathbin{\underline{\times}} tt \mid tt \mathbin{\overline{\rightarrow}} tt \mid tt \mathbin{\underline{\rightarrow}} tt$$

The essential intuition will be that objects of type $tt \mathbin{\overline{\rightarrow}} tt$ are to be evaluated at compile-time whereas objects of type $tt \mathbin{\underline{\rightarrow}} tt$ are to be evaluated at run-time. So from the point of view of the compiler it must perform the computations of type $tt \mathbin{\overline{\rightarrow}} tt$ and generate code for those of type $tt \mathbin{\underline{\rightarrow}} tt$.

A similar distinction is made for the expressions by having two copies of the λ-notation. So we shall e.g. have a λ-abstraction $\overline{\lambda} x_i[tt]\ldots$ for building functions of type $tt \mathbin{\overline{\rightarrow}} tt'$ and another

*Department of Computer Science, The Technical University of Denmark, DK-2800 Lyngby, Denmark.
†Department of Mathematics and Computer Science, AUC, Strandvejen 19, DK-9000 Aalborg, Denmark.

λ-abstraction $\underline{\lambda} x_i[tt]$.... for building functions of type tt $\underline{\rightarrow}$ tt'. The idea is here that we want the compiler to generate code for the functions specified by $\underline{\lambda}$-abstractions whereas those specified by $\overline{\lambda}$-abstractions should be interpreted at compile-time. Thus we shall be interested in transforming the λ-calculus specifying run-time computations into combinator form while leaving the λ-calculus for the compile-time computations untouched. This process will be called 2-level λ-lifting (as we do not want to distinguish inherently between combinators and supercombinators [4]).

Let us illustrate the approach by an example. In the λ-calculus the function select returning the n'th element of a list l may be defined by

$$\text{select} \equiv \text{fix}\ (\lambda S.\ \lambda n.\ \lambda l.\ (=\cdot\ 1\cdot\ n) \rightarrow (\text{hd}\cdot\ l),\ (S\cdot\ (-\cdot\ n\cdot\ 1)\cdot\ (\text{tl}\cdot\ l)))$$

Assume now that the first parameter always will be known at compile-time and that the second will not be known until run-time. In [11] we give an algorithm that will transform select into

$$\text{select'} \equiv \overline{\text{fix}}(\overline{\lambda} S.\ \overline{\lambda} n.\ \underline{\lambda} l.(=\overline{\cdot}\ 1\overline{\cdot}\ n) \overline{\rightarrow} (\text{hd}\underline{\cdot}\ l),(S\overline{\cdot}\ (-\overline{\cdot}\ n\overline{\cdot}\ 1)\underline{\cdot}\ (\text{tl}\underline{\cdot}\ l)))$$

where again overlining indicates that the computations are performed at compile-time and underlining that they are performed at run-time. The purpose of the 2-level λ-lifting will be to get rid of the variable l but to keep S and n since they will be bound at compile-time. So we shall aim at an expression like

$$\text{select"} \equiv \overline{\text{fix}}(\overline{\lambda} S.\ \overline{\lambda} n.\ (=\overline{\cdot}\ 1\overline{\cdot}\ n) \overline{\rightarrow} \text{hd},(S\overline{\cdot}\ (-\overline{\cdot}\ n\overline{\cdot}\ 1))\ \Box\ \text{tl})$$

where $\Box$ denotes functional composition at the run-time level.

In our previous work we have studied the efficient implementation of two-level functional languages where the compile-time actions are expressed in λ-notation and the run-time actions in combinator notation. In [8] we show how to generate code for abstract machines based on the von Neumann architecture and in [6,9] we study the application of data flow analyses within the framework of abstract interpretation. The present paper can therefore be seen as filling in the gap between these results and the techniques of [10,11] for imposing a 2-level structure on λ-expressions. Finally, the algorithms presented in this paper have been implemented in a test bed system designed to experiment with various ideas related to 2-level functional languages.

2 Review of the 1-level case

As an introduction to our approach to 2-level λ-lifting we first review the usual concept of λ-lifting (or bracket abstraction). This does not add much to the explanations given in [1] but allows us to fix our notation by means of the familiar case.

First we define the typed λ-calculus DML_e that has the types

$$t ::= A_i \mid t \times t \mid t \rightarrow t$$

and expressions

$$e ::= f_i[t] \mid (e,e) \mid e \downarrow j \mid \lambda x_i[t].e \mid e \cdot e \mid x_i \mid \text{fix } e \mid e \rightarrow e\ ,\ e$$

Here the $f_i[t]$ (for $i \in I$) are constants of the type indicated. Next we have pairing, projection, λ-abstraction, application, variable, fixed point and conditional. As we are in a typed language these expressions are subject to certain well-formedness conditions. The well-formedness predicate has the form tenv $\vdash$ e:t where tenv is a type environment (i.e. a map from a finite set of variables to types) and says that e has type t. It is defined by

$$\text{tenv} \vdash f_i[t]{:}t$$

$$\frac{\text{tenv} \vdash e_1{:}t_1,\ \text{tenv} \vdash e_2{:}t_2}{\text{tenv} \vdash (e_1,e_2){:}t_1 \times t_2}$$

$$\frac{\text{tenv} \vdash e{:}t_1 \times t_2}{\text{tenv} \vdash e \downarrow j{:}t_j} \qquad \text{if } j = 1,2$$

$$\frac{\text{tenv}[x_i \mapsto t] \vdash e{:}t'}{\text{tenv} \vdash \lambda x_i[t].e{:}t \rightarrow t'}$$

$$\frac{\text{tenv} \vdash e_1{:}t' \rightarrow t,\ \text{tenv} \vdash e_2{:}t'}{\text{tenv} \vdash e_1 \cdot e_2{:}t}$$

$$\text{tenv} \vdash x_i{:}t \qquad \text{if tenv}(x_i) = t$$

$$\frac{\text{tenv} \vdash e{:}t \rightarrow t}{\text{tenv} \vdash \text{fix } e{:}t}$$

$$\frac{\text{tenv} \vdash e{:}A_{\text{bool}},\ \text{tenv} \vdash e_1{:}t,\ \text{tenv} \vdash e_2{:}t}{\text{tenv} \vdash e \rightarrow e_1,e_2{:}t}$$

Fact 1 Expressions are uniquely typed, i.e. if tenv $\vdash$ e:t_1 and tenv $\vdash$ e:t_2 then $t_1 = t_2$. □

The proof is by induction on the inference of tenv $\vdash$ e:t_1 and $t_1 = t_2$ means that the types are syntactically equal.

In a similar way we define the typed combinator language DML_m. It has types

$$t ::= A_i \mid t \times t \mid t \rightarrow t$$

and expressions

$$e ::= f_i[t] \mid \text{tuple}(e,e) \mid \text{take}_j[t] \mid \text{curry } e \mid \text{apply}[t] \mid e \,\square\, e \mid \text{fix}[t] \mid \text{cond}(e,e,e) \mid \text{const}[t]\ e \mid \text{id}[t]$$

Here tuple and take_j relate to the product type and the intention is that tuple(f,g)(v) is (f(v),g(v)) and $\text{take}_j[t](v_1,v_2)$ is v_j. For the function space we have curry and apply and here curry(f)(u)(v) is f(u,v) and apply[t](f,v) is f(v). Function composition is denoted by □, fix[t] is the fixed point operator and the intended meaning of the conditional is that cond(f,g,h)(v) is g(v) if f(v) holds and otherwise h(v). Finally const[t] ignores one of its arguments so const[t](f)(v) is f and id[t] is the identity function.

The well-formedness predicate has the form $\vdash$ e:t and is defined by

$$\vdash f_i[t]{:}t$$

$$\frac{\vdash e_1{:}t \rightarrow t_1,\ \vdash e_2{:}t \rightarrow t_2}{\vdash \text{tuple}(e_1,e_2){:}t \rightarrow (t_1 \times t_2)}$$

$$\vdash \text{take}_j[t]{:}t \rightarrow t_j \qquad \text{if } t = t_1 \times t_2 \text{ and } j=1,2$$

$$\frac{\vdash e{:}(t_1 \times t_2) \rightarrow t_3}{\vdash \text{curry } e{:}t_1 \rightarrow (t_2 \rightarrow t_3)}$$

$$\vdash \text{apply}[t]{:}((t_1 \rightarrow t_2) \times t_1) \rightarrow t_2 \qquad \text{if } t = t_1 \rightarrow t_2$$

$$\frac{\vdash e_1{:}t_2 \rightarrow t_3,\ \vdash e_2{:}t_1 \rightarrow t_2}{\vdash e_1 \,\square\, e_2{:}t_1 \rightarrow t_3}$$

$$\vdash \text{fix}[t]{:}(t \rightarrow t) \rightarrow t$$

$$\frac{\vdash e_1{:}t \rightarrow A_{\text{bool}},\ \vdash e_2{:}t \rightarrow t',\ \vdash e_3{:}t \rightarrow t'}{\vdash \text{cond}(e_1,e_2,e_3){:}t \rightarrow t'}$$

$$\frac{\vdash e{:}t'}{\vdash \text{const}[t]\ e{:}t \rightarrow t'}$$

$$\vdash \text{id}[t]{:}t \rightarrow t$$

We have added sufficient type information to the combinators that we have the following analogue of Fact 1:

Fact 2 Expressions are uniquely typed, i.e. if $\vdash$ e:t_1 and $\vdash$ e:t_2 then $t_1 = t_2$. □

From a pragmatic point of view one might consider to constrain the type t of a constant $f_i[t]$ to be of the form $t_1 \rightarrow t_2$. We shall not do so as for the subsequent development to make sense we would either have to impose a similar constraint on constants of DML_e or else we should change the functionality of constants in the transformation to follow.

We now turn to the relationship between DML_e and DML_m. The transformation from DML_m to DML_e amounts to the expansion of the combinators into λ-expressions. A minor complication is that not all the necessary type information is explicitly present and we shall rely on Fact 2 in order to obtain it. We therefore formulate the process as the definition of a function

$$\varepsilon\colon \{\, e \in DML_m \mid \exists t.\ \vdash e{:}t \,\} \rightarrow \{\, e \mid e \in DML_e \,\}$$

by means of the following equations which merely restate the intuitions about the combinators tuple, $take_j[t]$ etc. in a formal way:

$$\varepsilon[\![f_i[t]]\!] = f_i[t]$$

$$\varepsilon[\![tuple(e_1, e_2)]\!] = \lambda x_a[t].\ (\varepsilon[\![e_1]\!]\cdot x_a, \varepsilon[\![e_2]\!]\cdot x_a) \qquad \text{where} \vdash e_1{:}t \rightarrow t_1$$

$$\varepsilon[\![take_j[t]]\!] = \lambda x_a[t].\ x_a \downarrow j$$

$$\varepsilon[\![curry\ e]\!] = \lambda x_a[t_1].\ \lambda x_b[t_2].\ \varepsilon[\![e]\!]\cdot (x_a, x_b) \qquad \text{where} \vdash e{:}\ (t_1 \times t_2) \rightarrow t$$

$$\varepsilon[\![apply\ [t]]\!] = \lambda x_a[(t_1 \rightarrow t_2) \times t_1].\ (x_a \downarrow 1)\cdot (x_a \downarrow 2) \qquad \text{where } t = t_1 \rightarrow t_2$$

$$\varepsilon[\![e_1 \square e_2]\!] = \lambda x_a[t].\ \varepsilon[\![e_1]\!]\cdot (\varepsilon[\![e_2]\!]\cdot x_a) \qquad \text{where} \vdash e_2{:}t \rightarrow t'$$

$$\varepsilon[\![fix[t]]\!] = \lambda x_a[t \rightarrow t].\ fix\ x_a$$

$$\varepsilon[\![cond(e_1, e_2, e_3)]\!] = \lambda x_a[t].\ \varepsilon[\![e_1]\!]\cdot x_a \rightarrow \varepsilon[\![e_2]\!]\cdot x_a, \varepsilon[\![e_3]\!]\cdot x_a \qquad \text{where} \vdash e_1{:}\ t \rightarrow A_{bool}$$

$$\varepsilon[\![const[t]\ e]\!] = \lambda x_a[t].\ \varepsilon[\![e]\!]$$

$$\varepsilon[\![id[t]]\!] = \lambda x_a[t].\ x_a$$

To see that this is a correct translation we note that

Fact 3 The transformation ε preserves the types of expressions, i.e. if $\vdash$ e:t then $\emptyset \vdash \varepsilon[\![e]\!]$:t. □

where $\emptyset$ denotes the empty type environment. Hopefully it is intuitively clear that it also preserves the semantics. If we were to be formal about this we could define reduction rules for DML_e and DML_m and use this as a basis for relating the semantics (see [1]). Alternatively, we could define a denotational semantics with a suitable notion of interpretation of the primitives (along the lines of [8,9]). However, we shall not pursue this further here.

Concerning the translation from DML_e to DML_m we consider an expression e of DML_e that has type t, i.e. that satisfies tenv $\vdash$ e:t. Assuming that tenv has a nonempty domain $\{x_1, \cdots, x_n\}$ and maps x_i to t_i the type of the translated term will be of the form $(\cdots(t_1 \times t_2) \times t_3 \cdots \times t_n) \rightarrow t$. To make this precise we shall let a *position environment* penv be a list of pairs of variables and types. The underlying type environment then is

$$\rho(penv) = \lambda x_i. \begin{cases} \text{undefined} & \text{if no } penv{\downarrow}j{\downarrow}1 \text{ is } x_i \\ penv{\downarrow}j{\downarrow}2 & \text{if } j \text{ is minimal s.t. } penv{\downarrow}j{\downarrow}1 \text{ is } x_i \end{cases}$$

and the product of the variable types is

$$\Pi(penv) = \begin{cases} \text{undefined} & \text{if } penv = () \\ t & \text{if } penv = ((x,t)) \\ \Pi(penv') \times t & \text{if } penv = ((x,t))\hat{\ }penv' \end{cases}$$

So if penv is $((x_1,A_1)(x_2,A_2)(x_3,A_3))$ then ρ(penv) maps x_i to A_i and Π(penv) is $(A_3 \times A_2)\times A_1$. The intention is that the transformed version $\Lambda^{\text{penv}}[\![e]\!]$ has type $\Pi(\text{penv}) \rightarrow t$ whenever $\rho(\text{penv}) \vdash e{:}t$. We shall not allow the case where penv = () and so if $\emptyset \vdash e{:}t$ we must artificially add a dummy variable and a dummy type. (This is in line with [1] but we shall need to be more careful when we come to 2-level λ-lifting!) To assist in the definition of Λ^{penv} we need the function

$$\pi_j^{\text{penv}} = \begin{cases} \text{undefined} & \text{if no penv}\downarrow j\downarrow 1 \text{ is } x_j \\ \text{id}[\Pi(\text{penv})] & \text{if penv} = ((x_j,t)) \\ \text{take}_2[\Pi(\text{penv})] & \text{if penv} = ((x_j,t))\hat{\ }\text{penv'} \\ \pi_j^{\text{penv'}} \,\Box\, \text{take}_1[\Pi(\text{penv})] & \text{if penv} = ((x_i,t))\hat{\ }\text{penv' and } i \neq j \end{cases}$$

for locating the component in Π(penv) that corresponds to x_j. For the example above we have

$$\pi_1^{\text{penv}} = \text{take}_2[(A_3 \times A_2)\times A_1],$$
$$\pi_2^{\text{penv}} = \text{take}_2[A_3 \times A_2] \,\Box\, \text{take}_1[(A_3 \times A_2)\times A_1]$$
$$\pi_3^{\text{penv}} = \text{id}[A_3] \,\Box\, \text{take}_1[A_3 \times A_2] \,\Box\, \text{take}_1[(A_3 \times A_2) \times A_1]$$

In analogy with the definition of ε we shall use Fact 1 to define a function

$$\Lambda^{\text{penv}}\colon \{ e \in \text{DML}_e \mid \exists t.\ \rho(\text{penv}) \vdash e{:}t \} \rightarrow \{ e \mid e \in \text{DML}_m \}$$

whenever penv $\neq$ () by

$$\Lambda^{\text{penv}}\ [\![f_i[t]]\!] = \text{const}[\Pi(\text{penv})]\ f_i[t]$$

$$\Lambda^{\text{penv}}\ [\![(e_1,\ e_2)]\!] = \text{tuple}(\Lambda^{\text{penv}}\ [\![e_1]\!],\ \Lambda^{\text{penv}}\ [\![e_2]\!])$$

$$\Lambda^{\text{penv}}\ [\![e\downarrow j]\!] = \text{take}_j[t] \,\Box\, \Lambda^{\text{penv}}\ [\![e]\!] \quad \text{where } \rho(\text{penv}) \vdash e{:}t$$

$$\Lambda^{\text{penv}}\ [\![\lambda x_i[t].e]\!] = \text{curry}\ \Lambda^{((x_i,t))\hat{\ }\text{penv}}\ [\![e]\!]$$

$$\Lambda^{\text{penv}}\ [\![e_1 \cdot e_2]\!] = \text{apply}\ [t_1\rightarrow t_2] \,\Box\, \text{tuple}(\Lambda^{\text{penv}}\ [\![e_1]\!],\ \Lambda^{\text{penv}}\ [\![e_2]\!]) \qquad \text{where } \rho(\text{penv}) \vdash e_1{:}t_1\rightarrow t_2$$

$$\Lambda^{\text{penv}}\ [\![x_i]\!] = \pi_i^{\text{penv}}$$

$$\Lambda^{\text{penv}}\ [\![\text{fix } e]\!] = \text{fix}[t] \,\Box\, \Lambda^{\text{penv}}\ [\![e]\!] \quad \text{where } \rho(\text{penv}) \vdash e{:}t \rightarrow t$$

$$\Lambda^{\text{penv}}\ [\![e_1 \rightarrow\ e_2,\ e_3]\!] = \text{cond}(\Lambda^{\text{penv}}\ [\![e_1]\!],\ \Lambda^{\text{penv}}\ [\![e_2]\!],\ \Lambda^{\text{penv}}\ [\![e_3]\!])$$

That this is a well-behaved definition that lives up to the claims is expressed by

Fact 4 If penv $\neq$ () and $\rho(\text{penv}) \vdash e{:}t$ then $\vdash \Lambda^{\text{penv}}\ [\![e]\!]{:}\Pi(\text{penv}) \rightarrow t$. □

Hopefully, it is also intuitively clear that Λ^{penv} preserves the semantics and as above we shall not be more formal about this. Because of the lack of space we must refer to any standard textbook, e.g. [1], for examples of the translation.

3 2-level λ-calculi and combinator languages

After the above review we can now approach 2-level λ-lifting. In the 2-level notations we replace the type system of the previous section with

$$tt ::= \overline{A}_i \mid \underline{A}_i \mid tt \mathbin{\overline{\times}} tt \mid tt \mathbin{\underline{\times}} tt \mid tt \mathbin{\overline{\rightarrow}} tt \mid tt \mathbin{\underline{\rightarrow}} tt$$

as was already mentioned in the Introduction. Here overlining is used to indicate early binding and our prime example of this is compile-time and similarly underlining is used to indicate late binding and here the prime example is run-time. The considerations of compile-time versus run-time motivate defining the following well-formedness predicate $\vdash tt{:}k$ for when a type tt is well-formed of kind $k \in \{c,r\}$. Clearly c will correspond to compile-time and r to run-time. The definition is

tt	$\vdash$ tt:c	$\vdash$ tt:r
$\overline{A}_i$	true	false
$\underline{A}_i$	false	true
$tt_1 \mathbin{\overline{\times}} tt_2$	$\vdash tt_1{:}c \wedge \vdash tt_2{:}c$	false
$tt_1 \mathbin{\underline{\times}} tt_2$	false	$\vdash tt_1{:}r \wedge \vdash tt_2{:}r$
$tt_1 \mathbin{\overline{\Rightarrow}} tt_2$	$\vdash tt_1{:}c \wedge \vdash tt_2{:}c$	false
$tt_1 \mathbin{\underline{\rightarrow}} tt_2$	$\vdash tt_1{:}r \wedge \vdash tt_2{:}r$	$\vdash tt_1{:}r \wedge \vdash tt_2{:}r$

Here no compile-time types can be embedded in run-time types; this is motivated by the fact that compile-time takes place before run-time. A run-time type of the form $tt_1 \mathbin{\underline{\rightarrow}} tt_2$ is also a compile-time type; this is motivated by the fact that a compiler may manipulate code (and code corresponds to run-time computations) but not the actual values that arise at run-time. One may of course consider variations in this definition but the present definition has been found useful for abstract interpretation and code generation [6,8].

The idea with the 2-level notations is that we have a choice of using λ-expressions or combinators at the compile-time level and a similar choice at the run-time level. This gives a total of four languages but we shall restrict ourselves to the case where we always use λ-expressions at the compile-time level. The notation where we use λ-expressions at both levels will be called TML_e and has expressions given by

$$\begin{array}{lllllllll} te ::= & f_i[tt] \mid & x_i \mid & \overline{(te,\ te)} \mid & te \mathbin{\overline{\downarrow}} j \mid & \overline{\lambda} x_i[tt].te \mid & te \mathbin{\overline{\cdot}} te \mid & \overline{\text{fix}}\ te \mid & te \mathbin{\overline{\Rightarrow}} te,\ te \\ & & \mid & \underline{(te,\ te)} \mid & te \mathbin{\underline{\downarrow}} j \mid & \underline{\lambda} x_i[tt].te \mid & te \mathbin{\underline{\cdot}} te \mid & \underline{\text{fix}}\ te \mid & te \mathbin{\underline{\rightarrow}} te,\ te \end{array}$$

Again overlining is used for the compile-time level and underlining is used for the run-time level. For the well-formedness predicate we propose the following generalization of the one for DML_e. The form of the predicate is tenv $\vdash$ te:tt and the definition is

$$\text{tenv} \vdash f_i[tt]{:}tt \qquad \text{if } \exists k.\ \vdash tt{:}k$$

$$\text{tenv} \vdash x_i{:}tt \qquad \text{if } \text{tenv}(x_i) = tt \text{ and } \exists k.\ \vdash tt{:}k$$

$$\frac{\text{tenv} \vdash te_1{:}tt_1,\ \text{tenv} \vdash te_2{:}tt_2}{\text{tenv} \vdash \overline{(te_1,\ te_2)}{:}tt_1 \mathbin{\overline{\times}} tt_2} \qquad \text{if } \vdash tt_1{:}c \text{ and } \vdash tt_2{:}c$$

$$\frac{\text{tenv} \vdash te{:}tt_1 \mathbin{\overline{\times}} tt_2}{\text{tenv} \vdash te \mathbin{\overline{\downarrow}} j{:}tt_j} \qquad \text{if } j = 1,2$$

$$\frac{\text{tenv}[x_i \mapsto tt] \vdash te{:}tt'}{\text{tenv} \vdash \overline{\lambda} x_i[tt].te{:}tt \mathbin{\overline{\Rightarrow}} tt'} \qquad \text{if } \vdash tt{:}c \text{ and } \vdash tt'{:}c$$

$$\frac{\text{tenv} \vdash te_1{:}tt' \mathbin{\overline{\Rightarrow}} tt,\ \text{tenv} \vdash te_2{:}tt'}{\text{tenv} \vdash te_1 \mathbin{\overline{\cdot}} te_2{:}tt}$$

$$\frac{\text{tenv} \vdash te{:}tt \mathbin{\overline{\Rightarrow}} tt}{\text{tenv} \vdash \overline{\text{fix}}\ te{:}tt}$$

$$\frac{\text{tenv} \vdash te{:}\overline{A}_{bool},\ \text{tenv} \vdash te_1{:}tt,\ \text{tenv} \vdash te_2{:}tt}{\text{tenv} \vdash te \mathbin{\overline{\Rightarrow}} te_1,\ te_2{:}tt}$$

$$\frac{\text{tenv} \vdash te_1{:}tt_1,\ \text{tenv} \vdash te_2{:}tt_2}{\text{tenv} \vdash \underline{(te_1,\ te_2)}{:}tt_1 \mathbin{\underline{\times}} tt_2} \qquad \text{if } \vdash tt_1{:}r \text{ and } \vdash tt_2{:}r$$

$$\frac{\text{tenv} \vdash te{:}tt_1 \mathbin{\underline{\times}} tt_2}{\text{tenv} \vdash te \mathbin{\underline{\downarrow}} j{:}tt_j} \qquad \text{if } j = 1,2$$

$$\frac{tenv[x_i \mapsto tt] \vdash te:tt'}{tenv \vdash \underline{\lambda} x_i[tt].te:tt \underline{\rightarrow} tt'} \quad \text{if } \vdash tt:r \text{ and } \vdash tt':r$$

$$\frac{tenv \vdash te_1:tt' \underline{\rightarrow} tt,\ tenv \vdash te_2:tt'}{tenv \vdash te_1 \ \underline{:}\ te_2:tt}$$

$$\frac{tenv \vdash te:tt \underline{\rightarrow} tt}{tenv \vdash \underline{fix}\ te:tt}$$

$$\frac{tenv \vdash te:\underline{A}_{bool},\ tenv \vdash te_1:tt,\ tenv \vdash te_2:tt}{tenv \vdash te \underline{\rightarrow} te_1,\ te_2:tt}$$

With respect to the rules for DML_e one may note that essentially we have two copies of these but we need to add additional side conditions of the form ⊢ tt:k in order for the constructed types to be well-formed. From an intuitive point of view it is unclear whether one should add the constraint that ⊢ tt:r in the rule for te $\underline{\rightarrow}$ te, te; however, in Section 4 we shall see a formal reason for imposing this constraint. We have

Fact 5 Expressions have well-formed types, i.e. if tenv ⊢ te:tt then ∃k. ⊢ tt:k. □

and in analogy with Fact 1 we also have

Fact 6 Expressions are uniquely typed, i.e. if tenv ⊢ te:tt_1 and tenv ⊢ te:tt_2 then $tt_1 = tt_2$. □

Furthermore we claim that TML_e is a natural analogue of DML_e but for the 2-level case. Clearly one can translate an expression in TML_e into one in DML_e (by removing all underlining and overlining) and it is shown in [10,11] that it is also possible to translate expressions in DML_e into TML_e.

Another 2-level notation is TML_m where we use combinators at the run-time level. The types tt are as above and so is the well-formedness predicate for types. For expressions the syntax is

$$\begin{aligned} te ::= {} & f_i[tt] \mid x_i \mid \overline{(te, te)} \mid te\ \overline{\downarrow j} \mid \overline{\lambda} x_i[tt].te \mid te\ \overline{\cdot}\ te \mid \overline{fix}\ te \mid te \overline{\Rightarrow} te, te \\ & \mid \underline{tuple}(te,te) \mid \underline{take_j}[tt] \mid \underline{curry}\ te \mid \underline{apply}[tt] \mid te \,\square\, te \\ & \mid \underline{fix}\ te \mid \underline{cond}(te,te,te) \mid \underline{const}[tt]\ te \mid \underline{id}[tt] \end{aligned}$$

The well-formedness predicate has the form tenv ⊢ te:tt and is defined by

$$\left.\begin{array}{l} tenv \vdash f_i[tt]:tt \quad \text{if } \exists k.\ \vdash tt:k \\ \quad\vdots \\ \dfrac{tenv \vdash te:\overline{A}_{bool},\ tenv \vdash te_1:tt,\ tenv \vdash te_2:tt}{tenv \vdash te \overline{\Rightarrow} te_1,\ te_2:tt} \end{array}\right\} \text{as above}$$

$$\frac{tenv \vdash te_1:tt \underline{\rightarrow} tt_1,\ tenv \vdash te_2:tt \underline{\rightarrow} tt_2}{tenv \vdash \underline{tuple}(te_1,te_2):tt \underline{\rightarrow} (tt_1 \underline{\times} tt_2)}$$

$$tenv \vdash \underline{take_j}[tt]:tt \underline{\rightarrow} tt_j \quad \text{if } \vdash tt:r \text{ and } tt = tt_1 \underline{\times} tt_2 \text{ and } j=1,2$$

$$\frac{tenv \vdash te:(tt_1 \underline{\times} tt_2) \underline{\rightarrow} tt_3}{tenv \vdash \underline{curry}\ te:tt_1 \underline{\rightarrow} (tt_2 \underline{\rightarrow} tt_3)}$$

$$tenv \vdash \underline{apply}[tt]:((tt_1 \underline{\rightarrow} tt_2) \underline{\times} tt_1) \underline{\rightarrow} tt_2 \quad \text{if } \vdash tt:r \text{ and } tt = tt_1 \underline{\rightarrow} tt_2$$

$$\frac{tenv \vdash te_1:tt_2 \underline{\rightarrow} tt_3,\ tenv \vdash te_2:tt_1 \underline{\rightarrow} tt_2}{tenv \vdash te_1 \,\square\, te_2:tt_1 \underline{\rightarrow} tt_3}$$

$$tenv \vdash \underline{fix}[tt]:(tt \underline{\rightarrow} tt) \underline{\rightarrow} tt \quad \text{if } \vdash tt:r$$

$$\frac{tenv \vdash te_1:tt \underline{\rightarrow} A_{bool},\ tenv \vdash te_2:tt \underline{\rightarrow} tt',\ tenv \vdash te_3:tt \underline{\rightarrow} tt'}{tenv \vdash \underline{cond}(te_1,te_2,te_3):tt \underline{\rightarrow} tt'}$$

$$\frac{\text{tenv} \vdash \text{te:tt'}}{\text{tenv} \vdash \underline{\text{const}}[\text{tt}]\ \text{te:tt} \underline{\rightarrow} \text{tt'}} \quad \text{if} \vdash \text{tt:r and} \vdash \text{tt':r}$$

$$\text{tenv} \vdash \underline{\text{id}}[\text{tt}]\text{:tt} \underline{\rightarrow} \text{tt} \quad \text{if} \vdash \text{tt:r}$$

The rules for well-formedness of the top-level terms are as in TML_e. In particular we do not constrain the types tt of the constants $f_i[tt]$ although it might seem unfit to have constants of run-time types that are not function types. (However, one may introduce the constraint $\vdash$ tt:c if desired and if also the type tt of a conditional $te_1 \overline{\Rightarrow} te_2,te_3$ is constrained in this way then TML_m would be a subset of the language considered in [8].) In analogy with the results for TML_e we have

Fact 7 Expressions have well-formed types, i.e. if tenv $\vdash$ te:tt then $\exists$k. $\vdash$ tt:k. □

Fact 8 Expressions are uniquely typed, i.e. if tenv $\vdash$ te:tt_1 and tenv $\vdash$ te:tt_2 then $tt_1 = tt_2$. □

As in the case of DML_e and DML_m the expansion of combinators is rather straight-forward. So we define a function

$$\varepsilon_{tenv}\text{: } \{ \text{ te} \in TML_m \mid \exists\text{tt. tenv} \vdash \text{te:tt } \} \rightarrow \{ \text{ te} \mid \text{ te} \in TML_e \}$$

for each type environment tenv. We need the type environment because we shall rely on Fact 8 in order to infer missing type information (just as we used Fact 2 in the 1-level case). The definition is

ε_{tenv} $[\![f_i[tt]]\!]$= $f_i[tt]$

ε_{tenv} $[\![x_i]\!]$= x_i

ε_{tenv} $[\![\overline{(}te_1,\ te_2\ \overline{)}]\!]$= $\overline{(}\varepsilon_{tenv}$ $[\![te_1]\!]$, ε_{tenv} $[\![te_2]\!]\overline{)}$

ε_{tenv} $[\![te\overline{\downarrow}\ j]\!]$= ε_{tenv} $[\![te]\!]\overline{\downarrow}$ j

ε_{tenv} $[\![\overline{\lambda}x_i[tt].te]\!]$= $\overline{\lambda}x_i[tt]$. $\varepsilon_{tenv[x_i \mapsto tt]}$ $[\![te]\!]$

ε_{tenv} $[\![te_1\ \bar{:}\ te_2]\!]$= ε_{tenv} $[\![te_1]\!]\bar{:}$ ε_{tenv} $[\![te_2]\!]$

ε_{tenv} $[\![\overline{\text{fix}}\ te]\!]$= $\overline{\text{fix}}$ ε_{tenv} $[\![te]\!]$

ε_{tenv} $[\![te_1 \overline{\Rightarrow} te_2,\ te_3]\!]$= ε_{tenv} $[\![te_1]\!]$ $\overline{\Rightarrow}$ ε_{tenv} $[\![te_2]\!]$, ε_{tenv} $[\![te_3]\!]$

ε_{tenv} $[\![\underline{\text{tuple}}(te_1,te_2)]\!]$= $\underline{\lambda}x_a[tt]$. $\underline{(}\varepsilon_{tenv}$ $[\![te_1]\!]\underline{:}$ x_a, ε_{tenv} $[\![te_2]\!]\underline{:}$ $x_a\ \underline{)}$ where tenv $\vdash$ te_1:tt$\underline{\rightarrow}$$tt_1$

ε_{tenv} $[\![\underline{\text{take}}_j[tt]]\!]$= $\underline{\lambda}x_a[tt]$. $x_a \underline{\downarrow}\ \underline{j}$

ε_{tenv} $[\![\underline{\text{curry}}\ te]\!]$= $\underline{\lambda}x_a[tt_1]$. $\underline{\lambda}x_b[tt_2]$. ε_{tenv} $[\![te]\!]\underline{:}$ $\underline{(}x_a,\ x_b\underline{)}$ where tenv $\vdash$ te:$(tt_1\underline{\times}tt_2)\underline{\rightarrow}$tt

ε_{tenv} $[\![\underline{\text{apply}}[tt]]\!]$= $\underline{\lambda}x_a[(tt_1\underline{\rightarrow}tt_2)\underline{\times}tt_1]$. $(x_a\underline{\downarrow}\ 1)\ \underline{:}\ (x_a\underline{\downarrow}\ 2)$ where tt = $tt_1\underline{\rightarrow}tt_2$

ε_{tenv} $[\![te_1\ \square\ te_2]\!]$= $\underline{\lambda}x_a[tt]$. ε_{tenv} $[\![te_1]\!]\underline{:}$ $(\varepsilon_{tenv}$ $[\![te_2]\!]\underline{:}$ $x_a)$ where tenv $\vdash$ te_2:tt$\underline{\rightarrow}$tt'

ε_{tenv} $[\![\underline{\text{fix}}[tt]]\!]$= $\underline{\lambda}x_a[tt\underline{\rightarrow}tt]$. $\underline{\text{fix}}$ x_a

ε_{tenv} $[\![\underline{\text{cond}}(te_1,\ te_2,\ te_3)]\!]$= $\underline{\lambda}x_a[tt]$. ε_{tenv} $[\![te_1]\!]\underline{:}$ x_a $\underline{\Rightarrow}$ ε_{tenv} $[\![te_2]\!]\underline{:}$ x_a, ε_{tenv} $[\![te_3]\!]\underline{:}$ x_a
where tenv $\vdash$ te_1: tt $\underline{\rightarrow}$ $\underline{A}_{bool}$

ε_{tenv} $[\![\underline{\text{const}}[tt]\ te]\!]$= $\underline{\lambda}x_a[tt]$. ε_{tenv} $[\![te]\!]$

ε_{tenv} $[\![\underline{\text{id}}[tt]]\!]$= $\underline{\lambda}x_a[tt]$. x_a

In these rules we have taken the liberty of assuming that x_a and x_b are not in the domain of tenv. To be precise we should have replaced a by m+1 and b by m+2 where m is the largest index i such that x_i is in the domain of tenv. We may note that

Fact 9 The transformation ε preserves the types, that is, if tenv $\vdash$ te:tt holds in TML_m then tenv $\vdash$ ε_{tenv} $[\![te]\!]$: tt will hold in TML_e. □

Hopefully it is intuitively clear that the semantics is preserved.

4 2-level λ-lifting

The translation from TML_e to TML_m, i.e. 2-level λ-lifting, is not so straight-forward. To illustrate the problem consider the well-formed TML_e expression

$$\underline{\lambda}x_1[\underline{A_1 \rightarrow A_1}].(\overline{\lambda}x_2[\underline{A_1 \rightarrow A_1}].x_1)\,\bar{\cdot}\,x_1 \tag{1}$$

Although this intuitively will be equivalent to $\underline{\lambda}x_1[\underline{A_1 \rightarrow A_1}].x_1$ that corresponds to $\underline{\mathrm{id}}[\underline{A_1 \rightarrow A_1}]$ in TML_m it would seem that one cannot translate (1) in a compositional way into a combinator expression of TML_m. The problem is that a variable, here x_1, that is bound by a (underlined) $\underline{\lambda}$ is passed inside the scope of overlined operators, here $\overline{\lambda}$ and $\bar{\cdot}$. It would seem that there are no ingredients in TML_m that could facilitate this. In fact, by looking at the definition of ε in the previous section it would appear that an expression like (1) will never be produced.

To make these rather vague impressions more precise we shall define a suitable subset TML_l of TML_e. This subset will be defined so as not to allow that $\underline{\lambda}$-bound variables are used inside the scope of overlined operators (although there will be one exception). It will emerge that the expression (1) will not be a well-formed expression of TML_l. We shall show that ε of the previous section only produces well-formed expressions of TML_l and that λ-lifting is possible when we restrict our attention to TML_l. This then will be the formal version of our claim that for 2-level λ-notations the λ-calculus (TML_e) and the combinator language (TML_m) are not equally expressive.

The types and expressions of TML_l are as for TML_e and we only define a new well-formedness predicate. Since we must distinguish between the variables bound by $\underline{\lambda}$ and those bound by $\overline{\lambda}$ the well-formedness predicate will have the form

$$\text{cenv, renv} \vdash \text{te:tt}$$

where cenv is the type environment for $\overline{\lambda}$-bound variables and renv is the one for $\underline{\lambda}$-bound variables. We shall enforce that the domains of cenv and renv are disjoint. The rules are adapted from those for TML_e by "emptying" the type environment for $\underline{\lambda}$-bound variables when we pass inside the "scope" of (most) overlined operators. They are

$$\text{cenv, renv} \vdash f_i[\text{tt}]\text{:tt} \qquad \text{if } \exists k.\ \vdash \text{tt:k and dom(cenv)} \cap \text{dom(renv)} = \emptyset$$

$$\text{cenv, renv} \vdash x_i\text{: tt} \qquad \text{if } \exists k.\ \vdash \text{tt:k, cenv}(x_i)\text{=tt or renv}(x_i)\text{=tt and dom(cenv)} \cap \text{dom(renv)} = \emptyset$$

$$\frac{\text{cenv}, \emptyset \vdash \text{te}_1\text{:tt}_1,\ \text{cenv}, \emptyset \vdash \text{te}_2\text{:tt}_2}{\text{cenv, renv} \vdash \overline{(\text{te}_1, \text{te}_2)}\text{:tt}_1 \overline{\times} \text{tt}_2} \qquad \text{if} \vdash \text{tt}_1\text{:c and} \vdash \text{tt}_2\text{:c}$$

$$\frac{\text{cenv}, \emptyset \vdash \text{te:tt}_1 \overline{\times} \text{tt}_2}{\text{cenv, renv} \vdash \text{te} \overline{\downarrow} \text{j:tt}_j} \qquad \text{if j} = 1{,}2$$

$$\frac{\text{cenv}[x_i \mapsto \text{tt}], \emptyset \vdash \text{te:tt'}}{\text{cenv, renv} \vdash \overline{\lambda} x_i[\text{tt}].\text{te:tt} \overline{\rightarrow} \text{tt'}} \qquad \text{if} \vdash \text{tt:c and} \vdash \text{tt':c}$$

$$\frac{\text{cenv}, \emptyset \vdash \text{te}_1\text{:tt'} \overline{\rightarrow} \text{tt},\ \text{cenv}, \emptyset \vdash \text{te}_2\text{:tt'}}{\text{cenv, renv} \vdash \text{te}_1\, \bar{\cdot}\, \text{te}_2\text{:tt}}$$

$$\frac{\text{cenv}, \emptyset \vdash \text{te:tt} \overline{\rightarrow} \text{tt}}{\text{cenv, renv} \vdash \overline{\text{fix}}\ \text{te:tt}}$$

$$\frac{\text{cenv}, \emptyset \vdash \text{te:}\overline{A}_{\text{bool}},\ \text{cenv, renv} \vdash \text{te}_1\text{:tt},\ \text{cenv, renv} \vdash \text{te}_2\text{:tt}}{\text{cenv, renv} \vdash \text{te} \overline{\rightarrow} \text{te}_1, \text{te}_2\text{:tt}}$$

$$\frac{\text{cenv, renv} \vdash \text{te}_1\text{:tt}_1,\ \text{cenv, renv} \vdash \text{te}_2\text{:tt}_2}{\text{cenv, renv} \vdash \underline{(\text{te}_1, \text{te}_2)}\text{:tt}_1 \underline{\times} \text{tt}_2} \qquad \text{if} \vdash \text{tt}_1\text{:r and} \vdash \text{tt}_2\text{:r}$$

$$\frac{\text{cenv, renv} \vdash \text{te:tt}_1 \underline{\times} \text{tt}_2}{\text{cenv, renv} \vdash \text{te} \underline{\downarrow} \text{j:tt}_j} \qquad \text{if } j = 1,2$$

$$\frac{\text{cenv}\lceil(\text{dom(cenv)}-\{x_i\}),\ \text{renv}[x_i \mapsto \text{tt}] \vdash \text{te:tt'}}{\text{cenv, renv} \vdash \underline{\lambda} x_i[\text{tt}].\text{te:tt}\underline{\rightarrow}\text{tt'}} \qquad \text{if} \vdash \text{tt:r and} \vdash \text{tt':r}$$

$$\frac{\text{cenv, renv} \vdash \text{te}_1\text{:tt'}\underline{\rightarrow}\text{tt},\ \text{cenv, renv} \vdash \text{te}_2\text{:tt'}}{\text{cenv, renv} \vdash \text{te}_1 \ \underline{:}\ \text{te}_2\text{:tt}}$$

$$\frac{\text{cenv, renv} \vdash \text{te:tt}\underline{\rightarrow}\text{tt}}{\text{cenv, renv} \vdash \underline{\text{fix}}\ \text{te:tt}}$$

$$\frac{\text{cenv, renv} \vdash \text{te:}\underline{\text{A}}_{\text{bool}},\ \text{cenv, renv} \vdash \text{te}_1\text{:tt},\ \text{cenv, renv} \vdash \text{te}_2\text{:tt}}{\text{cenv, renv} \vdash \text{te} \ \underline{\rightarrow}\ \text{te}_1,\ \text{te}_2\text{:tt}} \qquad \text{if} \vdash \text{tt:r}$$

In the rule for overlined conditional we have not emptied the type environment for $\underline{\lambda}$-bound variables for the "then" and "else" branches. This is connected with the fact that we have not restricted the type of the conditional to be of compile-time type and this is of importance when we come to λ-lifting. In the rule for underlined conditional we have restricted the type of the conditional to be of run-time type. This is in accord with the restrictions implicit in the rule for $\underline{\text{cond}}$ in TML_m. Finally we note that in analogy with Fact 7 and 8 we have

Fact 10 Expressions have well-formed types, i.e. if cenv, renv $\vdash$ te:tt then $\exists$k. $\vdash$ tt:k. □

Fact 11 Expressions are uniquely typed, i.e. if cenv, renv $\vdash$ te:tt$_1$ and cenv, renv $\vdash$ te:tt$_2$ then tt$_1$=tt$_2$. □

In Fact 10 (and similarly in Fact 7) the kind k will be unique unless tt is of the form tt$_1$ $\underline{\rightarrow}$ tt$_2$ in which case k may be c as well as r. It is straightforward to verify that the expression (1) is not well-formed in TML_l. It is also easy to see that any expression that is well-formed in TML_l also will be well-formed in TML_e. That we have not gone too far in the definition of TML_l may be expressed by

Fact 12 The expansion ε of combinators in TML_m only produces expressions in TML_l, i.e. if tenv$\vdash$ te:tt in TML_m then tenv, $\emptyset \vdash \varepsilon_{\text{tenv}}$ [[te]]:tt in TML_l . □

Turning to 2-level λ-lifting the intention will be to define a function

$$\Lambda^{\text{cenv}}_{\text{penv}}\text{: } \{ \text{ te} \in \text{TML}_l \mid \exists\text{tt. cenv}, \rho(\text{penv}) \vdash \text{te:tt } \} \rightarrow \{ \text{ te} \mid \text{ te} \in \text{TML}_m \}$$

whenever cenv is a type environment, penv is a position environment and the domains of cenv and ρ(penv) are disjoint. Looking back to the 1-level case we note that there we demanded that the position environment could not be the empty list. It is evident from the well-formedness rules for TML_l that the emptying of the type environment for $\underline{\lambda}$-bound variables means that we cannot take a similar cavalier attitude here. So the idea will be to demand that cenv, ρ(penv) $\vdash$ te:tt satisfies that

$$\text{penv} = () \Rightarrow\ \vdash \text{tt:c}$$

$$\text{penv} \neq () \Rightarrow\ \vdash \text{tt:r}$$

This means that when tt is tt$_1$ $\underline{\rightarrow}$tt$_2$ the position environment will tell us whether we want to regard tt$_1$ $\underline{\rightarrow}$ tt$_2$ as a run-time data object (in case penv $\neq$ ()) or as a run-time computation (in case penv=()). Thus we do not need to follow D.Schmidt [12] in making these distinctions in a syntactic manner (by having essentially three kinds of function arrows rather than just two).

The definition of $\Lambda^{\text{cenv}}_{\text{penv}}$[[te]] will closely follow the inference that cenv,ρ(penv)$\vdash$ te:tt for some tt. We have already pointed out that in this inference we shall replace the type environment ρ(penv) by the empty map $\emptyset$ when we move inside the "scope" of (most) overlined operators. In the definition of

$\Lambda^{\mathrm{cenv}}_{\mathrm{penv}}[\![\mathrm{te}]\!]$ the analogue will be to replace the position environment penv by the empty list (). Since this will entail ignoring some (run-time) arguments we define

$$\delta(\mathrm{penv})\ \mathrm{te} = \begin{cases} \mathrm{te} & \text{if penv} = () \\ \underline{\mathrm{const}}[\Pi(\mathrm{penv})]\ \mathrm{te} & \text{if penv} \neq () \end{cases}$$

where $\Pi(\mathrm{penv})$ is defined as in Section 2 but now uses $\underline{\times}$ in stead of $\times$. If we also define

$$\Delta(\mathrm{penv},\mathrm{tt}) = \begin{cases} \mathrm{tt} & \text{if penv} = () \\ \Pi(\mathrm{penv}) \underline{\rightarrow}\ \mathrm{tt} & \text{if penv} \neq () \end{cases}$$

we may note that if $\mathrm{tenv} \vdash \mathrm{te{:}tt}$ holds in TML_m then also $\mathrm{tenv} \vdash \delta(\mathrm{penv})\ \mathrm{te}{:}\Delta(\mathrm{penv},\mathrm{tt})$ holds in TML_m.

Similarly we may move into the "scope" of an underlined operator and there we cannot allow the position environment to be the empty list (as is witnessed by our insistence on penv $\neq$ () in the case of 1-level λ-lifting). This motivates defining

$$\varphi(\mathrm{tt},\mathrm{penv}) = \begin{cases} \mathrm{penv} & \text{if penv} \neq () \\ ((\mathrm{x_a},\mathrm{tt})) & \text{if penv} = () \end{cases}$$

for a dummy variable $\mathrm{x_a}$ so that $\varphi(\mathrm{tt},\mathrm{penv})$ is never the empty list. In connection with this we need

$$\omega(\mathrm{tt},\mathrm{penv})\ \mathrm{te} = \begin{cases} \mathrm{te} & \text{if penv} \neq () \\ \underline{\mathrm{apply}}[\mathrm{tt_1} \underline{\rightarrow} \mathrm{tt_2}] \ \Box\ \underline{\mathrm{tuple}}(\mathrm{te},\underline{\mathrm{id}}[\mathrm{tt_1}]) & \\ \quad \text{if penv} = () \text{ and tt} = \mathrm{tt_1} \underline{\rightarrow} \mathrm{tt_2} \end{cases}$$

where we shall take care that the first argument to ω always will have the proper form. One may note that if penv = () and $\emptyset \vdash \mathrm{te{:}tt_1} \underline{\rightarrow} \mathrm{tt_1} \underline{\rightarrow} \mathrm{tt_2}$ then $\emptyset \vdash \omega(\mathrm{tt_1} \underline{\rightarrow} \mathrm{tt_2},\mathrm{penv})\ \mathrm{te{:}tt_1} \underline{\rightarrow} \mathrm{tt_2}$ and it will be clear from below that ω will be used when we want to escape from the effects of having used φ. (This will be done by taking an argument and supplying it to the function twice so that the additional argument needed because of the introduction of the dummy variable will be catered for.)

Turning to the definition of $\Lambda^{\mathrm{cenv}}_{\mathrm{penv}}$ we use a version of $\pi^{\mathrm{penv}}_{\mathrm{j}}$ that is as in Section 2 but that uses underlined combinators. It may be helpful to take a look at Fact 13 while reading through the following equations

$$\Lambda^{\mathrm{cenv}}_{\mathrm{penv}}\ [\![\mathrm{f_i[tt]}]\!] = \delta(\mathrm{penv})\ \mathrm{f_i[tt]}$$

$$\Lambda^{\mathrm{cenv}}_{\mathrm{penv}}\ [\![\mathrm{x_i}]\!] = \begin{cases} \delta(\mathrm{penv})\ \mathrm{x_i} & \text{if } \mathrm{x_i} \in \mathrm{dom(cenv)} \\ \pi^{\mathrm{penv}}_{\mathrm{i}} & \text{if } \mathrm{x_i} \in \mathrm{dom(penv)} \end{cases}$$

$$\Lambda^{\mathrm{cenv}}_{\mathrm{penv}}\ [\![\overline{(}\mathrm{te_1},\ \mathrm{te_2}\overline{)}]\!] = \overline{(}\Lambda^{\mathrm{cenv}}_{()}\ [\![\mathrm{te_1}]\!],\ \Lambda^{\mathrm{cenv}}_{()}\ [\![\mathrm{te_2}]\!]\overline{)}$$

$$\Lambda^{\mathrm{cenv}}_{\mathrm{penv}}\ [\![\mathrm{te}\ \overline{\downarrow \mathrm{j}}]\!] = \delta(\mathrm{penv})\ (\Lambda^{\mathrm{cenv}}_{()}\ [\![\mathrm{te}]\!]\overline{\downarrow \mathrm{j}})$$

$$\Lambda^{\mathrm{cenv}}_{\mathrm{penv}}\ [\![\overline{\lambda}\mathrm{x_i[tt].te}]\!] = \overline{\lambda}\mathrm{x_i[tt]}.\Lambda^{\mathrm{cenv[x_i \mapsto tt]}}_{()}\ [\![\mathrm{te}]\!]$$

$$\Lambda^{\mathrm{cenv}}_{\mathrm{penv}}\ [\![\mathrm{te_1}\ \overline{\cdot}\ \mathrm{te_2}]\!] = \delta(\mathrm{penv})\ (\Lambda^{\mathrm{cenv}}_{()}\ [\![\mathrm{te_1}]\!]\overline{\cdot}\ \Lambda^{\mathrm{cenv}}_{()}\ [\![\mathrm{te_2}]\!])$$

$$\Lambda^{\mathrm{cenv}}_{\mathrm{penv}}\ [\![\overline{\mathrm{fix}}\ \mathrm{te}]\!] = \delta(\mathrm{penv})\ (\overline{\mathrm{fix}}\ \Lambda^{\mathrm{penv}}_{()}\ [\![\mathrm{te}]\!])$$

$$\Lambda^{\mathrm{cenv}}_{\mathrm{penv}}\ [\![\mathrm{te_1}\ \overline{\Rightarrow}\ \mathrm{te_2},\ \mathrm{te_3}]\!] = \Lambda^{\mathrm{cenv}}_{()}\ [\![\mathrm{te_1}]\!]\overline{\Rightarrow}\ \Lambda^{\mathrm{cenv}}_{\mathrm{penv}}\ [\![\mathrm{te_2}]\!],\ \Lambda^{\mathrm{cenv}}_{\mathrm{penv}}\ [\![\mathrm{te_3}]\!]$$

$$\Lambda^{\mathrm{cenv}}_{\mathrm{penv}}\ [\![\underline{(}\mathrm{te_1},\ \mathrm{te_2}\underline{)}]\!] = \underline{\mathrm{tuple}}(\Lambda^{\mathrm{cenv}}_{\mathrm{penv}}\ [\![\mathrm{te_1}]\!],\ \Lambda^{\mathrm{cenv}}_{\mathrm{penv}}\ [\![\mathrm{te_2}]\!])$$

$$\Lambda^{\mathrm{cenv}}_{\mathrm{penv}}\ [\![\mathrm{te}\ \underline{\downarrow \mathrm{j}}]\!] = \omega(\mathrm{tt_j},\mathrm{penv})(\underline{\mathrm{take}}_{\mathrm{j}}[\mathrm{tt_1} \underline{\times} \mathrm{tt_2}]\ \Box\ \Lambda^{\mathrm{cenv}}_{\varphi(\mathrm{tt_j},\mathrm{penv})}\ [\![\mathrm{te}]\!])$$

where $\mathrm{cenv},\ \rho(\mathrm{penv}) \vdash \mathrm{te{:}tt_1} \underline{\times} \mathrm{tt_2}$

$$\Lambda^{\mathrm{cenv}}_{\mathrm{penv}}\ [\![\underline{\lambda} x_i[tt].te]\!] = \begin{cases} \Lambda^{\mathrm{cenv}\lceil(\mathrm{dom(cenv)}-\{x_i\})}_{((x_i,tt))}\ [\![te]\!] & \text{if penv} = () \\ \underline{\mathrm{curry}}\ (\Lambda^{\mathrm{cenv}\lceil(\mathrm{dom(cenv)}-\{x_i\})}_{((x_i,tt))\hat{}\,\mathrm{penv}}\ [\![te]\!]\ ) & \text{if penv} \neq () \end{cases}$$

$$\Lambda^{\mathrm{cenv}}_{\mathrm{penv}}\ [\![te_1 \underline{:}\ te_2]\!] = \omega(tt_2,\mathrm{penv})(\underline{\mathrm{apply}}[tt_1 \underline{\rightarrow} tt_2] \,\square\, \underline{\mathrm{tuple}}(\Lambda^{\mathrm{cenv}}_{\varphi(tt_2,\mathrm{penv})}\ [\![te_1]\!],\ \Lambda^{\mathrm{cenv}}_{\varphi(tt_2,\mathrm{penv})}\ [\![te_2]\!]))$$

where cenv, ρ(penv) $\vdash$ te_1:$tt_1 \underline{\rightarrow} tt_2$

$$\Lambda^{\mathrm{cenv}}_{\mathrm{penv}}\ [\![\underline{\mathrm{fix}}\ te]\!] = \omega(tt,\mathrm{penv})(\underline{\mathrm{fix}}[tt] \,\square\, \Lambda^{\mathrm{cenv}}_{\varphi(tt,\mathrm{penv})}\ [\![te]\!]) \qquad \text{where cenv, } \rho(\mathrm{penv}) \vdash te{:}tt \underline{\rightarrow} tt$$

$$\Lambda^{\mathrm{cenv}}_{\mathrm{penv}}\ [\![te_1 \underline{\rightarrow}\ te_2,\ te_3]\!] = \omega(tt,\mathrm{penv})\ \underline{\mathrm{cond}}(\Lambda^{\mathrm{cenv}}_{\varphi(tt,\mathrm{penv})}\ [\![te_1]\!],\ \Lambda^{\mathrm{cenv}}_{\varphi(tt,\mathrm{penv})}\ [\![te_2]\!],\ \Lambda^{\mathrm{cenv}}_{\varphi(tt,\mathrm{penv})}\ [\![te_3]\!])$$

where cenv, ρ(penv) $\vdash$ te_2:tt

In these equations the intention is that the greek-letter operations should be "macro-expanded" as they are really a shorthand for their defining equation and are not parts of TML_m. To illustrate the use of δ we shall consider the expression

$$\underline{\lambda} x_1[\underline{A_1 \rightarrow A_1}].f_1[\underline{A_1 \rightarrow A_1}]$$

When processing $f_1[\underline{A_1 \rightarrow A_1}]$ the position environment will not be empty and so we must use the construct $\underline{\mathrm{const}}[\underline{A_1 \rightarrow A_1}]$ (via δ) to get rid of the run-time argument corresponding to x_1. To illustrate the use of ω we shall consider the expression

$$(\underline{\lambda} x_1[\underline{A_1}].x_1,\ \underline{\lambda} x_1[\underline{A_1}].x_1\ )\underline{\downarrow 1}$$

which is well-formed and of the compile-time type $\underline{A_1 \rightarrow A_1}$. So it would be natural to use an empty position environment but then we cannot sequence the operations. (This is the same problem as in Section 2.) Consequently, we use ω and φ to translate the expression as if the position environment had not been empty and then later to get rid of the extra element in the position environment. It is vital for this technique to succeed that if $\vdash$ tt:k holds for k = c as well as k = r then tt is of the form $tt_1 \underline{\rightarrow} tt_2$ as may be seen from the definition of ω. By way of digression it is worth observing that $\delta(\cdots)$ te roughly corresponds to $te^{>}$ in [1] and similarly $\omega(\cdots)$ te roughly corresponds to $te^{<}$.

The relationship between an expression and its λ-lifted version is given by

Fact 13 Whenever the domains of cenv and ρ(penv) are disjoint the above equations define a function of the stated functionality and it satisfies

$$\mathrm{cenv} \vdash \Lambda^{\mathrm{cenv}}_{\mathrm{penv}}\ [\![te]\!]{:}\Delta(\mathrm{penv},tt)$$

whenever cenv,ρ(penv) $\vdash$ te:tt and penv = () $\Rightarrow$ $\vdash$ tt:c and penv $\neq$ () $\Rightarrow$ $\vdash$ tt:r. □

Furthermore we shall claim that the semantics has been preserved. The importance of this fact is that the combinator notation of TML_m is equivalent in expressive power to the proper subset TML_l of the λ-notation TML_e.

Example: As an example of the use of the 2-level λ-lifting consider the TML_l expression

$$\begin{aligned} \mathrm{select'} \equiv\ & \overline{\mathrm{fix}}(\overline{\lambda} S[\overline{\mathrm{Int}} \overline{\rightarrow} \underline{\mathrm{List} \rightarrow \mathrm{Int}}].\ \overline{\lambda} n[\overline{\mathrm{Int}}].\ \underline{\lambda} l[\underline{\mathrm{List}}]. \\ & \quad (=[\overline{\mathrm{Int}} \overline{\rightarrow} \overline{\mathrm{Int}} \overline{\rightarrow} \overline{\mathrm{Int}}]\,\overline{:}\ 1[\overline{\mathrm{Int}}]\,\overline{:}\ n) \overline{\rightarrow} (\mathrm{hd}[\underline{\mathrm{List} \rightarrow \mathrm{Int}}]\,\underline{:}\ l), \\ & \qquad (S\,\overline{:}\ (-[\overline{\mathrm{Int}} \overline{\rightarrow} \overline{\mathrm{Int}} \overline{\rightarrow} \overline{\mathrm{Int}}]\,\overline{:}\ n\,\overline{:}\ 1[\overline{\mathrm{Int}}])\,\underline{:}\ (\mathrm{tl}[\underline{\mathrm{List} \rightarrow \mathrm{List}}]\,\underline{:}\ l))) \end{aligned}$$

where we e.g. write $\overline{\mathrm{Int}}$ for $\overline{A}_{\mathrm{Int}}$, $1[\overline{\mathrm{Int}}]$ for $f_1[\overline{A}_{\mathrm{Int}}]$ and n for x_n. First we get

$$\Lambda^{\emptyset}_{()}[\![\mathrm{select'}]\!] = \overline{\mathrm{fix}}\ \Lambda^{\emptyset}_{()}[\![\overline{\lambda} S[\ldots].\ldots]\!]$$

because the initial position environment is empty. The equation for compile-time λ-abstraction then gives

$$
\begin{aligned}
&\Lambda^{\emptyset}_{()}[\![\overline{\lambda}\mathrm{S}[\overline{\mathrm{Int}\Rightarrow}\underline{\mathrm{List}\to\mathrm{Int}}].\ \overline{\lambda}\mathrm{n}[\overline{\mathrm{Int}}].\ \underline{\lambda}\mathrm{l}[\underline{\mathrm{List}}]\ldots]\!] = \\
&\quad \overline{\lambda}\mathrm{S}[\overline{\mathrm{Int}\Rightarrow}\underline{\mathrm{List}\to\mathrm{Int}}].\ \Lambda^{[\mathrm{S}\mapsto\ \ldots]}_{()}[\![\overline{\lambda}\mathrm{n}[\overline{\mathrm{Int}}].\ \underline{\lambda}\mathrm{l}[\underline{\mathrm{List}}]\ldots]\!] = \\
&\quad \overline{\lambda}\mathrm{S}[\overline{\mathrm{Int}\Rightarrow}\underline{\mathrm{List}\to\mathrm{Int}}].\ \overline{\lambda}\mathrm{n}[\overline{\mathrm{Int}}].\ \Lambda^{\mathrm{cenv}}_{()}[\![\underline{\lambda}\mathrm{l}[\underline{\mathrm{List}}]\ldots]\!]
\end{aligned}
$$

where cenv abbreviates $[\mathrm{S}\mapsto \overline{\mathrm{Int}\Rightarrow}\underline{\mathrm{List}\to\mathrm{Int}};\ \mathrm{n}\mapsto \overline{\mathrm{Int}}]$. Since the position environment still is empty the equation for run-time λ-abstraction gives

$$\Lambda^{\mathrm{cenv}}_{()}[\![\underline{\lambda}\mathrm{l}[\underline{\mathrm{List}}].(\ldots)\overline{\Rightarrow}(\ldots),(\ldots)]\!] = \Lambda^{\mathrm{cenv}}_{\mathrm{penv}}[\![(\ldots)\overline{\Rightarrow}(\ldots),(\ldots)]\!]$$

where penv is $((\mathrm{l},\underline{\mathrm{List}}))$. Using the equation for compile-time conditional we see that

$$\Lambda^{\mathrm{cenv}}_{()}[\![=[\overline{\mathrm{Int}\Rightarrow\mathrm{Int}\Rightarrow\mathrm{Int}}]\bar{:}\ 1[\overline{\mathrm{Int}}]\bar{:}\ \mathrm{n}]\!],$$

$$\Lambda^{\mathrm{cenv}}_{\mathrm{penv}}[\![\mathrm{hd}[\underline{\mathrm{List}\to\mathrm{Int}}]\underline{:}\ \mathrm{l}]\!]$$

and

$$\Lambda^{\mathrm{cenv}}_{\mathrm{penv}}[\![\mathrm{S}\bar{:}\ (-[\overline{\mathrm{Int}\Rightarrow\mathrm{Int}\Rightarrow\mathrm{Int}}]\bar{:}\ \mathrm{n}\bar{:}\ 1[\overline{\mathrm{Int}}])\underline{:}\ (\mathrm{tl}[\underline{\mathrm{List}\to\mathrm{List}}]\underline{:}\ \mathrm{l})]\!]$$

must be calculated.

For the condition we get

$$
\begin{aligned}
&\Lambda^{\mathrm{cenv}}_{()}[\![=[\overline{\mathrm{Int}\Rightarrow\mathrm{Int}\Rightarrow\mathrm{Int}}]\bar{:}\ 1[\overline{\mathrm{Int}}]\bar{:}\ \mathrm{n}]\!] = \Lambda^{\mathrm{cenv}}_{()}[\![=[\ldots]]\!]\bar{:}\ \Lambda^{\mathrm{cenv}}_{()}[\![1[\overline{\mathrm{Int}}]]\!]\bar{:}\ \Lambda^{\mathrm{cenv}}_{()}[\![\mathrm{n}]\!] = \\
&\quad =[\overline{\mathrm{Int}\Rightarrow\mathrm{Int}\Rightarrow\mathrm{Int}}]\bar{:}\ 1[\overline{\mathrm{Int}}]\bar{:}\ \mathrm{n}
\end{aligned}
$$

so the expression is unchanged. For the true-branch of the conditional we get

$$
\begin{aligned}
&\Lambda^{\mathrm{cenv}}_{\mathrm{penv}}[\![\mathrm{hd}[\underline{\mathrm{List}\to\mathrm{Int}}]\underline{:}\ \mathrm{l}]\!] = \underline{\mathrm{apply}}[\underline{\mathrm{List}\to\mathrm{Int}}]\ \Box\ \underline{\mathrm{tuple}}(\Lambda^{\mathrm{cenv}}_{\mathrm{penv}}[\![\mathrm{hd}[\ldots]]\!],\ \Lambda^{\mathrm{cenv}}_{\mathrm{penv}}[\![\mathrm{l}]\!]) = \\
&\quad \underline{\mathrm{apply}}[\underline{\mathrm{List}\to\mathrm{Int}}]\ \Box\ \underline{\mathrm{tuple}}(\underline{\mathrm{const}}[\underline{\mathrm{List}}]\ \mathrm{hd}[\underline{\mathrm{List}\to\mathrm{Int}}],\underline{\mathrm{id}}[\underline{\mathrm{List}}])
\end{aligned}
$$

The false-branch of the conditional is more interesting. Similar to above we get

$$\Lambda^{\mathrm{cenv}}_{\mathrm{penv}}[\![\mathrm{tl}[\underline{\mathrm{List}\to\mathrm{List}}]\underline{:}\ \mathrm{l}]\!] = \underline{\mathrm{apply}}[\underline{\mathrm{List}\to\mathrm{List}}]\ \Box\ \underline{\mathrm{tuple}}(\underline{\mathrm{const}}[\underline{\mathrm{List}}]\ \mathrm{tl}[\underline{\mathrm{List}\to\mathrm{List}}],\underline{\mathrm{id}}[\underline{\mathrm{List}}])$$

Concerning $\Lambda^{\mathrm{cenv}}_{\mathrm{penv}}[\![\mathrm{S}\bar{:}\ (-[\ldots]\bar{:}\ \mathrm{n}\bar{:}\ 1[\ldots])]\!]$ the expression should be computed at compile-time but the position environment is non-empty so it is supposed to take a run-time parameter. We use the $\underline{\text{const}}$ expression (via δ) to get rid of the run-time parameter:

$$
\begin{aligned}
&\Lambda^{\mathrm{cenv}}_{\mathrm{penv}}[\![\mathrm{S}\bar{:}\ (-[\overline{\mathrm{Int}\Rightarrow\mathrm{Int}\Rightarrow\mathrm{Int}}]\bar{:}\ \mathrm{n}\bar{:}\ 1[\overline{\mathrm{Int}}])]\!] = \\
&\quad \underline{\mathrm{const}}[\underline{\mathrm{List}}]\ (\Lambda^{\mathrm{cenv}}_{()}[\![\mathrm{S}]\!]\bar{:}\ \Lambda^{\mathrm{cenv}}_{()}[\![-[\overline{\mathrm{Int}\Rightarrow\mathrm{Int}\Rightarrow\mathrm{Int}}]\bar{:}\ \mathrm{n}\bar{:}\ 1[\overline{\mathrm{Int}}]]\!])
\end{aligned}
$$

and it is now straightforward to show that

$$\Lambda^{\mathrm{cenv}}_{()}[\![\mathrm{S}]\!] = \mathrm{S}$$

and

$$\Lambda^{\mathrm{cenv}}_{()}[\![-[\overline{\mathrm{Int}\Rightarrow\mathrm{Int}\Rightarrow\mathrm{Int}}]\bar{:}\ \mathrm{n}\bar{:}\ 1[\overline{\mathrm{Int}}]]\!] = -[\overline{\mathrm{Int}\Rightarrow\mathrm{Int}\Rightarrow\mathrm{Int}}]\bar{:}\ \mathrm{n}\bar{:}\ 1[\overline{\mathrm{Int}}]$$

so for the false-branch we get

$$
\begin{aligned}
&\Lambda^{\mathrm{cenv}}_{\mathrm{penv}}[\![\mathrm{S}\bar{:}\ (-[\overline{\mathrm{Int}\Rightarrow\mathrm{Int}\Rightarrow\mathrm{Int}}]\bar{:}\ \mathrm{n}\bar{:}\ 1[\overline{\mathrm{Int}}])\underline{:}\ (\mathrm{tl}[\underline{\mathrm{List}\to\mathrm{List}}]\underline{:}\ \mathrm{l})]\!] = \\
&\quad \underline{\mathrm{apply}}[\underline{\mathrm{List}\to\mathrm{Int}}]\ \Box\ \underline{\mathrm{tuple}}(\underline{\mathrm{const}}[\underline{\mathrm{List}}]\ (\mathrm{S}\bar{:}\ (-[\overline{\mathrm{Int}\Rightarrow\mathrm{Int}\Rightarrow\mathrm{Int}}]\bar{:}\ \mathrm{n}\bar{:}\ 1[\overline{\mathrm{Int}}])), \\
&\qquad\qquad \underline{\mathrm{apply}}[\underline{\mathrm{List}\to\mathrm{List}}]\ \Box\ \underline{\mathrm{tuple}}(\underline{\mathrm{const}}[\underline{\mathrm{List}}]\ \mathrm{tl}[\underline{\mathrm{List}\to\mathrm{List}}],\underline{\mathrm{id}}[\underline{\mathrm{List}}]))
\end{aligned}
$$

Putting things together we get

$$
\begin{aligned}
&\Lambda^{\emptyset}_{()}[\![\text{select'}]\!] = \\
&\quad \overline{\text{fix}}(\overline{\lambda} S[\overline{\text{Int}}\overline{\Rightarrow}\underline{\text{List}\rightarrow\text{Int}}].\ \overline{\lambda} n[\overline{\text{Int}}].\ (=[\overline{\text{Int}}\overline{\Rightarrow}\overline{\text{Int}}\overline{\Rightarrow}\overline{\text{Int}}]\,\bar{\cdot}\ 1[\overline{\text{Int}}]\,\bar{\cdot}\ n)\overline{\Rightarrow} \\
&\qquad\quad \underline{\text{apply}}[\underline{\text{List}\rightarrow\text{Int}}] \,\square\, \underline{\text{tuple}}(\underline{\text{const}}[\underline{\text{List}}]\ \text{hd}[\underline{\text{List}\rightarrow\text{Int}}],\underline{\text{id}}[\underline{\text{List}}]), \\
&\qquad\quad \underline{\text{apply}}[\underline{\text{List}\rightarrow\text{Int}}] \,\square\, \underline{\text{tuple}}(\underline{\text{const}}[\underline{\text{List}}]\ (S\,\bar{\cdot}\ (-[\overline{\text{Int}}\overline{\Rightarrow}\overline{\text{Int}}\overline{\Rightarrow}\overline{\text{Int}}]\,\bar{\cdot}\ n\,\bar{\cdot}\ 1[\overline{\text{Int}}])), \\
&\qquad\qquad \underline{\text{apply}}[\underline{\text{List}\rightarrow\text{List}}] \,\square\, \underline{\text{tuple}}(\underline{\text{const}}[\underline{\text{List}}]\ \text{tl}[\underline{\text{List}\rightarrow\text{List}}],\underline{\text{id}}[\underline{\text{List}}])))
\end{aligned}
$$

The λ-lifting is specified in a syntax directed manner and this is the reason for the complicated form of the expression above. Semantically

$$\underline{\text{apply}}[\text{tt}\underline{\rightarrow}\text{tt'}] \,\square\, \underline{\text{tuple}}(\underline{\text{const}}[\text{tt}]\ \text{te},\underline{\text{id}}[\text{tt}]) \equiv \text{te}$$

and

$$\underline{\text{apply}}[\text{tt}\underline{\rightarrow}\text{tt'}] \,\square\, \underline{\text{tuple}}(\underline{\text{const}}[\text{tt}]\ \text{te},\text{te'}) \equiv \text{te} \,\square\, \text{te'}$$

so by performing a little partial evaluation [10] we can replace the expression above by

$$
\begin{aligned}
&\overline{\text{fix}}(\overline{\lambda} S[\overline{\text{Int}}\overline{\Rightarrow}\underline{\text{List}\rightarrow\text{Int}}].\ \overline{\lambda} n[\overline{\text{Int}}].\ (=[\overline{\text{Int}}\overline{\Rightarrow}\overline{\text{Int}}\overline{\Rightarrow}\overline{\text{Int}}]\,\bar{\cdot}\ 1[\overline{\text{Int}}]\,\bar{\cdot}\ n)\overline{\Rightarrow} \\
&\qquad\qquad \text{hd}[\underline{\text{List}\rightarrow\text{Int}}],\ (S\,\bar{\cdot}\ (-[\overline{\text{Int}}\overline{\Rightarrow}\overline{\text{Int}}\overline{\Rightarrow}\overline{\text{Int}}]\,\bar{\cdot}\ n\,\bar{\cdot}\ 1[\overline{\text{Int}}])) \,\square\, \text{tl}[\underline{\text{List}\rightarrow\text{List}}])
\end{aligned}
$$

which is the expression called select" in the Introduction.

5 Applications in denotational semantics

In our previous work [7] we have studied the application of a variant of TML_m as a meta-language for denotational semantics. One motivation for this is that the informal semantics of a language often makes a distinction between those computations that are performed at compile-time and those that are performed at run-time. An example is Tennent's distinction between static expression procedures and expression procedures in Pascal-like languages [14]. Another motivation is that the automatic generation of compilers from denotational definitions will benefit from the distinction between binding times in that code only will be generated for the run-time level [8].

In [7] we study a Pascal-like language with e.g. declarations, commands and expressions. We do not have the space to give all the details so let us concentrate on the important semantic domains:

Dv	$= A_{\text{Loc}} + \cdots$	denotable values
Env	$= A_{\text{Ide}} \rightarrow \text{Dv}$	environments
Ev	$= A_{\text{Loc}} + \cdots$	expressible values
S	$= A_{\text{Loc}} \rightarrow \cdots$	stores
Ans	$= \cdots$	answers
Cc	$= \text{S} \rightarrow \text{Ans}$	command continuations
Ec	$= \text{Ev} \rightarrow \text{Cc}$	expression continuations

As an example, in a standard continuation style semantics the semantic function $\mathcal{E}$ for expressions (Exp) could have the functionality

$$\mathcal{E}\colon \text{Exp} \rightarrow \text{Env} \rightarrow \text{Ec} \rightarrow \text{Cc}$$

As mentioned above we want to distinguish between compile-time and run-time. The idea will therefore be to rewrite the semantics using the 2-level meta-language TML_e because this will make the binding times explicit. The operational intuition is that environments and denotable values will be compile-time objects whereas stores, answers and expressible values will be run-time objects. This gives rise to the following semantic domains

$$\begin{array}{lll}
\mathrm{Dv} & = \overline{\mathrm{A}}_{\mathrm{Loc}} \overline{+} \overline{\cdots} & \text{(kind c)} \\
\mathrm{Env} & = \overline{\mathrm{A}}_{\mathrm{Ide}} \overline{\rightarrow} \mathrm{Dv} & \text{(kind c)} \\
\mathrm{Ev} & = \underline{\mathrm{A}}_{\mathrm{Loc}} \underline{+} \underline{\cdots} & \text{(kind r)} \\
\mathrm{S} & = \underline{\mathrm{A}}_{\mathrm{Loc}} \underline{\rightarrow} \underline{\cdots} & \text{(kind r)} \\
\mathrm{Ans} & = \underline{\cdots} & \text{(kind r)} \\
\mathrm{Cc} & = \mathrm{S} \underline{\rightarrow} \mathrm{Ans} & \text{(both kind r and c)} \\
\mathrm{Ec} & = \mathrm{Ev} \underline{\rightarrow} \mathrm{Cc} & \text{(both kind r and c)}
\end{array}$$

and the semantic function $\mathcal{E}$ will now have the functionality

$$\mathcal{E}\colon \mathrm{Exp} \overline{\rightarrow} \mathrm{Env} \overline{\rightarrow} \mathrm{Ec} \overline{\rightarrow} \mathrm{Cc}$$

The semantic equations of DML_e can now be rewritten in a similar way. As an example consider the following semantic equation (from [7])

$$\mathcal{E}[\![\mathrm{e}_1+\mathrm{e}_2]\!] = \lambda \mathrm{r}[\mathrm{Env}].\lambda \mathrm{k}[\mathrm{Ec}].\mathcal{E}[\![\mathrm{e}_1]\!] \cdot \mathrm{r} \cdot (\lambda \mathrm{v}_1[\mathrm{Ev}].\mathcal{E}[\![\mathrm{e}_2]\!] \cdot \mathrm{r} \cdot (\lambda \mathrm{v}_2[\mathrm{Ev}].\mathrm{k} \cdot (\mathcal{O}[\![+]\!] \cdot (\mathrm{v}_1,\mathrm{v}_2))))$$

where $\mathcal{O}[\![+]\!]$: $\mathrm{Ev} \times \mathrm{Ev} \rightarrow \mathrm{Ev}$. It may now be replaced by the following semantic equation of TML_e:

$$\mathcal{E}[\![\mathrm{e}_1+\mathrm{e}_2]\!] = \overline{\lambda} \mathrm{r}[\mathrm{Env}].\overline{\lambda} \mathrm{k}[\mathrm{Ec}].\mathcal{E}[\![\mathrm{e}_1]\!] \overline{\cdot}\, \mathrm{r} \,\overline{\cdot}\, (\underline{\lambda} \mathrm{v}_1[\mathrm{Ev}].\mathcal{E}[\![\mathrm{e}_2]\!] \overline{\cdot}\, \mathrm{r} \,\overline{\cdot}\, (\underline{\lambda} \mathrm{v}_2[\mathrm{Ev}].\mathrm{k} \,\underline{\cdot}\, (\mathcal{O}[\![+]\!] \underline{\cdot}\, \underline{(}\mathrm{v}_1,\mathrm{v}_2\underline{)})))$$

We note that the environment and the expression continuation are passed as compile-time arguments whereas the "intermediate values" v_1 and v_2 occur at the run-time level. In [11] we have given algorithms that will perform this transformation given information about the 2-level type of the semantic function. We refer to that paper for the details.

In the compiler we shall want to generate code for the run-time computations and the technique of 2-level λ-lifting will show us how to generate combinator code. This code can then be transformed into code for other abstract machines as described in [8]. Thus the remaining step will be to transform the semantic equations in TML_e into semantic equations in TML_m. As witnessed by the results of Section 4 this will only be straightforward if the semantic equations are in TML_l rather than TML_e. For the example language this will indeed be the case for most semantic equations (see [7]), but the above equation for $\mathcal{E}[\![\mathrm{e}_1+\mathrm{e}_2]\!]$ will be an exception. To see this note that the compile-time function application in the body of $\underline{\lambda}\mathrm{v}_1[\mathrm{Ev}].\cdots \overline{\cdot}\, (\underline{\lambda}\mathrm{v}_2[\mathrm{Ev}].\cdots)$ implies that v_1 must not occur free in the subexpression $\underline{\lambda}\mathrm{v}_2[\mathrm{Ev}].\cdots$ but unfortunately it does! So the well-formedness conditions of TML_l are not fulfilled. This then explains that our inability in [7] to provide semantic equations in TML_m is a necessary (although undesired) consequence of the nature of TML_m. Thus one would have to study ***heuristics*** for how to pass from TML_e to TML_l. Possible candidates are the rewriting of a continuation style semantics into a direct style semantics (as done in [7]) or the rewriting of a continuation style standard semantics into a continuation style store semantics (in the sense of [5]).

6 Conclusion

We have extended the notion of λ-lifting to 2-level languages using λ-notation at the top-level and λ-notation or combinator-notation at the bottom-level. The development has been performed for a 2-level type system with products and function spaces but recursive types and sum types may be incorporated as well. Unlike the 1-level case it turns out that the natural formulations of the two sorts of 2-level languages are not equally expressive in that the mixed notation (TML_m) corresponds to a proper subset of the pure λ-notation (TML_e). For the purposes of the implementation of functional languages in general, and semantics directed compiling in particular, this gives a clear formulation of some of the problems involved in achieving efficiency: The efficient implementation of a functional language (or a semantic notation) inevitably involves making a distinction between run-time and compile-time. In [11] it is shown how this distinction may be introduced in a mostly automatic way into a λ-calculus. However, this paper shows that the result (which is an expression in TML_e) is not necessarily in a form (namely TML_l) where one may vary the interpretations of the combinators (as in e.g. [8]). This calls for further research into how TML_m can be extended so as to correspond more closely to TML_e.

References

[1] P.-L.Curien: Categorical Combinators, Sequential Algorithms and Functional Programming, Pitman, London, 1986.

[2] H.B.Curry, R.Feys: Combinatory Logic, vol.1, North-Holland, Amsterdam, 1958.

[3] R.J.M.Hughes: Super-combinators, a new implementation method for applicative languages, Conf. Record of the 1982 ACM Symposium on LISP and functional programming, 1982.

[4] T.Johnson: Lambda lifting - transforming programs to recursive equations, Functional Programming Languages and Computer Architecture, Springer LNCS 201, 1985.

[5] R.Milne, C.Strachey: A Theory of Programming Language Semantics, Halstead Press, 1976.

[6] F.Nielson: Abstract interpretation of denotational definitions, STACS 1986, Springer LNCS 210, 1986.

[7] H.R.Nielson, F.Nielson: Pragmatic aspects of two-level denotational meta-languages, ESOP 1986, Springer LNCS 213, 1986.

[8] H.R.Nielson, F.Nielson: Semantics directed compiling for functional languages, Proceedings of the 1986 ACM Conf. on LISP and Functional Programming, 1986.

[9] F.Nielson: Strictness analysis and denotational abstract interpretation (extended abstract), Proceedings from the 1987 ACM Conf. on Principles of Programming Languages, 1987. A full version is to appear in Information and Computation.

[10] F.Nielson: A formal type system for comparing partial evaluators, The Technical University of Denmark, 1987. To appear in proceedings from Workshop on Partial Evaluation and Mixed Computation, North Holland, 1988.

[11] H.R.Nielson, F.Nielson: Automatic binding time analysis for a typed λ-calculus, to appear in Proceedings from the 1988 ACM Conf. on Principles of Programming Languages, 1988.

[12] D.Schmidt: Static properties of partial reduction, Kansas State University, 1987. To appear in proceedings from Workshop on Partial Evaluation and Mixed Computation, North Holland, 1988.

[13] M.Schoenfinkel: Über die Bausteine der mathematischen Logik, Mathematische Annalen, vol.92, 1924.

[14] R.D.Tennent: Principles of Programming Languages, Prentice Hall, 1981.

[15] D.A.Turner: A new implementation technique for applicative languages, Software - Practice and Experience, vol.9, 1979.

[16] D.A.Turner: Another algorithm for bracket abstraction, The Journal of Symbolic Logic, vol.44, 1979.

Deforestation: Transforming programs to eliminate trees

Philip Wadler
University of Glasgow*

Intermediate lists—and, more generally, intermediate trees—are both the basis and the bane of a certain style of programming in lazy functional languages. For example, to compute the sum of the squares of the numbers from 1 to n, one could write the following program:

$$sum\ (map\ square\ (upto\ 1\ n)) \tag{1}$$

A key feature of this style is the use of functions (*upto*, *map*, *sum*) to encapsulate common patterns of computation ("consider the numbers from 1 to n", "apply a function to each element", "sum a collection of elements").

Intermediate lists are the basis of this style—they are the glue that holds the functions together. In this case, the list $[1, 2, \ldots, n]$ connects *upto* to *map*, and the list $[1, 4, \ldots, n^2]$ connects *map* to *sum*.

But intermediate lists are also the bane—they exact a cost at run-time. For each list, time is required to allocate it, examine it, and deallocate it. Transforming the above to eliminate the intermediate lists gives

$$\begin{array}{lcl} h\ 0\ 1\ n & & \\ \textbf{where} & & \\ h\ a\ m\ n & = & \textbf{if}\ m > n \\ & & \quad \textbf{then}\ a \\ & & \quad \textbf{else}\ h\ (a + square\ m)\ (m + 1)\ n \end{array} \tag{2}$$

This program is more efficient because all operations on list cells have been eliminated.

This paper presents an algorithm that transforms programs to eliminate intermediate lists—and intermediate trees—called the Deforestation Algorithm. We characterise a form of function definition, *treeless form*, that uses no intermediate trees. An algorithm is given that can transform any term composed of functions in treeless form into a function that is itself in treeless form. For example, *sum*, *map square*, and *upto* all have treeless definitions, and applying the algorithm to program (1) yields a program equivalent to (2).

The algorithm appears suitable for inclusion in an optimising compiler. Treeless form is easy to identify syntactically, and the transformation applies to any term (or sub-term) composed of treeless functions.

Treeless form and the Deforestation Algorithm are presented in three steps. The first step presents "pure" treeless form in a first-order lazy functional language; in this form, no intermediate

*This work was in part performed at Oxford University, under a research fellowship funded by ICL.

Author's address: Department of Computing Science, University of Glasgow, Glasgow G12 8QQ, Scotland

values whatsoever are allowed. This is too restrictive for most practical uses, so the second step extends treeless form by allowing one to use "blazing" (marking of trees according to type) to indicate where intermediate values may remain. Finally, the third step extends the results to some higher-order functions, by treating such functions as macros. These "higher-order macros" may also be of use in other applications.

A prototype of the transformer has been added the LML compiler [Aug87,Joh87] by Kei Davis [Dav87]. The prototype handles blazed treeless form, and demonstrates that the transformer does work in practice. However, a thorough evaluation of the utility of these ideas must await an implementation that handles higher-order functions (as macros or otherwise).

This paper is the outgrowth of previous work on "listlessness"—transformations that eliminate intermediate lists [Wad84,Wad85]. The new approach includes several improvements. First, the definition of treeless form is simpler than the definition of listless form. Second, the Deforestation Algorithm applies to *all* terms composed solely of treeless functions, whereas the corresponding algorithm in [Wad85] applies only when a semantic condition, pre-order traversal, can be verified. Third, the treeless transformer is source-to-source (it converts functional programs into functional programs), whereas the listless transformer is not (it converts functional programs into imperative "listless programs"). However, the class of treeless functions is not the same as the class of listless functions. In some ways it is more general (it allows functions on trees, such as the *flip* function defined later), but in other ways it is more restricted (it does not apply to terms that traverse a data structure twice, such as *sum xs/length xs*). Whereas listless functions must evaluate in constant bounded space, treeless functions may use space bounded by the depth of the tree.

The remainder of this paper is organised as follows. Section 1 describes the first-order language. Section 2 introduces treeless form. Section 3 outlines the Deforestation Algorithm and sketches a proof of its correctness. Section 4 extends treeless form to include blazing. Section 5 describes how to treat some higher-order functions as macros. Section 6 concludes.

1 Language

We use a first-order language with the following grammar:

t	$::=$	v	variable
	$\mid$	$c\ t_1\ \ldots\ t_k$	constructor application
	$\mid$	$f\ t_1\ \ldots\ t_k$	function application
	$\mid$	$\textbf{case}\ t_0\ \textbf{of}\ p_1 : t_1 \mid \cdots \mid p_n : t_n$	case term
p	$::=$	$c\ v_1\ \ldots\ v_k$	pattern

In an application, $t_1, \ldots, t_k$ are called the *arguments*, and in a case term, t_0 is called the *selector*, and $p_1 : t_1, \ldots, p_n : t_n$ are called the *branches*. Function definitions have the form

$$f\ v_1\ \ldots\ v_k\ =\ t$$

Example definitions are shown in Figure 1.

The patterns in case terms may not be nested. Methods to transform case terms with nested patterns to ones without nested patterns are well known [Aug85,Wad87a].

We assume that the language is typed using the Milner polymorphic typing system [Mil78,DM82,Han87], found in LML and Miranda[1] [Tur85], among others. Familiarity with this type system is assumed.

[1] Miranda is a trademark of Research Software Limited.

$$
\begin{array}{lcl}
\mathit{list}\ \alpha & ::= & \mathit{Nil} \mid \mathit{Cons}\ \alpha\ (\mathit{list}\ \alpha) \\
\mathit{tree}\ \alpha & ::= & \mathit{Leaf}\ \alpha \mid \mathit{Branch}\ (\mathit{tree}\ \alpha)\ (\mathit{tree}\ \alpha) \\
 & & \\
\mathit{append} & : & \mathit{list}\ \alpha \rightarrow \mathit{list}\ \alpha \rightarrow \mathit{list}\ \alpha \\
\mathit{append}\ \mathit{xs}\ \mathit{ys} & = & \mathbf{case}\ \mathit{xs}\ \mathbf{of} \\
 & & \quad \mathit{Nil} \quad\quad : \mathit{ys} \\
 & & \quad \mathit{Cons}\ x\ \mathit{xs} : \mathit{Cons}\ x\ (\mathit{append}\ \mathit{xs}\ \mathit{ys}) \\
 & & \\
\mathit{flip} & : & \mathit{tree}\ \alpha \rightarrow \mathit{tree}\ \alpha \\
\mathit{flip}\ \mathit{zt} & = & \mathbf{case}\ \mathit{zt}\ \mathbf{of} \\
 & & \quad \mathit{Leaf}\ z \quad\quad : \mathit{Leaf}\ z \\
 & & \quad \mathit{Branch}\ \mathit{xt}\ \mathit{yt} : \mathit{Branch}\ (\mathit{flip}\ \mathit{yt})\ (\mathit{flip}\ \mathit{xt})
\end{array}
$$

Figure 1: Example definitions

Each constructor c and function f has a fixed arity k. For example, the constructor *Nil* has arity 0, the constructor *Cons* has arity 2, and the function *append* has arity 2. Although the language is first-order, terms and types are written in the same notation as for a higher-order language, to facilitate the extension in Section 5.

Traditionally, a term is said to be *linear* if no variable appears in it more than once. For example, (*append xs* (*append ys zs*)) is linear, but (*append xs xs*) is not. We must extend this definition slightly for linear case terms: no variable may appear in both the selector and a branch, although a variable may appear in more than one branch. For example, the definition of *append* is linear, even though *ys* appears in each branch.

The intended operational semantics of the language is normal order (leftmost outermost first) graph reduction. We say one term is more efficient than another if, for every possible instantiation of the free variables, the first requires fewer steps to reduce than the second.

2 Treeless form

Let F be a set of function names. A term is *treeless* with respect to F if it is linear, it only contains functions in F, and every argument of a function application and every selector of a case term is a variable.

In other words, writing tt for treeless terms with respect to F, we have

$$
\begin{array}{rcl}
tt & ::= & v \\
 & | & c\ tt_1\ \ldots\ tt_k \\
 & | & f\ v_1\ \ldots\ v_k \\
 & | & \mathbf{case}\ v_0\ \mathbf{of}\ p_1 : tt_1 \mid \cdots \mid p_n : tt_n
\end{array}
$$

where, in addition, tt is linear and each f is in F.

Given a collection of function definitions F, we say that F is treeless if each right-hand side in F is treeless with respect to F. The definitions of *append* and *flip* in Figure 1 are both treeless.

What is the rationale for this definition? The restriction that every argument of a function or selector of a case term must be a variable guarantees that no intermediate trees are created. It outlaws terms such as

$$\mathit{flip}\ (\mathit{flip}\ zt)$$

where $(\mathit{flip}\ zt)$ returns an intermediate tree. On the other hand, constructor applications are not subject to the same restrictions. This allows terms such as

$$\mathit{Branch}\ (\mathit{flip}\ yt)\ (\mathit{flip}\ xt)$$

where the trees returned by $(\mathit{flip}\ yt)$ and $(\mathit{flip}\ xt)$ are not intermediate: they are part of the result.

The linearity restriction guarantees that certain program transformations do not introduce repeated computations. Burstall and Darlington use the term *unfolding* to describe the operation of replacing an instance of a left-hand side of an equation by the corresponding instance of the right-hand side [BD77]. Whenever we unfold a definition with a non-linear right-hand side, we risk duplicating a term that is expensive to compute, making the program less efficient. For instance, a classic example of a non-linear function is $\mathit{square}\ x = x \times x$. If t is some term that is expensive to compute, we would prefer our program to contain $\mathit{square}\ t$ rather than its unfolded equivalent $t \times t$. On the other hand, if we define $\mathit{square}\ x = \mathit{exp}\ (2 \times \log x)$ then square is linear, and there is no harm in unfolding $\mathit{square}\ t$ to get $\mathit{exp}\ (2 \times \log t)$. By insisting that treeless definitions are linear, we guarantee that we can unfold them without sacrificing efficiency.

Being treeless is a property of a definition, not of the function defined. Figure 2 gives two definitions of the function *flatten*. The definition of $\mathit{flatten}_1$ is treeless, while the definition of $\mathit{flatten}_0$ is not. (Unfortunately, the function to flatten a tree, rather than a list of lists, has no treeless definition; but see Section 6.)

We can now present our main result.

Deforestation Theorem. Every linear term, containing only occurrences of functions with treeless definitions, can be effectively transformed to an equivalent treeless

$$
\begin{array}{lcl}
\mathit{flatten}_0 & : & \mathit{list}\ (\mathit{list}\ \alpha) \rightarrow \mathit{list}\ \alpha \\
\mathit{flatten}_0\ xss & = & \textbf{case}\ xss\ \textbf{of} \\
 & & \quad \begin{array}{lcl} \mathit{Nil} & : & \mathit{Nil} \\ \mathit{Cons}\ xs\ xss & : & \mathit{append}\ xs\ (\mathit{flatten}_0\ xss) \end{array} \\
\\
\mathit{flatten}_1 & : & \mathit{list}\ (\mathit{list}\ \alpha) \rightarrow \mathit{list}\ \alpha \\
\mathit{flatten}_1\ xss & = & \textbf{case}\ xss\ \textbf{of} \\
 & & \quad \begin{array}{lcl} \mathit{Nil} & : & \mathit{Nil} \\ \mathit{Cons}\ xs\ xss & : & \mathit{flatten}_1'\ xs\ xss \end{array} \\
\\
\mathit{flatten}_1' & : & \mathit{list}\ \alpha \rightarrow \mathit{list}\ (\mathit{list}\ \alpha) \rightarrow \mathit{list}\ \alpha \\
\mathit{flatten}_1'\ xs\ xss & = & \textbf{case}\ xs\ \textbf{of} \\
 & & \quad \begin{array}{lcl} \mathit{Nil} & : & \mathit{flatten}_1\ xss \\ \mathit{Cons}\ x\ xs & : & \mathit{Cons}\ x\ (\mathit{flatten}_1'\ xs\ xss) \end{array}
\end{array}
$$

Figure 2: A non-treeless and a treeless definition of *flatten*

term, without loss of efficiency.

We will name the algorithm that carries out the effective transformation the Deforestation Algorithm. Although the statement above only guarantees no loss of efficiency, there will in fact be a gain whenever the original term contains an intermediate tree.

For example, both *append* (*append xs ys*) *zs* and *flip* (*flip zt*) satisfy the hypothesis of the theorem. Applying the Deforestation Algorithm transforms these functions as shown in Figure 3. The transformation of *append* (*append xs ys*) *zs* is particularly noteworthy, since this term takes time $2m + n$ to compute, whereas the transformed version takes time $m + n$ to compute (where m is the length of *xs* and n is the length of *ys*). The transformation of this term introduces two new (treeless) definitions, h_0 and h_1; observe that h_1 is equivalent to *append*. Incidentally, *append xs* (*append ys zs*) is transformed into exactly the same term, modulo renaming; so, as a by-product, the Deforestation Algorithm provides a proof that *append* is associative.

The characterisation of treeless definitions and the hypothesis of the Deforestation Theorem are both purely syntactic, so it is easy for the user to determine when deforestation applies. The user need not be familiar with the details of the Deforestation Algorithm itself.

append (*append xs ys*) *zs*

transforms to

```
h0 xs ys zs
where
h0 xs ys zs  =  case xs of
                  Nil        :  h1 ys zs
                  Cons x xs  :  Cons x (h0 xs ys zs)
h1 ys zs     =  case ys of
                  Nil        :  zs
                  Cons y ys  :  Cons y (h1 ys zs)
```

flip (*flip zt*)

transforms to

```
h0 zt
where
h0 zt  =  case zt of
            Leaf z        :  Leaf z
            Branch xt yt  :  Branch (h0 xt) (h0 yt)
```

Figure 3: Results of applying the Deforestation Algorithm

3 The Deforestation Algorithm

The heart of the Deforestation Algorithm is the seven rules shown in Figure 4. We write $T[\![t]\!]$ to denote the result of converting term t to treeless form. We must have that

$$t = T[\![t]\!]$$

That is, t and $T[\![t]\!]$ should compute the same value.

Simple examination shows that the rules cover all possible terms: of the four kinds of term (variable, constructor application, function application, case term) three are covered directly, and for case terms, all four possibilities for the selector are considered.

It is clear that each of the rules preserves equivalence. In rules (1), (2), and (4), the basic form already matches treeless form, and the components are converted recursively. In rules (3) and (6), a function application is unfolded, yielding an equivalent term that is converted recursively. For rules (5) and (7), the case term is simplified, and the result is converted recursively. (Rule (7) is valid only if no variable in $p_1, \ldots, p_m$ occurs free in any of $t'_1, \ldots, t'_n$. It is always possible to rename the bound variables so that this condition applies.)

There is one problem: the algorithm as given does not terminate! An example of applying rules

$$
\begin{array}{lll}
(1) & T[\![v]\!] & = v \\
(2) & T[\![c\ t_1\ \ldots\ t_k]\!] & = c\ (T[\![t_1]\!])\ \ldots\ (T[\![t_k]\!]) \\
(3) & T[\![f\ t_1\ \ldots\ t_k]\!] & = T[\![t[t_1/v_1, \ldots, t_k/v_k]]\!] \\
 & & \quad \text{where } f \text{ is defined by } f\ v_1\ \ldots\ v_k = t \\
(4) & T[\![\textbf{case}\ v\ \textbf{of}\ p'_1 : t'_1 \mid \cdots \mid p'_n : t'_n]\!] & \\
 & & = \textbf{case}\ v\ \textbf{of}\ p'_1 : T[\![t'_1]\!] \mid \cdots \mid p'_n : T[\![t'_n]\!] \\
(5) & T[\![\textbf{case}\ c\ t_1\ \ldots\ t_k\ \textbf{of}\ p'_1 : t'_1 \mid \cdots \mid p'_n : t'_n]\!] & \\
 & & = T[\![t'_i[t_1/v_1, \ldots, t_k/v_k]]\!] \\
 & & \quad \text{where } p'_i = c\ v_1\ \ldots\ v_k \\
(6) & T[\![\textbf{case}\ f\ t_1\ \ldots\ t_k\ \textbf{of}\ p'_1 : t'_1 \mid \cdots \mid p'_n : t'_n]\!] & \\
 & & = T[\![\textbf{case}\ t[t_1/v_1, \ldots, t_k/v_k]\ \textbf{of}\ p'_1 : t'_1 \mid \cdots \mid p'_n : t'_n]\!] \\
 & & \quad \text{where } f \text{ is defined by } f\ v_1\ \ldots\ v_k = t \\
(7) & T[\![\textbf{case}\ (\textbf{case}\ t_0\ \textbf{of}\ p_1 : t_1 \mid \cdots \mid p_m : t_m)\ \textbf{of}\ p'_1 : t'_1 \mid \cdots \mid p'_n : t'_n]\!] & \\
 & & = T[\![\textbf{case}\ t_0\ \textbf{of} \\
 & & \qquad p_1 : (\textbf{case}\ t_1\ \textbf{of}\ p'_1 : t'_1 \mid \cdots \mid p'_n : t'_n) \\
 & & \qquad \cdots \\
 & & \qquad p_m : (\textbf{case}\ t_m\ \textbf{of}\ p'_1 : t'_1 \mid \cdots \mid p'_n : t'_n)]\!]
\end{array}
$$

Figure 4: Transformation rules for the Deforestation Algorithm

(1–7) is shown in Figure 5. This shows transformation of the term

$$\mathit{flip}\ (\mathit{flip}\ zt)$$

After the steps shown, we finally reach the form

$$\begin{array}{lll} \textbf{case}\ zt\ \textbf{of} & & \\ \quad \mathit{Leaf}\ z & : & \mathit{Leaf}\ z \\ \quad \mathit{Branch}\ xt\ yt & : & \mathit{Branch}\ (T[\![\mathit{flip}\ (\mathit{flip}\ xt)]\!])\ (T[\![\mathit{flip}\ (\mathit{flip}\ yt)]\!]) \end{array} \qquad (*)$$

This contains two instances of the original expression, and so the same rules may be applied again without end.

The key trick to avoid this infinite regress is to introduce appropriate *new* function definitions. For the example above, we introduce a function h_0 that satisfies the equation

$$h_0\ zt \quad = \quad T[\![\mathit{flip}\ (\mathit{flip}\ zt)]\!]$$

Now when the expansion of $T[\![\mathit{flip}\ (\mathit{flip}\ zt)]\!]$ reaches the form $(*)$ above, we can recognise that the two occurrences of $T[\![\ldots]\!]$ match the right-hand side of this equation, and replace them by the corresponding left-hand side, giving

$$\begin{array}{lllll} h_0\ zt & = & \textbf{case}\ zt\ \textbf{of} & & \\ & & \quad \mathit{Leaf}\ z & : & \mathit{Leaf}\ z \\ & & \quad \mathit{Branch}\ xt\ yt & : & \mathit{Branch}\ (h_0\ xt)\ (h_0\ yt) \end{array}$$

This completes our task; we have translated the term $\mathit{flip}\ (\mathit{flip}\ zt)$ to the equivalent treeless term $h_0\ zt$, where h_0 has the treeless definition we have just derived.

When should we introduce new definitions? The answer is that *every* term of the form $T[\![\ldots]\!]$ encountered in the course of applying rules (1–7) is a potential right-hand side for a new definition. We keep a list of all such terms. Whenever we encounter a term for a second time, we create the appropriate function definition and replace each instance of the term by a corresponding call of the function. It is sufficient if the new term is a *renaming* of a previous term. For example, in the transformation above, $(\mathit{flip}\ (\mathit{flip}\ xt))$ was a renaming of $(\mathit{flip}\ (\mathit{flip}\ zt))$, and was replaced by the corresponding call $(h_0\ xt)$. We insist that the new term is a renaming, rather than a more general instance, of the previous term; this guarantees that the resulting function call has the form $(f\ v_1\ \ldots\ v_k)$, and hence is a treeless term.

It is a simple inductive proof to show that if the computation of $T[\![t]\!]$ terminates then we get a term in treeless form, and that this term will itself be equivalent to t. Below we sketch a proof that whenever t satisfies the hypothesis of the Deforestation Theorem, then there is a bound on the size of the terms of the form $T[\![\ldots]\!]$ encountered while applying rules (1–7). Since the terms are bounded in size, and there are only a finite number of constructor and function symbols involved, then there are only a finite number of different terms (modulo renaming). Thus, eventually a renaming of a previous term must be encountered, and the algorithm is guaranteed to terminate.

As mentioned previously, linearity guarantees that unfolding (rules (3) and (6)) never introduces a repeated computation. It is easy to verify that the other rules also do not duplicate computations, and hence the derived treeless term is at least as efficient as the original term.

It remains to show that if t contains only occurrences of treeless functions, then there is a bound on the size of the terms encountered by the Deforestation Algorithm. Define the *nesting* of

```
T[[flip (flip xt)]]

 = T[[case (flip xt) of                                            (by (3))
         Leaf z       : Leaf z
         Branch xt yt : Branch (flip yt) (flip xt)]]

 = T[[case (case xt of                                             (by (6))
              Leaf z'         : Leaf z'
              Branch xt' yt'  : Branch (flip yt') (flip xt')) of
         Leaf z       : Leaf z
         Branch xt yt : Branch (flip yt) (flip xt)]]

 = T[[case xt of                                                   (by (7))
         Leaf z       : (case Leaf z of
                            Leaf z'        : Leaf z'
                            Branch xt' yt' : Branch (flip yt') (flip xt'))
         Branch xt yt : (case Branch (flip yt) (flip xt) of
                            Leaf z'        : Leaf z'
                            Branch xt' yt' : Branch (flip yt') (flip xt'))]]

 = case xt of                                                      (by (4))
     Leaf z       : T[[(case Leaf z of
                            Leaf z'        : Leaf z'
                            Branch xt' yt' : Branch (flip yt') (flip xt'))]]
     Branch xt yt : T[[(case Branch (flip yt) (flip xt) of
                            Leaf z'        : Leaf z'
                            Branch xt' yt' : Branch (flip yt') (flip xt'))]]

 = case xt of                                                      (by (5), (5))
     Leaf z       : T[[Leaf z]]
     Branch xt yt : T[[Branch (flip (flip xt)) (flip (flip yt))]]

 = case xt of                                                      (by (2), (1), (2))
     Leaf z       : Leaf z
     Branch xt yt : Branch (T[[flip (flip xt)]]) (T[[flip (flip yt)]])
```

Figure 5: Deforestation of *flip* (*flip* *xt*)

a term t, written $N[\![t]\!]$, as follows:

$$\begin{array}{lcl} N[\![v]\!] & = & 0 \\ N[\![c\ t_1\ \ldots\ t_k]\!] & = & max(N[\![t_1]\!],\ldots,N[\![t_k]\!]) \\ N[\![f\ t_1\ \ldots\ t_k]\!] & = & 1 + max(N[\![t_1]\!],\ldots,N[\![t_k]\!]) \\ N[\![\mathbf{case}\ t_0\ \mathbf{of}\ p_1 : t_1 \mid \cdots \mid p_n : t_n]\!] & = & max(N[\![t_0]\!],N[\![t_1]\!],\ldots,N[\![t_k]\!]) \end{array}$$

It is easy to verify that the nesting of a treeless term is at most 1, and that unfolding a treeless definition never increases the nesting of a term. So the nesting of any term encountered by the Deforestation Algorithm is bounded by the nesting of the initial term; call this N. Further, let M be the maximum of the size of the initial term and the size of any right-hand side of a function definition referred to (directly or indirectly) from the initial term. Then the size of any term encountered by the Deforestation Algorithm can be shown to be bounded by MN. This guarantees that the Deforestation Algorithm terminates whenever the hypothesis of the Deforestation Theorem is satisfied, and so completes the proof of the theorem.

Even if the given term does not satisfy the hypothesis of the Deforestation Theorem, the algorithm may still terminate, and when it does it will return an equivalent treeless term. For example, applying the algorithm to the non-treeless definition of $flatten_0$ in Figure 2 yields (a renaming of) the treeless definition of $flatten_1$.

4 Blazed treeless form

The definition of treeless form given in the previous section, which we will henceforth call *pure* treeless form, is quite restrictive. Consider the definition

$$\begin{array}{lcl} upto & : & int \rightarrow int \rightarrow list\ int \\ upto\ m\ n & = & \mathbf{case}\ (m > n)\ \mathbf{of} \\ & & \quad True\ :\ Nil \\ & & \quad False\ :\ Cons\ m\ (upto\ (m+1)\ n) \end{array}$$

For example, *upto* 1 4 returns [1,2,3,4]. Here we write $t_1 + t_2$ as an abbreviation for $(+)\ t_1\ t_2$, where $(+)$ is considered a function name; and similarly for other infix operators.

This definition is not in pure treeless form: first, because it contains a selector $(m > n)$ and a function argument $(m + 1)$ that are not variables; and, second, because it is not linear (m appears once in the selector and twice in the second branch). But in all cases, the offending intermediate "tree" is really an integer.

To accommodate definitions such as *upto*, we will divide all terms into two kinds, marked with either a $\oplus$ or a $\ominus$. In forestry, *blazing* is the operation of marking a tree by making a cut in its bark, so we will call the mark $\oplus$ or $\ominus$ the blazing of the term. The idea is that deforestation should eliminate ("fell") all intermediate terms ("trees") blazed $\oplus$, but that intermediate terms blazed $\ominus$ may remain. Blazing will be assigned solely on the basis of type, and all terms of the same type must be blazed the same way. In the following, we will blaze all terms of type ($list\ \alpha$) or ($tree\ \alpha$) with $\oplus$, and all terms of type *int* or *bool* with $\ominus$. If t stands for an arbitrary term, we will write $t^{\oplus}$ to indicate that t is of a type blazed $\oplus$, and $t^{\ominus}$ to indicate that t is of a type blazed $\ominus$.

In the definition of pure treeless form, the places where intermediate values can appear (function arguments and case selectors) are restricted to be variables, and terms are required to be linear. For *blazed treeless form*, the places where intermediate values can appear are restricted either to be variables or to be blazed $\ominus$, and terms are required to be linear only in variables blazed $\oplus$.

This yields the following new grammar for treeless terms with respect to a set of function names F:

$$\begin{array}{rcl} tt & ::= & vv \\ & | & (c\ tt_1\ \ldots\ tt_k)^{\oplus} \\ & | & (f\ vv_1\ \ldots\ vv_k)^{\oplus} \\ & | & (\mathbf{case}\ \ vv_0\ \ \mathbf{of}\ \ p_1 : tt_1 \mid \cdots \mid p_n : tt_n)^{\oplus} \\ vv & ::= & v \\ & | & (c\ vv_1\ \ldots\ vv_k)^{\ominus} \\ & | & (f\ vv_1\ \ldots\ vv_k)^{\ominus} \\ & | & (\mathbf{case}\ \ vv_0\ \ \mathbf{of}\ \ p_1 : vv_1 \mid \cdots \mid p_n : vv_n)^{\ominus} \end{array}$$

where in addition tt and vv are linear in variables blazed $\oplus$, and each f is in F. Note that $tt^{\ominus}$ is equivalent to $vv^{\ominus}$, and $vv^{\oplus}$ is equivalent to $v^{\oplus}$. As before, a collection of definitions F is treeless if each right-hand side in F is treeless with respect to F. The definition of *upto* and all the definitions in Figure 6 are treeless.

The Deforestation Theorem carries over virtually unchanged:

Blazed Deforestation Theorem. Every term linear in variables blazed $\oplus$, con-

```
sum            :  list int → int
sum xs         =  sum' 0 xs

sum'           :  int → list int → int
sum' a xs      =  case xs of
                    Nil            :  a
                    Cons x xs      :  sum' (a + x) xs

squares        :  list int → list int
squares xs     =  case xs of
                    Nil            :  Nil
                    Cons x xs      :  Cons (square x) (squares xs)

sumtr          :  tree int → int
sumtr xt       =  case xt of
                    Leaf x         :  x
                    Branch xt yt   :  sumtr xt + sumtr yt

squaretr       :  tree int → tree int
squaretr xt    =  case xt of
                    Leaf x         :  Leaf (square x)
                    Branch xt yt   :  Branch (squaretr xt) (squaretr yt)
```

Figure 6: More example definitions

taining only occurrences of functions with blazed treeless definitions, can be effectively transformed to an equivalent blazed treeless term, without loss of efficiency.

Two examples of applying the Blazed Deforestation Algorithm are shown in Figure 7.

To accommodate blazing, the Deforestation Algorithm is extended as follows. If during the course of transformation a sub-term arises that is blazed $\ominus$, this sub-term may be extracted and transformed independently. It is convenient to introduce the notation **let** $v^{\ominus} = t_0^{\ominus}$ **in** t_1 to represent the result of such an extraction. We will only introduce **let** terms through extraction, so the bound variable will always be blazed $\ominus$.

For example, applying extraction to the term

$$sum'\ 0\ (squares\ (upto\ 1\ n))$$

yields the term

$$\begin{array}{l}\textbf{let}\ \ u_0 = 0\ \ \textbf{in} \\ \quad \textbf{let}\ \ u_1 = 1\ \ \textbf{in} \\ \quad\quad sum'\ u_0\ (squares\ (upto\ u_1\ n))\end{array}$$

Later in the same transformation, applying extraction to the term

$$sum'\ (u_0 + square\ x)\ (squares\ (upto\ (u_1 + 1)\ n))$$

$$sum\ (squares\ (upto\ 1\ n))$$

transforms to

$$\begin{array}{lcl} h_0\ 0\ 1\ n & & \\ \textbf{where} & & \\ h_0\ u_0\ u_1\ n & = & \textbf{case}\ (u_0 > n)\ \textbf{of} \\ & & \quad True \ :\ a \\ & & \quad False\ :\ h_0\ (u_0 + square\ u_1)\ (u_1 + 1)\ n \end{array}$$

$$sumtr\ (squaretr\ xt)$$

transforms to

$$\begin{array}{lcl} h_0\ xt & & \\ \textbf{where} & & \\ h_0\ xt & = & \textbf{case}\ xt\ \textbf{of} \\ & & \quad Leaf\ x \quad\quad\ \ :\ square\ x \\ & & \quad Branch\ xt\ yt\ :\ h_0\ xt + h_0\ yt \end{array}$$

Figure 7: Results of applying the Blazed Deforestation Algorithm

yields the term

$$\begin{array}{l} \textbf{let } u_2 = u_0 + square\ x \textbf{ in} \\ \quad \textbf{let } u_3 = u_1 + 1 \textbf{ in} \\ \quad\quad sum'\ u_2\ (squares\ (upto\ u_3\ n)) \end{array}$$

The inner term here is a renaming of the inner term of the previous expression, and will cause the appropriate new function to be defined:

$$h_0\ u_0\ u_1\ n = T[\![sum'\ u_0\ (squares\ (upto\ u_1\ n))]\!]$$

Calls to h_0 will now replace the inner terms above.

Extraction forces all arguments of a function blazed $\ominus$ to be variables. This is why it is not necessary for terms to be linear in variables blazed $\ominus$: since unfolding only replaces such variables by other variables, no duplication of a term that is expensive to compute can occur.

We must also add to the definition of $T[\![t]\!]$ in Figure 4 the four additional rules in Figure 8. Rules (8) and (9) supersede rules (3) and (6), respectively, in the case where the result and all arguments of a function are blazed $\ominus$. In this case it is not necessary to unfold the application: it can be simply left in place unchanged. In particular, rules (8) and (9) cover all applications of primitive functions, such as $t_0 > t_1$ or $t_0 + t_1$, which cannot be unfolded anyway. Rules (10) and (11) manage occurrences of let. (Rule (11) is only valid if v does not occur in any of $p'_1, \ldots, p'_m$. It is always possible to rename the bound variables so that this condition applies.)

After the transformation is complete, all terms of the form

$$\textbf{let } v^{\ominus} = tt_0^{\ominus} \textbf{ in } tt_1$$

may be removed as follows. If v occurs at most once in tt_1, the term may be replaced by $tt_1[tt_0/v]$. If v occurs more than once, we may introduce a new function h defined by $h\ v = tt_1$, and the term may be replaced by $h\ tt_0$. Since tt_0 is blazed $\ominus$, this application is a treeless term. (Alternatively, we can simply add **let** terms to the language, and just extend the definition of treeless term to include terms in the above form.)

It is a straightforward extension of the previous results to show that the modified Deforestation Algorithm satisfies the requirements of the Blazed Deforestation Theorem.

$$\begin{array}{ll}
(8) & T[\![(f\ t_1^{\ominus}\ \ldots\ t_k^{\ominus})^{\ominus}]\!] \\
 & \quad = \ (f\ (T[\![t_1^{\ominus}]\!])\ \ldots\ (T[\![t_k^{\ominus}]\!]))^{\ominus} \\
(9) & T[\![\textbf{case } (f\ t_1^{\ominus}\ \ldots\ t_k^{\ominus})^{\ominus} \textbf{ of } p'_1 : t'_1 \mid \cdots \mid p'_n : t'_n]\!] \\
 & \quad = \ \textbf{case } (f\ (T[\![t_1^{\ominus}]\!])\ \ldots\ (T[\![t_k^{\ominus}]\!]))^{\ominus} \textbf{ of } p'_1 : T[\![t'_1]\!] \mid \cdots \mid p'_n : T[\![t'_n]\!] \\
(10) & T[\![\textbf{let } v^{\ominus} = t_0^{\ominus} \textbf{ in } t_1]\!] \\
 & \quad = \ \textbf{let } v^{\ominus} = T[\![t_0^{\ominus}]\!] \textbf{ in } T[\![t_1]\!] \\
(11) & T[\![\textbf{case } (\textbf{let } v^{\ominus} = t_0^{\ominus} \textbf{ in } t_1) \textbf{ of } p'_1 : t'_1 \mid \cdots \mid p'_n : t'_n]\!] \\
 & \quad = \ \textbf{let } v^{\ominus} = T[\![t_0^{\ominus}]\!] \textbf{ in } T[\![\textbf{case } t_1 \textbf{ of } p'_1 : t'_1 \mid \cdots \mid p'_n : t'_n]\!]
\end{array}$$

Figure 8: Additional rules for the Blazed Deforestation Algorithm

5 Higher-order macros

From the user's point of view, one of the most attractive features of programming in a functional style is the use of higher-order functions. However, for the implementor of a program transformation system, such as the Deforestation Algorithm, first-order languages may be easier to cope with. This section shows how much (but not all) of the expressiveness of higher-order functions can be achieved in a first-order language, by treating higher-order functions as macros. The same idea may be useful for a variety of applications where it is easier to deal with a first-order language, but the power of a higher-order language is desirable.

The first step is to add **where** terms to the language. These have the form

$$t \textbf{ where } d_1; \ldots; d_n$$

where t is a term and $d_1, \ldots, d_n$ are function definitions. This can be translated back into our equation language in a straightforward manner, by use of a technique called *lambda lifting* [Joh87,Pey87]. In particular, if $d_1, \ldots, d_n$ contain no free variables then the term above is just equivalent to t, where the definitions $d_1, \ldots, d_n$ are added to the top-level list of definitions, with systematic renaming of functions (according to the scope of the **where** clause) to avoid any name conflicts.

The second step is to add higher-order macro definitions. These have the form

$$f\ v_1\ \ldots\ v_k\ \hat{=}\ t$$

That is, they are like ordinary definitions, but we write $\hat{=}$ instead of $=$. The term t may now contain variables in place of function names, and applications are no longer restricted by arity. The same Milner polymorphic type system is used. The formal parameters $v_1, \ldots, v_n$ may now have a ground type, like *int* or (*list* α), or a function type, like (*int* $\rightarrow$ *int*), or even a higher-order type, like ((*int* $\rightarrow$ *int*) $\rightarrow$ *int*). The only restriction is that *higher-order macros cannot be recursive.*

The lack of recursion, combined with the Milner type discipline, guarantees that all higher-order definitions can be expanded out at compile-time, with no risk of a non-terminating expansion. But at first the lack of recursion may seem overly restrictive. Doesn't it rule out our favourite higher-order functions, such as *map* and *fold*? As it turns out, it doesn't: we get the recursion back by using the **where** facility defined above. Definitions of *map* and *fold* are given in Figure 9; recursion is limited to the first-order functions g and h.

Given the definitions in Figure 9 we can write terms such as

$$\begin{gathered} sum\ (map\ square\ (upto\ 1\ n)) \\ map\ sum\ (map\ (map\ square)\ xss) \\ (map\ square \circ map\ cube)\ xs \\ map\ (square \circ cube)\ xs \end{gathered}$$

Each of these expands out to a first-order program, which can then be transformed using the Deforestation Algorithm of the preceding sections.

The mechanism defined here covers many, but not all, uses of higher-order functions. For instance, using this mechanism it is not possible to define or manipulate a list of functions, as one could in a true higher-order language.

Higher-order macros provide one way to extend the Deforestation Algorithm from a first-order language, and they may be valuable for other applications as well. However, their worth is not yet proven. An alternative would be to formulate a version of the Deforestation Theorem that applies to higher-order functions directly, without the need to treat them as macros.

$$\begin{array}{lcl}
map & : & (\alpha \rightarrow \beta) \rightarrow list\ \alpha \rightarrow list\ \beta \\
map\ f\ xs & \hat{=} & g\ xs \\
 & & \textbf{where} \\
 & & g\ xs\ =\ \textbf{case}\ xs\ \textbf{of} \\
 & & \qquad Nil \quad : \ Nil \\
 & & \qquad Cons\ x\ xs \ : \ Cons\ (f\ x)\ (g\ x) \\
 & & \\
fold & : & (\alpha \rightarrow \beta \rightarrow \alpha) \rightarrow \alpha \rightarrow list\ \beta \rightarrow \alpha \\
fold\ f\ a\ xs & \hat{=} & h\ a\ xs \\
 & & \textbf{where} \\
 & & h\ a\ xs\ =\ \textbf{case}\ xs\ \textbf{of} \\
 & & \qquad Nil \quad : \ a \\
 & & \qquad Cons\ x\ xs \ : \ h\ (f\ a\ x)\ xs \\
 & & \\
sum & : & list\ int \rightarrow int \\
sum & \hat{=} & fold\ (+)\ 0 \\
 & & \\
(\circ) & : & (\beta \rightarrow \gamma) \rightarrow (\alpha \rightarrow \beta) \rightarrow \alpha \rightarrow \gamma \\
(f \circ g)\ x & \hat{=} & f\ (g\ x)
\end{array}$$

Figure 9: Example higher-order definitions

6 Conclusion

An oft-repeated justification for the study of functional programming is that functional programs are eminently suited for program transformation. And indeed, program transformation is a star member of the repertoire for writers of functional compilers. For example, many key steps in the LML compiler involve transformation techniques [Aug87,Joh87]. Deforestation appears to be an attractive candidate for the next application of program transformation to compiler technology.

An important feature of the Deforestation Algorithm is that it is centred on an easily recognised class of definitions, treeless form. This eases the task of the compiler writer. Perhaps even more importantly, it eases the task of the compiler user, because it is easy to characterise what sort of expressions will be optimised and what sort of optimisations will be performed.

Further work is desirable in two directions.

First, treeless form may be generalised. One possible generalisation rests on the observation that some function arguments, such as the second argument to *append*, appear directly in the function result. These arguments might be treated in the same way as arguments to constructors in the definition of treeless form. It was previously noted that the function to flatten a tree has no treeless definition; with this generalisation, it would. Related ideas are discussed in [Wad87b].

Second, further practical experience should be acquired, in order to assess better the utility of the ideas presented here.

Acknowledgements. I am grateful to Kei Davis for acting as a sounding board and undertaking to implement some of the ideas reported here, and to Cordelia Hall and Catherine Lyons for their comments on this paper.

comments on this paper.

References

[Aug85] L. Augustsson, Compiling pattern matching. In *Proceedings of the Conference on Functional Programming Languages and Computer Architecture*, Nancy, France, September 1985. LNCS 201, Springer-Verlag, 1985.

[Aug87] L. Augustsson, Compiling lazy functional languages, Part II. Ph.D. dissertation, Department of Computer Science, Chalmers Tekniska Högskola, Göteborg, Sweden, 1987.

[BD77] R. M. Burstall and J. Darlington, A transformation system for developing recursive programs. *Journal of the ACM*, 24(1):44–67, January 1977.

[Dav87] M. K. Davis, Deforestation: Transformation of functional programs to eliminate intermediate trees. M.Sc. dissertation, Programming Research Group, Oxford University, September 1987.

[DM82] L. Damas and R. Milner, Principal type schemes for functional programs. In *Proceedings of the ACM Symposium on Principles of Programming Languages*, January 1982.

[Joh87] T. Johnsson, Compiling lazy functional languages. Ph.D. dissertation, Department of Computer Science, Chalmers Tekniska Högskola, Göteborg, Sweden, 1987.

[Han87] P. Hancock, Polymorphic type-checking. In [Pey87].

[Mil78] R. Milner, A theory of type polymorphism in programming. *Journal of Computer and System Sciences*, 17:348–375, 1978.

[Pey87] S. L. Peyton Jones, *The Implementation of Functional Programming Languages*, Prentice Hall, 1987.

[Tur85] D. A. Turner, Miranda: A non-strict functional language with polymorphic types. In *Proceedings of the Conference on Functional Programming Languages and Computer Architecture*, Nancy, France, September 1985. LNCS 201, Springer-Verlag, 1985.

[Wad84] P. L. Wadler, Listlessness is better than laziness: Lazy evaluation and garbage collection at compile-time. In *Proceedings of the ACM Symposium on Lisp and Functional Programming*, Austin, Texas, August 1984.

[Wad85] P. L. Wadler, Listlessness is better than laziness II: Composing listless functions. In *Proceedings of the Workshop on Programs as Data Objects*, Copenhagen, October 1985. LNCS 217, Springer-Verlag, 1985.

[Wad87a] P. L. Wadler, Efficient compilation of pattern-matching. In [Pey87].

[Wad87b] P. L. Wadler, The concatenate vanishes. Note distributed to FP electronic mailing list, December 1987.

On implementing logic programming languages on a dataflow architecture

Patrick Weemeeuw[1]
Maurice Bruynooghe[2]
Marleen De Hondt[3]

K.U.Leuven
Department of Computer Science
Celestijnenlaan 200 A
B-3030 Heverlee
Belgium

Abstract

An implementation scheme for a logic programming language on the Manchester Dataflow Computer is presented. The Manchester Dataflow Computer is a parallel data-driven computer based on the tagged-token model. The logic programming language is derived from PROLOG, with addition of modes and types. The cut operator has been replaced by guards. The implementation scheme supports OR-parallel evaluation of don't-know and don't-care non determinism.

Introduction

Exploiting parallelism is currently one of the major research goals in computer science. At the hardware level, an important approach is the development of dataflow architectures. A well known example is the Manchester Dataflow Computer [Gurd et al. 85]. At the software level, logic programming is a promising approach. In this paper, we explore how a simple logic programming language can be executed on the Manchester Dataflow Computer. We concentrate on aspects of OR-parallelism.

In section 1, we give a brief survey of the Manchester Dataflow Computer. This is followed by a description of our simple logic programming language in section 2. The implementation scheme is presented in section 3, and some experimental results are discussed in section 4. In section 5, we refer to some related work, and we finish with some discussion in section 6.

1. Survey of the Manchester dataflow computer

We briefly summarize the main features of the Manchester Dataflow Computer, for more details, the reader is referred to [Gurd et al. 85] and [Kirkham 84]. A recent survey of dataflow machine architectures is in [Veen 86].

A dataflow graph is a directed graph; the nodes represent functions and the arcs represent data paths between these functions. A state of the computation is represented by a set of tokens on the arcs of the graph. A node is activated as soon as each input arc contains a token. The active node removes the tokens from its input arcs and puts tokens on (some of) its output arcs.

Due to hardware limitations, a node has one or two input arcs, and zero, one or two output arcs. Multiple copies of a token can be obtained by a tree of DUP nodes: the DUP (DUPlicate) operation produces two copies of its only input.

Conditional computation is possible with the BRR (BRanch on boolean - Repeat) node, which copies its left (or first) input token to its left or right output arc, according to the boolean value of its right (or second) input token.

---

1. Currently supported by CEE Biotechnology Action Programme
2. Supported as research associate by the Belgian National Fund For Scientific Research
3. Currently at BIM, Kwikstraat 4, B 3078 Everberg

The graph structure has only an implicit representation in the hardware, all tokens travel on the same ring structure. Besides a (typed) data value, tokens also contain their destination specifying the address and input port of the node which has to process the token. Arcs are usually static and the destinations are known at compile time, however, to allow e.g. returning the result of a procedure to the caller, one has also dynamic arcs, the destination of tokens on such arcs is only known at run-time. Finally, to allow multiple simultaneous activations of the same node (*reentrant code*), tokens also contain a label (*tag*) consisting of an index, an iteration level and an activation name. A node *fires* only when there are tokens with the same label on each input port. A fatal error, called a token clash occurs when there is more than one token with the same label on some edge of the graph (input port of a node). Graphs which are free from token clashes are called *safe*.

The index differentiates between different parts of the same data structure (e.g. an array); the iteration level differentiates between the (possibly parallel) activations of the body of a loop, and the activation name is intended to differentiate between (possibly parallel) activations of a procedure body.

Iteration level and activation name together form the *colour* of a token; the *context* of a token consists of its destination and its colour. Instructions involving labels or destinations will be introduced when needed.

To introduce the notion of matching functions, we first explain the matching unit. The matching unit is a sort of associative memory, where tokens destinated for a node with two input ports wait for the arrival of a token with a corresponding (*matching*) label. This is the standard use of the matching unit, achieved with the matching function EW (Extract/Wait).

The matching function is also included in the destination field. If the destination is a unary operator, the matching function is always BY (BYpass): the token passes the matching store and the operator is activated. The success action prescribes what happens to the already stored *matching* token before activating the operator, the fail action prescribes what happens to the arriving token when a matching token is not available. So, EW means: if the matching token is in the matching unit, then extract it, otherwise wait (i.e. store the arriving token in the matching unit).

Other matching functions are: ED, DD, ID, DD and PG. We only explain here those that are needed for our purposes.

- PD (Preserve/Defer): preserve as success action leaves a copy of the matching token in the matching unit; defer as fail action does not store the token in the matching unit but put it back on the ring structure for another cycle.
- DD (Decrement/Defer): decrement as success action leaves a copy of the matching token in the matching unit with the value decremented; defer as fail action.
- ID (Increment/Defer): analogous to DD.

Note: it is the matching function of the arriving token that determines the action to be performed.

A dataflow graph is *well formed* if no tokens are left in the matching unit after execution. This is an important property, because the capacity of the matching unit is finite and the performance decreases quickly when overflow occurs.

It is often necessary, for reasons of efficiency, to store some data structures (see [Bowen 81],[Veen 86]). For the time being, this is done in the matching unit by means of special matching functions. A special unit, called the *structure store*, is announced to cope with this needs without burdening the matching unit.

2. Description of the source language

Our source language is derived from PROLOG. The language is different from PROLOG in three major points:

- guards as a means of control instead of cuts;
- modes;
- types.

We do not allow cuts in our source language because the effect of the cut-operator depends on the sequential execution of the program. Instead of this, we introduce don't-care non determinism by means of guards. We distinguish between don't-know and don't-care predicates.

Don't-know procedures do not contain any guards; all clauses can be initiated in parallel, and several clauses may succeed.

A don't-care procedure has in each clause one (possibly empty) guard. The guards of the different clauses can be started in parallel; only one of the clauses with succeeding guard commits and is selected for further execution. A procedure call fails if either all guards fail or the remainder of the body of the commited clause fails. Procedures occurring in a guard are not allowed to produce side-effects; but may bind variables.

To simplify compilation in this first attempt, we have also used type and mode declarations; this avoids real unification. We distinguish between modes in and out: an argument on an in-position must be ground at run-time before executing the call; an argument on an out-position must be free at-run time before executing the call, ground after. This mode restriction is often made and a lot of practical programs obey it. [Drabent 87] has a thorough discussion on this topic. Both types and modes can often be inferred with sufficient precision by abstract interpretation, see a.o. [Bruynooghe et al 87].

Currently we handle only types built from the primitive "integer" and the structure "list".

As an illustration, we show some well known examples:

A. **append**: concatenates two (generic) lists to form a new list.

```
modes: in/in/out
types: List(T)/List(T)/List(T)

append ( L1, L2, L3 ) :-
        L1 = nil | L3 <== L2 ;
        L1 <> nil | L1 ==> ( X . L1' ),
                append( L1', L2, L3' ),
                L3 <== ( X . L3' ) .
```

Notes: - we use the infix notation for lists.
- '<==' means construction, '==>' means selection.
- '=' is a test for equality.
- '|' is the commit sign.

B. **delete**: takes one element (the first argument) out of a list of integers (the second argument) and returns also the remainder of the list(the third argument).

modes: out/in/out
types: Integer/List(Integer)/List(Integer)

```
delete ( E, L, R ) :-
        L <> nil, L ==> ( E . R );
        L <> nil, L ==> ( X . L' ),
                    delete ( E, L', R' ),
                    R <== ( X . R' ).
```

C. **perm**: generate a permutation (second argument) of the list given in the first argument.

modes: in/out
types: List(T)/List(T)

```
perm ( L, PL ) :-
        L = nil | PL <== nil;
        L <> nil | delete ( E, L, R ),
                 perm ( R, PL' ),
                 PL <==  ( E . PL' ).
```

In the remainder of the text, we mean by 'in line code' all code associated with (explicitly written) unification, i.e. tests, selections and constructions.

3. Implementation scheme

In this section we present our implementation scheme. This is done in an incremental way: we start with introducing the chosen data representation. This is followed by a discussion of the implementation of the basic building blocks and an example. Then we discuss the extensions needed to include garbage collection and to abort the guards.

The figures below are drawn according to the following conventions:

— nodes are indicated by boxes; macro-nodes are drawn with double lines at the sides of the box.

— continuous arrows represent static arcs; dashed arrows represent dynamic arcs.

— matching functions, if different from the default values, are written close to the arc they refer to.

— a literal on an input arc is represented between double quotes at a T symbol; a ⊥ represents a cutted output arc (no tokens are produced).

— tokens are indicated with their symbolic name or their type and value followed (if necessary for good understanding) by (a part of) their label between '<' and '>'. E.g. L <col(c)> means the token representing the value of L with the colour c in its label; cxt(dest(d),col(c0)) stands for a context token consisting of the destination d and the colour c0, with concealed label.

— when an input port of a node is explicitly labeled in a figure (because there is a destination token referring to it), then that label is in italics.

— DUP nodes are usually indicated by the splitting of an arc.

3.1 Implementation of data structures

In [Bowen 81] a profound justification of possible implementation schemes can be found.

For objects of a scalar type, the implementation is straightforward: they are represented by a token with an appropriate data value.

The representation of structured objects (only lists in our case) is more complex. An empty list is a scalar object whose data value type is *null*, nonempty lists are represented by a token whose data value type is a *context*-type; the data value itself consists of a context: a colour-destination pair *c-d.r*; the destination *d.r* is always the right input port of a SCD node (Set Colour and Destination, see below). The information stored in the list is represented by three distinct tokens, which have colour *c*, destination *d.l* and which have as index respectively 1, 2 and 3. The first token is a reference count, the data value is an integer, it is used for garbage collection (see below). The second token represents the head, the data value represents either a scalar or another structured object. The third token represents the tail, which is either the empty list or again a structured object. These three tokens reside on the left input port (*d.l*) of a SCD node, which means that they occupy the matching unit, waiting for a matching token to arrive on the other port of the SCD node. (Thus a n-element list occupies 3 n entries in the matching unit, these are the tokens to be moved to the announced "structure store".) One of these tokens can be selected by sending an appropriate token to the other port of the SCD node, this is illustrated in fig. 3.1.

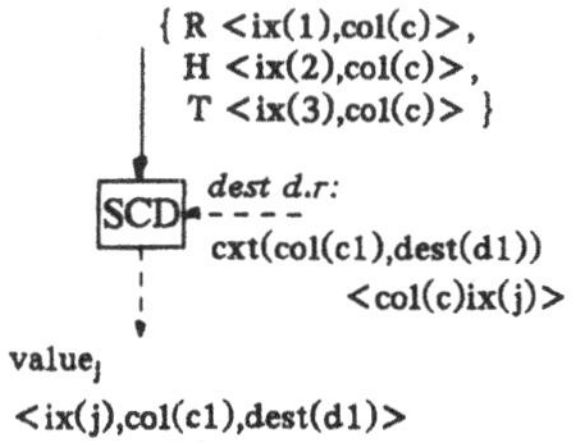

Figure 3.1: Selection of a token residing on a SCD node
SCD node with address d; *three tokens representing a list are on the left input port. Arrival of a context token with the same color* c *selects the token with index* j, *gives it the color* c1 *and forwards it to destination* d1 *(value$_j$ is either* R, H *or* T*). If the matching function of the context token is PD, the selection is non destructive.*

3.2 List operators

The macros we use, resemble very much the macros given in [Bowen 81]. The only difference is that we use the information that there are exactly 3 fields needed for a list cell; this allows to optimise the COLLECT-macro described there. For details, we refer to [Bowen 81], we only show a specification of the macro's we will use.

3.2.1 Construction

As a list construction always succeeds, we can use the (slightly modified) STORE-macro of [Bowen 81]. Consequently, ..., L <— (X.L'), ... is represented as shown in fig. 3.2.

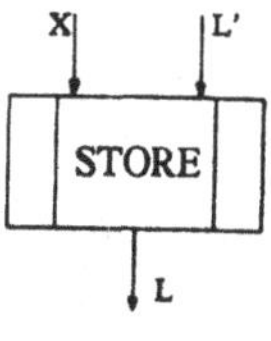

Figure 3.2: List construction X *and* L' *have the same color c; a token* L *with color c is created whose data value is cxt(col(c),dest(d.r)), with d.r the address of the right input port of a SCD node. Also the three list tokens (reference count, head and tail) with colour c and destination d.l are created by the STORE macro.*

3.2.2 Testing for an empty list

Fig. 3.3 shows the graph for this test. Failure of the test must absorb all tokens related to the clause under consideration, so, all these tokens are inputs for the macro BRR. The test is done with the CET (Compare Equal Type) node which compares the type of the data value with the type *null*. The result of the test is fed into a BRR node and decides whether the inputs are forwarded on the F branch or absorbed on the T branch.

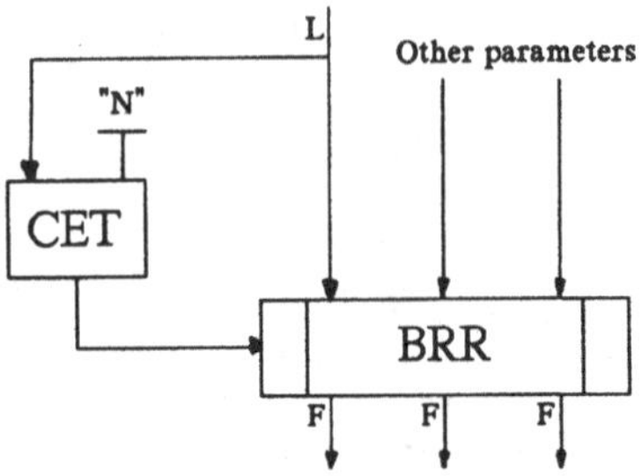

Figure 3.3: Test L <> nil (type of nil is "N")

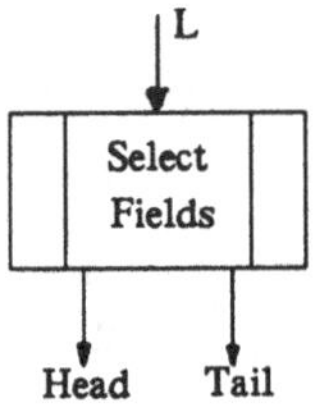

Figure 3.4: Selection L ==> (Head.Tail)

3.2.3 Selection

Selection of the head or the tail of a list is accomplished by sending the index of the corresponding field of the first list cell, together with the context-token representing the list to the SELECT macro as given in [Bowen 81]. For the sake of simplicity, we will always select both the head and the tail, and we represent this by the single macro 'select-fields' as shown in figure 3.4. If the list is possibly empty, a test on nil has to be inserted before the selection.

3.3 Procedure calls

3.3.1 Non tail-recursive calls

To execute a procedure call, all tokens representing input parameters are sent to the body of the procedure; for each output parameter, the destination for that parameter is sent. Some other values are also passed to the procedure; they are explained in fig. 3.5. All tokens passed to the procedure have the same unique colour.

As a procedure may be non deterministic and may produce multiple solutions, all solutions have a distinct colour to distinguish between them. This colour is an extra output parameter of the procedure (the "colour token"). For each solution, a copy in the correct colour has to be produced of all values still alive after the procedure call, because together with the result of the procedure they activate the remainder of the body in that branch. As a result, all this values have to be stored, as can be seen in fig. 3.5. This is the general scheme without garbage collection for non tail-recursive calls.

3.3.2 Tail-recursive calls

Problems arise if, ignoring in-line instructions, the last call of a procedure is a recursive call as in the second alternative of delete. The results of a call delete (E,L',R') at recursion level n are E, R' and a result color ci. These results are fed into the in-line instruction R <== (X.R') of delete at level n-1. This in-line instruction does not change the color, thus we obtain a result at level n-1 having also the color ci. This cannot yield clashes for R' tokens in the instruction R <== X.R' because the level n result with color ci is consumed before the level n-1 result with the same color is produced. However, the result colour ci is produced independently from R and is used to colour the X token required by the instruction R <== X.R'. Thus the result color ci at level n-1 and the X token with color ci at level n-1 can be produced before the X token with color ci is consumed at level n. In such a case we have a token clash.

Two solutions are possible, we can delay the creation of the result colour until the in-line instructions have finished, or we can take care that colours become different. We have opted for the last solution: we change the colour. Before entering such problematic calls, we increment the iteration level of the colour, after returning, we decrement the iteration level. This assures that the results of the two levels have a different colour.

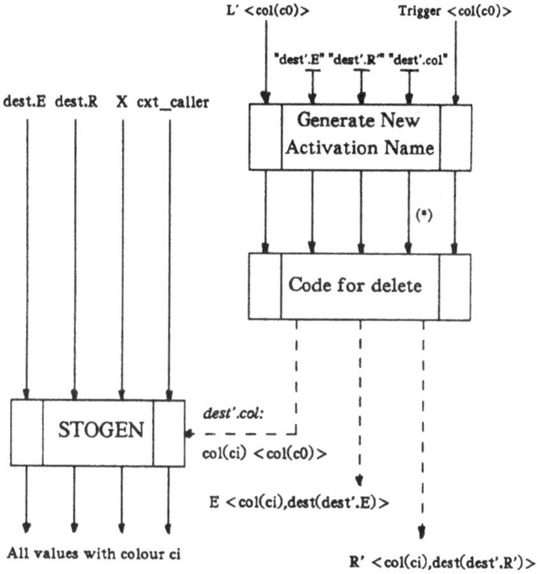

Figure 3.5: Procedure call for delete (E, L', R')
L' is an input parameter. A trigger token **Trigger** *is also sent to the procedure, to activate parts of the dataflow graph that are not activated automatically by the data. As* E *and* R' *are output parameters, the destination for each of them is sent to the procedure, together with the destination of the colour token* (**dest'.col**) *and the colour of the caller* (**c0**)*, both combined in one context token cxt(col(c0)dest(dest'.col)) at (*). All outputs of generate new activation name have a new color c1. For each solution, delete returns the tokens* E *and* R' *as results. They have colour* ci*); also a colour token is returned, it has as value* col(ci) *and as colour the initial colour* c0*. This token is fed into STOGEN, where it matches the other tokens of the clause. STOGEN forwards its other inputs with new colour* ci*. These tokens, combined with the results of delete are used to complete the computation (the statement R <== (X.R')).*

This problem of clashing arises in all cases where, after finishing a call P, an ancestor P' of the same predicate can be completed only by executing in-line code.

3.4 The generate block

At the end of each branch, the results, and the colour of each of them, are returned to the calling procedure by the generate block. For each result we have to return, we use a SDS (Set DeStination) node to send the result to its proper destination (fig. 3.6). The scheme of fig. 3.7 produces the resulting colour token and sends it to its proper destination.

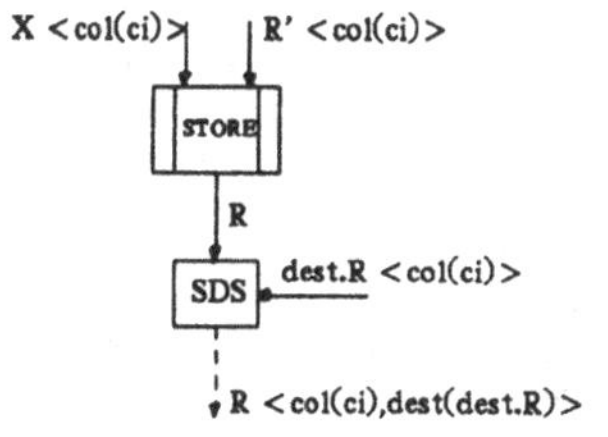

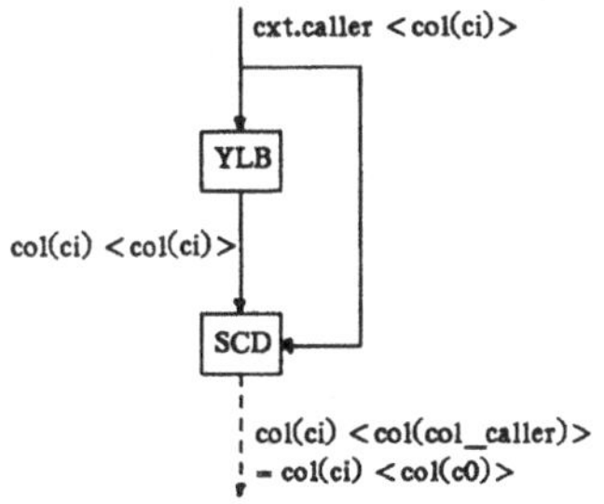

Figure 3.6: R <== (X.R') and returning of R

Figure 3.7: Part of generate block
The YLB (Yield LaBel) node returns the label field of the incoming token.

3.5 Or-parallelism

The branches in a procedure body are activated in parallel. Branches without procedure calls are given a new activation name, except the first one. Because procedure calls start with giving a new activation name (fig. 3.5), this assures that solutions computed in different branches have different activation names.

The duplication of incoming values, and the computation of new activation names for the branches which need it, is done by a split block at the beginning of each branch.

Our scheme for assigning new activation names is as in fig 3.9 (where '&' indicates the generation of a new activation name, and '...' in-line code). This scheme is equivalent with the scheme in figure 3.8, but more economical in activation names, because the third and the fourth branch may fail in the in-line part before generating a new activation name. For procedures which are recursive in more than one branch (as our example), the difference becomes more important, because the difference in use of activation names at the bottom level of recursion is multiplied for each level of recursion. For branches without procedure calls, it would be better to generate new activation names at the end of the branch instead of at the beginning, but this has not been implemented.

```
Query: ..., a, ... .

a :- & ... ;
     & ... ;
     & ..., a, ... ;
     & ..., a, ... .
```

Figure 3.8: A simple scheme for the generation of new activation names.

```
Query: ..., & a, ... .

a :- ... ;
     & ... ;
     ..., & a, ... ;
     ..., & a, ... .
```

Figure 3.9: A more economical scheme for the generation of new activation names.

3.6 An example: delete

Here follows the complete scheme for the procedure delete without garbage collection (see fig. 3.10).

3.7 Garbage collection

Up till now, we didn't pay any attention to make our programs well formed. In fact, there are two sources of tokens which remain in the matching store after execution of the program: i.e. lists and the values that have to survive a procedure call.

The garbage collection on lists can be done automatically by introducing a reference count for each cell of the lists, as can be found in [Bowen 81]. This introduces some synchronisation constraints when manipulating lists, in order to guarantee that the counters should not be decremented to soon. This is not further discussed here.

On the other hand, stored values are deleted when the called procedure sends a finish signal to the calling procedure, which means that no more solutions will be generated (see fig 3.11: partial expansion of the modified macro STOGEN). The value to be stored comes on the left input part of the SCD node. Each arriving colour token combines with the destination of the stored value to send a copy of the stored value to the desired destination in the right colour. The finish signal extracts the stored value and sends it to a kill node (this is the reason why the outcoming arc is dynamic). To generate this finish signal, several other synchronisation signals are necessary, but let us first mention the implementation goals for this garbage collection:

- garbage should be removed as soon as possible;
- its effect on performance should be minimal.

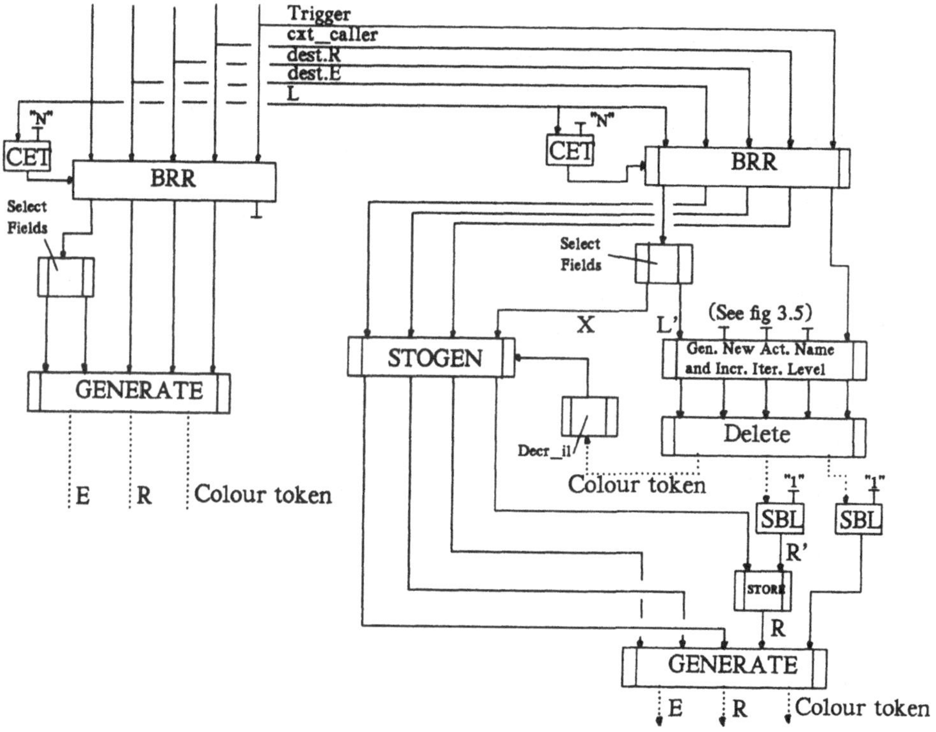

Figure 3.10: Delete without garbage collection
Remark: SBL subtracts 1 from the iteration level in the label, *the "Decr_il" macro subtracts 1 from the iteration level in the* value *of the colour token.*

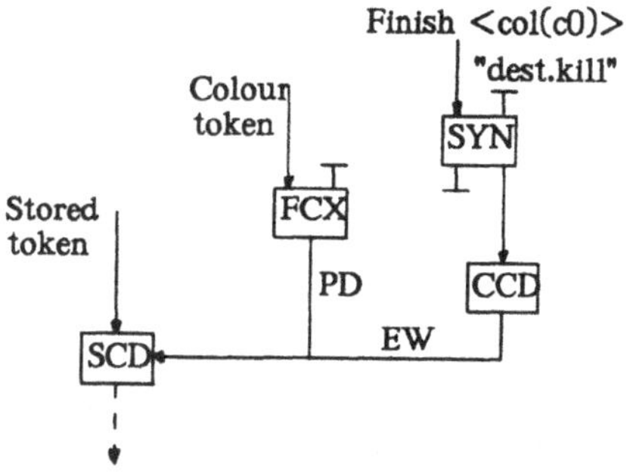

Figure 3.11: Part of STOGEN with garbage collection
The FCX node (Form ConteXt) combines the colour of the solution of the called procedure with the destination of the node where the stored token is further processed. When the finish signal arrives, it triggers the literal **"dest.kill"**, *which is the address of a KIL node (a KIL node consumes its input tokens without producing any output tokens). This destination token has the same colour as the finish token:* **c0**. *The CCD node (Combine Colour and Destination) transforms the destination token in a context token, which is sent to the SCD node with matching function* **EW** *to remove the stored token.*

3.7.1 *Principle*

A procedure call is finished when all branches are finished, so for each branch we need an end-of-branch signal. Further, we do not generate a finish signal for a procedure until we know that all produced solutions are accepted by the calling procedure, because the copies of the stored values at the call may be destroyed as soon as the finish signal arrives. So we need two auxiliary signals: a generate signal that indicates that some branch has produced a solution, and an accept signal that indicates that the calling procedure has processed the solution.

To synchronise this exchange of messages between caller and callee, the callee increments a counter before sending a solution and decrements a counter when the accept signal is received. The finish signal is only forwarded when all solutions are sent and the counter has its initial value.

An end-of-branch signal is derived from the finish signals of the calls or in-line code in the branch. The finish signals travel from right to left in the branch.

When a test fails, a finish signal is generated. When a solution is produced at the end of the branch, a finish signal is released as soon as the generate signal has been registered. Each procedure call in the body of the branch sends a finish signal to its left when

- the called procedure is terminated, i.e. it will produce no more solutions;
- for each solution produced by the called procedure, the part of the branch to the right has been terminated, i.e. it has received a finish signal for each of them.

3.7.2 *Algorithm*

The behaviour described above is accomplished by extending the function of the already defined blocks. We sum up the functions of each of them here.

The call block

For each activation the call block performs the following functions:

— storage of tokens representing values needed for the activation of the remainder of the branch;

— generation of a copy of those tokens for each solution of the called procedure;

— delivery of an accept signal to the called procedure for each received solution after the generation of the copies of the stored values (i.e.: the activation of the remainder of the branch);

— counting the number of the generated solutions of the called procedure;

— accepting the finish signal of the called procedure;

— accepting a finish signal for each activation of the remainder of the branch;

— sending a finish signal for this activation of the call block to the previous call block (or the split block if there are no previous procedure calls), when the called procedure has finished and the remainder of the branch has finished for each activation initiated by this activation of the call block.

Split block

All the split blocks perform the following functions:

— duplication of all parameters to activate this branch (if not the last branch);

— placing a new activation name on all parameters if necessary;

— accepting an end-of-branch signal from this branch and a finish signal of the next branch; when both are received, a finish signal is transmitted to the previous branch. (The n-th split block doesn't wait of course for the finish signal generated by the next branch).

The first split block performs in addition the following functions:

- counting the generate signals received from the generate blocks of this procedure; and returning a respond signal.
- counting the accept signals of the corresponding call block in the calling procedure;
- generation of a finish signal for this activation of the procedure if 1) the first branch has finished; and 2) a finish signal is received form the second split block (if any); and 3) the number of generate signals equals the number of accept signals.

The generate block

The functions of the generate block are as follows:

- for each solution of this branch, a generate signal is sent to the first split block of this procedure;
- upon receipt of the respond signal of the first split block, the solution of the procedure is sent to the calling procedure and the finish signal is sent to the previous call block (or the split block for this branch if there are no procedure calls in this branch).

The following points are noteworthy in this implementation scheme:

- for each generated solution, the generate signal is guaranteed to arrive before the accept signal: this is the function of the respond signal;
- when a branch fails (because of failing unification), it generates also a finish signal;

3.11 Guards

Up to now, we have ignored the guards. Although a straightforward solution is not difficult to implement (only one partial solution may proceed after the commit-tokens), we aim at aborting all guard evaluations as soon as one partial solution is computed. For the moment, we have an implementation scheme for this, but it has not yet been tested.

There are two kinds of abort signals in a don't-care procedure: internal and external ones. The internal abort signal is generated at a commit-token in the procedure itself, and has to be propagated to all procedures called in the guards (in the form of an external abort signal). The external abort signal is generated at a commit-token of an ancestor procedure and has reached this procedure due to propagation. The processing of the two types of abort signals is the same, but the followed path in the procedure is different. For don't care procedures, we have only external abort signals.

To accomplish this abortion, we associate with each call block a stream of colours. This stream indicates every activation of the procedure associated with the call block.

When a procedure receives an abort signal, it first checks if this is the first abort signal, and if it has not already finished all activity for the activations with the colour of the abort signal (the abort signal and the finish signal may cross each other). If this is the case, then we send recursively one or more abort signals to every directly activated procedure, by using the stream of colours associated with each call block. Further solutions of the procedure are also deleted.

4. Discussion of some experiments

We have tested some small programs with the Manchester simulator [Sargeant 85]. We derived the number of executed instructions, the length of the critical path and the average parallelism as a function of the number of elements of the list. Tables with the results for *quicksort* (deterministic) and *delete* (nondeterministic) are shown in figures 4.1.a and 4.1.b. A first conclusion is that garbage collection introduces much overhead: the average parallelism remains the same, but the number of instructions is multiplied roughly by 3 à 3.5. This is not astonishing, because, to guarantee a correct execution, we had to introduce a lot of (local) synchronization. It is also an indication that this synchronization did not destroy the OR-parallelism of the program.

quicksort						
#elem.	without g.c.			with g.c.		
	#instr.	cr.p.	par.	#instr.	cr.p.	par.
10	7469	1932	3.9	22693	3846	5.9
20	19279	4872	4.0	58193	9669	6.0

Figure 4.1.a: Results for quicksort
number of instructions, length of critical path and average parallelism (with and without garbage collection)

delete						
#elem.	without g.c.			with g.c.		
	#instr.	cr.p.	par.	#instr.	cr.p.	par.
0	33	10	3.3	84	30	2.8
5	792	136	5.8	2656	374	7.1
10	2402	276	8.7	8041	794	10.1
15	4862	416	11.7	16176	1214	13.3
20	8172	556	14.7	27061	1634	16.6

Figure 4.1.b: results for delete

The number of executed instructions compares rather unfavourable with an implementation on a sequential machine with backtracking: we found a ratio of 1 instruction on a sequential architecture for 7 instructions on a dataflow architecture for delete with garbage collection (9 elements). According to [Gurd et al. 85] a dataflow MIPS has the potential to match the power of a conventional sequential MIPS (for an integration program), so this result seems rather bad. A major explanation is that we store a lot of tokens in the matching store, which have to be destroyed when no longer needed. The structure store might provide a partial solution for this problem. As the structure store appears colourless, some instructions manipulating the colours of the stored tokens might be avoided. However, we will still need the finish signal to decide when the stored tokens can be destroyed.

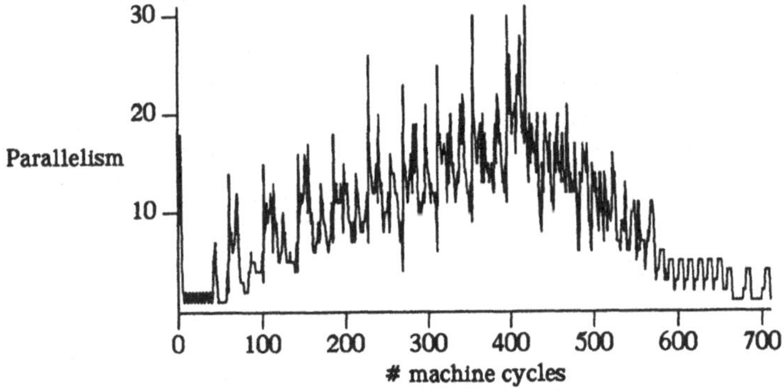

Figure 4.2: parallelism during execution of delete (9 elements)

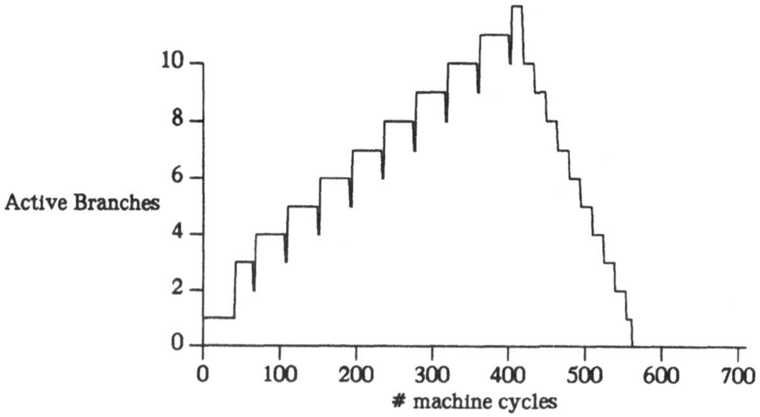

Figure 4.3: active branches during execution of delete (9 elements)

In fig. 4.2 we show the parallelism during the execution of delete with garbage collection for 9 elements. This parallelism is rather unevenly balanced, and may cause for other programs such as 'perm' too high peak values (with the related problems of matching store performance and token queue occupancy).

In fig. 4.3 we show the number of active branches during execution (an active branch is a branch that has received a trigger signal and not yet generated an end-of-branch signal). The procedure delete is activated at cycle 42 (the main activity before is the building of the lists, which is mainly sequential) and terminates at cycle 554. The query finishes at cycle 561, the remaining activity is to remove the lists.

5. Related work

Parallelism in logic programming has grown into a vast research area and it is outside the scope of this paper to attempt a survey. See for example the recent books [Conery 87] and [Wise 86]. Especially the latter gives a dataflow perspective on the field. Another survey focussing on OR-parallelism can be found in [Warren 87].

The only research effort we are aware of having some points in common with our approach is the implementation of flat PARLOG on the parallel reduction architecture ALICE [Lam & Gregory 87]. Both source languages have mode declarations. Flat PARLOG supports AND-parallelism, and thus suspension when trying to access unavailable variables. Our approach doesn't support full AND-parallelism, but there might be some overlapped execution of successive calls. Suspension is provided automatically when no values are available (the hardware is data driven). Our guards are not restricted to non-recursive procedures.

The ALICE architecture supports priority levels, which are used to perform garbage collection in parallel with other activities, but at a higher priority. This might improve the processing of finish and abort signals.

6. Discussion

We have spent a modest effort in exploring the possibilities of executing a logic programming language on the Manchester Dataflow Computer. The results obtained so far are not very encouraging. They indicate that the gains due to parallel execution of instructions are undone by the increased number of instructions to be executed.

Of course, there are several areas for improvement. First, the procedure calling scheme is too complex for deterministic procedures that always succeed exactly once. In that case, we do not have to store values in the call block, neither does such a procedure need a finish signal. We also expect that the handling of tail recursion can be improved. For the time being, we failed to find a scheme equivalent to an implementation on a sequential machine. For example, the in-line instruction after the tail recursive call of delete causes a major problem; if not present, it might be possible to skip all recursive levels between the first and the last recursive step for certain tokens.

On the other hand, the language was substantially simplified, the most significant restricion being that we excluded full unification by assuming modes. It is expected that the handling of full unification will increase the overhead.

Based on our effort, we are tempted to conclude that the realisation of an efficient PROLOG system on a dataflow machine is an undertaking at least as challenging as it has been for the conventional Von Neumann architecture. Only the widespread availability of such machines can make it a worthwile undertaking.

Acknowledgement

We are indebted to the dataflow research group at Manchester for providing us with the simulator and documentation.

References

— *[Bowen 81]* Bowen, D. L., Implementation of Data Structures on a Data Flow Computer, Ph. D. thesis, University of Manchester, April 1981

— *[Bruynooghe et al. 87]* Bruynooghe, M., G. Janssens, A. Callebaut and B. Demoen, Abstract interpretation, towards the global optimisation of Prolog programs, *Proc. Fourth IEEE Symposium on Logic Programming, San Francisco, september 1987*

— *[Catto 81]* Catto, A. J., Nondeterministic Programming in a Dataflow Environment, Ph. D. thesis, University of Manchester, june 1981.

— *[Catto & Gurd 80]* Catto, A. J. and J. R. Gurd, Nondeterministic Dataflow Graphs, *IFIP 1980*, p. 251 - 256.

— *[Conery 87]* Conery J. S., Parallel execution of logic programs, Kluwer Academic Publishers, 1987

— *[Drabent 87]* Drabent, W., Do logic programs resemble programs in conventional languages? *Proc. Fourth IEEE Symposium on Logic Programming, San Francisco, september 1987*

— *[Gurd et al. 85]* Gurd, J. R., Kirkham C. C. and Watson I., The Manchester Prototype Dataflow Computer, *Communications of the ACM*, January 1985 Volume 28 Number 1, 34 - 52

— *[Kirkham 84]* Kirkham, C. C., The Manchester Prototype Dataflow System, Basic Programming Manual, November 1984

— *[Lam & Gregory 87]* Lam, Melissa and Steve Gregory, PARLOG and ALICE: a Marriage of Convenience, *Proc. Fourth International Conference on Logic Programming*, Melbourne, p.294 - 310

— *[Sargeant 85]* Sargeant, J., Simulator Users Guide, University of Manchester, january 1985

— *[Veen 86]* Veen, A. H., Dataflow machine architecture, *ACM Computing Surveys*, Vol. 18, No 4 (december 1986), p. 365 - 396

— *[Warren 87]* Warren, D. H. D., Or-Parallel Execution Models of Prolog, *TAPSOFT 87: Proceedings of the international joint conference on theory and practice of software development*, Pisa, Italy, March 87, Lecture Notes in Computer Science 250, p. 243 - 259.

— *[Wise 86]* Wise, M. J., Prolog multiprocessors, Prentice-Hall, 1986

Systems Exhibition

---

* Abstract not received in time for publication

The PSG System: From Formal Language Definitions to Interactive Programming Environments

Rolf Bahlke, Gregor Snelting
Fachgebiet Praktische Informatik
Fachbereich Informatik
Technische Hochschule Darmstadt
Magdalenenstr. 11c, D-6100 Darmstadt

Overview

The PSG system developed at the University of Darmstadt generates interactive, language-specific programming environments from formal language definitions. All language-dependent parts of the environment are generated from an entirely nonprocedural specification of the language's syntax, context conditions and dynamic semantics. The generated environment consists of a language-specific hybrid editor, an interpreter and debugging system, and a library system.

The editor allows structure editing as well as text editing. Both modes are fully integrated and may be mixed freely. The user determines the granularity of incremental analysis: at one end of the spectrum there is pure text editing, while pure structure editing is the other extreme. When analysing textual input, PSG editors guarantee immediate detection of syntactic and static semantic errors. In structure mode, they even guarantee prevention of such errors. The editor will however not insist on immediate error correction; it tolerates incorrect or inconsistent programs. The user interface heavily utilizes raster graphics and mouse in order to achieve fast and ergonomic interaction.

PSG editors employ a novel algorithm for incremental semantic analysis, namely the concept of context relations. This concept is based on type inference rather than type checking. The context conditions of the language are described by inference rules. During editing, these rules are evaluated using a unification algorithm for order-sorted algebras. Change propagation is used to achieve fast incremental behaviour, and structure sharing avoids excessive memory requirements. The algorithm is language independent and guarantees immediate error detection in arbitrary incomplete program fragments. Error prevention is achieved by dynamically filtering all menus with respect to inferred context information.

The interactive interpreter is generated from a denotational semantics definition. It allows execution of incomplete program fragments. In order to generate an interpreter, semantic functions must be written in a functional language. The terms of this language are compiled into abstract machine code. This code is interpreted during fragment execution.

The debugger, which is currently available only as a prototype, is generated from an extension of the semantics definition. It offers additional features such as tracing, single-stepping, displaying variable values, setting conditional breakpoints etc. Interaction with the debugger is always on language level rather than on machine level.

The library is language-independent and stores programs as abstract trees. Usually, interaction with the library is invoked automatically by the editor resp. the interpreter. It is possible to import and export external text files into/from the environment.

PSG has been used to generate environments for Fortran 77, Lisp, Modula-2, Pascal, and the formal language definition language itself. PSG is also used to generate the programming environments of the German supercomputer SUPRENUM.

The PSG system is currently available on PCS Cadmus and SUN Workstations. Research institutions may obtain a copy for a nominal fee.

References

Bahlke, R., Snelting, G. : The PSG System: From Formal Language Definitions to Interactive Programming Environments. ACM TOPLAS, Vol. 8, No. 4 (October 1986), pp. 547-576.

Bahlke, R., Snelting, G.: Context-Sensitive Editing with PSG Environments. Proc. Advanced Programming Environments, Trondheim, June 1986, Springer Lecture Notes in Computer Science, Vol. 244, pp. 26-38.

Bahlke, R., Moritz, B., Snelting, G.: A Generator for Language-Specific Debugging Systems. Proc. SIGPLAN '87 Symposium on Interpreters and Interpretive Techniques, ACM Sigplan Notices, Vol. 22, No.7, July 1987, pp. 92-101.

Bahlke, R., Hunkel, M.: The User Interface of PSG Programming Environments. Proc. 2nd IFIP Conference on Human-Computer Interaction, September 1987, North Holland, pp. 311-315.

LPG: A generic, logic and functional programming language

D. Bert, P. Drabik, R. Echahed

Av. Félix Viallet, 46
F-38000 Grenoble (FRANCE)

O. Declerfayt, B. Demeuse, P-Y. Schobbens, F. Wautier

Unité d'Informatique, Université Catholique de Louvain
Place Sainte-Barbe, 2
B-1348 Louvain-La-Neuve (BELGIQUE)

LPG is a programming language designed to implement and experiment new concepts in the field of specification languages. In LPG, programs are theories in Horn clause logic with equality [3] [4]. Syntactically, a program is a theory presentation $TP = (S, \Sigma, \Pi, E, C)$ in which sorts (S), operators (Σ) and predicates (Π) can be declared; operators are specified by conditional equations (E), and predicates are specified by Horn clauses (C). Literals of a clause body may be equalities on terms. There are three kinds of presentations:

- properties (i.e. class of structures like group theory, ring theory, etc.);
- data types where the semantics is given by initial models;
- enrichments (i.e. hierarchical definitions of new operators and predicates on previously defined data types).

Moreover, data type and enrichment presentations may be parameterized by properties [1], thus providing generic data types and generic enrichments. It is also possible to relate theories between themselves by declaring theory morphisms. Those declarations are used by the instantiation mechanism, which is needed because of genericity.

Up to now, the following tools are available:

- An interpreter: this tool is designed to reduce ground terms to their normal form, with respect to the rewriting system deduced from the equations. This interpreter uses an abstract machine which deals with compiled programs. It also uses built-in procedures for operators over predefined data types like natural numbers, strings, etc. Taking advantage of the instantiation mechanism of generic operators, the interpreter is a good tool for testing specifications, prototyping, and functional programming.
- A logical evaluator (called "solver"): given a list of literals and/or equalities on terms, called a goal, the solver attempts to find the values of the variables which satisfy the goal. The underlying algorithm combines the resolution principle and conditional narrowing [2]. It has been shown sound and complete for a canonical rewrite rule system, but termination is not guaranteed for every goal.
- An interactive theorem prover: an interface with the OASIS system [5] has been developed in order to prove theorems. Implemented strategies are equational rewriting, case analysis, and proofs by induction. This system is also used to verify semantic correctness of specifications, like the validity of theory morphisms. (Multics version only.)
- A completer: this tool uses the Knuth-Bendix completion algorithm [7] to derive confluent systems of equational rewrite rules.
- A syntax-directed editor: this tool, based on [6], guides the user in the syntax of the LPG language (Sun version only), and performs context-dependent checks.

Two versions of the system are available, one written in Pl/1 and running under the Multics operating system, the other written in Ada and running on Sun workstations under Unix BSD 4.3. It is planned to port the Ada version to other machines, and to extend the language and its environment, in collaboration between LIFIA, UCL, Cert/DERI (Toulouse), CISI Ingénierie (Toulouse).

The presentation of LPG can be sketched as follows:

- Generic and functional programming: presentation of the instantiation mechanism, examples of interpretations.
- Generic and logic programming: examples of evaluations of goals.
- Demonstration of the auxiliary tools (syntax-directed editor, etc.)

References

[1] D. Bert, R. Echahed, Design and Implementation of a Generic, Logic and Functional Programming Language, Proc. of the European Symposium on Programming (ESOP'86), LNCS 213, Springer, 1986, pp. 119-132

[2] R. Echahed, Prédicats et sous-types en LPG. Réalisation de la E-unification, RR-IMAG-550-LIFIA-29, July 1985.

[3] J.A. Goguen, J. Meseguer, Introducing institutions, Proc. Logic for Programs, LNCS 164, Springer, 1984, pp. 115-125

[4] J.A. Goguen, J. Meseguer, Equality, Types, Modules and (Why not?) Generics for Logic Programming, Proc. Int. Conf. on Logic Programming, Uppsala, 1984, pp. 115-125 (also in J. Logic Programming, Vol.1 n.2, 1984, pp.179-210)

[5] E. Paul, Manuel OASIS, Note technique NT/PAA/CLC/LSC/959, CNET, 1985

[6] T. Teitelbaum, Th. Reps, Synthesizer Generator (2nd edition), Departement of Computer Science, Cornell University, Ithaca, 1987

[7] D.E. Knuth, P.B. Bendix, Simple word problem in universal algebra, in Computable problems in abstract algebra, J. Leech (ed.), Pergamon Press, 1970, pp. 263-297.

CEC: A System for the Completion of Conditional Equational Specifications†

Hubert Bertling, Harald Ganzinger, Renate Schäfers

Fachbereich Informatik, Universität Dortmund
D-4600 Dortmund 50, W. Germany, uucp, bitnet: hg@unido

The CEC-system has been developed to support various operational aspects of software specifications by conditional equations. It is part of the efforts in the PROSPECTRA-project to support the development of programs from specifications. CEC is implemented in Prolog and runs under C-Prolog 1.5 and Quintus-Prolog 1.6 and 2.0. The present system is a successor of a system that has been presented at STACS '87, Passau, and at the Workshop on Conditional Term Rewriting, Orsay 1987. The old version was based on a concept of completion relative to constraints as described in [1] whereas the new version is based on ideas investigated in [2].

The Specification Language

A specification consists of a many-sorted signature and conditional equations. Operators may be specified as constructors, with the understanding that different constructor ground terms must not be identified in the equational theory. Linear notation of terms as in C-Prolog is possible. Additional parsing and pretty-printing functions can be provided by the user.

The Termination Proof System

CEC supports two concepts for proving the termination of rewrite systems, recursive path orderings in the version of Kapur, Narendran and Sivakumar [3] and polynomial interpretation with the techniques described by Ben Cherifa and Lescanne [4].

The Completion Procedure

The main feature of CEC is a completion procedure for conditional equations. The theory behind the procedure is described in [2]. It can handle nonreductive conditional equations by a kind of narrowing technique in which nonreductive conditions are superposed by reductive rewrite rules.

In order to make completion terminate on nontrivial examples, CEC has implemented two powerful techniques for simplifying critical pair peaks and superposition instances of nonreductive conditional equations. One technique we call rewriting in contexts, meaning that the equations of a condition are oriented into rules as far as possible, and these (skolemized) rules are used when reducing a conditional equation to normal form. The second technique uses the nonreductive equations for simplification of other equations by a forward chaining derivation. If the condition of a nonreductive equation is instance of a subset of the condition of an equation to be considered for simplification, the corresponding instance of the conclusion is added as a further condition to the equation to be simplified. This forward chaining is allowed as long as the complexity of the resulting equation does not exceed a bound that is defined during the creation of the equation to be simplified. Accompanied by a subsumption test and by rewriting in these enriched contexts, the procedure is therefore able to detect a quite large class of loops in the narrowing process.

The completion can be run automatically or through manual guidance of the user. For that purpose, CEC makes the basic completion inference rules visible at the user level. The system automatically keeps

† This work is partially supported by the ESPRIT-project PROSPECTRA, ref#390.

track of the fairness constraints so that arbitrary changing between automatic and manual mode is possible. The procedure can also be applied to theories with associative-commutative operators.

The Rewrite Rule Compiler

Reductive conditional rewrite rules are upon creation immediately compiled into Prolog-code. The Prolog-code performs the matching and rewriting for the rule. In the non-AC case, matching is mapped to the matching in Prolog. Otherwise, the techniques are similar to what has been described by Kaplan. In addition, we exploit the specific properties of constructors and partially evaluate the matching procedure in the AC-case.

Support of Modular Specifications

CEC allows for (injective) renaming of signatures and for forming the union of two specifications. If possible, termination proofs for the old system(s) are carried over to the resulting specification. Also, overlaps between any two axioms of one module will not be recomputed upon enrichment or combination. CEC incorporates some specific optimization techniques in order to perform acceptably on large specifications acc

Environment-related Facilities

CEC offers to save and restore the state of specifications internally, as well as to and from external files. Moreover, user decisions may be taken back via a general undo mechanism.

The Data Base

In order to facilitate changes to the basic data structures, CEC contains a frame-oriented data base kit. The structure of the primitive objects can be specified so that computation of dependent attributes and objects are invoked automatically upon any creation of an object. Dependencies between objects can be specified, allowing e.g. to automatically dispose dependent objects upon deletion of an object.

Some Benchmarks

The following figures are for Quintus-Prolog 2.0 on a Sun 3/260.

Completion of integers with s, p, and $<$ (8 equations generating 25 superpositions): 18 sec.

Completion of ordered lists with $\leq$, $\neq$, *has*, *insert*, *delete*, *isordered* (about 25 equations including some inductive properties, generating 21 superpositions): 35 sec.

Completion of binary representations of natural numbers with $<$, $\neq$, $+$, $-$, $*$: In this example only the "true"-cases of $<$ and $\neq$ have been specified such that the negative case have to be inferred "by failure" through the narrowing process. The final system contains more than 50 axioms, including 12 nonoperational (nonreductive) equations; 85 superpositions are being computed): 200 sec. Computing 123456789*123456789 in the generated system: 0.1 sec.

Acknowledgements

H. Baumeister, U. Waldmann, and U. Wertz have helped in implementing major parts of the system.

References

[1] Ganzinger, H.: Ground term confluence in parametric conditional equational specifications. Proc. STACS 1987, LNCS 247, 1987.

[2] Ganzinger, H.: A completion procedure for conditional equations. Report 234, U. Dortmund, 1987, to appear in Proc. 1st Int'l Workshop on Conditional Term Rewriting, LNCS, 1988.

[3] Kapur, D., Narendran, P., and Sivakumar, G.: A path ordering for proving termination of term rewrite systems. LNCS 186, 1985, 173-187.

[4] Ben Cherifa, A. and Lescanne, P.: An actual implementation of a procedure that mechanically proves termination of rewriting systems based on inequalities between polynomial interpretations. Proc. CADE-8, LNCS 230, 1986.

A Functional Language for the Specification of Complex Tree Transformations

Reinhold Heckmann

Universität des Saarlandes
D-6600 Saarbrücken, W. Germany

The implementation of the language TrafoLa was developed on a VAX 11/780 computer with operating system UNIX. It consists of two processes running together and linked to a circle by two UNIX pipes. The first process is the front end for TrafoLa, and the second one an ML interpreter acting as TrafoLa interpreter.

The front end is concerned with file handling and user input/output. It reads concrete TrafoLa text and translates it into abstract syntax trees that are submitted to the real interpreter as concrete ML text through the first pipe.

The ML interpreter evaluates this ML expression and converts the result into a string by unparsing, and sends it back to the front end that refines and displays it. Example:

TrafoLa input: [1, 2] . [3]
ML expression sent to the ML interpreter:
ip(valof(edot(eseq([enum 1 ,enum 2]),eseq([enum 3]))));
where 'ip' is the function implementing the TrafoLa interpreter
and its argument is the abstract form of the TrafoLa expression
to be evaluated
Answer of the ML interpreter: > "[1, 2, 3]" : string
Output of the whole system: > [1, 2, 3]

The front end was mainly generated by a combined scanner, LL (2) parser, and tree generator generator from a specification of the concrete syntax of TrafoLa and of its translation into abstract syntax. To this generated code, some functions for converting the abstract trees into ML text, for user interaction and file handling were added. The front end is completely written in the programming language C.

The denotational semantics of TrafoLa was translated into an ML program and compiled into abstract ML machine code. When the TrafoLa interpreter is started, the ML interpreter is invoked with this code as argument, and is then able to evaluate ML expressions standing for TrafoLa terms.

The ML program consists of modules for

- the semantic values (sequences, trees, and functions) of TrafoLa and their operations (concatenation, insertion, application, etc.)
- environments implemented as sequences of pairs of variables and values, and their operations (look up, superposition etc.)
- sets of environments with union and superposition
- the abstract syntax of TrafoLa as ML data type
- the interpreting functions 'match' and 'eval'
- the initialization and update of the global environment

Both components of the TrafoLa interpreter are essentially generated: the front end from a specification of the concrete syntax of TrafoLa and its translation into abstract syntax, and the real interpreter from the denotational semantics of TrafoLa. This is advantageous for an experimental implementation since both syntax and semantics of TrafoLa may easily be updated or extended, but implies that the interpreter is quite slow.

We intend to design an abstract machine for TrafoLa and to compile it to code of this machine. The emphasis will lie on the patterns of TrafoLa since the expressions are similar to those in other functional languages.

Author Index

Vol. 270: E. Börger (Ed.), Computation Theory and Logic. IX, 442 pages. 1987.

Vol. 271: D. Snyers, A. Thayse, From Logic Design to Logic Programming. IV, 125 pages. 1987.

Vol. 272: P. Treleaven, M. Vanneschi (Eds.), Future Parallel Computers. Proceedings, 1986. V, 492 pages. 1987.

Vol. 273: J.S. Royer, A Connotational Theory of Program Structure. V, 186 pages. 1987.

Vol. 274: G. Kahn (Ed.), Functional Programming Languages and Computer Architecture. Proceedings. VI, 470 pages. 1987.

Vol. 275: A.N. Habermann, U. Montanari (Eds.), System Development and Ada. Proceedings, 1986. V, 305 pages. 1987.

Vol. 276: J. Bézivin, J.-M. Hullot, P. Cointe, H. Lieberman (Eds.), ECOOP '87. European Conference on Object-Oriented Programming. Proceedings. VI, 273 pages. 1987.

Vol. 277: B. Benninghofen, S. Kemmerich, M.M. Richter, Systems of Reductions. X, 265 pages. 1987.

Vol. 278: L. Budach, R.G. Bukharajev, O.B. Lupanov (Eds.), Fundamentals of Computation Theory. Proceedings, 1987. XIV, 505 pages. 1987.

Vol. 279: J.H. Fasel, R.M. Keller (Eds.), Graph Reduction. Proceedings, 1986. XVI, 450 pages. 1987.

Vol. 280: M. Venturini Zilli (Ed.), Mathematical Models for the Semantics of Parallelism. Proceedings, 1986. V, 231 pages. 1987.

Vol. 281: A. Kelemenová, J. Kelemen (Eds.), Trends, Techniques, and Problems in Theoretical Computer Science. Proceedings, 1986. VI, 213 pages. 1987.

Vol. 282: P. Gorny, M.J. Tauber (Eds.), Visualization in Programming. Proceedings, 1986. VII, 210 pages. 1987.

Vol. 283: D.H. Pitt, A. Poigné, D.E. Rydeheard (Eds.), Category Theory and Computer Science. Proceedings, 1987. V, 300 pages. 1987.

Vol. 284: A. Kündig, R.E. Bührer, J. Dähler (Eds.), Embedded Systems. Proceedings, 1986. V, 207 pages. 1987.

Vol. 285: C. Delgado Kloos, Semantics of Digital Circuits. IX, 124 pages. 1987.

Vol. 286: B. Bouchon, R.R. Yager (Eds.), Uncertainty in Knowledge-Based Systems. Proceedings, 1986. VII, 405 pages. 1987.

Vol. 287: K.V. Nori (Ed.), Foundations of Software Technology and Theoretical Computer Science. Proceedings, 1987. IX, 540 pages. 1987.

Vol. 288: A. Blikle, MetaSoft Primer. XIII, 140 pages. 1987.

Vol. 289: H.K. Nichols, D. Simpson (Eds.), ESEC '87. 1st European Software Engineering Conference. Proceedings, 1987. XII, 404 pages. 1987.

Vol. 290: T.X. Bui, Co-oP A Group Decision Support System for Cooperative Multiple Criteria Group Decision Making. XIII, 250 pages. 1987.

Vol. 291: H. Ehrig, M. Nagl, G. Rozenberg, A. Rosenfeld (Eds.), Graph-Grammars and Their Application to Computer Science. VIII, 609 pages. 1987.

Vol. 292: The Munich Project CIP. Volume II: The Program Transformation System CIP-S. By the CIP System Group. VIII, 522 pages. 1987.

Vol. 293: C. Pomerance (Ed.), Advances in Cryptology – CRYPTO '87. Proceedings. X, 463 pages. 1988.

Vol. 294: R. Cori, M. Wirsing (Eds.), STACS 88. Proceedings, 1988. IX, 404 pages. 1988.

Vol. 296: R. Janßen (Ed.), Trends in Computer Algebra. Proceedings, 1987. V, 197 pages. 1988.

Vol. 297: E.N. Houstis, T.S. Papatheodorou, C.D. Polychronopoulos (Eds.), Supercomputing. Proceedings, 1987. X, 1093 pages. 1988.

Vol. 298: M. Main, A. Melton, M. Mislove, D. Schmidt (Eds.), Mathematical Foundations of Programming Language Semantics. Proceedings, 1987. VIII, 637 pages. 1988.

Vol. 299: M. Dauchet, M. Nivat (Eds.), CAAP '88. Proceedings, 1988. VI, 304 pages. 1988.

Vol. 300: H. Ganzinger (Ed.), ESOP '88. Proceedings, 1988. VI, 381 pages. 1988.